New South Wales

Jon Murray
Tom Smallman
David Willett

New South Wales

2nd edition

Published by
   Lonely Planet Publications
   Head Office: PO Box 617, Hawthorn, Vic 3122, Australia
   Branches: 155 Filbert St, Suite 251, Oakland, CA 94607, USA
                 10 Barley Mow Passage, Chiswick, London W4 4PH, UK
                 71 bis rue du Cardinal Lemoine, 75005 Paris, France

Printed by
   Pac-Rim Kwartanusa Printing
   Printed in Indonesia

Photographs by

Glenn Beanland	David Collins	David Curl	Richard I'Anson	Mark Kirby
Ron & Viv Moon	Jon Murray	Bernard Napthine	Richard Nebesky	Denis O'Byrne
Tom Smallman	Paul Steel	Richard Timbury	Tony Wheeler	

Front cover: Surfer, Lennox Head, North Coast (Mark Kirby)

First Published
   October 1994

This Edition
   November 1997

National Library of Australia Cataloguing in Publication Data

   Smallman, Tom
   New South Wales

   2nd ed.
   Includes index
   ISBN 0 86442 464 7

   1. New South Wales – Guidebooks. 2. Australian Capital
   Territory – Guidebooks. I. Willett, David, 1955– .
   II. Murray, Jon. New South Wales & the ACT. III. Title.
   IV. Title: New South Wales and the Australian Capital Territory.
   V. Title: New South Wales & the ACT

919.4404

text & maps © Lonely Planet 1997
photos © photographers as indicated 1997

Jon Murray

Jon Murray spent time alternating between travelling and working with various publishing companies in Melbourne before joining Lonely Planet as an editor. He was soon travelling again, this time researching the guidebooks. He wrote the original *Sydney* and co-authored Lonely Planet's *Africa, Lesotho & Swaziland* and updated several other guides including *Papua New Guinea*, *Bangladesh* and parts of *Australia*. He shares a bush block near Daylesford, Victoria, with quite a few marsupials.

Tom Smallman

Tom was born and raised in the UK and currently lives in Melbourne, Australia. He had a number of jobs before joining Lonely Planet as an editor and now works full time as an author. He has worked as co-author on Lonely Planet's *Canada, Ireland, Dublin, Sydney* and *New York, New Jersey & Pennsylvania*.

David Willett

David grew up in Hampshire, England and wound up in Australia in 1980 after stints working on newspapers in Iran and Bahrain. He spent two years working as a sub-editor on the *Sun* in Melbourne before opting to live somewhere warmer. David is now a freelance journalist based on the mid-north coast of NSW with his partner Rowan and their seven-year-old son Tom. Between jobs, he has travelled extensively in Europe, the Middle East and Asia. David updated the NSW section of LP's *Australia* and has worked on *Greece, Tunisia, Africa, Indonesia, South-east Asia, Mediterranean Europe* and *Western Europe*.

From the Authors

Tom Smallman My thanks to Sue Graefe for her patience and tolerant support; to Lindy Mark for her invaluable information; to Brian McKenna, who told me more about Kings Cross than he ought to have known; to Narelle Graefe and Lindy Spindler for their hospitality in Canberra; to Gisèle Etienne for her insights; to the Denson family; to the Countrylink staff at Central Station; to all those other people in the travel industry who patiently answered my questions; to Bruce Cameron for writing the Disabled Travellers section; and to Mary Neighbour, Steve Womersley and Jane Fitzpatrick at Lonely Planet who fed me new information.

A special thanks to Stuart, Kerry and Rob in Cobar, who picked me up after I totalled my car somewhere south of Nymagee.

My work on this edition is dedicated to the memory of Manfred (Mick) Peters, who grew up in Tumut and whose travels finished far too soon.

David Willett My thanks go to Rowan and Tom for their help and company on the long haul around the western regions of NSW and to Mon and Julie from Ballina for their hospitality. Thanks also to co-author Tom Smallman for his support and good humour and to the crew at LP Melbourne (Rob, Mary and Wendy).

This Book

The 1st edition of Lonely Planet's *New South Wales* was written by Jon Murray. This 2nd edition was coordinated by Tom Smallman who also updated the Sydney chapters and most of the Central West, Riverina, South East, South Coast and ACT chapters. David Willett worked on the Hunter Valley, North Coast, New England, some parts of the Central West, North West, Far West and the Islands chapters.

From the Publisher

This edition was edited by Wendy Owen with Paul Harding, Janet Austin, Craig McKenzie, Peter Cruttenden and Sue Harvey. Rebecca Turner and Janet Austin helped with proofreading and Mary Neighbour helped with just about everything. Most of the indexing was done by Kerrie Williams. Michelle Lewis coordinated the mapping and layout and Mark Griffiths was drawing the maps until he had a car accident which left him in hospital where he had to concentrate on drawing breath. He was finally allowed to go home, and we'll be delighted to see him back in the office. Jacqui Saunders, Lyndell Taylor and Tony Fankhauser helped out with mapping. New illustrations were drawn by Trudi Canavan and Adam McCrow designed the cover.

Warning & Request

Things change – prices go up, schedules change, good places go bad and bad places go bankrupt – nothing stays the same. So, if you find things better or worse, recently opened or long since closed, please tell us and help make the next edition even more accurate and useful.

We value all of the feedback we receive from travellers. Julie Young coordinates a small team who read and acknowledge every letter, postcard and email, and ensure that every morsel of information finds its way to the appropriate authors, editors and publishers.

Everyone who writes to us will find their name in the next edition of the appropriate guide and will also receive a free subscription to our quarterly newsletter, *Planet Talk*. The very best contributions will be rewarded with a free Lonely Planet guide.

Excerpts from your correspondence may appear in new editions of this guide; in our newsletter, *Planet Talk*; or in updates on our Web site – so please let us know if you don't want your letter published or your name acknowledged.

Thanks

Many thanks to the following travellers who used the last edition and wrote to us with useful advice and interesting anecdotes: Lisa Beringer, Wendy Blythe, Nicole Hills, Fiona K, R Lewis, Zina McIlraith, Doug McKenzie, Natalie Mundy, Lyn Murphy, Margaret Toohey and Catherine Wiles.

Contents

Boxed Asides

Map Legend

BOUNDARIES

.... International Boundary
.... Regional Boundary

ROUTES

.... Freeway
.... Highway
.... Major Road
.... Unsealed Road or Track
.... City Road
.... City Street
.... Railway
.... Underground Railway
.... Monorail
.... Walking Track
.... Walking Tour
.... Ferry Route
.... Cable Car or Chairlift

AREA FEATURES

.... Parks
.... Built-Up Area
.... Pedestrian Mall
.... Market
.... Cemetery
.... Forest
.... Beach or Desert
.... Rocks

HYDROGRAPHIC FEATURES

.... Coastline
.... River, Creek
.... Intermittent River or Creek
.... Rapids, Waterfalls
.... Lake, Intermittent Lake
.... Canal
.... Swamp

SYMBOLS

○ CAPITAL	.... National Capital	
◉ Capital	.... Regional Capital	
◍ CITY	.... Major City	
● City	.... City	
● Town	.... Town	
● Village	.... Village	
■ ▼	.... Place to Stay, Place to Eat	
☒ ♈	.... Cafe, Pub or Bar	
✉ ☎	.... Post Office, Telephone	
❶ ❸	.... Tourist Information, Bank	
◒ 🅿	.... Transport, Parking	
🏛 ⌂	.... Museum, Youth Hostel	
🚐 Å	.... Caravan Park, Camping Ground	
⛪ ✚	.... Church, Cathedral	
☪ ✡	.... Mosque, Synagogue	
卍 卐	.... Buddhist Temple, Hindu Temple	
✚ ★	.... Hospital, Police Station	

◔ 🅿	.... Embassy, Petrol Station	
✈ ✝	.... Airport, Airfield	
▬ ✿	.... Swimming Pool, Gardens	
◈ ➶	.... Shopping Centre, Zoo	
⚲ ▣	.... Winery or Vineyard, Picnic Site	
◄— 25	.... One Way Street, Route Number	
🏛 ⚱	.... Stately Home, Monument	
⛳ ⚐	.... Golf Course, Ski Field	
⌒ ✕	.... Cave, Mine	
▲ ✳	.... Mountain or Hill, Lookout	
🗼 ⚓	.... Lighthouse, Shipwreck	
)(◉	.... Pass, Spring	
➴ ⚑	.... Beach, Surf Beach	
∴	.... Archaeological Site or Ruins	
⌢⌢⌢⇒ ⇐	.... Cliff or Escarpment, Tunnel	
Ⓤ	.... Underground Railway Station	
╫╫╫╫	.... Railway Station	

Note: not all symbols displayed above appear in this book

Map Index

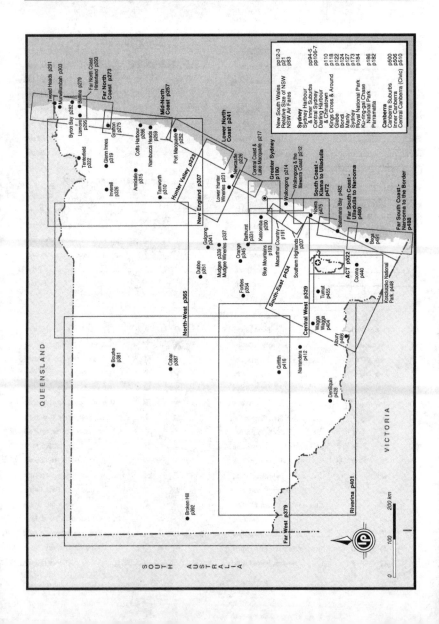

QUEENSLAND

VICTORIA

SOUTH AUSTRALIA

Tweed Heads p291
Murwillumbah p303
Byron Bay p282
Lismore p296
Ballina p279
Far North Coast Hinterland p283
Far North Coast p273
Tenterfield p322
Glen Innes p319
Grafton p275
Coffs Harbour p286
Nambucca Heads p259
Mid-North Coast p257
Inverell p326
Armidale p315
Port Macquarie p252
Lower North Coast p241
Tamworth p310
Hunter Valley p223
New England p307
Lower Hunter Wineries p231
Newcastle p226
Central Coast & Lake Macquarie p217
Greater Sydney p180
Wollongong & the Illawarra Coast p212
Wollongong p214
South Coast – Kiama to Ulladulla p172
Gulgong p341
Mudgee p339
Mudgee Wineries p337
Bathurst p331
Katoomba p200
Orange p345
Blue Mountains p193
Macarthur Country p191
Southern Highlands p207
Nowra p475
Batemans Bay p482
South Coast – Ulladulla to Narooma p480
Far South Coast – Narooma to the Border p488
Bega p91
North-West p365
Dubbo p351
Forbes p354
South-East p329
ACT p522
Cooma p440
Tumut p455
Kosciuszko National Park p448
Bourke p381
Cobar p387
Griffith p416
Central West p434
Wagga Wagga p404
Albury p406
Narrandera p412
Deniliquin p428
Riverina p401
Broken Hill p392
Far West p379

0 100 200 km

Introduction

Cosmopolitan Sydney with its beautiful setting and easy-going lifestyle is one of the world's great cities and will be a great venue for the 2000 Olympics. Within easy reach are many beaches and forests, the spectacular Blue Mountains and the wineries of the Hunter Valley.

The coastal route from Sydney to Queensland is deservedly popular. It passes through resort towns like Byron Bay, an endless string of superb, often deserted beaches, and offers access to the national parks of the Great Dividing Range. Australia's largest ski-fields are in the Snowy Mountains, in the south-east of NSW, and nearby is the Australian Capital Territory, containing Canberra, the national capital.

The south coast is just as scenic as the north coast but less developed. On the Great Dividing Range is a series of high tablelands, including New England, with its spectacular gorges and waterfalls. West of the range you'll meet rural Australia. There are some fine old towns in the rich farmlands of the western slopes and another winery area around Mudgee. Further west are the vast landscapes of the great plains, merging into the red soil of the baking outback in the north-west. South of the plains is the Riverina with its lazy rivers and redgum forests.

Many national parks have World Heritage status; some are wilderness areas where possibilities for adventure activities abound.

From ancient Aboriginal sites to picturesque country pubs, practically everything that's considered 'typically Australian' can be found in NSW.

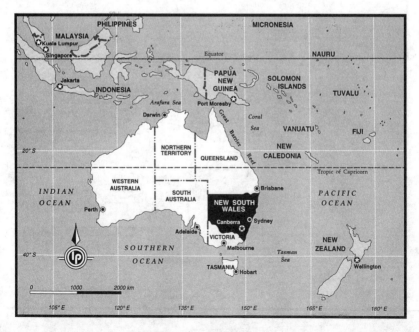

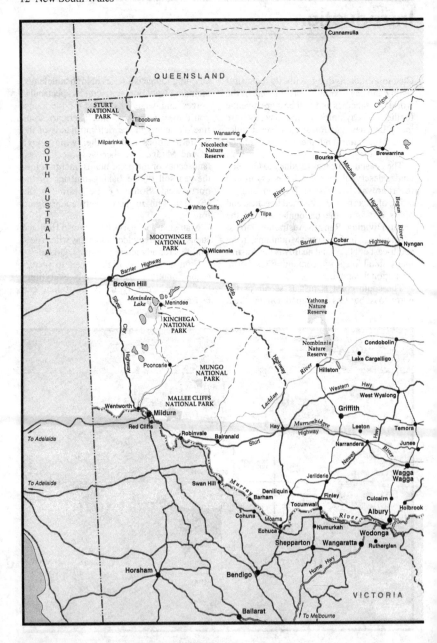

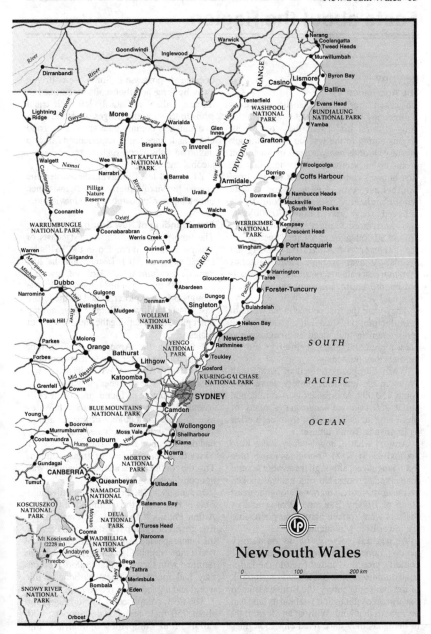

New South Wales

Facts about the Region

HISTORY
The Aborigines

Australian Aboriginal (which literally means 'indigenous') society has the longest continuous cultural history in the world, with origins dating to the last Ice age. Although mystery shrouds many aspects of Australian prehistory, it seems almost certain that the first humans came here across the sea from South-East Asia. Heavy-boned people whom archaeologists call 'Robust' are believed to have arrived around 70,000 years ago, and more slender 'Gracile' people around 50,000 years ago. Gracile people are the ancestors of Australian Aboriginal people. Archaeological evidence suggests that the descendants of these settlers colonised the entire continent within a few thousand years.

They were the first people in the world to manufacture polished edge-ground stone tools, cremate their dead and engrave and paint representations of themselves and the animals they hunted.

When Europeans arrived in New South Wales in the late 18th century, there were some 750,000 Aborigines in Australia and about 250 regional languages – many of these languages as distinct from each other as English is from Chinese.

Around what is now Sydney, there were approximately 3000 Aborigines using three main languages, although there were several dialects and groups. Ku-ring-gai was spoken on the north shore, Dharawal along the coast south of Botany Bay, and Dharug and its dialects were spoken across the plains into the lower Blue Mountains.

Aboriginal society, based on family groups rather than large political units, couldn't present a united front to the European colonisers, and in the crude realpolitik of the late 18th century, the British assumed that a people which didn't defend its land had no right to that land. Without any legal right to the lands they once lived on, Aborigines became dispossessed. Some were driven away by force and thousands succumbed to disease. Others voluntarily left their tribal lands to travel to the fringes of settled areas to obtain new commodities such as steel and cloth, and, once there, experienced hitherto unknown substances such as tea, tobacco, alcohol and opium.

At a local level, individuals resisted the encroachment of settlers, but such resistance only temporarily postponed the inevitable.

The Founding of New South Wales

The inhospitable north and west coasts of Australia had been charted in the 1640s by Dutch explorer Abel Tasman and he had named the continent New Holland. It wasn't until 1770 that Captain James Cook, the famous British explorer, sailed up the fertile east coast, landing at Botany Bay (among other places) and naming the area New South Wales.

Following the American Revolution, Britain was no longer able to transport convicts to North America. With jails and prison hulks already overcrowded, it was essential that an alternative be found quickly. In 1779 Joseph Banks suggested New South Wales as a fine site for a colony of thieves and in 1786 Lord Sydney announced that the king had decided upon Botany Bay as a place for convicts under sentence of transportation. That the continent was already inhabited was not considered significant.

In January 1788, the First Fleet sailed into Botany Bay under the command of Captain Arthur Phillip, who was to be the colony's first governor. Phillip was disappointed with the landscape and sent a small boat north to find a more suitable landfall. The crew soon returned with the news that in Port Jackson they had found the finest harbour in the world and a good sheltered cove.

The fleet, comprised of 11 ships carrying about 750 male and female convicts, 400 sailors, four companies of marines and enough livestock and supplies for two years, weighed anchor again and headed for Sydney Cove to begin establishing a settlement.

The early settlement did it hard. The soils around Sydney Cove proved to be poor and the tools were worse, so the settlers were dependent on their stores and supply ships from England. None came for 2½ years.

Shortly after a supply ship relieved the threat of famine in 1790, the Second Fleet struggled into Sydney Cove, bringing few supplies but another 740 convicts.

For the convicts, New South Wales was a harsh and horrible place. The reasons for transportation were often minor, and the sentences, of no less than seven years with hard labour, were tantamount to life sentences as there was little hope of returning home. Whippings were common and were designed to break the spirit.

Hunger to the point of weakness afflicted most of the convicts, while the need for strong labourers to grow food remained urgent. A farm was established at Parramatta (today's Parramatta Rd basically follows the old cart track) where the soil was more fertile, and gradually the situation improved. However, it was more than a decade until enough food was grown in the colony for the threat of famine to disappear completely.

The Early Colony

As crops began to yield, New South Wales became less dependent on Britain for food. There were still, however, huge social gulfs in the fledgling colony: officers and their families were in control and clinging desperately to a modicum of civilised British living; soldiers, free settlers and even emancipated convicts were beginning to eke out a living; yet the majority of the population was still in chains, regarded as the dregs of humanity and living in squalid conditions.

Little of the country was explored during those first years, and few people ventured further than Sydney Cove.

Phillip believed New South Wales wouldn't progress if the colony continued to rely solely on the labour of convicts, who

Harsh beginnings: cuffs and leg fetters kept convicts working for the new colony

were already busy constructing government roads and buildings. He believed prosperity depended on attracting free settlers, to whom convicts could be assigned as labourers, and on granting land to officers, soldiers and worthy emancipists (convicts who had served their time).

Phillip returned to England in 1792 and his second-in-command, Major Grose, took over. In a classic case of 'jobs for the boys', Grose tipped the balance of power further in favour of the military by granting land to officers of the New South Wales Corps. With money, land and cheap labour at their disposal, the officers became exploitative, making huge profits at the expense of the small farmers.

To encourage convicts to work, the officers were given permission to pay them in rum. The officers quickly prospered and were soon able to buy whole shiploads of goods and resell them at huge profits. The colony was becoming an important port on trade routes, and whaling and sealing were increasing. The officers, who became known as the Rum Corps, met little resistance and continued to do virtually as they pleased, all the while getting richer and more arrogant.

A new governor, William Bligh, was appointed to restore order, but the bad temper which had already caused him to suffer a mutiny on the *Bounty* again caused his downfall, and he suffered another rebellion and was arrested by the Rum Corps. This rebellion, known as the Rum Rebellion, was the final straw for the British government, which in 1809 dispatched Lieutenant-Colonel Lachlan Macquarie with his own regiment and orders for the return to London of the New South Wales Corps.

John Macarthur, one of the officers involved in the Rum Rebellion, was already a successful farmer and was to have far-reaching effects on the colony's first staple industry. He saw the country's wool-growing potential and set about breeding a strain of merino sheep that could prosper here. His wife, Elizabeth, did much of the work, as John remained in England for nearly a decade for his part in the rebellion.

Governor Macquarie, having broken the stranglehold of the Rum Corps, set about putting the colony to rights. He instituted a building programme, employing talented convict architect Francis Greenway, several of whose buildings remain today (see the Sydney and Around Sydney chapters). Because hamlets along the riverflats of the Hawkesbury were repeatedly flooded, Macquarie established five well-planned towns on higher ground around Windsor – the Macquarie towns (see the Around Sydney chapter). He encouraged explorers to find a route across the Blue Mountains and, when they did, had a road across completed in just six months, then established the town of Bathurst on the plains beyond.

However, Macquarie also had the strange idea that convicts who had served their time should be allowed rights as citizens, and he began appointing emancipists to public positions.

The gentry of Sydney Cove wanted nothing to do with ex-cons or their children. Anti-emancipists, including the irascible John Macarthur, were outraged at what they saw as a social perversion and began carping about Macquarie's expensive public works programmes and creating the impression that the colony was ungovernable. Many wealthier colonists were also simply annoyed that Macquarie's building programmes were using all the available convicts, leaving them no free labour for their farms.

Macquarie, generally agreed to have been the best of the early governors, returned to England under a cloud in 1821. His reign had been a watershed for the colony. When he arrived it was a struggling penal settlement; when he left there was little doubt that a permanent and potentially wealthy colony had been established.

A New People

From the earliest days of New South Wales, Australian-born colonials saw themselves as different from the upper-crust British officers who ran the colony, who they regarded as effete. Anyway, with an increasing number of Irish political prisoners and their descendants, it wasn't likely that an affection for the Old Dart would burn brightly.

Before long, the free-born children of the convicts became a sizeable proportion of the population. They were called Currency Lads and Lasses. Little is known about these first white Australians and it's unlikely that anyone but they themselves considered them to be Australians. The power and money in the colony rested with people who had their sights set on making their name or their fortune and returning home. For the free-born, Australia *was* home.

Astoundingly, the lowest crime-rate in the early colony was among the free-born, lower even than that among the free settlers.

Exploration & Expansion

By 1800 there were only two small settlements in Australia – at Sydney and on Norfolk Island. While unknown areas on world maps were shrinking, most of Australia was still one big blank. It was even suspected that it might be two large, separate islands, and it was hoped that there might be a vast sea in the centre.

George Bass charted the coast south of Sydney almost down to the present location of Melbourne during 1797-98, and in the following year, with Matthew Flinders, he sailed around Van Diemen's Land (Tasmania), establishing that it was an island. Flinders went on in 1802 to sail right around Australia – he suggested that the continent should be called Australia rather than New Holland.

The Blue Mountains at first proved an impenetrable barrier, limiting the size of the colony, but in 1813 a path was finally forced through and the western plains were reached by the explorers Blaxland, Wentworth and Lawson. Soon after, George Evans led two expeditions across the mountains and found the Macquarie and Lachlan rivers.

In 1817, John Oxley's party set out from the newly-founded town of Bathurst down the Lachlan River in search of more good land and perhaps an inland sea. The river petered out into swamps so they headed south-west across arid plains then turned north, crossing the Lachlan and reaching the Macquarie River, which they followed upstream to Bathurst. Oxley was unenthusiastic about the country he had found, but he had been unlucky. If he had persisted through the swamps on the Lachlan, he would have soon reached the Murrumbidgee River.

The following year, Oxley was sent to find the mouth of the Macquarie River, only to find that it too flowed through poor country and ended in great marshes. The party headed east to the coast, crossing the Liverpool Plains (which were to prove to be some of the best grazing land in the world), found a way across the Great Divide and followed the fertile Hastings Valley to the rivermouth, which Oxley named Port Macquarie. This country was much more promising.

In 1819 a route to Bathurst from Cow Pastures (around Camden) was found by Charles Throsby, thereby opening up the southern highlands to graziers, and James Meehan explored a route from the southern highlands to the coast near Jervis Bay (now called Booderee), finding still more fertile land.

In 1824 the explorers Hume and Hovell, starting from near present-day Canberra, made the first overland journey southwards, reaching the western shores of Port Phillip Bay. On the way they discovered a large river and named it after Hume, although it was later renamed the Murray by another great

Father of the Murray: explorer Charles Sturt, who dispelled the myth of an inland sea

explorer, Charles Sturt. By 1830, Sturt had established that the Murrumbidgee and Darling River systems tied in with the Murray, and had followed the Murray to its mouth, finally dispelling the inland sea theory.

By the mid-1830s the general layout of present-day New South Wales was understood, and settlers with their herds and flocks eagerly followed the explorers' routes. The settlers often pushed into territory that was outside the defined 'limits of settlement', but the government inevitably expanded those limits in reaction to the new settlements.

The colony was increasingly seen as a promising place in which to make money. The British government and the wealthier colonials began to envisage a rich pastoral colony to which British society could be transplanted.

The increasing number of large landholders began to debate whether convicts (cheap but unreliable) or the free-born (good workers but uppity and expensive) made better farm labourers. A growing minority wanted an end to transportation altogether. This view eventually prevailed and the last ship bringing convicts to New South Wales arrived in 1848.

When Arthur Phillip arrived in 1788, New South Wales comprised about half of the continent and Tasmania. The western half of the continent (which became Western Australia after some shifting of borders) was claimed by Britain in 1829 and Tasmania became a separate colony in 1825. The mainland colonies were progressively carved from New South Wales – South Australia (1834), Victoria (1850) and Queensland (1859). From *being* Australia, New South Wales became one of several Australian colonies.

New South Wales was granted responsible government in 1855 and two years later all males in the colony were given the vote. Women had to wait until 1902 before they were allowed to vote, but both men and women were given the vote here much earlier than in many other countries.

Gold!

The discovery of gold in the 1850s brought about the most significant changes in the social and economic structure of the colony.

The large quantities of gold found at Ophir (near Orange) in 1851 caused a rush of hopeful miners from Sydney, and for the rest of the century there were rushes throughout New South Wales and much of Australia. The influx of miners from around the world and the independence of life on the diggings swept away any hope of the Australian colonies remaining strictly controlled pastoral societies.

Besides the population and economic growth that came with the goldrushes, they also contributed greatly to the development of a distinctive Australian folklore. The music brought by the British and Irish, for instance, reflected life on the diggings, while poets, singers and writers began telling stories of the people, the roaring gold towns and the boisterous hotels, the squatters and their sheep and cattle stations, the swagmen, and the derring-do of the notorious bushrangers, many of whom became folk heroes.

Although few people actually made their fortunes on the goldfields, many stayed to settle the country, as farmers, workers and shopkeepers. At the same time, the Industrial Revolution in Britain produced a strong demand for raw materials. With the agricultural and mineral resources of such a vast country, Australia's economic base became secure.

Early 20th Century

During the 1890s, calls for the separate colonies to federate became increasingly strident. Supporters argued that it would improve the economy (which was undergoing a severe depression) by removing intercolonial tariffs. Also, a sense of an Australian identity, spurred by painters and writers, had grown. Sydney was by now a vigorous city of nearly 500,000 people and a great port.

With Federation, which came about on 1 January 1901, New South Wales became a state of the new Australian nation. But Australia's loyalties and many of its legal ties to Britain remained. When WWI broke out in Europe, Australian troops were sent to fight in the trenches of France, the Gallipoli fiasco and the Middle East.

The site for Canberra, the new national capital, was chosen in 1908 (after much bickering between Sydney and Melbourne), and the Australian Capital Territory (ACT) was created in 1911. See the ACT chapter for the story of Canberra's development.

There was great economic expansion in the 1920s, but all this came to a halt with the Great Depression, which hit Australia hard. In 1931 almost a third of breadwinners were unemployed and poverty was widespread.

Sydney's population was approaching one million and conditions in the crowded inner suburbs were desperate. NSW premier Jack Lang ('the Big Fella') attempted to raise money to alleviate the suffering by defaulting on the state's loans from Britain. This made him enormously popular, but he was soon sacked as premier and expelled from the Labor party.

By 1932, however, the economy was starting to recover as a result of rises in wool prices and a rapid revival of manufacturing. With the opening of the Harbour Bridge in that same year, Sydney's building industry picked up again.

'Protection' of Aboriginal People

By the early 1900s, legislation designed to segregate and 'protect' Aboriginal people imposed restrictions on Aborigines' rights to own property and to seek employment; and the Aboriginals Ordinance of 1918 even allowed the state to remove children from Aboriginal mothers if it was suspected that the father was non-Aboriginal. Many Aborigines are still bitter about having been separated from their families and forced to grow up apart from their people.

An upside of the ordinance was that it gave a degree of protection for 'full-blood' Aboriginal people living on reserves, as non-Aboriginal people could enter only with a permit, and mineral exploration was forbidden.

WWII & Postwar NSW

When WWII broke out, Australian troops again fought beside the British in Europe, but after the Japanese bombed Pearl Harbour Australia's own national security finally began to take priority. In May 1942, four midget Japanese submarines were destroyed in Sydney Harbour, and a week later a Japanese submarine surfaced off the coast and lobbed shells into the suburbs of Bondi and Rose Bay. Australia's location in Asia, a long way from Europe, suddenly became frighteningly relevant. The Japanese advance was stopped by Australian and US forces in Papua New Guinea and ultimately it was the US, not Britain, that helped protect Australia from the Japanese.

In the postwar years, construction boomed again in Sydney and the city spread west rapidly. The new immigration programmes brought growth and prosperity to Australia and living conditions improved.

Australia came to accept the US view that it wasn't so much Asia but communism in Asia that threatened the increasingly Americanised Australian way of life, so it was no surprise that in 1965 the conservative government committed troops to serve in the Vietnam War.

During the Vietnam War years, Sydney's face changed as American GIs flooded the city for their R&R (rest and recreation) leave. Kings Cross flaunted its sleaziness – and the hippie and peace movements became established in Australia.

'Assimilation' of Aboriginal People

The process of social change for Aboriginal people was accelerated by WWII. After the war, 'assimilation' of Aboriginal people became the stated aim of the government. To this end, the rights of Aboriginal people were subjugated even further – the government had control over everything, from where Aborigines could live to whom they could marry. Many children were taken from their families and put in white foster homes or missions and people were forcibly moved from their homes to townships. The idea was that they would adapt to European culture, which would in turn aid their economic development. This policy was a dismal failure.

In the 1960s the assimilation policy came under scrutiny, and non-Aboriginal Australians became increasingly aware of the inequity of their treatment of Aborigines. In 1967 non-Aboriginal Australians voted to give Aborigines and Torres Strait Islanders the status of citizens, and gave the federal government power to legislate for them in all states. The states had to provide them with the same services as were available to other citizens, and the Federal government set up the Department of Aboriginal Affairs to identify and legislate for the special needs of Aboriginal people.

The assimilation policy was finally dumped in 1972, to be replaced by the government's policy of self-determination, which for the first time brought Aborigines into the decision-making processes.

In 1976 the Aboriginal Land Rights Act gave Aborigines in the Northern Territory indisputable title to all Aboriginal reserves and a means for claiming other crown land.

It also provided for mineral royalties to be paid to Aboriginal communities. This legislation was supposed to be extended to cover all of Australia, but the removal of the reformist Labor government in 1975 (see later) put paid to that prospect.

The 1970s & Beyond

Support for involvement in Vietnam was far from absolute, and conscripting 18-year-olds to fight a foreign war troubled many Australians. Even during the two world wars Australians had voted to reject sending conscripts to foreign battlefields. Civil unrest eventually contributed to the rise to national power, in 1972, of the Australian Labor Party for the first time in 20 years. The Whitlam government withdrew Australian troops from Vietnam and instituted many reforms, such as free tertiary education and free universal health care.

Labor, however, was hampered by a hostile Senate and talk of mismanagement. On 11 November 1975, the governor general dismissed Parliament and installed a caretaker government led by the leader of the Opposition, Malcolm Fraser. Such action was unprecedented in the history of the Commonwealth of Australia, and the powers that the governor general had been able to invoke had long been regarded by many as an anachronistic vestige of Australia's now remote British past, the office itself as that of an impotent figurehead.

See the Politics Since Federation section in the ACT chapter for more on the Federal political scene.

In NSW, long years of conservative rule ended in 1976 with the election of Labor under Neville Wran. He instituted reforms and presided over the clean-up of a state that had been slipping into corruption. Wran left politics in 1986 and, without his charismatic presence, Labor lost the next election. Liberal premiers Nick Greiner and his successor, John Fahey, proved to be a lot less colourful than 'Nifty Nev' Wran, concentrating on balancing the budget. In 1995 Labor was re-elected under the leadership of Bob Carr.

After the 80s boom, which saw a lot of development in Sydney, Australia found itself in recession again in the early 90s – which left some big holes in the ground in Sydney after construction projects folded. The recession is now over, according to the government, but recovery will take some time. Sydney is gearing itself up for the Olympic Games in 2000 but unemployment remains high and many farmers continue to be forced off the land because they can't keep up mortgage payments.

Aborigines Today

Many Aborigines in south-eastern Australia now identify themselves as Kooris.

Only relatively recently has the non-Aboriginal community come to realise that a meaningful conciliation between indigenous and non-indigenous Australia was vital to the psychological well-being of all Australians. In 1992 the High Court handed down what became known as its Mabo ruling. It was the result of a claim by a Torres Strait Islander, Eddie Mabo, challenging the established concept of *terra nullius* – the idea that Australia belonged to no-one when Europeans first arrived. The court ruled that Aborigines did once own Australia and that where there was continuous association with the land they had the right to claim it back.

In 1993 the Federal government introduced its native title legislation, which formalised the High Court's Mabo ruling. Then, in 1996 the High Court handed down the Wik decision, which established that pastoral leases don't necessarily extinguish native title. The ruling has resulted in some fairly hysterical responses and threatens to undermine the reconciliation process between Aboriginal and non-Aboriginal Australians.

This reconciliation has been further undermined by the emergence of the right-wing independent federal MP, Pauline Hanson. She wants to roll back gains achieved by Aborigines and abolish the Aboriginal and Torres Strait Islander Council (ATSIC) and what she calls 'handouts' to Aborigines.

Another issue that remains unresolved is that of the 'stolen generations'. Aboriginal communities are still suffering the psychological, emotional and social consequences of the assimilation policy. There is a growing movement to persuade the prime minister to apologise for the policies and actions of previous federal and state governments and other authorities.

Meantime, many Aborigines still live in appalling conditions, they're more likely to be jailed than non-Aborigines, Aboriginal deaths in custody remain high and substance abuse is a big problem.

GEOGRAPHY & GEOLOGY

Australia is an island continent whose landscape is the result of gradual changes wrought over millions of years. Although there's still seismic activity in the eastern and western highland areas, Australia is one of the world's most stable land masses and for about 100 million years has been free of the mountain-building forces that have given rise to huge ranges elsewhere.

There are four main areas of NSW, handily falling into an east-to-west pattern.

The Coast

The strip of land between the sea and the Great Divide runs from Tweed Heads on the Queensland border to Cape Howe on the Victorian border. The entire coast is lined with superb beaches and Australians' love-affair with 'The Beach' has plenty of opportunity for consummation. Right along the coast but especially in the southern half, there are many bays, lakes and meandering estuaries backing the beaches.

The Great Dividing Range

This great mountain range runs the length of Australia's east coast. In the south of NSW the range rears up to form the Snowy Mountains, with Australia's highest peak, Mt Kosciuszko (2228m). The enormous Kosciuszko National Park protects much of the 'Snowies'.

The eastern side of the range tends to form a steep escarpment and is usually heavily

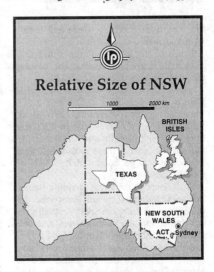

Relative Size of NSW

forested. The cool-climate rainforests in the south and the subtropical rainforests in the north are some of the most beautiful places in the world.

Most of the ancient range's peaks have been worn down to a series of plateaus or tablelands, the largest ones being the New England tableland, the Blue Mountains, the southern highlands and the Monaro tableland.

The Western Slopes

The western side of the Great Dividing Range is less steep than the eastern and dwindles into a series of foothills and valleys which provide some of the most fertile farmland in the country.

The Western Plains

The western slopes of the Great Divide peter out about 300km inland from the coast, and from here west the state is almost entirely flat, with only the odd undulation and hill (generally honoured with the title of 'mountain') to break the huge horizon. Right on the western edge of NSW, Broken Hill sits at the end of a long, low range which juts into the state from South Australia and is rich with minerals.

North of the Darling River, which cuts diagonally across the plains, the country takes on the red soil of the outback.

Rivers

There are two types of rivers in NSW. Short, swift and bountiful rivers rise in the Great Dividing Range and flow east to the sea. In the north of the state these eastward-flowing rivers have large coastal deltas and are mighty watercourses.

Also rising in the Great Dividing Range, but meandering westward across the dry plains to reach the sea in South Australia, are the Darling and the Murray rivers, and their significant tributaries such as the Lachlan and the Murrumbidgee. These rivers have often changed their sluggish courses, and the Murray-Darling basin takes in nearly all of the state west of the Great Divide. The plains are riddled with creeks, swamps and lakes which were once part of the river system but are now usually dry – except when they are in flood.

Land Use

Most of the state is farmland, much of it pretty marginal. By the mid-19th century sheep-farming had been at least attempted throughout the entire state, with ponderous bullock wagons hauling the wool clip across hundreds of kilometres of tough country to river ports such as Bourke, Wilcannia and Hay. Today there are still sheep stations in the most unlikely terrain.

There has been a lot of diversification since then, with wheat, rice, cotton and beef becoming important export products. The wide range of climates means that just about every fruit and vegetable imaginable is grown here.

Despite the wholesale clearing of forests, the economic importance of native timber was recognised fairly early and the Forestry Commission was allocated vast tracts of forest. Many state forests have since become national parks.

Most of the dense forest is in the Great Dividing Range, partly because there was less incentive to clear such steep country for sheep stations, and partly because that's where much of the forest was in the first place.

CLIMATE

Australia's seasons are the antithesis of those in Europe and North America. It's hot in December and many people spend Christmas at the beach, while in July and August it's midwinter. Summer starts in December, autumn in March, winter in June and spring in September.

The climate in NSW varies depending on the location, but the rule of thumb is that the further north you go the warmer it'll be. Geographical factors tend to make it hotter (and drier) the further west you are.

Although there's more likelihood of cloudy weather in midwinter, rainfall is generally sparse and unpredictable.

Sydney is blessed with a temperate climate. The temperature rarely falls below 10°C except overnight in the middle of winter and, although temperatures can hit 40°C during summer, the average summer maximum is a pleasant 25°C. Average monthly rainfall ranges from 75 mm to 130 mm. However, torrential downpours are not uncommon, especially October to March. When it's hot and the humidity skyrockets, the climate can become quite oppressive, day and night.

Canberra suffers the more extreme climate of the high country, with harsh frosts and some snow in winter, and baking days in summer. Spring and autumn are the best times to visit the national capital.

Summer

The whole state is hot, with temperatures rising above 40°C in the north-west corner, and not much less on the rest of the baking plains. The air quivers and shakes above the boiling horizon, and mirages are common. Bourke holds the record for the state's highest recorded temperature, a blistering 51.7°C in the shade (that's 125° F) and shares an old record of 37 consecutive days over

100°F (38°C). Tibooburra, in the north-western corner, is regarded as the state's hottest town. Of course, there are a lot of empty spaces in the far west, and who knows how hot it gets out there?

Luckily, the places with extreme temper-atures are also very dry, and the heat can be bearable if you drink lots of water – without water, the heat quickly becomes life-threat-ening. If you're travelling in remote regions you *must* carry water.

In the Great Dividing Range, the days can be hot but the nights are often pleasantly cool. Summer on the south coast is as hot as you could want for a seaside holiday, but when a cool change arrives the temperature drops lower than it would on the north coast. Sydney and the north coast can be humid, with spectacular thunderstorms. Although you get the odd very hot day, coastal temper-atures are usually below the mid-30s.

Autumn

In the Great Dividing Range and the south-ern parts of the western slopes, the days become cool, deciduous trees turn red and gold, and the clear nights often bring frosts. In Sydney the humidity recedes and the warm, clear days make this an ideal time to visit. On the coast the water temperature stays quite warm until the beginning of winter.

Winter

Temperatures in the far west drop to a com-fortable level and the skies are often blue and clear. There can be frosts at night out on the plains, but this is the best time to visit the outback.

Up on the Great Dividing Range it's chilly, with heavy frosts and occasional snowfalls, but it's only in the Snowy Mountains that the snow accumulates.

Sydney slips into winter gradually, with sometimes gloomy weather in June and July but nothing like a dismal European (or Mel-bourne) winter.

Spring

You don't have to look hard to be aware of

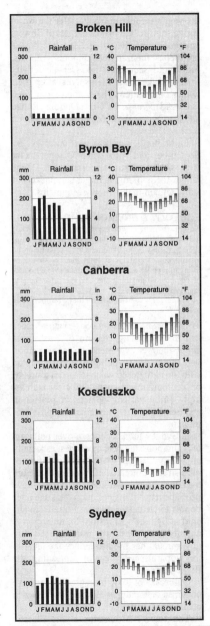

the year's turning in NSW. After the warm spring rains on the plains, carpets of flowers emerge among the tall grasses, and on the north coast the frangipani blooms. Animals, birds and insects burst into frenetic activity – and snakes sun themselves after their winter hibernation. The wattle blooms, and in the old towns of the Great Dividing Range and the Central West, deciduous trees put on their new leaves.

In the north, spring is well underway by September, and by the end of October the far west is becoming uncomfortably hot. On the ranges the cool nights linger and pockets of snow remain in the Snowy Mountains.

ECOLOGY & ENVIRONMENT

No-one thought of conserving anything ... When jellied, fly-blown human backs had the sanction of society, there was no tenderness towards animals, no artistic or scientific realisation that in Australia's living unique flora, fauna and avifauna were masterpieces beyond anything she can ever contribute to museums and galleries.

Miles Franklin, *All that Swagger,* **1936**

With growing focus on conservation issues and the increasing concern of Australians about their environment, the conservation vote is important to political parties. Coupled with the recognised value in 'green tourism' or 'ecotourism', many natural areas increasingly enjoy varying degrees of protection and management. Nevertheless, problems remain.

In Sydney there's concern over pollution of its harbour and ocean beaches, especially after heavy rainfall when billions of litres of rubbish and untreated effluent emerge from overflow points. Millions of dollars have been spent installing pollution traps and litter booms to clean stormwater. Noise from aircraft at Sydney's Kingsford Smith airport is a major issue for nearby residents; the state government has tried to reduce the level in the worst affected areas by 'spreading' the flight paths.

Outbreaks of toxic blue-green algae have occurred on the upper Hawkesbury River in recent years.

The Snowy Mountains Hydro-Electric Scheme was hailed as a marvel of engineering when completed in 1974. Its dams capture the waters of a number of rivers including the Snowy, Murrumbidgee and Murray. The wine producing and rice and fruit growing industries benefited enormously from the secure water supply. But little account was taken of the environmental impact of diverting water for irrigation and electricity. Fish populations in the Snowy River have dwindled and salinisation of the land, caused by tree clearing and irrigation, has grown rapidly. Trees, like the red river gum, that depended on regular flooding for survival, have also declined.

See also Introduced Species and Endangered Species under the Flora & Fauna section below.

On a more positive note, after long-running discussions involving the state government, environmentalists and the logging industry the 90,000 hectare South East Forests National Park near Eden was created in 1997. There's a moratorium on logging of another 30,000 hectares.

If you would like to find out more, the government-run Australian Environmental Resource Information Network has information on many aspects of the environment on the Internet at kaos.erin.gov.au/erin.html.

Australian Conservation Foundation

The Australian Conservation Foundation (ACF; ☎ 9247 1206), 33 George St, the Rocks, Sydney, is the largest nongovernment organisation involved in protecting the environment. It covers a wide range of issues including the greenhouse effect and depletion of the ozone layer, the negative effects of logging, the preservation of rainforests and the problems of land degradation.

Wilderness Society

The Wilderness Society also is a large nongovernment organisation, but more directly focused on protection of wilderness and the designation of wilderness areas. There are Wilderness Society shops where you can buy books, T-shirts, posters, badges etc. Its NSW office (☎ 9552 2355) is on the 1st floor at 263 Broadway, Glebe, Sydney.

National Trust of Australia
The National Trust is dedicated to preserving historic buildings. It owns a number of them throughout the country which are open to the public. Many other buildings are 'classified' by the National Trust to try to ensure their preservation. It also owns and manages a number of museums and galleries and is actively involved in conservation programmes.

The National Trust produces some excellent literature, including a fine series of walking-tour guides to many cities. These guides are often available from local tourist offices or from National Trust offices and are usually free even to nonmembers. Membership is worth considering, however, because it entitles you to free entry to National Trust properties for your year of membership. Addresses of the National Trust offices are:

Australian Capital Territory
    2 Light St, Griffith, ACT 2603 (☎ 6239 5222)
New South Wales
    Observatory Hill, Sydney, NSW 2000 (☎ 9258 0123)

Greenpeace
Greenpeace is a global organisation that campaigns on a diverse range of environmental issues from the dumping of toxic waste to commercial whaling. Over the next few years one of Greenpeace Australia's main goals is to ensure that Sydney meets its commitment to a 'green' Olympic Games in 2000. Its national office (☎ 9261 4666) is at 35-9 Liverpool St, Sydney.

Environment Centres
In many towns you'll find environment centres, run by volunteers and concerned with local issues. It's always worth dropping in as the people are friendly and can be a good source of information, both about the natural environment of the area and on local events such as markets and fundraising dances.

Australian Trust for Conservation Volunteers
The Australian Trust for Conservation Volunteers (ATCV; ☎ 9564 1244), 2 Holt St, Stanmore in Sydney, runs a large number of conservation projects around the country. It provides transport, food and accommodation for volunteers in return for a contribution to help cover costs. Most projects are either for a weekend or a week. It's an excellent way to get involved with the conservation movement and, at the same time, visit some of the more interesting areas of the country.

You can organise a stint with the ATCV from overseas, on a package with World Travellers Network (☎ 9264 2477), 14 Wentworth Ave, Sydney, NSW 2010.

WWOOF
Willing Workers on Organic Farms (WWOOF) has been operating in Australia since 1981 and is well established. The idea is that you do a few hours' work each day on a farm in return for bed and board. Becoming a WWOOFer is a great way to meet people and to travel cheaply. There are about 750 WWOOF associates in Australia, mostly in Victoria, NSW and Queensland.

To join WWOOF (☎ 5155 0218) send $25 for one person or $30 for two people travelling together and a photocopy of your driver's licence or passport data page to WWOOF, Box LP, Buchan, Victoria 3885 and you'll receive a membership number and a booklet listing WWOOF places in Australia.

FLORA & FAUNA
Native Plants
Australia has an enormous diversity of plant species – more than Europe and Asia combined.

Australia's distinctive vegetation began to take shape about 55 million years ago when it broke from the supercontinent of Gondwanaland, drifting away from Antarctica to warmer climes. At this time, Australia was completely covered by cool-climate rainforest, but due to its geographic isolation and the gradual drying of the continent, rainforests retreated, plants like eucalypts and wattles (acacias) took over and grasslands expanded. Eucalypts and wattles were able to adapt to warmer temperatures, the increased natural occurrence of fire and the later use of fire for hunting and other purposes by Aborigines. Now many species actually benefit from fire (or, more correctly, from the smoke from fires).

The gum tree, or eucalypt, is ubiquitous except in the deepest rainforests and the most arid regions. Of the 700 species of the genus *Eucalyptus*, 95% occur naturally in Australia, the rest in New Guinea, the Philippines and Indonesia.

Gum trees vary in form and height from the tall, straight hardwoods such as mountain ash *(Eucalyptus regnans)* and river red-gum *(E. camaldulensis)* to the stunted, twisted snow gum *(E. pauciflora)* with its colourful trunk striations. Other distinctive gums are the spotted gum *(E. maculata)* of NSW's coast; the scribbly gum *(E. haemastoma)*, which has scribbly insect tracks on its bark; and the ghost gum *(E. papuana)*, with its distinctive white trunk. Many varieties flower, the wood is prized and its oil is used for pharmaceutical and perfumed products.

Around 600 species of wattle are found in Australia. Many wattles have deep green leaves and bright yellow to orange flowers. Most species flower during late winter and spring, when the country is ablaze with wattle and the reason for the choice of green and gold as the national colours is obvious. Wattle is Australia's floral emblem.

Other common natives include grevilleas, hakeas, banksias, waratahs (telopeas), bottlebrushes (callistemons), paperbarks (melaleucas), tea-trees (leptospermums), boronias and native pines (casuarinas).

Mammals

Native animals you're most likely to see in the wild are wallabies and kangaroos, possums and koalas. However, there's a huge range of small, mainly nocturnal animals going about their business unobserved. Part of the reason for Australia's appalling record of animal extinction is that many species died out before anyone (anyone European, that is) knew they existed. This process continues today.

Australia's most distinctive fauna are the marsupials and monotremes. Marsupials such as kangaroos and koalas give birth to partially developed young which they suckle in a pouch. Monotremes – platypuses and echidnas – lay eggs but also suckle their young.

Kangaroos The extraordinary breeding cycle of the kangaroo is well adapted to Australia's harsh, often unpredictable environment.

The young kangaroo, or joey, just millimetres long at birth, claws its way unaided to the mother's pouch where it attaches itself to a nipple that expands inside its mouth. A day or two later the mother mates again, but the new embryo doesn't begin to develop until the first joey has left the pouch permanently.

Grey Kangaroo, cuter than his brother Red

At this point the mother produces two types of milk – one formula to feed the joey at heel, the other for the baby in her pouch. If environmental conditions are right, the mother then mates again. If food or water is scarce, however, the breeding cycle is interrupted until conditions improve.

As well as many species of wallabies (some endangered), there are two main species of kangaroos in NSW, the western grey and the majestic red kangaroo, which is common in the far west and can stand two metres tall. Unlike most cute kangaroos, the red has a facial expression which suggests that it don't take no aggravation. Reds have been known to disembowel dogs that are bothering them.

Possums There's a wide range of possums – they seem to have adapted to all sorts of conditions, including those of the city, where you'll find them in parks especially around dusk. Some large species are found in suburban roofs and eat cultivated plants and food scraps. If you're camping, the weird noises that squabbling possums make can be spooky.

Wombats Wombats are slow, solid, powerfully built marsupials with broad heads and short, stumpy legs. These fairly placid, easily tamed creatures are legally killed by farmers, who object to the damage done to paddocks by wombats digging large burrows and tunnelling under fences.

The common wombat, slow and stumpy but a good undercover agent. An Australian mole!

Koalas Distantly related to the wombat, koalas are found along the eastern seaboard. Their cuddly appearance belies an irritable nature, and they'll scratch and bite if sufficiently provoked.

Koalas initially carry their babies in pouches, but later the larger young cling to their mothers' backs. They feed only on the leaves of certain types of eucalypt (found mainly in the forests of the Great Dividing Range) and are particularly sensitive to changes to their habitat.

Platypuses & Echidnas The platypus and the echidna are the only living representatives of the monotremes, the most primitive group of mammals. Both lay eggs, as reptiles do, but suckle their young on milk secreted directly through the skin from mammary glands.

The amphibious platypus has a duck-like bill, webbed feet and a beaver-like body. Males have poisonous spurs on their hind feet. The platypus is able to sense electric currents in the water and uses this ability to track its prey. Platypuses are shy creatures, but they occur in many rivers.

The echidna is a spiny anteater that hides from predators by digging vertically into the ground and covering itself with dirt, or by rolling itself into a ball and raising its sharp quills.

Dingoes Australia's native dog is the dingo, domesticated by the Aborigines and a stable breed for at least 3000 years, possibly much longer. Its ancestor is the Indian wolf. After the Europeans arrived and Aborigines could no longer hunt freely, dingoes again became 'wild', and by preying on sheep they earned the wrath of graziers. These sensitive, intelligent dogs are legally considered to be vermin. Some are still found in the high country.

Birds
Emus The only bird larger than the emu is the African ostrich, also flightless. The emu is a shaggy-feathered bird with an often curious nature. After the female emu lays the

eggs, the male hatches them and raises the young. Emus are common in the Riverina and the far west.

Parrots & Cockatoos There's an amazing variety of these birds. The noisy pink and grey galahs are among the most common, although the sulphur-crested cockatoos have to be the noisiest. Rainbow lorikeets have one of the most brilliant colour schemes and in some parks they're not backward in accepting a free feed from visitors.

Kookaburras A member of the kingfisher family, the kookaburra is heard as much as it is seen – you can't miss its loud, cackling laugh, usually at dawn and sunset. Kookaburras can become quite tame and pay regular visits to friendly households.

Lyrebirds The lyrebird, found in moist forest areas, is famous for both its vocal abilities and its beauty. Lyrebirds are highly skilled mimics which copy segments of other birds' songs to create unique hybrid compositions. During the courting season, with his colourful fern-like tailfeathers spread like a fan, the male puts on a sensational song-and-dance routine to impress potential partners.

Magpies The black-and-white magpie (no relation to the European bird of the same name) has a distinctive and beautiful warbling call. Magpies can be aggressively territorial when nesting (around September). Being 'swooped' by a magpie is an unnerving experience as it dives at you silently from behind.

Reptiles
Snakes There are many species of snake in NSW, all protected. Many are poisonous, some deadly, but few are aggressive and they'll usually get out of your way before you realise that they're there. See Dangers & Annoyances in the Facts for the Visitor chapter for ways of avoiding being bitten and what to do in the unlikely event that you are.

Lizards There's a wide variety of lizards,

from tiny skinks to prehistoric-looking goannas which can grow up to 2.5m long, although most species in NSW are much smaller. Goannas can run very fast and when threatened use those big claws to climb the nearest tree – or perhaps the nearest leg!

Bluetongue lizards, slow-moving and stumpy, are children's favourites and are sometimes kept as pets. Their even slower and stumpier relations, shinglebacks, are common in the outback.

Introduced Species
The Acclimatisation Society was a bunch of do-gooders in the Victorian era who devoted themselves to 'improving' the countries of the British Empire by introducing plants and animals. On the whole, their work was disastrous.

Exotic animals thriving in NSW include rabbits, cats (big, bad feral versions of the domestic moggie), pigs (now bristly black razorbacks with long tusks) and goats. In the alps and towards the Queensland border you might see wild horses, mean brutes which travel in bad-tempered packs. These have all been disastrous for native animals, as predators and as competitors for food and water.

Probably the biggest change to the ecosystem has been caused by another exotic animal: the sheep. To make room for sheep there was wholesale clearing of the bush, and the plains were planted with exotic grasses. Many small marsupials became extinct when their habitats changed, and major reasons for the incarceration and massacre of Aborigines were that they hunted sheep and resisted the theft of their land by graziers.

Disruption of Aboriginal land-management meant that there was no longer regular burning of the bush and plains, causing less-frequent but disastrous bushfires which fed on the accumulated growth, and a change in an ecosystem which depended on regular low-intensity fires for germination.

Sheep were the first hoofed animals to tread NSW's light, fine topsoil, and in a remarkably short time they had trodden it into a hard-packed mass which couldn't

support many species of native flora and was
vulnerable to erosion.

Animal Rescue

You see a lot of native animals killed by the
roadside. They have no road sense at all. You
might find injured animals, especially young
marsupials which often survive road trauma
that kills their mothers, hidden in the pouch.
Essentially, baby animals separated from
their mothers will be cold (so wrap them up),
stressed (disturb them as little as possible)
and dehydrated (but don't give them cow's
milk).

Wildlife Information & Rescue (WIRES)
is a voluntary organisation which cares for
native animals. There are WIRES branches
in many places, but for current addresses
contact the Sydney head office (☎ 9975
1633/5567), 5 Darley St, Forestville. Alternatively, a vet will know of local animal
welfare organisations.

Endangered Species

The yellow-footed rock wallaby was thought
to be extinct until a group was found in
western NSW in the 1960s. National parks
were created to protect them and local
farmers agreed to protect them on their properties. But the wallabies can't compete with
feral goats for food and shelter and their
numbers are decreasing. They can still be
seen in Mootwingee National Park north-
east of Broken Hill.

Since the late 1980s the numbers of
Kosciuszko National Park's yellow-and-
black corroboree frog have declined rapidly
and no-one knows why. In 1997, in an
attempt to save the species, 500 eggs were
collected and sent to Melbourne for hatch-
ing, after which the tadpoles were released
back into the park.

Overfishing, off the southern coast of
NSW and elsewhere, has brought the southern bluefin tuna to the edge of extinction.
Industrial fishing methods used to catch the
tuna and other fish have also reduced the
numbers of albatross who feed off them.
Greenpeace has launched a campaign to try
to save them.

Golden Bell Frog

The first winner in the Sydney Olympics is the
golden bell frog, a colony of which was discovered in a disused brickpit in the early 1990s in
what is now Sydney Olympic Park. The frogs
are an endangered species and only a few
colonies are thought to exist in Australia. Plans
to build tennis courts and a multistorey car park
on the brickpit site were shelved. Instead, in
order to protect the frogs, a series of tunnels
and ponds were built at a cost of $400,000. The
tunnels are intended to allow them to travel
safely from the brickpit site to nearby Millen-
nium Park. ■

Along the north coast around Port Macquarie, urban expansion, traffic and the rise
in domestic animals is putting enormous
pressure on koalas and their habitats.

Urban expansion north of Sydney is
threatening the extinction of the native plant,
grevillea caleyi. They can still be seen in
Ku-ring-gai Chase National Park and along
the roadsides near Mona Vale.

National Parks

There are over 80 national parks in NSW,
covering about four million hectares and
protecting environments as diverse as the
peaks of the Snowy Mountains, the subtropical rainforest of the Border Ranges and the
vast arid plains of the outback.

Many parks are World Heritage areas of
exceptional beauty and significance. Some
parks include designated wilderness areas
which offer outstanding remote-area
walking. The most recent addition to the park
list is the 90,000-hectare South-East Forests
National Park in the south-east corner of the
state.

The National Parks & Wildlife Service
(NPWS) does a good job, and many national
parks have visitor centres where you can
learn about the area, as well as campsites and
often walking tracks. Where there isn't a
visitor centre, visit the nearest NPWS office
for information. Bush camping (ie, heading
off into the bush and camping where you

please) is allowed in many national parks, but not all – check before you go.

The NPWS head office is at 43 Bridge St, Hurstville in Sydney. It has an information line (☎ 9584 6333) open 8.30 am to 4 pm, although there are often long delays and the information is pretty general. For information on specific parks, it's better to call the ranger or district office.

There is, at least theoretically, an entrance fee for all national parks: generally around $5 to $7.50 per car, and $12 *per day* for Kosciuszko National Park. Camping fees are about $5 to $8, often less for bush camping.

There's a $50 annual pass which gives free entry (but not free camping) to all parks except Kosciuszko. It probably isn't worth buying unless you plan a systematic coverage (not a bad idea, as there are some magnificent parks), but the $60 pass which includes Kosciuszko is definitely worthwhile if you plan to visit Kosciuszko plus a few other parks.

The NPWS is also responsible for some other reserves. State recreation areas (SRAs) are set aside for recreation activities. They often contain bushland, but the quality of the forest might not be as good as in national parks. Many are centred on lakes or large dams where watersports are popular and they can be crowded in summer. There's often commercial accommodation (usually a caravan park), and bush camping is usually not permitted. There are exceptions to this, however.

Nature reserves are generally smaller reserves, usually with day-use facilities, protecting specific ecosystems.

Historic sites protect areas of historical significance, such as the ghost town of Hill End near Bathurst and Aboriginal rock-art sites.

State Forests

State forests are timber reserves, most of which are systematically logged. They cover around three million hectares and can be beautiful, although logging often means that the bush is young and of poor quality. Bush camping (free) is allowed in most state forests, but so are trail bikes, 4WDs, pets …

GOVERNMENT & POLITICS

Australia has a federal system of government, with elements of both the US and Westminster systems. The various state governments have no control over national defence, foreign affairs, immigration, the postal service or income tax, and they're dependent on the federal government for a lot of their funding. The High Court can overrule a state's Supreme Court. Apart from this, state governments are pretty much autonomous Westminster-style governments, with premiers occupying positions equivalent to that of prime minister. There are upper and lower houses in most states, both elected.

Australia's head of state is the governor general, and each state has a governor. Governors are technically the British monarch's representative, although they are appointed by the various Australian governments.

Political Parties

There are three main parties. The Liberal Party isn't especially liberal – it's the party of the conservatives and stands for free enterprise, law and order, 'family values' and the like. The Liberal's minority coalition partner is the National Party, once the National Country Party, which mainly represents country seats.

The Australian Labor Party (ALP) is a social-democratic party that has been in existence for over 100 years and grew out of the great shearers' strikes last century.

The ALP was narrowly returned to power in NSW in 1995 and the current premier is Bob Carr.

The only other party of substance is the Australian Democrats, which has largely carried the flag for the growing green movement. At the federal level it holds the balance of power in the senate.

The NSW state parliament includes several independents, including Fred Nile, religious-fundamentalist leader of the Festival of Light party. Fred and his Christian

An Australian Republic for 2000?

One of the issues Australia is debating is whether or not it should become a republic. Republican murmurings have always been a part of the political scene, but it was the governor general's dismissal of the Whitlam government in 1975 which caused many people to take the idea seriously. In recent years the desire for change has become widespread, as more people feel that constitutional ties with Britain are no longer relevant.

This is especially true with Sydney having been awarded the Olympic Games in the year 2000. Although there has been strong debate over whether Australia should become a republic, it's probable that Australia's head of state will still be the British monarch at the time of the Olympics. Traditionally, a country's head of state opens the games, but many people feel that an Australian should open them. Although the governor general, the British monarch's representative, is now always an Australian he (there hasn't been a 'she' yet) is still the representative of a foreign head of state. And the election in 1996 of a conservative federal government means it may be a long time before the ties to the British monarch are done away with. So who will open the games? ■

supporters are against just about everything; Sydney's Gay & Lesbian Mardi Gras really gets their blood boiling.

ECONOMY

Australia is a relatively affluent industrialised nation, but much of its wealth still comes from agriculture and mining. NSW fits this pattern, with coal exports being the greatest earner of foreign exchange. Other important minerals are gold, silver, copper and lead.

Over 65% of NSW is farmland. The main crops are wheat, barley, oats and rice (about 90% of the rice is exported to Asia). Fruit and timber are important in the south-east, and the Hunter Valley north of Newcastle is the state's principal wine region. Wool and livestock are also significant money earners.

In manufacturing, some of NSW's chief industries are iron, steel, chemicals and textiles.

As in the rest of Australia (and the world), tourism is gaining more importance especially in the lead-up to the Olympic games. It's estimated that the games will bring in about $7 billion from TV rights, sponsorships, licensing fees, marketing royalties and ticket sales.

Most of Australia's foreign trade is conducted in NSW.

The main industry in the ACT is bureaucracy, although there is a growing private sector and in rural areas sheep-grazing is significant. Canberra is also the national pornography centre!

POPULATION & PEOPLE

The population of NSW is just over six million, more than a third of Australia's total. With well over four million people living within 100km or so of Sydney, the rest of the state is sparsely populated. More than half the state has a population density of less than two people per sq km.

The ACT's population is around 282,000, with almost everyone living in Canberra.

If you come to Australia in search of a real Australian, you'll find one quite easily. He or she may be a Lebanese cafe-owner, an English used-car salesperson, an Aboriginal musician, a Malaysian architect or a Greek greengrocer.

Like the rest of Australia, NSW has a diverse population. Mass migration since WWII has profoundly changed Australia. Approximately 20% of people in NSW were born in other countries and many more are children of people who were born in other countries.

About 70,000 people in NSW considered themselves to be Aborigines or Torres Strait Islanders in the 1991 census. In south-east Australia, the word Aborigines use to describe themselves is Koori.

Although many Australians have British

or Irish ancestors, nearly all regard themselves as Australians.

The Chinese have been here since the 19th century, but kept a low profile until after WWII, when mass immigration began. After WWII, many Jewish survivors of the Holocaust came to Australia, along with many other European refugees. Subsequent large scale immigration has drawn many people from Italy, Greece, Turkey, Lebanon, Yugoslavia, the Pacific and, more recently, from South-East Asia (especially Vietnam). Many people from Hong Kong now live in Australia as do significant minorities from many other countries.

Although more recent immigrants tend to stay in the larger cities, you'll find non-Anglo-Celtic people all over the state. Where there are orchards or vineyards, chances are you'll find people of Italian descent, often Australians of many generations' standing. Most country towns have a Chinese restaurant, while some have Vietnamese or Thai restaurants. As soon as you cross the Great Dividing Range, however, you enter Anglo-Celtic country.

Note that Asia means the countries of the 'far east' to most Australians; people from the Indian subcontinent, the 'near east' and the 'middle east' are not commonly considered to be Asian. (Eurocentric terms are still often used, although the term 'our northern neighbours' is replacing 'far east'.)

ARTS
Aboriginal Art
Aboriginal art has undergone a major revival in the last two decades. Artists throughout the country have found both a means to express and preserve ancient dreaming values, and a way to share this rich cultural heritage with the wider community.

While the so-called dot paintings of the central deserts are the most readily identifiable and probably most popular form of contemporary Aboriginal art, there's a huge range of material being produced – bark paintings from Arnhem Land, wood carving and silk-screen printing from the Tiwi Islands north of Darwin, batik printing and wood carving from central Australia, and more.

The initial forms of artistic expression were rock carvings, body painting and ground designs, and the earliest engraved designs known to exist date back at least 30,000 years. Art has always been an integral part of Aboriginal life, a connection between past and present, the supernatural and the earthly, people and the land.

Earthly art was a reflection of the various peoples' ancestral Dreaming – the 'Creation', when the earth's physical features were formed by the struggles between powerful supernatural ancestors such as the Rainbow Serpent. Not only was the physical layout mapped but codes of behaviour were also laid down. Although these laws have been diluted and adapted in the last 200 years, they still provide the basis for today's Aborigines. Ceremonies, rituals and sacred paintings are all based on the Dreaming.

Painting
It's interesting to see what the first European landscape painters made of Australia. The colours seem wrong and the features they chose to depict aren't what would now be regarded as 'typically Australian'. Colonial artists such as Conrad Martens painted Turneresque landscapes of Sydney Harbour in the 1850s that now startle many Sydneysiders.

In the 1880s, artists discovered that the Australian landscape had its own moods and that the quality of light in Sydney was radically different from Europe. Major Australian artists, such as Arthur Streeton and Tom Roberts in Melbourne, came to Sydney and established an artist's camp at Little Sirius Cove in Mosman in 1891 which became a focal point for Sydney artists. Their paintings have virtually defined all subsequent reactions to the harbour and its surrounding bushlands. Similarly, Grace Cossington-Smith's paintings of the Harbour Bridge under construction in the 1930s also created enduring images of the city.

At the turn of the century, Australian

painters began to flirt with Art Nouveau. Sydney Long painted bush scenes peopled with fairies in a strange attempt to mythologise and personify the landscape, something Aborigines had been doing successfully for thousands of years.

In the 1940s, a flowering of predominantly expressionist art began. The main practitioners were mostly from Melbourne, but painters such as Sidney Nolan, Arthur Boyd, Albert Tucker and Russell Drysdale transcended locale to approach all Australians on the level of myth.

Less academic, but vigorous and distinctively Australian, the Brushmen of the Bush of Broken Hill, such as Pro Hart and Jack Absalom, produce naive works that are well worth seeing. Broken Hill, a mining town, is, somewhat surprisingly, a major art centre.

Sydney artist, Brett Whitely, who died in 1992, was an internationally celebrated *enfant terrible* who painted luscious, colourful canvases, often with distorted Bacon-like figures. His paintings of Sydney Harbour are unsurpassed; a gallery dedicated to his work is in Surry Hills. Probably Sydney's most famous – and commercially successful – living artist is Ken Done whose simple, vivid works adorn everything from coasters to T-shirts.

Other modern artists include Ian Fairweather, Keith Looby and Sandy Bruch.

Literature

While Tom Roberts and his mates were developing a distinctive art style, there were a number of writers doing similar things with the written word.

Two of the first distinctively Australian writers to achieve popular acclaim were Henry Lawson (1867-1922) and A B ('Banjo') Paterson (1864-1941).

Paterson's generally cheerful poems and short stories have to some extent been hijacked by the nostalgia industry, but they're worth reading if only to understand the myths being pushed by advertising agencies. Think of him as a distant relation of Kipling and you'll be on the right track.

Lawson is a different matter. A gloomy alcoholic for much of his life, he nevertheless wrote some extremely funny short stories, such as *The Loaded Dog*, as well as bitter reflections on the Australian way of life, such as *The Drover's Wife*. His poetry tends to be mawkish but it remains popular.

Less well known, Joseph Furphy (1843-1912) wrote only one book, but one that is arguably among the best ever written in Australia. *Such is Life* is on the surface a rambling, funny series of bush yarns, but is surprisingly modern in its construction and attitude.

Miles Franklin (1879-1954) made a decision early in her life to become a writer rather than a traditional wife and mother. Her best-known book, *My Brilliant Career*, was also her first. It was written at the turn of the century when the author was only 20, and brought her both widespread fame and criticism. She endowed an annual award for an Australian novel; today the Miles Franklin Award is the most prestigious in the country.

Another well known writer of this century is Eleanor Dark, who in the 1940s wrote the historical trilogy *The Timeless Land*, *Storm of Time* and *No Barrier*. These covered the period 1788-1914, and were highly unusual at the time for the sympathetic treatment they gave to the Aboriginal culture.

The works of Nobel Prize-winner Patrick White are some of the best to come out of Australia. His better-known books include *Voss* (1957), which contrasts the outback with colonial life in Sydney.

A reading list focused on Sydney and NSW might include the following. *Seven Poor Men of Sydney* (1934) is a poetic account of a cross-section of Sydneysiders by expatriate author Christina Stead. *The Harp in the South* (1948) and *Poor Man's Orange* (1949) are Ruth Park's autobiographical accounts of growing up in Surry Hills. David Ireland's *The Glass Canoe* is an excellent novel exploring urban life in general and pub culture in particular. Frank Moorhouse's *Days of Wine and Rage* (1980) evokes 1970s Sydney. *They're a Weird Mob* (1955) by Nino Culotta was a humorous tale of an Italian migrant in Sydney. Rosa

Cappiello's *Oh Lucky Country* (1984) is a harrowing account of the modern migrant experience.

Less serious but offering an insight into the seamier side of Sydney is the work of crime writer Peter Corris. The genre has produced several other authors, including John Baxter and Marele Day.

Kate Grenville's *Lilian's Story*, loosely based on the life of Sydney eccentric, Bea Miles, was made into a film. Other books worth reading are Dorothy Porter's *Monkey Mask* set in the Blue Mountains, Janetter Turner Hospital's *The Last Magician*, set in part around Newtown railway station, and Justin Ettler's *River Ophelia*.

Music

In NSW you can hear everything from world-class opera to grungy pub bands. As with the other arts, most Australian music derives from foreign forms but often has a distinctive local twist.

Australian folk music is a mixture of English, Irish and Scottish roots, in much the same way as American folk music. Bush bands, playing fast-paced and high-spirited folk music for dancing, can be anything from performers trotting out standards such as *Click Go the Shears* to serious musicians who happen to like a rollicking time. Fiddles and banjos feature, plus the indigenous 'lagerphone', a percussion instrument made from a great many beer-bottle tops nailed to a stick and shaken or banged on the ground. If you have a chance to go to a bush dance, take it! Aboriginal music is a strong influence on contemporary folk music. The Bush Music Festival in Glen Innes is a good place to sample a range of folk music.

Country music, of the American variety, is popular west of the Great Dividing Range, and Tamworth's big festival is the place to be.

The rock music scene is pretty interesting and although Sydney isn't such a breeding-ground for innovative groups as Melbourne is (introspection isn't a popular Sydney pastime), everyone who's anyone will play in Sydney eventually. See the Entertainment section in the Sydney chapter for some venues.

Recent years have seen a merging of Aboriginal music with rock. This music is really different and has probably made the greatest contribution to non-Aboriginal understanding of contemporary Aboriginal culture. Notable Aboriginal rock musicians include the group Yothu Yindi, Archie Roach and Christine Anu. Not only do they play good music but they're uncompromisingly Aboriginal in their outlook.

Theatre & Dance

The prestigious Sydney Theatre Company (STC) provides a balanced programme of modern, classical, local and foreign drama. The National Institute of Dramatic Art (NIDA) in Sydney is a breeding ground for new talent. The institute stages performances of students' work.

The leading contemporary Australian playwright is Sydney-based David Williamson, whose dissections of Australian middle-class rituals began in 1971 with *The Removalists* and *Don's Party*. Recent Williamson plays include *Money & Friends* and *Sanctuary*, an examination of the ethics of journalism and the dynamics of political correctness. Other interesting contemporary playwrights include Louis Nowra and Michael Gow.

The Australian Ballet, the national ballet company, is considered one of the finest companies in the world. It tours Australia's major cities, performing a mixed programme of classical and modern ballets. It usually presents four ballets a year during its season at the Opera House.

Under the guidance of artistic director, Graeme Murphy, the Sydney Dance Company (SDC) has become Australia's leading contemporary-dance company.

The internationally acclaimed Bangarra Dance Theatre fuses traditional Aboriginal and modern dance.

Cinema

The Australian film industry began as early as 1896, a year after the Lumière brothers opened the world's first cinema in Paris. Australia's first cinema was opened in Sydney in 1896. Maurice Sestier, one of the LumiSres' photographers, came to Australia and made the first films in the streets of Sydney.

Cinema historians regard an Australian film, *Soldiers of the Cross*, as the world's first 'real' movie. It was first screened in 1901, cost £600 to make and was shown throughout America in 1902. A flourishing industry developed and over 250 silent feature films were made before the 1930s, when the talkies and Hollywood took over.

In the 1930s, film companies such as Cinesound, based at Bondi Junction in Sydney, sprang up. Cinesound made 17 features between 1931 and 1940, many based on Australian history or literature. *Forty Thousand Horsemen*, directed by Cinesound's great film-maker Charles Chauvel, was a highlight of this era of locally made and financed films which ended in 1959, the year of Chauvel's death. The cinema in Sydney's Paddington Town Hall is named after him. Chauvel is also noted for giving Errol Flynn his first film role.

Before the introduction of government subsidies in 1969, the Australian film industry found it difficult to compete with US and British interests. The creation of the Australian Film Commission in 1975 helped establish a renaissance of Australian cinema, which is still continuing and today Sydney is a major centre of film production. New South Wales, and Sydney in particular, have formed the backdrop to numerous movies. Recent ones include *Young Einstein* (Palm Beach, *Sweetie* (Willoughby), *Strictly Ballroom* (Pyrmont and Marrickville), *Muriel's Wedding* (Parramatta, Oxford St, Darling Point, Ryde), *Priscilla, Queen of the Desert* (Eskineville), *Lilian's Story* (Sydney Harbour) and *Babe* (the Southern Highlands.)

Architecture

Although NSW has some fine Georgian architecture, mainly in and around Sydney, the Victorian era has left the larger legacy.

Any country town worth its salt has an impressive town hall complete with Corinthian columns. Older courthouses are also in neo-Renaissance style, with domes and colonnaded porticos, but those built around the turn of the century have a distinctive, heavy look to them.

Lands Department buildings are always worth looking out for (some are now state government offices). They're quite different from the more imposing public buildings, being often made of wood with shutters and fanciful fretwork. They seem to be the only large buildings which have attempted to beat the hot climate by cunning rather than sheer bulk.

Railway stations, post offices and banks are also often worth seeing.

The only private buildings to rival these shrines of government and business are pubs, but they make a pretty good fist of it. Although many country pubs are past their prime (the ubiquitous clubs have stolen their customers), many are still spectacularly grand buildings, and all dedicated to the thirst of workers.

Buried in most urban subconscious is a myth about grand old homesteads commanding the plains, their broad verandahs dripping with iron lace. Unfortunately, it *is* a myth. The average farm might contain a roughly-built barn that was once the first homestead, a wooden cottage falling into disrepair or housing the retired patriarch, and a modern brick veneer house which is home to his son, the current farmer (yep; not many daughters get to inherit the family farm). There are exceptions in the districts settled early, but not many.

Around the turn of the century, Australia developed its own style of domestic architecture. Houses of the Federation style, as it is known, were built to make life in a hot climate comfortable, unlike the previous Victorian-era houses which were basically boxes with verandahs tacked on.

California Bungalow and Art Deco became the dominant styles in the 1920s, and there are fine examples of Art Deco apartments still standing in Sydney.

In the 1960s the so-called Sydney School pioneered a distinctively Australian organic architecture that used over-burnt brick and native landscaping to blend into the local environment.

Modern Australian architecture struggles to maintain a distinctive style, with overseas trends dominating large projects and the lowest common denominator applied most to suburban housing. As well as the Sydney Opera House there are some notable modern buildings, such as the Convention Centre at Darling Harbour and the Sydney Football Stadium (both designed by Philip Cox). The museum in Kempsey is a little gem, designed by Glenn Murcutt.

Art Deco is enjoying a resurgence in popularity as can be seen in the design of the Coopers & Lybrand building in Sydney.

At the Museum of Sydney, a modern office tower sits atop the sandstone foundations of Australia's first Government House and has won several architectural awards.

For information on some grand old buildings contact the National Trust (☎ 9258 0123), Observatory Hill in Sydney. The Historic Houses Trust of NSW (☎ 9692 8366), 61 Darghan St, Glebe in Sydney, publishes a useful booklet, *Identifying Australian Houses*.

See the ACT chapter for the distinctive architecture of Canberra.

SOCIETY & CONDUCT
Aboriginal Society
Many non-Aboriginal perceptions of Aboriginal cultures are just wrong. For example 'going walkabout' was not shiftless, irresponsible wandering as it has been so often portrayed by non-Aboriginal people. Complex systems of trade, seasonal food gathering and religious duties meant travel was regular and social and economic ties between widely separated groups were maintained by regular meetings, a process developed over hundreds of centuries.

This lack of understanding is in part due to the fact that the initial, disastrous contact between whites and blacks was often undertaken by avaricious settlers who were hellbent on grabbing land without regard for the British laws, much less the rights of the Aborigines. Not only were these whites likely to act inhumanely but they weren't interested in recording information about the cultures they were destroying.

Non-Aborigines who oppose what they call 'the guilt industry' trot out the maxim that you can't judge historical events by today's standards, but even by 19th-century standards the treatment of Aborigines was bad. And many abuses continued well into the 20th century.

Whites who were interested in other cultures, or were at least prepared to see blacks as people, didn't arrive in most areas until Aboriginal cultures had been severely disrupted by disease and the loss of land. That's why northern Australia, which was settled by Europeans relatively recently, remains the stronghold of traditional cultures.

For a long time even enlightened whites saw Aborigines as a pathetic, childlike race, doomed to extinction. White appreciation of the richness and complexity of Aboriginal cultures is a recent phenomenon and came too late to save the cultures of many peoples in the areas which were settled early. However, much remains and even in NSW, the first area to be settled, Aborigines retain their links with the past.

Places in NSW where you can see concrete remains of traditional culture include rock-art sites in the Sydney area (such as Ku-ring-gai Chase National Park), the Goulburn River National Park in the Hunter Valley, the Grenfell Historic Site near Cobar and Mootwingee National Park near Broken Hill. At Brewarrina there are the remains of large scale stone fish-traps. On the far north coast, for example near Tweed Heads, there are *bora* rings, large ceremonial grounds, and all along the coast there are middens, piles of shells accumulated after centuries of shellfish feasts. Mungo National Park, south-east of Broken Hill, is a treasure house of human history.

The NSW Central Mapping Authority produces an interesting map, *Aboriginal New South Wales*. It shows which peoples

Traditional Aboriginal Culture

The Aborigines have a rich and complex culture, which flourished in Australia for over 40,000 years prior to the arrival of Europeans.

Society & Lifestyle Aborigines were traditionally tribal people living in extended family groups, or bands. Each band had a defined territory, within which were a number of spiritually significant places, known as sacred sites. It was the responsibility of the clan, or particular members of it, to maintain and protect the site in the correct way so that ancestral beings were not offended and would continue to look after the clan. Traditional punishments for those who failed in these responsibilities were often severe, as their actions could affect the whole clan's wellbeing – food and water shortages, natural disasters and mysterious illnesses could all be attributed to disgruntled or offended ancestral beings.

Many Aboriginal communities were semi-nomadic, while others were sedentary. Where food and water were readily available, the people tended to remain in a limited area. When they did wander, it was to visit sacred places to carry out rituals, or perhaps take advantage of seasonal foods available elsewhere. The traditional role of the men was that of hunter, tool-maker and custodian of male law; women reared the children, and gathered and prepared food. There was also female law and ritual which the women would be responsible for.

Environmental Awareness Wisdom and skills obtained over millennia enabled Aborigines to use their environment to the maximum. An intimate knowledge of the behaviour of animals and the correct time to harvest the many plants they utilised ensured that food shortages were rare. They never hunted an animal species or harvested a plant species to the point where it was threatened with extinction. Like other hunter-gatherer peoples of the world, the Aborigines were true ecologists.

Although Aborigines in northern Australia had been in regular contact with the farming peoples of Indonesia for at least 1000 years, the farming of crops and domestication of livestock held no appeal. The only major modification of the landscape practised by the Aborigines was the selective burning of undergrowth in forests and dead grass on the plains. This encouraged new growth, which in turn attracted game animals to the area. It also prevented the build-up of combustible material in the forests, making hunting easier and reducing the possibility of major bushfires. Dingoes were domesticated to assist in the hunt and to guard the camp from intruders.

Technology & Trade Similar technology – for example the throwing-stick (boomerang) and spear – was used throughout the continent, but techniques were adapted to the environment and the species being hunted. In the wetlands of northern Australia, fish-traps hundreds of metres long were built from bamboo and used to catch fish at the end of the wet season. In the area now known as Victoria, permanent stone weirs many km long were used to trap migrating eels, while in the tablelands of Queensland finely woven nets were used to snare herds of wallabies and kangaroos.

Various goods found their way along the long trade-routes which criss-crossed the continent. Many of the items traded, such as certain types of stone or shell, were rare and had great ritual significance. Boomerangs and ochre were other important trade items. Along the trading networks large numbers of people often met for 'exchange ceremonies', where not only goods but also songs and dance styles were passed on. Near Brewarrina in north-west NSW you can still see ingenious stone fish-traps which caught fish to feed the huge gatherings there.

Cultural Life The simplicity of the Aborigines' technology is in contrast with the sophistication of their cultural life. Religion, history, law and art are integrated in complex ceremonies which depict the activities of the ancestral beings, and prescribe codes of behaviour and responsibilities for looking after the land and all living things. The link between the Aborigines and the ancestral beings is totems, and each person has his or her own totem, or Dreaming. These totems take many forms, such as caterpillars, snakes, fish and magpies. Songs explain how the landscape contains these powerful creator ancestors, who can still exert either a benign or a malevolent influence. They also tell of the best places and times to hunt and where to find water in drought years, and specify kinship relations and correct marriage partners.

Ceremonies are still performed in many parts of Australia. Many of the sacred sites are believed to be dangerous, and entry to them is prohibited under traditional Aboriginal law. These restrictions may seem to be based on superstition, but in many cases have a pragmatic origin. For example, one site in northern Australia was believed to cause sores to break out all over the body of anyone visiting the area. Subsequently, the area was found to have a dangerously high level of radiation from naturally occurring radon gas. ∎

lived where at the time of European settlement and gives a rough idea as to the distribution of the various sites.

Today most Aborigines in NSW live an urban life in towns, yet they remain distinctively Aboriginal. In the Sydney suburb of Glebe the Tranby Aboriginal Co-operative College is run by and for Aborigines and Redfern has a large, vital Koori population. Across the state you'll find Koori communities whose voices are beginning to be heard in the political process.

Assimilation policies have been discredited, but there are moves by many Koori communities to participate in the Australian economy on their own terms. Small industries producing Aboriginal-designed fashions are appearing, and in a few places in NSW (such as near Ulladulla) Aboriginal-run tours show the country from the Koori perspective.

Mainstream Society

Australians' self-image as a resourceful, self-reliant people at home in the bush has never been strictly correct. That's not to say that the hardy pioneers, the lusty shearers, the tough bullockies with hearts of gold and the 'lithe, laughing girls, as handy with a horse as a teacup' didn't exist. They did, but they were objects of bemused admiration for the majority, who lived in towns. 'True blue' Aussie values, such as egalitarianism and willingness to give anyone a 'fair go', are still strong. While today's multicultural society has seen narrowness and intolerance diminish, there are still plenty of rednecks out there.

The popular myths about hard riding, hard drinking Australians obscure the fact that there has always been a strong streak of free thinking. Henry Lawson is well known for his idealisation of mateship in the bush, but fewer people remember that his mother, Louisa, began publishing a feminist magazine, *The Dawn*, in 1888.

Out of the Mainstream

Although good ol' Aussie culture seems all-pervasive, there's a lot of cultural diversity.

For a start, there are the immigrants who maintain their cultures – the Queen's Birthday, Greek Easter and Chinese New Year are some of the events which are recognised by the wider community. Gay and lesbian culture is so strong, especially in Sydney, that it's almost mainstream, though there's still a strong streak of homophobia among 'dinkum' Aussies.

'Back to the land' movements began in the late 60s around Nimbin and continue quite strongly today. State legislation legalised hamlet development in the 70s and throughout the Great Dividing Range there are communities whose lifestyles bear little relation to mainstream Australia's. Some even have their own barter systems.

RELIGION

Australia is a secular country but almost all religions are represented and given equal official recognition.

A shrinking majority of people in NSW are at least nominally Christian. Most Protestant churches merged to become the Uniting Church, although the Anglican Church of Australia remains separate. The Roman Catholic Church is the largest Christian group (about 30%), with the original Irish adherents boosted by large numbers of Mediterranean immigrants.

Non-Christian minorities abound, the main ones being Buddhist, Jewish and Muslim. Islam is the second largest religion in Australia and Buddhism is one of the fastest growing. About 13% of Australians have no religion.

Aboriginal Religion

Aboriginal religious beliefs centre on the continuing existence of spirit beings that lived on Earth during the Dreamtime, which occurred before the arrival of humans. These beings created the features of the natural world and were the ancestors of all living things. They took different forms but behaved as people do, and as they travelled about they left signs to show where they had passed.

Despite being supernatural, the ancestors

were subject to ageing and eventually they returned to the sleep from which they'd awoken at the dawn of time. Here their spirits remain as eternal forces that breathe life into the newborn and influence natural events. Each ancestor's spiritual energy flows along the path it travelled during the Dreamtime and is strongest at the points where it left physical evidence of its activities, such as a tree, hill or claypan. These features are sacred sites. (See also the box on page 37; Traditional Aboriginal Culture.)

Every person, animal and plant is believed to have two souls – one mortal and one immortal. The immortal soul is part of a particular ancestral spirit and returns to the sacred sites of that ancestor after death, while the mortal soul fades into oblivion. Each person is spiritually bound to the sacred sites that mark the land associated with his or her ancestor. It is the individual's obligation to help care for these sites by performing the necessary rituals and singing the songs that tell of the ancestor's deeds. By doing this, the order created by that ancestor is maintained.

Unfortunately, Aboriginal sacred sites are not like Christian churches, which can be desanctified before the bulldozers move in. Neither can they be bought, sold or transferred. Other Australians find this difficult to accept because they regard land as belonging to the individual, whereas in Aboriginal society land is regarded as belonging to the community. In a nutshell, Aboriginal people believe that to destroy or damage a sacred site threatens not only the living but also the spirit inhabitants of the land. It's a distressing, dangerous act that no responsible person would condone.

Throughout much of Australia, when pastoralists were breaking the Aboriginal peoples' subsistence link to the land, and sometimes shooting them, many Aboriginal people sought refuge on missions and became Christian. However, becoming Christian has not, for most Aboriginal people, meant renouncing their traditional religion. Many senior Aborigines are also devout Christians, and in many cases they are ministers.

LANGUAGE

Visitors from abroad who think Australian (that's 'Strine') is simply a weird variant of English/American will have a few surprises. For a start, many Australians don't even speak Australian – they speak Italian, Lebanese, Turkish, Greek or Vietnamese. English is the official and dominant language, but about 15% of people in NSW use a different language at home.

There's a slight regional variation in the Australian accent, while the difference between city and country speech is mainly a matter of speed. Some of the most famed Aussie words are hardly heard at all – 'mate' is far more common than 'cobber'. If you want to pass for a native, try speaking slightly nasally, shortening any word of more than two syllables and then adding a vowel to the end of it, making anything you can into a diminutive (even the Hell's Angels can become mere 'bikies') and peppering your speech with expletives. Lonely Planet's *Australian Phrasebook* is an introduction to Australian English and Aboriginal languages; the list below may also help.

arvo – afternoon
avagoyermug – traditional rallying call, especially at cricket matches
award wage – minimum pay rate

back o' Bourke – back of beyond, middle of nowhere
bail up – hold up, rob, earbash
barbie – barbecue
barrack – cheer on team at sporting event, support (as in 'who do you barrack for?')
battler – hard trier, struggler
beaut, beauty, bewdie – great, fantastic
bikies – motorcyclists
billabong – water hole in dried-up riverbed, more correctly an ox-bow bend
billy – tin container used to boil tea in the bush
bitumen road – surfaced road
black stump – where the 'back o' Bourke' begins
bloke – man
blowies – blowflies

bludger – lazy person, one who won't work

blue – argument or fight (as in 'have a blue')

bluey – swag, or nickname for a red-haired person

bonzer – great, ripper

boomer – very big, a particularly large male kangaroo

boomerang – a curved flat wooden instrument used by Aborigines for hunting

booze bus – police van used for random breath-testing for alcohol

bottle shop – liquor shop

Buckley's – no chance at all

bunyip – Australia's yeti or bigfoot

bush – country, anywhere away from the city

bushbash – to force your way through pathless bush

bushranger – Australia's equivalent of the outlaws of the American Wild West (some goodies, some baddies)

bush tucker – native foods, usually in the outback

BYO – Bring Your Own (booze to a restaurant, meat to a barbecue, etc)

camp oven – large, cast-iron pot with lid, used for cooking on an open fire

cask – wine box (a great Australian invention)

chook – chicken

chuck a U-ey – do a U-turn

cocky – small-scale farmer, cockatoo, cockroach

compo – compensation such as workers' compensation

counter meal, countery – pub meal

cozzie – swimming costume (togs, trunks)

crook – ill, badly made, substandard

cut lunch – sandwiches

dag, daggy – dirty lump of wool at back end of a sheep, also an affectionate or mildly abusive term for a socially inept person

daks – trousers

damper – bush loaf made from flour and water and cooked in a camp oven

deli – delicatessen, milk bar in South Australia

didgeridoo – cylindrical wooden musical instrument played by Aboriginal men

dill – idiot

dinkum, fair dinkum – honest, genuine

dinky-di – the real thing

divvy van – police divisional van

dob in – to tell on someone

donk – car or boat engine

drongo – worthless person

dunny – outdoor lavatory

earbash – talk nonstop

esky – large insulated box for keeping beer etc cold

fair go! – give us a break

flake – shark meat, used in fish & chips

fossick – hunt for gems or semiprecious stones

galah – noisy parrot, thus noisy idiot

garbo – person who collects your garbage

gibber – Aboriginal word for stony desert

give it away – give up

g'day – good day, traditional Australian greeting

good on ya – well done

grazier – large scale sheep or cattle farmer

grog – general term for alcohol

hoon – idiot, hooligan, yahoo

how are ya? – standard greeting (expected answer: 'good, thanks, how are *you*?')

icy-pole – frozen lolly water or ice cream on a stick

jackaroo – young male trainee on a station (farm)

jillaroo – young female trainee on a station

jocks – men's underpants

journo – journalist

Koori – Aboriginal term for Aborigines of south-east Australia

lair – layabout, ruffian

lairising – acting like a lair

lamington – square of sponge cake covered in chocolate icing and coconut

larrikin – a bit like a lair

lay-by – put a deposit on an article so the shop will hold it for you
lollies – sweets, candy
lurk – a scheme

manchester – household linen
mate – general term of familiarity, whether you know the person or not
middy – 285ml beer glass
milk bar – general store
mozzies – mosquitoes

no hoper – hopeless case
no worries – she'll be right, that's OK
nulla-nulla – a wooden club, used by Aborigines

ocker – an uncultivated or boorish Australian
off-sider – assistant or partner
outback – remote part of the bush, back o' Bourke, byond the black stump

paddock – field
pastoralist – large scale grazier
pavlova – meringue and cream dessert, named after Anna Pavlova
perve – to watch, to gaze with lust
pissed – drunk
pissed off – annoyed
pom – English person
pokies – poker machines
postie – mailperson
push – group or gang of people, such as shearers

ratbag – friendly term of abuse
ratshit – lousy
rapt – delighted, enraptured
reckon! – you bet!, absolutely!
rego – registration, as in 'car rego'
ridgy-didge – original, genuine
ripper – good (also 'little ripper')
root – have sexual intercourse
rooted – tired
ropable – very bad-tempered or angry
rubbish (ie *to rubbish*) – deride, tease

Salvo – member of the Salvation Army
sanger – sandwich

scallops – fried potato cakes in NSW; shell-fish elsewhere
schooner – large beer glass
sealed road – surfaced road
sea wasp – deadly box jellyfish
semi-trailer – articulated truck
sheila – woman
shellacking – comprehensive defeat
she'll be right – no worries
sickie – day off work ill (or malingering)
smoko – tea break
snag – sausage
squatter – pioneer farmer who occupied land as a tenant of the government
squattocracy – Australian 'old money' folk, who made it by being first on the scene and grabbing the land
station – large farm
stickybeak – nosy person
stoush – fight, argument
stubby – small bottle of beer
sunbake – sunbathe (well, the sun's hot in Australia)
surfies – surfing fanatics
swag – canvas-covered bed-roll used in the outback; also a large amount

tall poppies – achievers (knockers like to cut them down)
tinny – can of beer
too right! – absolutely!
trucky – truck driver
true blue – dinkum
tucker – food
two-up – traditional heads/tails gambling game

uni – university
ute – utility, pickup truck

wag (ie *to wag*) – to skip school or work
walkabout – lengthy walk away from it all
weatherboard – wooden house
wharfie – docker
whinge – complain, moan
wowser – spoilsport, puritan
wobbly – disturbing, unpredictable behaviour (as in throw a wobbly)
woomera – stick used by Aborigines for throwing spears

yabby – small freshwater crayfish
yahoo – noisy and unruly person
yakka – work (from an Aboriginal language)
yous – the plural of 'you'. English needs a
  second-person plural, and 'yous' supplies
  it beautifully. However, because of snob-
  bery you won't hear anyone with any pre-
  tension to education using the word. If you
  think that Australia is an egalitarian
  society, try using 'yous' in an upmarket
  situation!

Aboriginal Language

At the time of European settlement there
were around 250 separate Australian languages spoken by the 600 to 700 Aboriginal
'tribes', and some were as distinct from each
other as English and Chinese. Often three or
four adjacent tribes spoke what amounted to
dialects of the same language, but another
adjacent tribe might speak a completely different language.

It's believed that these languages evolved
from a single language family as the Aborigines gradually moved out over the continent
and split into new groups. There are a
number of words that occur right across the
continent, such as *jina* (foot) and *mala*
(hand), and similarities also exist in the often
complex grammatical structures.

The number of Aboriginal languages has
been drastically reduced. At least eight separate languages were spoken in Tasmania
alone, but none of these were recorded
before the native speakers either died or were
killed. Only around 30 languages are today
spoken on a regular basis and taught to children.

There are a number of terms which Aborigines use to describe themselves, and these
vary according to the region. The term for
the people of south-eastern Australia is
Koori. The Koori word for a non-Aborigine
is Gubbah.

Facts for the Visitor

PLANNING

When to Go

There's warm weather and clear skies somewhere in NSW at any time of the year. Generally speaking, however, the winter months of June, July and August are cool and sometimes dreary through much of the state. Winter is the best time to visit the outback and the only time you'll be able to ski.

Summer in Sydney can be sticky and unpleasant, although you can cool off at the beaches, but the major Sydney festivals are held at that time. Summer is Sydney's peak season for visitors, so there are few accommodation bargains. Autumn is probably Sydney's best season, at the start of which in early March is the Gay & Lesbian Mardi Gras (see Special Events). For more information on climate see the Facts about NSW chapter.

The other major consideration is school holidays. Families take to the road (and air) en masse at these times, many places (especially at beach resorts) are booked out, prices rise considerably and things generally get a bit crazy. The main holiday period is mid-December to late January; the other two-week periods are roughly early to mid-April, late June to mid-July and late September to early October.

What Kind of Trip?

Your particular interests have a large bearing on the kind of trip it'll be, as will the amount of time and money at your disposal. The longer you stay, the more likely you are to step outside the often superficial world of the tourist, and the lower your relative daily expenses will be. If you're visiting from abroad and you're able to work or study in Australia, make the most of the opportunity.

If your time is limited, try to leave enough to do a walk or two in the bush and spend a couple of days somewhere off the beaten track. Sydney is a great city, but only represents part of what there is to experience.

Public transport to many places outside the main cities is limited, so you may want to consider hiring or buying a car. On the other hand, most attractions can be visited as part of a guided tour. This is often a good way to get a quick overview of areas you're unfamiliar with and allows you to consider your options should you want to return.

Travelling alone is fine, provided you follow the normal precautions, and is a great way to meet new people. Hostels and camping grounds are good places to meet fellow travellers, and B&Bs are a good way to meet locals who may offer the kind of insights unavailable at the local tourist office.

Maps

The maps in this book provide a useful first reference; supplemented by a road map of NSW, you'll be able to get by using them. If you're planning to bushwalk, cycle or explore minor roads, however, you'll need more detailed maps.

The Department of Conservation & Land Management (DCLM) is the main publisher of maps in the state, with a wide range of topographic maps and also some informative maps designed for tourists, focusing on popular areas and individual national parks. Its series of 1:25,000 maps cover most of the Great Divide and are essential for bushwalking. The DCLM's head office (☎ 9228 6111) is at 23-33 Bridge St, Sydney; its main mapping office is at the Land Information Centre (☎ 6332 8200), Panorama Ave, Bathurst. You can make telephone orders with a credit card. The Land Information Centre used to be called the Central Mapping Authority (CMA), and some of its maps are still known as CMA maps.

The Australian Surveying & Land Information Group (AUSLIG) is the national mapping authority and also has credit-card phone sales. Contact AUSLIG (☎ 6201

4300), Maps & Publication Sales, Scrivener Building, Dunlop Court, Bruce, ACT 2617.

Shops selling outdoor equipment and some of the larger tourist information centres often carry topographic maps. Most tourist offices can provide a map of their town or area, but the quality varies greatly.

If you're planning to do a lot of driving, take along the NRMA's series of regional roadmaps which show almost every road and track in the state. Their descriptions of road conditions are accurate and up to date. Take a general roadmap of the whole state as well (the NRMA has one of these, too) because the detailed maps show so many alternative routes that it can be difficult to work out which is the most direct. All NRMA offices (and some associated garages) will have the maps to their area, and probably the whole set. They're free to members, and to members of motoring organisations in other states.

The NRMA maps are detailed enough for cyclists, but they don't show topography. If you want to avoid steep hills you'll need to investigate the DCLM's range of topographic maps.

What to Bring

You can buy just about anything along the way, so it's better to pack light and pick up extras as you need them. A travelpack – a combination of backpack and shoulder bag – is a good item for carrying gear. It also looks smart and can be made reasonably thief-proof with small combination locks.

Bring at least one warm jumper (pullover, sweater) or jacket, even if visiting during the summer, to cope with air-conditioning or a cool spell. Sydney's rainfall tends to come in drenching downpours, so wet-weather gear and an umbrella are handy.

Australia gets a lot of UV radiation, and a sunhat, sunglasses and sunscreen are essential. Lathering zinc cream onto your nose is a socially acceptable way to be safe.

If you're intending to bushwalk, bring strong, comfortable walking boots. Thongs (rubber sandals) are fine for the beach or a barbecue, but not for sightseeing or bushwalking.

Generally, Australians are casual dressers, although men may be required to wear jackets and ties in Sydney's more expensive hotels and restaurants.

SUGGESTED ITINERARIES

How much of NSW you see will largely depend on how much time you have. The following suggestions may help:

One week
  You can easily spend a week in Sydney. During the first three or four days explore Sydney's sights around Circular Quay, the Rocks, Sydney Harbour Bridge and Darling Harbour, the historic buildings of Macquarie St, the Botanic Gardens and take a ferry ride to Manly. In the next few days you could explore Oxford St, the inner suburbs of Paddington and Glebe, then the beachside suburbs of Bondi and Coogee or Balmoral on the North Shore. You might also fit in a day trip to the national parks to the north, to the wineries of the Hunter Valley or to the Blue Mountains. Sometime during the week take in a performance at the Opera House.

Two weeks
  In the second week visit the Blue Mountains, where you can go bushwalking for two or three days. Then head south to visit the national capital, Canberra, for a couple of days and onto Kosciuszko National Park for some skiing, bushwalking or boating depending on the season.

Four weeks
  In the third week you could head west through the Riverina as far as Wentworth (with a side trip to Mildura in Victoria), stopping off at some of the country towns along the way. Then head north to Broken Hill via the magical Mungo National Park. After two days absorbing Broken Hill, you could make a day trip to Mootwingee National Park north of town.

Six weeks
  In week five head east to visit country towns like Wilcannia, Cobar, Dubbo, Coonabarabran and Tamworth before hitting the coast at Port Macquarie. Then head north along the coast, stopping for a beer in Taylors Arms near Nambucca Heads, whitewater rafting near Coffs Harbour or Grafton and swimming at Byron Bay. If you have two or three days left you could head inland to see the alternative-lifestyle town of Nimbin and the World Heritage site of Border Ranges National Park on the Queensland border.

HIGHLIGHTS

Sydney has enough highlights of its own to keep you occupied for some time, and the nearby national parks (Royal, Ku-ring-gai Chase and Blue Mountains) offer great escapes, as do the wineries in the Hunter Valley. Further afield there are many more places worth visiting.

The whole coastline is a string of wonderful beaches, and a visit to Byron Bay is a must. While you're there, check out the alternative lifestyles of the hinterland.

With such diversity of landscapes, it's hard to say which of the national parks are the best. You can choose between the alpine forests of Kosciuszko, the rainforests of Border Ranges, the eerie outback expanses of Mungo or Sturt, the jagged peaks of Warrumbungle, the lush bush and idyllic beaches of Murramarang – or one of the other 60 or so parks!

Canberra is an intriguing place with plenty of attractions, but then so is Broken Hill, a city in the outback. Smaller towns are also fascinating, such as the near ghost town of Hill End, prosperous old towns like Mudgee, the outback mining settlements of Lightning Ridge and White Cliffs, sleepy riverside centres like Deniliquin, the planned towns of the Murrumbidgee Irrigation Area, fishing ports like Eden, the timber towns of Bombala and Wauchope, outback hamlets like Mt Hope or Ivanhoe ...

There's no shortage of adventure activities either: sailing on Sydney Harbour, abseiling in the Blue Mountains, surfing at Coffs Harbour, cattle-droving on horseback in the north-west, whitewater rafting in New England, bushwalking through the Great Divide, tandem hang-gliding on the north coast or just dropping a line in a river and waiting for a 50-kg Murray cod to take the bait.

Most roads from the coast up the escarpment of the Great Dividing Range climb through superb forests and offer dramatic views. Two of the best are the road between Batemans Bay and Canberra and the long but rewarding trip from Gloucester to Scone, skirting Barrington Tops National Park. The steep climb from Bellingen to Dorrigo is also spectacular, as is the drive from Grafton to Glen Innes. In complete contrast, the lonely outback roads in the far west offer unlimited horizons, huge skies and a surprising amount of wildlife.

TOURIST OFFICES
Local Tourist Offices

The government-run NSW Travel Centre (☎ 132077), 11-13 York St, Sydney, has a range of publications, some with quite detailed information on prices and deals on accommodation and packages. However, places have to pay for the space, so many aren't listed. It's always worth checking out the NSW Travel Centre's accommodation deals, as it often has bargains at middle and top-end places, especially in Sydney.

At the next level down are the local or regional tourist offices. Almost every major town (and many minor ones) maintains a tourist office with local information not readily available from the larger state offices. In smaller towns these often operate from a small local business like a craft shop.

Interstate Tourist Offices

The NSW Travel Centre has three offices interstate:

South Australia
  45 King William St, Adelaide 5000 (☎ (08) 8231 3167)
Queensland
  40 Queen St, Brisbane 4000 (☎ (07) 3229 8833)
Victoria
  388 Bourke St, Melbourne 3000 (☎ (03) 9670 7461)

Tourist Offices Abroad
Australian Tourist Commission (ATC)

The ATC is the federal government body which informs potential visitors about the country. ATC offices have some useful free magazine-style booklets and fact sheets, plus a map available for a small fee. These are intended for distribution overseas only; if you want copies, get them before you come to Australia. The ATC maintains Helplines, which independent travellers can ring or fax to get specific information about Australia. Alternatively, check the ATC Internet web site (www.aussie.net.au). Addresses of ATC offices include:

Hong Kong
> Suite 1501, Central Plaza, 18 Harbour Rd, Wanchai (☎ 2802 7700)
> Helpline: ☎ 2802 7817; fax 2802 8211

Japan
> Australian Business Centre, New Otani Garden Court Bldg 28F, 4-1 Kioi-cho, Chiyoda-ku, Tokyo 102 (☎ (03) 5214 0720)
> Helpline: ☎ (03) 5214 0730; fax 5214 0719
> Twin 21 MID Tower 30F, 2-1-61 Shiromi, Chuo-ku, Osaka 540 (☎ (06) 946 2503)
> Helpline: ☎ (06) 946 2500; fax 946 2473

New Zealand
> Level 13, 44-48 Emily Place, Auckland 1 (☎ (09) 379 9594; fax 307 3117)
> Helpline: ☎ (09) 527 1629; fax 377 9562

Singapore
> Suite 1703, United Square, 101 Thomson Rd, Singapore 1103 (☎ 255 4555)
> Helpline: ☎ 250 6277; fax 253 8431

UK
> Gemini House, 10-18 Putney Hill, London SW15 6AA (☎ (0181) 780 2227; fax 780 1496)

USA
> Suite 1200, 2121 Ave of the Stars, Los Angeles, CA 90067 (☎ (310) 552 1988; fax 552 1215)
> 25th floor, 100 Park Ave, New York, NY 10017 (☎ (212) 687 6300; fax 661 3340)
> Helpline: ☎ (708) 296 4900; fax 635 3718

Tourism NSW This body operates along the same lines as the ATC but at a state level. It has offices in the following locations:

Japan
> New Otani Garden Court Bldg 28F, 4-1 Kioi-cho, Chiyoda-ku, Tokyo 102 (☎ (03) 5214 0777; fax 5214 0780)

New Zealand
> Level 13, 44-48 Emily Place (PO Box 1921), Auckland 1 (☎ (09) 379 9118; fax 366 6173)

Singapore
> Unit 13-04, United Square, 101 Thomson Rd, Singapore (☎ 253 3888; fax 352 4888)

UK
> Gemini House, 10-18 Putney Hill, London SW15 6AA (☎ (0181) 789 1020; fax 789 4577)

USA
> 13737 Fiji Way, Suite C-10, Marina Del Rey, CA 90292 (☎ (310) 301 1903; fax 301 0913)

VISAS & DOCUMENTS
Passport

Your most important travel document is a passport, which should remain valid for at least six months after your intended stay. If it's about to expire, renew it before you go. This may not be easy to do away from your home country.

Applying for or renewing a passport can take from a few days to several months, so don't leave it till the last minute. Things will probably happen faster if you do everything in person, but check first on what you need to take with you. Once you start travelling, carry your passport at all times and guard it carefully.

Visas

All visitors to Australia need a visa. Only New Zealand nationals are exempt, and even they receive a 'special category' visa on arrival.

Visa application forms are available from either Australian diplomatic missions overseas or travel agents. There are several different types of visas, depending on the reason for your visit.

There are two main types of visitor visas.

Tourist Visas Tourist visas are issued by Australian consular offices abroad This type of visa is the most common and they are generally valid for a stay of either three or six months. The three-month visas are free; for the six-month visa there's a $35 fee. The visa is valid for use within 12 months of the date of issue and can be used to enter and leave Australia several times within that 12 months.

When you apply for a visa, you need to present your passport and a passport photograph, as well as sign an undertaking that you have an onward or return ticket and 'sufficient funds' – the latter is obviously open to interpretation.

You can also apply for a long-stay visa, which is a multiple-entry, four-year visa which allows for stays of up to six months on each visit. These also cost $35.

Working Visas Young, single visitors from the UK, the Republic of Ireland, Canada, Korea, Holland and Japan may be eligible for a 'working holiday' visa. 'Young' is fairly loosely interpreted as between 18 and 26, although exceptions are made and people up to 30, and young married couples without children, may be given a working holiday visa.

A working holiday visa allows for a stay of up to 12 months, but the emphasis is on casual employment rather than a full-time job, so you're only supposed to work for three months. This visa can only be applied for from outside Australia (preferably but not necessarily in your country of citizenship), and you can't change from a visitor visa to a working holiday visa.

Conditions attached to a working holiday visa include having sufficient funds for a ticket out, and taking out private medical insurance; a fee of about $140 is payable when you apply for the visa.

See also the Work section later in this chapter.

Visa Extensions The maximum stay is one year, including extensions.

Visa extensions are made through Department of Immigration & Ethnic Affairs offices in Australia and, as the process takes some time, it's best to apply about a month before your visa expires. There's an application fee of $135 – and even if they turn down your application they can still keep your money! To qualify for an extension you are required to take out private medical insurance to cover the period of the extension, and have a ticket out of the country.

There's an office of the Commonwealth Department of Immigration & Ethnic Affairs (☎ 9258 4555) at 88 Cumberland St, the Rocks, Sydney. There are other offices in Sydney and in Canberra, Newcastle and Wollongong.

Photocopies
You should make two photocopies of your most valuable documents before leaving home. Make sure you include your passport and visa, driver's licence, airline ticket, travel insurance and a list of your travellers cheque numbers. Keep one copy at home. Carry the second copy with you, but separate from the originals. If your documents are lost or stolen, replacing them will be much easier.

Travel Insurance
This not only covers you for medical expenses and luggage theft or loss, but also for cancellations or delays in your travel arrangements under certain circumstances (you might fall seriously ill two days before departure, for example) – and everyone should be covered for the worst possible case, such as an accident requiring hospital treatment and a flight home. Cover depends on your insurance and type of ticket, so ask both your insurer and your ticket-issuing agency to explain where you stand. Ticket loss is also (usually) covered by travel insurance. Buy travel insurance as early as possible. If you buy it the week before you fly, you may find, for example, that you're not covered for delays to your flight caused by strikes or industrial action.

Check the fine print: some policies exclude 'dangerous activities' like scuba diving or motorcycling. If such activities are on your agenda, you don't want that policy. Finally, make sure the policy includes health care and medication in the countries you may visit to/from Australia.

Driving Licence & Permit
Foreign driving licences are valid for the first three months of your visit. If you're staying longer, it's worth obtaining an International Driving Permit (IDP) from your local automobile association before you leave – you'll need a passport photo and a valid licence. IDPs are valid for one year.

While you're there, ask your automobile association for a Letter of Introduction or other proof of membership, which will give you reciprocal rights to the services of the NRMA, including free maps, breakdown services and technical advice.

Student & Hostel Cards

Carrying a student card entitles you to a wide variety of discounts throughout NSW. The most common card is the International Student Identity Card (ISIC). It is issued by student unions, hostelling organisations or 'alternative style' travel agencies.

It's also worth bringing a youth hostel membership card (Hostelling International, Youth Hostel Association etc). As well as entitling you to discounts, it's valid for membership of the YHA in NSW.

EMBASSIES & CONSULATES

Australian diplomatic missions overseas include:

Canada
    Suite 710, 50 O'Connor St, Ottawa (☎ (613) 236 0841); also in Toronto and Vancouver
China
    21 Dongzhimenwai Dajie, Sanlitun, Beijing 100600 (☎ (10) 532 2331); also in Guangzhou and Shanghai
Denmark
    Kristianagade 21, DK 2100 Copenhagen (☎ 3526 2244)
France
    4 Rue Jean Rey, Paris 75724 (☎ 01 40 59 33 00)
Germany
    Godesberger Allee 107, 53175 Bonn (☎ (0228) 81 030); also in Frankfurt and Berlin
Greece
    37 Dimitriou Soutsou, Ambelokipi, Athens 11521 (☎ (01) 644 7303)
Hong Kong
    23/F Harbour Centre, 25 Harbour Rd, Wanchai, Hong Kong Island (☎ 2827 8881)
India
    Australian Compound, No 1/50-G Shantipath, Chanakyapuri, New Delhi 110021 (☎ (11) 688 8223); also in Bombay
Indonesia
    Jalan H R Rasuna Said Kav C 15-16, Jakarta Selatan 12940 (☎ (021) 522 7111)
    Jalan Prof Moh Yamin 51, Renon, Denpasar, Bali (☎ (0361) 23 5092)
Ireland
    Fitzwilton House, Wilton Terrace, Dublin 2 (☎ (01) 676 1517)
Italy
    Via Alessandria 215, Rome 00198 (☎ (06) 852 721); also in Milan
Japan
    2-1-14 Mita, Minato-ku, Tokyo 108 (☎ (03) 5232 4111)

Malaysia
    6 Jalan Yap Kwan Seng, Kuala Lumpur 50450 (☎ (03) 242 3122); also in Kuching and Penang
Netherlands
    Carnegielaan 4, 2517 KH The Hague (☎ (070) 310 8200)
New Zealand
    72-78 Hobson St, Thorndon, Wellington (☎ (04) 473 6411)
    Union House, 32-38 Quay St, Auckland 1 (☎ (09) 303 2429)
Papua New Guinea
    Independence Drive, Waigani NCD, Port Moresby (☎ 325 9333)
Philippines
    Dona Salustiana Ty Tower, 104 Paseo de Roxas, Makati, Metro Manila (☎ (02) 817 7911)
Singapore
    25 Napier Rd, Singapore 1025 (☎ 737 9311)
South Africa
    292 Orient St, Arcadia, Pretoria 0083 (☎ (012) 342 3740); also in Cape Town
Sweden
    Sergels Torg 12, Stockholm (☎ (08) 613 2900)
Switzerland
    29 Alpenstrasse, CH-3006 Berne (☎ (031) 351 0143); also in Geneva
Thailand
    37 South Sathorn Rd, Bangkok 10120 (☎ (02) 287 2680)
UK
    Australia House, The Strand, London WC2B 4LA (☎ (0171) 379 4334); also in Edinburgh and Manchester
USA
    1601 Massachusetts Ave NW, Washington DC 20036 (☎ (202) 797 3000); also in Atlanta, Boston, Chicago, Denver, Honolulu, Houston, Los Angeles, New York and San Francisco
Vietnam
    66 Ly Thuong Kiet, Hanoi (☎ (04) 25 2763); also in Ho Chi Minh City
Zimbabwe
    4th floor, Karigamombe Centre, 53 Samora Machel Ave, Harare (☎ (04) 75 7774)

Foreign Embassies & Consulates

Canberra is home to most foreign embassies, but many countries maintain consulates in Sydney as well – see the Sydney and ACT chapters for addresses.

CUSTOMS

When entering Australia you can bring most articles in free of duty, provided that Customs is satisfied they're for personal use and that you'll be taking them with you when you leave. There's also the usual duty-free per-person quota of one litre of alcohol, 250 cigarettes and dutiable goods up to the value of A$400.

Two issues need particular attention. Number one is drugs. Customs has a mania about the stuff and can be extremely efficient when it comes to finding it. Unless you have a real desire to investigate prison conditions, don't bring any in with you.

Issue two is animal and plant quarantine. You'll be asked to declare all goods of animal or vegetable origin and show them to an official. Authorities are naturally keen to prevent weeds, pests or diseases getting into the country – Australia has so far managed to escape many of the agricultural pests and diseases prevalent in other parts of the world. Fresh food is also unpopular, particularly meat, sausage, fruit and vegetables, as well as flowers.

Weapons and firearms are either prohibited or require a permit and safety testing. Other restricted goods include products (such as ivory) made from protected wildlife species, non-approved telecommunications devices and live animals.

When you leave, don't take any protected flora or fauna with you. Australia's unique birds and animals fetch big bucks from overseas collectors, and Customs comes down hard on animal smugglers.

MONEY
Costs
With low inflation over the past few years, prices in Australia have remained fairly stable.

Compared with other western countries, Australia is cheaper in some ways and more expensive in others. Manufactured goods like clothes tend to be more expensive, but food and wine are both high in quality and low in cost.

Accommodation is also reasonably priced. In virtually every town where backpackers are likely to stay there'll be a backpackers' hostel with dorm beds for around $14, or a caravan park with on-site vans for around $25 for two people. An average-to-good motel room costs around $45/55 (more in Sydney), with plenty of cheaper places and a lot of regional and seasonal variation – you'll pay a lot more on the coast in summer, for example.

Transport isn't expensive in terms of dollars per kilometre, but the distances are great so fares are high.

Food is reasonably priced. Even the smallest town has a cafe where you can get a large hamburger for about $3. Local bowling or ex-servicemen's clubs often have the best-value meals. A good restaurant meal can be found for around $10.

Unless otherwise indicated, prices in this book are given in Australian dollars.

Carrying Money
Carry the money you'll need for the day somewhere inside your clothing rather than in a handbag or an outside pocket. Put the money in several places. Most hotels and hostels provide safekeeping, so you can leave your money and other valuables with them.

Cash
Carry some Australian currency in the form of cash – it's useful for small transactions, and some cheaper hotels and places to eat may not accept credit cards. Set aside a small sum for emergencies.

Travellers Cheques
American Express, Thomas Cook and other well-known brands of travellers cheques can be changed at most banks in the state. A passport is usually adequate for identification, but it would be sensible to carry your driver's licence, credit cards or a plane ticket in case of problems.

Buying Australian dollar travellers cheques is an option worth looking at. These can be exchanged immediately at the bank cashier's window without being converted from a foreign currency and incurring commissions, fees and exchange rate fluctuations.

Fees for changing foreign currency travellers cheques seem to vary from bank to bank. Of the 'big four', Westpac doesn't charge any fee, while at the National Australia and Commonwealth banks it costs $5 and at the ANZ bank it's $6.50 per transaction, regardless of amount or number of cheques.

ATMs

There are automatic teller machines (ATMs) at the branches of most banks throughout the state. ATMs can be used day or night, and it's possible to use the machines of some other banks: Westpac ATMs accept Commonwealth Bank cards and vice versa; National Bank ATMs accept ANZ cards and vice versa.

There's a limit on how much you can withdraw each day from your card account. This varies from bank to bank, but is usually $400 to $600 per day.

Credit Cards

Visa, MasterCard, Diners Club and American Express are widely accepted. Cash advances from credit cards are available over the counter and from many ATMs, depending on the card.

Credit cards makes renting a car much simpler. They're looked upon with greater favour than nasty old cash, and many agencies simply won't rent you a vehicle if you don't have a card.

Local Bank Accounts

Opening an account at an Australian bank isn't easy, especially for overseas visitors. A points system operates and you need to score a minimum of 100 points before you can have the privilege of letting the bank take your money. Passports, driver's licences, birth certificates and other 'major' IDs earn you 40 points; minor ones such as credit cards get you 20 points. However, if you apply to open an account during the first six weeks of your visit, then just showing your passport will suffice.

The four major national banks are ANZ, the Commonwealth Bank, National Australia Bank and Westpac. The other banks with a NSW profile are the State Bank of New South Wales and St George. Post offices act as agencies for the Commonwealth Bank, which can be handy if you're planning to visit remote areas.

Most travellers these days opt for an account which includes a cash card that can be used to access cash from ATMs.

Many businesses, such as service stations, supermarkets and convenience stores, are linked into the Electronic Funds Transfer at Point of Sale (EFTPOS) system which allows you to use your card to pay for services or purchases and withdraw cash directly from your account. Cards (either credit cards or bank account debit cards) can be used to make local, STD and international phone calls in special public phones.

Currency

The unit of currency is the Australian dollar, which is divided into 100 cents. There are $100, $50, $20, $10 and $5 notes, and $2, $1, 50c, 20c, 10c and 5c coins. The 2c and 1c coins have been taken out of circulation, although prices can still be set in odd cents. Shops round prices up (or down) to the nearest 5c on your total bill.

There are no notable restrictions on importing or exporting currency or travellers cheques, except that you may not take out more than A$5000 in cash without prior approval.

Currency Exchange

The Australian dollar fluctuates quite markedly against the US dollar, but seems to stay pretty much in the 70c to 80c range – a disaster for Australians travelling overseas but a real bonus for inbound visitors. Approximate exchange values are:

Canada	C$1	=	A$0.95
France	FF1	=	A$0.22
Germany	DM1	=	A$0.77
Japan	¥100	=	A$1.17
Korea (South)	W100	=	A$0.14
New Zealand	NZ$1	=	A$0.91
UK	UK£1	=	A$2.17
USA	US$1	=	A$1.33

Changing Money

Changing foreign currency or travellers cheques is no problem at almost any bank or licensed moneychanger, such as Thomas Cook or American Express.

Tipping

While tipping is becoming more common, and might be expected in more upmarket restaurants and cafes, it isn't yet an entrenched practice. A tip of around 10% is average, but feel free to vary the amount depending on your satisfaction with the level of service. Taxi drivers don't expect to be tipped, but 'rounding up' the fare to the nearest dollar is common.

POST & COMMUNICATIONS
Post

Australia Post (☎ 131318 for general enquiries) runs the country's mail system. Most post offices open Monday to Friday from 9 am to 5 pm, but you can often get stamps from local post offices operating from newsagencies or from Australia Post retail outlets on Saturday mornings (9 am to noon) as well.

Sending Mail It costs 45c to send a standard letter or postcard within Australia.

Aerogrammes are 70c and air-mail letters/postcards cost 75/70c to New Zealand, 85/80c to Singapore and Malaysia, 95/90c to Hong Kong and India, $1.05/95c to the USA and Canada, and $1.20/1 to Europe and the UK.

The rates for posting parcels aren't too extortionate. By sea mail a 1/2/5-kg parcel costs $14.50/18/28.50 to New Zealand and India, and $15/19/31 to the USA, Europe and the UK. Each kilogram over 5 kg costs $3.50 for New Zealand and India, and $4 for the USA, Europe and the UK, with a maximum of 20 kg for all destinations. Air-mail rates are considerably more expensive.

Receiving Mail All post offices hold mail for visitors. American Express and Thomas Cook offices in big cities provide mail services for their clients.

Telephone

Area Codes The area code for most of NSW and the ACT is ☎ 02. The exceptions are Broken Hill which has the South Australia ☎ 08 area code, Tweed Heads with the Queensland ☎ 07 area code and several towns in the Riverina along the Murray River with the ☎ 03 Victoria area code. You must use the ☎ 02 area code when calling from outside NSW or when making STD calls within the state (eg when calling Newcastle from Tamworth).

Local Calls Local calls from public phones cost 40c for an unlimited amount of time. You can make local calls from gold or blue phones – often found in hotels, shops, bars etc – and from payphone booths. Local calls from private telephones cost 30c.

STD Calls It's also possible to make long-distance (STD – Subscriber Trunk Dialling) calls from virtually any public phone. Many public phones accept Telstra phonecards, which come in $5, $10, $20 and $50 denominations, and are available from retail outlets such as newsagents and pharmacies which display the phonecard logo. Otherwise, use coins and be prepared to feed them through at a fair old rate. STD calls are cheaper in off-peak hours – see the front of a local telephone book for the different rates.

Some public phones are set up to take only bank cash cards or credit cards, and these too are convenient, although you need to keep an eye on how much the call is costing as it can quickly mount up. The minimum charge for a call on one of these phones is $1.20.

STD calls are cheaper at night. In ascending order of cost:

Economy – from 6 pm Saturday to 8 am Monday; 10 pm to 8 am every night
Night – from 6 to 10 pm Monday to Friday
Day – from 8 am to 6 pm Monday to Saturday

International Calls From most STD phones you can also make ISD (International Subscriber Dialling) calls. Dialling ISD you can get through to overseas numbers almost as quickly as you can access local numbers and if your call is brief it needn't cost very much.

Dial ☎ 0011 for overseas, the country code (44 for Britain, 1 for North America, 64 for New Zealand), the city code (dropping the initial zero if there is one, eg 171 or 181 for London, 212 for New York etc) and then the telephone number. Have a phonecard, credit card or plenty of coins to hand.

It's possible to make ISD calls with either of Australia's two main telecommunications companies, Optus and Telstra. The fee structure varies slightly between the two, and if you're phoning one country constantly it may be worth comparing them. This option is only available from private phones in certain areas. Phone Optus (☎ 1800 500 002) for details on how to access their services.

International calls from Australia are among the cheapest you'll find anywhere. A Telstra call to the USA or Britain costs $1.35 a minute ($1.03 off peak); New Zealand is $1.09 a minute ($0.72 off peak). Off-peak times, if available, vary depending on the destination – see the back of any white pages telephone book, or call ☎ 0102 for more details. Sunday is often the cheapest day to ring.

Country Direct is a service which gives travellers in Australia direct access to operators in nearly 50 countries, to make collect or credit-card calls. For a full list of the countries hooked into this system, check the local white pages telephone book. They include: Canada (☎ 1800 881 150), Germany (☎ 1800 881 490), Ireland (☎ 1800 881 353), Japan (☎ 1800 881 810), New Zealand (☎ 1800 881 640), the UK (☎ 1800 881 440) and the USA (☎ 1800 881 011).

Free & Low Fee Calls Many businesses and some government departments operate a toll-free service, so no matter where you're ringing from around the country, it's a free call. These numbers have the prefix 1800. Many companies, such as the airlines, have six-digit numbers beginning with 13, which are charged at the rate of a local call. Often these numbers are Australia-wide, or may be

applicable to a specific STD district only. Unfortunately, there's no way of telling without actually ringing the number.

Mobile Phones Phone numbers with the prefixes 014, 015, 016, 018 or 041 are mobile or car phones. The three mobile operators are the government's Telstra and the privately run Optus and Vodaphone. Calls from mobile numbers are charged at special STD rates and can be expensive.

Information Calls Other odd numbers you may come across are those starting with 0055 and 190. The 0055 numbers, usually recorded information services and the like, are provided by private companies, and your call is charged in multiples of 25c (40c from public phones) at a rate selected by the provider. These rates are: Premium, 70c per minute; Value, 55c per minute; and Budget, 35c per minute.

Numbers beginning with 190 are also information services, but they're charged on a fixed-fee basis, which can vary from as little as 35c to as much as $30!

Fax & Telegram
Faxes All post offices (but few agencies) send faxes. It costs $4 to send a fax to another fax machine or to a postal address. If the fax is sent to a postal address, it is sent to the local post office and either delivered in the normal mail service, usually the next day, or the post office will telephone you and ask you to come and collect it. You can send a same-day fax to a postal address for $12 if you send it by 1 pm. There's also a two-hour courier delivery service open until 4 pm ($20). These rates apply to the first page of any fax. Subsequent pages cost $1, no matter which service you use.

Overseas faxes, either to a fax machine or delivered in the local mail service, cost $10 for the first page and $5 for following pages.

If you're sending a fax to a fax machine it's worth seeing if any businesses offer a fax service, as they're often cheaper than the post office. The international code for sending fax messages is 0015.

Telegrams Local telegrams (cables) have been replaced by faxes, but you can send an international telegram at a flat rate of $7.50 plus 60c per word, including the address. The telegram is delivered by the country's normal postal system (so it's usually next day), but in countries where the post office can arrange courier delivery you can pay an extra $16 for same-day delivery. It's almost always cheaper to send a fax.

E-mail & Internet Access

If you want to send or receive e-mails, there are service providers in Sydney which can allow you access to your existing POP e-mail account and to other Internet services. On-line costs vary, but a typical price structure is a $25 joining fee then $5 per hour on-line, with no minimum charge. A few of the current major players include:

Australia On Line
    ☎ 1800 621 258; www.ozonline.com.au
On Australia (Microsoft Network)
    ☎ (02) 9934 9000
OzEmail
    ☎ (02) 9391 0480; www.ozemail.com.au
Pegasus Networks
    ☎ 1800 812 812; www.peg.apc.org

Users of CompuServe (☎ 1800 025 240) who want to access the service locally should phone to get the local log-in numbers.

If you don't have your own hardware you can log on at most public libraries or at Internet cafes.

BOOKS
Lonely Planet

The information in Lonely Planet's *Sydney* city guide is similar to the information in this guidebook, but if you're reading this in a bookshop and plan to visit only Sydney, check it out. *Bushwalking in Australia* by John & Monica Chapman details, among others, the walk in the Blue Gum Forest in the Blue Mountains.

For travel elsewhere in Australia, Lonely Planet publishes the *Australia* guide, as well as individual guides to the other states, the *Melbourne* city guide, *Islands of Australia's*

Great Barrier Reef, *Outback Australia* and the *Australian Phrasebook*.

Guidebooks

Burnum Burnum's Aboriginal Australia, subtitled 'a traveller's guide', explores Australia from the Aboriginal point of view.

Gregory's *National Parks of NSW* is a handy guide to the state's national parks, popular nature reserves, state recreation areas and historic sites.

The NRMA publishes star-rated accommodation guides to caravan parks and motel-style accommodation. Nonmembers pay about $10, and members (and members of other states' motoring organisations) pay a reduced fee. The guides are handy but they don't list most pubs and you'll miss the simpler, cheaper places if you rely on them.

Guide to B&Bs & Rural Retreats in NSW by Wendy Robinson lists places across the state.

Travel Literature

A great book to read while visiting Sydney is *Sydney* by Jan Morris, one of the best travel writers around. In *Sean & David's Long Drive*, an offbeat road book by Sean Condon and one of the titles in Lonely Planet's 'Journeys' series, the protagonists visit NSW.

Aborigines

The Australian Aborigines by Kenneth Maddock is a good cultural summary. The award-winning *Triumph of the Nomads* by Geoffrey Blainey is also good. For accounts of what's happened to the original Australians since whites arrived, read *Aboriginal Australians* by Richard Broome. *A Change of Ownership*, by Mildred Kirk, covers similar ground to Broome's book, but does so more concisely, focusing on the land-rights movement.

The Other Side of the Frontier, by Henry Reynolds, uses historical records to give a vivid Aboriginal view of the arrival of Europeans in Australia. His *With the White People* identifies Aboriginal contributions to the survival of the early white settlers. *My Place*,

Sally Morgan's prize-winning autobiography, traces her discovery of her Aboriginal heritage. *The Fringe Dwellers*, by Nene Gare, describes just what it's like to be an Aborigine growing up in a white-dominated society.

Don't Take Your Love to Town by Ruby Langford and *My People* by Oodgeroo Noonuccal (formerly Kath Walker) are also recommended reading for people interested in Aborigines' experiences.

Day of the Dog, by Aboriginal writer Archie Weller, has been made into a film, *Blackfellas*.

History

For a good introduction to Australian history, read *A Short History of Australia* by the late Manning Clark, a much-loved Aussie historian. A single-volume condensation of Clark's definitive (and controversial) six-volume *History of Australia* is also available.

The Fatal Shore, Robert Hughes' best-selling account of the convict era, is a very good read.

Finding Australia, by Russel Ward, traces the early days from the first Aboriginal arrivals up to 1821. His *Concise History of Australia* is another quick introduction.

The Exploration of Australia, by Michael Cannon, is a fascinating reference book about the gradual European uncovering of the continent. An intriguing combination of history and nature study is Eric Rolls' excellent *A Million Wild Acres*. It tells the story of the Pilliga Scrub in north-western NSW, but in the context of the state's history and largely from the viewpoint of the farmers and timber-cutters who pioneered white settlement.

Children's Books

Two classics for younger children which are essential reading are Norman Lindsay's *The Magic Pudding* and May Gibbs' *Snugglepot & Cuddlepie*. Lindsay's home, now open as a museum, is near Springwood in the Blue Mountains. There are displays relating to *The Magic Pudding*, although more space is devoted to his sculpture and painting, much

of which is cheerfully erotic. Nutcote, May Gibbs' house in North Sydney, is also a museum.

Flora & Fauna

Identifying the state's strange and beautiful plants and trees is rewarding but difficult. Handy guides include the *Field Guide to Native Plants of Australia* (Bay Books), *Key Guide to Australian Trees* (Reed) and *Key Guide to Australian Wildflowers* (Reed). These will help, but the range of flora is so wide that becoming familiar with it all takes years.

Guides to fauna include *Key Guide to Australian Mammals* (Reed).

ONLINE SERVICES

The World Wide Web is a major source of information. Although things on the Internet change rapidly, some sites which provide a range of information on Australia include:

Guide to Australia
> This site, maintained by the Charles Sturt University in NSW, is a mine of information, with links to Australian government departments, weather information, books, maps etc. (www.csu.edu.au/education/australia.html)

The Aussie Index
> A fairly comprehensive list of Australian companies, educational institutions and government departments which maintain web sites. (www.aussie.com.au/aussie.htm)

Australian Government
> The Federal government has a site, which is predictably unexciting, but it is wide-ranging and a good source for things like visa information. (gov.info.au)

Lonely Planet
> Our own site covers Australia, as well as many other places, and is definitely worth a look. Well, we would say that, wouldn't we? (www.lonelyplanet.com.au)

NEWSPAPERS & MAGAZINES

The *Sydney Morning Herald* is one of the best newspapers in the country. It's a serious broadsheet, but it captures some of Sydney's larrikinism as well. The other Sydney paper is the *Telegraph Mirror*, a tabloid but much tamer than other products of the Rupert Murdoch stables.

Two national newspapers are available in NSW: the *Australian*, a conservative daily which has an interesting weekend edition; and the business-oriented *Australian Financial Review*.

Local newspapers are published throughout rural NSW. Many are produced by and for the various ethnic groups, some in English, and appear only weekly.

The *Bulletin* is a venerable, conservative weekly newsmagazine, first published in 1880, which carries a condensed version of *Newsweek*.

Widely available international papers include the *International Herald Tribune*, the *European* and the *Guardian Weekly*. *Time* produces an Australian edition.

RADIO & TV

The largest broadcaster in the country is the government-funded (less and less), commercial-free (so far) Australian Broadcasting Corporation (ABC). There are two main services: Radio National, heard just about everywhere (sometimes on AM and sometimes via FM relays), and lighter regional services, generally only around major centres. Fine Music is the ABC's classical music station and Triple J is its excellent 'youth' station; neither is available everywhere. Pick up a copy of the free *Travellers Guide to ABC Radio* from ABC shops or radio stations.

Outside Sydney, which has more than 20 radio stations, you'll usually be able to pick up an ABC station, a local commercial station and often a local public station. You might also be able to tune into the foreign-language programmes of the Special Broadcasting Service (SBS), the multi-cultural network.

Local tourist information is broadcast in most places on 88 FM.

There are five main TV networks in NSW: the ABC, SBS and the three commercial networks, channels 10, 9 and 7. The ABC and at least one commercial station can be received almost everywhere in the state. SBS is only available in Sydney (and the other state capital cities) and several large centres like Broken Hill and Orange.

The commercial channels are just like commercial channels anywhere, with a diet of sport, soap operas, lightweight news, sensationalised current affairs and plenty of sit-coms (mainly American).

The ABC produces some excellent current affairs and documentaries, as well as showing a lot of sport, slightly heavier news and sit-coms (mainly British). The ABC also has a knack of making good comedy and drama programmes which receive critical acclaim and low ratings.

SBS invariably has the best news and movies, and some good arts and music programmes.

PHOTOGRAPHY & VIDEO

Australian film prices are similar to the rest of the western world, so if you arrive via Hong Kong or Singapore it's probably worth buying film there. A 36-exposure Kodachrome 64 or Fujichrome 100 slide film costs around $25 to $28, including developing. With a little shopping around, you might find it for around $23, or less if you buy it in quantity.

The more popular colour print films are sold everywhere, but outside Sydney slide or B&W film is hard to find.

There are plenty of camera shops, and standards of camera service are high. Developing standards are also high, with many places offering one-hour developing of print film.

Remember that film is susceptible to heat, so protect your film, keeping it cool and having it processed as soon as possible. Other camera and film hazards are dust and humidity. The best results are gained early in the morning and late in the afternoon, especially in summer.

As in any country, politeness goes a long way when taking photographs: ask before taking pictures of people. Note that most Aborigines don't like having their photographs taken, even from a distance.

At airports passengers must pass their luggage through x-ray machines. Today's technology doesn't jeopardize lower-speed film, but it's best to carry your film and camera with you and ask the x-ray inspector to check them visually.

Overseas visitors thinking of purchasing videos should remember that Australia uses the Phase Alternative Line (PAL) system, which isn't compatible with other standards unless converted.

TIME

NSW uses Eastern Standard Time (as do Queensland, Victoria and Tasmania), which is 10 hours ahead of GMT/UTC (Greenwich Mean Time).

Other time zones in Australia are Central Time (half an hour behind Eastern Standard Time and used in both South Australia and the Northern Territory) and Western Time (two hours behind Eastern Standard Time and used in Western Australia). Note that Broken Hill, in western NSW, uses Central Time.

At noon in Sydney it's 2 am in London, 3 am in Rome, 9 am in Bangkok, 2 pm in Auckland, 6 pm the previous day in Los Angeles and 9 pm the previous day in New York.

From the last Sunday in October to the first Sunday in March, NSW is on Eastern Summer Time, one hour ahead of standard time.

ELECTRICITY

Voltage is 220-240 V and plugs are flat three-pin, but they are not like British three-pin plugs. Other than in fancy hotels, it's difficult to find converters to take either US flat two-pin plugs or the European round two-pin plugs used with electric shavers or hair driers. Adaptors for British plugs are found in good hardware shops, chemists and travel agents.

WEIGHTS & MEASURES

Australia uses the metric system. In country areas you'll still hear people using imperial units and when you're receiving directions it's a good idea to make sure that they are talking about kilometres, not miles. See the back of this book for conversion tables.

Distances are often colloquially measured in the time it takes to drive them. For example, the question 'How far is it to Melbourne?' may be answered 'About 11 hours'.

LAUNDRY

Most hostels and cheaper hotels have self-service laundry facilities, while the more expensive hotels will return your clothes washed, dried and neatly folded. Otherwise there are self-service laundromats or dry-cleaning places, many of which open daily. Washing a load costs about $1.50 and drying it is another $2 for 30 minutes. Some laundromats have attendants who wash, dry and fold your clothes for an additional fee. To find a laundromat, look in the yellow pages under 'Laundries – Self-Service'.

HEALTH

Vaccinations aren't required for entry unless you've visited an infected country in the preceding 14 days (aircraft refuelling stops don't count).

Medical care in Australia is first-class and only moderately expensive. A typical visit to the doctor costs around $35. Health insurance cover is available, but there's usually a waiting period after you sign up before any claims can be made.

There is universal health care in Australia (for Australians and citizens of nations with reciprocal rights) and you can choose your own doctor. Visitors from Finland, Italy, Malta, the Netherlands, New Zealand, Sweden and the UK have reciprocal health rights and can register at any Medicare office. Seeing a doctor is simply a matter of finding one nearby – check the yellow pages under 'Medical Practitioners'.

If you have an immediate health problem, contact the casualty section at the nearest public hospital; in an emergency call an ambulance (☎ 000).

Medical Kit

It's always a good idea to travel with a basic medical kit even when your destination is a country like Australia where first-aid supplies are readily available. Don't forget any medication you're already taking. A small medical kit might include aspirin or paracetamol, antihistamine, antiseptic, multivitamins, cold and flu tablets, calamine lotion, bandages, Band-aids, scissors and insect repellent.

Health Precautions

The sun can be very intense in Australia and ultraviolet rays can burn you badly even on an overcast day. Australia has the world's highest incidence of skin cancer, so cover up and wear plenty of sunscreen. The sun is at its fiercest between 11 am and 3 pm, so be especially careful during this period.

Too much sunlight, whether direct or reflected (glare), can damage your eyes. If you're near water, sand or snow, good-quality sunglasses which filter out UV radiation are essential.

Dehydration or salt deficiency can cause heat exhaustion. Take time to acclimatise to high temperatures and make sure you drink sufficient liquids. Wear loose clothing and a broad-brimmed hat. Heat stroke occurs when the body's heat-regulating mechanism breaks down and the body temperature rises to dangerous levels. If you arrive during a hot period avoid excessive alcohol or strenuous activity.

Salbutamol inhalers (Ventolin) are available without prescription, but you must give your name and address to the chemist.

The contraceptive pill is available on prescription only, so a visit to a doctor is necessary. Condoms are available from chemists, convenience stores and vending machines in hotel toilets.

HIV/AIDS

The Human Immunodeficiency Virus (HIV) may develop into Acquired Immune Deficiency Syndrome (AIDS). Exposure to blood, blood products or bodily fluids may put the individual at risk. In industrialised countries like Australia transmission is mostly through contact between homosexual or bisexual males, or via contaminated needles shared by IV drug users. Apart from abstinence, the most effective preventative is always to practise safe sex using condoms. It's impossible to detect the HIV-positive status of an otherwise healthy-looking person without a blood test.

HIV/AIDS can also be spread through infected blood transfusions and by dirty needles – vaccinations, acupuncture, tattooing and ear or nose piercing can potentially be as dangerous as intravenous drug use if the equipment isn't clean. In Australia, although there may be a risk of infection, it's very small. Fear of HIV infection should never preclude treatment for serious medical conditions.

For advice call the 24-hour AIDS Information Line (☎ 9332 4000) or contact the AIDS Council of NSW (☎ 9206 2000, 1800 063 060), PO Box 350, Darlinghurst, NSW 2010.

WOMEN TRAVELLERS

NSW is generally a safe place for women travellers, although you should avoid walking alone in Sydney late at night. Sexual harassment is uncommon, although the Aussie male culture does have its sexist elements. Don't tolerate any harassment or discrimination. Female hitchhikers should exercise care at all times.

In Sydney some of the major women's organisations (which can direct you to local institutions) are:

Royal Hospital for Women
    188 Oxford St, Paddington (☎ 9339 4111)
Women & Girls Emergency Centre
    190 Elizabeth St (☎ 9281 1277)
Women's Legal Resources Centre
    (☎ 9637 4597, 1800 801 501)
Women's Liberation House
    63 Palace St, Petersham (☎ 9569 3819)

GAY & LESBIAN TRAVELLERS

Gay and lesbian culture is so strong in Sydney that it's almost mainstream. Oxford St, especially around Taylor Square, is the centre of what is probably the second-largest gay community in the world. The suburb of Newtown is home to Sydney's lesbian scene.

Sydney is one of the top three holiday destinations for North American gays and lesbians.

The Gay & Lesbian Mardi Gras (see Public Holidays & Special Events later) is the biggest annual tourist event in Australia. It culminates in a spectacular parade up Oxford St, watched by about 650,000 people, and a huge party at the Royal Agricultural Society's Showgrounds.

Despite all this, there's still a strong streak of homophobia among 'dinkum' Aussies, even in Sydney itself, and violence against homosexuals isn't unknown.

For the record, it's legal in NSW for a man to have sex with a man over the age of 18, and for a woman to have sex with a woman over the age of 16. Note that laws in other states differ.

The *g'day accommodation guide* gives listings of items of interest to gay travellers. National gay/lesbian magazines include

Travel in NSW for People with Disabilities
With the 2000 Olympics and Paralympics on the horizon the international spotlight will fall on Sydney, so local authorities are examining ways of ensuring access to all services for disabled people. The following resources are available at present.

Information
- NICAN (National Information & Communication Awareness Network), PO Box 407 Curtin 2605 ACT (☎ (02) 6285 3713 or Freecall 1800 806 769), provides accommodation and recreation information and has a list of access guides and maps available around the state. Contact the council at your intended destination to obtain a contact at the local Access Committee.
- ACROD (Australian Council for the Rehabilitation of the Disabled), 55 Charles St, Ryde 2112 (☎ (02) 9809 4488) also provides information on accommodation, activities and support organisations.
- Paraplegic & Quadriplegic Association of NSW (☎ (02) 9764 4166), Burlington Rd, Homebush
- Independent Living Centre (☎ (02) 9808 2233), 600 Victoria Rd, Ryde 2112 (for equipment hire options)
- Deaf Society of NSW (TTY (02) 9893 8858 or 9893 8555), Level 4, 169 Macquarie St, Parramatta 2150
- Royal Blind Society of NSW (☎ (02) 9334 3333), 4 Mitchell St, Enfield 2136
- Port Stephens Access Map, Port Stephens Council, (02) 4980 0255.

Publications
The following publications contain useful information on access for travellers with disabilities:
Easy Access Australia – A Travel Guide to Australia ($24.85, including postage): PO Box 218, Kew VIC 3101
Accessing Sydney ($19.95, includes accommodation): ACROD NSW (☎ (02) 9809 4488)
Visitors Guide – National Parks in NSW, and *Outdoor Access for Everybody:* National Parks & Wildlife Service (☎ (02) 9585 444)
Blue Mountains Access Guide (1996): PO Box 189, Katoomba 2780
Access Ilawarra – A Guide to Wollongong, Shell Harbour & Kiama for People with Disabilities & the Elderly (1990): Illawarra Disabled Persons' Trust. Available from Australian Quadriplegic Association (Illawarra), (02) 4272 9356

Getting There & Away
Travel options to Sydney or Canberra are by air, rail and road via private vehicle as buses are not an option for wheelchairs. Ansett and Qantas encourage people with disabilities to fly. NICAN in conjunction with Qantas has developed a Carer Concession Card where carers can travel half-price. Sydney and Canberra airports have dedicated parking spaces, drop-off points, accessible toilets, lifts and air bridges.

Countrylink trains (Freecall 13 2232 or (02) 6257 1576) operate to/from Brisbane, Melbourne, Sydney and Canberra and major regional centres in NSW, and have at least one accessible carriage (two wheelchair spaces and toilet).

OutRage, *Campaign*, *Lesbians on the Loose (LOTL)* and the art magazine *Blue*. In Sydney free gay papers such as *Capital Q Weekly* and the *Sydney Star Observer* have comprehensive listings of gay and lesbian events.

For advice, counselling and referral call the Gay & Lesbian Line (☎ 9207 2800), daily 4 pm to midnight; for information call the 24-hour information service (☎ 9207 2822). See also HIV/AIDS under Health.

SENIOR TRAVELLERS

Australian senior citizens are entitled to discounts on things like public transport, museum admission fees etc, provided they show an Australian Pensioners Card. Few of these apply to senior citizens from abroad, though some places may agree to give you a discount if you show your seniors card from home.

In your home country, a lower age may already entitle you to interesting travel pack-

---

Getting Around

Accessible cabs are available in Sydney through Sydney Cabs centralised booking system (Freecall 1800 043 187). Both Hertz (Freecall 133039) and Avis (Freecall 1800 225 533) provide hand-controlled rental cars.

Ferries are a great way to view Sydney Harbour, but stick to the terminals at Circular Quay, Manly, Parramatta and Darling Harbour, as smaller terminals have steep slippery ramps and even steps. Quayside Booking Centre (☎ (02) 9247 9371) at Circular Quay will book Sydney Ferries, JetCats, Captain Cook Cruises and Matilda Cruises (Manly and Parramatta JetCat may have accessible toilets.)

The monorail which runs above Darling Harbour into the CBD is an excellent way of seeing the city.

Countrylink trains (☎ (02) 9379 4850 or Freecall 132232) service all of NSW. There is at least one carriage per train which is wheelchair accessible and has an accessible toilet.

Things to See & Do

Darling Harbour (visitors centre ☎ (02) 9286 0111) has a number of accessible attractions including the Maritime Museum, Chinese Gardens, Sydney Aquarium and nearby Powerhouse Museum. There is a Mobility Map, but it is less informative than those in other cities.

Other Sydney attractions providing good access include Centrepoint Tower (☎ (02) 9229 7444), the Royal Botanic Gardens (☎ (02) 9231 8111) and the historic buildings in Macquarie St.

A regional attraction that provides excellent access is the Western Plains Zoo in Dubbo.

Accommodation

- NICAN and *Accessing Sydney* are good sources of information on accommodation options in Sydney.
- The new Sydney Central YHA (02) 9281 9111) opposite Central Station, has accessible rooms with twin single beds and ensuite bathrooms with wheel-in showers, grab rails etc. The cost is $26 per person per night.
- The Wheel Resort (☎ (02) 6685 6139) at Byron Bay on the north coast has seven cabins and is fully wheelchair accessible (including the pool and spa). Prices start at $80 per night or $500 per week for a single unit in the low season.
- Clark Bay Farm (☎ (02) 4476 1640) at Narooma on the south coast has three self-contained two-bedroom units (including one high-dependancy unit with ceiling hoist) and is fully wheelchair accessible. Prices start at $110 per night in the low season.

Organised Tours

- Barrier Free Travel, (☎ (02) 6655 1733), 36 Wheatly St, Nth Bellingen 2454
- Crossroads Disabled & Handicapped Travel Centre, (☎ (02) 6582 5910) 54 Vendul Crescent Port Macquarie 2444
- Special Care Travel, (☎ (02) 6564 7566), PO Box 229, Bowraville 244
- Ability Specialised Transport, (☎ (02) 6297 5517, Unit 17/14 King St, Queanbeyan 2620

Information for disabled travellers in Canberra is covered separately in the ACT chapter.

Quality Access International provides online information on hotels, tours etc at http: / /ww.qai.com.au

Bruce M Cameron

ages and discounts (on car hire, for instance) through organisations and travel agents that cater to senior travellers. Start hunting at your local senior citizens' advice bureau.

For information on recreational and other activities contact the Seniors Information Service (☎ 131244), 6th floor, 93 York St, Sydney 2000. In March, there's a seniors week with exhibitions, concerts, seminars etc.

TRAVEL WITH CHILDREN

Successful travel with young children requires effort, but it can certainly be done. Try not to overdo things and consider using some sort of self-catering accommodation as a base. Include children in the planning process; if they've helped to work out where you're going, they'll be more interested when they get there. Include a range of activities – for example, balance a visit to the Art Gallery of NSW with one to the Powerhouse Museum. During school holidays many places put on extra activities specifically for children.

In Sydney, look for a copy of *Sydney's Child*, a free monthly paper listing businesses and activities geared to ankle-biters.

For more general information see Lonely Planet's *Travel with Children*.

EMERGENCY

In the case of a life-threatening situation dial ☎ 000. This call is free from any phone and the operator will connect you with the police, ambulance or fire brigade. For other crisis and personal counselling services (eg sexual assault, poisons information, alcohol or drug problems), check the Community Information section of the local telephone book.

DANGERS & ANNOYANCES
Theft

NSW is a relatively safe place to visit, but you should still take reasonable precautions, especially in Sydney. Don't leave your hotel room or car unlocked; don't leave your money, luggage or valuables unattended or in full view through car windows.

If you're unlucky enough to have something stolen, immediately report it to the nearest police station. If your credit cards, cash card or travellers cheques have been taken, notify your bank or the relevant company immediately (most have 24-hour 'lost or stolen' numbers listed under 'Banks' or 'Credit Card Organisations' in the yellow pages).

Swimming

It seems unnecessary to mention it, but don't ever go swimming if you have been drinking alcohol. Swimming after a heavy meal is also unwise. See also Ecology & Environment in the Facts about the Region chapter.

Ocean-Beaches The surf lifesaving clubs that line the coast aren't there for show – many people are rescued from the surf each year.

To signal that you're in trouble in the water, *raise your arm* and keep it raised while treading water or floating. If you've been sensible enough to swim at a patrolled beach (indicated by flags), help will come quickly.

Dumpers, waves that break in shallow water, can cause spinal injuries, but most people who are rescued have been caught in rips. A rip is the 'river' by which water from the surf makes its way back to the sea. Being swept out in a rip can be terrifying, but keep your head. All you need do is stay afloat and raise your arm. Most rips lose momentum quickly.

To rescue yourself from a rip, wait until you seem to have slowed, then swim parallel to the shore for about 30 metres. By then you should be out of the rip and can swim back in. Never try to swim back to shore against a rip.

You can expect to find rips near river and lake mouths, especially after rain, but they can occur anywhere.

Rivers & Lakes Watch out for dead trees and the like which can tangle you up, and never jump or dive in if you're uncertain of the depth.

Sharks & Other Ocean-Going Nasties

Shark attacks are extremely rare – you're much more likely to be involved in a car accident. Some major beaches, especially around Sydney, have shark-netting. The nets usually don't actually stop sharks from approaching the beach – they run out from the shore to deter sharks from cruising along the beaches and checking out the menu. The more popular beaches also have shark-spotting planes at peak times.

There are various poisonous marine animals, such as stone fish (with poison spines) and deadly blue-ringed octopuses (they're small and hang out in rock pools). If you don't know what it is, don't touch it.

Snakes & Spiders

Snakes are protected. Although there are many venomous snakes, few are aggressive, and unless you have the bad fortune to stand on one it's unlikely that you'll be bitten. Taipans and tiger snakes, however, will attack if alarmed. Sea snakes can also be dangerous.

To minimise your chances of being bitten always wear boots, socks and long trousers when walking through undergrowth where snakes may be present. Don't put your hands into holes and crevices, and be careful when collecting firewood.

Snake bites don't cause instantaneous death and antivenenes are usually available. Keep the victim calm and still, wrap the bitten limb tightly, as for a sprained ankle, then attach a splint to immobilise it. Then seek medical help, if possible with the dead snake for identification. Don't attempt to catch the snake if there's even a remote possibility of being bitten again. Tourniquets and sucking out the poison are now comprehensively discredited.

There are a few nasty spiders too, including the funnel-web, the redback and the white-tail, so it's best not to play with any spider. The funnel-web bite is treated in the same way as snake bite. For redback bites, apply ice and seek medical attention.

Insects

Flies The swarms of bushflies that descend on you in outback areas are unbelievably annoying, but other than driving you demented they do no harm. Use insect repellent if you don't want to spend your whole day waving the little bastards from your face. Flies vanish at sunset, but that's when the mosquitoes come out ...

Mosquitoes Mozzies can be a problem. Fortunately, none of them are malaria carriers although every few years there are localised

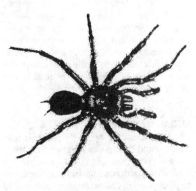

The funnel-web spider is named after the shape of the web it creates to trap its prey

The redback spider is actually only about half this size, but its bite can still be deadly

outbreaks of mosquito-borne fevers, such as Ross River fever.

Ticks The common bush-tick (found in the forest and scrub country along the eastern coast) can be dangerous if left lodged in the skin, as the toxin the tick excretes can cause paralysis and sometimes death. Check your body for lumps every night if you're walking in tick-infested areas. The tick should be removed by dousing it with methylated spirits or kerosene and levering it out, but make sure you remove it intact. Check children and dogs for ticks after a walk in the bush.

Cockroaches Sydney and some of the more humid coastal areas suffer from cockies. No, not the birds – cockroaches. Sydneysiders seem to get by with a mixture of tolerance and all-out chemical warfare, but if you haven't encountered a giant cockroach before, you're in for a surprise.

Leeches Leeches are quite common, and while they will suck your blood they are, however, not dangerous and they can usually be easily removed by the application of salt or water.

On the Road

Kangaroos and wandering stock can be a real hazard to drivers. A collision with one will badly damage your car and probably kill the animal. Unfortunately, other drivers are even more dangerous, especially those who drink. Australia has its share of fatal road accidents, particularly in the countryside, so don't drink and drive, and take care. The dangers posed by stray animals and drunks are greater at night, so avoid travelling after dark. See the Getting Around chapter for more on driving hazards.

Bushfire

In dry, hot weather, bushfires can raze thousands of hectares of eucalypt forests, with the volatile haze of eucalyptus oil exploding into a wall of flames 40 metres high. If a firestorm

develops, the inferno can devour the bush faster than you can drive away from it.

Most fires are started by people. Be *extremely* careful when camping in summer. Apart from a real risk of dying in a fire, the legal penalties for lighting one – accidentally or deliberately – on a Total Fire Ban day are severe. This includes camping stoves fuelled by gas or liquid. *Never* throw a cigarette butt out of a car. Australians don't like 'dobbing' people in to the police, but they make exceptions of those who light fires on Total Fire Ban days.

If there's a fire in the area, leave early – most bushfire deaths occur in the panic of last-minute evacuations.

If you're caught in a fire you must shelter from the intense radiant heat. It melts glass in seconds! Put a wall or just a dampened woollen jumper between you and the flames. In a crisis, stay in your car and park in as clear a space as you can find. Lie on the floor under the dashboard, covering yourself with a woollen blanket if possible. The fire front often passes quickly and it can be safer to head back into the burnt area than to run or drive away from the fire. Watch for falling trees.

Bushwalkers should take local advice before setting out. On a Total Fire Ban day, don't go – delay your trip until the weather has changed. Call the Country Fire Authority's recorded message service (☎ 131599) for current fire restrictions. If you're out in the bush and you see smoke, even at a great distance, take it seriously. Go to the nearest open space, downhill if possible. A forested ridge is the most dangerous place to be. Bushfires move quickly and change direction with the wind.

LEGAL MATTERS

The legal drinking age is 18 and you may need a photo ID to prove your age. Stiff fines, jail and other penalties could be incurred if you're caught driving under the influence of alcohol. During festive holidays and special events, random breath-testing stations (booze buses) are often set up to deter drunk drivers. The legal blood-alcohol limit is 0.05%.

Traffic offences (illegal parking, speeding etc) usually incur a fine for which you're allowed 30 days to pay. See also Road Rules in the Getting Around chapter.

The importation and use of illegal drugs is prohibited and could result in prison.

If you need legal assistance contact the Legal Aid Commission of NSW (☎ 9219 5000), 19 Castlereagh St, Sydney.

BUSINESS HOURS

Most offices and businesses open weekdays from 9 am to 5 pm, some until 5.30 pm. Banking hours are usually Monday to Thursday from 9.30 am to 4 pm, Friday to 5 pm.

Most shops open weekdays from 8.30 or 9 am to 5 or 5.30 pm, with extended hours on Thursday to 9 or 9.30 pm in larger towns. Many shops open all day Saturday but some still close at noon. Shopping hours are now more flexible and Sunday trading is becoming more common. Twenty-four-hour convenience stores are common in Sydney and other cities. On the major highways you'll come across 24-hour service stations, often with cafes attached.

Most pubs open at 10 am and close sometime around 11 pm or midnight, later on weekends. Some have 24-hour licenses.

PUBLIC HOLIDAYS & SPECIAL EVENTS

Public holidays in NSW and the ACT are:

New Year's Day
    1 January
Australia Day
    26 January
Trades & Labour Day (ACT only)
    1 March
Easter (Good Friday & Easter Monday)
    March/April
Anzac Day
    25 April
Queen's Birthday
    June (2nd Monday)
Bank Holiday (NSW only)
    August (1st Monday)
Labour Day
    October (1st Monday)

Christmas Day
    25 December
Boxing Day
    26 December

Most public holidays become long weekends, and if a fixed-date holiday such as New Year's Day falls on a weekend, the following Monday will usually be a holiday. Some country towns have holidays for local festivals, such as show day.

Annual special events include:

January
    Australia Day – this national holiday, commemorating the arrival of the First Fleet in 1788, is observed on 26 January
    Survival Festival – the Aboriginal version of Australia Day, also held on 26 January, marked by Koori music, dance and arts and crafts displays in Sydney
    Australasian Country Music Festival – Tamworth *is* country music in Australia, and this festival held on the Australia Day long weekend is the showcase for the country's top C&W artists
February
    Royal Canberra Show – held in late February
February/March
    Gay & Lesbian Mardi Gras – the most colourful event on the Sydney social calendar, culminating in a spectacular parade along Oxford St
March
    Hunter Valley Vintage Festival – wine enthusiasts flock to the Hunter Valley for wine tasting, and grape picking and treading contests
March to April
    Royal Easter Show – livestock contests and rodeos held in Sydney
    Canberra Festival – held over 10 days in mid-March, ending with a public holiday
    National Folk Festival – held in late March in Canberra
April
    Anzac Day – a national public holiday, on 25 April, commemorating the landing of Anzac troops at Gallipoli in 1915. Memorial marches by the returned soldiers of both world wars and the veterans of Korea and Vietnam are held all over the country.
June
    Ski season opens – Snowy Mountains
August
    Sydney City to Surf – Australia's biggest foot race
September
    Mudgee Wine Festival

October
> Australian Bush Music Festival – Aboriginal and non-Aboriginal singers, dancers and musicians perform at Glen Innes
> Bathurst 1000 – motor-racing enthusiasts flock to Bathurst for the annual 1000-km touring-car race on the superb Mt Panorama circuit

November
> Melbourne Cup – on the first Tuesday in November, Australia's premier horse race is run in Melbourne. The whole country shuts down for three minutes or so while the race is run. Many country towns schedule racing events to coincide with it.

December to January
> These are the busiest summer months, with Christmas, school holidays, lots of beach activities, rock and jazz festivals, international sporting events including tennis and cricket, a whole host of outdoor activities and lots of parties. The Sydney to Hobart Yacht Race is one of the major events.

Agricultural Shows

For a taste of rural life you should visit an agricultural show. Sydney's Royal Easter Show is by far the biggest, but it's a case of the city being given a glimpse of the country. If you would like to take a look at country people kicking up their heels in their own element visit a country show. There are plenty of them.

Field Days

Without the side-show-alley attractions of the agricultural shows, field days are aimed at farmers. Apart from the opportunity to see the big toys and latest developments in agribusiness at close hand, there are also sheepdog trials and other events of more general interest. The biggest field days are listed below, but other centres also hold them.

> Ag-Quip Field Days – Tamworth, mid-August; Gunnedah, August
> Henty Machinery Field Days – Henty, third week in September
> Australian National Field Days – range, in mid November

There are also small-farm field days, with less emphasis on big machinery and offering more chances of meeting alternative lifestylers. A popular small-farm field day is held at Mudgee in mid-July.

Livestock Sales

Just about every large country town west of the Great Dividing Range (and some east) has saleyards, and the local paper has the date of the next sales. It's well worth attend-

At the Livestock Sales

The graziers wear their best: the standard uniform for men is an Akubra hat (the good one, not the old one), moleskin trousers, boots and a sportscoat; women might be dressed similarly, or in their church-going gear. The sale offers a chance to catch up on district gossip, and tea is drunk amidst the Landcruisers, utes and Fairlanes parked in the shade. Later there might be a few beers at the pub.

Over at the yards, the dogs are working hard, responding to shrill whistles or, if something is going awry, furious yelling. The cattle bellow, the sheep set up a cacophony of baas and clattering hooves, semi-trailers growl in and out with loads of livestock and there might be a couple of drovers on horseback, cracking whips around a swirling mob of cattle. Up on the boardwalk, the auctioneer's quickfire patter is interspersed with lusty shouts from the bidders, and his clerk knows all the buyers by name. And that all-pervading smell? Big bucks. ■

ing one for an undiluted look at rural Australia.

Surf Lifesaving Carnivals

The volunteer surf lifesaver is one of Australia's icons, but despite the macho image about a third of lifesavers are female and the proportion is growing. Each summer, surf carnivals are held all along the coast where you can see the lifesavers in action. Check at a local surf lifesaving club for dates or contact Surf Lifesaving NSW (☎ 9663 4298).

ACTIVITIES

There are plenty of activities that you can take part in while travelling around the state. NSW has a flourishing skiing industry. Bushwalking is cheap and you can do it anywhere. There are many fantastic walks in the various national parks. If you're interested in surfing you'll find great beaches and surf, and there's good diving along the coast. You can go horseriding just about everywhere, from the high country to the outback plains. You can cycle all around NSW; for the athletic there are long, challenging routes and for the not-so-masochistic there are plenty of great day trips.

Cycling

There are possibilities for some great rides in NSW, from the endless western plains to the Snowy Mountains in summer. See the Getting Around chapter for information on long-distance cycling.

The Blue Mountains – A Guide for Cyclists by Jim Smith (paperback, $15) is pricey for its size but has been recommended for its detail. The experienced and adventurous could try *Cycle the Bush* by Sven Klinge (Hill of Content), which details 100 rides in NSW for mountain-bikers.

If you're having trouble finding these titles, Bicycle NSW (☎ 9283 5200), Level 2, 209 Castlereagh St, Sydney, may have copies. It publishes a handy book called *Cycling around Sydney* which details routes and cycle paths in Sydney, the Blue Mountains, Illawarra and the Central Coast. It also publishes other booklets on cycling in the state.

Skiing

Some excellent skiing is available in the Snowy Mountains. See the South-East chapter for details.

Bushwalking

Opportunities for bushwalking abound in NSW, with a huge variety of standards, lengths and terrains. Almost every national park either has walking trails or offers wilderness walking. Near Sydney there are popular walks in the Blue Mountains and Royal National Park, with the wilderness areas of Wollemi National Park not far away.

Longer routes include the three-day **Six Foot Track** to the Jenolan Caves and the 140-km **Ensign Barralier Track** from Katoomba to Mittagong. The **Great North Walk** from Sydney to Newcastle can be walked in sections or as a two-week trek. The *Great North Walk Kit* is available from various bushwalking suppliers and NPWS outlets, with more detailed tracknotes in *The Great North Walk* (Kangaroo Press) by McDougall & Shearer-Herlot. The **Hume & Hovell Walking Track** from Yass to near Albury follows the route of two early explorers and passes through some beautiful high country. It can be walked in sections or as a trek of up to 25 days. The DCLM publishes a guide to the track by Harry Hill.

The best way to find out about walking areas is to contact a bushwalking club – contact the Confederation of Bushwalking Clubs NSW (☎ 9548 1228) or check the yellow pages under 'Clubs – Bushwalking'. Outdoor stockists such as Paddy Pallin and Mountain Designs are also good sources of information. If you want to walk without the bother of carrying a pack, contact Great Australian Walks (☎ 9555 7580).

Lonely Planet's *Bushwalking in Australia* describes five walks in NSW.

Rock Climbing & Abseiling

The sheer cliffs of the Blue Mountains are very popular for climbing and abseiling, and a number of places in Katoomba run beginners' courses. See the Around Sydney chapter.

Surfing

With 1900 km of coastline, much of it surf beaches, it makes sense to get out there and surf. That isn't as easy as it sounds, though, and boogie-boarding or body-surfing is as far as most visitors get. You can learn to surf in Coffs Harbour and Byron Bay. North Coast Surfaris (☎ 1800 634 951) offers week-long surfing trips up the coast from Sydney to Byron Bay.

Tracks magazine provides good insights into Aussie surfing, and *Surfing Australia's East Coast* by Aussie surf-star Nat Young is a slim, cheap, comprehensive guide to the best breaks. He's also written the *Surfing & Sailboard Guide to Australia*, which covers the whole country. Surfing enthusiasts can also look for the expensive coffee-table book *Atlas of Australian Surfing* by Mark Warren.

Swimming

A visit to NSW will involve swimming at a beach sooner or later – there are just so many! – but there are also many lakes and rivers where you can cool off. Also, most towns have an Olympic-sized pool.

Whitewater Rafting

There are some excellent thrills to be had shooting rapids on the upper Murray and Shoalhaven rivers in the south and the Nymboida River in the north. See the Coffs Harbour section of the North Coast chapter, and the South-East and ACT chapters.

Canoeing & Kayaking

Many of the state's waterways are suitable for canoeing, with adventurous runs on the short, swift rivers flowing to the coast from the Great Dividing Range, and long, lazy treks on the meandering inland rivers.

The Canoe Association of NSW (☎ 9660 4597) can help you with general queries and point you towards clubs and hire places. It also has a recorded message (☎ 00555 0889) telling you river heights throughout the state.

You can rent sea kayaks in Sydney and on the south coast.

Hang-Gliding & Paragliding

Hang-gliding is popular near Wollongong and Byron Bay, and you can take tandem flights. Paragliding outfits are found at many beach resorts.

Horseriding & Trekking

Opportunities for horseriding abound, from hour-long jaunts to overnight (or longer) treks. Popular areas for organised horse treks include New England and the north-west.

Diving

There are plenty of places to go diving in Sydney, on the Central Coast and in the waters around Booderee (Jervis Bay), Ulladulla, Narooma and Merimbula on the South Coast. Outfits like Pro Dive run dive courses.

WORK

If you have a 12-month 'working holiday' visa, you can officially only work for three of those 12 months. Working on a regular tourist visa is *verboten*. To receive wages without being taxed at the maximum rate you need a Tax File Number, issued by the Taxation Department. Forms are available from post offices and you must show your passport and visa.

With unemployment in Australia high, it isn't easy finding casual work; make sure you have enough funds to cover yourself for your stay, or have a contingency plan if work isn't forthcoming. However, many travellers manage to find some work, especially in the peak season at major tourist centres. The best prospects for casual work include bar work, waiting on tables or washing dishes, nanny work, fruit picking and collecting for charities. People with office skills can often find temp work in Sydney. The Commonwealth Employment Service (CES) offices have in the past been able to provide good information on what is available where but the government has plans to privatise the service. Try the classified section of the daily papers under Situations Vacant. Hostels often have information about work.

Harvests are the main source of casual work in rural areas. The CES has in the past produced a booklet detailing harvest times and locations, but you should use this as a general guide only – call the local CES office or its privatised equivalent to confirm dates and availability of work before heading off into the sticks.

Grape harvests in the Hunter Valley and around Griffith begin around mid-February and last through March. Other fruit is picked around Griffith from November to March. The apple harvest near Orange and Batlow begins in early March. Cherry picking around Young begins in late spring. Hot work on the cotton harvest is sometimes available near Moree and Bourke in early summer. See the various sections in this book for more information.

With persistence and luck you might find a farm or station willing to give you board and lodging (and perhaps some pocket money) in return for work. This won't make you rich but it's a good way to experience the country. If you don't have any contacts, the only way is to turn up in person and see what's doing. Expect a lot of knock-backs.

See Ecology & Environment in the Facts about NSW chapter for information on voluntary conservation work and WWOOF.

ACCOMMODATION

NSW is well equipped with youth hostels, backpackers' hostels and caravan parks. A typical town of a few thousand people will have a basic motel at around $45/50 for singles/doubles, an old hotel with rooms (shared bathrooms) at $25/35 or less, and a caravan park – probably with tent-sites for around $10 and on-site vans or cabins for $30 for two people. If the town is on a main road or is bigger, it'll probably have several of each.

If there's a group of you, the rates for three or four people in a room are always worth checking. Often there are larger 'family' rooms or units with two bedrooms.

Camping & Caravanning

For many, camping in the bush is one of the highlights of a visit to Australia.

If you're using a tent as your main accommodation you'll find that almost every town has a caravan park. If you want to get around Australia on the cheap, then camping is the cheapest way of all, with nightly costs for two from around $10 (twice that in some beachside resorts in summer).

Caravan parks are, as the name says, intended more for caravans (trailers) than tents, but most have a lawn area set aside for tents. Apart from bathrooms and laundries, there are few communal facilities. In most big towns caravan parks are a long way from the centre, which means that if you're doing a lot of camping you'll need your own transport.

Many caravan parks also have on-site vans which you can rent for the night. These give you the comfort of a caravan without the inconvenience of actually having to tow one. Self-contained on-site cabins are also widely available. They usually have one bedroom, or an area which can be screened from the rest of the unit – just the thing if you have small kids. Cabins also have their own bathroom and toilet, although this is sometimes an optional extra. They're also much less cramped than caravans, and the price difference is not always that great – say $25 to $30 for an on-site van, $30 to $50 for a cabin.

Hostels

Hostels are great places for meeting people and great travellers' centres; in many busier hostels foreign visitors often outnumber Australians.

YHA Australia has an active Youth Hostel Association (YHA), with hostels in many parts of NSW. YHA hostels provide basic accommodation, usually in small dormitories or bunk rooms although more and more provide twin rooms for couples. The nightly charges are reasonable – usually $13 to $19 or $20 to $25 per person in a twin.

You must have a regulation sleeping-bag

sheet or bed linen – for hygiene reasons a regular sleeping bag will not do. If you don't have sheets they can be rented at many hostels (usually $3), but it's cheaper, after a few nights' stay, to have your own. YHA offices and some larger hostels sell the official YHA sheet bag.

All hostels have cooking facilities and 24-hour access, and there's usually a communal area. There are generally laundry facilities and often there are excellent noticeboards. Many hostels have a maximum-stay period – because some hostels are permanently full it would hardly be fair for people to stay too long when others are being turned away.

Accommodation can usually be booked directly with the manager or through the YHA Membership & Travel Centre (☎ 9261 1111), 422 Kent St, Sydney. The annual *YHA Accommodation Guide* tells all.

Few YHA hostels still have the old fetishes for curfews and chores, but many retain segregated dorms. Most also take non-YHA members, although there may be a small 'temporary membership' charge. To become a full YHA member in Australia costs $27 a year (there's also a $17 joining fee, although if you're an overseas resident joining in Australia you don't pay this). You can join at any youth hostel.

The YHA also has the Aussie Starter Pack, whereby Australian residents joining the YHA receive two vouchers worth $8.50 each to use at a hostel in their state. International visitors joining the YHA at a hostel receive their first night at that hostel for free. Under the scheme, the additional nightly fee charged to non-YHA members is $3 per night. Nonmembers receive an Aussie Starter Card, to be stamped each night by the YHA. Full membership is given when the card has nine stamps.

Youth hostels are part of Hostelling International, so if you're already a member of the YHA in your own country, you're entitled to use Australian hostels.

The YHA has an impressive Australia-wide list of discounts on everything from meals to hiking gear.

Other Backpacker Hostels Sydney has a large selection of backpacker hostels. You won't find many in the more out-of-the-way places, as they aren't philanthropic like the YHA. They're mostly on the lucrative backpacker trail up the coast.

The standards vary enormously: some are rundown inner-city hotels where the owners try to fill empty rooms; unless renovations have been done, these are generally gloomy and depressing. A few are former motels, so each unit, typically with four to six beds, will have fridge, TV and bathroom. The best in terms of facilities are purpose built, although sometimes they're simply too big.

In Sydney, especially, backpackers are often employed to run the hostels and usually it's not long before standards slip. The best places are often smaller hostels where the owner is also the manager.

Prices at backpackers' hostels are in line with YHA hostels, about $15, sometimes more in Sydney and Byron Bay.

VIP (aka Backpacker Resorts of Australia or BRA) is one backpacker organisation you can join to receive a discount card ($20, valid for 12 months) and a list of participating hostels. This is hardly a great inducement to join, but you receive useful discounts on other services like transport so it may be worth considering.

Nomads Backpackers (☎ 1800 819 883) runs a number of revamped pubs.

Colleges

University colleges in Sydney offer inexpensive accommodation during vacations. See the Sydney chapter for details.

Guesthouses & B&Bs

Choices include everything from converted barns and stables, renovated and rambling old guesthouses and upmarket country homes to simple bedrooms in family homes. Some are listed in this book, but for a greater selection contact Homestay International (☎ 9948 8384), 21 Bareena Drive, Balgowlah Heights 2093, or B&B Australia (☎ 9498 5344), 666 Pacific Highway, Killara 2071.

Tariffs cover a wide range but are typically in the $40 to $100 a double bracket.

Some places don't accept credit cards or cheques.

Farmstays

Across the state you'll find properties offering accommodation, and sometimes a programme of farm activities. Some are just B&Bs in farmhouses, others are cottages which happen to be on farms. Expect to pay around $300 for a week in a self-contained cottage and from about $70 (sometimes less) to about $180 per person per night for full board and activities.

Some farmstays are listed in this guide, but for a more complete list contact NSW Farm & Country Holidays (☎ 9436 4757, 1800 803 007), PO Box 772, Crows Nest 2065. It has a brochure and can make credit-card bookings. Packages which can be booked from overseas are arranged by Australian Farmstay Holidays (☎ 9369 5822), 355 Spring St, Bondi Junction 2022. Many overseas travel agents can make direct bookings with this organisation.

Pubs

Outside Sydney and a few big towns, hotel accommodation means pub accommodation. Although the grandest buildings in country towns are often the pubs, the standard of accommodation rarely lives up to the architecture. Many pubs prefer not to offer accommodation, but the licensing laws require them to do so.

Pub rooms are usually clean but basic, with not much more than a bed, a wardrobe and sometimes a wash-basin. The bathroom is usually shared. Despite the lack of luxury, it's worth considering staying in pubs rather than motels. Apart from the saving in cost (around $15/30 is average), staying at 'the pub' means that you have an entree to the town's social life. You'll already be known to the bar-person and you won't have trouble meeting people. The smaller the town, the friendlier the pub.

The two essentials in choosing a pub room are to get one which isn't directly above the noisy bar, and to check that the bed is in reasonable condition.

A big plus with pubs is that the breakfasts (sometimes included in the tariff, but increasingly an extra charge) can be quite enormous.

Motels

If you want a more modern place, with your own bathroom and other facilities, then you're moving into the motel bracket. Prices vary, and (unlike hotels) singles are often not much cheaper than doubles. The reason is quite simple – in the old hotels many of the rooms really are singles, relics of the days when single men travelled the country looking for work. In motels, the rooms are almost always doubles.

In most places you'll have no trouble finding a budget motel for around $45 to $55 a double; better motels cost around $60 to $70.

Hotels

As well as pubs, the upper end of the hotel spectrum is well represented, in Sydney and Canberra at least. There are many excellent four and five-star hotels and quite a few lesser places where standards vary. Outside the capitals, quality accommodation is offered by the more expensive motels or beach resorts.

Serviced Apartments

Restricted mainly to Sydney and Canberra, serviced apartments offer hotel-style convenience (the apartment is cleaned for you and there's a reception desk) with cooking facilities and a bit more room to move than a hotel room. They're increasingly popular in the upper-price brackets, the cheaper ones being attractive for families travelling on a budget. See the Sydney and ACT chapters for more information.

Holiday Flats

Holiday flats, found mainly in beachside towns, are geared to family holidays, so they fill up at peak times and often have minimum rental periods of a week. Outside peak times you might be able to rent one by the night. Standards and prices vary enormously, but if you have a group they can be affordable and might even be cheaper than hostels outside peak season.

Houseboats

The Hawkesbury River near Sydney, Port Stephens and the nearby Myall Lakes, the Clarence River and the Murray River are some of the waterways where you can hire houseboats. Houseboat hire rates are second only to those of ski lodges in complexity, but basically if you have a few people (say three or four) and hire midweek outside peak times, the cost can be comparable to motels.

FOOD

Fresh, high-quality ingredients make eating in NSW a pleasure. The state grows everything from tropical fruit to cold-climate vegetables and is even a major producer of rice. The beef and lamb are among the best in the world, and the Pacific Ocean supplies superb seafood. Add to this the huge variety of ethnic cuisines and you have the recipe for some memorable meals.

'Modern Australian' food has become a recognisable style – an amalgamation of Mediterranean, South-East Asian and Californian cuisines, with a look and taste that's distinctively Australian. Sydney has a multitude of excellent eateries for all budgets. Canberra is catching up, and in the larger towns, especially on the coast, there's a range of eating places.

In country areas you might find that steak and three veg is still the main item on the menu. In some small, remote country towns you might still be served canned vegetables.

Cafes & Restaurants

In Sydney, Canberra and the other large centres you'll find plenty of cafes and restaurants offering a myriad of cuisines, but in country towns you might be restricted to an old-style cafe (often just a takeaway shop with tables) and a Chinese restaurant.

If there are more than a couple of Chinese places you'll often find that they are in hot competition and offer good deals, with $5 lunch specials for example. Don't expect great cuisine though – the owners know that country people often judge food by the size of the serving.

Country motels sometimes have dining rooms but you're often paying restaurant prices for pub food. Order the least complicated dish on the menu.

This scenario is changing, and any place with the hint of a tourist industry, especially along the coast, is likely to have some good places to eat.

Pub & Club Food

For a sit-down meal in a country town, head for the pub, where you can almost always buy counter meals. These were once eaten at the bar, but nowadays there are usually tables. The quantities are usually large and prices are low, unless the pub serves meals in the dining room and calls it a bistro. Menus mostly have roasts, steaks, sausages, mixed grills and the like, although seafood and pasta dishes are common. There are usually set times for counter meals, say noon to 1.30 or 2 pm for lunch and 6 to 8.30 pm for dinner (or tea, as it's known).

Almost every town has an ex-servicemen's club, which uses profits from poker machines to provide an inexpensive dining room or bistro. Visitors are welcome, although there might be some basic dress restrictions. Bowling clubs are similar.

Takeaway Food

Australia's original takeaway food, the meat pie, is sold everywhere. While there are a few state-wide brands, most towns have a baker who makes pies. They can be pretty good.

Other fast food also abounds, and if you can't do without mass-produced, over-packaged junk food served by adolescents in uniform there are plenty of outlets. However, you're much better off seeing what the local takeaway shop has on offer (but avoid those where the food is pre-cooked). Even in country towns it's quite common for takeaway shops to have a selection of salads.

British visitors will barely recognise fish

& chips here. For a start, they're fried in vegetable oil, not lard, and the flavour and texture have more than a passing resemblance to fish and potatoes. Hamburgers from local takeaways are usually good. If you're a little hungrier, try a steak sandwich. In country towns your plain steak sandwich comes piled with salad. Note that what are called potato cakes in other states are called scallops (as in scalloped potatoes) in NSW.

As well as the fish & chip or hamburger shop (interchangeable terms, usually), you can get takeaway sandwiches, rolls etc at delis, milkbars (corner stores) and some bakeries. Many towns have Vietnamese (or Chinese) takeaways, or at least restaurants where you can buy takeaways.

Self-Catering

A wide range of produce is sold in supermarkets and (perhaps fresher) in neighbourhood shops. Prices are low. Some seasonal variation in prices and availability occurs, but with produce shipped in from all over Australia you can almost always find what you want at a reasonable price.

There are many excellent delis selling cheeses, processed meats and a wide range of delights such as pickled octopus or six varieties of olives. They often have tempting pastries, salads and other takeaways as well.

For more basic supplies, there are corner stores or milkbars stocking staples such as milk, bread, tinned food and maybe some fresh fruit and vegetables.

Even the old-fashioned butcher shops sell delicious pre-marinated, pre-seasoned, pre-portioned meats which you can cook with a minimum of fuss. Bakeries stock a wide range of products, although in small towns you'll still find some bakeries where lamingtons, cream buns, eclairs and elaborate wedding cakes fill the window displays.

In many coastal towns, fishing co-operatives sell seafood straight off the boat.

DRINKS
Nonalcoholic Drinks

Australians knock back Coke and flavoured milk like there's no tomorrow and also have some excellent mineral water brands. Coffee enthusiasts will find excellent coffee served all over Sydney. De-caf hasn't made much of an impression and is rarely offered in cafes or restaurants. Tea is of the tea-bag variety.

Alcohol

Beer Australian beer will be fairly familiar to North Americans; it's similar to what's known as lager in the UK. It may taste like lemonade to the European real-ale addict, but Australian beer has a higher alcohol content than British or American beers. Standard beer is generally around 4.9% alcohol, although most breweries now produce light beers, with an alcohol content of between 2% and 3.5%. Aussie beer is invariably chilled before drinking.

Once, buying a beer was simple. You decided whether you wanted 'new' or 'old'

Cooking Yabbies
You can catch yabbies at several farms in NSW, and just about every creek and dam in the Riverina yields them, but how do you cook them? Here's a recipe from Premier Yabbies (near Culcairn):

- Cool the yabbies in iced water and bring a large pot of water to the boil.
- Add a lemon cut into quarters and half a cup of brown sugar.
- Put the yabbies into the boiling water, up to 10 at a time.
- Return the water to the boil and wait for the yabbies to float to the top (about three minutes).
- Remove, rinse and drain the yabbies.
- Now you have to shell and clean them, a knack that's acquired through practice. It's similar to cleaning prawns: remove the shell and tail, then strip out the vein and the digestive tract. ■

(a heavier lager) and asked for a 'middy' (285 ml/10 oz glass) or a 'schooner' (450 ml/16 oz glass) and the bar-person filled one for you. Nowadays you have to stand there dithering between many fairly similar brands of lager and decide whether you want light or full-strength beer.

Toohey's is the largest brewer in the state, with Reschs maintaining a market, especially in rural areas. The Carlton brewery, an interloper from Victoria, has made big inroads, especially with their Victoria Bitter (VB or Vic). Carlton also brews Foster's, perhaps the best known of Australia's beer brands, but you don't see it often in NSW.

Small 'boutique' brewers have also been making a comeback and you'll find one-off brands such as Redback, Dogbolter and Eumundi. They're more expensive than the big commercial brands but definitely worth a try. Guinness is occasionally found on draught, usually in Irish pubs and rarely outside Sydney.

Wine European wine experts now realise just how good Australian wines can be – exporting wine is a multi-million dollar business. Wines need not be expensive. You're entering the 'pretty good' bracket if you pay over $10 for a bottle, and drinkable wines can be found for much less.

It takes a little while to become familiar with Australian wineries and their styles, but it's an effort worth making. Apart from browsing through bottle shops, the best way to sample a lot of styles is to visit wineries. The main areas are the Hunter Valley and the smaller Mudgee area. Most wineries welcome visitors for tastings.

You'll find some restaurants advertising that they're BYO ('Bring Your Own') and it means that they're not licensed to sell alcohol but you're permitted to bring your own with you. This is a real boon to wine-loving, budget-minded travellers, because you can bring your own bottle of wine from the local bottle shop or winery you visited and not pay any mark-up. There might be a small 'corkage' charge (typically about $1 per person) if you bring your own.

ENTERTAINMENT
Cinema
In the big cities there are commercial cinema chains, such as Village, Hoyts and Greater Union, and their cinemas are usually found in centres which will have anything from two to 10 screens in the one complex. Smaller towns have just the one cinema and many of these are almost museum pieces in themselves. Seeing a new-release mainstream film is expensive, around $12.50, maybe less in country areas. City cinemas often have one day a week when the price is lower.

In Sydney and Canberra you'll find art-house and independent cinemas and these places generally screen films that aren't made for mass consumption or specialise purely in re-runs of classics and cult movies.

Nightclubs
There's no shortage of these, but they're confined to the larger cities and towns. Clubs range from the exclusive 'members only' variety to barn-sized discos where anyone who wants to spend the money is welcomed with open arms. Admission charges range from around $6 to $12.

Some places have dress standards, but it's generally left to the discretion of the people at the door – if they don't like the look of you, bad luck. The more 'upmarket' night-clubs attract an older, more sophisticated and affluent crowd, and generally have stricter dress codes, smarter decor – and higher prices.

Live Music
Many suburban pubs have live music, and these are often great places for catching bands, either nationally well-known names or up-and-coming performers – most of Australia's popular bands started out on the pub circuit.

The best way to find out about the local scene is to get to know some locals, or travellers who have spent some time in the place. Otherwise, there are often comprehensive listings in newspapers, particularly on Friday.

Gambling

Despite the national propensity for gambling, it's strictly controlled.

Hardly a town in the state is without a horse-racing track or a Totalisator Agency Board (TAB) betting office. You can bet on the horses, the trots (harness racing) and the dogs (greyhound racing). Sydneysiders can also bet on some yacht races. For poker machines, all you have to do is step into one of the ubiquitous clubs; many pubs have them too. Lottery tickets and scratch cards are sold at newsagents. Canberra has a casino and Sydney has a temporary one in Pyrmont while a new one is being built.

SPECTATOR SPORTS

If you're an armchair – or wooden bench – sports fan, NSW has plenty to offer. Many of the following sports are best seen in Sydney – see the Entertainment section in the Sydney chapter for details.

Football

At least four types of football are played in NSW, each type being called 'football' by its aficionados. The season runs from about March to September.

Rugby is the main game in NSW and it's rugby league, the 13-a-side working-class version, that attracts the crowds. Most teams are in Sydney but there are others in Canberra, Wollongong and Newcastle. The main competition, run by the Australian Rugby League, is the Winfield Cup. A breakaway competition, the Super League, run by media giants Rupert Murdoch and Kerry Packer, began its first official season in 1997.

The other big rugby league series is the State of Origin clash with Queensland, which generates a lot of passion. These games are played in Sydney, Brisbane and Melbourne.

The more gentlemanly game of 15-a-side rugby union, originally for amateurs, has a less fanatical following, but the Australian rugby union team, the Wallabies, are world-beaters.

Aussie Rules football is a unique, exciting sport – only Gaelic football is anything like it. The Sydney Swans are NSW's only team so far in the Australian Football League.

Soccer is slowly gaining popularity thanks in part to the success of the national team, the appointment of England's Terry Venables as manager and the high profile of some Aussies playing for overseas clubs. The national league is only semi-professional and games attract a relatively small following. In the past most clubs were ethnically based, but they now appeal to the broader community. For information contact Soccer Australia (☎ 9380 6099).

Cricket

In Sydney you'll find the Sydney Cricket Ground, where international Test and one-day matches are played. There's also an interstate competition, the poorly attended Sheffield Shield, and hard-fought state-wide district cricket. The cricket season is October to March.

Other Sports

Basketball has grown phenomenally as a spectator sport since the formation of a national league. Baseball is another American sport slowly becoming more popular. Along the coast there are regular surf lifesaving carnivals and competitions. There's also yacht racing, some good tennis, including the NSW Open, and golf.

THINGS TO BUY

Avoid tacky souvenirs like plastic boomerangs, 'Aboriginal' ashtrays or cuddly koalas. They're all probably made abroad anyway. If you want to buy a souvenir of Australia, check to see that it was made here.

Aboriginal Art & Craft

The main forms of art were body painting, cave painting and rock engraving, and it's only in the last few decades that Aboriginal artists have begun using western materials like canvas and acrylic paints. These works have quickly gained wide appreciation. The paintings depict traditional Dreamtime stories and ceremonial designs, and each design has a particular spiritual significance.

Much of the Aboriginal art available in Sydney, especially the traditional styles, comes from other areas of Australia, but because they capture the essence of the Australian outback, they make a wonderful reminder of a trip to Australia.

The best works are out of reach of the average traveller, but among the cheaper artworks on sale are prints, baskets, small carvings and some beautiful screen-printed T-shirts produced by Aboriginal craft cooperatives – and a larger number of commercial rip-offs. It's worth shopping around and paying a few dollars more for the real thing.

Much of the Aboriginal art available in NSW, especially the traditional styles, comes from other areas of Australia and is sold in Sydney galleries. If you're travelling up the north coast, call in at Gurrigai Aboriginal Arts & Crafts at the New Italy site, off the Pacific Highway between Maclean and Ballina.

Australiana

The term 'Australiana' describes the things you buy as gifts for the folks back home or to remember your visit by, and are supposedly representative of Australia. Arts, crafts, T-shirts, designer clothing and bush gear are sold practically everywhere. Apart from the usual kitsch there's much that's of high quality, with prices to match, though you can pick up the odd bargain.

The seeds of many of Australia's native plants are on sale all over the place. Try growing kangaroo paws back home. Australian wines are well known overseas; but why not try honey (leatherwood honey is one of a number of local varieties), macadamia nuts or Bundaberg rum, with its unusual sweet flavour. You can also get exotic tinned witchetty grubs, honey ants and other bush tucker.

Aussie Clothing

Fit yourself out in some local clothes – made in Australia for Australian conditions. Start off with some Bonds undies and a singlet, a pair of Holeproof Explorer socks and Blundstone or Rossi boots. Then there's anything from the RM Williams line (boots, moleskin trousers, shirts), some Yakka or King Gee workwear, a shearer's top or bush shirt, a greasy-wool jumper, a Bluey (a coarse woollen worker's coat), a Driza-bone (an oilskin riding coat) – and top it off with an Akubra hat.

Australia also produces some of the world's best surfing equipment and clothing, including companies like Mambo, Hot Tuna and Quiksilver.

Outdoor Gear

Sydney's outdoor and adventure shops carry an excellent range of Australian-made and imported gear. In many cases, the locally made products are of equivalent quality to (and cheaper than) the imports. Paddy Pallin, Mountain Designs and Kathmandu are among the local firms.

Opals

The opal is Australia's national gemstone, and opals and opal jewellery are popular souvenirs. They are beautiful stones, but buy wisely and shop around – quality and prices can vary widely from place to place.

Antiques

Look for early-Australian colonial furniture made from cedar or huon pine; Australian silver jewellery; ceramics – either early factory pieces or studio pieces (especially anything by the Boyd family); glassware such as Carnival glass; and Australiana collectables and bric-a-brac such as old signs, tins, bottles etc. Updated annually, *Carter's Price Guide to Antiques in Australia* is an excellent price reference.

Crafts

You'll find many shops and galleries displaying crafts by local artists. The local craft scene is especially strong in the fields of ceramics, jewellery, stained glass and leathercraft. To see some of the best before you start travelling around the state, visit the Arts & Crafts Society of NSW (☎ 9241 1673), 80-84 George St, the Rocks, Sydney.

Getting There & Away

AIR

The majority of visitors to Australia arrive by air at Sydney's Kingsford-Smith airport, which is serviced by major international airlines.

Airfares to Australia are expensive – it's a long way from anywhere and flights are often heavily booked. If you're flying to Australia at a busy time of year (the middle of summer, ie Christmas time, is notoriously difficult) or on a particularly popular route (Hong Kong-Sydney or Singapore-Sydney), then plan well ahead. There are also a number of deals to ease the pain of ticket prices.

Travellers with Special Needs

If you've broken a leg, are vegetarian or require a special diet, are travelling in a wheelchair, taking a baby, terrified of flying, or whatever, let the airline staff know as soon as possible so that they can make the necessary arrangements. Remind them when you reconfirm your booking (at least 72 hours before departure) and again when you check in at the airport. It may also be worth ringing round the airlines before you make your booking to find out how they can handle your particular needs.

Airports and airlines can be helpful, but they need advance warning. Most international airports provide escorts from the check-in desk to the aeroplane where needed, and there should be ramps, lifts, accessible toilets and reachable phones. Aircraft toilets, on the other hand, are likely to present a problem; travellers should discuss this with the airline at an early stage and, if necessary, with their doctor.

Guide dogs for the blind often travel in a specially pressurised baggage compartment with other animals, away from their owner; smaller guide dogs, however, may be admitted to the cabin. All guide dogs are subject to the same quarantine laws as other animals

> **Warning**
> Prices for international travel are volatile, routes are introduced and cancelled, schedules change, rules are amended, special deals come and go, borders open and close. Airlines and governments seem to take a perverse pleasure in making price structures and regulations as complicated as possible and you should check directly with the airline or travel agent to make sure you understand how a fare (and ticket you may buy) works.
>
> In addition, the travel industry is highly competitive and there are many lurks and perks. The upshot of this is that you should get opinions, quotes and advice from as many airlines and travel agents as possible before you part with your hard-earned cash. The details given in this chapter should be regarded only as pointers and cannot be any substitute for your own careful, up-to-date research. ■

when entering or returning to countries free of rabies.

Deaf travellers can ask for airport and in-flight announcements to be written down for them.

Children under two travel for 10% of the standard fare (or free on some airlines) as long as they don't occupy a seat. They don't get a baggage allowance either. 'Skycots' should be provided by the airline if requested in advance; these will take a child weighing up to about 10kg. Children aged between two and 12 years can usually occupy a seat for half to two-thirds of the full fare, and get a baggage allowance. Pushchairs can often be taken as hand luggage.

Discount Tickets

For a cheap ticket, go to an agent not directly to the airline. The airline usually only quotes you the regular fare, but an agent can offer special deals, particularly on competitive routes. Occasionally, however, airlines make one-off special deals on particular routes in order to fill seats so watch the travel ads in the press.

What's available and what it costs depends on the time of year, the route you're flying and your choice of airline. If you're flying on a popular route (eg from Hong Kong) or one where the choice of flights is limited (eg from South America or Africa), the fare is likely to be higher or only the official fare will be available.

Similarly, dirt-cheap fares are often less conveniently scheduled, and go by less convenient routes or with less popular airlines.

Things to consider when choosing a ticket are its validity (you don't want to buy a return ticket that's only valid for two weeks) and the number of stopovers you want. As a rule of thumb, the cheaper the ticket the fewer stopovers you'll be allowed. Also think about how much of a hassle it'll be if you have to change planes on the way to Australia. Paying more for a ticket may be worth it to avoid delays or waiting for hours in a foreign departure lounge.

Round-the-World Tickets

Round-the-World (RTW) tickets are popular and many take you through Australia. The airline RTW tickets are often real bargains. Since Australia is at the other side of the world to Europe and North America, it can sometimes be cheaper to keep going in the same direction rather than return the way you came.

Air Travel Glossary

Apex Apex, or 'advance purchase excursion' is a discounted ticket which must be paid for in advance. There are penalties if you wish to change it.

Baggage Allowance This will be written on your ticket: usually one 20-kg item to go in the hold, plus one item of hand luggage.

Bucket Shop An unbonded travel agency specialising in discounted airline tickets.

Bumped Just because you have a confirmed seat doesn't mean you're going to get on the plane – see Overbooking.

Cancellation Penalties If you have to cancel or change an Apex ticket, there are often heavy penalties involved – insurance can sometimes be taken out against these penalties. Some airlines impose penalties on regular tickets as well, particularly against 'no show' passengers.

Check In Airlines ask you to check in at a certain time ahead of the flight departure (usually 1½ hours on international flights). If you fail to check in on time and the flight is overbooked, the airline can cancel your booking and give your seat to somebody else.

Confirmation Having a ticket written out with the flight and date you want doesn't necessarily mean you have a seat. Until the agent has checked with the airline that your status is 'OK' or confirmed, you could just be 'on request' (RQ), this being the code that would be written in place of OK on your ticket.

Discounted Tickets There are two types of discounted fares – officially discounted (see Promotional Fares) and unofficially discounted. The lowest prices often impose drawbacks like flying with unpopular airlines, inconvenient schedules, or unpleasant routes and connections. A discounted ticket can save you other things than money – you may be able to pay Apex prices without the associated Apex advance booking and other requirements. Discounted tickets only exist where there is fierce competition.

Full Fares Airlines traditionally offer 1st class (coded F), business class (coded J) and economy class (coded Y) tickets. These days, there are so many promotional and discounted fares available from the regular economy class that few passengers pay full economy fare.

Lost Tickets If you lose your ticket an airline will usually treat it like a travellers' cheque and, after inquiries, issue you with another one. Legally, however, an airline is entitled to treat it like cash and if you lose it then it's gone forever. Take good care of your tickets.

No Shows No shows are passengers who fail to show up for their flight, sometimes due to unexpected delays or disasters, sometimes due to simply forgetting, sometimes because they made more than one booking and didn't bother to cancel the one they didn't want. Full fare passengers who fail to turn up are sometimes entitled to travel on a later flight. The rest of us are penalised (see Cancellation Penalties).

On Request An unconfirmed booking for a flight, see Confirmation.

Open Jaws A return ticket where you fly out to one place but return from another. If available, this can save you backtracking to your arrival point.

Official airline RTW tickets are usually put together by two airlines and permit you to fly anywhere you want on their route systems as long as you don't backtrack. Other restrictions (usually) include booking the first sector in advance and cancellation penalties then apply. There may be restrictions on how many stops you're permitted and normally the tickets are valid from 90 days up to a year. Typical prices for RTW tickets with South Pacific stopovers are around £850 or US$2000.

An alternative RTW ticket is one put together by a travel agent using a combination of discounted airline tickets. A UK agent like Trailfinders can put together interesting London-to-London RTW combinations via Australia for around £895 to £1099.

Circle Pacific Tickets

Circle-Pacific fares are similar to RTW tickets, using a combination of airlines to circle the Pacific – combining Australia, New Zealand, North America and Asia. Some examples are Qantas-Northwest Orient and Canadian Airlines International-Cathay Pacific.

As with RTW tickets there are advance-purchase restrictions and limits on how many stopovers you can make. Typically fares range between US$2000 and US$2500. The Circle-Pacific route is Los Angeles-

Overbooking Airlines hate to fly empty seats and, since every flight has some passengers who fail to show up (see No Shows), they often book more passengers than they have seats. Usually the excess passengers balance those who fail to show up, but occasionally somebody gets bumped. If this happens, guess who it is most likely to be? The passengers who check in late.

Promotional Fares Officially discounted fares like Apex fares which are available from travel agents or direct from the airline.

Reconfirmation At least 72 hours prior to departure time of an onward or return flight you should normally contact the airline and 'reconfirm' that you intend to be on the flight. If you don't do this the airline can delete your name from the passenger list and you could lose your seat. You don't have to reconfirm the first flight on your itinerary or if your stopover is less than 72 hours. It doesn't hurt to reconfirm more than once.

Restrictions Discounted tickets often have various restrictions on them – advance purchase is the most usual one (see Apex). Others are restrictions on the minimum and maximum period you must be away, such as a minimum of 14 days or a maximum of one year. See Cancellation Penalties.

Standby A discounted ticket where you only fly if there is a seat free at the last moment. Standby fares are usually only available on domestic routes.

Tickets Out An entry requirement for many countries is that you have an onward or return ticket, in other words, a ticket out of the country. If you're not sure what you intend to do next, the easiest solution is to buy the cheapest onward ticket to a neighbouring country or a ticket from a reliable airline which can later be refunded if you do not use it.

Transferred Tickets Airline tickets cannot be transferred from one person to another. Travellers sometimes try to sell the return half of their ticket, but officials can ask you to prove that you are the person named on the ticket. This is unlikely to happen on domestic flights, but on international flights tickets may be compared with passports.

Travel Agencies Travel agencies vary widely and you should ensure you use one that suits your needs. Some simply handle tours, while full-service agencies handle everything from tours and tickets to car rental and hotel bookings. A good one will do all these things and can save you a lot of money, but if all you want is a ticket at the lowest possible price, then you really need an agency specialising in discounted tickets. A discounted ticket agency, however, may not be useful for other things, like hotel bookings.

Travel Periods Some officially discounted fares, Apex fares in particular, vary with the time of year. There is often a low (off-peak) season and a high (peak) season. Sometimes there's an intermediate or shoulder season as well. At peak times, when everyone wants to fly, not only will the officially discounted fares be higher, but so will unofficially discounted fares; or there may simply be no discounted tickets available. Usually, the fare depends on your outward flight – if you depart in the high season and return in the low season, you pay the high-season fare. ■

Hawaii-Auckland-Sydney-Singapore-Bangkok-Hong Kong-Tokyo-Los Angeles.

The UK

The cheapest tickets in London are provided by 'bucket shops' (discount-ticket agencies) which advertise in magazines and papers like *Time Out* and *TNT*. The magazine *Business Traveller* also has good advice on airfare bargains. Most bucket shops are trustworthy and reliable, but the occasional sharp operator appears – *Time Out* and *Business Traveller* give useful advice on precautions to take.

Trailfinders (☎ (0171) 938 3366), 194 Kensington High St, London W8, and STA Travel (☎ (0171) 937 9962), 86 Old Brompton Rd, London SW7 and 117 Euston Rd, London NW1 (☎ (0171) 465 0484), are good, reliable agents for cheap tickets.

The cheapest London to Sydney bucket-shop tickets are about £385/640 one way/return. Such prices are usually only available if you leave London in the low season – March to June. In September and mid-December, fares go up by about 30%; the rest of the year they're somewhere in between.

From Australia you can expect to pay around A$1200/1800 one-way/return to London and other European capitals, with stops in Asia on the way.

North America

There's a variety of connections across the Pacific from Los Angeles, San Francisco and Vancouver. These include direct flights, flights via New Zealand, island-hopping routes and more-circuitous Pacific-rim routes via Asia. Qantas, Air New Zealand and United fly USA-Australia; Qantas, Air New Zealand and Canadian Airlines International fly Canada-Australia. An interesting option from the west coast is Northwest Airlines' flight via Japan. Air Pacific flies via Fiji.

One advantage of flying Qantas or Air New Zealand is that on US airlines, if your flight goes via Hawaii, the west coast to Hawaii sector is treated as a domestic flight.

This means you pay for drinks and headsets, which are free on international sectors.

To find good fares to Australia, check the travel ads in the Sunday travel sections of papers like the *Los Angeles Times, San Francisco Chronicle-Examiner, New York Times* or Canada's *Globe & Mail*. You can typically get a one-way/return ticket from the west coast for around US$830/1000 or from the east coast for US$1050/1400. Council Travel and STA Travel, are good sources for discount tickets in the USA and have lots of offices around the country; in Canada, Travel CUTS offers a similar service. Fares from Vancouver are similar to US west coast prices. From Toronto, fares go from around C$1700 return.

If Pacific island-hopping is your aim, check out the airlines of Pacific island nations, some of which have good deals on indirect routings. Qantas can give you Fiji or Tahiti along the way, Air New Zealand can offer both and the Cook Islands as well. See Circle Pacific Tickets for more details.

One-way/return fares from Australia include San Francisco A$1000/1650, New York A$1150/2400 and Vancouver A$1150/1900.

New Zealand

Air New Zealand and Qantas operate a network of trans-Tasman flights linking Auckland, Wellington and Christchurch in New Zealand with most major Australian cities. You can also fly directly between a lot of other places in New Zealand and Australia.

From New Zealand to Sydney you're looking at around NZ$530/650 one-way/return. From Sydney to New Zealand expect to pay from A$490 one-way and between A$500 and A$700 return, depending on the time of year. The competition on this route means you'll find good discounts.

Asia

Ticket discounting is widespread in Asia, particularly in Singapore, Hong Kong, Bangkok and Penang. There are numerous fly-by-nighters on the Asian ticketing scene, so take care. Also, Asian routes fill up fast. Flights between Hong Kong and Australia are heavily booked, while flights to/from Bangkok and Singapore are often part of the longer Europe-Australia route, so they're sometimes full. Plan ahead. For more information on South-East Asian flights to Australia see Lonely Planet's *South-East Asia on a shoestring*.

Typical one-way fares to Sydney are S$1000 from Singapore, HK$6600 from Hong Kong.

From Australia's east coast, some typical return fares to Singapore, Kuala Lumpur and Bangkok range from A$900 to A$1100, and to Hong Kong from A$900 to A$1600.

You can pick up interesting tickets in Asia to include Australia on the way across the Pacific Ocean. Qantas and Air New Zealand offer discounted trans-Pacific tickets.

Africa

There's a number of direct flights each week between Africa and Australia, but only between Perth and Harare (Zimbabwe) or Johannesburg (South Africa). Qantas, South African Airways and Air Zimbabwe fly this route. Other airlines which connect southern Africa and Australia include Malaysia Airlines (via Kuala Lumpur) and Air Mauritius (via Mauritius), both of which have special deals from time to time.

Sydney to Harare costs about A$2000 return; to Johannesburg it's from about A$1600 return.

South America

Two routes operate between South America and Australia. The long-running Chile connection involves Lan Chile's Santiago-Easter Island-Tahiti twice weekly flight, from where you fly Qantas or another airline to Australia. Alternatively, there's a route which skirts the Antarctic Circle, flying from Buenos Aires to Auckland and Sydney, operated twice weekly by Aerolineas Argentinas. Sydney to Santiago or Buenos Aires costs about A$2000 return.

Domestic Flights

The major domestic carriers are Ansett (☎ 131300) and Qantas (☎ 131313), the international flag-carrier. Both fly between Sydney and other state capitals, and both have subsidiaries which fly smaller planes on shorter interstate and intrastate routes: Eastern Australia is part of Qantas; Ansett Express is part of Ansett. Smaller airlines include Hazelton (☎ 131713) and Impulse (☎ 131381).

You don't have to reconfirm domestic flights on Ansett and Qantas, but if you want to check flight details, the numbers to call are ☎ 131515 (Ansett) and ☎ 131223 (Qantas).

Qantas domestic flights with numbers QF001 to QF399 operate from the international terminal, flight numbers QF400 and above from its domestic terminal.

All airports and domestic flights are nonsmoking.

Fares Few people pay full fare on domestic travel because airlines offer a wide range of discounts. These discounts come and go and there are regular 'spot specials', so keep your eyes open. Because discounting is unpredictable, we quote full economy fares in this book.

Full-time university or other higher education students get 25% off the regular economy fare on production of student ID or an ISIC card, but you can usually find fares discounted by more than that.

Nonresident international travellers can get up to 40% discount on internal Qantas flights, and 25 % on Ansett flights simply by presenting their international ticket when booking. The discount applies only to the full economy fare, so in many cases it will be cheaper to take advantage of other discounts.

Air Passes If you can book two or three weeks in advance you'll find that some discounted fares are cheaper than an air pass and have fewer restrictions. However, air passes are worth checking out.

Qantas and Ansett each offers two types. The Qantas Australia Explorer Pass can only be purchased overseas and involves buying a coupon for each sector: a Sydney-Melbourne one-way flight costs $165, Sydney-Perth $417. The price varies depending on when you travel and for how long.

The Qantas Backpackers Pass can only be bought in Australia with identification such as a YHA membership or a VIP Backpackers or Independent Backpackers Card. You must purchase a minimum of four sectors, and stay a minimum of two nights at each stop. The discount is quite substantial; a sample fare using this pass is Sydney to Uluru for $265 one way, as against the full economy fare of $549.

Ansett's Kangaroo Airpass gives you two options – 6000km with a minimum/maximum of two/three stopovers for $949 ($729 for children) and 10,000km with a minimum/maximum of three/seven stopovers for $1499 ($1149 for children). Restrictions apply to these tickets, although they can be good value if you want to see a lot of the country in a short time. You don't need to start and finish at the same place.

LAND
Bus

It pays to shop around for fares. Students, YHA members and other backpacker card holders get discounts of at least 10% with many long-distance companies. On straight point-to-point tickets there are varying stopover deals. Some companies give one free stopover on express routes, others charge a small fee, which might be waived if you book through certain agents, such as hostels.

Greyhound Pioneer Australia (☎ 132030)

Interstate Distances
Travelling interstate from Sydney is a major journey. The nearest state capital is Melbourne, 870km away by the shortest road route. To Brisbane it's almost 1000km; to Adelaide at least 1400km; Darwin is 4000km; and Perth is 4100km. Sydney to Darwin via Adelaide is 4450km, and it's nearly 5000km via Townsville. ■

---

operates the only truly national bus network and McCafferty's (☎ 9361 5125) is the next largest. Pioneer Motor Service (☎ 9281 2233), a local company (no relation to Greyhound Pioneer), is also a large operator now that it runs Kirklands buses. There are quite a few other companies running less extensive routes.

Major interstate routes and fares from Sydney are as follows:

Melbourne
It's a 12 to 13-hour run (more if you go via Canberra) by the most direct route, the Hume Highway. Firefly Express (☎ 9211 1644) charges just $40, other companies charge around $55. Greyhound Pioneer also offers the prettier but longer (about 18 hours) Princes Highway coastal route ($64). For destinations along the Princes Highway within NSW, Pioneer Motor Service has the best fares.

Brisbane
It takes about 16 hours via the Pacific Highway and the standard fare is $69. You often need to book in advance. Some buses don't stop in all the main towns en route. Companies running the Pacific Highway route to Brisbane include Greyhound Pioneer Australia, Kirklands and McCafferty's.
Fares between Sydney and destinations in northern NSW include Port Macquarie $48 (seven hours), Coffs Harbour $55 (9½ hours) and Byron Bay $70 (13 hours).
McCafferty's, Greyhound Pioneer Australia and Border Coaches (☎ 6041 3255) also have services on the inland New England Highway which take an hour or two longer but cost about the same. Book at their offices or the Sydney Coach Terminal.

Adelaide
Sydney to Adelaide takes 18 to 25 hours and costs around $96. Services run via Canberra or Broken Hill. Travelling Sydney-Melbourne-Adelaide with Firefly is cheaper ($75) than travelling Sydney-Adelaide with other companies. Countrylink's daily Speedlink service consists of a train to Albury, then a bus to Adelaide; it costs $99.

Elsewhere
The 52 to 56-hour trip to Perth costs $277. To Alice Springs it's about 42 hours (plus some waiting in Adelaide) and $208, and all the way to Darwin it's 67 hours and $308, via Mt Isa.

Bus Passes If you're planning to travel around Australia, Greyhound Pioneer Australia and McCafferty's have a variety of useful passes so it's a matter of deciding which suits your needs.

As an example, McCafferty's has a Sun & Centre pass which runs from Sydney to Cairns then inland to Darwin and Uluru. Valid for six months and with unlimited stops it costs $575.

Alternative Buses Oz Experience (☎ 9907 0522) is a backpackers' bus line offering frequent service along the east coast with off-the-beaten track detours to cattle stations and national parks. It has 18 passes (with unlimited stops) ranging in price from $121 to $833 depending on distance and valid for six to 12 months.

Straycat (☎ (03) 9481 2993, 1800 800 840) has three-day Sydney to Melbourne trips via the Snowy Mountains and Victoria's High Country for $149, or two-day trips via the coast for $79. The prices include meals but not accommodation, which is booked for you and costs about $12 a night. The Wayward Bus (☎ 1800 882 823) offers similar four-day trips between Sydney and Melbourne via Victoria's High Country for $180.

Pioneering Spirit (☎ 1800 672 422), 2/127 Blair St, Bondi, runs a six-day bus trip from Sydney to Brisbane via the coast for $220. It describes itself as a mobile hostel. It leaves Sydney every Friday and you need to book two weeks in advance. You can book the bus as far as Byron Bay for $175.

Train

Australia's railway system is less comprehensive than the bus networks and train services are less frequent and more expensive. However, they're as fast as or faster than buses and special fares make the prices competitive. Individual states run their own railway services; in NSW it's Countrylink.

For information about, and to make bookings on, interstate services call the Central Reservation Centre (☎ 132232 daily 6.30 am to 10 pm) or contact a Countrylink Travel Centre.

Fares There are three standard fare levels for interstate rail travel – economy, 1st class and sleeping berths, although sleeping berths aren't available on all trains. Depending on availability, a limited number of discounted fares are offered on most trains. These cut 10% to 40% off the standard fares.

On interstate journeys you can make free stopovers – you have two months to complete your trip on a one-way ticket and six months on a return ticket.

Interstate routes and fares from Sydney are:

Melbourne
> A nightly XPT, 10 hours: $90/125/215 in economy/1st class/1st class sleeper.

Brisbane
> A nightly XPT, about 12½ hours: $90/125/215 in economy/1st class/1st class sleeper. This train connects with a bus at Casino for passengers travelling to the far north coast of NSW and Queensland's Gold Coast. You can also take the train between Sydney and Murwillumbah, just south of the Queensland border from where there's a connecting bus to the Gold Coast.

Adelaide & Perth
> The twice-weekly Indian Pacific goes to Perth via Adelaide. The 26-hour trip to Adelaide costs $140/394 in economy/1st class sleeper. There's also a daily bus/train connection to Adelaide called Speedlink, which is cheaper at $99/149.50 for economy/1st class and five or six hours faster. The 70-hour trip to Perth costs $360/1116 in economy/1st class sleeper. The 1st class fares include meals.

Rail Passes A number of rail passes allow unlimited rail travel either across the country or just in one state. The national passes are only available to international visitors. With the Austrail Pass you can travel anywhere on the Australian rail network for a set number of days beginning with 14 days for $485. The Austrail Flexipass differs in that it allows a set number of travelling days within a six-month period beginning with eight days for $400.

Car & Motorcycle

See the Getting Around chapter for details of road rules, driving conditions and information on buying and renting vehicles.

The main road routes into NSW are the Hume Highway from Melbourne to Sydney (a freeway in Victoria but much of it pretty narrow in NSW); the Princes Highway from Melbourne to Sydney via the coast (longer than the Hume but prettier and carrying less traffic until you reach the Shoalhaven area, beginning near Ulladulla); the Pacific Highway between Brisbane and Sydney via the coast (passing through or near all the north-coast beach resorts, but not a fun road to drive); and the route from Adelaide to Sydney via Broken Hill and Dubbo (wide open spaces and empty roads – except for kangaroos). The Newell Highway is a good road from Victoria to Brisbane, crossing much of rural NSW along the way.

SEA

Cruise liners regularly call at Sydney, as do yachts. The liners aren't really a feasible way of travelling from point A to point B, but yachts looking for crew might be, especially if point B is a Pacific island. Ask around at yacht clubs and check hostel noticeboards. *Sydney Afloat* is a free monthly paper which occasionally has ads for crew. You'll find a copy at most yacht clubs. If you're determined to try yacht-crewing and have some spare time and money, it might help to do one of the sailing courses offered in Sydney.

Cargo ships are more expensive than flying (although cheaper than a cruise ship), but could be interesting. Try agents such as the Sydney Sea & Air Centre (☎ 9283 1199) or Freighter Travel (☎ 9484 6100).

DEPARTURE TAXES

There's a departure tax of $27 payable by everyone leaving Australia which is incorporated into your airfare. Sydney also has a noise tax of $3.40; again, this is added to your airfare.

Getting Around

AIR

Ansett Express (☎ 131300) and Impulse (☎ 131381), which are subsidiaries of Ansett and Qantas, have intrastate flights and there are several regional operators such as Hazelton (☎ 131713) and Kendell (☎ 6922 0100). Most flights are between Sydney and major country centres (see the chart for fares), with few flights linking country centres. It would be difficult to put together a tour of the state by scheduled flights without a lot of backtracking to Sydney.

BUS

The most comprehensive bus network is Countrylink's system of coordinated buses and trains.

The major bus lines also serve many towns on their express runs from Sydney to other capitals – see the Getting There & Away chapter for routes and fares. However, travelling short distances within NSW on an interstate bus is often expensive, and because of regulations interstate lines might not be allowed to take you on some sectors. Also, even though a town may be listed on their schedule, interstate buses may only stop there if there has been a confirmed booking.

Countrylink and a few local services fill the gaps.

Once you arrive at a major town there's usually a local service to smaller places nearby, but these are rarely frequent.

From Sydney to Canberra, Murrays (☎ 9252 3590) has three daily express buses which take under four hours and cost $32. Greyhound Pioneer has the most frequent Canberra service and also charges $32. With McCafferty's it's $28.

TRAIN
Countrylink

The NSW government's Countrylink rail network is the most comprehensive in Australia. The trains, in conjunction with connecting buses, take you quite quickly (if not always frequently) to most sizeable towns.

As well as the high-speed XPT trains (some with sleepers) there are nippy Explorer trains. Trains run as far as Albury (and on to Melbourne), Armidale, Canberra, Broken Hill (and on to Adelaide and Perth), Dubbo, Kyogle (and on to Brisbane), Moree and Murwillumbah.

On point-to-point tickets, Countrylink's prices can be comparable to the private bus lines and there are sometimes special deals. You can make free stopovers, but they must be booked when you buy the ticket. With a one-way ticket you have to complete the journey within a week and on a return ticket the outward half must be completed in a week and the return half within two months.

Most Countrylink services have to be booked (☎ 9217 8812, or 132232 outside Sydney, 6.30 am to 10 pm daily).

New South Wales Air Fares

All fares in Australian dollars
One-way economy air fares

Coolangatta

Coffs Harbour 291

Dubbo

Port Macquarie

Broken Hill 226

Newcastle 185

174

359 97

SYDNEY

158

221 175

CANBERRA

Cooma

Albury

Fares Between Sydney and Canberra two trains run daily (4½ hours, $40/54 economy/1st class).

Within NSW, Countrylink one-way economy fares from Sydney include:

Destination	Distance	Fare
Albury	643km	$70
Armidale	530km	$65
Bathurst	240km	$30
Bourke	841km	$79
Broken Hill	1125km	$95
Byron Bay	883km	from $79
Coffs Harbour	608km	$65
Cooma	446km	$53
Dubbo	431km	$53
Orange	323km	$37
Tamworth	455km	$58

Rail Passes The NSW Discovery Pass allows you to travel anywhere in the state, is valid for one month and costs $249; there's a discount of $50 for YHA members.

CityRail

CityRail (☎ 131500), the Sydney metropolitan service, runs frequent electric trains south through Wollongong ($6.60 one way) to Bomaderry ($12.40); west through the Blue Mountains to Katoomba ($9.40) and Lithgow ($14.20); north to Newcastle ($14.20); and south-west through the Southern Highlands to Goulburn ($22). Some services duplicate Countrylink services, but they're a little slower and much cheaper, especially if you buy a day-return ticket. You can't book seats on CityRail trains. Off-peak return fares are available after 9 am weekdays and all day on weekends.

CAR

You can get around Sydney and between main country centres easily enough using train and bus, but many of NSW and the ACT's finest features are not readily accessible by public transport. For many visitors this means buying or renting a car.

Road Rules

Driving in NSW and the ACT holds few real surprises for overseas visitors. Australians drive on the left-hand side of the road just like in the UK, Japan and most countries in south and east Asia and the Pacific. A main road rule is 'give way to the right' – if an intersection is unmarked (unusual), you must give way to vehicles entering the intersection from your right.

Although overseas licences are acceptable in Australia, an International Driving Permit is preferred.

Speed Limits The speed limit is 100km/h (roughly 60 mph), except where otherwise indicated. On freeways, other divided roads and some rural highways this is sometimes raised to 110km/h. Some dangerous sections of rural roads have a limit of less than 100km/h. The usual limit in towns is 60km/h, sometimes rising to 80km/h on the outskirts and dropping to 40km/h in residential areas. Speeding in towns isn't uncommon (if stupid), but near schools *everyone* observes the 40km/h limit.

Speed cameras and radar guns catch people who exceed these limits, but they generally operate only in cities and on major roads, which leaves country drivers to speed unhindered on narrow back roads where head-on collisions are a real possibility.

Seat Belts New cars have seat belts back and front, and if your seat has a belt you're required to wear it. You're liable to a fine if you don't. Small children must be belted into an approved safety seat.

Alcohol The blood alcohol limit in NSW is 0.05%, which most people reach after drinking two full-strength beers in an hour (although there is a lot of variation between individuals). Bus drivers must not have any alcohol in their system when they get behind the wheel. These limits are enforced with random breath tests; penalties for exceeding them are heavy, which accounts for the popularity of low-alcohol beer.

Parking Parking in Sydney can be a nightmare – there are just too many cars for those narrow streets. Beware of tow-away zones!

A lot of cheaper accommodation in Sydney has no parking, so you're left with the choice of paying for commercial parking or constantly shifting your car to avoid fines.

Outside Sydney, parking meters are rare. Many country towns insist on rear-to-kerb angle parking. This takes a while to master, and also means that the car in front of you will signal a left turn then move to the middle of the road, hopefully stopping to see that you're behind them before reversing into the parking space.

On the Road

Australia isn't crisscrossed by multi-lane highways, and although the east of NSW is reasonably closely settled (well, compared with the Northern Territory, not compared with Sussex), don't expect to find major roads everywhere you want to go.

You'll certainly find stretches of divided road, particularly on roads out of Sydney, but elsewhere highways are usually only two lanes wide.

Between cities, signposting on the main roads is generally OK, but once you enter the maze of rural backroads you'll need a map – the NRMA's series of regional roadmaps should see you right. In towns the street-signing can be poor.

Fuel Service stations generally stock diesel, super and unleaded fuel. Liquid petroleum gas (LPG, Autogas) is usually available in major centres, but harder to find elsewhere. Prices vary from place to place and from price war to price war, but generally they're in the 70c to 80c per litre range. In remote areas the price can soar, and some outback service stations are not above exploiting their monopoly position. Distances between fill-ups can be long in the far west, so make sure you have enough fuel.

Outback Driving

There are very few sealed roads in the state's far west, but there are plenty of unsealed tracks. Some are in good condition and carry a relatively large amount of traffic (you might see a car every hour or so), but others

are lonely, remote and potentially dangerous if you break down. You often don't need 4WD to tackle these roads, but you do need to be prepared. Backtracking hundreds of kilometres to pick up a replacement for some minor malfunctioning component or, much worse, to arrange a tow, is unlikely to be easy or cheap.

You need to carry a fair amount of water in case of disaster. Food is less important – the space might be better allocated to an extra spare tyre.

If you run into trouble in the back of beyond, *stay with your vehicle*. It's much easier to spot a car than a human being from the air. Also, the heat can quickly kill you once you leave the shelter of your car.

The number one rule of outback driving is to seek local advice, preferably from the police. They know the road conditions (sections of road can still be boggy many days after the last rain) and can advise you whether your vehicle is suitable for a particular track. Many outback routes are OK for 2WD vehicles, but you might need high clearance to cope with ruts and washouts if the road hasn't been graded since the last rains, for example.

The DCLM's tourist map of the outback is informative, but if you plan to drive on the minor unsealed roads you should supplement it with more detailed maps. There's a recorded message (☎ 11571) detailing road conditions for all of NSW. You should still contact a local police station before setting out.

For the full story on safe outback travel see Lonely Planet's *Outback Australia*.

4WD or 2WD? You can get to most places in a conventional car. Having said that, a 4WD gives you full access to the more remote national parks and state forests.

You see a lot of 4WDs, but many never leave the sealed roads and fewer still do any serious rough-terrain work. If you stick to regularly maintained routes, a 4WD's main advantage is its high clearance which can cope with minor flooding and deep ruts. Of course, they're also designed not to fall apart under the strains of outback travel, and they're generally big bastards, so you can carry a lot of fuel and luggage.

After rain, some outback roads are closed, not necessarily because 4WDs can't get through but because they'll damage the road. Some drivers see a Road Closed sign as a challenge and stuff things up for everyone else. 'Bush-bashing' (making your own road through the bush) is definitely a no-no.

Hazards

Local drivers on little-used rural roads often speed, and they often assume that there's no other traffic. Be wary of oncoming cars at blind corners on country roads.

Animals Animals are common hazards on country roads, and a collision is likely to kill the animal, seriously damage your vehicle and possibly injure or kill you and others. Kangaroos are most active around dawn and dusk, and they travel in groups. If you see one hopping across the road in front of you, slow right down – its friends are probably just behind it. In remote areas many people avoid travelling altogether between 5 pm and 8 am, because of the hazards posed by animals.

If an animal appears in front of you, hit the brakes (gently if you're on dirt) and only swerve to avoid the animal if it's safe to do so. The number of people who have been killed in accidents caused by swerving to miss an animal is high.

Other animals with no road sense include cows, sheep (they're incredibly stupid) and emus. Once again, if you see one you can expect more to be following.

In the country, even on quite major roads, it's fairly common to meet a herd of sheep or cattle being driven (droved?) along the road. Sometimes you'll have been warned by signs placed on the roadside, but often you'll come around a corner and find the road crammed with animals. Stop and assess the situation (drovers won't appreciate it if you scatter a herd that they and the dogs have just rounded up), then drive through *very* slowly. Beware

of stragglers – and impatient drivers in other vehicles.

Dirt Roads You don't have to get far off the beaten track to find yourself on dirt roads. The coating of fine dust gives little or no traction if you have to brake or swerve (especially when wet). Most are regularly graded and reasonably smooth (although rain can alter that), and it's often possible to travel at high speed – *don't*.

If you're travelling along a dirt road at 100km/h and you come to a corner, you won't go around that corner – you'll sail off into the bush. If you put on the brakes to slow down you'll probably spin or roll or both. If you swerve sharply to avoid a pot-hole or an animal you'll go into an exciting four-wheel drift then find out what happens when your car meets a gum tree. Worst of all, if another car approaches and you have to move to the edge of the road, you'll lose control and may collide head on.

On dirt roads that are dry, flat, straight, animal free, traffic-free and wide enough to allow for unexpected slewing as you hit pot-holes and drifted sand, you could, with practice, drive at about 80km/h. Otherwise, treat dirt like ice.

Gates & Grids Rural roads, especially access roads to national parks and out-of-the-way waterfalls etc, sometimes run through private property where you might encounter closed gates and cattle grids.

The essential rule about gates is: *always leave a gate as you find it*. If it's open, leave it open; if it's closed, close it after you.

Cattle grids (usually sections of railway tracks laid across a pit) stop stock from wandering. They're usually no hassle to drive across, unless the road has been washed out on either side, in which case you'll get an almighty jolt. It always pays to slow down.

One-Lane Bridges These are fairly common on minor roads. They're usually signposted, but not always.

Buying a Car

If you're buying a second-hand vehicle (which is what nearly all travellers do) reliability is all-important.

You can buy through a dealer (you'll probably pay more, but you'll get a guaranteed title and help with paperwork), or privately by checking classified newspaper ads or hostel noticeboards. If you're buying an old car, remember that the further you get from big towns, the better it is to be in a Holden or a Ford Falcon. Life is simpler when you can get spare parts anywhere from Bourke to Bulamakanka, and every scrapyard in Australia is full of good ol' Holdens and Falcons. This isn't so much of a problem in NSW unless you have a very exotic car, but elsewhere in the country it might be.

Sydney is the best place to buy a car. Parramatta Rd is lined with used-car lots, and there are other setups geared especially to travellers. The Kings Cross Car Market (☎ 9358 5000), on the corner of Ward Ave and Elizabeth Bay Rd, is for private sellers and charges $35 a week. This place can help with paperwork and insurance and is something of a travellers' rendezvous. The Flemington Sunday Car Market (☎ 0055 21122) near Flemington Station charges sellers $60.

Several dealers, such as Travellers Auto Barn (☎ 9360 1500), 177 William St, Kings Cross, will sell you a car with an undertaking to buy it back at an agreed price. Always read the small print. A buy-back deal with a private seller (such as a hostel manager) is risky, as they might not have enough ready cash when you want to sell.

Before you buy it's worth having the car checked by a mechanic. The NRMA (☎ 132132) will do this for $105/125 for members/nonmembers. It costs $88 to join the NRMA, but members of interstate and some overseas motoring organisations pay only $44. Many garages do inspections for much less.

For full details of the paperwork required to buy a car, pick up a copy of the Roads & Traffic Authority (RTA) pamphlet 'Six Steps to Buying a Secondhand Motor Vehicle', available at RTA and NRMA offices. Motor Registry offices also have information and there are many of them. If you're buying privately it's essential to check that the registration is still valid, that the vehicle isn't stolen or owned by a finance company, and that there are no outstanding fines – the pamphlet tells you how to do this.

Every registered vehicle has third-party insurance – a Green Slip. This covers you against injuries you might cause, but not damage to other people's property, so it's a good idea to have third-party property insurance. The major insurance companies don't sell third-party property insurance to travellers, but the Kings Cross Car Market (and some dealers) can arrange it, even if you didn't buy the car there.

When the time comes to sell the car, fill in a Notice of Disposal card (available from a Motor Registry office), or you might be liable for fines incurred by the new owner.

Renting a Car

There are some places where if you haven't got your own wheels you have to choose between a tour and a rented vehicle since there is no public transport and distances are too great for walking or even bicycles. Competition is fierce, so rates tend to vary and lots of special deals pop up and disappear again. Whatever your mode of travel on the long stretches, it can be useful to have a car for some local travel. Between a group of people, it can even be reasonably economical.

The three major companies, Budget, Hertz and Avis, have agents everywhere. Thrifty is a second-string outfit which also has a wide network. Then there is a vast number of local firms. The big operators often have higher rates than the local firms, but not always. You'll need to calculate insurance, per km rates and all the other fine print. The big companies usually allow one-way rentals, although there might be a drop-off charge and other restrictions.

Insurance usually has an excess – if you have a prang, the excess is the amount you pay before the insurance company takes over. With some of the small companies this can be very high. Most companies prefer to rent to people over 21, and some require you to be over 25, although there are a few who will rent to 18-year-olds (often with higher insurance premiums or a greater excess).

The major companies offer unlimited km rates in Sydney and some other major centres, but in country areas it's usually a flat charge plus so many cents per km. Straightforward city rentals are all much the same price. It's on special deals, odd rentals or longer periods that you find the differences. Weekend specials – usually three days for the price of two – are usually good value.

Daily rates are typically about $65 a day for a small car (eg Ford Laser); about $75 a day for a medium car (eg Holden Camira); and about $100 a day for a big car (eg Holden Commodore, Ford Falcon), all including insurance. Prices start to drop if you hire for more than a day or two.

'Rent-a-wreck' companies specialise in renting older cars, typically around $35 a day. If you want to travel around the city, or not too far out, they're worth considering.

4WDs Renting a 4WD vehicle is within the budget range if a few people get together. Something small like a Suzuki costs around $80 per day; for a Toyota Landcruiser you're looking at around $115, which should include insurance and some free kilometres (typically 100km). Check the insurance conditions, especially the excess, as they can be onerous.

Hertz has 4WD rentals, with one-way rentals possible between the eastern states and the Northern Territory. Brits Australia (☎ 9667 0402), 182 O'Riordan St, Mascot 2020, hires 4WD vehicles fitted out as campervans. These aren't too badly priced at $74 per day with unlimited km, plus collision damage waiver ($15 per day).

NRMA

The National Roads & Motorists Association (NRMA) is the NSW motoring association and provides emergency breakdown service, literature, excellent maps and detailed guides to accommodation. It has reciprocal arrangements with other state associations and with some organisations overseas. Bring proof of membership with you. The NRMA's head office (☎ 9260 9222) is at 151 Clarence St, Sydney 2000. There are other offices around the state and most towns have a garage affiliated with the NRMA.

MOTORCYCLE

Motorcycles are a popular way of getting around. The climate is almost ideal for biking much of the year and the many small trails from the road into the bush often lead to perfect spots to spend the night in the world's largest camping ground.

A fuel range of 350km will cover most fuel stops. You'll need a rider's licence – a car licence isn't enough – and a helmet.

To bring your own motorcycle into Australia you'll need a *carnet de passages*, and if you try to sell it you'll get less than the market price because of restrictive registration requirements (not so severe in Western and South Australia and in the Northern Territory). Shipping from just about anywhere is expensive.

Unfortunately, renting a bike is expensive. In Sydney try Ace Sydney (☎ 9633 1000), 68-74 Wentworth Ave in the city or All Bike Hire (☎ 9707 1691), 21 Moxon Rd, Punchbowl. Ace Sydney charges $99/560 a day/week for a Honda V25; the deposit is a hefty $750.

Buying your own two wheels is quite feasible. Australian newspapers and the local bike press have extensive classified advertisements where $2500 gets you something that will take you around the country if you know a bit about bikes. The main drawback is trying to sell it again afterwards.

An easier option is a buy-back arrangement with a large motorcycle dealer, although this isn't common and the major disasters that can befall bikes make agreeing on a buy-back price very much a matter for negotiation. Holiday Wheels Motorcycles (☎ 9718 6668), 589 Canterbury Rd, Belmore, Sydney, has buy-back deals and can help arrange insurance (sometimes a problem for foreign visitors).

Take some spares and tools even if you can't use them, because someone else often can. The basics include: a spare tyre tube (front wheel size, which will fit on the rear but usually not vice versa); puncture repair kit with levers and a pump (or tubeless tyre repair kit with two or three carbon dioxide cartridges); a spare tyre valve; the bike's standard toolkit for what it's worth (after-market items are better); spare throttle, clutch and brake cables; tie wire, cloth tape ('gaffer' tape) and nylon 'zip-ties'; a handful of bolts and nuts in the usual emergency sizes (M6 and M8), along with a few self-tapping screws; one or two fuses; a bar of soap for fixing tank leaks (knead to a putty with water and squeeze into the leak); and, most important of all, a workshop manual for your bike (even if you can't make sense of it, the local motorcycle mechanic can).

If you hit an animal you could suffer serious injuries. It's wise to stop riding around 5 pm. Keep an eye out for cattle grids. As with car driving, outback travel demands that you carry plenty of water (and drink it even when you don't feel thirsty, as you dehydrate rapidly on a bike). If you break down, park your bike where it's clearly visible and stay with it.

BICYCLE

NSW is a great place for cycling and it's possible to plan rides of any duration and through almost any terrain. There are thousands of kilometres of good roads which carry so little traffic that the biggest hassle is waving back to the drivers.

Bicycle helmets are compulsory, as are front and rear lights for night riding.

Cycling has always been popular and not only as a sport: some shearers rode for huge distances between jobs, rather than use less reliable horses. It's rare to find a reasonably sized town that doesn't have a shop stocking at least basic bike parts.

If you're coming specifically to cycle, it

Long-Distance Cycling

Until you get fit you should be careful to eat enough to keep you going – remember that exercise is an appetite suppressant. It's easy to be so depleted of energy that you end up camping under a gum tree just 10 km short of a shower and a steak. No matter how fit you are, water is still vital. Dehydration can be life-threatening.

It can get very hot in summer, and you should take things slowly until you're used to the heat. Cycling in 30°C-plus temperatures isn't too bad if you wear a hat and plenty of sunscreen, and drink *lots* of water. Be aware of the blistering 'hot northerlies', the prevailing winds that make a north-bound cyclist's life uncomfortable in summer. In April, when the south-east region's clear autumn weather begins, the 'southerly trades' prevail.

Check with locals if you're heading to remote areas, and notify the police if you're about to do something particularly adventurous. That said, you can't rely too much on local knowledge of road conditions, as most people have no idea of what a heavily loaded touring-bike needs. What they think of as a great road may be pedal-deep in sand or bull dust. ■

makes sense to bring your own bike. Check with your airline for costs and the degree of dismantling/packing required. Within Australia you can load your bike onto a bus or train to skip the boring bits. Bus companies require you to dismantle your bike, and some don't guarantee that it will travel on the same bus as you. Trains are easier, but supervise the loading and if possible tie your bike upright, otherwise you may find that the guard has stacked crates of Holden spares on your fragile alloy frame.

See Activities in the Sydney chapter for some bike rental places.

Much of eastern Australia seems to have been settled on the principle of not having more than a day's horse-ride between pubs, so it's possible to plan even ultra-long routes and still get a shower at the end of the day. Most people carry camping equipment, but it's feasible to travel from town to town staying in pubs or on-site vans.

You can get by with roadmaps but they don't show topography, so if you care about hills, buy DCLM maps. The scale you need depends on the terrain – mountain biking through a national park demands a detailed map; following a major road across the western plains doesn't. The 1:250,000 series is good for road work, but you'll need a lot of maps if you're covering much territory.

Bicycle NSW (☎ 9283 5200), 209 Castlereagh St, Sydney, has more information and publishes a series of booklets on cycling throughout the state. Some bike shops listed in the Sydney chapter can also help with information on routes and suggested rides.

HITCHING

Hitching is never entirely safe in any country, and we don't recommend it. Travellers who decide to hitch should understand that they're taking a small but potentially serious risk. However, many people do choose to hitch, and the advice that follows should help to make their journeys as fast and safe as possible.

Successful hitching depends on several factors, all just good sense. The most important is numbers – two people is ideal and these should be one female and one male. Any more makes things very difficult and two guys hitching together can expect long waits. It's not advisable for women to hitch alone, or even in pairs.

Factor two is position – look for a place where vehicles will be going slowly and where they can stop easily. Junctions and freeway slip roads are good places if there's stopping room. Position goes beyond just where you stand. The ideal location is on the outskirts of a town – hitching from way out in the country is as hopeless as from the centre of a city. Take a bus out to the edge of town.

Factor three is appearance. The ideal appearance for hitching is a sort of genteel poverty – threadbare but clean. Looking too good can be as much of a bummer as looking too bad! Don't carry too much gear – if it looks like it's going to take half an hour to pack your bags aboard, you'll be left on the roadside.

Factor four is knowing when to say no. Saying no to a car-load of drunks may be pretty obvious, but it can be time-saving to say no to a short ride that might take you from a good hitching point to a lousy one. Your best bet is to wait for the right, long ride to come along.

Trucks are often the best lifts, but they only stop if they're going slowly and can get started easily again. Thus the ideal place is at the top of a hill where they have a downhill run. Truckies often say they're going to the next town and, if they don't like you, will drop you anywhere. As they often pick up hitchers for company, the quickest way to create a bad impression is to jump in and fall asleep.

If you're visiting from abroad, a nice prominent flag on your pack helps, and a sign announcing your destination is also useful. University and hostel notice boards are good places to look for hitching partners.

The main law against hitching is 'thou shalt not stand in the road' – so when you see the law coming, step back.

Just as hitchers should be wary when

accepting lifts, drivers who pick up travellers should also be aware of the risks.

WALKING

Most long-distance walking is recreational (see the Activities section of the Facts for the Visitor chapter), but 'humping your bluey' (walking with a swag, or bedroll) is a time-honoured way of getting around rural roads. You don't see many swaggies (people who carry swags) these days, but they do still exist. They resemble Britain's tramps or America's hobos, but their social status is traditionally a little higher: if you are down on your luck it is considered no disgrace to 'go on the wallaby' (hit the road) and look for work.

LOCAL TRANSPORT
Bus & Train

Sydney has a good public transport network run by the State Transport Authority (STA). In Canberra, Wollongong and Newcastle it's also possible to get around by public transport. Anywhere else it becomes a bit problematic. There are buses in cities such as Wagga Wagga and Dubbo, but they're fairly infrequent.

The Kindness of Strangers

If you're totally stuck in an out-of-the-way place with no bus for another week and you don't want to hitch, there are a few last-resort options. Chances are there's a school bus taking students to a high school in the area's nearest large town. The bus probably isn't licensed to take you along, but your charm might get you on board. The mail-run is usually let out to private contractors who just might let you go along, maybe for a fee, maybe not. The post office knows contractors and their routes. Finally, there's probably some sort of carrier in town who might be persuaded to give you a lift on a delivery-run.

Don't count on these options. Country people might be hospitable but they can also be wary of strangers. Arranging a lift in the pub the night before is likely to be more successful than turning up out of the blue. ■

Taxi

Sydney has a lot of taxis, but you won't see many plying for trade on the streets of country towns. That doesn't mean they aren't there – even small towns often have at least one taxi. Taxi fares vary through the state, but shouldn't differ much from Sydney fares, unless there are local considerations such as dirt roads.

ORGANISED TOURS

There are some interesting tours, although few cover much of the state. Most are connected with a particular activity (eg bushwalking or horseriding) or area (eg outback tours from Broken Hill). See Activities in the Facts for the Visitor chapter and the various chapters of this book for suggestions.

It's worth checking with the Sydney YHA, as it often runs good tours or knows about others available. Hostel noticeboards are also good sources of information.

Major tour companies in Sydney have programmes of tours to Canberra, the Blue Mountains, the Hunter Valley and the Hawkesbury River; see the Sydney chapter.

A good way of travelling between Sydney and Byron Bay is with Ando's Opal Outback Tours (☎ 9559 2901), which takes a week for the trip and travels inland via Lightning Ridge. Tours leave Sydney every two weeks and include opal, sapphire and gold mining, optional horse riding, and accommodation in miners' cabins, outback pubs and cotton plantations. Ando is quite a character and his tour gets good feedback from backpackers. At $390, it's a bargain. Ando sometimes has other tours; ring and check.

See Alternative Buses in the Getting There & Away chapter for trips between Sydney and Melbourne and along the east coast to Brisbane.

Breakout Tours (☎ 9558 8229), 10 Roseby St, Marrickville in Sydney, has tours catering specifically to gays and lesbians.

Sydney

Sydney is a glittering, lively city with a fabulously beautiful harbour at its centre. The citizens of Australia's largest city (population 3.7 million) pursue fashion and trends with a vigour not found elsewhere in the country. Sydneysiders aren't noted for their reserve, perhaps because they live among some reassuringly large and constant natural features: the harbour, the Pacific Ocean and the encircling mountains.

Barriers which restricted the growth of the early colony still affect the city's outlook. Like the convicts who thought that China was on the other side of the impassable Blue Mountains, Sydneysiders behave as though the outback begins at Lithgow, and as though Newcastle and Wollongong are the limits of civilisation. You're more likely to hear the latest news from New York or Paris than Adelaide or Melbourne.

Despite Sydney's cosmopolitan population, there's a strong streak of Australian larrikinism (saying to hell with formality and 'good manners') and egalitarianism.

Sydneysiders are often open and friendly. If you need help, you'll either be ignored or shown amazing solicitude. Don't expect queuing or other formal signs of politeness, though. When the train doors slide back or the ferry ramp slams onto the deck, step lively or you might be left behind.

ORIENTATION

The harbour divides Sydney in half, with the Sydney Harbour Bridge and the Harbour Tunnel joining north and south. Central Sydney and most places of interest are south of the harbour. To explore beyond the inner suburbs, a street directory is essential.

City Centre

The central city area is relatively long and narrow, and only George and Pitt Sts (the main commercial and shopping streets) run the three km from the waterfront at Circular Quay south to Central Station.

HIGHLIGHTS

- Taking a cruise or ferry on Sydney Harbour, one of the best ways to view the city
- Enjoying the view from an alfresco cafe or restaurant table at Campbells Cove in the Rocks or Circular Quay
- Sydney Harbour National Park – not many cities can boast a national park in their centre, and certainly none with a setting like this
- Seeing a performance at the Sydney Opera House
- The excellent displays at the Powerhouse Museum and Art Gallery of NSW
- The Gay & Lesbian Mardi Gras
- Superb harbour and ocean beaches
- Eating a pie at Harry's Cafe de Wheels in Woolloomooloo

The historic Rocks and Circular Quay, where you'll find the Opera House and the Harbour Bridge, mark the northern boundary of the centre; Central Station is on the southern edge; the inlet of Darling Harbour is the western boundary; and a string of parks borders Elizabeth and Macquarie Sts on the eastern side.

Inner Suburbs

Most of Sydney's inner suburbs have undergone some gentrification and their Victorian workers' terraced houses are now spruce – and expensive. Cafes, restaurants, interesting shops and good pubs are scattered throughout the inner suburbs.

East of the city centre are Kings Cross, Woolloomooloo, Potts Point and Elizabeth Bay. Farther east again are exclusive suburbs such as Double Bay and Vaucluse. South-east of the city centre are the interesting suburbs of Darlinghurst, Surry Hills and Paddington. At the city's eastern extreme are the ocean-front suburbs of Bondi Beach and Coogee.

West of the centre is the radically changing suburb of Pyrmont and to the south-west of here Glebe, a bohemian suburb famous for its eateries. West of Pyrmont is Rozelle and the arty suburb of Balmain.

Kingsford Smith airport is in Mascot, which juts into Botany Bay 10 km south of the city centre.

North Shore

The suburbs north of the bridge are known collectively as North Shore. Mainly middle-class enclaves, they lack the vibrancy and diversity of the areas south of the harbour, but there are some excellent views, beaches and pockets of bushland.

Directly across the Harbour Bridge from the city centre is North Sydney, the city's second business district. Military Rd runs east from North Sydney through the harbourside suburbs of Neutral Bay, Cremorne and Mosman. Hunters Hill, west of the bridge, is one of Sydney's most expensive suburbs.

To the north-east, Manly sits on a narrow peninsula near the entrance to Sydney Harbour, fronting both ocean and harbour. A string of ocean beaches runs north from Manly to Palm Beach, another of Sydney's wealthy suburbs. Palm Beach fronts the Pacific Ocean and backs onto Pittwater. On the western side of Pittwater is Ku-ring-gai Chase National Park (see Around Sydney chapter).

Greater Sydney

Westward, Sydney's suburbs stretch for more than 50 km, encompassing Parramatta, once a country retreat for the colony's governor, and ending at Penrith at the foot of the Blue Mountains. South-west of the city, there's a similar sprawl of housing developments, swamping old towns such as Campbelltown and Liverpool.

Maps

Most tourist brochures contain a map of the city centre. These are OK, but usually limited in scope or legibility. For a handy map of the city centre and many nearby suburbs, including Kings Cross, look for the UBD Sydney City Pocket Map ($4.95).

The NRMA has a good map of the whole city, free to members. It's too unwieldy for use in a car but good for orientation. If you're planning on doing a lot of driving or exploration beyond the city centre, a street directory is indispensable. Companies such as UBD and Gregory's charge $25 to $30 for their full-sized directories, although there are smaller versions.

For maps of country areas, see the NRMA. For topographic maps, visit the Department of Conservation & Land Management (DCLM), 23-33 Bridge St; you can make credit-card telephone orders (☎ 9228 6111).

INFORMATION
Tourist Offices

The NSW Travel Centre (☎ 132077) and the Countrylink Travel Centre share the same office at 11-13 York St, open weekdays from 9 am to 5 pm. It's always worth checking the travel centre's deals on accommodation because it often has bargains at middle and top-end places. The Sydney Information Booth (☎ 9235 2424) is nearby in Martin Place (sharing a booth with Halftix), open the same hours as the travel centre.

The Tourist Information Service (☎ 9669 5111) answers phone enquiries from 8 am to 6 pm daily. In the Sydney Coach Terminal on Eddy Ave (outside Central Station), the Travellers' Information Service (☎ 9281 9366) makes bus and accommodation bookings (not hostels).

Foreign Consulates

All foreign embassies are in Canberra, but

SYDNEY

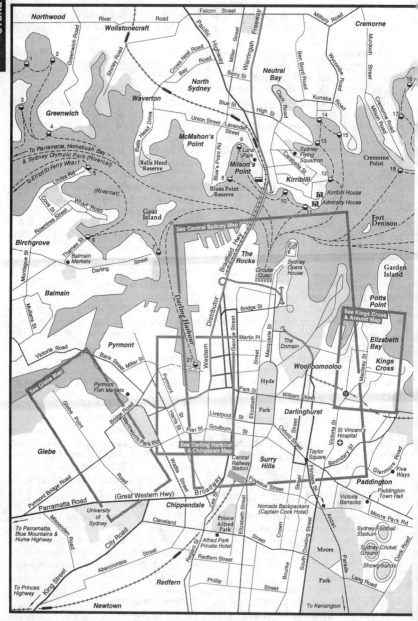

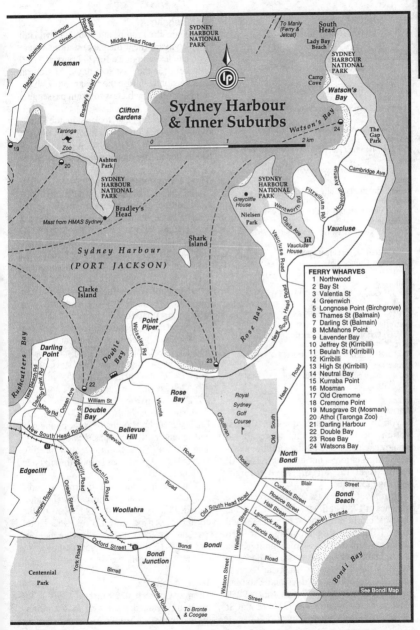

Sydney Harbour & Inner Suburbs

Sydney Harbour (PORT JACKSON)

FERRY WHARVES
1 Northwood
2 Bay St
3 Valentia St
4 Greenwich
5 Longnose Point (Birchgrove)
6 Thames St (Balmain)
7 Darling St (Balmain)
8 McMahons Point
9 Lavender Bay
10 Jeffrey St (Kirribilli)
11 Beulah St (Kirribilli)
12 Kirribilli
13 High St (Kirribilli)
14 Neutral Bay
15 Kurraba Point
16 Mosman
17 Old Cremorne
18 Cremorne Point
19 Musgrave St (Mosman)
20 Athol (Taronga Zoo)
21 Darling Harbour
22 Double Bay
23 Rose Bay
24 Watsons Bay

many countries maintain large consulates in Sydney as well. They include:

China
     539 Elizabeth St, Surry Hills (☎ 9698 7929)
France
     31 Market St, city (☎ 9261 5779)
Germany
     13 Trelawney St, Woollahra (☎ 9328 7733)
Greece
     15 Castlereagh St, city (☎ 9221 2388)
Indonesia
     236 Maroubra Rd, Maroubra (☎ 9344 9933)
Italy
     1 Macquarie St, city (☎ 9392 7900)
Japan
     52 Martin Place, city (☎ 9231 3455)
Malaysia
     67 Victoria Rd, Bellevue Hill (☎ 9327 7565)
Netherlands
     500 Oxford St, Bondi Junction (☎ 9387 6644)
New Zealand
     1 Alfred St, Circular Quay (☎ 9247 1999)
Papua New Guinea
     100 Clarence St, city (☎ 9299 5151)
Philippines
     301 George St, city (☎ 9299 6633)
Sweden
     350 Kent St, city (☎ 9262 6433)
Switzerland
     500 Oxford St, Bondi Junction (☎ 9369 4244)
USA
     19-29 Martin Place, city (☎ 9373 9200)
Vietnam
     489 New South Head Rd, Double Bay (☎ 9327 2539)

Money

If you're arriving in Sydney at Central Station, bear in mind that there are no foreign-exchange or banking facilities available at the station – not even an ATM. All terminals at the airport have foreign-exchange facilities.

Thomas Cook has foreign-exchange branches at 175 Pitt St (☎ 9229 6611), in the Queen Victoria Building (☎ 9264 1133) and in the Kingsgate shopping centre (☎ 9356 2211), beneath the Coca-Cola sign in Kings Cross. The Pitt St branch is open Monday to Saturday, the others daily. American Express branches are open weekdays and Saturday morning, and include 92 Pitt St (☎ 9239 0666) in the city centre and 73-79 Mount St (☎ 9957 2277) in North Sydney.

Left Luggage

There are cloakrooms at Central, Town Hall and Wynyard (near the park) stations where you can leave luggage for 24 hours at $1.50 per item for the first two days. At Central Station don't confuse the cloakroom with the luggage office, which is for train passengers only.

There are luggage lockers in the Greyhound Pioneer office on Eddy Ave outside Central Station. They cost $4 to $8 for 24 hours depending on the size of the luggage.

Post & Communications

Sydney's original general post office (GPO) was in the grand Victorian building on Martin Place, but business is now conducted around the corner at 159-171 Pitt St (☎ 9230 7834). The office is open weekdays from 8.15 am to 5.30 pm, Saturday 8.30 am to noon, and has poste restante and computer terminals where you can check to see if mail is waiting for you. Bring some ID. You can have mail redirected to any suburban post office for a small fee.

Several travel agencies offer mail-holding and forwarding services. American Express and Thomas Cook provide mail services for their clients or you can try Travellers Contact Point (☎ 9221 8744), Suite 11-15, 7th floor, 428 George St, or Travel Active (☎ 9264 2477), 14 Wentworth Ave.

Telstra Phone Centre (☎ 9233 1177), 231 Elizabeth St, has booths of coin, phonecard and credit-card telephones. It's open daily. The 24-hour Translating & Interpreting Service (☎ 131450) can help with language difficulties.

You can log onto the Internet at most public libraries or at Internet cafes. The latter include Paragon Hotel (☎ 9241 3522), on the corner of Alfred and Loftus Sts, Hotel Sweeney (☎ 9267 1116), 236 Clarence St, and Well Connected (☎ 9566 2655), 35 Glebe Point Rd, Glebe.

Travel Agencies

Thomas Cook (☎ 9229 6611), 175 Pitt St, has a travel agency as well as a foreign-exchange desk; it's open Monday to Friday from 8.45 am to 5.15 pm, Saturday 10 am to 1 pm. American Express (☎ 9239 0666), 92 Pitt St, opens Monday to Friday from 8.30 am to 5.30 pm, Saturday 9 am to 2 pm.

A number of travel agents cater to budget travellers/backpackers. STA Travel (not to be confused with the State Transit Authority) has its head office (☎ 9212 1255) at 855 George St, Ultimo, plus several branches. Others include Let's Travel Australia (☎ 9358 2295), 165 Victoria St near Kings Cross; Eden Travel (☎ 9368 1271), 2 Springfield Ave, Kings Cross; and Travellers Contact Point (☎ 9221 8744), 7th floor, 428 George St, above Dymocks bookshop.

Bookshops

Dymocks and Angus & Robertson are large Sydney chain stores. Dymocks' main branch (☎ 9235 0155), 424-30 George St, is an enormous shop with a huge range of stock and a coffee shop. You'll find an Angus & Robertson (☎ 9235 1188) in the Imperial Arcade, 168 Pitt St.

The Travel Bookshop (☎ 9241 3554), downstairs at 6 Bridge St, specialises in travel books and maps and is open weekdays 9 am to 6 pm, Saturday 10 am to 5 pm, and Sunday noon to 5 pm. The friendly Abbey's Bookshop (☎ 9264 3111), 131 York St, opposite the Queen Victoria Building, carries a wide range of literature, including many foreign-language titles. Green Books (☎ 9261 1919), 92 Liverpool St, has books and posters on environmental issues and indigenous cultures.

Oxford St has a handful of decent bookshops. The Bookshop Darlinghurst (☎ 9331 1103), 207 Oxford St, near Taylor Square, specialises in gay literature. Ariel (☎ 9713 4568), at No 42-44, Paddington, specialises in art and design. Berkelouw's Books (☎ 9360 3200), at No 19, opposite Ariel, has secondhand and antique books and a good travel section as well as a small cafe.

The Humanities Bookshop (☎ 9331 5514), 240 Oxford St, opposite Paddington Town Hall, sells interesting second-hand titles, including first editions. New Edition bookshop (☎ 9360 6913), at No 328, has general fiction.

In Glebe, Gleebooks (☎ 9660 2333), 49 Glebe Point Rd, is worth checking out, as is its other outlet (☎ 9552 2526), at No 191, for secondhand and children's books.

Libraries

The City of Sydney Library has its main branch (☎ 9265 9470) on the 3rd floor at the Town Hall and is open weekdays from 8 am to 7 pm, Saturday 10 am to noon. There's another smaller branch (☎ 9265 9472) farther south in a restored sandstone building at 744 George St, Haymarket. It's open Monday to Friday 8.30 am to 6 pm, Saturday 10 am to 1 pm. The libraries have public telephones, photocopiers and computers, a collection of CD-ROMs and Internet access.

Cultural Centres

Among the many foreign cultural centres in Sydney are:

Alliance Francaise
    257 Clarence St, city (☎ 9267 1755)
British Council
    203 New South Head Rd, Edgecliff (☎ 9326 2022)
Goethe Institute
    90 Ocean Institute, Woollahra (☎ 9238 7411)
Italian Institute of Culture
    1 Macquarie Place (☎ 9392 7939)
Japan Cultural Centre
    Level 14, 201 Miller St, North Sydney (☎ 9954 0111)

Laundry

There are dozens of convenient laundromats and dry-cleaning places around town, many of which are open daily.

While your clothes are washing at My Favourite Laundrette (☎ 9332 1843), 128 Darlinghurst Rd south of Kings Cross, you can pop next door to Fishface for a meal. You can do the same at Fitzroy Laundry (no phone), 61 Fitzroy St next to Johnnie's Seafood Cafe, Surry Hills. Wash on the Rocks (☎ 9247 4917) is at 9A Argyle Place, the Rocks; it's closed on Sunday.

Medical Services

Several places give vaccinations and advice, but you need to book an appointment. The Traveller's Medical & Vaccination Centre (☎ 9221 7133), Room 12, 7th floor, 428 George St, between King and Market Sts above Dymocks bookshop, is open Monday to Friday from 9 am to 5 pm, Saturday 9 am to noon. Kings Cross Travellers' Clinic (☎ 9358 3066), Suite 1, 13 Springfield Ave, is open Monday to Friday from 10 am to 1 pm and 2 to 6 pm, Saturday 10 am to noon.

Many of the city's public hospitals have casualty departments, including St Vincent's Hospital (☎ 9339 1111), on the corner of Victoria and Burton Sts, Darlinghurst, and Sydney Hospital (☎ 9382 7111), Macquarie St, in the city.

Some chemists with longer opening hours are:

Blake's Pharmacy
    28 Darlinghurst Rd, Kings Cross – daily 9 am to midnight (☎ 9358 6712)
Chemist Shop
    321 Glebe Point Rd, Glebe – daily 8 am to 8 pm (☎ 9552 3372)
Darlinghurst Prescription Pharmacy
    261 Oxford St, Darlinghurst – daily 8 am to 10 pm (☎ 9361 5882)
Wu's Pharmacy
    629 George St, city – Monday to Saturday 9 am to 9 pm, Sunday 9 am to 7 pm (☎ 9211 1805)

Emergency

Dial ☎ 000 for emergency help from the police, ambulance or fire brigade, from any telephone for free. Some other useful emergency numbers include:

Chemist
    Emergency Prescription Referral Service, 24 hours (☎ 9235 0333)
Dentist
    Dental Emergency Information Service (☎ 9369 7050)
Gay & Lesbian Line
    daily 4 pm to midnight (☎ 9207 2800)
Interpreter Service
    Telephone Interpreter Service, 24 hours, over 20 languages available, particularly useful in an emergency or when seeking medical treatment (☎ 131450)

Life Crisis
    Lifeline, 24 hours (☎ 131114)
    Salvo Care Line (Salvation Army), 24 hours (☎ 9331 6000)
    Youth Line, noon to midnight (☎ 9951 5522)
Poisons
    Poisons Information Centre, 24 hours (☎ 131126)
Rape
    Rape Crisis Centre, 24 hours (☎ 9819 6565/7842)

The Wayside Chapel (☎ 9358 6577, 24 hours), 29 Hughes St, Kings Cross, is a crisis centre which provides useful local information and can help solve many problems.

Police stations in the city include one at 192 Day St (☎ 9265 6499) near Darling Harbour, another in the Rocks on the corner of George and Argyle Sts (☎ 9265 6366) and one in Kings Cross at 1-15 Elizabeth Bay Rd (☎ 9265 6233).

See also Medical Services above.

Dangers & Annoyances

Sydney isn't an especially dangerous city, but you should remain alert. The usual big-city rules apply: never leave your luggage unattended, never show wads of money or get drunk in the company of strangers.

You may be hassled for small change in Kings Cross, George St near the cinema complex, Oxford St between Taylor Square and Hyde Park, and along Eddy Ave outside Central Station.

Harassment of gays/lesbians and non-Anglo-Celts isn't rife, but does happen. Use extra caution in Kings Cross, which attracts drifters from all over Australia and gutter-crawlers from all over Sydney.

Sydney is generally safe for women travellers, although you should avoid walking alone late at night. Gross sexual harassment is uncommon, but you should be a little wary, especially in pubs.

Some Sydney beaches are polluted after heavy rainfall.

Sydney drivers are noted for their aggressive driving, speeding and casual regard for road rules. Pedestrians should be careful when crossing at traffic lights. If you're driving, remember that there are many one-way streets.

Work

Many backpacker hostels boast that they can find work for guests though much of it involves collecting for charities or door-to-door sales. *TNT Magazine* has a list of employment agencies.

The government-run Commonwealth Employment Service (CES) has in the past been able to help find work for local and overseas visitors if they had work permits. At the time of going to press, the government was planning to privatise the CES so the situation may have changed by the time you read this book. The main city office (☎ 9379 8000) was at 477 Pitt St. In the same building was the CES's Temp Line service (☎ 9227 9333), which specialised in filling casual office vacancies.

SYDNEY HARBOUR

The harbour has moulded and shaped the Sydney psyche since settlement; today it's both a major port and the city's playground. Its waters, beaches, islands and waterside parks offer all the swimming, sailing, picnicking and walking you could wish for.

Officially called **Port Jackson**, Sydney's extravagantly colourful harbour stretches some 20 km inland to join the mouth of the Parramatta River. The headlands at the entrance are known as North Head and South Head and the most scenic area is on the ocean side. The harbour has multiple sandstone headlands, beautiful bays and beaches, numerous inlets and several islands. A couple of km inside the Heads is a large inlet called **Middle Harbour**. At weekends, the harbour is filled with the sails of hundreds of yachts.

The best way to view the harbour is to take

City Views

The highest view in Sydney is from **Sydney Tower** (☎ 9229 7444), the 300-metre needle which soars from the Centrepoint shopping centre at the corner of Market and Pitt Sts. The views extend west to the Blue Mountains and east to the ocean, as well as straight down to the streets of inner Sydney. The tower opens Sunday to Friday from 9.30 am to 9.30 pm (to 11.30 pm on Saturday), and the lift (elevator) to the top costs $9 ($4 children). To get to the tower's lifts, enter Centrepoint from Market St and take the lift to the podium level where you buy your ticket.

The **Harbour Bridge** offers excellent views. You can get onto the bridge from a stone staircase off Cumberland St in the Rocks or from near Milsons Point railway station on the North Shore. A footpath runs right across. If the view from the footpath isn't enough, you can climb the 200 stairs inside the south-east pylon for panoramic views of the harbour and city.

For a sea-level view of the Opera House, harbour and bridge, walk to **Mrs Macquarie's Point**, at the headland east of the Opera House. The point has been a lookout since at least 1810, when Elizabeth Macquarie, wife of Governor Lachlan Macquarie, had a stone chair hewn into the rock so she could watch ships entering the harbour and keep an eye on hubby's construction projects just across Farm Cove. The seat is still there today.

To get the best views, catch a **ferry**. The most spectacular are seen from the Manly ferries which traverse the length of the Harbour Bridge. The ferries which travel west of the bridge (such as the Hunters Hill ferry) are also worth catching, both for the experience of cruising under the bridge and to see the narrow waterways humming with workaday activity. ∎

a cruise or catch one of the numerous ferries that ply its waters. The Manly ferry offers vistas of the harbour east of the bridge, while the Parramatta RiverCats cover the west. You can also take trips to some of the small islands which are part of Sydney Harbour National Park (see below).

For details of Sydney Harbour's beaches, see the Beaches section.

Sydney Harbour National Park

This park protects scattered pockets of bushland around the harbour and includes several small islands. It offers some great walking tracks, scenic lookouts, Aboriginal carvings, beaches and a handful of historic sites. On the southern shore it incorporates South Head and Nielsen Park; on North Shore it includes North Head, Dobroyd Head, Middle Head and Ashton Park. Fort Denison, Goat, Clarke and Shark islands are also part of the park. Park headquarters (☎ 9337 5511) is at Greycliffe House in Nielsen Park, Vaucluse.

Islands Previously known as Pinchgut, **Fort Denison** is a small fortified island off Mrs Macquarie's Point. It was originally used as a punishment 'cell' to isolate troublesome convicts until it was fortified in the mid-19th century during the Crimean War amid fears of a Russian invasion. Hegarty's Ferries (☎ 9247 5033, 9206 1167) has daily 1½-hour tours to the island at 10 am, noon and 2 pm, departing from wharf 6 at Circular Quay, for $9 ($6.50 concession).

On weekends there are three-hour guided tours (☎ 9555 9844) of **Goat Island**, west of the Harbour Bridge, which has been a shipyard, quarantine station and gunpowder depot. Tours depart from the Harbourmaster's Steps at Circular Quay West and cost $12 ($8 concession).

Clarke Island, off Darling Point, and **Shark Island**, outside Rose Bay, make great picnic getaways, but you'll need to hire a water taxi or have access to a boat to reach them. You need to get a permit from the NPWS to visit the islands; these cost $3 per person and bookings should be made several

weeks in advance at Cadman's Cottage (☎ 9555 9844).

Walks At the entrance to the harbour, near Watsons Bay, there's a fine, short walk round **South Head**. It begins at Camp Cove and passes Lady Bay, Inner South Head and **The Gap**, ending at Outer South Head. Bus No 325 from Circular Quay runs past Nielsen Park to Watsons Bay. Ferries run to Watsons Bay on weekends.

On North Shore, the four-km **Ashton Park track** begins below Taronga Zoo and heads east round Bradleys Head, skirting Taylors Bay to reach Clifton Gardens. Take the Taronga Zoo ferry from Circular Quay to get to Ashton Park. From Taronga you can walk west to **Cremorne Point** via a combination of parks, stairways, streets and bush. Either way you get good views of the harbour and the southern shore. George's Head, Obelisk Bay and Middle Head, northeast of Taylor's Bay, are also part of the national park.

One of the best walks in the park is the eight-km **Manly Scenic Walkway**, which follows the harbour shore from Manly to Spit Bridge and takes about four hours. Collect a leaflet detailing the walk from Manly's Visitors' Information Bureau. For more information call the NPWS (☎ 9977 6229) or Manly Municipal Council (☎ 9976 1500).

THE ROCKS

Sydney's first non-Aboriginal settlement was made on the rocky spur of land on the western side of Sydney Cove, from which the Harbour Bridge now crosses to North Shore. It became known as the Rocks because of the prominent outcrops of sandstone on the hillside. Soon after settlement the Rocks became the centre of the colony's maritime and commercial enterprises. Warehouses and bond stores were built and the area was filled with convicts, officers, ticket-of-leavers, whalers and sailors. Brothels and inns soon followed.

In the 1820s and 30s the nouveaux riches built three-storey houses on what is now Lower Fort St (which overlooked the slums), but the area remained notorious until the 20th century. In the 1870s and 80s, the infamous Rocks 'pushes' (street gangs) used to haunt the area, snatching purses, holding up pedestrians, feuding and generally creating havoc. The area fell into decline as modern shipping and storage facilities moved away from Circular Quay. It declined further following an outbreak of bubonic plague in 1900 which led to whole streets being razed. The construction of the Harbour Bridge which began two decades later resulted in further demolition.

Redevelopment, which began in the 1970s under the auspices of the Sydney Cove Redevelopment Authority, has turned the area into a sanitised, historical tourist precinct, full of narrow, cobbled streets, fine colonial buildings, converted warehouses and tea-rooms. If you ignore the kitsch, it's a delightful place to stroll around.

Orientation & Information

George St leads into the Rocks from the city centre. It curves under the Harbour Bridge and meets Lower Fort St, which leads south to Observatory Park and north to the waterfront near Pier One. Cumberland St parallels George St and almost all of the area's attractions are crammed into the narrow paths and alleyways between the two. Argyle Cut in Argyle St is the short cut between the eastern and western sides of the peninsula.

The Rocks Visitor Centre (☎ 9255 1788, 1800 067 676), 106 George St, is open daily from 9 am to 5 pm. There you can buy the Rocks Ticket ($40, $26.50 children) which gives visitors entry to a couple of attractions, and includes a meal, a walking tour and a harbour cruise. You can also buy a ticket which includes admission to Taronga Zoo.

The visitor centre has a good range of publications and souvenirs, and there are maps of self-guided walking tours in the area for 50c.

The Rocks isn't large, but there are many small streets and hidden corners, so a map is handy. At Millers Point on the western side of the Bradfield Highway (the elevated Harbour Bridge approach road), you'll find

some charming, old terraced houses and the Sydney Observatory.

Things to See & Do

The oldest house in Sydney is **Cadman's Cottage** (1816), 110 George St, close to the visitor centre. It was once the home of the last government coxswain, John Cadman. When the cottage was built it was actually on the waterfront and the arches to its south housed longboats. The cottage is now an office of the NPWS (☎ 9555 9844), open daily 9 am to 5 pm. Its staff help organise tours of the harbour islands.

Susannah Place, 58-64 Gloucester St, is a terrace of tiny houses dating from 1844. It's one of the few remaining examples of the modest housing which was once standard in the area.

The Rocks has several interesting shopping centres. They include the **Argyle Centre** on Argyle St, which was a bond store between 1826 and 1881 but today houses shops, studios and the Woolshed theatre restaurant; the **Rocks Centre**, also on Argyle St, and the **Metcalfe Arcade** on George St.

The work of Sydney artist Ken Done is on show at the **Ken Done Gallery** (☎ 9247 2740), 1 Hickson Rd, off George St, in a converted warehouse. It's open daily from 10 am to 5.30 pm.

A short walk west along Argyle St through **Argyle Cut**, an old tunnel excavated through the hill by convicts, takes you to the other side of the peninsula and **Millers Point**, a delightful district of early colonial homes. It was named after the flour mill which once stood on what is now Observatory Hill in Observatory Park.

At the far end of the cut is **Garrison Church** (1848), the first church in Australia. Nearby is **Argyle Place**, an English-style village green, and the Lord Nelson and the Hero of Waterloo hotels which vie for the title of Sydney's oldest pub (see Entertainment section).

Farther north, at 53 Lower Fort St, is the **Colonial House Museum** (☎ 9247 6008), a private house fitted out with colonial-era furniture. It's open daily 10 am to 5 pm; admission is just $1 (50c children).

Built in the 1850s, the historically and architecturally interesting **Sydney Observatory** (☎ 9217 0485) has a commanding position atop **Observatory Hill** overlooking Millers Point and the harbour. The observatory has an interesting little museum with interactive displays and videos. Daytime admission is free and the observatory is open weekdays from 2 to 5 pm, weekends and school holidays 10 am to 5 pm. A small planetarium has shows ($2) on weekends at 11.30 am and 3.30 pm. The observatory is also open on Thursday to Tuesday at 6.15 and 8.15 pm for a tour of the building, videos and telescope viewing. These must be booked and cost $6 ($3 children, $15 family).

The **National Trust Centre** (☎ 9258 0123) in the old military hospital houses the SH Ervin Gallery which has changing exhibitions; it's open Tuesday to Friday from 11 am to 5 pm (from noon on weekends) and admission is $6 ($3 concessions).

Although Darling Harbour has been redeveloped there are still many wharves and warehouses around Dawes Point. **Pier One**, at the tip of Dawes Point, has been renovated but is still an under-used shopping and leisure complex. By contrast, **Pier Four** is home to the renowned Sydney Theatre and Sydney Dance companies. Hour-long tours of the complex are held on the last Thursday of each month and cost $5 – bookings are advisable (☎ 9250 1700) or enquire at the box office.

South of the Rocks on Essex St, up towards St Patrick's Church, you'll find the site of the **public gallows**, which were in use until 1804, and Sydney's first jail.

Walking Tour

The Rocks Walking Tours (☎ 9247 6678) offers guided 75-minute walks starting from the visitor centre on weekdays at 10.30 am, 12.30 and 2.30 pm, weekends at 11.30 am and 2.30 pm; they cost $10 (children under 10 free).

SYDNEY HARBOUR BRIDGE

From the northern end of the Rocks the imposing 'old coat hanger' crosses the harbour at one of its narrowest points, linking the southern and northern shores. Considered ugly by some, it has, however, always been a popular icon. The two halves of the mighty arch were built out from each shore, supported by cranes. After nine years of work, when the ends of the arches were only centimetres apart and ready to be bolted together, a gale blew up and winds of over 100 km/h set them swaying. But the bridge survived and the arch was completed.

The bridge cost $20 million, a bargain in modern terms, but it wasn't paid off until 1988. It took nine years to build, and normally it takes 10 years to completely repaint it, but the city authorities are speeding up the process in time for the Olympics.

You can climb inside the south-eastern stone pylon which houses the small **Harbour Bridge Museum**. Admission to the pylon is $2 ($1 children), and it's open daily from 10 am to 5 pm. The pylons supported the cranes used to build the bridge but today they're purely decorative.

Cars, trains, cyclists, joggers and pedestrians use the bridge. The cycleway is on the western side, the pedestrian walkway on the eastern; stair access is from Cumberland St

Cutting 'Red' Tape

The Sydney Harbour Bridge was opened in 1932 – twice.

Before the NSW Premier, Jack Lang, could cut the ribbon, a Captain de Groot charged up on horseback and cut it with his sword, declaring the bridge open on behalf of 'decent and loyal citizens'. The captain was a member of the New Guard, a mob of right-wing revolutionaries who were outraged that Lang was shepherding NSW through the Depression with 'socialist ideas', such as feeding the poor. After de Groot was led away, Lang opened the bridge on behalf of 'the people of New South Wales', 750,000 of whom were in attendance. ■

in the Rocks and near Milsons Point Station on North Shore.

The best way to experience the bridge is undoubtedly on foot; don't expect much of a view if you cross by car or train. When driving south you will have to pay a $2 toll; there's no toll in the other direction.

The bridge shares Sydney's massive trans-harbour traffic with the **Harbour Tunnel**. It begins about half a kilometre south of the Opera House, crosses under the harbour east of the bridge and meets the Warringah Freeway (the road leading north from the bridge) on the northern side. There's also a $2 southbound-only toll. From the North Shore to the eastern suburbs, it's easier to use the tunnel.

SYDNEY OPERA HOUSE

Australia's most recognisable icon sits dramatically on Bennelong Point on the eastern headland of Circular Quay. The Opera House's soaring shell-like roofs were actually inspired by palm fronds but look a little like white turtles in congress. Started in 1959, the Opera House was officially opened in 1973 after a tumultuous series of personality clashes, technical difficulties and delays.

It's a truly memorable experience to experience a performance, listen to a free Sunday afternoon concert or sit at an outdoor cafe and watch harbour life go by. The Opera House itself looks fine from any angle but the view from a ferry coming into Circular Quay is one of the best.

The Opera House (☎ 9250 7111) has four auditoriums and stages dance, theatre, concerts and films, as well as opera. It's also home to the Performing Arts Library & Archives, open weekdays 9 am to 5 pm.

There are tours (☎ 9250 7250) of the building which are worth taking, although the inside isn't as spectacular as outside. Tours are held daily every half-hour (approximately, depending on what's happening) between 9 am and 4 pm for $9 ($6 children). Not all tours can visit all theatres at any given time because of the various activities. You're more likely to see everything if you take a tour early in the day or go on Sunday, often the quietest day.

You can often catch a free lunchtime film or organ recital in the concert hall. On Sunday there's free light entertainment outside on the 'prow', jazz near the Concourse restaurant and a market selling arts and crafts near the front entrance.

The bi-monthly *Opera House Diary* details forthcoming performances and is available free at the Opera House. The box office (☎ 9250 7777) is open Monday to Saturday from 9 am to 8.30 pm and 2½ hours before a Sunday performance.

The Soap Opera House

The hullabaloo surrounding construction of the Sydney Opera House was an operatic blend of personal vision, long delays, bitter feuding, cost blowouts and narrow-minded politicking.

The NSW government held an international design competition in 1956, which was won by Danish designer Jorn Utzon with a $7-million plan. Construction of Utzon's uniquely shaped design began in 1959, but the project soon became a nightmare of cost overruns and construction difficulties. After political interference and disagreements with his consultants about construction methods, Utzon quit in disgust in 1966, leaving a consortium of three Australian architects to design a compromised interior. The parsimonious state government financed the eventual $102-million cost in true-blue Aussie fashion through a series of lotteries. The building was completed in 1973.

After all the hullabaloo, brawling and political bickering, the first public performance staged at the Opera House was, appropriately, Prokofiev's *War & Peace*. The preparations were reported to be a debacle and a possum appeared on stage during one of the dress rehearsals.

More recently, the resident Australian Opera Company staged *The Eighth Wonder*, which dramatised the events surrounding the building of the Opera House. ∎

SYDNEY

CIRCULAR QUAY

Circular Quay, built around Sydney Cove, is one of the city's major focal points. Sydney Cove was the landing place of the First Fleet and the first European settlement grew up around the Tank Stream, which now runs underground into the harbour near wharf 6. Circular Quay was for many years the shipping centre of Sydney; early photographs and paintings show a forest of masts crowding the skyline. Today it's both a commuting centre and a recreational space.

Circular Quay is the departure point for all harbour ferries, the starting point of many city bus routes and a railway station on the City Circle. It has ferry and bus information booths and a Countrylink Travel Centre (☎ 9241 3887). The elevated Cahill Expressway, running above Alfred St behind the ferry wharves, rather isolates the quay from the rest of the city.

The grand, old **Customs House** (1885) on Alfred St is currently being redeveloped, but its future role is as yet uncertain.

Circular Quay East runs out beside the Royal Botanic Gardens to Bennelong Point with the Opera House perched on the end. Along Circular Quay West is the small **First Fleet Park**, a good place to rest after you've pounded the pavements; the **Overseas Passenger Terminal**, where liners moor; and the little bay of **Campbells Cove**, backed by the low-rise Park Hyatt Hotel.

The **Museum of Contemporary Art** (MCA; ☎ 9241 5892), 140 George St fronting Circular Quay West, is in a stately Art Deco building. It has a fine collection of modern art and temporary exhibitions of the sublime and the ridiculous. Admission is $8 ($5 children) and it's open daily from 10 am to 6 pm.

MACQUARIE PLACE & AROUND

Narrow lanes lead south from Circular Quay towards the city centre. On the corner of Loftus and Bridge Sts, under the shady Moreton Bay figs in Macquarie Place, are a cannon and anchor from the First Fleet flagship, HMS *Sirius*. Other pieces of colonial memorabilia in this interesting square include gas lamps, an ornate drinking fountain (1857), a National Trust-classified gentlemen's convenience (not open) and an **obelisk** (1818), indicating road distances in miles to various points in the nascent colony.

The square has a couple of pleasant outdoor cafes and is overlooked by the rear facade of the imposing 19th-century **Lands Department building**, on Bridge St, whose statues are of surveyors, explorers and politicians.

Museum of Sydney

The excellent Museum of Sydney (☎ 9251 5988), 37 Phillip St, stands on the site of the colony's first and infamously fetid Government House, built in 1788. The museum uses multiple-perspective and installation art to explore Sydney's early history – including the early natural environment, the culture of the indigenous Eora people and convict life. It's open daily 10 am to 5 pm; admission is $6 ($4 children).

Justice & Police Museum

The museum (☎ 9252 1144) is in the old

The Bureaucrats who Won the West

The various ways in which crown land has been allotted, leased and sold have both reflected and caused major changes in the development of NSW. It was bureaucrats and barristers who settled land disputes in the Australian colonies, not sheriffs and six-guns. This is reflected in the imposing proportions of the Lands Department building (built 1876-1891) on Bridge St, a neo-Renaissance pile complete with statues of explorers, surveyors and others connected with the spread of white settlement. More than half the 48 niches intended to contain statues remain unfilled, perhaps because politicians began squabbling over whose statues should be erected. ■

Water Police Station at 8 Phillip St, which was designed by colonial architect James Barnet and completed in 1886. It's now set up as a 19th-century police station and court and has various exhibits on criminal activity, once a major industry in the nearby Rocks. You can take part in mock trials. Most of the year the museum only opens on Sunday from 10 am to 5 pm; in January it is open Sunday to Thursday. Admission is $6 ($3 children).

CITY CENTRE

Central Sydney stretches from Circular Quay in the north to Central Station in the south. The business hub is towards the northern end near Circular Quay, but most redevelopment is occurring at the southern end and this is gradually shifting the focus of the city.

Sydney lacks a true civic centre, but **Martin Place** lays claim to the honour, if only by default. This grand pedestrian mall extends from Macquarie St to George St and is impressively lined by the monumental buildings of financial institutions and the colonnaded Victorian former general post office (GPO). The Commonwealth Bank on the corner of Martin Place and Elizabeth St, and the Westpac on George St, opposite the western end of Martin Place, have impressive old banking chambers.

The street has a couple of fountains, plenty of public seating and an amphitheatre – a popular lunchtime entertainment spot, especially in January during the Festival of Sydney when there's free entertainment daily.

Near the George St end of Martin Place is the **Cenotaph** commemorating Australia's war dead. This is where Sydney's Christmas tree is placed in December's summer heat.

Barrack St, west of Martin Place, another pedestrian area, has fruit barrows and good views of Martin Place and the GPO. The delightful historic buildings of **Macquarie St** and the parks and gardens on the city centre's eastern edge (detailed later) are east of Martin Place.

The old civic locus a few blocks south used to be the plaza containing the Town Hall and St Andrew's Cathedral but traffic and insensitive development have diminished the area's authority. The ornate exterior of the **Town Hall** (1874), on the corner of George and Druitt Sts, is matched by the elaborate chamber room and concert hall inside. The concert hall contains an impressive organ and is a venue for lunchtime and evening concerts (☎ 9265 9554). Across the open space to the south, **St Andrew's Cathedral** (☎ 9265 1661), built in the same period, is the oldest cathedral in Australia. It holds free organ recitals on Thursday at 1.15 pm.

The huge, sumptuous **Queen Victoria Building** (QVB), opposite the Town Hall, takes up an entire block bordered by George, Market, York and Druitt Sts. It houses about 200 shops, cafes and restaurants. It was built in 1898 in the style of a Byzantine palace to house the city's fruit and vegetable market. There are guided tours (☎ 9265 6864) twice daily.

Opposite the QVB, underneath the Hilton Hotel and the Royal Arcade, is the **Marble Bar**, an extravagant piece of Victoriana. The bar was built by George Adams, who founded Tattersalls lotteries. When the old Adams Hotel was torn down to build the Hilton the bar was carefully dismantled and reassembled. The city's other ostentatious building is the **State Theatre**, to the north at 49 Market St. It was built as a movie palace during Hollywood's heyday and is now a National Trust-classified building. Except during the Sydney Film Festival in June, it stages only live shows. It's worth attending a performance just to marvel at the decor.

On Pitt St, a block south of Martin Place, is the busy **Pitt St Mall**, with shopping arcades and department stores nearby. The lovingly restored **Strand Arcade**, which houses speciality and designer shops, runs west off the mall to George St. On the eastern side of the mall is the modern **Skygarden** arcade; take the long 'express' escalator straight to the top. **Centrepoint**, at the bottom of the Sydney Tower (see City Views), is another large complex. Two large department stores, Grace Brothers and the more upmarket David Jones, are nearby on

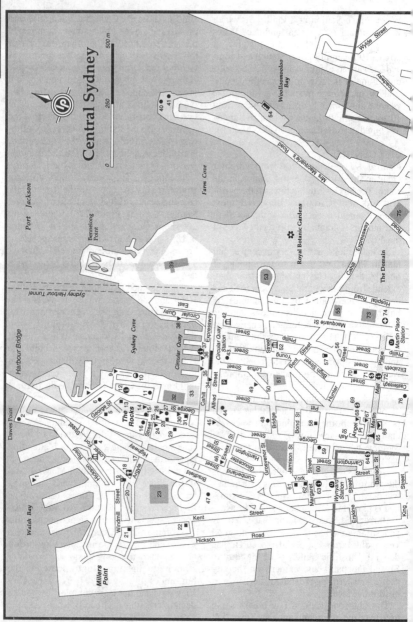

Central Sydney

Port Jackson

Harbour Bridge

Dawes Point

Walsh Bay

Millers Point

Sydney Cove

Bennelong Point

Sydney Harbour Tunnel

Farm Cove

Woolloomooloo Bay

Royal Botanic Gardens

The Domain

The Rocks

Circular Quay

Circular Quay Station

Circular Quay East

Macquarie St

Martin Place Station

Wynyard Station

Hickson Road

Kent Street

George Street

York Street

Pitt Street

George St

Mrs Macquarie's Road

Cahill Expressway

Hospital Road

0 250 500 m

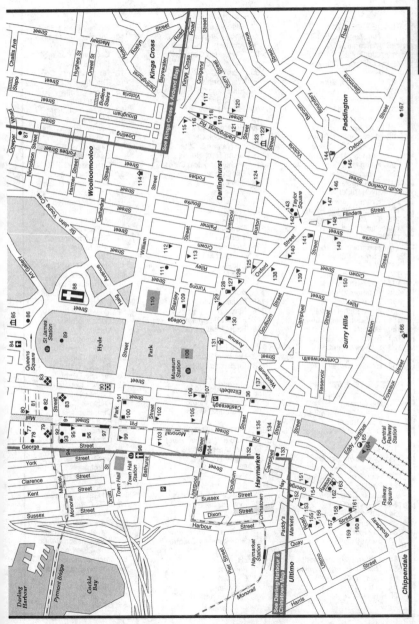

PLACES TO STAY
4 Harbour View Hotel
5 Mercantile Hotel
13 Old Sydney Parkroyal
21 Lord Nelson Brewery Hotel
22 The Observatory Hotel
28 Harbour Rocks Hotel
29 The Stafford
31 The Russell Hotel
58 Grand Hotel
61 York Apartment Hotel
62 Wynyard Vista Hotel
70 Sydney City Centre Serviced Apartments
96 Hilton Hotel
100 Criterion Hotel
101 Park Regis
107 Hyde Park Inn
109 Sydney Park Inn
114 Forbes Terrace Hostel
116 Top Of The Town Hotel
119 L'Otel
127 Parkridge Corporate Apartments & The Park All-Suite Hotel
131 YWCA
132 CB Private Hotel
135 Westend Hotel
136 Southern Cross Hotel
150 Crown Lodge International Motel
155 Travellers Rest Hotel
160 Country Comfort Hotel
161 Crystal Palace Hotel
163 Sydney Central YHA Hostel
166 Excelsior Hotel

PLACES TO EAT
1 Pier Four (Wharf Restaurant)
7 Italian Village, Wolfies & Waterfront
9 Doyle's at the Quay & Bilson's
14 G'Day Cafe
24 Clocktower Square Shopping Centre
25 Gum Nut Tea Garden
26 Phillip's Foote & Rocks Cafe
30 Ox on the Rocks
34 Nulbom Oriental Food
35 Cafe Rossini
36 City Extra
38 Sydney Cove Oyster Bar
45 Kable's (Regent Hotel)
46 The Rocks Teppanyaki
49 Bar Paradiso
67 El Sano
68 Merivale

77 Old Sydney Coffee Shop (Strand Arcade)
80 Skygarden Complex (cafes & bars)
95 Arizona's
99 Woolworth's
102 Edinburgh Castle & Pitt St Bistro
103 Planet Hollywood
105 Diethnes Restaurant
106 Hellenic Club
112 Hard Rock Cafe
113 No Names & Other Italian Restaurants
115 Michaelangelo's Cafe
117 Bar Coluzzi
118 Govinda's & The Movie Room
120 Una's Coffee Lounge
122 Laurie's Vegetarian Diner
124 Dov Cafe
125 1 Burton
126 Metro Cafe (Vegetarian)
129 Burdekin Hotel
134 Chamberlain Hotel
138 Hanovers
139 Betty's Soup Kitchen
140 Maltese Cafe
146 Kim
147 Balkan Restaurant
148 Bagel House
149 Riberries
151 Cafe Inn
152 House of Guangzhou
153 Emperor's Garden BBQ
154 Mekong
156 Prince Centre
158 Malaya on George
164 Wildfood Cafe

ENTERTAINMENT
19 Hero of Waterloo Hotel
57 Wentworth Hotel & Legends
121 Darlo Bar
128 Exchange Hotel
130 DCM
133 Capitol Theatre
141 Kinselas
144 Albury Hotel
145 Academy Twin Cinema
159 Her Majesty's Theatre

OTHER
2 Pier One
3 Colonial House Museum
6 Metcalfe Arcade

8 Sydney Opera House
10 Overseas Passenger Terminal
11 Cadman's Cottage (NPWS Office)
12 Rocks Visitors' Centre
15 The Rocks Centre
16 Argyle Centre
17 Argyle Cut
18 Garrison Church
20 Argyle Place
23 Sydney Observatory
27 Ken Done Design
32 Museum of Contemporary Art
33 First Fleet Park
37 Ferry Information
39 Government House
40 Mrs Macquarie's Point
41 Mrs Macquarie's Chair
42 Justice & Police Museum
43 Old Customs House
44 Goldfields House (Australian Wine Centre)
47 National Trust Centre
48 Travel Bookshop
50 Macquarie Place
51 Lands Department Building
52 Museum of Sydney
53 Conservatorium of Music
54 Boy Charlton Pool
55 State Library
56 Chifley Square
59 Paxtons Cameras
60 Wynyard Park
63 NSW & Countrylink Travel Centres
64 Westpac Bank
65 Cenotaph
66 Post Office
69 American Express
71 Commonwealth Bank
72 Sydney Information Booth, Halftix & Ticketek
73 Parliament House
74 Sydney Hospital
75 Art Gallery of NSW
76 MLC Centre & Theatre Royal
78 Dymocks Bookshop & Traveller's Medical & Vaccination Centre
79 Grace Brothers
81 Imperial Arcade
82 Centrepoint & Sydney Tower
83 David Jones
84 St James Church
85 Sydney Mint Museum

86	Hyde Park Barracks	97	Town Hall Monorail	142	Darlinghurst
87	The Gunnery		Station		Courthouse
88	St Mary's Cathedral	98	St Andrew's Cathedral	143	Old Darlinghurst Gaol
89	Archibald Fountain	104	World Square	157	CES City Casuals
90	Great Synagogue		Monorail Station	162	Thomas Cook
91	City Centre Monorail	108	Anzac Memorial		Outdoor Clothing
	Station	110	Australian Museum	165	Coach Station
92	State Theatre	111	Watters Gallery	167	Victoria Barracks
93	Gowings	123	Sydney Jewish		
94	Queen Victoria		Museum		
	Building	137	Women & Girls		
			Emergency Centre		

Market St. Gowings, on the corner of Market and George Sts, is a big menswear shop from a previous era.

To the south-west are the lively **Chinatown** and the much smaller **Spanish Town**. Chinatown, west of George St between Liverpool and Quay Sts, is booming, fuelled by an influx of money from Hong Kong. This colourful area encompasses Dixon St and **Haymarket** and includes the restored Paddy's Markets. Spanish Town is along Liverpool St between George and Sussex Sts. A block east, **World Square**, once a big hole in the ground, is beginning to take shape.

The dynamism of this part of the city is spreading south to breathe life back into the zone around **Central Station** (1906) and **Railway Square** at the intersection of Broadway, George and Regent Sts on the city centre's southern periphery. At the turn of the century this was Sydney's business district. Running beneath Central from Railway Square is a long pedestrian subway, emerging on the east side at Devonshire St in Surry Hills. It's usually crowded with commuters (and buskers), but late at night can be spooky.

DARLING HARBOUR & PYRMONT

This huge, purpose-built waterfront leisure park on the city centre's western edge was opened in 1988 but hasn't been the success that was hoped for. Recent developments like Darling Walk will no doubt attract more visitors. Another $50 million is being spent on upgrading the Harbourside shopping centre. This is the supposed centrepiece but the real attractions are the aquarium, maritime museum, IMAX Theatre, Chinese Garden, Darling Walk and casino.

Darling Harbour Visitors Centre (☎ 9286 0111), under the elevated freeway near the IMAX Theatre, is open daily from 9 am to 5.30 pm. You can also call the Infoline (☎ 1902 260 568) for recorded information.

Although the complex covers a large area it's possible to see it all on foot. If you're bent on seeing everything consider the Darling Harbour Superticket, which costs $29.90 ($19.50 children) and gives you a harbour cruise, entry to the aquarium, a restaurant meal, entry to the Chinese Garden, a monorail ride and discount on a tour of Sydney Olympic Park. You can buy the Superticket at the aquarium, monorail stations, the Chinese Garden or through Matilda Cruises. The ticket is valid for one month from the date of purchase.

Harbourside

Harbourside (☎ 9281 3999), a large, graceful structure, is basically a shopping mall. There are two sections, known as the north and south pavilions. Most shops stay open till 7 pm Sunday to Wednesday, till 9 pm Thursday to Saturday. **Gavala** (☎ 9212 7232), as well as exhibiting Aboriginal arts and crafts, puts on cultural performances including storytelling, traditional dancing and didgeridoo playing.

Sydney Aquarium

This aquarium (☎ 9262 2300), which displays the richness of Australian marine life,

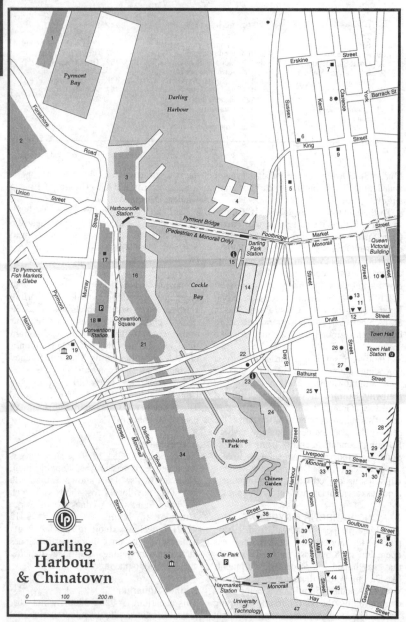

Darling
Harbour
& Chinatown

consists of three 'oceanariums' moored in the harbour, with sharks, rays and big fish in one and Sydney Harbour marine life and seals in the others. There are also transparent underwater tunnels, informative and well-presented exhibits of freshwater fish and coral gardens. The aquarium opens daily from 9.30 am to 9 pm; admission costs $14.90 ($7 children).

Australian National Maritime Museum
It's hard not to spot the maritime museum (☎ 9552 7777) at the western end of Pyrmont Bridge because its roofs appear to billow like sails. This thematic museum tells the story of Australia's relationship with the sea, from Aboriginal canoes and the First Fleet to surf culture and the America's Cup. Different types of vessels stand inside or are moored at the wharves, including the destroyer HMAS *Vampire* and a submarine from the former Soviet Union. There's an audiovisual display of sailing life, maritime craft demonstrations and entertainment.

The admission price varies depending on how much you want to see. To see the lot – the museum, HMAS *Vampire* and the sub-marine – costs $15 ($9 children). Prices include guided tours which take place on the hour from 11 am to 2 pm. The complex is open daily from 9.30 am to 5 pm.

Powerhouse Museum
Sydney's most spectacular museum (☎ 9217 0111), 500 Harris St, is housed in a vast building which was once the power station for Sydney's trams.

The museum covers the decorative arts, social history, science and technology. The collections are superbly displayed and the emphasis is on interaction and education. There's a variety of free tours from Monday to Friday at 1.30 pm, weekends at 11.30 am and 1.30 pm.

The museum is open daily from 10 am to 5 pm. Admission is $8 ($2 children); entry is free on the first Saturday of every month.

IMAX Theatre
The IMAX Theatre (☎ 133462 for group bookings), with its yellow-and-black chequered facade, rises up between two elevated freeways. It shows 45-minute feature films daily on its giant six-storey screen. The

screenings begin on the hour from 9 am to 10 pm but are not cheap – admission costs $13.95 ($8.50 children). The films are so realistic that a sign warns patrons that they may experience physical discomfort.

Chinese Garden

The exquisite 10-hectare Chinese Garden (☎ 9281 6863/6352), between Harbour St and Pier St, is the biggest outside China and an oasis of tranquility. It was designed by landscape architects from NSW's Chinese sister province, Guangdong, to commemorate Australia's bicentenary in 1988. The garden has several distinct geographical features, such as mountains, wilderness, forest and lake, interspersed with pavilions, waterfalls and lush plants.

It is open daily from 9.30 am to sunset; admission is $3 ($1.50 children).

Around Tumbalong Park

The pleasant grassy area in the centre of the Darling Harbour complex is Tumbalong Park. The park has an amphitheatre which hosts free entertainment most lunchtimes and weekends.

The **Sydney Convention Centre** and **Sydney Exhibition Centre** on the western edge of the park were designed by Australian architect Philip Cox, who also designed the aquarium, the maritime museum and the Sydney Football Stadium. The centres' roofs are suspended from steel masts, continuing Darling Harbour's maritime theme.

South of the Chinese Garden the old pumphouse, which used to supply hydraulic power to Sydney's lifts, is now the **Pumphouse Tavern Brewery**, which brews its own beer. Farther south again, on the edge of Chinatown, is the **Sydney Entertainment Centre**, a venue for rock concerts and sporting events.

Darling Walk, on the eastern side of the park, is a new development containing **Sega World**, Australia's first indoor theme park. It uses the latest in computer graphics and virtual technologies and there are live stage shows. Beneath Sega World is a complex of cafes, restaurants, shops and a performing-arts space.

Olympic Showcase & Information Centre

This centre (☎ 9267 0099) is on Australia's oldest steam ferry, the SS *South Steyne*, on the eastern side of the harbour. Inside is an electronic clock counting down to the Olympic opening ceremony on 15 September 2000. There's also a history of Sydney's bid to host the games, a video of the various venues and interactive computers with information on different aspects of the games. It's open daily from 9 am to 7 pm; entry is $2 ($1 children).

Motor Vehicle Museum

A short walk from the Powerhouse Museum, this museum (☎ 9552 3375), Level 1, 320 Harris St, has over 150 vehicles on display, from vintage beauties to Morris Minors. It's open Wednesday to Sunday and school holidays, 10 am to 5 pm; admission is $8 ($4 children).

Sydney Harbour Casino

This enormous complex is being built on a waterfront site in Pyrmont on the north-eastern headland of Darling Harbour. It's scheduled to open in 1998. In the meantime, a temporary casino operates at wharves 12 and 13 at Darling Harbour. For information call ☎ 1300 300 711.

Pyrmont Fish Markets

Fish auctions are held on weekdays at these markets west of Darling Harbour, on the corner of Pyrmont Bridge Rd and Bank St beside the approach roads to Glebe Island Bridge. They begin at 5.30 am and last three to six hours, depending on the size of the catch. The complex includes eateries and several fabulous fish shops.

Call ☎ 9660 1611 for information about tours.

Getting There & Around

The two main pedestrian approaches to Darling Harbour are footbridges from

Market St and Liverpool St. The one from Market St leads onto the lovely old Pyrmont Bridge, a pedestrian and monorail-only route. It was famous in its day as the first electrically operated swing-span bridge in the world. Town Hall is the closest railway station, then it's a short walk down either Druitt St or Market St.

Monorail The monorail (☎ 9552 2288) circles Darling Harbour and links it to the city centre. As a transport system the monorail isn't great but for sightseeing it's worth the $2.50. Get off at Haymarket for the Powerhouse Museum or at Harbourside for Harbourside shopping centre, the National Maritime Museum and Pyrmont Bridge.

Bus & LRT Bus No 456 connects Circular Quay with the Powerhouse Museum and the casino. The Sydney Explorer bus (see Getting Around) stops at five points around Darling Harbour every 20 minutes.

The light-rail transit (read tram) system runs from Central Station to Darling Harbour and Pyrmont.

Ferry Ferries leave Circular Quay's wharf 5 every 30 minutes from 8 am to 7.30 pm and cost $2.80 ($1.40 children). They stop at Darling Harbour's Aquarium wharf. Matilda Cruises (☎ 9264 7377) operates the Darling Harbour Rocket ferry which leaves the Harbourmaster's Steps at Circular Quay West every 20 minutes and costs $3.10 ($1.55 children).

People Mover The People Mover (☎ 018 290 515) is an incongruous, trackless mini-train which makes a 20-minute loop around Darling Harbour's sights from 10 am to 5 pm for $2.50 ($1.50 children).

MACQUARIE ST
Sydney's greatest concentration of early public buildings grace Macquarie St, which runs along the eastern edge of the city from Hyde Park to the Opera House. The street is named after Lachlan Macquarie, the first governor to have a vision of the city as something more than a convict colony. In the early 19th century he commissioned convicted forger Francis Greenway to design a series of public buildings.

Hyde Park Barracks Museum & St James Church
These two Greenway gems on Queens Square at the northern end of Hyde Park face each other across Macquarie St. The barracks (1819) were built originally as convict quarters, then became an immigration depot and later a women's asylum. They now house a museum on the history of the building and Sydney's social history. The museum (☎ 9223 8922) is open daily from 10 am to 5 pm; admission is $5 ($3 children). The church (1819-24) contains traditional stained glass but also the more modern, striking 'creation window' in the Chapel of the Holy Spirit.

Sydney Mint Museum
This lovely building (1816), which now has exhibits on the gold rush, coins, stamps, minting and a collection of decorative arts, was originally the southern wing of the infamous Rum Hospital. It became a branch of the Royal Mint in 1854, the first to be established outside London. It's open daily from 10 am to 5 pm. Admission is $5 ($2 children); the first Saturday of every month is free.

Parliament House
Parliament House (1810), used by the Legislative Council of the colony from 1829, is still used by the NSW Parliament. This simple but elegant two-storey, sandstone building, surrounded by verandahs, is the world's oldest continuously ally operating parliament building and was originally the northern wing of the Rum Hospital. It's open Monday to Friday from 9.30 am to 4 pm and admission is free. There are free tours (☎ 9230 2111) at 10 and 11 am and 2 pm on non-sitting weekdays and a tour at 1.30 pm on sitting days, including question time, usually booked out several months in advance.

Sydney Hospital

This hospital (☎ 9382 7111), south of Parliament House on the site of the Rum Hospital's central wing, dates from the 1880s. A tour of its historic features begins at 11 am on the first Wednesday of the month; meet at the top of the main entrance stairway. There's a pleasant cafe in the courtyard. In front of the hospital is the **Little Boar** statue. Rubbing its snout – coupled with a donation that goes to the hospital – is supposed to grant you a wish.

State Library of NSW

The state library (☎ 9230 1414) is more of a cultural centre than a traditional library. It has one of the best collections of early works on Australia, including the journals of Captain Cook and Joseph Banks and Captain Bligh's log from the *Bounty*. Many items are displayed in the library's exhibition galleries, open weekdays 9 am to 5 pm, weekends 11 am to 5 pm.

Conservatorium of Music

The conservatorium (☎ 9230 1222), at the northern end of Macquarie St, was built by Greenway as the stables and servants' quarters of Lachlan Macquarie's planned new government house. However, Macquarie was replaced as governor before the rest of the new house could be finished. Francis Greenway's life ended in poverty because he couldn't recoup the money he had invested in the building.

The conservatorium is now a centre of musical studies where students come to fine-tune their jazz, classical music and singing, and it hosts free lunchtime concerts on Wednesday and Friday during term.

ROYAL BOTANIC GARDENS

The Royal Botanic Gardens encompass Farm Cove, the first bay east of Circular Quay. They have a magnificent collection of South Pacific plant life and a beautiful, old-fashioned, formal rose garden. The visitors centre (☎ 9231 8125) is open daily from 9.30 am to 4.30 pm.

The gardens were established in 1816 and include the site of the colony's first vegetable patch. There's a fabulous tropical display housed in the interconnecting Arc and Pyramid glasshouses, well worth the $5 admission ($2 children). It's open daily 10 am to 6 pm in summer, 10 am to 4 pm the rest of the year. A great place to visit on a cool, grey day.

The gardens are open daily 6.30 am to sunset. The free guided walks, daily at 10.30 am from the visitors centre, are extremely informative.

The Trackless Train (similar to Darling Harbour's People Mover) does a circuit of the gardens for $3 ($2 children).

THE DOMAIN

The Domain, a large grassy area south of Macquarie St, is separated from the Royal Botanic Gardens by the Cahill Expressway, but you can cross the expressway on the Art Gallery Rd bridge. The Domain is used by workers for lunchtime sports and as a place to escape the bustle of the city. On Sunday afternoons it's the gathering place for impassioned soapbox speakers who do their best to entertain or enrage their listeners. It's also the setting for free events staged during the Festival of Sydney in January as well as for the popular Carols by Candlelight at Christmas.

ART GALLERY OF NSW

The Art Gallery of NSW (☎ 9225 1790) is in the north-eastern corner of the Domain, a short walk from the city centre. It has an excellent permanent display of Australian, European, Japanese and tribal art, and has some inspired temporary exhibits.

There are beautiful views of the harbour and Woolloomooloo from the ground floor. It's open 10 am to 5 pm daily, and free guided tours are held at 11 am and 2 pm. Admission is free, but you have to pay to see some temporary exhibitions.

AUSTRALIAN MUSEUM

Established only 40 years after the First Fleet dropped anchor, the Australian Museum (☎ 9320 6000, 0055 29408 for recorded

Galleries

The Art Gallery of NSW, at Circular Quay West, and the Museum of Contemporary Art shouldn't be missed. Other galleries abound, especially in the inner eastern suburbs.

Index is a free monthly pamphlet which has gallery listings and you can get it at most bookshops, cafes and galleries in the eastern suburbs. The *Sydney Morning Herald*'s Friday 'Metro' section lists galleries and art exhibitions, but for more detailed information look for the monthly Art Almanac ($2) at galleries and newsagents; it covers all of Australia. There are many galleries in Paddington; pick up a copy of *Paddington Galleries & Environs* at one of these galleries or at the New Edition bookshop (☎ 9360 6913), 328 Oxford St, Paddington. You can also call the Art Gallery Info Line (☎ 0055 20437) for recorded information.

The Art Gallery of NSW – not to be missed

The many galleries include the following:

Artspace
   The Gunnery, 43-51 Cowper Wharf Rd, Woolloomooloo – Tuesday to Saturday, 11 am to 6 pm; has changing contemporary avant-garde exhibitions (☎ 9368 1411)
Australian Centre for Photography
   257 Oxford St, Paddington – Wednesday to Saturday (☎ 9331 6253)
Australian Galleries
   15 Roylston St, Paddington – Monday to Saturday (☎ 9360 5177)
Boomalli Aboriginal Artists Cooperative
   27 Abercrombie St, Chippendale – Tuesday to Friday and Saturday afternoon (☎ 9698 2047)
The Cartoon Gallery
   Level 2, Queen Victoria Building – open daily; specialising in animation and comic-strip art (☎ 9267 3022)
Coo-ee Aboriginal Art Gallery
   98 Oxford St, Paddington – open daily (☎ 9332 1544)
Ken Done Gallery
   1 Hickson Rd, on the corner of George St – open daily; colourful, naive art by a popular designer (☎ 9247 2740)
Stills Gallery
   16 Elizabeth St, Paddington – Wednesday to Saturday, 11 am to 6 pm; photography (☎ 9331 7775)
Tin Sheds Gallery
   154 City Rd, University of Sydney – daily (from 1 pm on weekends); contemporary (☎ 9351 3115)
Wagner Art Gallery
   9 Gurner St, Paddington – Tuesday to Saturday, 11 am to 5.30 pm; famous Australian art (☎ 9360 6069)
Watters Gallery
   109 Riley St, East Sydney – Tuesday and Saturday 10 am to 5 pm, Wednesday to Friday 10 am to 8 pm; contemporary (☎ 9331 2556)
Wentworth Galleries
   31 Norfolk St, Paddington – Wednesday to Saturday, 11 am to 5 pm; contemporary (☎ 9331 8633)
Brett Whitely Gallery
   2 Raper St, Surry Hills – weekends 10 am to 4 pm, Thursday by appointment (☎ 9225 1740/1744)

information), 6 College St across from Hyde Park, is a natural-history museum with an excellent Australian wildlife collection. One gallery traces Aboriginal history from the Dreamtime to the present. The museum has a good bookshop; proceeds from purchases help fund environmental research at the museum.

Guided 30-minute tours occur on the hour from 10 am to 3 pm and an impressive

SYDNEY

gamelan orchestra plays twice a week. There are plenty of activities to keep children amused. The museum opens daily 9.30 am to 5 pm; admission is $5 ($2 children).

HYDE PARK & AROUND

The pleasant Hyde Park is large enough to offer a break from traffic and crowds but retains a city-centre feel.

At the northern end is the richly symbolic Art Deco **Archibald Memorial Fountain**. Near Liverpool St, at the southern end, is the dignified **Anzac Memorial** (1934) which has a small free exhibition containing photographs and exhibits covering the wars in which Australians have fought. There are daily tours at 11.30 am and 1.30 pm. Pine trees near the memorial were grown from seeds gathered at Gallipoli.

St Mary's Cathedral (1882), across College St from the park's north-eastern corner, took 14 years to build. Though you can hardly tell from the outside, it is one of the world's largest cathedrals. There's a free tour of the cathedral and crypt at noon on Sunday, departing from the College St entrance.

The impressive 1873 **Great Synagogue** (☎ 9267 2477) is diagonally opposite St Mary's on Elizabeth St, north of Park St. There's a free 45-minute tour at noon on Tuesday and Thursday leaving from the entrance at 166 Castlereagh St.

You can enter **Museum Station** from the south-western corner of Hyde Park, near the cafe. Many people dislike Museum, others find it a charming period piece; it depends on whether those dim tunnels of glazed tiles remind you of *film noir* or a public toilet. Museum Station and nearby renovated St James date from the 1920s and were Sydney's first underground stations.

KINGS CROSS & AROUND

The Cross is a bizarre cocktail of strip joints, prostitution, crime and drugs with a handful of classy restaurants, designer cafes, international hotels and backpacker hostels thrown in. It attracts an odd mix of low-life, sailors, travellers, Japanese tourists, inner-city trendies and suburbanites looking for a night out.

The Cross has always been a bit raffish, from its early days as a centre of bohemianism to the Vietnam-war era when it became the vice centre of Australia. Today the Cross retains its risque aura, with a hint of menace and more than a touch of sleaze. Sometimes the razzle-dazzle has a sideshow appeal; Darlinghurst Rd can be about as appetising as finding a cockroach in your cornflakes.

However, there's more to the Cross than sleaze. It's the travellers' headquarters of Sydney and many people begin and end their Australian travels here. It has Australia's greatest concentration of hostels and there are also many good (and increasingly fashionable) places to eat as well as plenty of entertainment that doesn't involve the sex industry. You don't have to walk far from the neon lights to find gracious, old terraces in tree-lined streets.

Darlinghurst Rd is the main trashy drag. This dog-legs into Macleay St which continues into the more upmarket suburb of Potts Point. Most hostels are on Victoria St, which diverges from Darlinghurst Rd north of William St, near the iconic Coca-Cola sign.

Kings Cross Tourist Information Booth (☎ 9368 0479), 60 Macleay St in the Fitzroy Gardens, is open Monday to Friday 8.30 am to 5 pm. A police station (☎ 9265 6233) is bunkered down in the Fitzroy Gardens. The Cross is a good place to swap information and buy or sell things. Noticeboards can be found in hostels, shops and along Victoria St. At Kings Cross Car Market (☎ 9358 5000), on the corner of Ward Ave and Elizabeth Bay Rd, travellers buy and sell vehicles.

The most notable landmark in Kings Cross is the thistle-like **El Alamein Fountain** in the brick-paved Fitzroy Gardens. The fountain is known locally as the 'elephant douche'.

To the north, in the suburb of Elizabeth Bay is the 1839 **Elizabeth Bay House** (☎ 9358 2344), 7 Onslow Ave. Once known as 'the finest house in the colony', it has fine views of the harbour. Designed in English neoclassical revival style, it has been meticulously restored and refurbished with early 19th-century furniture. The house is open Tuesday to Sunday 10 am to 4.30 pm; admission costs $5 ($3 children).

If you follow Victoria St north from the Cross you enter leafy **Potts Point** and at the end of the point is **Garden Island**, a large naval base – is it a happy coincidence that the lurid delights of the Cross are only a short stroll away?

In the dip between the Cross and the city is **Woolloomooloo**, one of Sydney's oldest areas; it extends from William St north to the waterfront. Reasonably sensitive urban restoration has made the area pleasant to stroll around. Its huge disused wharf is awaiting redevelopment. Harry's Cafe de Wheels, next to the wharf, must be one of the few pie carts in the world to be a tourist attraction. It opened in 1945, stays open 18 hours a day and is *the* place to go for a pie any time of day. The innovative **Artspace** gallery is opposite.

East of the Cross is **Rushcutters Bay**, both a small suburb of apartment blocks and a pretty bay backed by a sizeable park.

Getting There & Away

The simplest way to get to the Cross is on a CityRail eastern suburbs train from Martin Place, Town Hall or Central stations. It's the first stop outside the city loop on the line to Bondi Junction.

The STA's Airport Express bus No 350 runs to Kings Cross, as does the private Kingsford Smith Transport (see Getting Around). From Circular Quay, bus Nos 324, 325 and 327 run to Kings Cross; from Railway Square take bus No 311.

You can walk from Hyde Park along William St in 15 minutes. A prettier, longer route involves crossing the Domain, descending the hill behind the Art Gallery of NSW, walking past Woolloomooloo's wharf and climbing McElhone Stairs to the northern end of Victoria St.

INNER EAST

The lifeblood of Darlinghurst, Surry Hills and Paddington, **Oxford St** is one of the more exciting places for late-night action, with its strip of shops, cafes, bars and nightclubs. Its flamboyance and spirit are largely attributed to its vibrant, vocal gay community, and the route of the Sydney Gay & Lesbian Mardi Gras parade passes this way.

The main section of Oxford St runs from the south-eastern corner of Hyde Park to the north-western corner of Centennial Park. Taylor Square, at the junction of Oxford, Flinders and Bourke Sts, is the hub of social life in the area. In Oxford St the numbers restart west of the junction with South Dowling and Victoria Sts on the Darlinghurst-Paddington border. South-east of Taylor Square, Darlinghurst Rd and Victoria St run north off Oxford St to Kings Cross, while Oxford St continues on through Paddington and Woollahra, eventually reaching Bondi Junction. Bus Nos 380 and 382 from Circular Quay, and No 378 from Railway Square, run the length of the street.

Darlinghurst

This is the inner-city mecca for bright young things who want to be close to the action. It's a vital area of trendy, self-conscious, urban cool that's fast developing a cafe culture. There's no better way to soak up the ambience than to loiter in a few sidewalk cafes. Darlinghurst encompasses the vibrant 'Little Italy' of Stanley St in East Sydney and is wedged between Oxford and William Sts.

Facing Taylor Square is **Darlinghurst Courthouse** (1842) and behind it is the old **Darlinghurst Gaol**, where author Henry Lawson was incarcerated several times for debt. Today it houses East Sydney TAFE College.

Sydney Jewish Museum (☎ 9360 7999), 148 Darlinghurst Rd on the corner of Burton St, has exhibits on the Holocaust and Australian Jewish history. It's open Monday to Thursday 10 am to 4 pm, Friday 10 am to 2 pm, Sunday 11 am to 5 pm. Admission is $6 ($4 children).

Surry Hills

South of Darlinghurst, Surry Hills, squeezed between the east side of Central Station and

SYDNEY

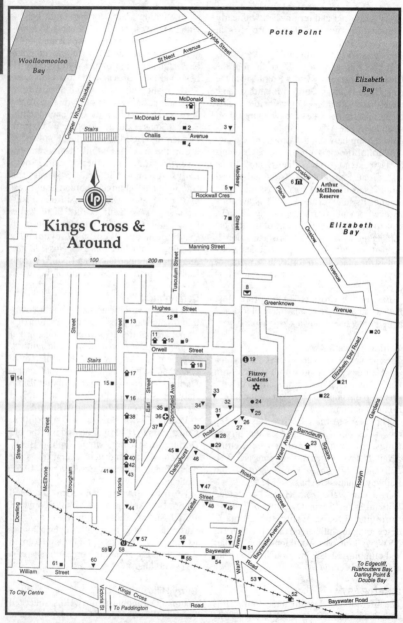

Woolloomooloo Bay

Potts Point

Elizabeth Bay

Elizabeth Bay

Kings Cross & Around

0   100   200 m

Fitzroy Gardens

To Edgecliff, Rushcutters Bay, Darling Point & Double Bay

To City Centre

To Paddington

Bayswater Road

PLACES TO STAY
1   Rucksack Rest
2   Simpsons of Potts Point
4   Challis Lodge
7   Landmark Parkroyal
9   Orwell Lodge
10 Jolly Swagman Back-
    packers (Orwell St)
11 Eva's Backpackers
12 Gala Private Hotel
13 Victoria Court Hotel
15 Kanga House
17 Jolly Swagman Back-
    packers (Victoria St)
18 Jolly Swagman Back-
    packers (Springfield
    Mall)
20 Montpelier Private Hotel
21 The Sebel
22 17 Elizabeth Bay Rd
23 Barncleuth House
    (Pink House)
    Travellers' Rest
28 Kingsview Motel
29 Kingsview Hotel
30 Fountain Plaza Hostel
35 Springfield Lodge

37 Bernly Private Hotel
38 Travellers' Rest
39 Original Backpackers
40 Highfield House
42 Plane Tree Lodge
45 Maksim Lodge
51 Metro Motor Inn
52 Backpackers'
    Headquarters
54 Crescent on Bayswater
    Hotel
55 Barclay Hotel
61 O'Malley's Hotel

PLACES TO EAT
3   Moran's Restaurant &
    Cafe
5   Macleay St Bistro
16 Mère Catherine
25 Fountain Cafe,
    Restaurant & Bar
26 Fountain Cafe,
    Restaurant & Bar
27 Bourbon & Beefsteak
31 Astoria
32 Nick's Seafood
33 Yakitori

34 Pad Thai
43 Roy's
44 Joe's Cafe Deluxe
46 Oporto
47 Lime & Lemon Grass
    Brasserie
48 Dean's Cafe
49 Cafe Iguana
50 Bayswater Brasserie
53 Cafe 59
56 Waterlily Cafe
57 Action Pizza & House
    Kebab
60 Williams on William

OTHER
6   Elizabeth Bay House
8   Post Office
14 Old Fitzroy Hotel
19 Tourist Information
    Booth
24 El Alamein Fountain
36 Kings Cross Travellers'
    Clinic
41 Let's Travel
58 Kings Cross Station
59 Kings Cross Hotel

South Dowling St, is a former working-class neighbourhood that's undergoing gentrification. It's a multicultural area and is the centre of Sydney's rag trade and print media. The main attraction is the **Brett Whitely Gallery** (☎ 9225 1740/1744), 2 Raper St, in a small lane in a quiet part of the suburb. The gallery, in the former studio of this renowned modern Australian painter, contains a selection of his paintings and drawings. It's open weekends 10 am to 4 pm, Thursday by appointment. Admission is $6.

Surry Hills is a short walk south of Oxford St. Catch bus Nos 301, 302 and 303 from Circular Quay.

Paddington
Paddington, four km east of the city centre, is an attractive inner-city residential area of leafy streets and tightly packed terrace houses. It was built for aspiring artisans in the later years of the Victorian era but during the lemming-like rush to the dreary outer suburbs after WWII the area became a slum. A renewed interest in Victorian architecture,

combined with a sudden recollection of the pleasures of inner-city life, led to the restoration of Paddington during the 1960s. Today the area is a fascinating jumble of often beautifully restored terraces which tumble down the steeply sloping streets which are full of trendy shops and restaurants, fine art galleries, bookshops and interesting people.

You can wander through Paddington's streets and winding laneways any time but the best time is from around 10 am on Saturday when the **Paddington Village Bazaar** in the grounds of the Uniting Church on the corner of Newcombe and Oxford Sts is in full swing.

At the Victoria Barracks on Oxford St between Oatley and Greens Rds, the **Army Museum** (☎ 9339 3000), which contains military memorabilia, is undergoing refurbishment but should be open by the time you read this.

There are many **art galleries** in Paddington; pick up a copy of *Paddington Galleries & Environs* at one of them or at the New

Paddington terraces – built for artisans,
declined to slums, now restored and trendy

Edition bookshop (☎ 9360 6913), 328
Oxford St.

The **Australian Centre for Photography**
(☎ 9332 1455), 257 Oxford St, has regular
exhibitions.

The utilitarian **Moore Park**, south of Paddington on South Dowling Rd, bordering
Surry Hills, has walking, cycling and skating
tracks; horse trails; playing fields; a golf-
driving range and grass skiing. It's also home
to the historic **Sydney Cricket Ground
(SCG)** and the **Sydney Football Stadium**.
Much of the **Royal Agricultural Society's
(RAS) Showgrounds** are to become a 20th
Century Fox film studio and entertainment
complex in 1999. Sportspace (☎ 9380 0383)
offers behind-the-scenes guided tours of the
facilities including historic displays featuring great players (and commentators)
associated with sports played at the park.
Tours are held daily at 10 am, 1 and 3 pm
(except match days when times change and
tours may be shortened) and cost $18 ($12
children) for 1½ hours.

Centennial Park, Sydney's biggest park,
is further east again, south of Woollahra. It
has running, cycling and horse tracks, barbecue sites, football pitches and more. You can
hire bicycles and inline skates from several
places on Clovelly Rd, Randwick, near the
southern edge of the park, or hire horses from
the RAS Showgrounds on Lang Rd. At the
southern edge of the park is **Randwick
Racecourse** and south of there is the **University of NSW**. The university is on Anzac
Parade, which becomes Flinders St and runs
into Taylor Square. Many buses run along
Anzac Parade, including No 336 from Circular Quay.

EASTERN SUBURBS

The harbourside suburbs east of Kings Cross
are some of Sydney's most expensive. The
main road through this area is New South
Head Rd, the continuation of William St.

Darling Point, east of Rushcutters Bay,
was a popular place for the city's first mer-
chants to build mansions. Inland is the
suburb of **Edgecliff**. The wealthy harbourside suburb of **Double Bay** is further east.
Double Bay's main shopping street is Bay St,
which runs north off New South Head Rd. It
eventually leads to a quiet waterfront park
and the ferry wharf. Double Bay is worth a
visit. There are plenty of cafes and patisseries
that don't necessarily cost a fortune, and you
can at least window shop for some designer
clothes.

There's a small beach near the ferry wharf
and a saltwater pool to the east, near Seven
Shillings Beach. The latter is actually part of
Point Piper, the headland which separates
Double Bay from **Rose Bay**. Rose Bay has
a pair of longer beaches, visible at low tide,
though people rarely swim here. It's also
served by ferries. Inland, behind the wharf
area, is the Royal Sydney Golf Course.

Rose Bay curves north onto the peninsula
which forms the southern side of the
entrance to Sydney Harbour. On the harbour
side of the peninsula is **Vaucluse**, the most
exclusive suburb of all. Vaucluse was a desirable address even in the colony's early days,
but it's ironic that **Vaucluse House** (1828),
one of its finest mansions, was built by
William Wentworth, an outcast from high
society because of his democratic leanings.

Vaucluse House (☎ 9337 1957) is open
Tuesday to Sunday from 10 am to 4.30 pm;
admission is $5 ($3 concession). It's an

imposing, turreted example of 19th-century Australiana, in fine grounds. You can get there on bus No 325 from Circular Quay; get off a couple of stops past **Nielsen Park**, which is part of the Sydney Harbour National Park (see Sydney Harbour).

Watsons Bay is nestled on the harbour side of the peninsula as it narrows toward South Head. On the ocean side is **The Gap**, a dramatic cliff-top lookout. On the harbour north of Watsons Bay are the small fashionable beaches of **Camp Cove** and **Lady Bay**. At the tip of the peninsula is **South Head**, with great views across the harbour to North Head and Middle Head.

Getting There & Away
The closest suburb to a rail link is Double Bay, which is north-east of the Edgecliff railway station on the eastern suburbs line. Take the New South Head Rd exit from the station, turn right and follow New South Head Rd to the nearby corner of Ocean Ave, turn left and head down to the corner of Cooper St, which leads to Bay St. Alternatively you could stay on New South Head Rd until you meet Bay St, but it's a less pleasant walk.

Infrequent ferries run from Circular Quay to Double Bay, Rose Bay and, on weekends, Watsons Bay. See Places to Eat for private boats to Watsons Bay. Bus Nos 324 and 325 run from Circular Quay to Watsons Bay.

INNER WEST
Balmain & Birchgrove
Once a tough, working-class neighbourhood, Balmain attracted artists in the 1960s and has been prime real estate for some time, rivalling Paddington in Victorian-era trendiness. There's nothing special to do or see, but there are some pleasant walks and good places to eat.

Most construction in Balmain occurred between 1855 and 1890, although there are Georgian and early Victorian houses still standing. Most streets worth visiting are north of Darling St, towards Birchgrove. A stroll around the wharf area at the end of Darling St, and through the park and the

maze of tiny streets behind, is also worthwhile.

Darling St, Balmain's spine, runs the length of the peninsula. It has bookshops, restaurants, antique stores, bakeries and boutiques. There's a market every Saturday from 8.30 am to 4 pm at St Andrew's Congregational Church.

The suburbs between Balmain and Glebe – **Annandale** and **Leichhardt** (its lesbian population dubs it 'dyke-heart') – also attract interesting people and have some good places to eat.

A major attraction when visiting Balmain is the journey on the Hunters Hill ferry from Circular Quay; it stops at Thames St, Darling St and Birchgrove wharves. Bus Nos 441, 442, 445 and 446 also come here.

Glebe
Glebe is south-west of the city centre, close to the University of Sydney. It has been going up the social scale in recent years but still has a bohemian atmosphere. The main thoroughfare, Glebe Point Rd, runs the length of the suburb and offers affordable restaurants, recycled clothing shops and secondhand bookshops. There are several good places to stay and Glebe's proximity to the city makes it an interesting alternative to the Cross.

The **Buddhist Temple**, on Edward St, was built by Chinese immigrants during the 1850s goldrush, and has been fully restored by Sydney's Chinese community. It welcomes visitors, but remember that it's a holy place. At the northern tip of Glebe Point Rd is **Jubilee Park**, with views across the bay to Rozelle and back towards the city.

Getting There & Away From the airport you can take the KST bus; from the city and Railway Square, bus Nos 431-4 run along Glebe Point Rd.

On foot, head south on George St and Broadway, turning right into Glebe Point Rd about a km south-west of Central Station. A more interesting walk begins at Darling Harbour's Pyrmont Bridge, which leads to Pyrmont Bridge Rd. After passing **Pyrmont**

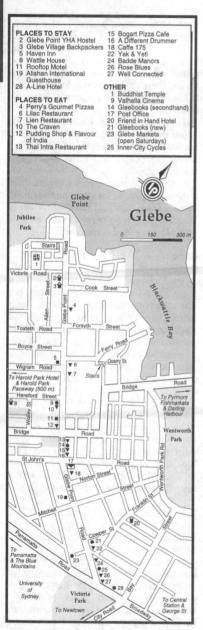

PLACES TO STAY		15	Bogart Pizza Cafe
2	Glebe Point YHA Hostel	16	A Different Drummer
3	Glebe Village Backpackers	18	Caffe 175
5	Haven Inn	22	Yak & Yeti
8	Wattle House	24	Badde Manors
11	Rooftop Motel	26	Rose Blues
19	Alishan International	27	Well Connected
	Guesthouse		
28	A-Line Hotel	OTHER	
		1	Buddhist Temple
PLACES TO EAT		9	Valhalla Cinema
4	Perry's Gourmet Pizzas	14	Gleebooks (secondhand)
6	Lilac Restaurant	17	Post Office
7	Lien Restaurant	20	Friend in Hand Hotel
10	The Craven	21	Gleebooks (new)
12	Pudding Shop & Flavour	23	Glebe Markets
	of India		(open Saturdays)
13	Thai Intra Restaurant	25	Inner-City Cycles

Fish Markets on Blackwattle Bay, follow the road past Wentworth Park. Turn right onto Burton St, and take the steps up to Ferry Rd which leads into Glebe Point Rd. Parts of this route are quiet after hours so you mightn't feel like walking it at night.

Rozelle

This suburb lies across Rozelle Bay from Glebe. The main attraction is the **Sydney Maritime Museum Restoration Site** (☎ 9818 5388), at James Craig Rd, beside the bay. Moored here is the 1874 windjammer *James Craig*. After many years of painstaking restoration it will be open to the public in 1998. Two harbour ferries, the *Kanangra* and *Waratah*, built early this century, are also being restored. The museum has a 'Fish & Ships' tour of the vessels which includes a 20-minute boat trip across Blackwattle Bay to Pyrmont Fish Markets.

The site is open daily from 10 am to 5 pm (later in summer) and admission costs $2 ($1 children). Take bus No 440 from Circular Quay.

Newtown

On the southern border of the University of Sydney, Newtown is a melting pot of social and sexual subcultures, students and home renovators. King St, its relentlessly urban main drag, is full of funky clothes stores, bookshops, cafes and Thai restaurants. While it's definitely moving up the social scale, Newtown comes with a healthy dose of grunge and political activism and harbours several of Sydney's live-music venues. The best way to get there is by train, but bus Nos 422, 423, 426 and 428 from the city run along King St.

Leichhardt

Predominantly Italian, Leichhardt, south-west of Glebe, is increasingly popular with students, lesbians and young professionals. Its Italian eateries on Norton St have a city-wide reputation. Bus No 440 runs here from the city.

INNER SOUTH

South-west of Central Station, the small suburb of **Chippendale** is a maze of Victorian terraced houses; an unscrubbed version of Paddington. South of Railway Square, near the corner of Lee (George) and Regent Sts, is the quaint neo-Gothic **Mortuary Station**, where coffins and mourners once boarded funeral trains bound for Rookwood Cemetery, now in the city's western suburbs.

Chippendale borders the east of the **University of Sydney**, Australia's oldest tertiary institution. **Nicholson Museum** (☎ 9351 2812), at the university, displays Greek, Assyrian, Egyptian and other antiquities.

Redfern, south of Central Station but on the eastern side of the tracks, is one of the few inner suburbs to escape gentrification and remains predominantly working class. A few sections come close to being Australia's only real slum. Redfern tends to buck the system and relations between the police and the community (especially the large Koori community) are at times bad.

The site of the former Eveleigh Locomotive Workshops, at the corner of Garden and Boundary Sts, is home to the National Technology Park and National Innovation Centre. Some buildings contain Victorian steam-powered blacksmithing equipment, used by **Wrought Artworks** (☎ 9319 6190) to manufacture artefacts. Call Wrought Artworks for an appointment and they'll show you around.

BONDI BEACH

Although it's Australia's most famous beach, Bondi Beach isn't as glamorous as this fame or the tourist brochures might suggest. It's still largely working class and successive waves of migrants have made it their home. In recent years it has become more fashionable and has received a huge facelift. Today, its unique flavour is blended from the mix of old Jewish and Italian communities, dyed-in-the-wool Aussies, New Zealand, Irish and UK expats, working travellers and surf rats, all bonded by their love for the beach.

Orientation & Information

Campbell Parade, the main beachfront road, is where most shops, hotels and cafes can be found. The corner of Campbell Parade and Hall St is the hub. The main road into Bondi Beach is Bondi Rd which branches off from Oxford St east of the mall in Bondi Junction. This is the same Oxford St that begins at Hyde Park and runs through Darlinghurst and Paddington.

The post office is on the corner of Jacques Ave and Hall St. A little further up Hall St you enter a small Jewish area where you will find kosher shops and the Hakoah Club.

Although Bondi Beach is usually referred to simply as Bondi, the suburb of Bondi is actually inland, between Bondi Junction and Bondi Beach.

Things to See & Do

The main reason for coming is the beach, where you can swim, surf or just hang out. If the water's too rough for swimming there are sea-water swimming pools. Accessible **Aboriginal rock engravings** are a short walk north of Bondi Beach on the golf course in North Bondi. A beautiful coastal walking path travels south to the beaches at Tamarama, Bronte and Coogee (see below).

Getting There & Away

Bondi Junction is the terminus of the eastern suburbs CityRail line and the nearest railway station to Bondi Beach. From there you can take bus No 380, 382 or 389 to Bondi and Bondi Beach. Alternatively, you can take these buses from Circular Quay or bus No 378 from Railway Square which continues south to Bronte; bus Nos 378 and 380 run along Oxford St.

Buses stop along Campbell Parade, terminating at Brighton Blvd in North Bondi.

TAMARAMA & BRONTE

South of Bondi, Tamarama is a lovely cove with strong surf that's popular with Sydney's 'beautiful' people. Get off the bus just before it reaches Bondi Beach; Tamarama is a five-minute walk down the hill.

At Bronte, south of Tamarama, there's a

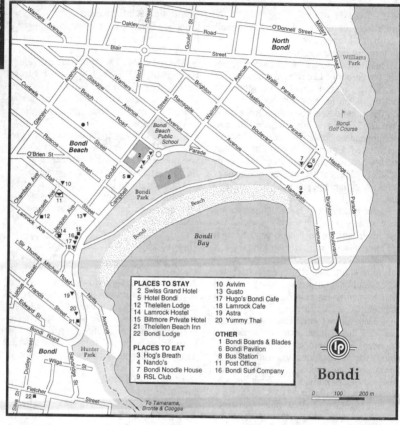

PLACES TO STAY
2 Swiss Grand Hotel
5 Hotel Bondi
12 Thelellen Lodge
14 Lamrock Hostel
15 Biltmore Private Hotel
21 Thelellen Beach Inn
22 Bondi Lodge

PLACES TO EAT
3 Hog's Breath
4 Nando's
7 Bondi Noodle House
9 RSL Club

10 Avivim
13 Gusto
17 Hugo's Bondi Cafe
18 Lamrock Cafe
19 Astra
20 Yummy Thai

OTHER
1 Bondi Boards & Blades
6 Bondi Pavilion
8 Bus Station
11 Post Office
16 Bondi Surf Company

Bondi

0   100   200 m

To Tamarama,
Bronte & Coogee

superb family-oriented beach. Cafes with outdoor tables, picnic areas and barbecues make the place perfect for a day of rest and relaxation. Catch bus No 378 from the city or a train to Bondi Junction and pick up the bus there. You can walk along the wonderful clifftop footpath from Bondi Beach or from Coogee via Gordon's Bay, Clovelly and the sun-bleached Waverley Cemetery.

COOGEE
Coogee, about four km south of Bondi Beach, is almost a carbon copy, minus the crowds or increasingly glitzy development.

It has a relaxed air, few graces and a good sweep of sand.

The main beachfront street is Arden St and the junction of Arden St and Coogee Bay Rd is the commercial centre. Like Bondi, Coogee's main attraction is its beach and this is a great spot for a snorkel. From Coogee, the spectacular clifftop footpath runs north along the coast to Bondi Beach passing Gordon's Bay, Clovelly, Bronte and Tamarama.

Getting There & Away
Bus Nos 373 and 374 run from Circular

Quay; Nos 371 and 372 run from Railway Square; and Nos 314 and 315 run from Bondi Junction.

THE NORTH SHORE

The North Shore is the unofficial but universally recognised name applied to the suburbs north of the harbour. The area's pretty bays and beaches, good shopping and places to eat make it worthwhile leaving the cosmopolitan delights of the southern side to see how wealthier Sydneysiders live.

Kirribilli & Milsons Point

The Sydney residences of the governor general and the prime minister are on Kirribilli Point, east of the Harbour Bridge. The prime minister stays in **Kirribilli House** (1854) and the governor general in **Admiralty House** (1846).

To the north of Kirribilli Point is the **Royal Sydney Yacht Squadron** headquarters. Yachting has been popular on the harbour since the 1830s and the Australian Yacht Club was formed in 1862.

Luna Park amusement park, at Milsons Point on the edge of Lavender Bay, immediately west of the Harbour Bridge, was at its peak in the 1930s when thousands of people flocked across the harbour via the new bridge. The park has opened and closed a couple of times in recent years; owing to disputes with nearby residents, it's currently closed and its future is uncertain.

McMahons Point is a pleasant, sleepy suburb on the next headland west. It's tipped by **Blues Point Reserve**, named after the Jamaican-born Billy Blue who ferried people across from Dawes Point in the 1830s. If you follow Blues Point Rd north from the ferry wharf it'll bring you to North Sydney.

Kirribilli, Lavender Bay and Blues Point are all serviced by ferries from Circular Quay. Other ways of getting here include walking across the bridge or taking a North Shore line train to Milsons Point.

North Sydney & Crows Nest

North Sydney, north-west of the Harbour Bridge, is Sydney's second business district. Along Mount St at No 7 is **Mary MacKillop Place** (☎ 9954 9900), a museum that tells the life story of a girl from the bush who became a nun – and Australia's first saint. It's open Sunday to Friday from 10 am to 4 pm, Saturday noon to 4 pm. Admission is $5 ($2 children) which includes a tour.

A km or so north along the Pacific Highway from North Sydney is the suburb of Crows Nest, which has a number of good places to eat. The 1880s **Sexton's Cottage Museum** (☎ 9936 8400), in St Thomas' Rest Park at 250 West St, has displays relating to early life in the area. It's open on Thursday from 1 to 4 pm and the first Sunday of the month from 2 to 4 pm. Entry is free.

Balls Head Reserve

Balls Head Reserve not only has great views of the harbour but also boasts old Aboriginal rock paintings and carvings, although they're not easy to discern. The park is two headlands west of the Harbour Bridge. Take a train to Waverton, turn left when you leave the station and follow Bay Rd, which becomes Balls Head Rd.

Hunters Hill & Woolwich

The elegant suburbs of Hunters Hill and Woolwich, on a spit at the junction of the Parramatta and Lane Cove rivers, are full of Victorian houses. The National Trust **Vienna Cottage** (☎ 9258 0123), 38 Alexandra St, Hunters Hill, built of stone in 1871 by Jacob Hellman, is typical of the era. It's open on the second and fourth weekends of the month (Saturday 2 to 4 pm, Sunday 11 am to 4 pm); entry is $2.

Hunters Hill ferries from Circular Quay stop at Woolwich's Valentia St wharf.

Mosman & Around

East of the Harbour Bridge, **Mosman**, **Neutral Bay** and **Cremorne** have good shopping centres and some beautiful foreshore parks and walks. Mosman is on the large chunk of land separating Middle Harbour from the main harbour. Cremorne and Neutral Bay are farther west. The beachside suburb of **Balmoral**, north of Mosman, faces Manly across Middle Harbour. It has three fine beaches and some good restaurants.

In Neutral Bay you'll find **Nutcote** (☎ 9953 4453), 5 Wallaringa Ave, the former home of well-known Australian children's author May Gibbs. It's now a museum containing exhibits on her life and work and is open from Wednesday to Sunday from 11 am to 3 pm; entry is $6 ($3 children). It's a short walk from the Neutral Bay ferry wharf.

To the south is Kurraba Point. Off Bogata Ave you can pick up a footpath that runs through bushy gardens to the end of **Cremorne Point**. This is an excellent spot to picnic or go for a swim, with great views of the harbour.

The main road through this area is Military Rd, which branches east off the Warringah Freeway (the northern side of the Harbour Bridge) near North Sydney. Military Rd crosses Middle Harbour at Spit Bridge then runs north, changing names several times. It bypasses Manly, eventually reaching **Palm Beach**, Sydney's northernmost beachside suburb.

Bus No 190 runs a limited-stop route from Wynyard in the city to Palm Beach via Military Rd; bus No 182 from Wynyard runs to Cremorne and Mosman. Buses also run to Military Rd from the North Shore suburb of St Leonards.

Taronga Zoo

The 30-hectare Taronga Zoo (☎ 9969 2777), a short ferry ride from Circular Quay, has an attractive hillside setting overlooking the harbour. It houses over 4000 critters, including a substantial number of Australian ones. Children will like the Friendship Farm where they get the chance to pat the animals.

Ferries to the zoo depart from Circular Quay's wharf 2 every half-hour from 7.15 am on weekdays, 8.45 am on Saturday and 9 am on Sunday. The zoo is at the top of a hill; if you can't be bothered walking, take a bus or the 'Aerial Safari' cable car ($2.50; $1.50 children) to the top entrance. It's open daily from 9 am to 5 pm and admission is

$14.95 ($7.50 children). A ZooPass ticket, sold at Circular Quay and elsewhere, costs $21 ($10.50 children) and includes return ferry rides, the bus to the entrance, zoo admission and the 'Aerial Safari'.

MANLY

The jewel of North Shore, Manly was one of the first places in Australia to be named by Europeans – Arthur Phillip named it after the 'manly' physique of the Aborigines he saw here in 1788. Sun-soaked Manly boasts all the trappings of a full-scale holiday resort and a sense of community identity, but isn't afraid to show a bit of tack and brashness to attract visitors. It makes a refreshing change from the prim, upper-middle class harbour enclaves nearby.

It's half an hour by ferry from Circular Quay (15 minutes by JetCat) and the trip offers fantastic views of the city.

Orientation & Information

Manly straddles the narrow peninsula leading to North Head and has both ocean and harbour beaches. The ferry wharf is on Manly Cove, on the harbour side. From here the Corso (the main commercial strip) runs to the ocean, where you'll find Manly Beach, lined with Norfolk Pines. Most of the Corso is a pedestrian mall.

Manly Visitors Information Bureau (☎ 9977 1088), open daily from 10 am to 4 pm, is on Manly Beach (South Steyne) near the Corso. It has useful, free pamphlets on the eight-km Manly Scenic Walkway and sells Manly Heritage Walk booklets ($3.50). There are small lockers where you can leave your things while you go for a swim. A craft market is held near the bureau on weekends. There's a bus information booth at the entrance to the wharf.

Things to See & Do

The long ocean beach north of the Corso is **North Steyne Beach**; the shorter stretch of beach running south is usually called **Manly Beach** but it's technically South Steyne Beach. The beachfront road is called North Steyne and South Steyne. At the southern

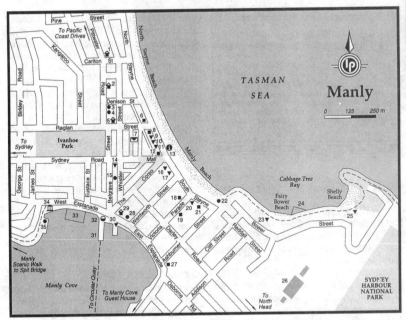

TASMAN SEA

Manly

0   125   250 m

Cabbage Tree Bay

Fairy Bower Beach

Shelly Beach

Manly Beach

Manly Cove

Manly Scenic Walk to Spit Bridge

To Sydney

To Pacific Coast Drives

To Circular Quay

To Manly Cove Guest House

To North Head

SYDNEY HARBOUR NATIONAL PARK

PLACES TO STAY
1 Manly Beach Resort Backpackers & Motel
2 Manly Astra Backpackers
5 Manly Backpackers Beachside
6 Manly Pacific Parkroyal Hotel
8 Paradise Motel
12 Steyne Hotel
18 Eversham Private Hotel
19 Manly Lodge
21 Radisson Kestrel Hotel
27 Periwinkle Guest House
29 The Wharf Backpackers

PLACES TO EAT
9 The BarKing Frog
10 Wi Marn
11 Lui's
14 Malacca Straits Satay Restaurant
16 Cafe Tunis
17 Pan Thip Thai
20 Cafe Steyne
23 Bower Restaurant
25 Le Kiosk Restaurant & Shelly Beach Kiosk
30 Armstrong's

OTHER
3 Aloha Surf
4 Manly Cycle Centre
7 Post Office
13 Manly Visitors Information Bureau
15 Dive Centre
22 Manly Life Saving Club
24 Rockpool
26 St Patrick's Seminary
28 Manly Twin Cinema
31 Manly Wharf
32 Bus Interchange
33 Netted Swimming Area
34 Manly Art Gallery & Museum
35 Oceanworld

end of Manly Beach is the Manly Life Saving Club and from there a path leads around the rocky headland to tiny **Fairy Bower Beach**, which has a small swimming pool. Further around is beautiful **Shelly Beach**. The large building on the hill south-east of the town

centre is **St Patrick's College** (1889). Manly Hospital is nearby.

North Steyne Beach runs up to **Queenscliff Beach** near the steep Queenscliff headland. There's a lifesaving club here as well. Around the headland (although not

Daylight Swimming Legal!

While you're enjoying Manly Beach, thank William H Gocher that you're not breaking the law by swimming in daylight. Such immorality was illegal until Gocher, a local newspaper editor, announced in 1902 that he would take a dip in daylight, defying the authorities to arrest him. He had to swim three times before he was arrested, but the subsequent court case led to the legalisation of daylight bathing. ■

simple to get to on foot) is **Freshwater Beach**.

There's another stretch of sand on the harbour side at **Manly Cove**, backed by the East and West Esplanade. In the centre is **Manly Wharf**, which has cafes, restaurants, shops and a small amusement park.

Oceanworld (☎ 9949 2644), West Esplanade, is on the headland at the western end of Manly Cove. It's a good oceanarium and its programme includes turtle and shark feeding. It's open daily from 10 am to 5.30 pm and admission is $13 ($7 children). You can also dive with the sharks! Shark dives must be booked and cost $99 for non-divers (the fee includes a lesson), $65 for certified divers. Dives are held in the evening about three times a week, depending on numbers. Friends of divers can watch for $5.

Manly Art Gallery & Museum (☎ 9949 2435), next to Oceanworld, has exhibitions on beach themes and local history (much the same thing in Manly). It's open Tuesday to Sunday, 10 am to 5 pm; admission is $2 (children free).

You can continue past Oceanworld to join the eight-km **Manly Scenic Walkway** which follows the shoreline to Spit Bridge at Middle Harbour (see Sydney Harbour National Park). It takes about three hours. Buses run from Spit Bridge to the city centre.

North Head Spectacular North Head, at the Sydney Harbour entrance, about three km south of Manly, offers good views of the ocean, harbour and city skyline. Most of the headland is in the Sydney Harbour National Park; contact the NPWS office (☎ 9977 6522) near the Quarantine Station for information. The **Quarantine Station** housed disease carriers from 1832 to 1984. The station is run by the NPWS and you have to book a guided tour if you want to visit. These 1½-hour tours are held daily at 1.10 pm and cost $9.50 ($7 children).

The centre of the headland is an off-limits military reserve, but you can visit the **National Artillery Museum** (☎ 9976 1138) in North Fort, Manly. It's open Wednesdays and weekends from noon to 4 pm and at other times by appointment; admission is $4 ($2 children).

Manly Coach Tours (☎ 9938 4677), 40 Chard Rd, Brookvale, runs passenger services around North Head from outside Manly wharf. The return fare is $3.20.

Getting There & Away

See the Getting Around section for details on ferries to Manly. Alternatively, bus No 169 runs from Wynyard Park in the city.

SYDNEY OLYMPIC PARK

Sydney Olympic Park, in the suburb of Homebush Bay, 14 km west of the city centre, will be the main venue for the 2000 Olympics. It will also contain the Olympic Village where the athletes will be staying. **Sydney International Athletic Centre** and **Sydney International Aquatic Centre** are open to visitors. You can go swimming at the aquatic centre or walk through the **Leisure Garden** which depicts Australia's different natural habitats. There are guided tours weekdays at 10 am, noon and 2 pm, weekends by appointment; call ☎ 9752 3666. Also here is the **Sydney Showground**, new home of the Royal Easter Show.

To visit the park, take a train to Strathfield ($2.40 off-peak return), then bus No 401, 402, 403 or 404. Bus No 401 also does a tour ($5; $2.50 children) of Sydney Olympic Park from outside Strathfield station at 9.30 and 10.30 am and 12.30 pm; call the Homebush Bay Corporation (☎ 9735 4800) for bookings. See also Organised Tours.

SYDNEY

The 2000 Olympics

In 1993 Sydney was chosen to host the Olympic Games in the year 2000. The partying that followed the announcement was quickly replaced by political squabbling and predictions of economic doom (this seems to be essential for Sydneysiders to get anything done). Now, as the games approach, life in the city has moved up several gears.

Preparations are under the control of the Sydney Organising Committee for the Olympic Games (SOCOG), which has had its share of personnel problems. Except for the all-important media centre, construction for the games seems to be on track, but costs look like being way above original projections. Hardly a day goes by without an update or some controversy in the media.

Sydney's successful bid to host the games was partly because of its environmental proposals and the Olympic village in Homebush will be entirely solar powered. The environmental watchdog, Greenpeace has objected to the use of PVC pipes and electrical insulation, which it claims cause toxic waste. The city will also need to clean up its waterways and beaches.

Sydney has learnt from the transport problems in Atlanta in 1996; it's upgrading the road network, a new ferry wharf in Homebush should be operational soon and a train station is being built in the centre of Sydney Olympic Park.

The games are expected to attract about 1.5 million tourists and a TV audience of four million. They're also expected to add $7 billion to the Australian GDP. Some of that money will come from the merchandise displaying the games' mascots – Syd the platypus, Millie the echidna and Olly the kookaburra.

Most tickets are available for purchase from 1998 but to help finance preparations, platinum tickets ($34,000 each) and gold tickets ($10,000 each) went on sale much earlier. Some lucky people will have the best accommodation in the world for the games – on one of the 10 cruise liners which will be moored in the harbour. The QE II will have the prize location of Circular Quay.

For more information contact SOCOG (☎ 9297 2000), 207 Kent St. Its postal address is GPO Box 2000, Sydney 2001. For recorded information call ☎ 1900 957 402, or visit the web site at http://www.sydney.olympic.org on the Internet. You can also visit the Olympic Showcase & Information Centre in the former ferry boat SS South Steyne in Darling Harbour, or visit Sydney Olympic Park itself. ■

Call Sydney Ferries to see if the new RiverCat service to Homebush Bay has begun operating. A CityRail link to the park is under construction.

BEACHES

Sydney's beaches are some of its greatest assets. They're easily accessible and usually good, although some post warnings about swimming is inadvisable after heavy rains because of stormwater runoff.

There are two types – harbour beaches (sheltered, calm and generally smaller) and ocean beaches (which often have good surf).

Although they get busy on hot summer weekends, Sydney's beaches are never really packed. Swimming is generally safe. At ocean beaches you're only allowed to swim within the 'flagged' areas patrolled by the famed lifesavers. Efforts are made to keep surfers separate from swimmers. High points of Sydney's beach life are the surf lifesaving

competitions held at various beaches during summer.

Shark patrols operate during summer, and ocean beaches are generally netted – Sydney has only had one fatal shark attack since 1937.

Many of Sydney's beaches are 'topless' but some aren't: do as the locals do. There are also a couple of nude beaches.

Harbour Beaches

Immediately inside the Heads, on the southern side, is tiny **Lady Bay Beach**, a nude beach, mainly gay. South of Lady Bay is **Camp Cove**, a small but pleasant sliver of sand popular with families and topless bathers. This is where Arthur Phillip first landed in Sydney. South of Camp Cove is **Watsons Bay**, which hosts two of the delightful Doyle's outdoor seafood restaurants. Another popular harbour beach is the family-oriented **Shark Beach** at Nielsen

Park in Vaucluse. These beaches can be reached by bus No 324 or 325 from Circular Quay.

On the North Shore there are harbour beaches at **Manly Cove** (suburban beach), **Reef Beach** (nudist), **Clontarf** (families), **Chinaman's Beach** (quiet hideaway) and **Balmoral** (popular daytrip for North Shore residents). The Manly ferry docks at Manly Cove and Reef Beach is a two-km walk along the Manly Scenic Walkway. The other beaches are accessible, with a bit of walking, by catching bus No 178, 180 or 182, which depart from Wynyard Park, travel along Military Rd and cross Spit Bridge.

Southern Beaches

South of the Heads there's a string of ocean beaches all the way to Botany Bay. **Bondi Beach**, with its crowds and surfies, is Australia's best-known beach. It's a favourite with young visitors to Sydney and has a selection of cheap accommodation.

Tamarama, a little south of Bondi, is a pretty cove with strong surf. Take bus No 391 from Bondi Junction or catch a Bondi Beach bus and walk from the bottom of Bondi Rd. Next south is **Bronte**, a broader beach popular with families. Take bus No 378 from Railway Square or Bondi Junction. The tiny inlet of **Clovelly** is nestled between Bronte and Coogee. It has a breakwater which makes it safe for swimming. Catch bus No 339 from George St in the city or No 329 from Bondi Junction. **Coogee** has a wide, sweeping beach. Take bus No 373 or 374 from Circular Quay. **Maroubra** is further south again and can be reached by bus Nos 395-398 from Circular Quay. Botany Bay is more for sailing than swimming, due to its large shark population.

Northern Beaches

A string of ocean-front suburbs stretches 30 km north along the coast from Manly, ending at beautiful, well-heeled Palm Beach and spectacular Barrenjoey Head at the entrance to Broken Bay. There are plenty of beaches along the way. **Freshwater**, the first north of Manly, attracts a lot of teenagers; then there's

Curl Curl (families and surfers); **Dee Why** and **Collaroy** (families); and the long sweep of **Narrabeen** (surfers). The most spectacular are **Whale Beach** and **Bilgola**, near Palm Beach, which both have dramatically steep headlands. The northern end of **Palm Beach** is for nude bathers. Several of the northernmost beach suburbs also back onto **Pittwater**, a lovely inlet off Broken Bay and a favoured sailing spot.

Bus Nos 136 and 139 run from Manly to Freshwater and Curl Curl. Bus No 190 from Wynyard Park runs to Newport and north to Palm Beach. From Manly, take bus No 155 or 157 to Mona Vale and pick up No 190 there.

Surf Beaches

With so many good beaches it's easy to see why surfing is a popular pastime in Sydney. Serious surf beaches include Bondi, Tamarama, Maroubra and, beyond Botany Bay, Cronulla. North of Manly there are another dozen; the best are Narrabeen, North Avalon and Palm Beach.

PARKS & GARDENS

Sydney has plenty of parks, many with harbour views, making it a wonderful city for a picnic or a stroll.

The Royal Botanic Gardens, the Domain and Hyde Park (see earlier) border the eastern side of the city centre. There are also a few smaller parks in the city centre which provide respite from the cement. **Wynyard Park** is a wedge of Victoriana on York St outside Wynyard Station; **Lang Park** is a few blocks north and **First Fleet Park** is north again, at Circular Quay. **Observatory Park**, on the western side of the Bradfield Highway, is a pleasant place with old trees and good views.

There are two small parks at Elizabeth Bay, north-east of Kings Cross: the delightful **Arthur McElhone Reserve** opposite Elizabeth Bay House and **Beare Park**, down by the water. The nearest swathe of green to the Cross is **Rushcutters Bay Park**, a pretty waterfront area to the east.

East of Surry Hills and south of Paddington are the adjacent **Moore** and **Centennial** parks, both large recreational areas (see Paddington).

Many headlands and bays on the North Shore have small parks, including Blues Point, Kirribilli (Careening Cove), Neutral Bay (Anderson Park), Cremorne Point and Mosman (Reid Park). Finding them without a street directory can be difficult.

On the North Shore there's an eight-km corridor of bushland called **Garigal National Park** stretching from Bantry Bay on Middle Harbour north to Ku-ring-gai Chase National Park at St Ives. **Lane Cove National Park**, between the suburbs of Ryde and Chatswood, is also on North Shore. Both parks have extensive walking tracks and Lane Cove has lots of picnic areas.

See also Sydney Harbour National Park.

ACTIVITIES

The *Sydney Morning Herald*'s Friday 'Metro' guide lists activities in the Out & About section. Noticeboards at hostels are usually crammed with suggestions and travel agents often have good information on day trips.

Swimming

Sydney's harbour beaches offer sheltered water conducive to swimming. At the ocean beaches swimming is safe if you follow instructions and swim within the 'flagged' areas patrolled by lifeguards. There are some notorious but clearly signposted rips even at Sydney's most popular beaches so don't underestimate the surf just because it doesn't look threatening. Efforts are made to keep surfers separate from swimmers.

There are more than 100 public swimming pools in Sydney, including the saltwater Andrew 'Boy' Charlton pool in the Domain on the edge of Woolloomooloo Bay; the Prince Alfred Park pool, near Central Station; the small pool at Fairy Bower Beach, Manly; and the two oceanside pools at Coogee, one of which, McGiver's Pool, is for women only. The Boy Charlton and Alfred Park pools close during winter.

Surfing

South of the Heads, the best spots are Bondi, Tamarama, Coogee and Maroubra. Cronulla, south of Botany Bay, is also a serious surfing spot. On the North Shore, there are a dozen surf beaches between Manly and Palm Beach; the best are Manly, Curl Curl, Dee Why, North Narrabeen, Mona Vale, Newport Reef, North Avalon and Palm Beach itself.

In Manly, Aloha Surf (☎ 9977 3777), 44 Pittwater Rd, rents surf and boogie boards (including wetsuits) for $15/25 for a half/full-day's hire (until 7 pm). In Bondi Beach you can hire surfboards and body boards from Bondi Surf Company (☎ 9365 0870) ⌐t 72 Campbell Pde, for $20 or $40 for three hours, depending on the board. This includes a wetsuit.

In Coogee, Surfworld (☎ 9664 1293) is at 250 Coogee Bay Rd, near the corner of Arden St.

Sailing & Boating

There are plenty of sailing schools in Sydney and an introductory lesson is a fun way of getting onto the harbour.

The sociable East Sail Sailing School (☎ 9327 1166) at d'Albora Marina, New Beach Rd, Rushcutters Bay, runs a range of courses from introductory to racing level.

The friendly Sunsail (☎ 9955 6400), 23A King George St on McMahon's Point in Lavender Bay, has an introductory course of four three-hour lessons for $350.

If you want to learn to sail a dinghy see Northside Sailing School (☎ 9969 3972) at the southern end of Spit Bridge in Mosman. You'll pay $230 for four three-hour lessons. Dinghies cost $15 per hour to hire.

If you'll be in Sydney for a while and you'd like to learn how to sail a yacht contact the Australian Sailing School (☎ 9960 3999), The Spit, not far from Northside Sailing School. It has 10-week lessons for beginners.

Pittwater and Broken Bay offer some of the world's best sailing. Scotland Island Schooners at Church Point has a sailing school (☎ 9999 2285) specialising in ocean-going boats. It takes some months to earn the

SYDNEY

internationally recognised Certificate of Competency – but what a qualification to have!

Diving
The best shore dives in Sydney are the Gordons Bay Underwater Nature Trail, north of Coogee; Shark Point, Clovelly; and Ship Rock, Cronulla. Popular boat dive sites are Wedding Cake Island, off Coogee; around the Sydney Heads; and off the Royal National Park. In Manly you can make beach dives from Shelly Beach.

Plenty of outfits will take you diving and many run courses. Pro Dive has a number of outlets in and around Sydney, including in the city at 428 George St (☎ 9264 6177) and in Coogee at 27 Alfreda St (☎ 9665 6333). It runs four-day diving courses for $345 and rents snorkelling gear for $15 a day. In Manly, the Dive Centre (☎ 9977 2095), 10 Belgrave St, has one-day courses for $95. It also hires snorkelling gear for $15, wetsuits for $12. Pacific Coast Divers (☎ 9977 5966), 169 Pittwater Rd, Manly, is similar.

You can also dive with sharks at Manly's Oceanworld (see Manly section).

Canoeing & Kayaking
The Canoe Association of NSW (☎ 9660 4597), Wentworth Park Complex, Ultimo, has information on clubs which provide lessons. Call Tuesday to Thursday, 9 am to 5 pm.

Canoe Specialists (☎ 9969 4590) at the southern end of Spit Bridge in Mosman rents sea kayaks to paddle on Middle Harbour, or onto Sydney Harbour if it isn't too rough. Single kayaks cost $10 for the first hour, $5 for subsequent hours. Double kayaks cost twice that.

Natural Wanders (☎ 9555 9788), 45 Wharf Rd, Beechgrove, has weekend kayak tours of the harbour. From Lavender Bay they head under Sydney Harbour Bridge to Bradley's Head, stopping in secluded bays for short walks. Patrick, the tour operator, who'll tailor a tour to suit you, relates the history and architecture of the area. The tour includes a 'gourmet' lunch, takes 5½ hours

and costs $75. No kayaking experience is necessary.

Inline Skating
The beach promenades at Bondi and Manly are the most favoured spots for skating.

Manly Blades (☎ 9976 3833), in Manly Beach Plaza on North Steyne, hires out skates for $10 for the first hour, $5 for subsequent hours. It also offers lessons. Bondi Boards & Blades (☎ 9365 6555), 148 Curlewis St, back from Campbell Parade, rents skates for $10 for the first hour, $5 for subsequent hours. Protective gear is free.

Golf
The most central of Sydney's 40-odd public golf courses is Moore Park (☎ 9663 3960) on Centennial Ave, which charges $24 for 18 holes on weekends, $21 on weekdays. Other public courses include Bondi (☎ 9130 3170), on Military Rd in North Bondi, and Barnwell Park (☎ 9713 9019), on the corner of William St and Lyons Rd in Five Dock.

In the city centre, City Golf Driving Range (☎ 9223 2600), 117 Pitt St, is open daily and charges $8 for 50 balls, $13 for 100. It's rather bizarre to see a driving range in the heart of the city, but there it is.

Horseriding
Several outfits offer rides in Centennial Park, such as Blue Ribbon Riding School (☎ 9361 3859), Centennial Park Horse Hire (☎ 9361 4513) and Eastside Horse Riding Academy (☎ 9360 7521). They're based at the RAS Showgrounds (enter on the corner of Lang and Cook Rds). Prices are $40 per hour and bookings are necessary.

Tennis
There are tennis courts for hire all over the city. Some are:

Coogee South Squash & Tennis
    222 Malabar Rd, Coogee (☎ 9344 7976)
Darling Harbour Tennis Centre
    On the corner of Day and Bathurst Sts (☎ 9212 1666)
Millers Point Tennis Court
    Kent St, the Rocks (☎ 9256 2222)

Parklands Tennis Centre
   On the corner of Anzac Parade and Lang Rd,
   Moore Park, Paddington (☎ 9662 7033)
Prince Alfred Park Tennis Centre
   Next to Central Station (☎ 9698 9451)

Running/Jogging
The foreshore from Circular Quay around
Farm Cove to Woolloomooloo Bay and
through the Royal Botanic Gardens and the
Domain are popular routes with joggers.
North Shore inhabitants often choose to
commute to work in the city by running
across the Harbour Bridge.

Centennial Park and the promenades at
Bondi Beach and Manly are the best jogging
spots. The cliff trail between Bondi Beach
and Bronte is also good.

Cycling
See Getting Around at the end of the chapter.

ORGANISED TOURS
There's a vast array of city and area coach
tours. Ask at the NSW Travel Centre
(☎ 132077), 11-13 York St, for details and
check the free magazines at hotels.

Australian Pacific (☎ 9247 7222), AAT
King's (☎ 1800 334 009), Clipper Grayline
(☎ 9241 3983), Newmans (☎ 9247 7222),
Murrays (☎ 132259) and Great Sights Tours
(☎ 9241 2294) carry most tourists around
town. You can join a half-day city or koala-
cuddling tour from $35 to $45, or a full-day
city tour from around $60.

If you'd like to learn more about Aboriginal culture, Australian Pacific has a
5¼-hour tour to Pittwater and Ku-ring-gai
Chase National Park. The guide will tell you
about Aboriginal engravings, the Dreamtime, bush tucker and the ecology of the
bush. The tour, including morning tea, costs
$72 ($62 children).

The NPWS runs tours of Sydney's historic
forts and islands. See Sydney Harbour
National Park earlier.

Blue Thunder Bike Tours (☎ 9977 7721)
and Eastcoast Motorcycle Tours (☎ 9555
2700) show you Sydney from the back of a
Harley-Davidson. With Eastcoast a one-hour
tour of the harbour costs $65; they also offer
daytrips out of the city. Both organisations
have set tours or you can plan your own
itinerary.

Another interesting way to see Sydney is
from the air. South Pacific Seaplanes
(☎ 9544 0077) has 15-minute scenic flights
of the harbour for $45 or 75-minute flights
of the harbour, beaches and mountains for
$195.

Harbour Cruises
A wide range of cruises from Circular Quay
offer relatively inexpensive excursions on
the harbour. You can book most of these at
the Quayside Booking Centre (☎ 9247 5151,
24 hours) at Circular Quay's wharf 2.
Captain Cook Cruises (☎ 9206 1111) has its
own booking office at wharf 6.

Tours to Sydney Olympic Park
As preparations for the Olympics in 2000 continue, a number of companies have begun to run guided
tours from the city centre to Sydney Olympic Park in Homebush Bay.

From Circular Quay, Matilda Cruises (☎ 9264 7377) offers a two-hour cruise of Sydney Harbour
and up the Parramatta River to the Olympic site. There you can opt to take a two-hour coach tour
which visits the Sydney International Aquatic Centre, State Sports Centre, Athletic Centre and other
venues. The combined cruise and coach tour costs $30 ($20 children); the harbour cruise by itself
costs $20 ($12 children).

Murrays (☎ 132259) has a day tour to the Sydney International Aquatic Centre, where you can get
an underwater view of the competition pool and visit the leisure area. It costs $35.

Red Terra Tours (☎ 015 434 936) also visits the aquatic centre, then the Yiribana gallery with its
huge collection of Aboriginal art; the tour culminates in Aboriginal dance and story telling. It takes
4½ hours and costs $55 ($35 children). ■

STA ferries offer some good-value cruises, such as the 2½-hour trip which departs at 1 pm weekdays, 1.30 pm weekends, and visits Middle Harbour. Tickets cost $16 ($12 children) and can be bought from the ferry information office under the Cahill Expressway opposite wharf 4.

The Sydney Harbour Explorer, run by Captain Cook Cruises, is a hop-on, hop-off service which stops at the Opera House, Watsons Bay, Taronga Zoo and Darling Harbour. Boats run every two hours from 9.30 am to 3.30 pm; the fare is $19 ($11 children).

Matilda Cruises (☎ 9264 7377) offers two-hour harbour sailing cruises on *Solway Lass*, a restored 40-metre schooner, twice daily from Darling Harbour's Aquarium Wharf. Tickets cost $25 ($12.50 children), or $38 ($19 children) with a buffet lunch. Their three-hour daily evening cruise with dinner costs $60 ($45 children). Bookings are essential.

Sail Venture Cruises (☎ 9262 3595) sails big catamarans around the harbour several times a day. They depart from Darling Harbour's Aquarium Wharf and also pick up at Circular Quay's East Pontoon (you get a longer cruise for the same price if you start at Darling Harbour). The cruise takes about two hours and costs $27 ($13.50 children). There's a lunch option for $44 ($22) and a dinner cruise for $70 ($35).

Sailing cruises are also offered on the *Bounty* (☎ 9247 1789), a replica of the ship lost by Captain Bligh in the famous mutiny. It was made for the film starring Mel Gibson and sails twice daily, Monday to Friday, three times on weekends. Prices range from $39 for the 1½-hour Sunday-morning brunch sail to $70 for the 2½-hour daily evening dinner cruise. The ship leaves from Campbell's Cove, the Rocks, as does the *Svanen* (☎ 9698 4456).

There are also tours of harbour islands – see Sydney Harbour earlier.

Walking Tours

Several people offer guided walks in Sydney. Maureen Fry (☎ 9660 7157), 15 Arcadia Rd, Glebe, caters mainly for groups of about eight people but she can take individuals or perhaps fit you in with a group. For a walking tour of the Rocks see that section earlier.

Bicycle Tours

M&J Sydney Bike Tours (☎ 9967 3030) has a daily 2½-hour bike ride at 10 am and 2 pm (and 5.30 pm October to March) around Sydney's sights. Tours leave from the Overseas Passenger Terminal at Circular Quay and cost $40.

SPECIAL EVENTS

In addition to the state-wide holidays and events, Sydney has some major celebrations of its own.

Spring

September

> *Royal Botanic Gardens Spring Festival* – mid-September; includes concerts, brass bands and a plant market; display of spring flowers in David Jones' city store
>
> *Festival of the Winds* – second Sunday; Bondi Beach welcomes spring with a kite-flying festival with a multicultural theme; it includes a display of kites above the beach and competitions for best home-made kites
>
> *Taylor Square Arts Festival* – mid-September; week-long, wide range of events, many involving local Oxford St businesses
>
> *Rugby League Grand Final* – held at the Sydney Football Stadium

October

> *Manly Jazz Festival* – Labour Day long weekend; styles range from trad and big band to fusion, bop and contemporary
>
> *Sleaze Ball* – Labour Day long weekend; gay and lesbian dance party at the Royal Agricultural Showgrounds; a crowd of over 15,000 gathers to raise funds for the Gay and Lesbian Mardi Gras

November

> *Kings Cross Carnival* – first weekend; busking competition, food and wine tastings

Summer

December

> *Christmas Party* – 25 December; an impromptu party at Bondi Beach, a favourite with travellers; although alcohol-free restrictions have been introduced there has been media hype about Westies (people from the western suburbs) coming and inciting violence
>
> *Sydney to Hobart Yacht Race* – 26 December;

Sydney Harbour is crowded with boats farewelling yachts competing in the race
New Years Eve – 31 December; Circular Quay and Darling Harbour are popular; a huge fireworks display

January
Sydney Festival & Carnivale – most of January; wide range of events from inline skating and street theatre to huge, free concerts in the Domain
Great Ferry Boat Race – Australia Day, 26 January; contest by the city's ferries, decorated for the race with balloons and streamers; they race from the Harbour Bridge to Manly and back
Survival Festival – 26 January; Aboriginal version of Australia Day, marked by Koori music, dance, arts and crafts

January/February
Chinese New Year – January or February; celebrated in Chinatown

February/March
Gay & Lesbian Mardi Gras – February and early March; attracts more visitors and generates more tourist dollars than any other event in Australia; month-long festival includes a sports carnival, the Blessing of the Mardi Gras, theatre, an arts festival and *lots* of parties; culminates in an amazing parade (the first Saturday in March) and Mardi Gras Party. Tickets, normally sold out by mid-January, are usually only available to Mardi Gras members, though interstate and overseas visitors can get temporary membership. There are usually accommodation and tour packages to Sydney during the Mardi Gras. For information call the Mardi Gras office (☎ 9557 4332, 1900 957 800, http://www.geko.com.au/mardigras), 21-23 Erskineville Rd, Erskineville.

Autumn
March/April
Royal Easter Show – Sydney Showground in Homebush Bay; a 12-day event which traditionally begins with a massive parade of farm animals; has a distinctly agricultural flavour but there are plenty of events to entertain city slickers
Golden Slipper – March; Sydney's major horse race, held at Rosehill
Sydney Cup – April; the second major horse race, held at Randwick

Winter
June
Sydney Film Festival – at the magnificent State Theatre; you can subscribe to the whole season or buy tickets to individual screenings (☎ 9660 3844)
Sydney Biennale – in even years; international arts festival at the Art Gallery of NSW and other city venues

July
Yulefest – in the Blue Mountains, guesthouses and restaurants celebrate Christmas; if you're lucky there might be snow

August
City to Surf Run – second Sunday; more than 40,000 runners pound the 14 km from Park St in the city to Bondi Beach; some are deadly serious, others are in it for fun, and everyone gets their name and finishing position published in the *Sydney Morning Herald*; entry forms appear in the *Herald* months before the race, although you can enter on the day; there's a fee of about $20

PLACES TO STAY
There's a huge variety of accommodation in Sydney with good options in every price range.

Most hotels and hostels lift rates or cancel special deals during the busy summer period from November to February, and prices at beachside resorts can be as much as 40% higher. But in winter, when things are slow, it's worth phoning around to see if there are any bargains. Special deals are often available if you book through an agency such as the NSW Travel Centre (☎ 132077), 11-13 York St.

Many top-end hotels cater primarily to business people, so their rates might be lower on weekends. Some bigger hotels include breakfast and parking in their rates. Mid-range and top-end hotels publish 'rack' rates (standard rates) but often have special deals; it's worth ringing and asking. Prices are also often quoted per room, depending on the facilities and/or the view, not per the number of occupants.

For longer-term stays there are places in the 'flats to let' and 'share accommodation' ads in the *Sydney Morning Herald*, especially on Wednesday and Saturday. Many travellers find flat-shares through other travellers. Hostel noticeboards are good sources of information. Serviced apartments often sleep more than two people and with lower weekly rates they can be inexpensive for a group.

Places to Stay – bottom end
Camping Sydney's caravan parks, most of which have tent sites, are a fair way out of

SYDNEY

Taxing Times for City Sleepers

In September 1997 the NSW government introduced a controversial 10% inner-Sydney bed tax, added to the standard room rate of hotels, serviced apartments and B&Bs in the central business district. Add 10% to rates listed in this chapter to get a reasonable estimate and ask individual establishments for exact room rates. Rates at backpacker hostels and youth hostels are not affected by the tax.

Kings Cross, Paddington, the Rocks, Circular Quay, Milsons Point, Lavender Bay, North Sydney, Neutral Bay and parts of Surry Hills and Darlinghurst are included in the zoned area, but Glebe and Bondi are not. ∎

town. One of the closest is *Sheralee Tourist Caravan Park* (☎ 9567 7161), 88 Bryant St, Rockdale, 13 km south. It has sites from $12 to $18 and vans for $35 a double. The *Grand Pines Caravan Park* (☎ 9529 7329), 289 The Grand Parade, Sans Souci, is 17 km south. It has no tent sites; van sites are $19, and on-site vans/cabins cost from $30/40 a double. *East's Lane Cove River Van Village* (☎ 9805 0500), Plassey Rd, North Ryde, is 14 km north of the centre and has sites/vans/cabins from $15.50/43/48 a double.

Hostels Sydney has one of the highest number of hostels of any city in the world and there's a wide choice of location and standards. The largest concentration is in Kings Cross, but there are others in places like Bondi, Coogee, Glebe, Surry Hills and Manly. Facilities vary from dorms with ensuite, TV, fridge and cooking facilities to just a plain room with a couple of bunks; many also offer single and/or double accommodation. YHA hostels are often better run and cleaner than many backpacker places. Some hostels have set hours for checking in and out, though all have 24-hour access once you've paid.

The average price for a dorm bed is $15 but in the peak summer period this can rise to $20. Many hostels charge less by the week and most are acutely aware of the competition's rates. Prices quoted here could easily fluctuate by a few dollars depending on demand. Winter rates are often a little lower. Hostelling International and Youth Hostel Association members receive dis-

counts as do members of VIP Backpackers International.

Partly to stop locals using hostels as dosshouses and partly because of bad experiences with lecherous drunks, some Sydney hostels ban Australians altogether. Others are suspicious of Australians who aren't travelling (some demand a passport as ID), although in the off-season these quibbles sometimes vanish in the quest for a buck. YHA hostels take members of any nationality. The YHA's Membership & Travel Centre (☎ 9261 1111), 422 Kent St, can book you into any Australian YHA hostel, and many others around the world. The centre is also a travel agency. It's open Monday, Wednesday and Friday from 9 am to 5 pm, Thursday to 6 pm, Saturday from 10 am to 2 pm.

As well as the backpacker-only hostels, there are plenty of pubs and boarding houses which fill spare rooms with bunks. Some are OK but most lack the hostel atmosphere and the essential information grapevine.

City Centre The city centre has only two real hostels. One is the new 532-bed *Sydney YHA* (☎ 9660 5577), near Central Station in the renovated Daking House on the corner of Pitt St and Eddy Ave. It's the largest hostel in the world and has a heated rooftop pool, sauna and licensed cafe. Dorms cost $17, doubles $26 per person; there are no singles. Despite its size, its prime location means that it can fill up quickly, so book ahead.

The other is the *YWCA* (☎ 9264 2451), 5-11 Wentworth Ave, near the corner of Liverpool St. It has an enviable position, with Hyde Park, the city centre and Oxford St a short walk away and plenty of buses and trains nearby. The standard is high and there are simple but spotless, well-furnished rooms and an inexpensive cafeteria. Unfortunately, there's a fairly high price for this: $47/65/80 for singles/twins/triples or $65/90/100 with attached bathrooms. There are cheap weekly rates but you have to stay at least a month to qualify. There's also dorm accommodation at $22 a night but the maximum stay is three nights. Both men and women can stay.

Kings Cross & Around There are heaps of hostels in the Cross and little to distinguish between many of them. Eva's has the best reputation, followed by Backpackers Headquarters. Barncleuth House/Pink House is for those who like their hostels a little more lived-in and cosy. The Jolly Swagman hostels have the best organised social life.

North along Victoria St from Kings Cross station is *Plane Tree Lodge* (☎ 9356 4551) at No 172. This is a standard, large Kings Cross hostel with a variety of rooms; each room has a TV and fridge. Rates are $15/32/35 in a dorm/twin/double.

Highfield Private Hotel (☎ 9358 1552), at No 166, caters exclusively to overseas travellers and is run by friendly Swedes. It's secure, clean enough and has a good atmosphere. The rates stay much the same all year, with singles/doubles for $30/45 ($180/270

weekly). You can share a twin for $17 per person ($100 weekly) or a triple for $16 per person ($95 weekly). Bathrooms are shared.

Original Backpackers (☎ 9356 3232), at No 162, *is* the original backpacker hostel in this area and, having expanded to other houses nearby, is still going strong. The atmosphere is good, it's reasonably clean and there are good-sized common areas. Dorms cost $16/96 a day/week, twins and doubles $36/220. The noticeboard is full of ads and information. *Travellers Rest* (☎ 9358 4606), at No 156, has clean, well-equipped rooms (all have a sink, TV and – except for single rooms – a fridge), some with balconies overlooking Victoria St. This place is well run, with a resident owner. The rates tend to stay the same all year: (three-bed) dorms cost $16/90 a day/week, singles $25/125 or $30/145 with bath; twins $32/190 or $36/210 with bath.

At No 144 you'll find the busy *Jolly Swagman* hostel (☎ 9357 4733), also called *Sydney Central Backpackers*. There are two other Jolly Swagman hostels, at 16 Orwell St (☎ 9358 6600) and 14 Springfield Mall (☎ 9358 6400). The hostels have a good atmosphere, good security and someone at the desk 24 hours. Dorms cost $18, doubles $42; there are no single rooms. All rooms have fridges and cooking facilities.

Family owned and operated, *Eva's Backpackers* (☎ 9358 2185), 6-8 Orwell St, is

---

When is a pub not a pub?

First-time visitors to Australia may be confused by the distinction between hotels and ... well, hotels. There are three kinds.

Until relatively recently any establishment serving alcohol was called a hotel and was legally required to provide accommodation. These hotels are also known as pubs (public houses). Not surprisingly, the accommodation facilities at many were minimal, designed merely to satisfy the licensing authorities. A pub room is usually pretty basic – bathrooms are almost always shared and you probably won't have a phone in the room.

Private hotels are usually boarding houses with similar facilities to pubs, but without a bar. These often have 'private' in their name to distinguish them from a pub.

Hotels in the business of providing accommodation with all the usual facilities, such as room service etc, are usually rated at three stars or higher.

Sydney has a range of all these types of hotels. Pubs are generally the cheapest and most spartan, but can be good value, especially in country areas or on the fringes of the city. ■

SYDNEY

clean, friendly and well run. There's a rooftop barbecue area and a big kitchen/dining room. Dorms cost $17, doubles $20 per person. It's so popular that it's often full, even in winter. The desk is staffed from 7 am to 1 pm and from 5.30 to 8.30 pm.

The long-established *Rucksack Rest* (☎ 9358 2348), 9 McDonald St off Macleay St, in Potts Point, is quiet, clean and in fairly good condition and only accepts overseas travellers. The rooms are fairly small, but they're comfortable and the dorms don't house more than three people. Dorm beds cost $16, singles $25, twins $36 and doubles are $34 to $38. If you stay a week you only pay for six nights. There's also a self-contained four-bed family room opposite for $17 per person.

One of the most popular Kings Cross hostels is *Barncleuth House Travellers Hostel* (☎ 9358 1689), 6 Barncleuth Square, east of Darlinghurst Rd. Slightly away from the main drag, it's also called the Pink House Travellers Hostel. It has a courtyard garden and log fires. Dorm beds are $16 ($95 weekly), doubles $18 per person ($105 weekly).

The secure, squeaky-clean *Backpackers Headquarters* (☎ 9331 6180), 79 Bayswater Rd, has dorms for $16, doubles for $21 per person, and is often full.

One of the higher quality hostels is *Forbes Terrace* (☎ 9358 4327), 153 Forbes St in Woolloomooloo, north of William St and west of the Cross. It's clean, quiet and has a good courtyard area. It charges $17 for a dorm bed, $50 for doubles. Each room has a TV, fridge and tea and coffee-making facilities.

Surry Hills *Kangaroo Bakpak Map* (☎ 9319 5915), 665 South Dowling St, north of the corner of Cleveland St, is a friendly place which gets consistently good feedback. Dorm beds go for $15 ($90 weekly). To get here from Central Station, take bus No 372, 393 or 395. *Nomads Backpackers* (☎ 9331 6487), in the Captain Cook Hotel, 162 Flinders St, Surry Hills, has dorm beds for $16

and doubles or twins for $40; weekly rates are available. Its proximity to the cricket ground and football stadium means it gets booked out when big games are on. The pub downstairs is often packed (with people spilling out onto the street) before and after a game.

The VIP *Excelsior Hotel* (☎ 9211 4945), 64 Foveaux St, is only a few blocks from Central Station. Most rooms offer reasonable pub accommodation (with shared bathrooms), and there are a few large dorms. Dorm beds are $16 ($90 weekly) and doubles are $40 ($200 weekly).

Alfred Park Hotel (☎ 9319 4031), 207 Cleveland St, is also close to Central Station. It's a quality, low-cost place that concentrates on backpackers. It has a pleasant courtyard and kitchen and a balcony overlooking the park; all rooms have TV and fridge. Dorms with attached bathroom cost $16, singles $25 to $35, twins $40/50 without/with bathroom.

Glebe The variety of hostels, restaurants and entertainment options in Glebe make it a good area to stay in.

The large, clean and friendly *Glebe Point YHA Hostel* (☎ 9692 8418), 262-64 Glebe Point Rd, has five-bed dorms for $17, four-bed for $19 and twin/double rooms for $46/48. It offers a large range of activities, has luggage storage and deducts the airport bus fare from your bill.

The friendly *Glebe Village Backpackers* (☎ 9660 8133), 256-58 Glebe Point Rd, is a large ramshackle hostel in two big houses, suitable for travellers who place sociability above tidiness. It's well worn, but many people like the lively atmosphere. Dorms cost $13 to $18, doubles $44. There's a free bus shuttle to Central Station and the airport. There's also a small discount for VIP members.

The small *Wattle House* (☎ 9692 0879, 9552 4997), 44 Hereford St, is in a pleasant, old house. It's clean, renovated and has nice extras, such as free linen and doonas (duvets). The friendly owners live in – this is *not* a hostel for party animals. It has a minimum stay of three nights. The rates are a touch higher than at other hostels, but they're worth it and they don't deter guests – Wattle House is often full. A bunk in a three or four-bed dorm costs $18 ($110 weekly) and twin rooms are $22 per person ($150 weekly).

Dorm beds are available for $20 at the *Alishan International Guesthouse* (☎ 9566 4048), 100 Glebe Point Rd. See Places to Stay – Middle for more information.

Newtown The YHA operates a summer hostel at *St Andrews College* (☎ 9557 1133) at the University of Sydney, where dorms cost $17 and twins are $20 per person. Take bus No 422, 423, 426 or 428 from Railway Square.

Billabong Gardens (☎ 9550 3236), 5-11 Egan St, is a good hostel, purpose-built by one of Sydney's original hostel owners. It's clean and quiet and there's a small solar-heated pool. Dorm beds cost $16, twins/doubles $40, or $50 with an attached bathroom. Weekly rates are available.

The hostel picks up travellers at the airport between 9 am and 9 pm. To get here from Railway Square take bus No 422, 423, 426 or 428, which run up Newtown's King St, and get off at Missenden Rd. By train, go to Newtown station and turn right into King St; Egan St is about four blocks along, on the left.

Bondi Beach There's a range of accommodation in Bondi, not all of it particularly appealing, but with the beach on your doorstep you're unlikely to spend much time inside. This is a popular base for long-term, working travellers and there are plenty of inexpensive flats.

Lamrock Hostel (☎ 9365 0221) is at 7 Lamrock Ave, a block back from Campbell Parade. It's a well-worn but bright house with dorms at $15, singles/doubles $20/45 and studio flats for $70 per person per week. These rates stay the same all year, unlike most other budget accommodation in Bondi. This place has been running for years and it's friendly and popular.

Other places in Bondi have shared rooms; see Hotels & Guesthouses section.

Coogee It's further from the city than Bondi and other traveller centres but Coogee's relaxed atmosphere and off-season specials are popular with backpackers. It's worth phoning hostels before you arrive because some have limited office hours.

Surfside Backpackers Coogee (☎ 9315 7888), 186 Arden St (enter around the corner in Alfreda St), is close to the beach and main bus stop. It's a fine hostel with a five-backpack rating and has balconies, some with views of the beach. There are also lots of stairs! Rates are $16 ($90 weekly) in dorms, and doubles $38.

The popular *Coogee Beach Backpackers* (☎ 9315 8000), 94 Beach St, is a short but stiff walk up the hill at the northern end of the beach. It occupies a Federation-era house and a modern block next door. It's clean and has good common areas and a deck with great views of the ocean. Spacious dorms cost $16 to $18, doubles $35.

Indy's (☎ 9315 7644), 302 Arden St, is up the hill at the southern end of the beach. It's a smaller place in a pleasant, old Victorian-era house on the hill south of the beach. Four-bed dorms cost $18 for the first night, $15 for subsequent nights; rates include breakfast.

Manly Manly has great ocean and harbour beaches and few city hassles and is only 30 minutes by ferry (15 minutes by JetCat) from Circular Quay.

Manly Beach Resort Backpackers (☎ 9977 4188), 6 Carlton St, is part of a motel. Backpackers have their own section in a renovated house. The spacious, clean dorms cost $17, twin rooms $32. The long-running *Manly Astra Backpackers* (☎ 9977 2092) is nearby at 68 Pittwater Rd. Bunks in dorms go for $17 per person; doubles are $35 ($196 weekly). It's a pleasant but strictly-run place.

Manly Backpackers Beachside (☎ 9977 3411), 28 Raglan St, has beds in modern three-bed dorms for $16/105 per day/week

SYDNEY

and in four to six-bed dorms for $15/102. It also has twins/doubles for $36/42 and doubles with ensuite for $48.

The Wharf Backpackers (☎ 9977 2800), 48 East Esplanade, is another modern hostel conveniently close to Manly wharf. It has two kitchens, two TV rooms, a garden and barbecue area. Dorm beds cost $15 to $17, twin rooms $40.

The huge *Steyne Hotel* (☎ 9977 4977), 75 The Corso, has four-bed dorms for $25, which includes 'a big hearty Australian breakfast'. There are good, shared kitchen facilities, but with cheap food available in the bar there's little point in cooking.

North Shore The *Harbourside Hotel* (☎ 9953 7977), 41 Cremorne Rd, Cremorne Point, is a large hostel catering mainly for backpackers and young locals working in Sydney. There are good views and the atmosphere is something like a large shared house. It won't suit everyone but it's worth a look. Dorms cost $15 ($97 weekly), with singles/doubles for $25/30 ($150/194). Take a ferry to Cremorne wharf, turn left and walk 200 metres up the hill.

For a break from city life, try the relaxed northern beachside suburb of Avalon where you'll find the purpose-built *Avalon Beach Hostel* (☎ 9918 9709), 59 Avalon Parade. It's clean, friendly, well run and has an open-plan common area, couches around a fire and a big balcony. Avalon Beach is a couple of blocks away and the hostel has surfboards and bicycles for hire. It also arranges a variety of activities. Dorms cost $14 ($90 weekly) or $16 in a smaller dorm. Doubles are $36. Phone in advance because it's often full, even in winter.

Take bus No 190 from Wynyard Park on York St in the city and ask for Avalon Beach ($4.40, 1¼ hours).

University Colleges Many residential colleges accept casual guests. The places listed below accept non-students, both men and women. Unless otherwise stated, these rooms are available during vacations only, mainly the long break from mid-December

to late January. Some may also have rooms during shorter breaks.

The rates shown were quoted by the universities, but it isn't unusual for different staff members to quote different rates. Also, although most places quote B&B or full-board rates, it's often possible to negotiate a lower bed-only rate. Ask about weekly or fortnightly rates which, if available, might also be cheaper.

University of Sydney The uni is central, south-west of Chippendale, close to Glebe and Newtown.

International House, 96 City Rd, Chippendale – fully serviced B&B rooms for $70 for students or visitors connected with the university, $120 for others (☎ 9950 9800)

St Johns College, Missenden Rd, Camperdown – B&B ensuite rooms with for $55 a night or $220 a week (☎ 9394 5200)

Wesley College– charges students $32.50 for B&B, $45.50 full board; everyone else pays $40/51.50 (☎ 9565 3333)

Women's College, 15 Carillon Ave, Newtown – offers students and YHA members B&B for $33, dinner for $39 and full board for $44; everyone else pays $42/48/54; twin rooms go for $55/67/75 for students and YHA members, $62/74/84 for others (☎ 9516 1642)

Also worth trying are *St Paul's College* (☎ 9550 7444), 9 City Rd, Newtown, and *Sancta Sophia College* (☎ 9519 7123), 8 Missenden Rd, Camperdown.

University of New South Wales Although the University of NSW is further from the city centre, it's only a short bus ride from the uni to the southern-ocean beaches and Oxford St. The university is on Anzac Parade along which many buses run, including No 336 from Circular Quay.

International House, High St, Kensington – offers students full board for $40; for a few weeks around Christmas it offers B&B for $25 (☎ 9663 0418)

New College, Anzac Parade, Kensington – B&B for $40, full board $45; students get a $5 discount (☎ 9662 6066)

Kensington Colleges (☎ 9663 8111), The High St, Randwick, and *Shalom College* (☎ 9663 1366), Barker St, Kensington, are also worth trying.

Hotels & Guesthouses A wide variety of accommodation falls into this category and in some places you might find the tackiness a challenge. There are some fine budget hotels and guesthouses which work out only fractionally more expensive than hostels if you're travelling with friends. A refundable key deposit of $10 is often required.

City Centre The big *CB Private Hotel* (☎ 9211 5115), 417 Pitt St, near the corner of Goulburn St, first opened for business in 1908 and it's still going strong. It was once the largest residential hotel in the country, with over 200 rooms, mostly singles. It's plain, clean and reasonably well maintained, although it gets a lot of wear. There are two lounge rooms and one TV room. Daily rates are $30/49/59 for singles/doubles/triples with shared bathroom.

George Hotel (☎ 9211 1800), 700A George St, south of the corner of Goulburn St, is one of the best of the inner-city hotels. It's plain, clean, equipped with cooking and laundry facilities and doesn't have the slightest whiff of seediness. The rooms at the front are subject to traffic noise. Singles/doubles with common bathrooms are $32/48, and a double with TV and attached bathroom is $70. There are weekly rates.

Sydney Central Private Hotel (☎ 9212 1005), 75 Wentworth Ave, a short walk from Central Station and Oxford St, is a basic hotel with cooking and laundry facilities. Singles/doubles with shared bathroom cost $30/45; doubles/triples with ensuite are $50/65. Weekly rates are available.

Crystal Palace Hotel (☎ 9211 0957), 789 George St, near the corner of Valentine St, is a pub with singles/doubles for $45/65. All rooms have fridges, and double rooms (and some singles) have attached bathrooms. The *Criterion Hotel* (☎ 9264 3093) on the corner of Pitt and Park Sts is a large pub with rooms

from $50/60, or $70/80 with attached bathroom.

The Rocks The small *Harbour View Hotel* (☎ 9252 3769), 18 Lower Fort St, should have been renamed the 'Bridge View' back in 1932 because it's next to one of the pylons. There's some noise from trains, even more from the bands in the bar, but with clean singles/doubles at $45/55 (including a light breakfast), it's good value for the location.

The *Palisade Hotel* (☎ 9247 2272) stands like a sentinel at 35 Bettington St, Millers Point. It has basic pub rooms with shared bathroom, and city, bridge, harbour and dockyard views for $80 a double.

Pyrmont The *Woolbrokers Arms* (☎ 9552 4773), on the corner of Allen and Pyrmont Sts in Pyrmont, is close to Darling Harbour. It's a decent pub charging $60 a double for B&B.

Kings Cross There are some quite reasonable hotels in the heart of the Cross. The friendly *Bernly Private Hotel* (☎ 9358 3122), 15 Springfield Ave, has fairly modern singles/doubles with showers, but shared toilets, for $40/50. It also has 'deluxe' rooms with air-con and full ensuite for $75.

Springfield Lodge (☎ 9358 3222), 9 Springfield Ave, with its pink-painted exterior, is hard to miss. The reasonably well-maintained rooms have fridge, TV and tea/coffee-making facilities. Singles/doubles with shared bathrooms cost $35/44 ($175/224 weekly), with an attached bathroom $44/54 ($220/250). You're advised to book in advance.

Gala Private Hotel (☎ 9357 1199), 23 Hughes St, is a clean, quiet, welcoming guesthouse with TV lounge and communal kitchen. Reception is open from 8 am to 8 pm. It has singles/doubles for $35/40 with fridge and shared bathroom, and doubles with ensuite for $50; it's a good idea to book.

Montpelier Private Hotel (☎ 9358 6960), 39A Elizabeth Bay Rd, has rooms for $30/40 ($150/180 weekly) with shared bath. The

SYDNEY

rooms have tea/coffee-making facilities, TV and fridge.

Potts Point An accommodation bargain near the Cross is the low-key, well-maintained *Challis Lodge* (☎ 9358 5422), 21-3 Challis Ave, in a pair of cavernous renovated terraces. Rooms are simple but clean. Those on the upper floors are quieter and get better light. Singles/doubles cost $30/40 ($150/200 weekly) with shared bathrooms, $42/49 ($210/245) with attached bathrooms.

Round the corner, *Macleay Lodge* (☎ 9368 0660), 71 Macleay St, has good-value, bright rooms for $35/40 ($175/200 weekly). Nearby at No 55, *Holiday Lodge Hotel* (☎ 9356 3955) has rooms with air-con, TV, phone and fridge for $55. It's run by a German couple who also speak French (and English).

Newtown The clean, pleasant-looking *Australian Sunrise Lodge* (☎ 9557 4400), 485 King St, has motel-style singles/doubles with TV and fridge for $45/55, or ensuite rooms for $65. Turn left when you leave the station.

Bondi Beach Bondi's hotels are prone to summer price hikes like most beachside suburbs. Rates vary depending on demand; those listed below are for the busy summer season. However, these summer rates may rise on weekends and the bargain weekly rates may be dropped. There are better deals when trade is slow.

Thelellen Beach Inn (☎ 9130 5333), 2 Campbell Parade at the southern end, dates from the 1930s. It's a well-run place in a great location, with clean, acceptable rooms with TV and fridge and shared bathrooms. Singles cost $30, doubles $35 to $42. Some rooms sleep up to four people; an extra person costs $5. They let shared rooms for $15 per person. May to December there are cheap weekly rates (singles $140, doubles $150 to $170).

The renovated *Biltmore Private Hotel* (☎ 9130 4660), 110 Campbell Parade, has a TV lounge, kitchen and laundry. It charges $15 for dorm beds and $35/40 ($190/240 weekly) for singles/doubles.

Hotel Bondi (☎ 9130 3271) is the peach-coloured layer-cake at 178 Campbell Parade. It's a grand, old seaside hotel with reasonable accommodation and rates that stay the same year-round. This also means that vacancies can be scarce over summer. Singles/doubles cost $25/27.50, or $27.50/35 with attached bathroom. In the off-season, there are cheap weekly rates.

Thelellen Lodge (☎ 9130 1521), 11A Consett Ave, is run by the same people who manage the Thelellen Beach Inn. It's a modest operation in a renovated suburban house two blocks back from the beach. It's clean, has a good communal kitchen and singles/doubles for $37/49. Next door at No 11, *Bondi Beach Guesthouse* (☎ 9389 8309), which is slightly better, has dorms for $15 ($90 weekly) and singles/doubles for $20/40. The fully serviced rooms have a TV and fridge; there's some off-street parking.

Bondi Lodge (☎ 9365 2088), 63 Fletcher St, is a short walk up the hill from the southern end of the beach, but is well placed to get to neighbouring Tamarama Beach. It offers dinner, bed and breakfast for $30 in a dorm ($125 weekly), from $50/80 in singles/doubles.

Coogee *Grand Pacific Private Hotel* (☎ 9665 6301), at the bottom of Carr St, close to the beach, is at the southern end of Coogee. It has seen better days, but rooms have a TV, fridge and tea and coffee-making facilities. Bathrooms are communal, and there's a guests' kitchen and laundry. Singles/doubles cost $35/45 for the first night, less thereafter. *Metro Coogee Beach* (☎ 9665 1162), 171 Arden St at the northern end of the beach, has dorm beds for $20 ($120 weekly), singles/doubles for $40/50 ($240/300 weekly) including breakfast. Bus No 374 stops outside.

North Shore *St Leonards Mansions* (☎ 9439 6999), 7 Park Rd in St Leonards, occupies three old houses and has well-equipped, clean singles/doubles for $50/65, plus $15 for each extra person (up to six people). Most rooms have phones, fridges and cooking facilities. A light breakfast is free, and there are laundry and parking facilities. Some rooms have balconies with city views. From St Leonards station, head west along the Pacific Highway (towards the hospital); Park Rd is the second street on your left.

North Sydney Lodge (☎ 9955 1012), 310 Miller St in North Sydney, is opposite St Leonards Park. It's a pleasant guesthouse charging $68 to $95 for rooms, all with bathrooms and including breakfast.

The quiet suburb of Kirribilli, north-east of the bridge, has several guesthouses. *Tremayne Private Hotel* (☎ 9955 4155), 89 Carabella St, is a large, clean, quality guesthouse originally built as accommodation for country girls attending school in Sydney. Rates are $25/35 ($150/220 weekly) with shared bathroom. There are some units with bathrooms for $180/250 weekly.

Kirribilli Court Private Hotel (☎ 9955 4344) with its mock-Tudor frontage is nearby at 45 Carabella St. It has singles/doubles with shared bathroom for $30/40; weekly rates are $80 per person. *Glenferrie Private Hotel* (☎ 9955 1685), at No 12A to the south, is in a large old house. The hotel was closed for refurbishment but should be open by the time you read this.

Neutral Bay Motor Lodge (☎ 9953 4199), in Neutral Bay on the corner of Kurraba Rd and Hayes St, not far from the ferry wharf, is more of a guesthouse than a motel. It's a reasonable place and the rates are $55/65.

Manly Manly is a popular holiday resort and particularly susceptible to summer price rises.

The large *Eversham Private Hotel* (☎ 9977 2423), on Victoria Parade, is undergoing major renovation. Singles/doubles/triples cost $28/46/69 ($123/150/225 weekly). There's a dining room and some deals include meals.

Ask at Manly Lodge (see Places to Stay – middle) about the *Manly Cove Guest House*,

51 Wood St, where singles/doubles cost $39/49 ($160/180 weekly).

Places to Stay – middle

This section covers places charging about $70 to $170 for a double. It's a wide price span and standards vary accordingly.

B&Bs *B&B Sydneyside* (☎ 9449 4430), PO Box 555, Turramurra, NSW 2074, will find you accommodation in a private home in Sydney for about $45 to $65 a night for a single, $65 to $95 a double. This is a good way of meeting locals and getting inside advice on things to see and do. For those who don't want B&B accommodation, but still want to meet Sydneysiders, they can sometimes arrange lunches.

Hotels & Motels There are some mid-range hotels and guesthouses offering top-value facilities at little more than budget prices. Some hotels in this section are pubs providing slightly above-average accommodation.

City Centre Excellent value for the location, *Wynyard Hotel* (☎ 9299 1330), on the corner of Clarence and Erskine Sts, is a pleasant pub with singles/doubles with shared bathroom for $55/65. The rooms are plain, but clean and comfortable. Weekly rates are available and weekly guests can use the hotel's cooking facilities. There's a rooftop area where you can enjoy the view.

Another inner-city pub with accommodation is the quiet *Grand Hotel* (☎ 9232 3755), 30 Hunter St, where prices are a little higher at $60/80. Its rooms have TV, fridge and tea/coffee-making facilities.

The *Park Regis* (☎ 9267 6511, 1800 221 138), on the corner of Park and Castlereagh Sts, is a fairly sparse motel-style place with rooms for $130. It has free parking and a rooftop pool. The well-appointed *Hyde Park Inn* (☎ 9264 6001, 1800 221 030), 271 Elizabeth St, is being refurbished and charges $130/145 a single/double, $180 for an apartment. Prices include continental breakfast.

Convenient for Central Station, the redecorated *Westend Hotel* (☎ 9211 4822), 412

Pitt St , has 13 floors of small, fairly feature-less motel-style rooms, but all are clean with bathrooms, TV, fridge, air-con and phone. Singles are $60 to $80, doubles $90. There are weekly rates, but you have to stay a month and pay in advance – and it's strictly non-refundable. There's a bar and an inexpensive restaurant.

Wynyard Vista Hotel (☎ 9290 1840, 1800 652 090), 7-9 York St, has a good, central location. Although the rack rate for a room is $200, you can usually get one for around $140.

Not the bargain it used to be, *Sydney Travellers Rest Hotel* (☎ 9281 5555, 1800 023 071), 37 Ultimo Rd in Haymarket, is close to Chinatown and Darling Harbour. It has clean, quiet rooms with attached bathroom and TV for $98 to $115 (plus $10 for each extra person).

Country Comfort Hotel (☎ 9212 2544), on the corner of George and Quay Sts on Railway Square, is near Central Station and Darling Harbour and next to Her Majesty's Theatre. Rates are $141 per room, except Saturday when $15 is added to the tariff.

The *Southern Cross Hotel* (☎ 9282 0987), on the corner of Goulburn and Elizabeth Sts, has a rooftop pool, piano bar and 24-hour cafe; it's within walking distance of Hyde Park, Oxford St and Darling Harbour. The standard rate is $140 per night, but it often has specials.

Darling Harbour On the western side of Darling Harbour, the *Glasgow Arms Hotel* (☎ 9211 2354), 527 Harris St near the Powerhouse Museum, has rooms in a renovated old-style pub. B&B with bathroom and air-con costs $80/100.

Beside the Novotel (with which it shares its 1800 number) is *Hotel Ibis* (☎ 9563 0888, 1800 642 244), 70 Murray St, overlooking the harbour. Its rooms cost $150; $165 with a harbour (and city) view.

The Rocks *Lord Nelson Brewery Hotel* (☎ 9251 4044), 19 Kent St, Millers Point, is a boutique pub on the edge of the Rocks. Singles/doubles cost $60/80.

The *Mercantile Hotel* (☎ 9247 3570), 25 George St near the bridge, is a restored pub with a strong Irish connection. It has singles/doubles for $65/85 with shared bathroom; breakfast is included.

Kings Cross & Around *O'Malley's Hotel* (☎ 9357 2211), a friendly Irish pub at 228 William St, is a traditionally decorated, well-furnished hotel with air-con. Rooms are good value at $60/70 including breakfast. Some twins share a bathroom, but doubles have attached bathrooms. The only drawback is the noise – the traffic on William St rarely lets up.

Maksim Lodge (☎ 9356 3399), 37 Darlinghurst Rd, is another friendly place and has rooms for $60/70, all with bathroom, fridge, phone and television. Similar is *Orwell Lodge* (☎ 9358 1745), 18-20 Orwell St, which charges $60/70 ($350/420 weekly).

Barclay Hotel (☎ 9358 6133), 17 Bayswater Rd, has a wide range of air-con rooms with TV, telephone and bathroom for $65/75. The *Metro Motor Inn* (☎ 9356 3511), 40 Bayswater Rd, charges $80 for doubles with TV, kitchen and bathroom.

The hip *L'Otel* (☎ 9360 6868), 114 Darlinghurst Rd south of William St, is a stylish boutique hotel with individually designed rooms (some in retro 50s style, others more traditional). It charges $80 for a room with TV, telephone and attached bathroom.

At the renovated *Kingsview Motel* (☎ 9358 5599, 1800 805 108), 30 Darlinghurst Rd in the heart of the Cross, rooms with air-con, TV, telephone and attached bathroom cost $75. *Madison's Hotel* (☎ 9357 1155), 6-8 Ward Ave, Elizabeth Bay, in a converted 1930s building with a modern extension, has rooms with full facilities for $100 and suites for $110 to $125. Rates include breakfast and free parking.

Crescent on Bayswater (☎ 9357 7266, 1800 257 327) is a modern brick building at 33 Bayswater Rd. A room/suite costs $145/165 which includes breakfast and car parking.

Top of the Town Hotel (☎ 9361 0911), 227 Victoria St south of William St, has a rooftop restaurant and swimming pool. Singles/doubles with showers cost $145/160, or $160/170 with a spa.

Potts Point *De Vere Hotel* (☎ 9358 1211), 46 Macleay St, has rooms with TV, telephone and bathroom for $120. At the lovely Art Deco *Manhattan Hotel* (☎ 9358 1288), 8 Greenknowe Ave, the standard rate for doubles is $145 to $165 depending on the view, but it often has cheaper specials.

To the north is the *Chateau Sydney Hotel* (☎ 9358 2500), 14 Macleay St, where the rooms have balconies. Rooms with city views cost $160, those with views of Elizabeth Bay $180.

Victoria Court Hotel (☎ 9357 3200), 122 Victoria St, is a quiet retreat in a comfortable boutique hotel occupying two restored terrace houses. There's a large jacuzzi, security parking and a pleasant courtyard. The rates start from $120 up to $165 for rooms with a balcony, and include continental breakfast. More expensive is the *Parkroyal Plaza Hotel* (☎ 9368 4000), 203 Victoria St, which charges $155 for standard rooms, $170 for rooms with harbour views.

Edgecliff & Rushcutters Bay *Bersens Cosmopolitan Hotel* (☎ 9327 3207), 2B Mona Rd, is near the intersection with New South Head Rd (the eastward continuation of William St). Edgecliff train station is nearby. Rooms have a mini-kitchen with fridge and microwave, and some have good views. There's also a roof garden. Rooms are $75/85, but the place is due to be completely refurbished so expect rates to rise.

Metro Motor Inn (☎ 9238 7977), 230 New South Head Rd, has rooms with harbour views for $90.

In Rushcutters Bay, the three-star, four-storey *Bayside* (☎ 9327 8511), 85 New South Head Rd, has rooms for $139; call to check for any specials.

Double Bay The pleasant *Savoy Double Bay Hotel* (☎ 9326 1411, 1800 811 836) at 41-45 Knox St, is a small friendly, place but in a good location. The good-value rooms cost $109 to $165 single or double, which includes a light breakfast.

Watsons Bay To enjoy the harbour in a quiet locale and still be within a short ferry ride of the city, try the harbourside *Doyle's Watsons Bay Hotel* (☎ 9337 4299), 1 Military Rd, which has B&B for $50/80 with separate bathrooms.

Darlinghurst The 13-storey, three-star *Oxford Koala Hotel* (☎ 9269 0645, 1800 222 144) is on Pelican St near Oxford St. During the week rooms cost $99 to $109, apartments $119 including breakfast; weekend rates are higher but don't include breakfast.

Surry Hills *Crown Lodge International* (☎ 9331 2433), 289 Crown St a little south of Oxford St, offers standard motel accommodation and charges $75/80; there's a discount if you stay more than three nights.

More upmarket, *The Cambridge* (☎ 9212 1111, 1800 251 901), 212 Riley St, in a converted building, has a gym, sauna, heated pool and restaurant. Rooms with full facilities including kitchenette cost $175, but there are often cheaper specials.

Glebe *Alishan International Guesthouse* (☎ 9566 4048), 100 Glebe Point Rd, is both a guesthouse and an upmarket hostel. It boasts well-travelled, multilingual staff, good common areas, including kitchen and laundry facilities, and a small garden with a barbecue. Rooms with bathroom cost $70/85.

The *Rooftop Motel* (☎ 9660 7777, 1800 227 436), 146-148 Glebe Point Rd, is a fairly simple but friendly motel charging $80 to $87 per room. Further north, the *Haven Inn* (☎ 9660 6655), at No 196, is quite a good motel. It has large rooms (for an inner-city motel) from $109 for a standard room to $129 for one with a city view. There's a heated swimming pool, secure parking and a restaurant. The courtesy bus takes you into the city and other nearby destinations.

Closer to the city, the Chinese-run *A-Line Hotel* (☎ 9566 2111), 247-53 Broadway, has modest, clean rooms for $80 to $130.

Bondi Beach *Hotel Bondi* (☎ 930 3271), an impressive old pile on the corner of Campbell Parade and Curlewis St, has renovated suites for $60 to $80, and other rooms with beach views from $50.

Bondi Beach Motel (☎ 9365 5233), 68 Gould St, a block back from Campbell Parade, is a reasonable motel. Rooms cost $60/70, more in summer.

Bondi Beachside Inn (☎ 930 5311), 152 Campbell Parade, has older-style motel rooms, which are being upgraded. The rooms are small, but each has a kitchen and a balcony. It's fair value at $72 for an older single or double, up to $91 for a renovated room with beach views.

The refurbished *Beach Road Hotel* (☎ 9130 7247), 71 Beach Rd, is a large pub two blocks back from the beach. It has several bars, a couple of eateries and a nightclub. The rooms have air-con and bathrooms and go for $55/70.

Ravesi's (☎ 9365 4422) is an interesting three-star hotel in a renovated building on the corner of Campbell Parade and Hall St. There are only 16 rooms and suites, some with their own terraces. Rates start at $95; rooms with beach views cost $155. There are often special deals in winter and spring.

Coogee *Coogee Bay Hotel* (☎ 9665 0000), on the corner of Arden St and Coogee Bay Rd, has air-con rooms with fridge, TV, telephone and ensuite from $68/79.

Coogee Sands Motor Inn (☎ 9665 8588), on Dolphin St opposite the beach, charges $89 for a standard room, $110 for one overlooking the beach. There are a few other motels in the area, including *Corban International* (☎ 9665 2244), 183 Coogee Bay Rd, which charges from $80/90.

Manly This is a beach resort, so many places have seasonal and weekend deals; ring around to find out what's on offer.

The *Steyne Hotel* (☎ 9977 4977), is a pub

where you can also stay. It's at 75 The Corso, and most rooms have shared bathrooms. OK singles/doubles cost from $45/70.

Manly Lodge (☎ 9977 8514), 22 Victoria Parade, is a guesthouse with a holiday atmosphere. Most rooms are small, but they have TV, fridge, air-con and attached bathrooms and cost $69/89 to $145/160, including breakfast.

Manly Beach Resort (☎ 9977 4188), 6 Carlton St, is reasonable with rooms from $85/90 to $95/100 including continental breakfast.

Periwinkle Guest House (☎ 9977 4668), 18-19 East Esplanade, is an elegant restored Victorian house facing the harbour beach at Manly Cove. It has singles/doubles/triples for $70/85/100 with shared bathroom, $80/95/115 with bathroom. Kitchen and laundry facilities are available. The entrance is on Ashburner St.

Manly Paradise Motel (☎ 9977 5799), 54 North Steyne, is on the beachfront. It has a rooftop pool and air-con motel rooms with TV, fridge and bathroom for $75, or $95 with an ocean view.

Serviced Apartments Serviced apartments – anything from a hotel room with a fridge and a microwave, to a full-size apartment – can be good value, especially for families.

City Centre *Sydney City Centre Serviced Apartments* (☎ 9233 6677/3529), 7 Elizabeth St, in the heart of the financial district, offers some of the best value accommodation in the city. Each apartment is fully equipped, down to washing machine and drier. The apartments are bedsits but they're a reasonable size. Rates start at $70 to $90 a double.

Near Hyde Park and Oxford St, *Sydney Park Inn* (☎ 9360 5988, 1800 656 705), 2-6 Francis St, behind the NSW police headquarters, provides fully equipped studios complete with air-con, kitchenette, TV and personal safe. They cost $120 including a light breakfast.

Darling Harbour *Metro Inn* (☎ 9290 9200)

has good serviced apartments close to Darling Harbour, at 132 Sussex St, and nearby at 27-29 King St. The clean, bright rooms are split level and have great views. There's a kitchenette and a washer and dryer in the bathroom. Great value, especially for families, apartments cost $145 per night or $115 per night if you stay a week or more.

The nearby *Savoy Apartments* (☎ 9267 9211), 37-43 King St, is a little more expensive – an apartment costs $148 per night or $140 per night if you stay a week or more.

Downtown Serviced Apartments (☎ 9261 4333), 336 Sussex St, has a tennis court and swimming pool plus a rooftop garden with good views of the harbour. The apartments have two bedrooms, kitchen and living room and cost $150. A space in the car park is $10 extra.

The *Waldorf* (☎ 9261 5355, 1800 023 361), 57 Liverpool St, has a rooftop pool, spa, barbecue area and free parking. Single/doubles cost $185/220.

Potts Point *Oakford City West Apartments* (☎ 9358 4544, 1800 657 392), 10 Wylde St (the northern continuation of Macleay St) charges $160 to $205 for one-bedroom apartments. The more expensive ones have views of the harbour.

Elizabeth Bay In Elizabeth Bay, down the road from the Cross, *17 Elizabeth Bay Rd* (☎ 9358 8999) – that's the name as well as the address – has well-equipped, serviced apartments for $150; if you stay a week or more you're charged $20 less per night.

Medina Executive Apartments (☎ 9356 7400), 68 Roslyn Gardens, has bright, quiet rooms overlooking an atrium for $110.

Rushcutters Bay The four-storey *Lodge Studio Apartments* (☎ 9327 8511), 38-44 New South Head Rd, has studio apartments with TV, kitchenette and bathroom for $79 a double. Check-in is at the Bayside Motel opposite.

Places to Stay – top end

This section covers accommodation costing from $165 a night. Travel agents in other states or countries can book many of these places and probably have access to special deals and packages.

Hotels With a dozen five-star hotels and plenty of four-star establishments, there are lots of places to choose from.

Airport The *Sydney Airport Hilton* (☎ 9597 0122, 1800 222 255), 20 Levey St, Arncliffe, charges from $210/240 to $300/330 a single/double.

City Centre The *Sydney Hilton* (☎ 9266 6000, 1800 222 255), 259 Pitt St, is in the heart of the city. Its standard charges for singles/doubles are $250/280 to $320/350, but it often has cheaper weekend deals, especially in winter. The historic Marble Bar is downstairs.

Menzies Hotel (☎ 9299 1000, 1300 363 600), 14 Carrington St, across from Wynyard Park, has rooms for $159, or $189 with breakfast. The *Wentworth* (☎ 9230 0700, 1800 676 960), 61-101 Phillip St, is within walking distance of Circular Quay and the Macquarie St museums. It has rooms and suites from $270 to $650.

Several hotels overlook Hyde Park. *Sheraton on the Park* (☎ 9286 6000), 161 Elizabeth St, has a magnificent lobby with large, maroon-coloured marble columns. Rooms with views of the city/park cost $340/390.

Sydney Marriott Hotel (☎ 9361 8400, 1800 025 419), 36 College St, has rooms from $300 to $695 for up to three people. Rooms have three telephones! Next door, but with the same street number, is *Hyde Park Plaza Hotel* (☎ 9331 6933). Rooms cost $210, suites $230 to $420. Both hotels are close to Oxford St restaurants.

The Rocks & Circular Quay In a superb location, the *Russell* (☎ 9241 3543), 143A George St, is a pleasant, small, boutique-style hotel with traditionally decorated rooms, pleasant lounge areas and a roof garden. Depending on the views, rooms cost

$95/105 to $135/145 with shared bathrooms, $150/160 to $190/200 with attached bathrooms.

The *Stafford* (☎ 9251 6711), 75 Harrington St, is pleasant with self-contained studios and single-bedroom apartments (some in a row of restored terrace houses) from $185 to $250. Weekly rates are available. *Harbour Rocks Hotel* (☎ 9251 8944, 1800 251 210), diagonally opposite at 34-52 Harrington St, also occupies some restored 19th-century buildings. Rooms start at $185.

From the rooftop pool of the *Old Sydney Parkroyal* (☎ 9252 0524, 1800 221 493), 55 George St, there are great views of the Rocks, Sydney Harbour Bridge, the harbour itself and the Opera House. The rack rate for a room is $310 but the hotel offers specials with hefty discounts, such as weekend nights for $185.

The *Regent* (☎ 9238 0000), 199 George St, has great views from the upper floors. On weekdays singles/doubles cost $250/280 to $470/500 but on weekends they go for $215 to $400 single or double.

The three-storey *Observatory Hotel* (☎ 9256 2222, 1800 806 245), 89-113 Kent St, on the Millers Point side of the Bradfield Highway, is large for a boutique hotel, but small for a five-star one. It has singles/doubles for $340/365 including breakfast.

Nearby is the big *ANA Hotel Sydney* (☎ 9250 6000, 1800 801 080), 176 Cumberland St, which has 573 rooms and suites, all with harbour views. Rooms cost $290 to $480, most suites $470 to $520.

The luxurious *Park Hyatt* (☎ 9241 1234, 131234), 7 Hickson Rd, is in one of the best locations in Sydney – on the waterfront at the edge of Campbells Cove, in the shadow of the Harbour Bridge and facing the Opera House. It charges from $480 for a room, up to $850 for most suites.

The *Ritz-Carlton* (☎ 9252 4600, 1800 252 888), 93 Macquarie St, is in an elegant brick building. The staff are very courteous and rooms cost $279 to $369, suites $400 to $1200.

Next door, the *Hotel-Intercontinental* (☎ 9230 0200, 1800 221 828), 117 Mac-

quarie St, is in a beautiful sandstone building that once housed the treasury. It's one of the few hotels with an environmental 'mission statement' by which it maintains 'best-practice' use of resources. Rooms cost $325 to $375, suites from $675.

Darling Harbour The huge, 700-room *Hotel Nikko* (☎ 9299 1231, 1800 222 700) at 161 Sussex St normally charges $280 to $350, depending on the view, but often has specials.

A hotel with good views of Darling Harbour and the city is the 530-room *Novotel Sydney* (☎ 9934 0000, 1800 024 499), 100 Pyrmont St, behind Harbourside. It has a swimming pool, spa, gym and tennis court and charges $210 to $300. It's somewhat cut off from the harbour and you need to walk across covered footbridges (over Darling Rd) to get there.

The *Furama Hotel* (☎ 9281 0400, 1800 800 555), 68 Harbour St, in a renovated 19th-century woolstore (and a modern extension), is directly opposite Sydney Entertainment Centre. It has a walk-in rate of $165 for standard rooms, up to $235 for a deluxe room.

Potts Point *Simpsons of Potts Point* (☎ 9356 2199), 8 Challis Ave, is in a superb old house in a quiet secluded spot a short walk from Kings Cross. It offers large, well-furnished rooms with attached bathrooms for $140; breakfast is $10 extra. Definitely worth a look.

The 470-room *Landmark Parkroyal Hotel* (☎ 9368 3000), 81 Macleay St, has flight crews staying here as well as tourists. Spacious rooms with views of the city cost $165 to $195.

Elizabeth Bay The *Sebel* (☎ 9358 3244; fax 9357 1926), 23 Elizabeth Bay Rd, has a reputation for celebrity guests, especially from the music industry. It has some quality touches, including a gym and a heated pool on the roof. Rates are $189 to $459, with seasonal specials and good weekend deals.

Double Bay With its gold and deep purple decor the *Sir Stamford* (☎ 9363 0100), 22 Cross St, sits above the Cosmopolitan shopping centre. Reception is on the 3rd floor and rooms here cost $215 to $235, suites $315 to $395.

At the plush *Ritz-Carlton* (☎ 9362 4455), 33 Cross St, Double Bay, rooms cost $199 to $259, suites $350 to $1200. It's popular with the powerful and famous who require discretion. Princess Di stayed here on her 1996 visit.

Bondi Beach & Coogee The top-dollar place to stay in Bondi is the large, modern *Swiss Grand* (☎ 9365 5666, 1800 655 252), on Campbell Parade. The entrance is on Beach Rd. Suites are $190; those with beach views begin at $230.

In Coogee, the *Holiday Inn* (☎ 9315 7600, 1800 674 422), 242 Arden St, charges $199 for views of Coogee, $239 for ocean views.

North Shore *Duxton Hotel* (☎ 9955 1111, 1800 807 356), 11 Alfred St, is across from Milsons Point station. It's a stylish, modern, four-star hotel, oriented to business customers. It has rack rates from $235 to $310 but on weekends (from Friday night to Monday morning) there are specials from $145 including breakfast.

Manly There are two four-star hotels. *Manly Pacific Parkroyal* (☎ 9977 7666), 55 North Steyne, has a gym and swimming pool and rooms for $175 to $210. *Radisson Kestrel* (☎ 9977 8866), 8 South Steyne, has rooms with air-con, TV and bathroom for $179 to $269. At both, the more expensive rooms offer views of the ocean.

Serviced Apartments In the Rocks, *Quay West Sydney* (☎ 9240 6000, 1800 805 031), 98 Gloucester St, has quality apartments with views of Sydney Harbour or the city. Rates are $300 to $1300 for up to two people.

The 11-storey *Carrington Sydney City Centre Apartments* (☎ 9299 6556), 57-59 York St near the corner of Barrack St, has rooms for $180 to $230. The reception is on the 10th floor. From the 6th-floor swimming pool at *York Apartment Hotel* (☎ 9210 5000), 5 York St, you can see the approaches to Sydney Harbour Bridge. Rates for the spacious rooms are $200 to $305 and include free parking.

At 6-14 Oxford St, not far from Hyde Park, the swish *Parkridge Corporate Apartments* (☎ 9361 8600) has single/double suites for $160/190.

In Manly, *Manly Waterfront Apartment Hotel* (☎ 9976 1000), 1-3 Raglan St, has apartments from $215.

PLACES TO EAT

With great local produce, innovative chefs, inexpensive prices and BYO licensing laws, eating out is one of the great delights of Sydney. The city has a huge variety of restaurants and almost everywhere you'll find good places to eat.

Modern Australian food is an amalgam of Mediterranean, Asian and Californian cooking practices and emphasises lightness, freshness and healthy eating. This hybrid style has developed from migrant influences, climatic conditions and local produce. In Sydney, it has filtered down from sophisticated restaurants to modest corner bistros, so you can savour the style whatever your budget. Cafes tend to serve a near ubiquitous diet of focaccia, bagels, filled croissants and sandwiches.

You can save up for a big night out at one of the city's top restaurants and still eat well because there are scores of places serving decent food at reasonable prices. Modest Chinese, Indian and Vietnamese restaurants are almost as cheap as eating at home. Pub counter meals are also good for solid, inexpensive fare.

City Centre

There's no shortage of places for a snack or a meal in the city centre on weekdays, but many, especially north of Liverpool St, close in the evenings. They're clustered around railway stations, in shopping arcades and tucked away in the food courts at the base of office buildings.

Fast Food On Pitt St Mall there's reasonably priced food in the *Mid City Centre* food court on street level and in the *Centrepoint* food hall on the ground floor. They serve Mexican, Italian, Thai etc costing from $4 to $6. *Woolworth's*, on the corner of George and Park Sts, has a 2nd-floor cafeteria, open daily, which serves meals like roast lamb or pork from around $5.

The *YWCA* has a cafeteria serving sandwiches for around $2.80 and hot meals for $6. It's open weekdays from 7.30 am to 7 pm, weekends 8 am to 9 pm.

Cafes *Bar Paradiso* has a lovely aspect and outdoor tables in historic Macquarie Place. Focaccia, pizza and Turkish bread go for around $7; soup and bread for $5.50. *Bar Coluzzi* (☎ 9233 1651), 99 Elizabeth St behind Queens Square, serves good coffee; most food costs around $5.

For a quiet cup of tea or coffee away from the city bustle, try *Old Sydney Coffee Shop* on the ground floor of the elegant Strand Arcade, between the Pitt St Mall and George St. It has a wide choice of coffee or tea from around $2.

Farther south, drop into *Carruthers Vegetarian Food Centre* on Druitt St, near Clarence St, for a lunchtime vegetarian snack. It serves tasty sandwiches, salads and vegie burgers at low prices; breakfast specials are $2 to $2.60.

In the streets around Central Station is a diverse collection of inexpensive Asian places spilling over from Chinatown, older-style cafes and a few pubs with inexpensive counter meals.

Wildfood Cafe at 4 Eddy Ave serves organic food including Thai dishes, sandwiches and cakes; east meets west with scrambled tofu on toast for $4.50. Good-value takeaways can be had at the nearby *Central Park Cafe* next to the coach terminal; focaccia or gourmet sandwiches cost $4.

George St has plenty of cafes where you can buy breakfast for less than $7, such as the *Cafe Inn* at No 768, across from Ultimo Rd. Breakfast is $6 including tea or coffee.

Jackie's Espresso Bar, 86 Liverpool St,

around the corner from the George St cinemas, is popular and has a good vegetarian selection. Pasta is $6.

Pubs *Hotel Sweeney*, on the corner of Clarence and Druitt Sts, has a 3rd-floor cafe where you can get snacks from lunchtime onwards and surf the Internet. On the corner of Pitt and Bathurst Sts, *Pitt St Bistro* serves interesting and relatively inexpensive food upstairs at the Edinburgh Castle Hotel.

South of Pitt St Mall, *Arizona's* (☎ 9261 1077), 231-47 Pitt St on the 1st floor beside the City Centre monorail stop, is one of a small chain of 'western' bar/restaurants, popular for eating and drinking. It serves Tex-Mex food including quesadillas for $7.95.

The stylish *Merivale Restaurant & Bar* (☎ 9264 7711), in the old Angel Hotel at 125 Pitt St, has snacks for about $8, mains like smoked chicken with salad for $12.50. It's open weekdays from 7.30 am until late.

Restaurants In the Sydney Tower, the *International Revolving Restaurant,* on Level 1, has main courses from $26.50 to $39.50 and fixed-price lunch menus for $36 on weekdays. It's open weekdays for lunch, Monday to Saturday for dinner. *Level 2 Revolving Restaurant* has an all-you-can-eat buffet, offering a selection of meats, seafood and Asian dishes, but little for vegetarians. Prices depend on when you go – from $29.50 for lunch Tuesday to Saturday, to $37.50 for Saturday dinner (children less than half-price). Restaurant patrons aren't charged for the ride to the top of the tower, so you're $9 ahead. Bookings are recommended (☎ 9233 3722).

Merivale (☎ 9264 7000), 194 Pitt St, north of Pitt St Mall, serves meals such as grilled marinated mushrooms for $7.50 to $12.50, and a selection of cakes.

Substantial vegetarian meals with a South American flavour are sold at *El Sano*, downstairs on the north-west corner of Pitt St and Martin Place. Stuffed eggplant is $6.50. It's closed on weekends.

Diethnes (☎ 9267 8956), downstairs at

333 Pitt St, north of Liverpool St, is a large, friendly Greek restaurant where lamb specials cost $9.30. It's open for lunch and dinner Monday to Saturday.

Planet Hollywood (☎ 9267 7827), 600 George St, is hard to resist. The emphasis is on fun – the walls are crammed with movie memorabilia, unobtrusive video screens show film clips and there's music which isn't too loud. The food isn't bad either; burgers are $9.95.

Spanish Town consists of a cluster of Spanish restaurants and bars along Liverpool St, between George and Sussex Sts. *Captain Torres* (☎ 9264 5574) at No 73 has a great bar and good seafood for $14 to $18. *Casa Asturiana* (☎ 9264 1010), a few doors closer to George St, reputedly has the best tapas in Sydney, for which it charges $4.50 to $6.50. The *Grand Taverna* at the Sir John Young Hotel (☎ 9267 3608), on the corner of George St, is another popular place, and most main courses, like lemon sole, are $13 to $14.

The Vietnamese-run *Mekong* (☎ 9211 0221), 711 George St, is one of Sydney's cheapest eateries. It serves seafood laksa for $5 and a variety of vegetarian dishes for only $4. *Saigon* (☎ 9212 3822), on George St, is another Vietnamese restaurant which is busy at lunchtime; garlic beef with fried rice is $6.50.

Malaya on George (☎ 9211 0946), nearby on the corner of Valentine St, is a Malaysian/Chinese eatery, is more upmarket but has plenty of main courses $8.50 to $14, and cheaper vegetarian dishes. It's open Monday to Friday for lunch, nightly for dinner.

Mother Chu's Vegetarian Kitchen (☎ 9283 2828), 376 Pitt St, is a rare Chinese restaurant which serves vegan food. It doesn't use MSG, onion, garlic or chives! It's open for dinner daily, for lunch Monday to Friday; noodle dishes are $6.50, main courses around $8.50 to $10.50.

Chinatown

Chinatown is a dense concentration of mostly Chinese restaurants, cafes, takeaways and shops catering to the Chinese community. There are also Thai, Vietnamese, Japanese and Korean eateries. Officially, Chinatown consists only of the pedestrian mall on Dixon St but there are also good Chinese restaurants in the streets nearby, notably in the small Haymarket area at the southern end of Dixon St Mall.

You can spend a small fortune at some outstanding Chinese restaurants, or eat well for next to nothing in a food hall. Weekend yum cha brunch is popular; you may have to queue to get into some of the many places which offer it.

Fast Food The best place to start is the downstairs food hall, open daily 10 am to 10 pm, in *Harbour Plaza*, the pagoda-style building on the corner of Dixon and Goulburn Sts. There's a wide range of eateries with many dishes from $4 to $6. There's also a food hall on the top level of the *Sussex Centre*, diagonally across from the Harbour Plaza, fronting Dixon St and backing onto Sussex St; and another in the *Dixon Gourmet Food Centre* in Dixon House on the corner of Dixon St Mall and Little Hay St.

Cafes Open daily, *Emperor's Garden BBQ & Noodles*, on Thomas St, is a cafe-style Chinese eatery, popular with the Chinese community. Pork and rice is $5. A little along Thomas St, upstairs in the Prince Centre, the *Malay Chinese Takeaway* is also popular with the locals. It's a large, bright, cafeteria-style place with fried beef noodles for $6.

On the corner of Ultimo Rd and Thomas St, beneath the House of Guangzhou restaurant, is an inexpensive *Japanese cafe* with a few tables and most meals from $5 to $10; it also does takeaways.

Restaurants On the ground floor of the Prince Centre is the intimate, busy *Chinese Noodle Restaurant*. The noodles are made northern Chinese style; most meals cost around $6.

Hingara (☎ 9212 2169), 82 Dixon St, has interesting seafood dishes such as fried fish with corn sauce; mains are $10 to $15. Others worth checking out are the large *Tai*

Yuen (☎ 9211 3782), 110 Hay St, which has been around a long time and has a good reputation, and the *New Tai Yuen* (☎ 9212 5244) at 31 Dixon St – both have seafood noodles for $6.50, mains $11 to $15.

The popular, established *House of Guangzhou* (☎ 9281 2205), at 76 Ultimo Rd occupying two floors, has a reputation for good seafood; bookings are essential. Main courses cost around $14 to $20, though some seafood costs more.

The huge *Marigold* restaurant (☎ 9264 6744), 299-305 Sussex St, serves Cantonese food with great style and prices to match – mains cost $14 to $20 – and there's a good vegetarian selection. Despite its size you need to book. Another *Marigold* (☎ 9281 3388), on the 4th floor at 683-89 George St, serves lunchtime yum cha daily.

In the same price bracket, the upmarket *Regal* (☎ 9261 8988), 347-53 Sussex St, is another large place popular for Sunday yum cha.

Darling Harbour & Pyrmont

The biggest concentration of eateries is at Harbourside. Most are aimed at the tourist trade, but with a window or terrace table on a fine day, who cares? Stroll around and take your pick.

Fast Food, Cafes & Pubs There are heaps of fast-food outlets at Harbourside, particularly in the north pavilion which has a food court on the ground floor and more eateries on the 1st floor. Upstairs is the *Festival Cafe*, a large coffee lounge (but without views) serving sandwiches and burgers for around $5 and Devonshire teas.

Craig Bar & Grill in the north pavilion has pasta courses for around $9 and steak or fish dishes for $12.50. *Pumphouse Tavern Brewery*, 17 Little Pier St, near the Sydney Entertainment Centre, has above-average pub meals. Pasta is $7.50. There are tables outside.

Away from Darling Harbour proper you can eat with the locals at the *Glasgow Arms Hotel*, 527 Harris St, not far from the Pow-

erhouse Museum. It has a good bistro; burgers are $9.90.

Restaurants *Classis* (☎ 9281 3976) is a large restaurant on Harbourside's level 2 with traditional food like steak for $18.50 and good views of the harbour and city.

Jordon's (☎ 9281 3711) and *Jo Jo's* (☎ 9281 3888), both on the ground floor at Harbourside, are two of the more expensive joints and have some of the best views. Jordon's is a seafood restaurant. Its 'famous fish and chips' costs $17.50. It also has a bar. At Jo Jo's, starters such as calamari rings cost $9 to $19, mains like baked John Dory fillets $23 to $39.

Shipley's Restaurant (☎ 9281 0400) in the Furama Hotel, 68 Harbour St opposite Sydney Entertainment Centre, has two-course meals including a glass of wine for $25 and a breakfast buffet for $16.95.

Pyrmont Fish Markets have several places to eat. *Doyle's at the Markets* (☎ 9552 4339) is a bistro but also does takeaways. It serves fish of the day with chips for $9.80 and has seating outside.

Circular Quay

Many cafes and restaurants that line the quay, especially on the western side, have good views of the harbour, although you pay for the position. Most are aimed at tourists.

Fast Food If you want fuel rather than views there are lots of cheap stalls on the wharves as you head toward the ferries. You could also try the *Nulbom Oriental Food* kiosk, which sells reasonable Asian food for around $6. It's behind the quay on the Alfred St median strip at the corner of Pitt St.

Cafes Back from the wharves, amid the crowds and buskers, are the 24-hour *City Extra* and *Rossini*, which have reasonable coffee, snacks and meals. Grilled trout costs $16. The several cafes actually on the wharves aren't great value although they're OK for a cup of coffee – the floor may sway a little!

The *Museum of Contemporary Art* has a

stylish cafe in the cavernous foyer; the tables outside give good views of Circular Quay. The food is interesting and the service professional; poached chicken is $6.50.

On the eastern side of Circular Quay next to Sydney Cove Oyster Bar is *Portobello Caffe* which serves pastries and cakes for $3; it has some outdoor tables.

Restaurants *Doyle's at the Quay* (☎ 9252 3400) is a quality seafood restaurant in the Overseas Passenger Terminal at Circular Quay West. The seafood is good and prices reasonable, with mains from around $20. There's a surcharge of $6 per person on Sunday evenings and public holidays.

Bilson's (☎ 9251 5600), above Doyle's on the top floor of the terminal, is one of Sydney's most highly regarded seafood restaurants but is more formal than Doyle's. Starters are $16 to $24 and most mains cost $26.

There's a collection of restaurants with large outdoor areas and great views overlooking the quay farther north in the renovated Campbell's Storehouse complex. They include *Wolfie's* (☎ 9241 5577), which has seafood starters from $13 to $16 and Tasmanian salmon for $21.95. Others are the similarly priced *Waterfront* (☎ 9247 3666) and *Italian Village* (☎ 9247 6111).

Sydney Cove Oyster Bar (☎ 9247 2937), on the eastern side of Sydney Cove, near the Opera House, offers purely Australian produce including wine. Oysters cost from $18.50 a dozen, with other dishes from $13. It's open daily mid-morning until about 8 pm in winter, until 11 pm or later in summer. It has a surcharge on weekends.

There are three restaurants in the Opera House complex. On the western side the *Concourse* (☎ 9250 7300) is on the lower level where a wall protects you from the breeze. The menu is unadventurous but has mains such as duck from $17.50 to $20. It's open daily from 10 am, but not for dinner on Sunday. The *Harbour* (☎ 9250 7191), on the 'prow' of the Opera House, serves mostly seafood with main courses for around $20.

Upstairs is the classy *Bennelong Restau-*

rant (☎ 9250 7578), where you can expect to pay about $70 for a three-course meal. It's open Monday to Saturday for dinner only.

The Rocks
Here, too, the cafes and restaurants are aimed mainly at tourists but there are some good deals available, especially in the numerous pubs.

Fast Food, Cafes & Pubs There's a small food hall in the *Clocktower Square Shopping Centre*, a modern building on the corner of Harrington and Argyle Sts.

Gum Nut Tea Garden, 28 Harrington St, near Argyle St, is an old house with a courtyard where you can have coffee, cake and light meals for under $10.

Ox on the Rocks (☎ 9247 1920), 135 George St, in a Gothic building with a timber interior, has hamburgers for $6.50 and pasta dishes for $7.90. Upstairs is an à la carte restaurant. *Rock's Cafe*, at No 99, has snacks and light meals (with mains like Thai chicken curry for $15 to $17) from 8 am to 7 pm during the week and until late on Friday and Saturday nights. *G'Day Cafe*, at No 83, north of Argyle St, is similar, but cheaper still, with breakfast and focaccia for $4. It's open from 5.30 am to midnight.

Harbour View Hotel, 18 Lower Fort St, has basic but inexpensive meals; chicken avocado is $9. At the *Hero of Waterloo*, 81 Lower Fort St, you can get moussaka for $9. The *Lord Nelson Brewery Hotel*, 19 Kent St, also does decent pub grub.

Restaurants *Pancakes on the Rocks* (☎ 9247 6371) in Metcalfe Arcade is a member of the Pancake Parlour chain. It has the usual huge menu (pancakes are $13 to $15) and stays open long hours.

Phillip's Foote (☎ 9241 1485), 101 George St, has a pleasant outdoor barbecue area where you can cook your own steak or fish for $16. *Rockpool* (☎ 9252 1888), 109 George St, is one of Sydney's most highly regarded restaurants. It has a modern, stark Art Deco appearance and waiters rush around in white jackets. The seafood is superb. Crab costs $25.

There are two upmarket places on the corner of Cumberland and Essex Sts. *Rocks Teppanyaki* (☎ 9250 6020) is a Japanese restaurant in a painted sandstone building. It serves beef sashimi ($14) as a starter and tenderloin steak ($25) for main course. Next door, *Lilyvale* (☎ 9250 6019), 176 Cumberland St, in a brick building with shuttered windows, serves French/Modern Australian food; mains cost $26 to $29.

Kable's (☎ 9238 0000), at the Regent Hotel, 199 George St, is one of Australia's best restaurants, and the prices reflect this, but there's a three-course lunchtime special for $37.50.

There are several eating places at Pier One on Dawes Point, to the west of the Harbour Bridge. They include *Harbour Watch* (☎ 9241 2217), a seafood restaurant where most mains are $20 to $30. *Harbourside Brasserie* (☎ 9252 3000) nearby is cheaper, with soup for $7.50 and chicken chasseur $14.50. Dramatically situated in a converted warehouse at the end of Pier Four is the smart *Wharf Restaurant* (☎ 9250 1761), which serves modern Australian food for around $35 per person.

Kings Cross & Around

There are plenty of places where you can eat cheaply and watch Kings Cross life go by.

Fast Food & Cafes A great bargain and popular with backpackers are the pizzas available from *Action Pizza* at 72 Darlinghurst Rd (three slices for $1) and *House Kebab*.

Nick's Seafood, on the corner of Darlinghurst Rd, opposite the El Alamein Fountain, is mostly a takeaway but has a small eating area. It serves grilled fish, salad and chips for $5.

A number of cafes serve inexpensive fare on William St, around the corner from the Darlinghurst Rd/Victoria St intersection. You can usually find one offering a full breakfast for under $5. *Williams on William* (☎ 9358 5680), 242 Williams St, has breakfast specials for $3.90, pastas for $5. Across Brougham St is *O'Malley's Hotel*, which serves pasta for $6.

At the *Indian Home Diner*, 173 Darlinghurst Rd, most dishes are under $10.

Waterlily Cafe, 6 Bayswater Rd, has tables outside and large cushions on the seats inside. Pastas are $6.50 to $8.50. Try *Cafe 59*, 59 Bayswater Rd, for a coffee and good but inexpensive focaccia or fish and chips for $5. On Roslyn St the small, intimate *Cafe Cosmic*, at No 7, is good for breakfast; bagels are $5.50.

For cheap Thai food, try *Pad Thai*, 15 Llankelly Place. It's a tiny takeaway with a few tables and serves soups for $5, noodles $7. Opposite, the inexpensive *Yakitori* offers Japanese and Korean dishes for $4 to $5. Near Cafe 59 on Darlinghurst Rd, *Thai-Riffic* is another modestly priced Thai place with seafood dishes for $8.50.

Although a small section of Kellett St is devoted to the red-light trade, once you get to the corner and head toward Ward Ave the street quietens and there are several mid-range places catering to late-night eating and drinking. These include *Cafe Iguana* (☎ 9357 2609) at No 15, where beef or seafood mains cost $15.90, and *Dean's Cafe* (☎ 9368 0953) at No 5. You can sit outside at both. Opposite Cafe Iguana is *Zanzibar* (☎ 9358 3351), 58 Kellett St, a reasonably priced, popular cafe and bar; pasta is $8.

Restaurants One of the cheapest restaurants is the basic, brightly lit and busy *New York Restaurant*, on Kellett St near the corner with Bayswater Rd. It has filling meals for $5 to $7. *Astoria* (☎ 9358 6327), 7 Darlinghurst Rd, is also cheap and a rare, old-fashioned restaurant that serves honest tucker – roast lamb or beef costs $5.30.

Oporto (☎ 9368 0257), 3C Roslyn St, is one of a small chain that specialises in cooking chicken Portuguese style. Chicken burgers cost from $4.60.

There are several popular eateries near the El Alamein Fountain. The main attraction is the window seats or pavement tables where you can watch Kings Cross go by. The expanded *Bourbon & Beefsteak* (☎ 9358 1144), 24 Darlinghurst Rd, is open 24 hours. It serves breakfast all day – beans on toast $6.50, bacon and eggs $9.50 – steaks for $16 to $19, and many other dishes. Next door, the *Fountain Cafe, Restaurant & Bar* (☎ 9358 6009), at No 20, has something for everyone and seems intent on taking over Fitzroy Gardens. Sandwiches are $3.80, garlic steak $14.80.

Back on Kellet St, the mid-range *Lime & Lemon Grass Brasserie* (☎ 9358 5577), at No 42, is a Thai place with good tom yum soup for $12.50, curry mains for $13.50 to $18.

Bayswater Rd has several upmarket eateries. *Bayswater Brasserie* (☎ 9357 2177), 32 Bayswater Rd, is a classy but casual restaurant with excellent service, and if you choose carefully you needn't spend a fortune. Starters (mostly $10.50) include pickled herring, mains ($17.50 to $21.50) include Thai-style chicken.

Potts Point & Woolloomooloo

Victoria St, which leads north from the Kings Cross junction, is in the suburb of Potts Point and has some fashionable cafes and restaurants. There's also a group of more upmarket cafes and restaurants on Macleay St, the extension of Darlinghurst Rd, north of the Cross.

Fast Food, Cafes & Pubs *Harry's Cafe de Wheels*, next to the wharf in Woolloomooloo, has been operating since 1945. It stays open 18 hours a day and serves an assortment of pies and pasties with mushy peas and mashed potatoes.

Joe's Cafe Deluxe, 190 Victoria St near Kings Cross station, has a full breakfast of scrambled eggs, bread, tomatoes and mushrooms for $9.50. This is definitely a place to be seen and it has newspapers and magazines to read. Farther north is *Roy's*, at No 176, a slick Italian-style cafe with huge servings; focaccia is $7.50. It has some vegetarian dishes and is also good for a coffee or meal.

Popular with sailors from the nearby naval base, *Frisco Hotel* in Dowling St, Woolloomooloo, is a pub that's good for meals all day. It has a bistro downstairs and upstairs is a restaurant with a balcony. Spaghetti bolognese is $9.50.

Restaurants On Victoria St, near Roy's, *Out of India* (☎ 9357 7055), at No 178, is a reasonably priced Indian restaurant with three-course meals for $14.90.

Mère Catherine (☎ 9358 3862), 146 Victoria St, is a small, unpretentious French restaurant, serving filling meals for around $25 to $30. It's open Tuesday to Saturday from 7 pm. *Wockpool* (☎ 9368 1771), 155 Victoria St, is a modern restaurant and noodle bar offering delicious Chinese and Malaysian food. Chicken laksa costs $12. It's open daily for dinner only.

On Macleay St, the long-established BYO *Macleay St Bistro* (☎ 9358 4891), at No 73A, has a modern Australian menu with main dishes like roast salmon for $10 to $19. It also has delicious desserts. It's open nightly for dinner and for lunch Friday to Sunday (no bookings). Farther north, and with a similar menu, is the fashionable *Moran's Restaurant & Cafe* (☎ 9356 2223), 61-3 Macleay St. Duck and pea pie is $21.50.

The Pig & the Olive (☎ 9357 3745), 71A Macleay St, its walls decorated in a 'pig' theme, provides delicious pizza (from $11.50) with inventive toppings such as pumpkin, spinach and goat's cheese. It also does tasty pastas.

Darlinghurst & East Sydney

This area has the greatest concentration of cafes and restaurants in Sydney, ranging from the budget to the expensive. In Darlinghurst, most are either on Oxford St or Victoria St. In East Sydney, they're mainly on Stanley St between Riley and Crown Sts and are mostly Italian style.

Fast Food & Cafes The northern end of Victoria St, near Kings Cross, has plenty of cafes and restaurants. Most are trendy and probably won't last long but *Bar Coluzzi*, at No 322, is a caffeine institution. Another stayer is the BYO *Una's Coffee Lounge*

(☎ 9360 6885), 340 Victoria St south of Surry St. This Austrian-style cafe has solid, inexpensive fare and stays open until about 11 pm. Mains cost $7 to $9, breakfast $5.60.

At the busy *Fez Cafe*, 247 Victoria St, the food has a Middle-eastern flavour; couscous is $6.50, chicken dishes around $13.50. You can alse get good coffee.

The *Bandstand Cafe*, in Green Park, has a tranquil setting. It is squeezed into a renovated bandstand and serves coffees, cakes and light meals. Outdoor tables look across Victoria St to St Vincent's Hospital.

Le Petit Creme, 118 Darlinghurst Rd, is a popular Italian-style cafe with some alfresco tables. Breakfasts start from $6.20. The small *Fishface*, 132 Darlinghurst Rd, serves delicious seafood and fills quickly in the evening. Fish and chips cost $8.50.

Dov Cafe, 252 Forbes St, a popular BYO cafe in an old sandstone building, serves delicious Israeli/Mediterranean-inspired food. It has a long list of tasty cold dishes for $8, and good cakes for $4.50. It's also open for breakfast.

In East Sydney, on Stanley St, the ultra-cheap *No Name* is above the Arch Coffee Lounge; there's no sign outside indicating it's there. Go past the pool table and pinball machines at the front to the coffee lounge at the back, then up the stairs. Filling spaghetti meals cost $6. *Bill & Toni*, upstairs at 74 Stanley St, has croissants for $1.60, focaccia with a variety of fillings for $3 to $4.50.

For something more stylish try the licensed mid-range *Cafe Divino* (☎ 9360 9911), 70 Stanley St, where the menu is on blackboards and waiters are dressed in black. Spaghetti with chilli is $8. It also does breakfast. The BYO *Palati Fini* (☎ 9360 9121), at No 80, has similar prices and is popular at dinner time. Scallopine is $15.

The voluminous *Baraza Cafe* (☎ 9380 5197), 91 Riley St, is a casual place to drop in to for a savoury snack like tandoori chicken focaccia for $6.50 or a game of pool.

The atmosphere at the nearby *Hard Rock Cafe* (☎ 9331 1116), 121-129 Crown St, attracts a lot of people. It also has inexpensive food – burger and fries with salad costs

$10.75. The cafe is open daily from noon to at least midnight.

Restaurants *Laurie's Vegetarian Restaurant*, on the corner of Victoria and Burton Sts, is open for lunch and dinner daily. It has great soups for $5 and a tasty menu of vegetarian delights from about $6.50.

The smart Hare Krishna *Govinda's* (☎ 9380 4162), 112 Darlinghurst Rd, serves vegetarian food. It offers a $12.50 all-you-can-eat smorgasbord nightly from 6 to 10.30 pm; admission to the cinema upstairs is included (see Entertainment section).

In East Sydney the excellent, long-standing *Beppi's* (☎ 9360 4558), on the corner of Stanley and Yurong Sts, serves traditional Italian food. Expect to pay about $50 for a three-course meal. *Two Chefs* (☎ 9331 1559), 115 Riley St, is a stylish restaurant with mains at $12 to $20.

The huge *Atlas Bistro & Bar* (☎ 9360 3811), upstairs at 95 Riley St, between Stanley and Williams Sts, has good seafood and other dishes. Tuna steak is $17.50. *The Edge* (☎ 9360 1372), 60 Riley St on the opposite side of the block, is popular with Sydney foodies. It serves modern Australian food and has an outside seating area and bar.

Oxford St & Around

There's a wide variety of eateries along and near Oxford St.

Fast Food, Cafes & Pubs *North Indian Flavour*, 129 Oxford St, and *Tamana's Indian Diner* nearby both offer fast, good-value North Indian and tandoori meals, including their special of rice with three curries for $3.50.

Hanovers, 103 Oxford St between Crown and Riley Sts, has cakes for $6 and good coffee, plus meals. The retro *Roobar*, round the corner on Crown St, is a fine place to escape the hubbub of Oxford St. It serves open sandwiches for $8 and vegetarian burgers for $9. Cool jazz aids the digestion.

The area's prime people-watching spot is *Cafe 191*, on Taylor Square; you can just have a coffee or try its eclectic menu – Thai green curry is $11.90.

Bagel House Cafe, 2 Flinders St south of Taylor Square, is above a bakery which makes 'real' boiled bagels which you can sample for $1.80. Other food is available, including breakfasts. It's open daily, 8 am to 4 pm. The atmosphere is relaxed, the cakes are good and the staff friendly.

Back on Oxford St, *Buzz Cafe*, on the corner of Crown St, serves focaccia for $8.50 and has several computers for surfing the Internet.

Cafe Surreal, 197 Campbell St, is a small, relaxed place, good for a coffee or snack. Also small, the *Maltese Cafe*, 310 Crown St, serves pastas, including ravioli for $3. The bohemian *Mali Cafe*, one of Sydney's tiniest, is farther south on Crown St. It's a fine place for a chat over coffee on the weekend, when it expands onto the pavement with a few upturned milk crates for seating.

Burdekin Hotel, 2 Oxford St, near Hyde Park, has a restaurant upstairs with a varied and fairly pricey menu; soya burger is $8.50.

Restaurants *Betty's Soup Kitchen* (☎ 9360 9368), 269 Crown St between Campbell and Oxford Sts, is better than its name might suggest. It has soup and damper for $4.80 and lamb stew for $8.80.

1 Burton, off Oxford St by Oxford Square, is an Italian restaurant whose address, funnily enough, is 1 Burton St. It has a pleasant outdoor area. Mains cost $10.50 to $16.50. Opposite is the tiny but legendary *Metro Cafe* (☎ 9361 5356), a vegetarian restaurant at 26 Burton St. It's open for dinner Wednesday to Sunday, for lunch Wednesday to Saturday. Main courses cost from $7. You'll have to queue for a table.

Beside Gowings on the corner of Crown St are a couple of mid-range Indian places, including the popular *Tandoori Palace* (☎ 9331 7072) at No 86. Beef Vindaloo is $10.

Atomic Hair (☎ 9360 3746), 137 Oxford St, and *RamBaa* nearby are two recent additions to the strip; the first a brasserie, the latter a restaurant and cocktail bar. Avoid the outdoor tables unless you want to converse with the local drunks.

Along Oxford St, east of Taylor Square, is a clutch of medium-priced restaurants serving cuisine ranging from Cambodian to Californian. The long-established *Balkan* (☎ 9360 4970), 209 Oxford St, specialises in two basic Balkan dishes – raznjici and cevapcici. Ask for a pola-pola ($14.50) and you'll get half of each. The food is filling and definitely for meat eaters. *Kim* (☎ 9380 5429), 235 Oxford St, is a small, popular Vietnamese restaurant with seafood and beef mains for $9 to $13. It's only open for dinner and is closed on Monday and Tuesday.

For a taste of Australian flora and fauna try *Riberries* (☎ 9361 4929), 411 Bourke St, south of Taylor Square. It has an intriguing combination of exotic Australian produce and French cuisine, and a small menu offering four choices per course (including vegetarian). It costs $48 for three courses. It's open for dinner Monday to Saturday and it's a good idea to book; BYO alcohol, but leave your cigarettes at home.

Surry Hills

Surry Hills is an interesting multicultural dining area. Crown St is its main food thoroughfare but it's a long street and cafes and restaurants occur in clusters. The biggest concentration is between Cleveland and Devonshire Sts, both of which also have a number of eateries.

Cafes *Bills 2*, 355 Crown St, is a stylish urban cafe that's not as expensive as it looks; light meals cost around $7.

On the corner of Crown and Devonshire Sts is the vibrant *Rustic Cafe*, which has an extensive, varied menu at reasonable prices; beef vindaloo or gnocchi are $7.90. The *Elephant's Foot*, another bar and cafe across the road, offers pleasant fare including linguine for $11; there are tables outside.

Universal Deli Cafe, 555 Crown St, opposite Thai Orchid, has pumpkin and spinach quiche for $4 and excellent salads, sandwiches and coffee.

West along Devonshire St, *Mohr Fish* at

No 202 is a small but popular designer fish cafe; seafood mains are around $12.

La Passion du Fruit, on the corner of Bourke and Devonshire Sts, is an inexpensive, popular cafe, with snacks like focaccia for around $5.50 and main course dinners $10. It's closed on Monday. *Johnnie's Seafood Cafe*, on Fitzroy St, has grilled fish and chips for $4.

Restaurants *Prasit's Northside Thai* (☎ 9332 1792), 395 Crown St, is a nifty, box-like Thai restaurant with a good reputation, where you can get octopus stir fry for $12. A little south is the larger *Prasit's Northside on Crown* (☎ 9319 0748) at No 413. South again, the spacious *Thai Orchid* (☎ 9698 2097), 628 Crown St, is more upmarket but you can still dine for less than $20; meat mains cost around $10. Nearby, at No 622, is the simpler but busy *Thai Cotton* (☎ 9319 3206).

A group of Lebanese places line Cleveland St between Elizabeth and Wilton Sts. *Abdul's* (☎ 9698 1275) and *Nada's* have been there longest. Abdul's, on the corner of Elizabeth St, is basic, but it's relaxed and friendly. Many dishes are under $8. Most places charge similar prices, including *Fatima's* (☎ 9698 4895) and *Emad's* (☎ 9698 2631), east of Elizabeth St.

Turkish pide (sort of a pizza) is popular along Cleveland St, especially at *Erciyes*, diagonally opposite the junction with Crown St. Almost everything on the menu is $8. *Golden Pide* (☎ 9319 0706), on the corner of Bourke St, is also popular with pide for $6 to $7.

There's a number of inexpensive Indian restaurants on Cleveland St, including *Tandoori Rasoi* (☎ 9310 2470), on the corner of Bourke St. It serves decent Indian meals, such as chicken curry for $7.50. Nepal is represented by the *House of Kathmandu* (☎ 9319 2170); mains such as goat curry are around $10. Kathmandu serves seafood ($12) too – that's not bad for a land-locked country.

L'Aubbergade (☎ 9319 5929), 353 Cleveland St, has been serving good French food

for around 30 years. It has a $20 three-course set menu that's good value. It's open weekdays for lunch and dinner, and Saturday nights.

The Uruguayan *Casapueblo* (☎ 9319 6377), near the corner of Bourke and Cleveland Sts, is one of the few South American restaurants in the city. It's open for dinner from Tuesday to Saturday. Mains like pollo brasil (chicken in coconut sauce) cost $11 to $13.

Paddington

Oxford St continues east from Darlinghurst through Paddington. There are lots of places to eat west of Centennial Square.

Fast Food, Cafes & Pubs *Sloane Rangers*, 312 Oxford St, is a warm, intimate cafe with a large vegetarian selection and a courtyard. Baked potato with cheddar cheese and guacamole is $8.50. The *Golden Dog* (☎ 9360 1397), at No 388, opposite the site of the Saturday's Paddington Village Bazaar, has scrambled egg for $7.

Centennial Park Cafe, a five-minute walk inside the park from the Centennial Square entrance off Oxford St, is good for those who need a touch of the rural. It's a pleasant, open-sided cafe, surrounded by parkland and serves modern Australian lunch mains for around $12 to $15. It's open for breakfast and lunch daily and is busy on weekends.

The *Fringe Bar & Cafe*, on the corner of Oxford and Hopewell Sts, is a spartan, fashionable place in a renovated pub and offers delicious wood-fired pizzas.

At Five Ways (the junction of Glenmore Rd and Goodhope, Heeley and Broughton Sts), there are great views from the iron-lace balcony upstairs at the *Royal Hotel*, 237 Glenmore Rd. Beef curry is $14.80.

Noted for its fine dining, the *Bellevue Hotel*, 159 Hargreave St, is where meat lovers can dine on kangaroo pie for $14.50.

Restaurants There are several good restaurants at Five Ways. The BYO *Creperie Stivell* (☎ 9360 6191), 2B Heeley St, has a pleasant courtyard where you can eat crepes, pannequets and blintzes for $6.50 to $11. It's open for dinner daily from 6 pm and for lunch Wednesday to Sunday. *Paddo Cafe* (☎ 9360 1306), 222 Glenmore Rd, is an Italian-style eatery with pumpkin soup for $5.50 and lasagne for $7; it also does good cakes.

Paddington has a range of fine restaurants, many of them Italian and with long-standing reputations. They include *Darcy's* (☎ 9363 3706), 92 Hargreave St, which serves reputable Italian seafood such as fettucine with salmon for $15. At *Buon Ricordo Ristorante* (☎ 9360 6729), 108 Boundary St, you can enjoy authentic Italian food for around $50. Northern Italian cuisine is on offer at the large *Lucio's* (☎ 9380 5996), 47 Windsor St. Expect to pay around $45. It's open daily for lunch and dinner.

Glebe

Glebe Point Rd was Sydney's original 'eat street' and though it has been left behind by the food innovations sweeping the inner east, it has a laid-back, unfaddish atmosphere and varied food which is good value.

Cafes *Rose Blues Cafe*, 23 Glebe Point Rd near the intersection with Broadway, has a courtyard at the back and a balcony at the front overlooking the street. Lentil soup is $7, pasta dishes $10 to $11. *Badde Manors*, at No 37, is another old favourite, popular with locals and visitors alike. It's a relaxed place, sometimes chaotically so. Salads cost from $5.50, pasta around $7.50. Breakfasts, served 8 to 11.45 am, are popular, especially at weekends.

Farther along, at No 175, the brightly decorated *Caffe 175* has a huge menu which includes lunch specials of tomato and rosemary soup with tea or coffee for $6.

Bogart Pizza Cafe, at No 193 between Bridge and St Johns Rds, is reputed to have the best pizzas ($6 to $16) on the strip, and also does pasta. It's open from 5 pm.

Despite Glebe's 'students and bohemians' tag, many eateries have edged into higher price brackets, so it's good to see that *The Craven*, next door to the Valhalla Cinema,

remains a good, inexpensive place for a coffee or meal. Salads cost about $7.50 and other dishes are under $10. Most nights it's open until 10.30 pm.

Well Connected (☎ 9566 2655), 35 Glebe Point Rd, offers coffee, a modern Australian menu and access to the Internet, with two floors of terminals.

There are many places along Glebe Point Rd where counting calories would spoil the fun. Most cafes have a great selection of cakes and desserts and the *Pudding Shop*, at No 144B, is another source of the sweet and sticky; it also has hot pies.

Restaurants For tapas such as king prawns cooked with chilli and ginger and costing $6.80 to $10.80, try *A Different Drummer* (☎ 9552 3406), at No 185 Glebe Point Rd. It's open for dinner only and is closed on Monday.

Thai Intra (☎ 9660 4149), 207 Glebe Point Rd, is a fairly large, licensed Thai restaurant in a pleasantly decorated old house. The MSG-free food is good. Most mains are under $11.

Several Asian places offer excellent value. *Lien* (☎ 9566 4385), at No 331, provides Thai, Malaysian and Vietnamese food. It has vegetable dishes for $6.20, seafood for $9.50. More expensive is the nearby *Lilac Restaurant* (☎ 9660 5192), at No 333, which serves Chinese, Malaysian and Indonesian food. Beef mains cost $7.80 to $11.50; there's a good vegetarian selection.

Yak & Yeti (☎ 9552 1220), at No 41, is a Nepalese eatery with vegetable dishes for around $8.90, meat ones for $12 to $15.

Flavour of India (☎ 9692 0062) is at No142A. Starters like chicken tikka (chicken marinated in yoghurt and spices and grilled in the tandoor oven) are $5.50 to $7.50. It also has a good vegetarian selection.

The least expensive pizzas ($6 to $17) in the area are available from *Perry's Gourmet Pizzas* (☎ 9660 8440), at No 381, another block north.

Balmain

In Sydney's inner west, Balmain has some

good eating places. Because much of their trade is local, the service is usually friendly and the standards consistent. Most are on Darling St, a good place to visit at night. You can get here by ferry from Circular Quay or bus Nos 441, 442, 445 and 446.

Near the Darling St wharf, *Pelicans Fine Foods*, 81 Darling St, is open for breakfast and for snacks (including bagels, home-made pies and soups) during the day. At No 79, *Reveille* (☎ 9555 8874) has a short but select modern Australian menu and a select clientele. It opens at 7 pm and is closed Sundays. Fillet of beef is $19.

Sausolito (☎ 9810 9521), 246 Darling St, is open for lunch and dinner daily and serves modern Italian and Mediterranean cuisine; linguine or focaccia is $7.50. *La Lupa* (☎ 9818 1645), at No 332, is an Italian trattoria behind the Institute Arcade. Go through the main entrance to the arcade to the back or take the small alley to the left. Main courses, mostly chicken or fish, cost $14.50 to $17.

Jiyu No Omise (☎ 9818 3886), at No 342, offers Japanese food and is open for dinner. Teriyaki steak is $15.90. Next door, *The Totem*, at No 338-40, is a large restaurant and cafe which serves creole and cajun food. It has a 1st-floor balcony where you can eat and view the street below. Cajun steak is $16.

Word of Mouth (☎ 9810 8708), 493A Darling St, opposite the Cat & Fiddle Hotel, features a varied menu; pastas are $13, Bengal fish curry $13.95.

Leichhardt

Leichhardt, another interesting culinary centre in Sydney's inner west, has a reputation for Italian food. You'll find most cafes and restaurants on Norton St, which gets busy on weekend nights. Norton St is a short ride from George St on bus No 438 or 440.

Bar Italia (☎ 9560 9981), 169-71 Norton St, is an enormously popular restaurant, cafe and gelateria. It offers moderately priced pastas for $6.50 to $7.50 but one of its biggest drawcards is the delicious gelato, which costs from $2.50. Nearby, *Cafe Barzu*

(☎ 9550 0144) does excellent pizzas for $8.50 to $12.

On the other side of the road, the popular *Portofino's* (☎ 9550 0782), at No 166, is a cafe and bar with a large, diverse Italian menu. Pastas are around $10, seafood $15. The small *Mezzapica* (☎ 9568 2095), at No 128 on the corner of Macauley St, is also popular.

At the Parramatta Rd end, *Bar Baba* (☎ 9564 2044), 41 Norton St, is a pleasant, friendly Italian cafe and restaurant with good food. Gnocchi is $9, barbecued octopus $15. It's also good for breakfasts.

Newtown

Newtown's long King St has a huge range of eateries, many budget-priced. You'll find plenty of places which serve ethnic cuisine, from African to Vietnamese. They offer an interesting introduction to the suburb's community life.

Fast Food & Cafes The cheapest place to eat is the *Hare Krishna Centre* near the railway station (turn left as you come out), but it's only open weekdays 11 am to 3 pm, Saturday 5.30 to 7.30 pm. Sydney's Indian fast-food phenomenon is represented by *Tamana's Indian Diner*, which has two places on King St offering three curries with rice for $4.90.

At the convivial *Green Iguana Cafe*, which is at 6 King St (☎ 9516 3118), at the eastern end near the intersection with Darlington Rd, breakfast costs $6.50, spinach and mushroom flan $7.50. The noticeboard provides information on Newtown activities. *Hard Nox Cafe* (☎ 9550 1106), at No 45 a bit farther west on the other side of King St, is a reasonably priced vegetarian and seafood place. Vegetable curry is $5.80.

Restaurants *Le Kilimanjaro* (☎ 9557 4565) at 280 King St, is a bustling, East African restaurant with a high turnover. Coulombe (a Sudanese dip containing eggplants and peanuts) costs $4.50, mains are $7.50.

Ristorante Roman Latin, 111 King St, between Missenden Rd and tiny Elizabeth

MARK KIRBY

RICHARD NEBESKY

RICHARD NEBESKY

DAVID COLLINS

RICHARD I'ANSON

TOM SMALLMAN

A	B
C	D
E	F

Sydney

A: Sydney Harbour Bridge
B: Sailing past the Opera House
C: Surfing at Bondi Beach

D: Justice & Police Museum
E: Sydney Town Hall
F: Monorail, Liverpool Street

Sydney
Top: Sydney Harbour Bridge at sunset
Bottom: Sydney Harbour & the Opera House

St, is a mid-range Italian place with calamari for $10. It's open for dinner daily, for lunch Wednesday to Friday.

The Fish Tank (☎ 9557 5627), 119 King St, is a recommended upmarket seafood restaurant. Expect to pay around $35. Next door at No 115-117, *Ban Thai* (☎ 9519 5330) offers good Thai curries and vegetarian dishes.

Back at the Ranch (☎ 9519 7869), 175 King St on the corner of O'Connell St, is a Tex-Mex restaurant that's good value at lunchtime when meals cost almost half what they cost in the evening – enchiladas and burritos are $6.20.

Double Bay
This exclusive neighbourhood has some excellent places to eat, many on and around Bay St.

Peron's Health Cafe, 42 Bay St, is part of the Cosmopolitan shopping centre and has delicious salads and snacks. The nearby *Courtyard Cafe*, at No 37, serves good pasta dishes; fettucine with mushrooms in tomato sauce is $7.90. One of the city's top Italian restaurants is *Botticelli* (☎ 9363 3266), 21 Bay St where pasta mains are $10.50 to $15.50. It's a good place for a romantic dinner and is where former Australian prime minister Bob Hawke and his biographer Blanche d'Alpuget celebrated their nuptials.

Taste of India (☎ 9327 5712), 370 New South Rd near Knox St, is one of the best Indian restaurants in Sydney. Samosas are $5.50, mango chicken $13.50.

Bondi Beach & Around
Campbell Parade is one long string of takeaways, cafes and restaurants, many with sea views. Hall St, leading away from the beach, also has some interesting places.

Cafes The good-value *Gusto*, 16 Hall St near the corner of Jacques Ave, is a popular little deli. It has seating which faces the street and you can eat healthy snacks at fairly low prices; focaccia is $6.

Beneath the Swiss Grand Hotel, the wonderfully named *Hog's Breath Cafe*, on Campbell Parade, is part of a small chain selling reasonably priced food and drink. Chicken burgers are $7.95.

There's a strip of trendy cafe-bars at the southern end of the beach. Most have outdoor seating, ocean views and bistro fare influenced by the Mediterranean. At the reasonably priced *Lamrock Cafe*, at No 72, risotto or a vegetarian burger costs $9.80. *Hugo's Bondi Cafe*, at No 70, near Lamrock Ave, is stark, modern and a little more expensive, but it's a good place to show off your shades. Ravioli is $19.

Restaurants In North Bondi, the *RSL Club*, on Ramsgate Ave, has lunch specials for $3 and at the *Bondi Noodle House*, beside the bus terminal, most meals are under $7.

Yummy Thai, at the southern end of the parade, near the Thelellen Beach Inn, is a tiny place which sells inexpensive eat-in or takeaway dishes. Green curry is $7. Farther north is *Astra* (☎ 9130 5227), near the corner of Sir Thomas Mitchell Rd. It's modern, has brightly coloured paintings on the walls and a varied menu. Cajun chicken is $14. Next door, the popular *Bondi Trattoria* (☎ 9365 4303) has breakfast specials for $8.50.

Good-value Middle Eastern fare can be found at *Avivim* (☎ 9130 8302), 49 Hall St. It's BYO, but your wine must be kosher – luckily there's a deli selling kosher wine a block or so up Hall St. Grilled fish is $15.50.

There are a couple of good restaurants back towards the city. About 1km inland is *Indochine* (☎ 9387 4081) at 99 Bondi Rd, a popular Vietnamese restaurant serving braised pork for $9.80. At Bondi Junction, head for *Sennin* (☎ 9389 8081), 288 Oxford St. It has an attractive variety of meals. Antipasto is $8.90, cashew curry $12.90.

Coogee
Fast Food & Cafes There are numerous takeaways on Coogee Bay Rd which offer cheap eats, but you're better off hitting the cafes, which have healthier food, sunnier demeanours and outdoor tables. *Cafe Congo* on Arden St, north of Coogee Bay Rd, is popular, colourful and inexpensive. There's

nothing African about its menu, which is mostly Italian with a mix of Mexican. Nachos are $7, lasagne $8. The nearby *La Casa* is similarly priced with spaghetti or fish and chips for $7.

There are several bright, pleasant places on Coogee Bay Rd which serve standard cafe fare between $5 and $11, including *Coogee Cafe* at No 221 and *Cafe 242* at No 242.

Restaurants *Renato's* at 237 Coogee Bay Rd is a busy Italian restaurant which has good pastas for $7 to $8. Nearby at No 240 is *Erciyes 2*, an offshoot of the popular Erciyes Turkish restaurant in Surry Hills. The food is tasty and inexpensive with nothing over $8; doner kebabs are $7.

At the northern end of the beach, on Dolphin St, the Beach Palace Hotel has a couple of restaurants. *Seranata* has roast specials with five vegies for $7. On the 1st floor, the large *China Bowl* (☎ 9665 3308) is an upmarket Chinese restaurant specialising in seafood. Lobster goes for $18.80.

Nearby, *Fisherman's Net* (☎ 9665 5549), on the 1st floor of the Coogee Sands Motor Inn, has a three-course deal for $25.

Watsons Bay

The long-established *Doyle's on the Beach* (☎ 9337 2007), 11 Marine Parade, Watsons Bay, specialises in seafood, and main courses average around $25. Bookings are advisable. Next door at *Doyle's Watsons Bay*

Fish n' ships: Doyle's on the Beach, Watsons Bay

Hotel, which shares the fabulous view, there are cheaper bistro meals (Wednesday to Sunday nights); smoked Tasmanian salmon is $11.30.

Doyle's Wharf Restaurant (☎ 9337 1572) is nearby on Watsons Bay wharf. It's open daily for lunch, Wednesday to Saturday for dinner. Lobster is $35.

On the other side of Robertson Park in the beautiful, old Dunbar House, *Fisherman's Lodge* (☎ 9337 1226) is less expensive with John Dory fillets for $22.50.

Getting There & Away On weekday lunchtimes you can catch Doyle's own water taxi from the Harbour Master's Steps on the western side of Circular Quay. The taxi costs $4/7 one way/return, and services start at 11.30 am. An ordinary water taxi costs about $50 between four people. Ferries run from Circular Quay to Watsons Bay on weekends, but not frequently, and only until 3.45 pm. Bus Nos 324 and 325 run here from Circular Quay.

North Shore

Crows Nest Crows Nest, north-west of North Sydney, has many popular eating places. Most are on or near the three-way intersection of the Pacific Highway, Falcon St and Willoughby Rd.

At the *Wood Fire Pizza Company* (☎ 9439 3113), 308 Pacific Highway, the dish comes as close as it can to being a health food. The pizzas aren't cheap ($13.90 to $16) but the quality is good. West of the junction at 318 Pacific Highway is the *Afghan Authentic Restaurant* (☎ 9438 3592), which has lamb and beef mains for $11.90. It's open for dinner only and is closed on Sunday.

Along Willoughby Rd, a busy shopping precinct, try the *Blue Elephant* (☎ 9439 3468), upstairs at 36-38 Willoughby Rd; it has Sri Lankan food for around $10 but is closed on Sunday and Monday. *Talay Thai* (☎ 9906 3535), at No 88, has stir-fried dishes for $8 to $10.50; there are outside tables and it's open daily for dinner, Monday to Friday for lunch.

Borderland (☎ 9436 3918), at No 97, is a

Mexican restaurant with lunchtime specials for $5. The crowded *Ten-Sun* (☎ 9906 2956), at No 103 north of Albany St, is a Japanese noodles bar where meals are under $10.

A block west, Alexander St also has some good restaurants, including the large *Rangoon Racquet Club Restaurant* (☎ 9906 4091). It doesn't serve Burmese food, but the 'aromatic cuisine of British colonial India'. 'Elephant-boy curry' (beef marinated in a spicy sauce) is $14.95. It's open daily for dinner, Monday to Friday for lunch.

Across the road at No 57, *Montezuma's* (☎ 9901 3533), is a Mexican restaurant that's part of a chain and is open daily. Nachos cost $5.95 to $7.50, beef enchiladas $13.95.

North Sydney *North Sydney Noodle Market* (☎ 9417 3256) is a praiseworthy attempt to capture the atmosphere of Asian street-food markets. It's held in the park near the corner of Miller and McLaren Sts on Friday nights from 5.30 pm during the warmer months, Sunday lunchtimes from 11.30 am during winter. The numerous stalls serve Chinese, Indian, Malaysian, Nepalese and Vietnamese food.

Prasit's Northside Thai (☎ 9957 2271), in Mount St, on the corner of Elizabeth Plaza, is a good Thai restaurant and bar with spiced fish cakes for $7.50. It's open for lunch Monday to Friday, for dinner Tuesday to Saturday.

Balmoral In the quiet suburb of Balmoral, you'll find a number of good restaurants on East Esplanade, most with good views across the harbour.

Between Raglan St and Botanic Rd are some inexpensive cafes, including *Sam's Espresso Bar* which has filling sandwiches and rolls for $3 to $4. Nearby, *Bottom of the Harbour*, at No 21, has some of the best fish and chips ($5.50) in Sydney.

Two restaurants have prime locations on the foreshore itself – and prices to match. *Bathers Pavilion* (☎ 9968 1133), opposite No 59, is in a beautiful old building with views of North Head. Snapper costs $24.

Watermark (☎ 9968 3433), 2A East Espla-

nade at the junction with Botanic Rd, is a little more expensive but has views across to Manly. Queensland sea scallops are $17.90. It's open for breakfast, lunch and dinner.

Manly
Fast Food & Cafes You don't have to go any farther than the wharf to find eateries, many costing $4 to $7. The Corso is jammed with places to eat, and there are others along North and South Steyne.

Next to the Le Kiosk Restaurant on Shelly Beach east of the main beach is *Shelly Beach Kiosk*, where you can get sandwiches for $3.50 and ice creams.

Cafe Steyne, 14 South Steyne, has popular outdoor tables. It serves everything from daiquiris to melts, though an average dish on the large menu is pasta for $7 to $9. *Cafe Tunis*, on South Steyne, has good coffee and interesting food. Pita bread rolls with a choice of fillings are $9.50.

The *BarKing Frog*, 48 North Steyne, is a fashionable bar and cafe with starters like baked bruschetta for $9.50 and mains from $13.50.

Restaurants For a reasonably priced Thai meal, try *Wi Marn* (☎ 9976 2995), 47 North Steyne, which has starters for $5.50 and seafood dishes from $14. It doesn't use MSG. *Lui's* (☎ 9976 2111), 44 North Steyne, is a licensed Italian eatery with excellent pizzas from a wood-fired oven, and other Italian dishes for around $13. Next door is a seafood specialist, *Fishmongers* (☎ 9977 7513), with mains from $10 to $12.

Follow the foreshore path east from the main ocean beach to reach the small *Bower Restaurant* (☎ 9977 5451), 7 Marine Parade, pleasantly situated on Fairy Bower Beach. It has snacks and coffees, as well as main courses of modern Australian food for around $16. It's BYO and opens for breakfast and lunch daily. Farther around at Shelly Beach is the upmarket *Le Kiosk Restaurant* (☎ 9977 4122), 1 Marine Parade, which serves mostly Asian-influenced seafood. Expect to pay about $50.

The *Malacca Straits Satay Restaurant*

SYDNEY

(☎ 9977 6627), 49 Sydney Rd, has a good reputation and features reasonably priced Malay and Thai dishes. Main courses cost $7 to $13.

There's a seafood buffet at the *Manly Pacific Parkroyal Hotel*, on North Steyne, on Friday and Saturday nights for $29.50, or a champagne and jazz lunch on Sunday for $22.50.

On Manly Wharf, *Armstrong's* (☎ 9976 3835), at the western end, has a good reputation for modern Australian food, with the emphasis on seafood. Malaysian-style seafood curry is $19.90.

ENTERTAINMENT

The *Sydney Morning Herald*'s 'Metro' section, published on Fridays, lists most events in town during the week. For specialised music listings pick up one of the free weekly papers available around town such as *On the Street*, *Drum Media* or *Beat*.

Ticketek (☎ 9266 4800), 195 Elizabeth St, is the city's main booking agency for theatre, concerts, sports and other events. Phone bookings can be made weekdays from 9 am to 5 pm, Saturday noon to 4 pm. It also has agencies around town.

Halftix (☎ 0055 26655) sells half-price (or thereabouts) tickets to performances from a booth on Martin Place near Elizabeth St. It only sells tickets to that evening's performances and you can call after 11 am or check the posted list from noon to find out which shows have tickets available. The booth is also a Ticketek agency so if you miss out on cheap seats you can always buy full-price ones. Halftix is open weekdays from noon to 5.30 pm, Saturday noon to 5 pm.

Performing Arts

Sydney Opera House (☎ 9250 7111, 9250 7777 for bookings) is the performing arts centre of Sydney. The Australian Opera, Australian Ballet, Sydney Symphony Orchestra, Sydney Philharmonia Choir, Musica Viva Australia and the Sydney Theatre Company (see Theatre below) provide regular performances here.

For more information on companies' programmes contact:

Australian Ballet
    Level 15, 115 Pitt St (☎ 9223 9522)
Australian Opera
    480 Elizabeth St, Surry Hills (☎ 9319 1088)
Musica Viva Australia
    120 Chalmers St, Surry Hills (☎ 9698 1711)
Sydney Dance Company
    Pier Four, Hickson Rd, Millers Point (☎ 9221 4811)
Sydney Philharmonia Choir
    Pier Four, Hickson Rd, Millers Point (☎ 9251 2024)
Sydney Symphony Orchestra
    52 William St, East Sydney (☎ 9334 4644)

Aboriginal Performance You can see Aboriginal dancing, performed by the renowned *Bangarra Dance Theatre* (☎ 9569 4555), 40-76 William St, Leichhardt; the *Aboriginal Dance Theatre* (☎ 9699 2171), 88 Renwick St, Redfern, and the *Aboriginal Islander Dance Theatre* (☎ 9252 0199), Bond Store, 3 Windmill St, Millers Point.

At Darling Harbour in Harbourside, *Gavala* (☎ 9212 7232) presents the Doonooch Aboriginal dancers who perform traditional dances, play didgeridoos and recount stories on Friday and Saturday at 2 pm. Entry is $10.

Theatre

Sydney has numerous theatres and a vigorous calendar of productions.

The *Sydney Opera House* (☎ 9250 7111, 9250 7777 for bookings) has two theatres: the *Drama Theatre* regularly puts on plays by the Sydney Theatre Company, and the offerings at the *Playhouse* range from Aboriginal performances to Shakespeare. The Sydney Theatre Company is the city's top theatre company and has its own venue at the *Wharf Theatre* (☎ 9250 1777), Pier Four, Hickson Rd, Millers Point.

Major commercial theatres are the restored *Capitol Theatre* (☎ 9320 9122), 17 Campbell St, Haymarket; *Her Majesty's Theatre* (☎ 9212 3411), 107 Quay St near Railway Square; and the *Theatre Royal* (☎ 9320 9111) in the MLC Centre on King

St. A sight in itself is the wonderfully opulent *State Theatre* (☎ 9373 6655), 49 Market St between Pitt and George Sts – they don't make them like this any more! These theatres are often the venues for imported big-budget productions.

On North Shore, the small *Ensemble Theatre* (☎ 9929 0644), 78 McDougall St, Milsons Point, presents mainstream theatre in a great setting on the waterfront.

The *National Institute of Dramatic Art* (NIDA) (☎ 9697 7600), 215 Anzac Parade, Kensington, at the University of NSW, regularly stages excellent productions by its drama students. At the University of Sydney, the *Footbridge Theatre* (☎ 9320 9000), Parramatta Rd, Glebe, is also worth keeping an eye on.

The *Seymour Theatre Centre* (☎ 9364 9444), on the corner of Cleveland St and City Rd, Chippendale (near the University of Sydney), houses three theatres offering a variety of performances.

In experimental drama, the *Belvoir Street Theatre* (☎ 9699 3444), 25 Belvoir St, Surry Hills, and *Stables Theatre* (☎ 9361 3817), 10 Nimrod St, Kings Cross, feature interesting original Australian works. Although it has been around a long time, the *New Theatre* (☎ 9519 3403), 542 King St, Newtown, produces cutting-edge drama as well as traditional pieces.

Music & Dancing

Sydney doesn't have a dynamic pub music scene but there are enough pubs and plenty of clubs where you can hear something most nights. Five-star hotels often have famous cabaret artists. A few of the many venues are listed here; many places listed under Pubs & Bars also provide musical entertainment.

The Basement, 29 Reiby Place, Circular Quay – good food, good jazz, sometimes big international names (☎ 9251 2797)

The Bridge, 135 Victoria Rd, Rozelle – rock, sometimes big Aussie names, and DJs (☎ 9860 1260)

Cat & Fiddle Hotel, 456 Darling St, Balmain – jazz, R&B, usually Friday to Sunday nights (☎ 9810 7931)

DCM, 33 Oxford St, Darlinghurst – a big gay disco (☎ 9267 7380)

Golden Sheaf Hotel, 429 New South Head Rd, Double Bay – pub with free bands, good food, popular with travellers (☎ 9327 5877)

Grand Hotel, 89 Ebley St, Bondi Junction – several bars, bands (sometimes rock, sometimes Irish) or disco most nights (☎ 9389 3004)

Hopetoun Hotel, 416 Bourke St, Surry Hills – live music Wednesday to Saturday nights, comedy nights, small beer garden (☎ 9361 5257)

Kinselas, 383 Bourke St, Darlinghurst – a large venue with a cafe and bar downstairs and a nightclub upstairs; prices depend on who's playing on which level on which day of the week; worth checking out (☎ 9331 3299)

Lansdowne Hotel, 2 City Rd, Chippendale – lively young bands most nights (☎ 9211 2325)

Midnight Shift, 85-91 Oxford St, Darlinghurst – a popular gay nightclub that opens at 9 pm; it has a big dance floor and great lighting (☎ 9360 4319)

Mister GoodBar, 11 Oxford St, Paddington – popular dance club

Rose, Shamrock & Thistle Hotel, 'The Three Weeds', 193 Evans St on the corner of Belmore St, Rozelle – rock music (sometimes big names) plus jazz and folk (☎ 9810 2244)

Sandringham Hotel, 387 King St, Newtown – young bands most nights (☎ 9557 1254)

Selina's (in the Coogee Bay Hotel), Coogee Bay Rd, Coogee – rock, often top Australian bands, for which you can pay over $20; main nights Friday and Saturday, but cheaper bands most other nights (☎ 9665 0000)

Sight & Soho Lounge Bar, 171 Victoria St, Potts Point – dance club, funk, hip-hop, soul, from 9 pm, free (☎ 9358 4221)

Strawberry Hills Hotel, 453 Elizabeth St, Surry Hills – jazz most nights (☎ 9698 2997)

Pubs & Bars

Pubs and bars are an important part of Sydney's social scene. Many have a totally different atmosphere during the week from on weekends when the hordes are out on the town.

The Rocks & Circular Quay There are some nice old pubs in the Rocks. The *Fortune of War*, 137 George St, opposite the back of the Museum of Contemporary Art, claims to hold Sydney's oldest hotel licence – but a couple of other old pubs in nearby Millers Point make similar claims.

The *Hero of Waterloo*, 81 Lower Fort St

on the corner of Windmill St, and the *Lord Nelson Brewery Hotel*, 19 Kent St, both in Millers Point, are probably Sydney's best-known pubs and two of its busiest. They both vie for the title of Sydney's oldest pub. This isn't *quite* the same as claiming to have the oldest licence – other pubs lay claim to the title of 'oldest continuously operating pub'. The Hero of Waterloo has music on weekends, including traditional Irish music on Sunday nights, and the Lord Nelson brews its own beer.

One of Sydney's best places for a Guinness and live Irish music, rock or jazz is the *Mercantile Hotel*, 25 George St, near the bridge.

In the Opera House, the *Mozart Bar* near the box office is open before and after performances – it's intended for patrons so you might stand out without evening wear. *Legends*, on Bligh St beneath the Wentworth Hotel, is another upmarket bar, which sometimes has live entertainment.

City Centre A must for most visitors is the ornate *Marble Bar*, 259 Pitt St, underneath the Royal Arcade and Hilton Hotel; it has live music some nights, including blues and jazz.

Two contrasting pubs face each other on the corners of York and King Sts – the traditional *Forbes Hotel* and the trendy Art Deco *CBD Hotel*. Both are popular with office and shop workers.

The *Criterion Hotel*, on the corner of Pitt and Park Sts, has a basement bar open 24 hours. *Scruffy Murphy's*, 43 Goulburn St, near the corner of George St, is popular with young people, serves good Guinness and has music Tuesday to Sunday night.

Darling Harbour & Pyrmont *Craig Bar & Grill* in Harbourside offers $1 schooners of beer on Saturday from 8 to 9 pm. It's popular with backpackers, has good views of the harbour and often has entertainment of the fake-Elvis/Madonna variety. For real ale fans a good option is the *Pumphouse Tavern Brewery* near the Sydney Entertainment Centre.

Pyrmont Bridge Hotel, 96 Union St near Pyrmont Bridge, is pleasantly unpretentious beside the Darling Harbour and Sydney Harbour Casino glitz.

Kings Cross & Around Kings Cross and surrounding areas have plenty of places where you can go for a drink. The huge *Kings Cross Hotel* is recommended by many travellers as a reasonable place for a night out. More expensive places in the Cross include *Cafe Iguana* and *Dean's Cafe*, on Kellett St. Both have front courtyards.

The *Old Fitzroy Hotel* (☎ 9356 3848), on the corner of Cathedral and Dowling Sts in Woolloomooloo, is frequent by British backpackers and has music some nights. The *Woolloomooloo Bay Hotel*, 2 Bourke St, is popular at weekends both lunchtime and evenings.

Another popular place for a drink is the *Darlo Bar*, which takes up its own tiny block on the corner of Darlinghurst and Liverpool Sts. It's an interesting neighbourhood pub – this must be the narrowest in Sydney. Good food and cocktails are available (along with beer, of course) and the service is friendly.

Oxford St & Around A number of good pubs line Oxford St. These include the *Burdekin Hotel*, at No 2, which has a cafe and a stylish cocktail bar downstairs. The *Lizard Lounge* at the Exchange Hotel, 34 Oxford St, is a casual bar popular with lesbians and has house and garage music, bands and DJs nightly. Further east is the discreet *Q Cafe Bar*, 44 Oxford St, a cavernous bar and pool hall above Central Station Records.

On the other side of Taylor Square the *Albury Hotel*, 6 Oxford St in Paddington, is a gay pub which often has good entertainment. Other gay pubs in the area include the *Beauchamp Hotel*, on the corner of Oxford and South Dowling Sts; the *Flinders Hotel*, 63 Flinders St; and the *Beresford Hotel*, 354 Bourke St.

Lively pubs for twenty-somethings include the *Fringe Bar Cafe*, 106 Oxford St, near the Victoria Barracks, and the *Palace Hotel*, 122 Flinders St at the junction with South Dowling St.

Glebe The *Friend in Hand Hotel*, 58 Cowper St, full of old photos and bric-a-brac, has a reputation as a party pub. It stages events such as crab racing, has music on weekends and generous and frequent discounts on drinks and food. Glebe's other popular pub, the *Harold Park Hotel*, 115 Wigram Rd, also has a packed entertainment programme including regular comedy acts Thursday to Saturday; live bands perform at other times. It also has a sunny courtyard-cum-beer garden.

Surry Hills The *Cricketers Arms*, 106 Fitzroy St, Surry Hills, is popular with locals and British backpackers. In Woollahra, the *Lord Dudley Hotel*, on Jersey Rd, is as close as Sydney gets to an English pub atmosphere.

The *Dolphin Hotel*, 412 Crown St on the corner of Fitzroy St, is good for a quiet drink or a meal in the restaurant at the back. The *Bentley Bar*, 320 Crown St on the corner of Campbell St, is popular with young people.

Newtown The trendy *Bank Hotel*, 324 King St, has a beer garden and is a popular lesbian hangout. Another pub with a beer garden is the *Iron Duke Hotel*, on the corner of Botany and McEvoy Rds. The busy *Botany View Hotel*, 597 King St, serves decent Guinness and Cooper's ale on tap. The *Marlborough Hotel*, 145 King St, has live music Thursday to Saturday and a trivia quiz on Wednesday night.

Cinema

There's a cluster of mainstream multi-screen cinemas on George St, south of Town Hall between Bathurst and Liverpool Sts. New releases at these major cinemas cost a pricey $12.50, but they're cheaper on Tuesday.

One cinema that shows mainstream films but is inexpensive all the time is the *Ritz Theatre* (☎ 9399 9840), 43 St Pauls St, Randwick (not far from Coogee). It charges $7 ($4 children) daily.

For more unusual fare, try the independent *Dendy* (9264 1577), 624 George St (opposite the cinema complexes), which shows alter-

native as well as commercial films. It has other cinemas around town: at 19 Martin Place on the corner of Castlereagh St (☎ 9233 8166); and 261 King St (☎ 9550 5699) in Newtown (turn right out of the train station). Tickets are $11.50, cheaper on Tuesday.

Other cinemas showing foreign and alternative films are:

Academy Twin
  3A Oxford St on the corner of South Dowling St, Paddington (☎ 9361 4453)
Hayden Orpheum Picture Palace
  On Military Rd at the junction of Cremorne Rd, Cremorne – a fabulous Art Deco gem (☎ 9908 4344)
Third Eye Cinema
  64 Devonshire St, Surry Hills (☎ 9281 1191)
Valhalla Cinema
  166 Glebe Point Rd, Glebe (☎ 9660 8050)
Verona Cinema
  Upstairs at 17 Oxford St, Paddington – has an excellent Art Deco cafe and bar (☎ 9360 6099)
Walker Cinema
  121 Walker St, North Sydney (☎ 9959 4222)

In Darlinghurst, south of Kings Cross, the *Movie Room* (☎ 9380 5162), above Govinda's restaurant at 112 Darlinghurst Rd, shows mainstream blockbusters, art-house fare and old favourites. Admission costs $13.50 but includes an all-you-can-eat smorgasbord at Govinda's. Films screen nightly at 7 and 9.15 pm. Govinda's opens from 5.30 pm.

The Australian Film Institute (AFI; ☎ 9332 2111) screens interesting new work and classics at the *Sydney Film Centre/ Chauvel Cinemas* (☎ 9361 5398) in Paddington Town Hall on the corner of Oxford St and Oatley Rd.

The *State Theatre* (☎ 9373 6655), 49 Market St between Pitt and George Sts, is the main venue for the Sydney Film Festival in June.

RSL & Leagues Clubs

A lot of evening entertainment in Sydney takes place in Returned Services League (RSL) and football leagues clubs. Profits from poker machines – 'pokies' – enable the clubs to put on subsidised entertainment. This can include big-name acts (from old crooners to decent Australian rock), dance halls, snooker rooms and even cinemas.

The clubs may be 'members only' for locals but as an interstate or international visitor you would generally be welcome. Simply ring ahead and ask, then wave your interstate driving licence or passport at the door. The most lavish club is the *St George Leagues Club* (☎ 9587 1022), 124 Princes Highway, Kogarah. More centrally, there's the *City of Sydney RSL & Community Club* (☎ 9264 6281), 565 George St; the *South Sydney Leagues Club* (☎ 9319 4156), 263 Chalmers St, Redfern; *Balmain Leagues Club* (☎ 9555 1650), 138 Victoria Rd, Rozelle; or the *Sydney Aussie Rules Social Club* (☎ 9358 3055), 28 Darlinghurst Rd, Kings Cross.

Comedy

Sydney has several venues where comedy acts are performed regularly. The *Comedy Store* (☎ 9564 3900), 450 Parramatta Rd on the corner of Crystal St in Petersham, is open Tuesday to Saturday. Tuesday, when new comics try out, is the cheapest night.

Harold Park Hotel (☎ 9692 0564), 115 Wigram Rd, Glebe, describes itself as the 'Comedy Hotel' and provides regular stand-up comedy acts Thursday to Saturday.

Aussie comedian Austen Tayshus hosts comedy shows on Friday and Saturday nights at the *Double Bay Comedy Club* (☎ 9327 6560), 16 Cross St, Double Bay.

Gambling

Australians love to gamble and Sydney provides plenty of opportunity for punters to be separated from their money.

Sydney Harbour Casino A huge casino, theatre, restaurant and hotel complex is being built on the waterfront in Pyrmont on the north-eastern headland of Darling Harbour. It's scheduled to open in 1998. In the meantime, a temporary casino operates at wharves 12 and 13, beside Pyrmont Bay. For information call ☎ 1300 300 711.

Horse & Greyhound Racing Sydney has four horse-racing venues. These are:

Canterbury Park
    King St, Canterbury, south-west of the city centre (☎ 9930 4000)
Rosehill Gardens
    Grand Ave, Rosehill, near Parramatta (☎ 9930 4070)
Royal Randwick
    Alison Rd, Randwick, closest to the city, near Centennial Park (☎ 9663 8400)
Warwick Farm
    Hume Highway, Rosehill, near Liverpool (☎ 9602 6199)

Horse races are held alternately at these tracks throughout the year. But the most colourful and exciting time is during the spring and autumn carnivals, when major events like the Golden Slipper at Rosehill or the Sydney Cup at Randwick take place.

A little down the social scale are trotting/pacing (harness-racing) meetings at *Harold Park Paceway* (☎ 9660 3688), Ross St, Glebe, and greyhound racing at *Wentworth Park* (☎ 9552 1799), Wentworth Park Rd, also in Glebe.

Pokies Coin-fed gambling machines or 'pokies' (poker machines) are the most common form of gambling. They're everywhere. You'll find them in many pubs and in RSL, leagues and other clubs, which they help to keep profitable.

Free Entertainment

On summer weekends there's free music in many parks, especially in the Domain during the Festival of Sydney. There's often free lunchtime music in Martin Place, at Darling Harbour and also at the State Conservatorium of Music on Macquarie St on Wednesday and Friday during term. Free concerts are held in front of the Opera House every Sunday.

You can listen to buskers around the Opera House and Circular Quay, in the Rocks and Kings Cross and along the Corso in Manly. There's also free entertainment at many of Sydney's weekend flea markets.

Spectator Sports

You'll find vocal crowds and world-class athletes in action most weekends of the year.

Surf Lifesaving Carnivals The volunteer surf lifesaver is one of Australia's icons, but despite the macho image, many are female.

You can see lifesavers in action each summer at the surf carnivals held all along the coast. Check at a local surf lifesaving club for dates or contact Surf Life Saving NSW (☎ 9663 4298), 2 Epsom Rd, Rosebery.

Football The football season runs through autumn and winter, March to September. Rugby league games are played at various grounds but the main venue is the *Sydney Football Stadium* (☎ 9360 6601) in Moore Park, Paddington, where the sell-out finals are played in September. Tickets to most games cost $15 to $25.

You can occasionally see the Australian rugby union team, the Wallabies, in action against international teams in Sydney.

Aussie Rules football is represented by the Sydney Swans whose home ground is the *Sydney Cricket Ground* (SCG; ☎ 9360 6601), Moore Park, Paddington.

As well as at the Sydney Football Stadium, soccer games are played at the grounds of Sydney United (☎ 9823 6418), Edensor Rd, Edensor Park, and Marconi (☎ 9823 7161), Marconi Rd, Bossley Park, amongst others. For information contact Soccer Australia (☎ 9380 6099), Sydney Football Stadium.

Cricket The *Sydney Cricket Ground* (SCG; ☎ 9360 6601), Moore Park, Paddington, is the venue for sparsely attended Sheffield Shield (interstate) matches, well-attended Test (international) matches and sell-out World Series Cup (one-day, international) matches. Local district games are also played here. The cricket season is October to March.

Tennis Major tournaments are held at *White City* (☎ 9331 4144), 30 Alma St, Paddington; this is also the home of the NSW Tennis

Association. The year's biggest event is the NSW Open, held in the second week of January as a prelude to the Australian Open in Melbourne. Indoor games are played at the *Sydney Entertainment Centre* (☎ 9320 4200, 1900 957 333 recorded information), Harbour St, near Darling Harbour.

Yachting On weekends, hundreds of yachts weave around the ferries and ships on Sydney Harbour. Many are racing and the most spectacular yachts are the speedy 18-footers. The 18-footer races carry big prize money and the boats are covered in sponsors' logos, like racing cars. The 18-footer racing season runs from mid-September to late March. The oldest and largest 18-footer club is the Sydney Flying Squadron (☎ 9955 8350), 76 McDougall St, near Milson Park on Careening Cove on the northern side of Kirribilli Point.

The greatest yachting event on Sydney Harbour is the Boxing Day (26 December) start of the Sydney to Hobart Yacht Race. The harbour is crammed with competitors, media boats and a huge spectator fleet. Special ferries are scheduled by Sydney Ferries to follow them; call ☎ 131500 in November to find out when tickets go on sale.

Basketball Australia's basketball league has all the razzmatazz of US pro basketball (and quite a few US players as well), thanks largely to television coverage. The basketball season is from April to November and games are played on weekends at the Sydney Entertainment Centre (☎ 9320 4200, 1900 957 333 for recorded information), Harbour St, near Darling Harbour. The Sydney teams are the Kings (men) and the Flames (women).

THINGS TO BUY

Shopping centres in the city include the Queen Victoria Building (on George St), the Strand Arcade (between Pitt St Mall and George St), the Royal Arcade (beneath the Hilton Hotel), and the Imperial Arcade (connecting Pitt St Mall and Castlereagh St).

Next to the Imperial Arcade is the Centrepoint shopping centre, beneath Sydney Tower, and nearby is the sevenstorey Skygarden. Two of the newer shopping centres are Piccadilly, south of Pitt St Mall, and the upmarket Chifley Plaza, on the corner of Elizabeth and Hunter Sts. In the Rocks, there's the Argyle Centre, and at Darling Harbour there's Harbourside.

The biggest shopping centre in North Sydney is Greenwood Plaza, above North Sydney station.

Major department stores are Gowings, on the corner of Market and George Sts, Grace Brothers, 436 George St, and David Jones on Market St.

The most fashionable shops tend to be on Oxford St. Crown St has several fashionable shops. Newtown's King St is popular for grunge shopping. If you're looking for bargains, there are several factory outlets and seconds shops in Redfern, clustered around the corner of Regent and Redfern Sts.

See also Galleries earlier.

Aboriginal Art

A large range of traditional and contemporary Aboriginal art is available from the following: Aboriginal Art Shop (☎ 9247 4344), Upper Concourse, Sydney Opera House; Dreamtime Gallery (☎ 9247 1380), the Rocks Centre, the Rocks; Aboriginal & Tribal Art Centre (☎ 9241 5998), 117 George St, the Rocks.

Gavala Art Shop & Cultural Centre (☎ 9212 7232), in Harbourside in Darling Harbour, sells authentic Aboriginal art.

The Aboriginal Art Gallery (☎ 9290 3639), 1st floor, 203 Clarence St, displays and sells Jinta Aboriginal desert art from central Australia.

The Boomalli Aboriginal Artists Cooperative (☎ 9698 2047), 27 Abercrombie St, Chippendale, is open Tuesday to Friday and Saturday afternoons.

In Paddington, the Coo-ee Aboriginal Emporium & Art Gallery (☎ 9332 1544), 98 Oxford St, sells quality arts and crafts, as does Hogarth Galleries Aboriginal Art Centre (☎ 9360 6839), 7 Walker Lane.

Australiana

Arts, crafts, T-shirts, designer clothing and bush gear are sold practically everywhere. Apart from the usual kitsch there's much that's of high quality, with prices to match. Check out the huge range sold in the Rocks and Darling Harbour, then compare prices in other areas.

For Australian-made, environmentally friendly souvenirs visit the Wilderness Society Shop (☎ 9233 4674), on the 1st floor of Centrepoint, or the Australian Conservation Foundation (ACF) shop (☎ 9247 4754), 33 George St in the Rocks.

The *Australian Geographic* magazine has stores in Harbourside (☎ 9212 6539), Darling Harbour, and in Centrepoint (☎ 9231 5055), on Pitt St, full of Australian memorabilia.

At the Gardens Shop (☎ 9231 8125) in the Royal Botanic Gardens Visitors' Centre, there are souvenirs, posters and books on Australian flora.

Poster prints and silkscreen prints by Sydney artist Ken Done are available from the Ken Done Gallery (☎ 9247 2740), 1 Hickson Rd, the Rocks. There are also several Done & Design shops around town, including one nearby at 123 George St (☎ 9251 6099), which sell T-shirts, greeting cards etc.

The Australian Wine Centre (☎ 9247 2755), downstairs in Gold Fields House, behind Circular Quay at 1 Alfred St, is open daily and has wines from every Australian wine-growing region. Tastings for the general public take place Friday after 4 pm.

Aussie Clothing A must-buy item is an Akubra hat. These are sold everywhere tourists gather, but if you want good advice and the right size, try the Strand Hatters (☎ 9231 6884), 8 Strand Arcade on Pitt St Mall. This excellent shop sells a variety of hats, none very cheap, but the staff are friendly and knowledgeable.

RM Williams (☎ 9262 2228), 389 George St, is an established manufacturer and distributor of Aussie bush gear. Thomas Cook Boot & Clothing Company (☎ 9212 6616),

790 George St near Railway Square, is similar.

Opals The opal is a popular souvenir, but buy wisely and shop around – quality and prices vary widely.

Many Sydney jewellers and duty-free shops sell opals, especially in the Rocks. These include Opal Fields (☎ 9247 6800), 151 George St, Opal Minded (☎ 9247 9885), 36-64 George St, and Opal Beauty (☎ 9241 4050), 22 Argyle St in the Rocks Centre.

Outdoor Gear
There's a good selection of outdoor shops on Kent St near Bathurst St and the YHA Travel Centre. Among the Australian firms here are Kathmandu (☎ 9261 8901), Paddy Pallin (☎ 9264 2685) and Mountain Designs (☎ 9267 3822).

It's also worth checking out 'disposal' stores, which handle ex-army gear. They're good for rugged clothing and less hi-tech gear and can be a lot cheaper than the specialists. One of Sydney's many disposal stores is Mitchell King Camping & Disposals, which has several stores on Pitt St, including one at No 81 (☎ 9299 6321).

Antiques
Queen St in Woollahra is the main centre for antiques in Sydney. Woollahra Antiques Centre (☎ 9327 8840), 160 Oxford St (opposite the eastern end of Centennial Park), is a conglomeration of 50 shops. Sydney Antique Centre (☎ 9361 3244), 531 South Dowling St, Surry Hills, has 60 shops and is open daily from 10 am to 6 pm.

Crafts
Call into the Arts & Crafts Society of NSW (☎ 9241 1673), in the Metcalfe Arcade, 80-84 George St, which has a gallery and sales operation. You could also try Australian Craftworks (☎ 9247 7156), 127 George St, in the old police station.

Dinosaur Designs (☎ 9223 2953) in the Strand Arcade is noted for its excellent modern jewellery.

Duty Free
Duty-free shops abound in the city, especially on Pitt St, and include:

Allders Duty Free
    74 Pitt St (☎ 9233 8399)
City International Duty Free
    88 Pitt St (☎ 9232 1555)
Downtown Duty Free
    105 Pitt St (☎ 9221 4444)

Music
Big stores which sell recorded music include HMV Megastore (☎ 9221 2311) and Blockbuster Music (☎ 9223 8488), both on Pitt St Mall. Brashs' main city store (☎ 9261 2555) is at 244 Pitt St. For others see the yellow pages under 'Compact Discs, Records & Tapes'.

For guitars and stringed instruments, try the Guitar Centre (☎ 9380 9314), 30 Oxford St. The staff can often hunt up oddities and specialities.

Markets
Sydney has lots of weekend flea markets. The most interesting, Paddington Bazaar (☎ 9331 2646), St John's Church, 395 Oxford St, is held on Saturday from 10 am to 4.30 pm. It's quite a scene.

There are two Paddy's markets. The one on the corner of Hay and Thomas Sts in Haymarket, in the heart of Chinatown, is a Sydney institution where you'll find the usual market fare at rock-bottom prices. It's open Saturday and Sunday. The other, open Friday and Sunday, is on Parramatta Rd in Flemington near the Sydney Olympic Park.

In the Rocks, the top end of George St under the bridge is closed to traffic for a market (☎ 9255 1717) on weekends. There's also a Sunday craft market (☎ 018 286 320) outside the Opera House on Sunday.

Other good markets are Balmain Markets (☎ 9818 2674), St Andrew's Church, on Darling St, on Saturday; Glebe's weekend market (☎ 042 377 499), in Glebe Public School on Saturday; and Bondi Beach Market (☎ 9398 5486), in Bondi Beach Public School on Sunday.

SYDNEY

GETTING THERE & AWAY
Air
Sydney's Kingsford Smith airport is Australia's busiest and is inadequate to handle demand, so expect delays. It's only 10 km south of the city centre, which makes access easy but this also means that flights cease between 11 pm and 5 am due to noise regulations.

You can fly into Sydney from all the usual international points and from all over Australia. Both Qantas (☎ 131313) and Ansett (☎ 131300) have frequent flights to other capital cities and major airports. Smaller airlines, such as Ansett Express, Eastern Australia, Hazelton, Impulse and Kendell, fly within NSW.

Cheap international flights are advertised in the Saturday *Sydney Morning Herald*.

Bus
The private bus operators are competitive and service is usually efficient. Shop around for discounts. Compare private operator prices to the Countrylink network of trains and buses which has discounts of up to 40% on economy fares.

Sydney Coach Terminal (☎ 9281 9366), on Eddy Ave outside Central Station, is open daily 6 am to 10.30 pm. Greyhound Pioneer (☎ 132030) and McCafferty's (☎ 9361 5125) have an office on Eddy Ave, while Kirklands (☎ 9281 2233) and Firefly Express (☎ 9211 1644) have offices around the corner on Pitt St. Many lines stop in suburbs on the way in or out of the city, and some have feeder services from the suburbs.

See the Getting There & Away and Getting Around chapters for more information and some routes and fares.

Train
All interstate and principal regional services operate from Central Station. Call the Central Reservation Centre (☎ 132232 daily, 6.30 am to 10 pm) or contact a Countrylink Travel Centre. There are Countrylink Travel Centres on the main concourse at Central Station (☎ 9379 5036); at Circular Quay on Alfred St under the Cahill Expressway

behind wharf 5 (☎ 9241 3887); in the same office as the NSW Travel Centre at 11-31 York St (☎ 9224 4744); and in the Queen Victoria Building arcade near Town Hall (☎ 9267 1521). These centres are fully fledged travel agencies and keep to business hours but you can buy a train ticket at the Central Station office daily from 6 am to 9.35 pm. You can also make phone bookings and collect your tickets from a Countrylink Travel Centre or a railway station.

Call ☎ 1 1678 for recorded information on arrival/departure times.

See the Getting There & Away and Getting Around chapters for more information and some routes and fares.

Car & Motorcycle
Main Routes There are four main road routes out of Sydney: the Sydney-Newcastle Freeway/Pacific Highway, which runs north to Newcastle and eventually to Brisbane (cross the Harbour Bridge and follow the Pacific Highway to the start of the freeway in Hornsby); the Western Motorway (M4), running west to Penrith and the Blue Mountains, becoming the Great Western Highway (follow Parramatta Rd west to Strathfield); the Hume Highway, running south-west to Mittagong and Goulburn and on to Melbourne (follow Parramatta Rd west to Ashfield); and the Princes Highway, running south to Wollongong and the coast (follow South Dowling St south from Surry Hills).

Rental The major companies – Avis (☎ 9902 9292), Budget (☎ 132727) and Hertz (☎ 131918) – have offices at the airport and around the city. Thrifty is a smaller, national company which has desks (☎ 9669 6677) at the airport and an office (☎ 9380 5399) in the city at 75 William St. It offers small manual cars for $49 per day with insurance and unlimited km.

The Yellow Pages is crammed with other outfits. Many offer deals which appear better than those offered by the major companies, but advertisements may be misleading so read the small print carefully and ring around.

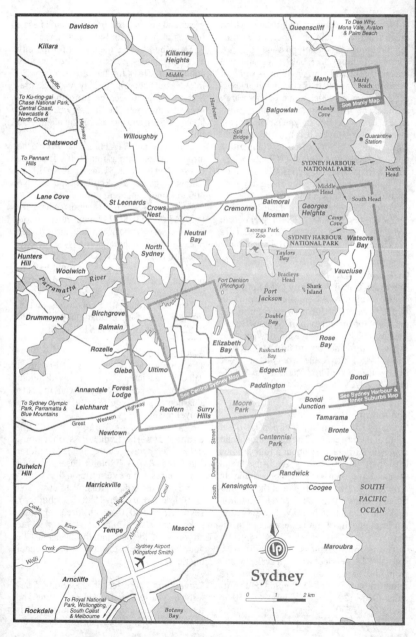

Sydney

0   1   2 km

Plenty of places rent older cars, which range from reasonable transport to frustrating old bombs. There are no huge bargains. Check for things like bald tyres and bad brakes *before* you sign anything – some of these outfits have all the compassion of used-car salespeople (which some of them are). Also, check the fine print regarding insurance excess – the amount you pay before the insurance takes over. It can be pretty high. One small company offering competitive rates is Bayswater Rental (☎ 9360 3622), 120 Darlinghurst Rd, Kings Cross, which rents small manual cars for $39 a day with insurance and 100 km free.

Motorcycle rentals are available from Ace Sydney (☎ 9633 1000), 68-74 Wentworth Ave, from $99 a day, or All Bike Hire (☎ 9707 1691), 21 Moxon Rd, Punchbowl.

GETTING AROUND

The State Transit Authority (STA) of NSW controls almost all public transport in Sydney. Call ☎ 131500 between 6 am and 10 pm daily for information on Sydney Buses, Sydney Ferries and CityRail, or visit their separate information booths at Circular Quay. Also, check the front of the A-K Yellow Pages. Children (under 16) pay half-price on STA services.

The Airport

Sydney's Kingsford Smith airport is 10 km south of the city centre. The international and domestic terminals are about a four-km bus trip apart ($2.50 with STA). Ansett and Qantas have their own separate domestic terminals. In the arrivals hall at the international terminal there's an airport information desk and a branch of the NSW Travel Centre. All terminals have foreign-exchange facilities.

The Airport Express (☎ 131500) is a special STA service which travels to and from the airport via Central Station (15 minutes), with bus No 300 going on to Circular Quay (30 minutes), bus No 350 to Kings Cross (30 minutes). Airport Express buses have their own stops and are painted

green and yellow. The one-way fare is $5; a return ticket, valid for two months, is $8.

These buses leave the airport for the city every 10 minutes. Buses leave Circular Quay and Kings Cross for the airport every 20 minutes but both stop on Eddy Ave at Central Station, so a bus leaves from the station every 10 minutes. The first service starts at about 5.15 am and the last runs at about 9.30 pm.

Some ordinary STA buses also service the airport but don't run as frequently. These are bus No 100 to North Sydney, bus No 305 to Railway Square (via Redfern) and bus No 400 to Bondi Junction.

Kingsford Smith Transport/Airporter (☎ 9667 0663/3800, 24 hours) runs a door-to-door service between the airport and places to stay (including hostels) in the city. The fare is $6/10 one way/return. If you are heading out to the airport, you will have to book at least three hours before you want to be collected.

Depending on traffic conditions, a taxi from the airport to Circular Quay costs $20 to $25, to Central Station $15 to $20.

STA Fare Deals

The composite SydneyPass offers great value if you intend to use many different forms of transport. If you just want to get to a particular place, you're better off buying a TravelPass.

SydneyPass The SydneyPass offers bus, rail and ferry travel on the Sydney Explorer and Bondi & Bay Explorer buses, harbour ferry cruises and a return trip on the Airport Express. A three-day SydneyPass costs $60 ($50 children), five days $80 ($70 children), seven days $90 ($80 children). Family tickets are also available. The trip to the airport is valid for a month but it must be your last trip because you have to surrender the ticket.

TravelPass This offers cheap weekly, quarterly or yearly travel on buses, trains and ferries. It's designed for commuters but is useful for visitors. There are various colour-coded tickets offering different combinations of distances and services. The Green TravelPass is valid for extensive bus and train travel and all ferries except the RiverCat and the Manly JetCat (before 7 pm). At $27 for a week, it's a bargain. If you buy a TravelPass after 3 pm, your week doesn't begin until the next day. Travel Passes are sold at newsagents, railway stations and STA offices.

TravelTen & FerryTen The colour-coded TravelTen ticket gives a sizable discount on 10 bus trips. The blue ticket is valid for two zones and costs $8.40. The FerryTen also allows 10 trips, beginning at $16, on the inner harbour.

Day Passes The BusTripper allows unlimited travel on Sydney bus routes for $7.80. The Bus/Ferry DayPass costs $12.

The CityHopper costs $6.60/5.20 peak/off-peak and gives you unlimited train travel within the city centre and on all normal buses. The DayRover ($20) adds unlimited travel on ferries.

Combination Passes Several transport-plus-entry tickets are available which are cheaper than paying separately. The ZooPass pays for your ferry to/from Taronga Zoo, the short bus ride from the wharf to the zoo entrance, zoo entry and the 'Aerial Safari' cable car ride. It costs $21 ($10.50 children). There are similar passes to the National Aquarium in Darling Harbour and Oceanworld in Manly.

The Rocks and Darling Harbour also have other composite tickets offering sightseeing, travel and admission to several attractions. See Things to See & Do earlier.

Bus
The bus information kiosk on the corner of Alfred and Loftus Sts (behind Circular Quay) is open daily. There are other offices on Carrington St (by Wynyard Park) and outside the Queen Victoria Building on York St.

Buses run almost everywhere but they're slow compared to trains. However, some places – including Bondi Beach, Coogee and North Shore, east of the Harbour Bridge – aren't serviced by trains. On the eastern suburbs line you can get a combination bus/rail ticket from some stations, which enables you to change from a train to a bus for a destination such as Bondi Beach. This works out cheaper than buying the tickets separately.

Sydney is divided into seven zones, with the city centre as zone 1. The main bus stops in the city centre are Circular Quay, Wynyard Park on York St and Railway Square. Nightrider buses provide a skeleton service after the regular buses and trains stop running.

Special Bus Services The red STA Sydney Explorer operates on a two-hour circular route from Circular Quay to Kings Cross, Chinatown, Darling Harbour and the Rocks, linking many inner-city attractions. It runs approximately every 20 minutes between 9.30 am and 9 pm daily. There's an on-board commentary, you can get on and off as often as you like, and your ticket entitles you to discounted entry to many attractions. This is a good way to familiarise yourself with the city and see a lot of sights.

The 22 Explorer stops are marked by green and red signs. You can use the Explorer ticket on ordinary buses between Central Station and Circular Quay or the Rocks until midnight and the ticket entitles you to big discounts on some tours – conditions apply. You can buy the ticket on the bus, from STA offices and elsewhere. Tickets cost $20 ($15 children).

The Bondi & Bay Explorer operates on similar lines but has a larger route which includes Circular Quay, Kings Cross, Paddington, Double Bay, Vaucluse, Watsons Bay, The Gap, Bondi Beach and Oxford St. Just riding the circular route takes two hours; if you want to get off at many of the 20 places of interest along the way, you'll need to start early. The bus runs half-hourly (hourly after 1.30 pm on weekdays) between 9 am and 6 pm daily. The ticket entitles you to travel on

SYDNEY

ordinary buses south of the harbour until midnight. Ticket prices are the same as the Sydney Explorer, or you can buy a two-day pass for $35 ($25 children) which gives you use of the Sydney Explorer as well.

Train
CityRail services a substantial portion of the city. It has frequent trains and is generally much quicker than the bus. Getting around the city centre by train is feasible (if disorienting). At Circular Quay, under the Cahill Expressway behind wharf 5, there is a CityRail booth which is open daily from 9 am to 5 pm.

The rail system consists of a central City Circle and a number of lines radiating out to the suburbs. The stations on the City Circle, in clockwise order, are Central, Town Hall, Wynyard, Circular Quay, St James and Museum. A single trip anywhere on the City Circle or to a nearby suburb such as Kings Cross costs $1.60. Most suburban trains stop at Central Station and at least one of the other City Circle stations. If you have to change trains, buy a ticket to your ultimate destination: it's cheaper.

Trains run from around 4 am to about midnight, give or take an hour. After the trains stop, Nightrider buses provide a skeleton service.

There are automatic ticket machines at most railway stations. They accept $5 and $10 notes and all coins, except 5c coins. You can buy an off-peak return ticket for not much more than a standard one-way fare after 9 am on weekdays and at any time on weekends.

Ferry
Sydney's ferries are one of the nicest ways of getting around. The picturesque old green-and-yellow boats are supplemented by speedy JetCats to Manly and sleek RiverCats running up the Parramatta River.

All the harbour ferries (and the Cats) depart from Circular Quay. The STA, which runs most ferries, has a ferry information office (which also sells tickets) on the concourse under the Cahill Expressway opposite the entry to wharf 4; it's open Monday to Friday 7 am to 6.45 pm, Saturday 8 am to 6.45 pm, Sunday 8 am to 5.45 pm. Many ferries have connecting bus services.

For Manly, you can choose a roomy ferry which takes about 30 minutes and costs $3.80 ($1.90 children), or a JetCat which does the trip in half the time and costs $5.20 (no concessions). The ferry trip is more pleasant because you can walk around and there's a snack bar. The JetCats have only a small outdoor area and you can be stuck inside, far from the windows. The JetCat is the only craft which runs to Manly after 7 pm, but you can take it for the normal ferry fare. If you're staying in Manly, consider buying a Manly FerryTen pass (10 trips for $26.60) or, better still, a Green TravelPass ($27 for a week of extensive train, bus and ferry travel).

Hegarty's Ferries (☎ 9206 1167) runs from wharf 6 at Circular Quay to wharves directly across the harbour: Lavender Bay, McMahons Point and two stops in Kirribilli. These services cater to peak-hour commuters and stop early in the evening.

For $3, most RiverCats travel upriver to Meadowbank, which is across the bridge from Sydney Olympic Park in Homebush Bay (a wharf is being built at Homebush Bay). Some RiverCats go to John St Wharf, near Parramatta.

Monorail
More a tourist attraction than a kosher form of public transport, the monorail (☎ 9552 2288) circles Darling Harbour and links it to the city centre. There's a train every four minutes and the full circuit takes 14 minutes. A single circuit costs $2.50 (free for children five and under) but with the $7 day pass you can ride as often as you like between 9 am and 7 pm.

Tram
In the 1930s Sydney had more than 250 km of tramway, but by the early 1960s the last tram had lowered its pantograph and that fine metaphor for a hasty departure, 'pulled out like a Bondi tram', became meaningless.

Is it a bird, is it a train? No, it's a monorail

However, in 1997 the tram made a return to Sydney's streets albeit with its name changed to light-rail transit (LRT). It's only another monorail in terms of usefulness to commuters and operates between Central Station and Pyrmont ($3.90 return) via Darling Harbour and Chinatown.

Car & Motorcycle

You'll need a street directory to drive around the city but with such good public transport, why bother? The city centre has an extensive one-way-street system.

Parking is hell in most of the inner city and tow-away zones lurk everywhere. Car parks in the inner area include: the Goulburn St Parking Station (☎ 9212 1522) on the corner of Goulburn and Elizabeth Sts; KC Park Safe (☎ 9283 4890), 581 George St near Chinatown; Grimes Parking (☎ 9247 3715), on Gateway Plaza at Circular Quay; the Rocks Space Station (☎ 9247 62222), 121 Harrington St, the Rocks; and Kings Cross Car Park (☎ 9385 5000) on the corner of Ward Ave and Elizabeth Bay Rd. Many maps indicate with a 'P' where you can park your car. See also the Yellow Pages under 'Parking Stations'.

If you have a car, make sure that your hotel has parking (many cheaper places don't) or you'll have to pay for commercial parking.

Taxi

Taxis are easily flagged down in the city centre and the inner suburbs. You'll also often find cabs in taxi ranks at Central, Wynyard and Circular Quay railway stations and at the large rank off George St in Goulburn St.

The four big taxi companies offer a reliable telephone service: Taxis Combined (☎ 9361 8222), 357 Glenmore Rd, Paddington; RSL Taxis (☎ 9581 1111), 20 O'Riordan St, Alexandria; Legion (☎ 131451), 7 Foveaux St, Surry Hills; and Premier Radio Cabs (☎ 131017), 33 Woodville Rd, Greenvale.

Taxi fares are: $1 booking fee, $3 flagfall, $1.07 per km. The waiting fee is $0.50 a minute and there's a luggage charge of $0.50 for up to 25 kg (often waived). These fares apply any time of the day or night. Tipping isn't mandatory but 'rounding-up' the bill is common: if the fare is $9.20 you might say 'call it $10, mate'; the driver may say the same to you if the fare is $10.20.

Water Taxi Water taxis are pricey but fun ways of getting around the harbour. Companies include Water Taxis (☎ 9955 3222) and Harbour Taxis (☎ 9555 1155). Up to four people can travel from Circular Quay to Watsons Bay for $35 for the first person, $5 for each extra person; to Clarke Island it's $25 for the first person, to Shark Island $30.

Bicycle

The steep hills, narrow streets and volume of traffic don't make Sydney a particularly bicycle-friendly city. Some roads have designated cycle lanes but these often run between parked cars and moving traffic. Bicycle NSW (☎ 9283 5200), Level 2, 209 Castlereagh St, publishes a handy book called *Cycling around Sydney* ($9.95). It details routes and cycle paths in and around the Sydney area. Another guide to cycling in Sydney is *Seeing Sydney by Bicycle* ($13) by Julia Thorne.

You can take your bicycle on suburban trains, but you have to buy it an adult fare ticket. Note that cycling is prohibited in

SYDNEY

Critical Mass

Sydney is full of bicycles on the last Friday of the month when hundreds of cyclists (plus joggers and inline skaters) gather to travel through the city during peak traffic time. The event is called Critical Mass and its aim is to raise awareness of the traffic conditions on Sydney's roads. Originating in San Francisco, the event gets its name from a scene in the film *Return to the Scorcher*, in which a lone cyclist at a four-way street can't make a left turn because of the motorised traffic. He waits patiently and is eventually joined by a sufficient number of other cyclists so that they're able to make the turn and the traffic is forced to stop.

Cyclists meet from 4.30 pm onwards at Hyde Park and everyone heads off at 5.30 pm. The route changes every month and the journey takes about an hour. For more information contact Green Books (☎ 9261 1919), 94 Liverpool St, or check out the website at http://www.physics.usyd.edu.au/eddie/cmass.html on the Internet. ■

Darling Harbour and Martin Place. With less hectic traffic and long cycle paths, Manly is one of Sydney's better places for cyclists. Centennial Park is also a popular cycling spot.

Unlike most bicycle shops, which are usually packed to the rafters, Innes (☎ 9264 9597), 222 Clarence St, has piped music and a spacious interior. It's a good place to go if you're thinking of buying a bicycle or if you need repairs done.

Bicycle Hire Check out Inner City Cycles (☎ 9660 6605), 31 Glebe Point Rd in Glebe, which rents quality mountain bikes for $30 a day, $60 for the weekend (from Friday afternoon to Monday morning); rental includes helmet, lock, water bottle and pump. They can also help with touring queries.

The Australian Cycle Company (☎ 9399 3475), 28 Clovelly Rd in Randwick (near the three-way intersection of Darley Rd, Clovelly Rd and Wentworth St), is one of several outfits in the area which rent bikes primarily for rides in Centennial Park.

Woolys Wheels (☎ 9331 2671), 82 Oxford St in Paddington, opposite the Victoria Barracks, rents hybrid bikes for $30 a day (24 hours). In Manly, you can hire bikes from the Manly Cycle Centre (☎ 9977 1189), 36 Pittwater Rd, for $10/25 an hour/day.

Most places require a hefty deposit but do accept credit cards.

Around Sydney

Sydney sprawls over a coastal plain, surrounded by rugged country on three sides and the South Pacific Ocean on the fourth.

The city is at the centre of the largest concentration of population in Australia, with at least 100 people per sq km from Wollongong to beyond Newcastle. More than two-thirds of the state's population is crammed into this area; about a quarter of all Australians live within 150 km of Sydney.

Most people live on the coast or around the lakes of the central coast – the slopes and forests of the Great Dividing Range have halted westward expansion, except along a ridge-top corridor through the Blue Mountains.

This might sound like a recipe for overcrowding but the region has historic small towns, stunning waterways, uncrowded beaches, superb national parks and vast tracts of forest. The proximity of Sydney means that public transport is often good, enabling you to see a lot of the area on day trips even if you don't have your own vehicle.

HIGHLIGHTS

- Walking the coastal trail in Royal National Park
- The spectacular water views in Ku-ring-gai Chase National Park
- Travelling the Hawkesbury River on the Riverboat Postman mail boat
- Bushwalking or cycling in the scenic Blue Mountains
- A tour of the limestone Jenolan Caves
- A drive along Bells Line of Road or Kangaroo Valley
- Horseriding in the Southern Highlands
- The surf beaches of the central coast

Greater Sydney

Sydney's sprawling suburbs have covered much of the coastal plain, with corridor development running out along the Great Western Highway to Penrith and south along the Hume Highway past Liverpool. In the hilly areas to the north-west, settlement is sparser but increasing.

BOTANY BAY

It's a common misconception among first-time visitors to Sydney that the city is built on the shores of Botany Bay. Sydney is actually built around the harbour of Port Jackson, some 10 to 15 km north of Botany Bay, although the city's southern suburbs now encompass the bay too.

Botany Bay is the stretch of water you sometimes see as you approach or depart from Sydney by plane. It was here that Captain Cook first stepped ashore in Australia. The bay was named by Joseph Banks, the naturalist who accompanied Cook, because of the many botanical specimens he found here. Cook's landing place is marked by monuments at Kurnell on the southern side of the bay in **Botany Bay National Park**.

The **Discovery Centre** in the park has material relating to Cook's life and expeditions and information on the surrounding wetlands. It's open from 10.30 am to 4.30 or 5 pm daily. There are bushland walking tracks and picnic areas in the park, which is

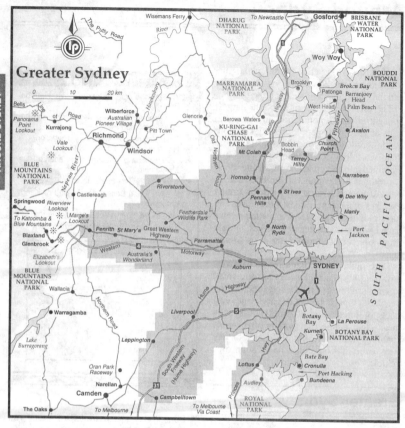

Greater Sydney

open 7.30 am to 7 or 8 pm. From Cronulla station (10 km away), take bus No 987. Entry costs $7.50 per car.

La Perouse is on the northern side of the bay entrance, at the spot where the French explorer of that name arrived in 1788, just six days after the arrival of the First Fleet. He gave the Poms a good scare because they weren't expecting the French to turn up quite so soon. La Perouse and his men camped at Botany Bay for a few weeks, then sailed off into the Pacific and were never seen again. It was not until many years later that the wrecks of their ships were discovered on a reef near

Vanuatu. There's a monument at La Perouse which was built in 1828 by French sailors to commemorate the explorer. You can also visit **La Perouse Museum** (☎ 9311 3379), which has relics from the French explorer's hapless expedition as well as a collection of antique maps. The museum is open daily from 10 am to 4.30 pm during school holidays, and on Wednesday to Sunday during the rest of the year; entry costs $2 ($1 children). You can book guided tours in English or French.

Bus Nos 394 and 398 run to here from Circular Quay.

WILDLIFE PARKS

In addition to the large national parks on the fringes of Sydney, there are several other places where you can see native animals – often at cuddling range. As well as the larger places listed below, you can meet native animals at **Australian Pioneer Village** near Wilberforce (see the following Macquarie Towns section). The **Australian Reptile Park**, near Gosford, has many native animals and birds as well as reptiles and is open daily.

Waratah Park

The popular Waratah Park on Namba Rd, Terrey Hills, on the edge of Ku-ring-gai Chase National Park, is a good place to see native fauna. The TV series *Skippy* was filmed here. It's open daily from 10 am to 5 pm and admission is $12.90 ($6.50 children). You can get here on Forest Coach Lines (☎ 9450 2277) bus No 284, which meets trains at Chatswood station on the North Shore line, but there are only three buses on weekdays and fewer on weekends. A recorded message (☎ 9450 1236) gives bus times. Forest Coach Lines also does tours from Circular Quay for $19 per person which includes entry.

Koala Park

Koala Park (☎ 9484 3141) on Castle Hill Rd in West Pennant Hills in north-west Sydney is open daily 9 am to 5 pm; admission is $9.50 ($5 children). The koalas are fed at 10.20 am, and at 2 and 3 pm. Take a train to Pennant Hills station, and from there catch bus Nos 661 to 665.

Featherdale Wildlife Park

Featherdale Wildlife Park (☎ 9671 4984 for recorded information) on Kildare Rd, Doonside, about halfway between Parramatta and Penrith, is a 'koala cuddlery' with a wide range of native fauna. Featherdale opens daily 9 am to 5 pm; entry costs $9.50 ($5 children). From the city, take a train to Blacktown, then bus No 725. Featherdale has its own bus tour from the city, the Aussie Wildlife Express (☎ 015 417 823 for book-

ings), which will pick you up and drop you off at your hotel; it costs $39 ($20 children).

Australia's Wonderland

This amusement park off the Western Motorway (M4), west of the city, also has the large **Australian Wildlife Park**. The wildlife park contains all sorts of native Australian animals as well as a replica of an outback woolshed where there's a 30-minute show. Entry to the wildlife park is $9.95 ($6 children).

There are pools and waterslides at the amusement park next door, so bring your cossie (swimsuit) in summer. Admission to both costs $31.95 ($21.95 children under 13, children under four free) and they're open daily 9 am to 5 pm. Call ☎ 9830 9187 for information.

PARRAMATTA

Sydney sprawls out well beyond Parramatta (population 130,000), 24 km west of the city centre, which was the second European settlement in Australia. Parramatta was selected as a site for a farm settlement because of the poor quality of the land around what is now Circular Quay.

Despite the suburb's modernisation, there's still a hint of a country-town atmosphere and it retains some beautiful, unique historic buildings.

Information

From the railway station, head north-west for half a block to the Church St pedestrian mall. The Parramatta Visitors' Centre (☎ 9630 3703), 353 Church St, is a couple of blocks north, just across the river. It has a walking-tour map and a good booklet, as well as other information. It's open Monday to Friday 10 am to 4 pm, Saturday 9 am to 1 pm, Sunday 10.30 am to 3 pm.

Historic Buildings

Parramatta's historic buildings are scattered but walking among them gives an insight into the more recent domestic architecture of this area. Not all the buildings are open to the

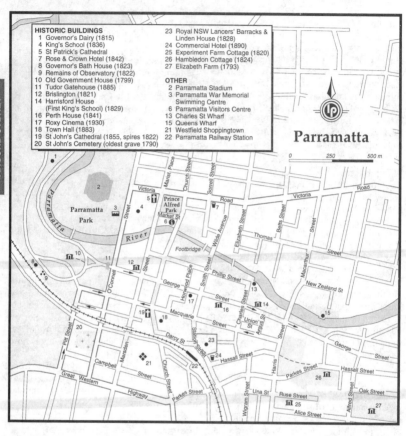

HISTORIC BUILDINGS
1 Governor's Dairy (1815)
4 King's School (1836)
5 St Patrick's Cathedral
7 Rose & Crown Hotel (1842)
8 Governor's Bath House (1823)
9 Remains of Observatory (1822)
10 Old Government House (1799)
11 Tudor Gatehouse (1885)
12 Brislington (1821)
14 Harrisford House
   (First King's School) (1829)
16 Perth House (1841)
17 Roxy Cinema (1930)
18 Town Hall (1883)
19 St John's Cathedral (1855, spires 1822)
20 St John's Cemetery (oldest grave 1790)

23 Royal NSW Lancers' Barracks &
   Linden House (1828)
24 Commercial Hotel (1890)
25 Experiment Farm Cottage (1820)
26 Hambledon Cottage (1824)
27 Elizabeth Farm (1793)

OTHER
2 Parramatta Stadium
3 Parramatta War Memorial
   Swimming Centre
6 Parramatta Visitors Centre
13 Charles St Wharf
15 Queens Wharf
21 Westfield Shoppingtown
22 Parramatta Railway Station

Parramatta

0   250   500 m

AROUND SYDNEY

public and the locations of those not listed below are shown on the map.

Parramatta Park was the site of the area's first farm and here you'll find **Old Government House** (☎ 9635 8149). It dates from 1799 and was originally a country retreat for the early rulers but is now a museum, open Tuesday to Friday 10 am to 4 pm, Saturday and Sunday 11 am to 4 pm. A guide shows you through. Admission is $5 ($3 concession). The **Governor's Bath House** (1823) nearby looks rather like an overgrown dovecote. The **Governor's Dairy** in the park wasn't a dairy at all but a labourer's cottage;

an important discovery because early humble homes are much rarer than grand ones. All that remains of an observatory built (1822) by governor Brisbane are the **transit stones** on which the telescope was placed.

St John's Cemetery, south of the park on O'Connell St, is one of the oldest in Australia.

There are more historic buildings east of the city centre. **Elizabeth Farm** (☎ 9635 9488), 70 Alice St, is the oldest surviving European home in the country. It was built in 1793 by John and Elizabeth Macarthur, whose sheep-breeding experiments formed the basis of Australia's wool industry. Elizabeth Farm is open daily 10 am to 5 pm; entry costs $6, ($3 concessions).

Hambledon Cottage (☎ 9635 6924), on Hassall St, was built for the Macarthur daughters' governess. It's open Wednesday, Thursday, Saturday and Sunday, 11 am to 4 pm; entry costs $2.50 ($1.50 children). **Experiment Farm Cottage** (☎ 9635 5655), 9 Ruse St, is a fine example of a homestead built in the early 1800s and is furnished in 1840s style. Run by the National Trust, it's open Tuesday to Thursday 10 am to 4 pm, Sunday 11 am to 4 pm; admission is $4 ($2 concessions).

The **Royal NSW Lancers Barracks** (☎ 9635 7822) are at the intersection of Station, Smith and Darcy Sts, near the railway station. The regiment is the oldest in Australia. There's a museum in Linden House (1828) open Sundays 11 am to 4 pm; entry is $2 (50c children).

Two blocks north, on George St west of Smith St, is the more recent, grand **Roxy Cinema**, dating from the 1930s.

Getting There & Away

CityRail trains run to Parramatta from Central Station or Town Hall, while ferries and JetCats run from Circular Quay. By car, follow Parramatta Rd west from the city centre and take either the Great Western Highway or the quicker Western Motorway (M4) toll road.

ROYAL NATIONAL PARK

This coastal park of dramatic cliffs, secluded beaches, scrub and lush rainforest is the oldest gazetted national park in the world. It begins at Port Hacking, 30km south of Sydney, and stretches 20km to the south. A road runs through the park with detours to the small township of Bundeena on Port Hacking, the beautiful beach at Wattamolla and the more windswept Garie Beach. The park has a large network of walking tracks, including a spectacular 26km coastal trail which runs the length of the park and is highly recommended.

The bushfires of 1994 devastated 95% of the park but all major picnic areas, beaches and the rainforest canopy in the southeastern corner were unaffected. The park is rapidly recovering and the walking tracks have re-opened.

The sandstone plateau at the northern end of the park is a sea of low scrub. You have to descend into the river valleys to find tall forest or go to the park's southern boundary on the edge of the Illawarra escarpment. In late winter and early spring the park is carpeted with wild flowers.

There's a visitors centre (☎ 9542 0648) at Audley, about 2km from the park's northeastern entrance, off the Princes Highway. It's open daily 9 am to 4 pm (closed 1 to 2 pm). It's a scenic spot, with picnic grounds on the Port Hacking River and is the starting point of many walks as well as the cycle track by the river. You can hire rowboats and canoes at the Audley Boat Shed (☎ 9545 4967) for $10/20 an hour/day. Bikes cost $6 an hour, $14 for four hours.

Garie, Era, South Era and **Burning Palms** are popular surf beaches; swimming or surfing at Marley Beach is dangerous (Little Marley is safe). Garie Beach has a surf lifesaving club and **Wattamolla Beach** has a picnic area and a lagoon for gentle swimming.

A walking and cycling trail follows the Port Hacking River south from Audley and other walking tracks pass tranquil freshwater swimming holes. You can swim in Kangaroo Creek but not in the Port Hacking River.

Park entry costs $7.50 per car but is free for pedestrians and cyclists. The road through the park and the offshoot to Bundeena are always open, but the detours to the beaches are closed at sunset.

The sizeable town of **Bundeena**, on the southern shore of Port Hacking, opposite Sydney's southern suburb of Cronulla, is surrounded by the park. Bundeena has its own beaches, or you can walk 30 minutes towards the ocean to **Jibbon Head** which has a good beach and Aboriginal rock art. Bundeena is the starting point of the 26km coastal walk. Coastline Dive (☎ 9523 2296) in Bundeena offers boat dives.

AROUND SYDNEY

Places to Stay

The only campsite accessible by car is at Bonnie Vale, near Bundeena, where sites cost from $10 for two people. Free bush camping is allowed in several other areas – one of the best places is Burning Palms Beach – but you must obtain a permit beforehand from the visitor centre. The small, basic (no electricity or phone) and secluded *Garie Beach YHA Hostel* is near one of the best surfing beaches and has beds for YHA members only for $6. You need to book; collect a key and get detailed directions from

the YHA Travel Centre (☎ 9261 1111), 422 Kent St, Sydney.

Getting There & Away

Train The Sydney-Wollongong railway line forms the western boundary of the park. The closest station is Loftus, 4km from the park entrance and another 2km from the visitors centre. Bringing a bike on the train is a good idea because there's a 10km ride through forest on a vehicle-free track about half an hour's ride from Sutherland station. The stations of Engadine, Heathcote, Waterfall and

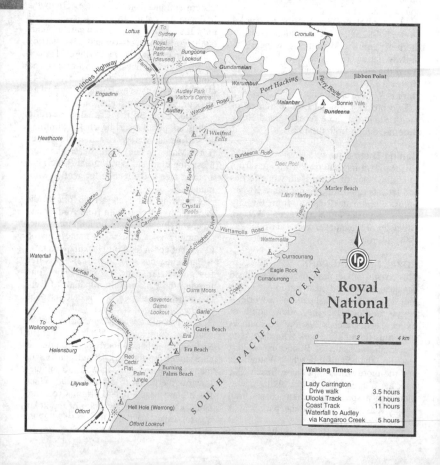

Walking Times:

Lady Carrington Drive walk	3.5 hours
Uloola Track	4 hours
Coast Track	11 hours
Waterfall to Audley via Kangaroo Creek	5 hours

Otford are on the park boundary and have walking trails into the park.

Train & Ferry A scenic way to reach the park is to take a train from Sydney to the suburb of Cronulla (changing at Sutherland on the way), then the Cronulla National Park Ferries (☎ 9523 2990) boat to Bundeena in the north-eastern corner of the park for $2.40 ($1.20 children). Ferries depart from the Cronulla wharf, just below the railway station. Cronulla Ferries also offers Hacking River cruises on Sunday, Monday and Wednesday for $8. The boats usually get as far as Audley (depending on the tide), but passengers cannot disembark.

If you're lucky you may witness the lyrebird's sensational song and dance courtship act in Ku-ring-gai Chase National Park

Car & Motorcycle From Sydney, take the Princes Highway and turn off south of Loftus to reach the northern end of the park. From the south, enter via Otford on the coast road north from Wollongong. It's a beautiful drive through thick bush and there are great views of the Illawarra escarpment and the coast from Bald Hill Lookout, just north of Stanwell Park, on the southern boundary of Royal National Park. There's a third entrance at Waterfall, just off the Princes Highway.

KU-RING-GAI CHASE NATIONAL PARK

This 15,000 hectare national park (☎ 9457 9322, 9457 9310 weekends), 24km north of the city centre, borders the southern edge of Broken Bay and the western shore of Pittwater. It has that classic Sydney mixture of sandstone, bushland and water vistas, plus walking tracks, horseriding trails, picnic areas, Aboriginal rock engravings and spectacular views of Broken Bay, particularly from West Head at the park's north-eastern tip. The park has over 100km of shoreline. There are several roads through the park and four entrances. Entry is $7.50 per car.

Large areas of Ku-ring-gai Chase, especially around West Head, were burned in the 1994 bushfires but the area is quickly regenerating. The camping area at the Basin and the Pittwater YHA Hostel were not affected.

Kalkari Visitors Centre (☎ 9457 9853), on Ku-ring-gai Chase Rd, about 4km into the park from the Mt Colah entrance, is open daily 9 am to 4.15 pm. The road descends from the visitor centre to the picnic area at Bobbin Head on Cowan Creek, then heads south to the Turramurra entrance. At Bobbin Head, Halvorsen (☎ 9457 9011) rents rowboats for $10 for the first hour, $4 for subsequent hours and motor boats that seat eight cost $30 for the first hour and $6 for subsequent hours.

The best places to see **Aboriginal engravings** are on the Basin Track and Garigal Aboriginal Heritage Walk at West Head.

It's unwise to swim in Broken Bay because of sharks but there are safe, netted swimming areas at Illawong Bay and the Basin.

Elevated parts of the park offer superb **views** across inlets such as Cowan Creek and Pittwater. From West Head there's a fantastic view across Pittwater to Barrenjoey Head at the end of Palm Beach. You may also see **lyrebirds** at West Head during their mating period (May to July).

Places to Stay

Camping is allowed only at the Basin on the western side of Pittwater. It's a 2km walk from the West Head road, or a ferry ride from Palm Beach. It costs $10 for two people, $15 in school holidays and you have to book two weeks in advance. Call ☎ 9451 8124 for

AROUND SYDNEY

Ku-ring-gai
Chase
National Park

0   2   4 km

To Newcastle
Patonga
Broken Bay
Hawkesbury River
Flint & Steel Beach
West Head
Barrenjoey Head
Gunyah Beach
Eleanor Beach
Hungry Beach
Garigal Picnic Area
Resolute Beach
Great Mackerel Beach
Palm Beach
Jerusalem Bay
Fishermans Beach
Refuge Bay
America Bay
Cowan
Hallets Beach
Whale Beach
Lambert Peninsula
Portuguese Beach
Towlers Bay
Avalon
Pacific Highway Freeway
Cowan Water
Cottage Point
Coal & Candle Creek
West Head Road
Lovett Bay
Scotland Island
Pittwater
Waratah Bay
Berowra
Smith Creek
Illawong Bay
Akuna Bay
Elvina Bay
Church Point
Bilgola
Appletree Bay
Coal & Candle Drive
McCarr's Creek Road
Barrenjoey Road
Mt Ku-ring-gai
Newcastle
Bobbin Head
Mona Vale
SOUTH
Kalkari Visitor Centre
Park Office
Duffys Forest
Booralie Road
Mona Vale Road
PACIFIC
Mt Colah
Sydney
Ku-ring-gai Chase Rd
Terrey Hills
Pittwater Road
OCEAN
Bobbin Head road
Sphinx War Memorial
Forest Way
Wakehurst Parkway
Narrabeen Lakes
Warrimoo Ave
North Turramurra
To Turramurra
To St Ives
To Belrose

Walking Times:
Berowra to Mt Ku-ring-gai — 3 hours
Garigal Aboriginal Heritage Walk (at West Head) — 1-1.5 hours

information about the ferry; call ☎ 9972 7378 for bookings.

The idyllic *Pittwater YHA Hostel* (☎ 9999 2196), a couple of km south of the Basin, is noted for its friendly wildlife. Beds cost $15, or $19 per person in a twin room; if you stay Saturday night only, rates are $20/24 respectively. Nonmembers pay $2 more. Book in advance and bring food.

Getting There & Away

There are four road entrances to the park: Mt Colah, on the Pacific Highway; Turramurra, in the south-west; and Terrey Hills and Church Point, in the south-east.

Bus From Wynyard Park in the city centre, take bus No 190 to Mona Vale where you pick up bus Nos 155, 157 or 159 to Church Point. Bus No 190 continues north to Palm Beach (the trip from Wynyard Park takes about an hour). Bus Nos 155 and 157 run from Manly.

Hornsby Buses (☎ 9457 8888) has a fairly frequent service from Turramurra railway station to the nearby park entrance ($2.10).

STA buses service the Terrey Hills and

Church Point entrances respectively, but it's quite a walk to the Pittwater YHA Hostel or the campsites from these entrances.

Boat The Palm Beach Ferry Service (☎ 9918 2747) runs to the Basin hourly from 8 am to 6 pm ($7 return). A ferry leaves Palm Beach for Bobbin Head (running via Patonga on the northern side of Broken Bay) daily at 11 am, returning at 3.30 pm. The one-way fare is $25 ($10 children).

To get to the Pittwater YHA Hostel, take a ferry from Church Point to Halls Wharf, from where the hostel is just a short walk. YHA members get ferry discounts. Scotland Island Schooners (☎ 9999 3954) at Church Point will drop you off at the Basin or the hostel by arrangement.

HAWKESBURY RIVER

The Hawkesbury River enters the sea 30km north of Sydney at Broken Bay. Dotted with coves, beaches, picnic spots and some fine riverside restaurants, it's one of Australia's most attractive rivers. The final 20-odd km of the Hawkesbury expands into bays and inlets like Berowra Creek, Cowan Water and Pittwater to the south, and Brisbane Water to the north before it enters the ocean. The river flows between Marramarra and Ku-ring-gai Chase national parks in the south and Dharug, Brisbane Water and Bouddi national parks to the north. Windsor and Richmond are about 120km upstream – see Macquarie Towns.

The **Riverboat Postman** (☎ 9985 7566) mail run is an excellent way to get a feel for the river. It does a 40km round trip weekdays, running upstream as far as Marlow, near Spencer. It leaves Brooklyn at 9.30 am and returns at 1.15 pm. A shorter afternoon run on Wednesday and Friday leaves at 1.30 pm and returns at 4 pm. It costs $25, ($10 children). The 8.16 am train from Central Station ($4.40 one way) gets you to Brooklyn's Hawkesbury River station in time to meet the morning boat. You may have to change at Hornsby. By car, take the Sydney-Newcastle Freeway or follow the old Pacific Highway.

The Riverboat Postman people also run a ferry service from Brooklyn to Patonga Beach five times a week for $10 return ($4 children). Bookings are necessary.

Wiseman Ferry Cruises (☎ 4566 4422) has two-hour cruises of the Hawkesbury, Colo and McDonald rivers for $37.50, including a food hamper.

There's also a daily ferry between Palm Beach, Patonga and Bobbin Head in Ku-ring-gai Chase National Park. From Patonga, Peninsula Bus Lines (☎ 4341 4133) has infrequent buses to Gosford where you can catch a bus or train going north.

You can hire **houseboats** in Brooklyn, Berowra Waters, Bobbin Head and Wisemans Ferry. These aren't cheap but renting midweek during low season is affordable for a group. There are different types and sizes and different deals for longer rentals and weekends. As a rough guide, *Holidays-A-Float* (☎ 9985 7368) in Brooklyn offers four midweek days (three nights) on a four-to six-berth boat for $550 between May and late September. Other companies include *Able Houseboats* (☎ 4566 4308), River Rd, Wisemans Ferry, and *Ripples on the Hawkesbury* (☎ 9985 7333), 31 Brooklyn Rd, Brooklyn.

Brooklyn & Berowra Waters

The settlements along the river have their own distinct character. Life in Brooklyn revolves totally around boats and the river. The town is on the Sydney-Newcastle railway line, just east of the Pacific Highway.

The small town of Berowra Waters, farther upstream on a narrow, forested waterway, is clustered around a free, 24-hour winch ferry which crosses Berowra Creek. It's a pretty location, with boat hire businesses and walking tracks through the bush. The main reason Sydneysiders come here on weekends is to eat at the *Berowra Waters Inn* (☎ 9456 1027), one of Australia's best-known restaurants. It's open for lunch and dinner on Friday and Saturday and for lunch only on Sunday. The excellent modern Australian set menu, including a glass of French champagne, costs $75 per person. Bookings are essential. There are also several cafes overlooking the water.

Berowra Waters is 5km west of the Pacific Highway; there's a railway station at Berowra, but it's a 6km hike down to the ferry.

Wisemans Ferry & Around

The tranquil settlement of **Wisemans Ferry** (see the central coast & Lake Macquarie map) is a popular spot on the Hawkesbury River, about halfway between Windsor and the mouth of the river. A free, 24-hour winch ferry is the only means of crossing the river here. A NPWS shop (☎ 4566 4382) has information on the area. The historic *Wisemans Ferry Inn* (☎ 4566 4301) has rooms for $55 a double. There are several caravan parks; one of the cheapest (sites $10 a double) being *Del Rio Riverside Resort* (☎ 4566 4330) 3km south-west of the village centre.

Unsealed roads on both sides of the river run north from Wisemans Ferry to the hamlet of **St Albans**. It's a pretty drive, with bush on one side and the serene flats of the Macdonald River on the other side, with the occasional old sandstone house. In St Albans the friendly *Settlers Arms Inn* (☎ 4568 2111) dates from 1848 and the public bar is worth a beer. It has a few pleasant rooms from $100 a double and there's a basic *campsite* opposite the pub. There's also B&B in the old *Court House* (☎ 4568 2042) for $75/95.

Note that it may be unwise to swim in the Hawkesbury River between Windsor and Wisemans Ferry during the summer due to blue-green algae. Call the EPA Pollution Line (☎ 9325 5555) for information.

National Parks Across the river, **Dharug National Park** (14,834 hectares) is a wilderness noted for its Aboriginal rock carvings dating back nearly 10,000 years. Forming the western boundary of the park is the **Old Great North Road**, built by convicts in the 1820s to link Sydney and Newcastle. Most of the road is badly dilapidated but a 2km section (running north into the national park from the sealed road across the river from

Wisemans Ferry) has been restored, although there's no vehicle access. There's camping in the park at Mill Creek and Ten Mile Hollow.

Yengo National Park (139,861 hectares), a rugged sandstone area covering the foothills of the Blue Mountains, stretches from Wisemans Ferry to the Hunter Valley. It's a wilderness area with no facilities and limited road access.

On the south side of the Hawkesbury is **Marramarra National Park** (11,760 hectares), with vehicle access from the Old Northern Rd south of Wisemans Ferry. You can bushcamp here. Contact the NPWS (☎ 4324 4911), 207 Albany St in Gosford, for more information.

Getting There & Away To reach Berowra Waters, turn off the Pacific Highway at Berowra. A scenic alternative is to take the road through the Galston Gorge north of Hornsby in Sydney's north-east.

A road leads to Wisemans Ferry from Pitt Town, near Windsor. You can also get there from Sydney on the Old Northern Rd, which branches off Windsor Rd north of Parramatta.

If you arrive at Wisemans Ferry by either of these routes, you have a choice of two ferries. The ferry in the west of town (at the bottom of the steep hill) takes you to St Albans Rd which runs up to St Albans; the ferry on the north-east side (a short way out of town, near the park) takes you to Settlers Rd which also runs up to St Albans. In the other direction, it goes to Central Mangrove and, eventually, to the Central coast or the Sydney-Newcastle Freeway.

From St Albans, an unsealed road runs north-east to Bucketty, from where you can get to Wollombi and Cessnock in the Hunter Valley.

The Sydney-Newcastle Freeway crosses the Hawkesbury River near Brooklyn. Trains run from Central Station to Brooklyn's Hawkesbury River railway station.

MACQUARIE TOWNS AREA

The riverflats of the upper Hawkesbury,

under the lee of the Blue Mountains, offered the young colony fertile land for growing much-needed food. After early settlements were flooded out several times, Governor Macquarie established the five 'Macquarie Towns' on higher ground in 1810 – Windsor, Richmond, Wilberforce, Pitt Town and Castlereagh. The area is still intensively cultivated.

The upper Hawkesbury is popular for water-skiing, but if you're tempted to get into the water, check that there isn't an algae problem. Call the EPA Pollution Line (☎ 9325 5555) for information.

Information

The Hawkesbury Visitors Centre (☎ 4588 5895), across from the Richmond RAAF base, on the road between Richmond and Windsor, is the main information centre for the upper Hawkesbury area. It's open daily from 9 am to 5 pm. Windsor has its own information centre (☎ 4577 2310) in the 1843 Daniel O'Connell Inn on Thompson Square, off Bridge St. You can book cruises on the Hawkesbury here.

In Richmond there's an NPWS office (☎ 4588 5247) at 370 Windsor St.

Windsor

Windsor, founded in 1810 on the banks of the Hawkesbury River, was the main settlement of Governor Macquarie's five towns and has many fine colonial buildings. The **Hawkesbury Museum** is in the same building as the information centre. It's open daily and admission is $2.50 ($1.50 children).

Windsor's other old buildings include the convict-built **St Matthew's Church** (1820), designed, like the old **courthouse** (1822), by convict architect Francis Greenway. George St has other historic buildings and the **Macquarie Arms Hotel** is reckoned to be the oldest pub in Australia, though there are a few 'oldest pubs'. This one was built in 1815 under orders from the governor. Happily, its history hasn't gone to its head and it's still very much a small-town pub.

On the edge of town is the **Tebbut Observatory**, featured on the $100 note. You can

look through the telescopes on Friday and Saturday night tours ($10), but you must book a fortnight in advance – contact the Clydesdale Horsedrawn Restaurant (☎ 4577 4544).

Wilberforce & Around

Wilberforce, 6km north of Windsor, is a tiny town on the edge of the riverflat farmland where the **Australian Pioneer Village** (☎ 4575 1457), a collection of old buildings gathered from around the district, forms a small historic park. It includes **Rose Cottage** (1811), probably the oldest surviving timber building in the country (occupied by the same family until 1961). There are also native animals and regular entertainment. The village is open daily from 10 am to 5 pm; admission is $15 ($6 children). Next to the village is a **butterfly farm**. You can get here by public transport – a CityRail train to Windsor and then by bus – but phone to check times, as the bus isn't frequent.

The originally Presbyterian (now Uniting) **Ebenezer Church** (1809) on Coromandel Rd, 5km north of Wilberforce, is said to be the oldest church in Australia still used as a place of worship. The old **Tizzana Winery** (☎ 4579 1150), 518 Tizzana Rd, near Ebenezer, is open weekends from noon to 6 pm.

Pitt Town & Around

Pitt Town, a few km north-east of Windsor, is another Macquarie Town, where the old buildings include the restored **Bird in Hand Hotel** (1825). North of Pitt Town, on the road to Wisemans Ferry, is the small **Cattai National Park** (☎ 4572 8404). There are two parts: Cattai Farm, containing the remains of an old homestead (c 1799), and, 2km east, Mitchell Park with pristine forest and walking trails. There's also canoe hire, horseriding and camping.

Richmond

Richmond is 6km west of Windsor, at the end of the CityRail line and at the start of the Bells Line of Road across the Blue Mountains. The town dates from 1810 and has some fine Georgian and Victorian buildings. These include the **courthouse** and **police station**, on Windsor St, and, around the corner in Market St, **St Andrew's Church** (1845). A number of notable pioneers are buried in the cemetery at **St Peter's Church** (1841).

Up the Putty Road
The Putty Rd (also called the Singleton Rd) is a scenic route from Windsor to the upper Hunter Valley via Wisemans Ferry (see Getting There & Away section). The road, flanked by Wollemi and Yengo national parks, runs through dense bush amid a sea of forest-covered ranges. On the Putty Rd, about 20km north of Windsor, there's a long descent to the lovely **Colo River**, a picturesque spot popular for swimming, canoeing and picnicking. It has a service station, shop and tourist information point and camping at the *Riverside Tourist Park* (☎ 4575 5253), where you can hire canoes for $7 an hour.

Getting There & Away
Train CityRail trains run from Sydney to Windsor and Richmond. Neither town is too large to see on foot, but getting to the other Macquarie towns involves connecting with an infrequent local bus service.

Car & Motorcycle From Sydney, the easiest routes to Windsor are on Windsor Rd (Route 40), the north-western continuation of Parramatta's Church St (you'll have to wind around the Church St mall), and via Penrith, heading north from either the Western Freeway or the Great Western Highway on Route 69 (Parker St and the Northern Rd).

The Putty Rd runs north from Windsor to Singleton, 160km north in the upper Hunter Valley. From Windsor, take Bridge St across the river then turn right onto the Wilberforce road (Route 69).

From Richmond, Bells Line of Road runs west up into the Blue Mountains. This is a more interesting (but considerably longer) route to Katoomba than the crowded Great Western Highway.

PENRITH & AROUND
Now Sydney's westernmost suburb, Penrith is bounded on the west by the serene Nepean River (which becomes the Hawkesbury a few km downstream). Across the river, the forested foothills of the Blue Mountains rise above the Nepean's riverflats and the plains of western Sydney come to an abrupt end. Europeans arrived here, soon after the colony was founded, in search of land to grow food. A road between Penrith and Parramatta was built in 1818.

The tourist information centre (☎ 4732 7671), open daily from 9 am to 4.30 pm, is in the car park of the Penrith Panthers complex.

Things to See & Do
The **Museum of Fire** (☎ 4731 3000), off Castlereagh Rd (the main road to Richmond), just east of the railway line, contains displays of historic fire-fighting equipment and some interesting educational items about fire and its dangers. There's a graphic display on the disastrous effects of fire. The museum is open Monday to Saturday from 10 am to 3 pm (until 5 pm on Sunday); admission is $3 ($2.50 children).

The huge **Penrith Panthers** complex is a leagues club with just about everything you could wish for: glitzy surroundings, plenty of pokies, flash restaurants, a free cinema, lavish amusements such as cable waterskiing and an expensive *motel* (☎ 4721 7700, 1800 024 911). A visit here on the way to the Blue Mountains may give you a better appreciation of the bush.

The *Nepean Belle* (☎ 4733 1274), a paddle wheeler, cruises the Nepean River several times a week.

In **Emu Plains**, on the highway west of Penrith, the **Arms of Australia Inn** (☎ 4735 4394) is an old pub (c 1840), now a small museum. It's open weekends from 1 to 5 pm; admission is $1.

Getting There & Away
Train Frequent CityRail trains stop at Penrith on the run between Sydney and the Blue Mountains.

Car & Motorcycle The Western Motorway (M4) from Sydney (a toll road) runs past Penrith and the Great Western Highway. The Northern Rd (Route 69) runs south from Penrith to the towns of Camden and Picton (see the Macarthur Country section) and north to Windsor (see the Macquarie Towns section).

MACARTHUR COUNTRY

The Hume Highway heads south-west from Sydney, flanked by the rugged Blue Mountains National Park to the west and the coastal escarpment on the east, following a rising corridor. This cleared and rolling sheep country contains some of the state's oldest towns, although many have been swallowed by Sydney's steamrolling suburbs. If you would prefer a closer look at the countryside, take the **Northern Rd** between Penrith and Narellan (just north of Camden).

Liverpool and, 20km further south, **Campbelltown** are unattractive outer suburbs of Sydney, though both do have some interesting old buildings.

Activities

Balloon Aloft (☎ 4655 9892, 1800 028 568) has early-morning hot-air flights from Camden for $130 including a champagne breakfast.

Camden & Around

Camden is a large country town (population 8700) that's almost a dormitory suburb of Sydney. The town retains its integrity but the surrounding countryside is fast filling up with weekend attractions for Sydneysiders. **John Oxley Cottage** on the northern outskirts houses the Camden Information Centre (☎ 4658 1370), open daily from 10 am to 3 pm. The **Camden Museum**, 40 John St, behind the library, is open on weekends between 1.30 and 4.30 pm (entry $1, 50c children).

The Macarthurs' home, **Camden Park House** (1835), is only open to the public on the last weekend in September.

Attractions around Camden are aimed pri-

marily at families and coach parties. **Gledswood** (☎ 9606 5111), Camden Valley Way in Catherine Field near Narellan, is an old homestead (1827) which now houses a winery and a restaurant. There's also sheep-shearing, boomerang-throwing and other activities. It's open daily from 10 am to 5 pm. **Struggletown** (☎ 4648 2424), on Sharman Close, is a collection of galleries and studios in historic cottages. Not far from Narellan, **Australiana Park** (also called El Caballo Blanco; in the floodlit arena at night there's a performance by dancing Andalusian stallions), Camden Valley Way, has a grab-bag of things to see and do, including sheep-shearing, water-sliding, horse-riding and koala-cuddling. The star attractions are the Andalusian Dancing Stallions; phone (☎ 9606 6266) for performance times. Admission is $14.95 ($7.95 children).

Midway between Camden and Campbelltown, **Mount Annan Botanic Garden** (☎ 4648 2477) is an offshoot of Sydney's

Cow Pastures & Sheep

The Macarthur Country area was originally called Cow Pastures because a herd of cattle which had escaped from Sydney Cove thrived here. But it was John and Elizabeth Macarthur's sheep, which arrived in 1805, which made the area famous. The couple's experiments with sheep-breeding led to the development of merino sheep suited to Australian conditions and these became the foundation of the Australian wool industry. ∎

botanic gardens and displays native flora on over 400 hectares. It's open daily October to March from 10 am to 6 pm, to 4 pm from April to September; admission is $5 per car or motorcycle, $2 for pedestrians. You can get here on bus No 896, which runs more or less hourly from Campbelltown railway station to Camden.

Picton & Around

South of Camden, pretty Picton is an old rural village which was originally called Stonequarry. Today coal is mined in the area (and there are subsidence problems under those rolling hills and sheep paddocks). A number of historic buildings still stand, including the railway station and the 1839 **George IV Inn** (☎ 4677 1415) which brews its own Bavarian-style beer and provides some modest accommodation. Upper Menangle St is listed by the National Trust.

Elizabeth Macarthur Agricultural Institute is a research station at 710 Morton Park Rd in Menangle, north-east of Picton. It takes in **Belgenny Farm** (☎ 4655 9651), the Macarthurs' first farm in the area and the oldest in Australia. It can be visited on organised tours; call for details. Most historians agree that Elizabeth supervised most of the sheep-breeding projects while the irascible John was embroiled in political disputes.

South of Picton in **Thirlmere**, the **Rail Transport Museum** (☎ 4681 8001), Barbour Rd, is worth visiting if you have an interest in old trains. Its collection of engines and rolling stock is huge, with many more

awaiting restoration. The museum opens weekdays from 10 am to 3 pm, weekends from 9 am to 5 pm. Admission is $8 ($2 children). There are steam-train excursions (☎ 9744 9999) on Sundays, public-holiday Mondays and Wednesdays during school holidays.

The small, 630 hectare **Thirlmere Lakes National Park** (☎ 9542 0666), south-west of Thirlmere, protects five small, interconnected, freshwater lakes and surrounding bush. It's home to 130 bird species and a rare waterlily called the woolly frogmouth.

Merigal Dingo Education Centre (☎ 4684 1156), 590 Arina Rd, near Bargo, about 20km south of Picton, is run by the Australian Native Dog Conservation Society, which aims to get a better deal for dingoes. Its first goal is to have them legally recognised as dogs, not vermin. The centre is open on weekends from 10 am to 3 pm; entry is $3.

The Blue Mountains

The Blue Mountains, part of the Great Dividing Range, have some truly fantastic scenery, excellent bushwalks and all the gorges, gum trees and cliffs you could ask for. The foothills begin 65km inland from Sydney and rise to 1100m but the mountains are really a sandstone plateau riddled with spectacular gorges formed over millenia by erosion.

The blue haze which gave the mountains their name is a result of the fine mist of volatile oil given off by eucalyptus trees – which is also why eucalypt forests can explode into firestorms.

For more than a century, the area has been a popular getaway for people seeking to escape the summer heat of Sydney. Despite the intensive tourist development, much of the area is so precipitous that it's still only open to bushwalkers.

During the 1994 fires large areas of the Grose Valley were burned but the Blue Gum Forest escaped almost intact.

The Blue Mountains offers two main

GLENN BEANLAND

DAVID COLLINS

JON MURRAY

Around Sydney
Top: The Three Sisters at Katoomba, Blue Mountains National Park
Middle: The Illawarra Escarpment from Bald Hill Lookout
Bottom: The Entrance, central coast

Top: Settlers' Arms Inn, St Albans, near Sydney
Bottom: Post Office, Maitland, Hunter Valley

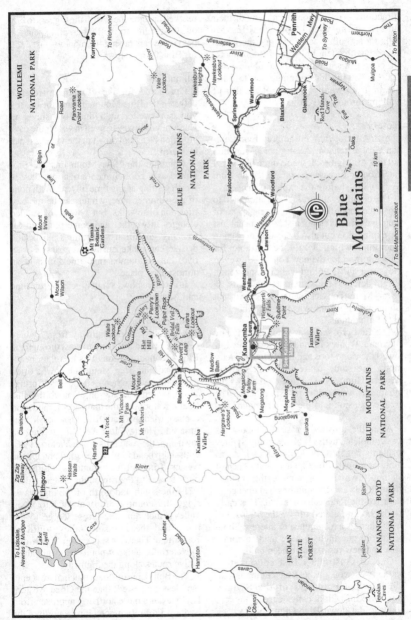

attractions – the national parks, with their superb scenery and opportunities for walking and other activities, and the guesthouses, with their hill-station atmosphere. Of course it's possible to combine both. There's nothing like coming back to a log fire in an Edwardian house after a day of walking through the bush.

History

The first Europeans in the area found evidence of extensive Aboriginal occupation but few Aborigines. It seems quite likely that catastrophic diseases had travelled up from Sydney long before the explorers arrived.

The colonists at Port Jackson attempted to cross the mountains within a year or so of their arrival, driven not just by the usual lust for exploration but also by an urgent need to find land which would be suitable for growing food for the new colony. However, the sheer cliffs, blind valleys and tough terrain defeated their attempts for nearly 25 years. Many convicts came to believe that China, and freedom, was just the other side of the mountains.

The first crossing was made in 1813, by Blaxland, Wentworth and Lawson. They followed the ridge-tops and their route is pretty much the same route of today's Great Western Highway. The first road across the mountains was built in just six months. The great expansion into the western plains had begun.

After the railway across the mountains was completed in the 1860s, wealthy Sydney residents began to build mansions here, as summer retreats from the heat and stench of Sydney town. By the turn of the century, grand hotels and guesthouses had opened to cater for the increasing demand. This early tourist boom tapered off by the 1940s, but today there is a resurgence of interest. Some of the old guesthouses have made a comeback and new resorts have been built.

One of Australia's first conservation battles was won in the Blue Mountains in 1931, when members of the Sydney Bushwalking Club came across loggers about to cut down Blue Gum Forest. They reached an agreement with the loggers to buy out their rights to the timber, and spent the next two years raising the money – just £150 for Blue Gum Forest!

Climate

Be prepared for the climatic difference between the Blue Mountains and the coast – you can swelter in Sydney but shiver in Katoomba. However, even in winter the days are often clear and down in the valleys it can be warm.

Although the Blue Mountains are promoted as a cool-climate attraction, they're worth visiting at any time of year. With none of the summer haze, winter can be the best time for bushwalks, but beware of sudden changes in weather and come prepared for freezing conditions. Autumn's mists and drizzle can make bushwalking less attractive, but Katoomba in a thick mist is an atmospheric place.

It usually snows some time between June and August.

Orientation

The Great Western Highway from Sydney follows a ridge from east to west through the Blue Mountains. Along this less-than-beautiful road, the Blue Mountains towns often merge into each other – Glenbrook, Springwood, Woodford, Lawson, Wentworth Falls, Leura, Katoomba (the main accommodation centre), Medlow Bath, Blackheath, Mt Victoria and Hartley. Just west of Mt Victoria township, the road falls down Victoria Pass, with sharp bends and a steep gradient. On the western fringe of the mountains is Lithgow, on a level with Penrith on the eastern side.

To the south and north of the highway's ridge the country drops away into steep valleys, including the Grose Gorge to the north and the Jamison Valley south of Katoomba. There's a succession of turn-offs to waterfalls, lookout points or scenic alternative routes along the highway.

The Bells Line of Road, much more scenic (and less congested) than the Great Western Highway, is a more northerly approach from Sydney. From Richmond it runs north of the

Grose Valley to emerge in Lithgow, although you can cut across from Bells Line of Road to join the Great Western Highway at Mt Victoria.

Information

There's a visitors information centre (☎ 4739 6266) on the Great Western Highway at Glenbrook and another (☎ 4782 0756) at Echo Point in Katoomba. The excellent NPWS Blue Mountains Heritage Centre (☎ 4787 8877) is on Govett's Leap Rd near Blackheath, about 3km north off the highway. On weekends a second NPWS visitors information centre (☎ 4739 2950) opens in Glenbrook on Bruce Rd.

Katoomba has its own tourist radio station (88 FM).

You can hire any camping gear from Mountain Designs (☎ 4782 5999), 190 Katoomba St, Katoomba.

Books & Maps The Blue Mountains Heritage Centre at Govett's Leap is the best place to ask about walks; it also sells maps and some books. Maps suitable for walking are also sold at information centres. Rockcraft (☎ 4782 2014), 182 Katoomba St, Katoomba, also has maps and books. Megalong Books (☎ 4784 1302), 82 Railway Parade in Leura, stocks books about the Blue Mountains. It's open daily.

How to See the Blue Mountains by Jim Smith (Megalong Books) is useful and has details of day walks as does Neil Paton's *Walks in the Blue Mountains* (Kangaroo Press). Lonely Planet's *Bushwalking in Australia*, by John and Monica Chapman, details the Blue Gum Forest walk.

National Parks

The **Blue Mountains National Park** protects large areas to the north and south of the Great Western Highway. It's the most popular and accessible of the three national parks in the area and offers great bushwalking, scenic lookouts, breathtaking waterfalls and Aboriginal stencils.

Wollemi National Park, north of Bells Line of Road, is the state's largest forested

wilderness area (nearly 500,000 hectares) and stretches as far as Denman in the Hunter Valley. It offers good rugged bushwalking and has lots of wildlife. Access is limited and the centre of the park is so isolated that a new species of tree, named the Wollemi Pine, was only discovered in 1994.

Kanangra Boyd National Park is southwest of the southern section of the Blue Mountains National Park. It has bushwalking, limestone caves and grand scenery including the spectacular Kanangra Walls Plateau, which is surrounded by sheer cliffs. The park can be reached by unsealed roads from Oberon or Jenolan Caves.

Entry to these national parks is free unless you enter the Blue Mountains National Park at Bruce Rd, Glenbrook, where it costs $7.50 per car; walkers are not charged.

Lookouts

Blue Mountains views have been cliches for so long that it's a little surprising to find that they *are* breathtaking. Don't miss **Echo Point** at Katoomba, where you'll see the famous Three Sisters. **Cliff Drive**, running along the edge of the Jamison Valley between Leura and Katoomba, also has some great views. Make sure you get to **Govett's Leap** (near Blackheath, close to the NPWS heritage centre) and **Evans Lookout** (north of the highway, turn off before Blackheath) for spectacular views. Less well-known but at least as spectacular are the viewpoints off Bells Line of Road, such as **Walls Lookout**. **Hawkesbury Heights**, on the road between Springwood and Bells Line of Road, is on the eastern face of the range and has views across the Nepean River to Sydney, sometimes muddied by a cloud of tan smog.

Farther from the main centres there are more views from **McMahon's Lookout** on Kings Tableland, 22km from the Queen Victoria Memorial Hospital (south of Wentworth) – for the last 10km you'll need a 4WD (or mountain bike).

Bushwalking

Bushwalking has been popular in the Blue Mountains for a long time. Myles Dunphy founded Australia's first bushwalking club in 1914 and the Blue Mountains was his favourite area.

There are walks lasting from a few minutes to several days. The two most popular areas, spectacular from both the tops of the cliffs and the bottoms of the valleys, are the **Jamison Valley** immediately south of Katoomba and the **Grose Valley** area north-east of Katoomba and Blackheath. South of Glenbrook is another good area.

Visit a NPWS visitor centre for information or, for shorter walks, ask at a tourist information centre. It's very rugged country and walkers sometimes get lost, so it's highly advisable to get reliable information, not to go alone, and to tell someone where you're going. Most Blue Mountains watercourses are polluted so you have to sterilise water or take your own. Be prepared for rapid weather changes.

Blue Mountains Backpackers in Katoomba takes guests to trailheads. There's free parking for bushwalkers' cars near the trailhead for the Grand Canyon walk on Evans Lookout Rd.

There's a fairly easy three-day walk from Katoomba to Jenolan Caves along the **Six Foot Track**. The Department of Conservation & Land Management (DCLM) has a brochure detailing the walk. More challenging is the 140km **Ensign Barralier Walking Track** from Katoomba to Mittagong in the Southern Highlands. See the Southern Highlands section for more information.

On weekends and public holidays the NPWS runs a series of guided walks, many with an historical or ecological theme. These have to be booked. Call ☎ 4787 8877 for information.

Adventure Activities

The cliffs, gorges and valleys of the Blue Mountains offer outstanding abseiling, rock climbing and canyoning (exploring gorges by climbing, abseiling, swimming, walking etc). **Narrow Neck**, **Mt Victoria** and **Mt Peddington** are among the popular sites. Most outfits offering guided adventure activ-

Social climbing: the Blue Mountains offer some outstanding sites for abseiling

ities and courses are based in Katoomba – see that section for more information.

Mountain Biking

Cycling is permitted on most of the national park trails and, notwithstanding the hassle of carrying your bike down to the valley floor and back up again, there is good riding. See Activities in the Katoomba sections for bike rentals and guided rides.

Horseriding

Several outfits in the Megalong Valley have trail rides – see that section.

Organised Tours

The major Sydney tour companies have day trips to the Blue Mountains for about $60.

On weekends the hop-on, hop-off Blue Mountains Explorer bus meets CityRail trains – see the Getting Around section under Katoomba.

The Wonderbus (☎ 9555 9800), popular

with backpackers, runs day tours of the Blue Mountains ($48) and overnight trips which include the Jenolan Caves ($111), dorm accommodation at the Katoomba YHA Hostel (you don't have to be a YHA member) and a visit to the Australian Wildlife Park. The tariff covers everything except discounted entry ($10) to the Jenolan Caves and meals other than breakfast on the overnighter. Book in person at the Sydney YHA Travel Centre or the YHA hostels in Sydney. The Martin Place information booth also takes bookings.

Another inexpensive tour operator which gets good feedback is Oz-Trek (☎ 9369 7055, 9360 3444), 448 Bourke St in Sydney's Surry Hills. From Sydney, Wayward Bus Company (☎ (08) 8232 6646, 1800 882 823), based in Adelaide, has two-day tours of the Blue Mountains, the Jenolan Caves, Sofala and Hill End for $75.

Fantastic Aussie Tours (☎ 9936 9133) has 2½-hour 4WD tours of the Blue Mountains from Sydney for $59 ($29 children). Cox's River Escapes (☎ 4784 1621), in Leura, offers 4WD day tours of the Cox's River Valley with swimming, bushwalking and picnicking for $240 for two people.

One way to see the area from the road is on the back of a Harley Davidson with Cliff-Edge Cruisers (☎ 4782 4462), starting at $35 for half an hour.

From the air, the mountains are even more spectacular and a short flight with Blue Mountain Helicopters (☎ 4788 1109) at Katoomba airfield, a few km from Medlow Bath, costs $49.

Yulefest

The region has a Yulefest in July, when many restaurants and guesthouses have good deals on 'Christmas' dinners.

Accommodation

Accommodation ranges from campsites and hostels to expensive guesthouses and resorts. Katoomba is the main accommodation centre. Most places charge more at weekends and guesthouses tend to be booked out on long weekends. Camping is banned in some

parts of the national parks and in others you need a permit, so check with the NPWS first.

There isn't room here to list all the accommodation options but information centres (including the NSW Travel Centre in Sydney) stock copies of the *Blue Mountains Holiday Book*, a free brochure listing mid-range and top-end places. Check prices before heading to the Blue Mountains because of the numerous packages available and seasonal price variations. Information centres (and some travel agents) book accommodation in the Blue Mountains and will know of current specials and packages.

Getting There & Away

Katoomba, 109km from Sydney's city centre, is almost a satellite suburb. CityRail trains run more or less hourly from Central ($9.40 one way, two hours). Countrylink buses meet trains at Mt Victoria on Tuesday, Friday and Sunday for the run to Oberon.

By car, exit the city via Parramatta Rd and detour onto the Western Motorway tollway (M4) ($1.50) at Strathfield. The motorway becomes the Great Western Highway west of Penrith. To reach the Bells Line of Road, exit the city on Parramatta Rd and from Parramatta head north-west on the Windsor Rd to Windsor. The Richmond Rd from Windsor becomes the Bells Line of Road west of Richmond.

See also Organised Tours earlier.

Getting Around

Mountainlink (☎ 4782 3333) buses run between Leura, Katoomba, Medlow Bath, Blackheath and Mt Victoria, with some services running down Hat Hill Rd and Govett's Leap Rd which lead respectively to Perry's Lookdown and Govett's Leap. The bus will take you to within about 1km of Govett's Leap, but for Perry's Lookdown you will have to walk about 6km from the last stop. Services are sparse, with only two buses running on Saturday to Hat Hill Rd and Govett's Leap, none on Sunday. In Katoomba the bus leaves from the top of Katoomba St, outside the Carrington Hotel.

On weekends and public holidays the Blue

Mountains Explorer Bus offers all-day travel for $16 ($8 children). It departs regularly from the railway station and visits the Scenic Railway, Skyway, Echo Point, Leura village and other places. It takes an hour to do the full circuit but you can get on or off and spend as much time as you like at a particular place. Contact Fantastic Aussie Tours, also called Golden West Travel (☎ 4782 1866), 283 Main St, Katoomba.

The Katoomba-Woodford Bus Company (☎ 4782 4213) runs between Katoomba, Leura, Wentworth Falls and east as far as Woodford. There's roughly one service an hour from Katoomba railway station.

There are railway stations in most Blue Mountains towns along the Great Western Highway. Trains run roughly hourly between stations east of Katoomba and roughly two hourly between stations to the west.

GLENBROOK TO KATOOMBA

From Marge's Lookout and Elizabeth's Lookout, just north of Glenbrook, there are good views back to Sydney. The section of the Blue Mountains National Park south of Glenbrook contains **Red Hand Cave**, an old Aboriginal shelter with hand stencils on the walls. It's an easy, 7km return walk southwest of the NPWS information centre.

Springwood

The famous (and infamous, for his cheerfully erotic art) artist and author Norman Lindsay lived in Springwood from 1912 until he died in 1969. His home at 14 Norman Lindsay Crescent is now the **Norman Lindsay Gallery & Museum** (☎ 4751 1067), with exhibits of his paintings, cartoons, illustrations and sculptures. It's open Wednesday to Monday from 11 am to 5 pm; admission costs $6 ($3 children). The streets in the housing developments nearby are named after characters from Lindsay's children's masterpiece *The Magic Pudding* – just the sort of kitsch that Lindsay hated.

Wentworth Falls

South of town there are views of the Jamison Valley and of the 300m Wentworth Falls

from **Falls Reserve**, the starting point for a network of walking tracks. In Wentworth Falls, **Yester Grange** (☎ 4757 1110) is the restored home of a 19th-century premier. It is open weekdays from 10 am to 4 pm, weekends from 10 am to 5 pm. Admission costs $5 ($2.50 children).

Leura

Leura is a quaint tree-lined centre full of country stores and cafes. **Leuralla** (☎ 4784 1169), 36 Olympian Parade, is an Art Deco mansion with a fine collection of 19th-century Australian art, as well as a toy and model-railway museum. The house is a memorial to HV 'Doc' Evatt, a former Labor Party leader and first president of the United Nations; it's open Wednesday to Sunday and admission is $6 ($3 children). In Leura Strand Arcade, the Candy Store has a huge range of lollies (sweets). South of Leura, **Sublime Point** is a great cliff-top lookout. **Gordon Falls Reserve** is a popular picnic spot; from there you can follow the road back past Leuralla, then take the Cliff Drive or the more scenic Prince Henry Cliff Walk to Katoomba's Echo Point.

Places to Stay

There are NPWS *camping areas* accessible by road at Euroka Clearing near Glenbrook, Murphys Glen near Woodford and Ingar near Wentworth Falls. You need a permit to camp at Euroka Clearing from the NPWS office (☎ 4588 5247) at Richmond. The tracks to Ingar and Murphys Glen may be closed after heavy rain.

Leura Village Caravan Park (☎ 4784 1552), on the corner of the Great Western Highway and Leura Mall, has tent sites (from $16), on-site vans (from $34) and cabins (from $45).

There's plenty of expensive hotel, motel and guesthouse accommodation. *Leura House* (☎ 4784 2035), 7 Britain St, is a grand Victorian home (c 1880) with a range of accommodation. Singles/doubles are $99/154 with breakfast, but there is a cheaper room ($58/96) and specials in summer. Mid-week packages are also available.

One of the top places to stay in the Blue Mountains is the big, 210-room *Fairmont Resort* (☎ 4782 5222) on Sublime Point Rd. It's right on the edge of the escarpment and charges from $155. You need to book on weekends.

Springwood YHA Hostel was destroyed in the 1994 bushfires, but there are plans to rebuild it. Contact the Sydney YHA Travel Centre (☎ 9261 1111).

KATOOMBA

Katoomba (population 8300) and the adjacent centres of Wentworth Falls and Leura form the tourist centre of the Blue Mountains. Katoomba is where the Sydney 'plains-dwellers' escape the summer heat, and has long catered to visitors. Despite the number of tourists and its closeness to Sydney, Katoomba has an uncanny atmosphere; another time, another place, accentuated by its Art Deco and Art Nouveau guesthouses and cafes, its thick mists and occasional snowfalls.

Information

The visitor information centre (☎ 4782 0756), at the end of Echo Point Rd, about 2km from the railway station down Katoomba St, is open daily from 9 am to 5 pm. Closer to the station, between Katoomba and Parke Sts, the post office is opposite the shopping centre.

Things to See

The major tourist attraction is **Echo Point**, near the southern end of Katoomba St, about a km from the shopping centre. Here you'll find some of the best views of the Jamison Valley and the magnificent **Three Sisters** rock formation.

The story goes that the three sisters were turned to stone to protect them from the unwanted advances of three young men, but the sorcerer who helped them died before he could turn them back into humans.

Floodlit at night, the rocks are an awesome sight. A walking track follows the road and goes even closer to the edge.

West of Echo Point, at the junction of Cliff

Drive and Violet St, are the **Scenic Railway** and **Scenic Skyway** (☎ 4782 2699). The railway drops 200m to the bottom of the Jamison Valley ($3/4 one way/return, extra for backpacks) where there's good bushwalking (see Activities). The railway was built in the 1880s to transport coal miners and its 45° incline is one of the steepest in the world. The Scenic Skyway cable car travels some 200m above the valley floor, traversing Katoomba Falls gorge ($4.50 return).

The **Explorers Tree**, just west of Katoomba near the Great Western Highway, was marked by Blaxland, Wentworth and Lawson, the first Europeans to find a way over the mountains in 1813.

If you want to experience the thrills of the Blue Mountains without leaving the comfort of a cushioned seat, **The Edge Cinema** (☎ 4782 3928), 225-37 Great Western Highway, shows a 38-minute Blue Mountains documentary, *The Edge*, and other films on a giant screen. Entry is $11.50 ($7.50 children).

Activities

The 12km-return **bushwalk** to the **Ruined Castle** rock formation on Narrow Neck Plateau, dividing the Jamison and Megalong valleys another couple of km west, is one of the best walks – watch out for leeches after rain. The **Golden Stairs** lead down from this plateau to more bushwalking tracks.

Several companies offer **abseiling, rock-climbing, canyoning** and **caving** adventure activities. The competition means that the deals are usually similar – expect to pay about $80 for a day's abseiling.

Rockcraft (☎ 4782 2014), 182 Katoomba St, runs the Australian School of Mountaineering and offers a two-day basic rock-climbing course for $180. There has been good feedback on this. The ASM's bush survival courses ($195 for two days) also sound interesting. Upstairs in the Mountain Designs shop, the Blue Mountains Adventure Company (☎ 4782 1271) organises similar activities (abseiling costs $79 a day)

AROUND SYDNEY

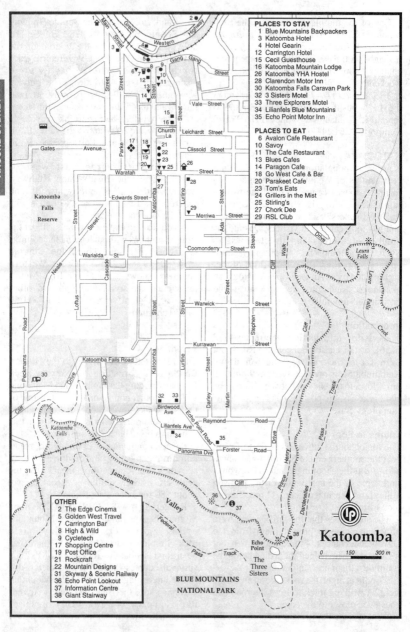

PLACES TO STAY
1 Blue Mountains Backpackers
3 Katoomba Hotel
4 Hotel Gearin
12 Carrington Hotel
15 Cecil Guesthouse
16 Katoomba Mountain Lodge
26 Katoomba YHA Hostel
28 Clarendon Motor Inn
30 Katoomba Falls Caravan Park
32 3 Sisters Motel
33 Three Explorers Motel
34 Lilianfels Blue Mountains
35 Echo Point Motor Inn

PLACES TO EAT
6 Avalon Cafe Restaurant
10 Savoy
11 The Cafe Restaurant
13 Blues Cafes
14 Paragon Cafe
18 Go West Cafe & Bar
20 Parakeet Cafe
23 Tom's Eats
24 Grillers in the Mist
25 Stirling's
27 Chork Dee
29 RSL Club

OTHER
2 The Edge Cinema
5 Golden West Travel
7 Carrington Bar
8 High & Wild
9 Cycletech
17 Shopping Centre
19 Post Office
21 Rockcraft
22 Mountain Designs
31 Skyway & Scenic Railway
36 Echo Point Lookout
37 Information Centre
38 Giant Stairway

Katoomba

0   150   300 m

Katoomba
Falls
Reserve

BLUE MOUNTAINS
NATIONAL PARK

and some interesting mountain-bike tours ($85 a day).

High 'n' Wild (☎ 4782 6224), 3/5 Katoomba St, across from the station, is run by an enthusiastic pair of ex-travellers. They concentrate mainly on abseiling but can help with other activities like wilderness walking and bushcraft.

Extreme Mountain Bike Tours (☎ 4787 7281) is a small outfit offering experienced mountain bikers some great riding. On weekends, Aussie Adrenalin Cycle Tours (☎ 019 92 4719), another small outfit, offers mountain-bike rides along a fire trail to the site of Aboriginal hand stencils and a swimming hole.

Blue Mountains Backpackers (see Places to Stay) organises guided walks and rock-climbing activities, often at a rate lower than other adventure companies. They'll drive you to any of the trail-heads in the area. The YHA hostel also organises activities.

Places to Stay – bottom end

Katoomba Falls Caravan Park (☎ 4782 1835) on Katoomba Falls Rd, about 2km south of the highway, has tent sites for $7 per person and on-site vans for $36.

Katoomba YHA Hostel (☎ 4782 1416) is in a nice old guesthouse on the corner of Lurline and Waratah Sts, near the centre of town. Dorm beds cost $15 and twins/doubles with ensuites are $24 per person. Nearby, *Katoomba Mountain Lodge* (☎ 4782 3933), 31 Lurline St, is a guesthouse and hostel which charges $10 for dorm beds and from $23 per person for singles/doubles with shared bathrooms. There are also more expensive rooms, which include breakfast, in the guesthouse section.

The VIP *Blue Mountains Backpackers* (☎ 4782 4226), 190 Bathurst Rd (the westward continuation of Main St), is close to the railway station and has large dorms for $15 (with a reduced rate for three nights or more) and good twins/doubles for $40. This is a popular place and receives consistently good reviews from travellers.

The Art Deco *Hotel Gearin* (☎ 4782 4395), always known as Gearin's Hotel, is a good local pub and has rooms for $25/45. Some of the rooms are much better than average pub rooms. The Gearin also has share rooms which are let to backpackers for $12 per person. The century-old *Katoomba Hotel* (☎ 4782 1106), a smoky Aussie local on the corner of Parke and Main Sts, has rooms for $30/45; the rate is reduced if you stay more than one night.

Places to Stay – middle & top end

There are many motels and even more guesthouses in and around Katoomba. Rates tend to rise at weekends and on long weekends accommodation can be scarce.

Clarendon Motor Inn (☎ 4782 1322), at the corner of Lurline and Waratah Sts, has guesthouse-style singles/doubles for $30/48 and motel rooms for $56/64.

Rates at most of the more expensive places vary widely, depending on the time of the week and the time of the year. The *3 Sisters Motel* (☎ 4782 2911), at the bottom end of Katoomba St, is an average cheaper motel, charging $50/56 to $80/90.

In the style of the grand guesthouses but with a lower tariff than many, the *Cecil Guesthouse* (☎ 4782 1411), 108 Katoomba St (there's a larger frontage on Lurline St), charges from $40/75 with breakfast.

At the top of the hotel scale is the *Hydro Majestic Hotel* (☎ 4788 1002), a few km west of Katoomba at Medlow Bath, a massive relic of an earlier era. Double rooms with views of the valley and light breakfast cost $120, or $200 with full breakfast and dinner. The equally grand *Carrington Hotel* (☎ 4782 1111) in the centre of Katoomba has begun a major refit. *Lilianfels Blue Mountains* (☎ 4780 1200, 1800 024 452) near Echo Point is one of the top places in the Blue Mountains and charges from $275 single or double.

Places to Eat

Katoomba St, between Gang Gang and Waratah Sts, has plenty of good places to eat. The bright, Art Deco *Savoy*, at No 12, has an interesting menu of the focaccia, pasta and Asian-inspired variety. It's pleasant and the prices are reasonable. Salads cost $6.90 and entree-size pastas from $8.50; the servings are large.

The *Blues Cafe*, at No 57, has mostly vegetarian (and vegan) food – a vegie burger is $6.90 – but also has some chicken dishes for $9.50. It also has Art Deco decor, but nearby is Katoomba's undisputed Art Deco masterpiece, the *Paragon Cafe*. While the menu offers only a little more than you'll find in NSW country-town cafes, the surroundings are wonderful – it's worth a visit if only for a cup of coffee. Check out the cocktail bar and the classical Greek figures in motif on the wood-panelled walls. Pasta is $9 and steak $12.50. The Paragon is open only during the day.

Back on the other side of the street, *Cafe Restaurant* is open for breakfast and serves burger and chips for $7.50, chicken sandwiches $4.80. Farther down Katoomba St, *Go West Cafe & Bar*, a small place with benches outside, has focaccia for $4.50, vegetable lasagne $5.

Towards the corner of Waratah St, *Tom's Eats*, 200 Katoomba St, has meals for well under $10. Chicken burgers are $7. It's open from 11 am to 11 pm during the week and until 1 am on weekends. Nearby, *Grillers in the Mist* (groan) sells fresh and frozen seafood and puts together some interesting takeaways, such as grilled sardine rolls for $4.50. The sociable *Parakeet Cafe* has tables outside and vegie burgers for $7.50, scotch fillet for $13.50. Across Waratah St, the Thai *Chork Dee* (☎ 4782 1913) has pad king (chicken with ginger) for $9.70, vegetarian dishes for around $7.50; it's open for dinner only.

Near the station, upstairs at 82 Main St and along some corridors, the *Avalon Cafe Restaurant* is a relaxed and pleasantly eccentric place, open for lunch and dinner Wednesday to Saturday and for dinner on Sunday. Pasta mains are $11 and other dishes around $17.

Entertainment

The Carrington Hotel on Katoomba St is closed for renovations but its revamped *Carrington Bar*, with a green-tiled facade, is

open. There are some dress regulations but that doesn't interfere with the events such as horizontal bungee-jumping that are held here. For local bands, try *Gearin's Hotel* or the *Katoomba Hotel* on weekends and there's a blues jam at Gearin's on Monday night. The *Blues Cafe* has jazz on Sunday night.

There's a theatre restaurant/cabaret at *Clarendon Motor Inn*, with shows on Friday and Saturday nights – some of the acts are big names.

See Mt Victoria for information on a night out at the Mt Vic Flicks.

Getting Around

Bus The Katoomba-Woodford Bus Company (☎ 4782 4213) runs from opposite the Carrington Hotel to the Scenic Railway, approximately hourly until about 4.30 pm on weekdays and a few times on Saturday ($1.60). Mountainlink (☎ 4782 3333) runs a service between Echo Point and Gordon Falls via Katoomba St and Leura Mall. There is roughly one service an hour midweek, fewer on weekends.

See also the Blue Mountains Explorer Bus under Getting Around at the start of the Blue Mountains section.

Car If you're driving, be aware of the parking restrictions, as they're strictly enforced. Cullen Utility Rental (☎ 4782 5535), 60 Wilson St, rents cars from $58 a day, including insurance and 250 free km.

Bicycle You can hire mountain bikes at the YHA hostel for $25 a day ($15 for guests). If all their bikes are out, try the Cecil Guesthouse, farther up Lurline St; the rates are similar. Cycletech (☎ 4782 2800), Gang Gang St, rents mountain bikes for $6 an hour or $15/25 for a half/full day. Katoomba Mountain Bike Hire (☎ 4782 6000), 38 Waratah St, has similar rates.

BLACKHEATH & AROUND

Blackheath (population 3800), 10km west of Katoomba on the Great Western Highway, is a good base for visiting the Grose and Megalong valleys. It has the closest railway station to the NPWS Blue Mountains Heritage Centre (☎ 4787 8877), about 3km north-east along Govett's Leap Rd. The centre is open daily from 9 am to 4.30 pm.

There are superb lookouts east of town, among them **Govett's Leap** with the adjacent **Bridal Veil Falls** (the highest in the Blue Mountains) and **Evans Lookout** (turn off the highway south of Blackheath). To the north-east, via Hat Hill Rd, are **Pulpit Rock, Perry's Lookdown** and **Anvil Rock**.

A long cliff-edge track leads from Govett's Leap to Pulpit Rock and there are walks down into the Grose Valley itself and floor of the valley. All involve at least a 300m descent and ascent. Get details on walks from the NPWS Heritage Centre. Perry's Lookdown is at the beginning of the shortest route to the beautiful **Blue Gum Forest** at the foot of the valley – about four hours return, but you'll want to spend longer.

To the west and south-west of Blackheath lie the Kanimbla and Megalong valleys, with yet more spectacular views from places like **Hargreaves Lookout**.

Places to Stay & Eat
The nearest NPWS campsite is Acacia Flat in the Grose Valley, near the Blue Gum Forest. It's a steep walk down from Govett's Leap or Perry's Lookdown. You can camp at Perry's Lookdown, which has a car park and is a convenient base for walks into the Grose Valley.

Blackheath Caravan Park (☎ 4787 8101), on Prince Edward St, off Govett's Leap Rd about 600 metres from the highway, has tent sites for $7 a single and vans from $36 a double (cash only). *Lakeview Holiday Park* (☎ 4787 8534) on Prince Edward St has cabins from $45 to $90 a double. The cosy *Gardners Inn* (☎ 4787 8347) on the Great Western Highway in Blackheath, is the oldest hotel (1831) in the Blue Mountains and charges $25/50, including breakfast.

On the road to Evans Lookout, *Federation Garden Lodge* (☎ 4787 7767) has two-bedroom apartments for $85 a double. The grounds are large and the facilities are good.

Jenby-Rimbah Lodge (☎ 4787 7622), 336 Evans Lookout Rd, is in bushland with good self-contained cabins from $90. It can organise activities with the NPWS.

Several cafes are clustered along the highway and Govett's Leap Rd, including *Wattle Cafe* which serves hamburgers for $2.50 and has a pot-belly stove you can warm yourself by. The *Banksia* has bagels with interesting fillings for $8.50 and good coffee. At the *Victory Theatre Cafe*, on Govett's Leap Rd, you can have egg on toast for $5 then spend hours looking at the antiques in the huge area at the back.

At the top of the price scale, *Cleopatra Country House* (☎ 4787 8456), on Cleopatra St, is an excellent restaurant, winner of many awards. There's also accommodation, with mid-week packages ranging from $175 to $220 per person including meals.

THE MEGALONG VALLEY
Unless you walk or take Katoomba's Scenic Railway, about the only chance you'll get to see what the gorges of the Blue Mountains look like from below is via the Megalong Valley. It feels like rural Australia there, a big change from the quasi-suburbs strung out along the ridge-tops. It is largely cleared farmland but still beautiful. The road down from Blackheath passes through pockets of **rainforest**; you can taste the Blue Mountains' beauty by following the 600m Coachwood Glen Nature Trail, a couple of km before the small settlement of Werribee.

Megalong Valley Farm (☎ 4787 8188) has shearing, milking and other activities as well as Clydesdale horses (you can book a ride) and native animals. It's open daily from 10 am to 5 pm; entry is $3, $2 children. There is also accommodation in bunkhouses, with dorm beds for $15.

There are several **horseriding** outfits, such as Werriberri Trail Rides (☎ 4787 9171), Megalong Rd near Megalong Valley Farm, and Packsaddlers (☎ 4787 9150), run by one of the district's longest-established families, at the end of the valley in Green Gully. Both offer riding by the hour and longer treks and accommodation.

MT VICTORIA

Mt Victoria is a small village (population 880), 16km north-west of Katoomba, with some historic old buildings and a semi-rural atmosphere. At 1043m, it's also the highest point in the mountains. It has been popular as a holiday spot for a long time and Henry Lawson worked here as a house-painter, decorating the new houses that his father had built. Today the town is classified by the National Trust.

Everything is an easy walk from the railway station where the **Mt Victoria Museum of Australiana**, open weekends from 2 to 5 pm. Interesting buildings include the Victoria & Albert guesthouse, the 1849 Tollkeeper's Cottage and the 1870s church.

Mt Vic Flicks (☎ 4787 1577) is a cinema of the old school, with 'usherettes', a piano player and door prizes. It shows mainstream films and the more popular arthouse releases. On Thursday and Friday nights it costs $5; on Saturday night $10 gets you a double feature plus supper at interval!

Off the highway at **Mt York** there's a memorial to the explorers who first crossed the Blue Mountains. A short stretch of the original road crosses the mountains here.

Places to Stay & Eat

The fine, old *Imperial Hotel* (☎ 4787 1233), on the Great Western Highway, arguably has the best backpackers' rooms in the region, at $20 for a dorm bed. It also has singles/doubles from $41/62 to $99/153, with various packages. The Imperial is the weekend watering hole of rock climbers, so this is a good place to make contacts.

Nearby, the *Victoria & Albert* (☎ 4787 1588), 19 Station St, is a guesthouse in the grand old style. B&B costs from $45/90, $15 more with attached bathroom. There's a cafe and in the evening a good restaurant offers two-course dinners for $24.50 and three courses for $30. Another old-style guesthouse is *Manor House* (☎ 4787 1369), on Montgomery St, with rooms for $79 to $155 per person, including dinner and breakfast. The Duke of York, later King George VI, had afternoon tea here in 1927.

HARTLEY HISTORIC SITE

In the 1830s, after the Victoria Pass route made it easier to travel inland from the coast, increasing numbers of travellers crossed the Blue Mountains. However, the discomforts of the old road via Mt York were soon replaced by the discomforts of being bailed up by bushrangers. The government established Hartley, 10km west of Mt Victoria, as a police post and the village became a popular place to break the journey, partly because it was safe and partly because of the pubs. Some fine sandstone buildings were constructed, notably the Greek Revival courthouse (1837). Many remain today, although the village is now deserted.

The NPWS information centre (☎ 6355 2117) in the Farmer's Inn is open daily from 10 am to 1 pm and 2 to 5 pm. You can wander around the village for free but to enter specific buildings you're given a guided tour which costs $3 ($2 children) per building. Countrylink buses stop nearby.

JENOLAN CAVES

South-west of Katoomba and on the western fringe of Kanangra Boyd National Park are the Jenolan Caves (☎ 6359 3311), the best-known limestone caves in Australia. One cave has been open to the public since 1867, although parts of the system are still unexplored. Three caves are open for independent viewing and you can visit a further nine by guided tour. There are about 10 tours daily from 10 am to 4 pm, with an evening tour at 8 pm. Tours last one to two hours and prices start from $12. At holiday time it's advisable to arrive early, as the best caves can be 'sold out' by 10 am.

Walks

There's a network of walking trails through the bush surrounding the Jenolan Caves.

The Six Foot Track from Katoomba to the Jenolan Caves is a fairly easy three-day walk. The DCLM has a detailed brochure. Great Australian Walks (☎ 9555 7580) has guided walks along the track with accommodation for $299. They carry everything for you.

Organised Tours

See Organised Tours at the start of the Blue Mountains section for information on the popular Wonderbus tour. Fantastic Aussie Tours (☎ 4782 1866, 9938 5714 in Sydney) has day-tours to the caves from Katoomba for $49 (plus cave entry). Walkers can be dropped off at and collected from the Six Foot Track at Jenolan for $32, but you have to book.

Places to Stay

You can camp near Jenolan Caves House for $10 per site. *Binda Bush Cabins* (☎ 6359 3311), on the road from Hartley, about 8km north of the caves, can accommodate six people in bunks for $75 for two people per night. The revamped 1889 *Jenolan Caves House* (☎ 6359 3304) is a big old-style guesthouse. Rooms cost from $55 to $150 single or double. Breakfast is an extra $16. It also has a motel section.

In Oberon, about 30km north-west of the caves, there are other, cheaper options – see the Central West chapter.

BELLS LINE OF ROAD

This back road between Richmond and Lithgow is the most scenic route across the Blue Mountains. It's highly recommended if you have your own transport. There are fine views towards the coast from Kurrajong Heights on the eastern slopes of the range, orchards around Bilpin and Shipley and sandstone cliff and bush scenery all the way to Lithgow. This road was constructed in 1841 by Archibald Bell, a local landowner, as an alternative route (to what is now the Great Western Highway) across the mountains.

Near the old village of Kurrajong Heights, about 15km from Richmond, **Kurrajong Heights Grass Ski Park** (☎ 4567 7184) has skiing and carting down a grassy slope. It costs $13 for two hours and the centre is open on weekends and holidays.

Mt Tomah Botanic Garden

Midway between Bilpin and Bell, Mt Tomah Botanic Garden (☎ 4567 2154) is a cool-climate annexe of Sydney's Royal Botanic Gardens. As well as native plants, there are exotic species including a magnificent display of rhododendrons. The gardens are open daily; admission is $5 per car or motorcycle, $2 for pedestrians and cyclists.

Mt Wilson

Mt Wilson is 8km north of Bells Line of Road; the turn-off is 7km east of Bell. Like Katoomba, Mt Wilson was settled by people with a penchant for things English, but unlike Katoomba, with its guesthouses and Art Deco cafes, Mt Wilson is a spacious village of hedgerows, lines of European trees and houses with big gardens. Near the Post House there's an information board with details of gardens open to the public and some short walks in the area.

A km or so from the village centre is a lovely remnant of rainforest thick with tree-ferns, the **Cathedral of Ferns**.

The *Post House* (☎ 4756 2000) serves teas and can arrange B&B accommodation or you could try *Blueberry Lodge* (☎ 4756 2022), with self-contained chalets sleeping up to six and costing $130 a double (more on weekends).

Zig Zag Railway

The Zig Zag Railway (☎ 6353 1795) is at Clarence, about 10km east of Lithgow. It was built in 1869 and was quite an engineering wonder in its day. Trains descended from the Blue Mountains by this route until 1910. A section has been restored and steam trains run daily. The fare for the 12km trip is $10 ($5 children).

LITHGOW

Nestled in the western foothills of the Blue Mountains, the Lithgow Valley was first settled by Europeans in the 1820s, but the town didn't begin to grow until the coal was mined in the 1870s to supply the trains which crossed the mountains on the Zig Zag Railway. Today, Lithgow (population 20,400) is an industrial town with a rural feel.

The Lithgow Visitors Centre (☎ 6353 18590) is in the old railway station on the

Great Western Highway just north of the turn-off into town. It's open daily from 9 am to 5 pm. There's a smaller information office (☎ 6351 2307) at 285 Main St.

Eskbank House (☎ 6351 3557) on Bennet St (off Inch St which is north of the railway line) is a gracious home built by the founder of Lithgow's coal industry in 1842 and now houses a museum. Admission is $2 and it's open Thursday to Monday between 10 am and 4 pm. Australia's first steelworks were established in Lithgow last century, but all that remain are a few crumbling buildings in **Blast Furnace Park** off Inch St, though there are plans to develop it.

There are fine views from **Hassan Walls Lookout**, 5km south of town.

Places to Stay

Lithgow Caravan Park (☎ 6351 4350), Cooerwull Rd, has tent sites for $8 for two people, on-site vans for $30 and self-contained cabins for $45.

Several pubs have accommodation, including the *Grand Central* (☎ 6351 3050) on the corner of Main and Eskbank Sts, with rooms for $20/36. Motels include the *Lithgow Valley Inn* (☎ 6351 2334), off the highway on Cooerwull Drive, with rooms from $36/52. More expensive is *Zig Zag Motel* (☎ 6352 2477), on the corner of Chifley Rd and Clwydd St, where rooms cost $62/72.

Getting There & Away

Bus Countrylink buses (☎ 6352 3099) connect with some trains and run to Orange, Bathurst, Dubbo, Coonabarabran, Mudgee, Gulgong, Forbes and Parkes, but not daily.

Train Lithgow is on the main western railway line to Bathurst, Orange and Dubbo. CityRail trains also run from Sydney ($14.20 one way).

Car & Motorcycle Lithgow is on the Great Western Highway which runs between Sydney and Bathurst. You can head south on smaller roads to Oberon (where still smaller

roads lead south to Goulburn) and north to Mudgee and Gulgong (turn off the highway about 7km on the Bathurst side of town).

AROUND LITHGOW

The road from Lithgow north towards Mudgee runs parallel to the western escarpments of the Blue Mountains and there are some good views, especially from **Pearsons Lookout**, 40km north of Lithgow. See the Bathurst to Mudgee section in the Central West chapter for information on places farther along this road.

At Lidsdale, on the Mudgee road, about 10 km north of Lithgow, a road which degenerates into a rough track runs 30-odd km to **Newnes**, a ghost town. There's a 5km walk to a disused railway tunnel full of glowworms and access to the wild Wollemi National Park. An 11km walking track leads north to the ghost town of **Glen Davis** where there's a museum open on weekends. There are camping areas at both Newnes and Glen Davis.

The Southern Highlands

The fertile Southern Highlands was one of the first inland areas to be settled. Most of it was quickly cleared of unruly native foliage to make way for agriculture and English-style villages. This development was early enough in Australia's history for the settlers to regard themselves as English landed gentry rather than Australian farmers and their unease at being so far from home can be understood from the landscape of bare hills, brooding pines and stone buildings.

As well as being of historical interest, the Southern Highlands gives access to the excellent Morton National Park (see below). The country north of the Hume expressway is more rugged and there's an interesting drive to the Wombeyan Caves (see below) and on to Bathurst (see the Central West chapter).

Information

The area's main source of information is the Southern Highlands Visitors Information Centre (☎ 4871 2888) in Mittagong; it's open daily from 8 am to 5.30 pm. It also provides a free accommodation booking service (☎ 1800 656 176). Craigie's *Visitors Map of the Southern Highlands* ($4.95) covers the area in detail.

Activities

There is some good bushwalking in the area, especially in Morton National Park. One of the longest trails is the **Ensign Barralier Walking Track** which begins near Mittagong at Lake Alexandra and winds 140km north through wild country to Katoomba. It takes a week to nine days and passes through the privately owned ghost town of **Yerranderie**. Robert Sloss has written a booklet which contains detailed tracknotes; it's available from the Southern Highlands Visitors Information Centre (they can mail credit-card orders) for $6.90. Information centres in the Blue Mountains may also stock it.

Horseriding is offered on many properties on the highlands. Caringal Holiday Farm (☎ 4886 4234), not far from Fitzroy Falls, charges $16 an hour for riding, $26 for lessons. Other outfits include Birrabongie (☎ 4877 1144), in Berrima, which has hourlong trail rides for $20 and Maple Downs Tourist Park (☎ 4861 6075) in Bowral.

Special Events

The Mittagong Country Fair is held in late March and the Bowral Tulip Festival is held in late September. Over the Queen's Birthday long weekend in June, the village of Burrawang holds a folk music festival.

Guesthouses

In the 1920s a bout of nostalgia for 'home' afflicted the area, resulting in lavish country guesthouses catering to wealthy Sydney residents. The few guesthouses that remain are popular. The highlands can be a bleak place in winter, with grey skies and winds off the snow, so log fires and hearty meals have their

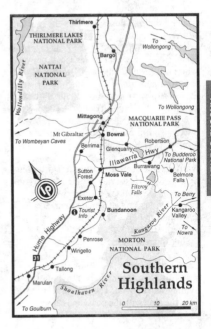

attraction and certainly offer a contrast to Sydney, not far away on the Hume Highway. As in the Blue Mountains, many guesthouses celebrate Christmas in winter.

The larger places are almost resorts and the words 'exclusive' and 'luxury' figure prominently in their advertising. The NSW Travel Centre and some travel agents in Sydney have brochures and will know about packages and special deals.

Getting There & Around

Bus Long-distance buses running on the Hume Highway between Sydney and Melbourne call in at Mittagong, but most don't go on to Bowral or Moss Vale. The Southern Highlands Visitors Information Centre in Mittagong sells tickets for most bus lines; you can buy Countrylink tickets at the railway station, a few blocks away. Buses don't come off the highway into Mittagong unless someone has booked a ticket. Except for Countrylink, whose buses stop at the railway station, buses stop at the visitors information centre.

Berrima Coaches (☎ 4871 3211) runs fairly frequent weekday services between Mittagong, Moss Vale and Bowral, with a few continuing on to Berrima, Sutton Forest, Exeter and Bundanoon. On Saturday morning, Berrima Coaches has services between Mittagong, Moss Vale and Bowral. Buses also link Wollongong and Moss Vale, some run via Bundanoon.

Train CityRail trains run to Mittagong, Bowral and Moss Vale. Some Countrylink trains on the Sydney-Canberra run stop at these stations and at Bundanoon; the XPT to/from Melbourne also stops at one or more of them. Check with CityRail and Countrylink for schedules.

Car & Motorcycle The Hume Highway runs past Mittagong, which is 1½ hours from Sydney, and Bowral. The Illawarra Highway links the area with the coast and runs through Moss Vale.

MITTAGONG & BOWRAL
These two large towns, surrounded by dairy farming and stud cattle country, have almost blended into each other. **Moss Vale**, just south of Bowral, may do the same. The total population of this area is approaching 20,000.

If you're driving between Bowral and Mittagong, take the scenic route over **Mt Gibraltar**, which gives good views down the valley.

Sir Donald Bradman began his cricketing career in Bowral. A large **Bradman Museum** (☎ 4862 1247) on St Jude St, a few blocks east of the main street, is in a purpose-built pavilion beside a cricket ground and contains plenty of memorabilia. You can see videos of the Don's career and other pieces of cricketing history. The museum is open daily from 10 am to 4 pm and admission is $5 ($2.50 children).

Places to Stay
Camping *Mittagong Caravan Park* (☎ 4871 1574), on the old highway, has tent sites for about $9, on-site vans for $25 and cabins from $31. *Moss Vale Village Park* (☎ 4868 1099), off Argyle St (the Illawarra Highway) south of the town centre, is a little more expensive.

Our Don Bradman
If you need to read this section, you must come from one of those barbaric nations which doesn't play cricket. If you come from a cricketing country, there's probably no need to read this section. Anyway...

Sir Donald Bradman is probably the greatest batsman cricket has ever seen. Born in Cootamundra in central west NSW in 1908, the young Bradman practised for his illustrious cricketing career by hitting a soft ball against a corrugated metal tank. In this way he developed his footwork, his quick eye and judgment of bowling. He became a brilliant outfieldsman and is considered by many to have been the greatest natural batsman in the history of cricket.

He scored 19 centuries in Test matches against England between 1928 and 1948 when he retired with a Test batting average of 99.9! The average would have been over 100 had Sir Donald not been dismissed for a duck (0) in his last innings, and it's a mark of the man's character that he didn't play another match to boost the average. ■

Hotels & Motels The *Mittagong Hotel* (☎ 4871 1923) on the old highway has accommodation for $35/50 a single/double. On the highway in Mittagong, motels include the *Melrose* (☎ 4871 1511) and the *Mittagong* (☎ 4871 1277), which charges from about $40/45. In Bowral there's a swag of expensive places, such as the *Oxley View* (☎ 4861 4211) on Moss Vale Rd which has singles/doubles with spa baths for $115/135; it also has cheaper rooms for $45/50.

Guesthouses *Braemar Lodge* (☎ 4871 2483) off the old highway just north of Mittagong is a big old mansion in large grounds with rooms for $100/160 including breakfast. There's also an Indian restaurant.

In Robertson, on the Illawarra Highway between Bowral and the coast, is *Ranelagh House* (☎ 4885 1111), built in 1924 as a big, exclusive guesthouse. Later it became a friary, a country club and a hotel, but is now back in business as a guesthouse, with 60 renovated rooms. Deer and peacocks roam through the extensive grounds and apparently a friendly ghost walks the hallways. B&B rates are $100/125.

Top-end places to stay include *Links House* (☎ 4861 1977), *Berida Manor* (☎ 4861 1177) and *Milton Park* (☎ 4861 1522), all in or near Bowral.

WOMBEYAN CAVES

These interesting limestone caves (☎ 4843 5976), 65km north-west of Mittagong, are reached by an even more interesting mountain road. The caves are in a pretty little valley with mown lawns shaded by poplars and pines. The surrounding bushland is a nature reserve with some walking trails and plenty of wildlife. You can walk to a swimming-hole at **Limestone Canyon**. Guided tours of the caves cost $12 ($6 children) and there's one cave which you can inspect by yourself for $10. Wombeyan is open daily from 8.30 am to 5 pm.

Places to Stay

At the Wombeyan *camping reserve* there are tent sites for $10, caravan sites at $15, on-site vans for $40 and cabins with ensuites for $55. There's a kiosk and a well-equipped communal kitchen for campers.

On the Mittagong road, just before the steep ascent into the Wombeyan Nature Reserve, *Wollondilly Camping Ground* (☎ 4888 9239) has some lovely camping areas on the banks of a broad, shallow river, for $5 per person ($3 children). They also rent out tents. Off the road, a bit further back towards Mittagong, is *River Island Nature Retreat* (☎ 4888 9236) with camping and cabins. There's a small store here.

Getting There & Away

From Canberra or Melbourne, the Goulburn/Taralga route is quickest and involves only 4km of narrow, winding road. From Sydney, take the road running west from Mittagong. This route is direct but it involves about 45km of narrow, steep and winding mountain road – very scenic but slow. It's a popular drive; watch out for oncoming cars at blind corners, especially on weekends.

Fuel is available at the camping reserve.

BERRIMA

The first Europeans travelled through the Berrima area early in the 19th century on an expedition to prove to Sydney's convicts that China (and thus freedom) did *not* lie on the other side of the Great Dividing Range.

The site for Berrima was chosen by explorer Thomas Mitchell and the town was founded in 1829. It blossomed as a stopping-place on the way to the wide lands west of the mountains. However, the road proved too steep for easy travel, bushrangers infested the route and eventually the railway bypassed the town. Berrima's population dropped to just eight people by 1900, and consequently the town suffered little from further development. Today its population is under 800 and the whole village is heritage classified.

The best of its old buildings is the neo-classical **Berrima Courthouse,** built in 1838. The court now houses an excellent little museum (☎ 4877 1505) and for $2.50

($2 children) you can see an audiovisual show on Berrima's history and visit the courtroom set up – complete with dummies and a soundtrack – as it was during the trial of a woman who murdered her husband with an axe. The courthouse is open daily from 10 am to 4 pm and also has tourist information.

Berrima Museum (☎ 4868 2230), at the other end of the main street, opposite the Alpaca Centre, houses a local history collection. It's open on weekends from 10 am to 4 pm and admission is $1 (20c children). The nearby **Surveyor General Inn** claims to be Australia's oldest continuously operating hotel (ho-hum). The first owner of the pub built himself a large house on Wilkinson St, **Harper's Mansion** (☎ 4861 2402), which is open at weekends from 11 am to 4 pm; entry is $2.

Places to Stay

The *White Horse Inn* (☎ 4877 1204) on Market Place was built in 1832 but has much more recent motel units for $65. So too does the *Berrima Bakehouse Motel* (☎ 4877 1381), which charges $50/65. The *Surveyor General Inn* (☎ 4877 1226) on the main street has doubles for $50 midweek ($70 on weekends), including breakfast. Ask the information centre about other places offering B&B, most of which are pricey.

BUNDANOON & AROUND

Bundanoon (population 1500) is a village off the Hume Highway, midway between Sydney and Canberra. Tourists discovered the town early and in the 1920s Bundanoon was the guesthouse capital of the Southern Highlands, with over 50 guesthouses. There are far fewer today but you can still experience some of that stuccoed charm.

Ye Olde Bicycle Shoppe (☎ 4883 6043), next to the post office and not far from the railway station, has a tea room and tourist information and rents bikes from $15 per day; cycling is a popular way to get around the area's villages. The shoppe is closed Tuesday and Wednesday.

Bundanoon's main attraction is its proximity to the northern escarpments of **Morton**

National Park and there are a number of lookouts and walking trails within easy reach of the town.

Exeter, a hamlet 7km north of Bundanoon, will satisfy Anglophiles in search of walled parks, gloomy lanes of pine trees and stone houses.

Places to Stay

Bundanoon YHA Hostel (☎ 4883 6010), on Railway Ave (the main street) about 1km east of the station, is an old boarding-house in a large, leafy yard. The manager might not be around during the day but the common areas are left unlocked. Dorm beds are $13, twins/doubles are $17 per person.

Most other places are cheaper midweek than on weekends, when you might have to take a package, including meals. *Bundanoon Country Hotel* (☎ 4883 6005), on Erith St across the tracks from the railway station, is a well-equipped place charging from $50/90 and has weekend packages for $125. The 1897 *Killarney Guesthouse* (☎ 4883 6224) on Ellsmore Rd is in 6 hectares of garden. It's a big setup, with a theatre restaurant and various accommodation options, with B&B for $40 to $55 per person midweek. *Mildenhall* (☎ 4883 6643), 10 Anzac Parade, has B&B from $50/75 and also offers weekend packages.

Getting There & Away

Bus Countrylink runs to Wollongong daily, via Moss Vale. Taking a train to Wollongong then a bus through Macquarie Pass National Park is a long but interesting way to get here from Sydney.

Train Bundanoon is on the Sydney-Canberra line.

MORTON NATIONAL PARK

This wilderness area in the Budawang Range, which covers 162,386 hectares, has magnificent sandstone cliffs and waterfalls which fall to the forests deep in the valleys below.

The NPWS Visitors Centre (☎ 4887 7270) is at Fitzroy Falls. Ask here about camping in the valleys below the escarpments – you'll probably have to walk in. The closest road access to the park is around Bundanoon and Fitzroy Falls and on the road from near Kangaroo Valley to Tallowa Dam on the Shoalhaven River. There's also the road which runs to Sassafras (surrounded by the park) from either Nowra or Braidwood.

The spectacular **Fitzroy Falls** have an 82m drop and the less well-known **Twin Falls** are a km or so from here along the eastern track. **Glow-worm Glen**, best visited at night, is a half-hour walk from the end of William St in Bundanoon. In the south of the park is the **Pigeon House**, a curiously shaped mountain. See the South Coast chapter for information on climbing it.

Twin Falls Bush Cottages (☎ 4887 7333) are self-contained and sleep six people in two bedrooms or up to four in a single-bedroom cabin. They are on their own patch of bushland. Nightly rates are $95 a double up to $180 for six people, plus a linen hire charge unless you bring your own. Weekend rates are higher.

On the north-east edge of Morton is the smaller **Budderoo National Park**, with more waterfalls, lookouts and walking trails. On the west side of the park is the **Minnamurra Rainforest Area** (see the Kiama section of the South Coast chapter). Access to both is from Robertson to the north or from Jamberoo near Kiama.

KANGAROO VALLEY

From Fitzroy Falls to Kangaroo Valley the road climbs down the steep escarpment. Kangaroo Valley is a lovely place, largely cleared but with steep, forested mountains and escarpments encroaching onto the valley floor.

You enter the valley through the castellated **Hamden Bridge** (1897), a few km north of the township of Kangaroo Valley. Near the bridge is **Pioneer Farm Settlement** (☎ 4465 1306), an old homestead with historic displays and some native animals in a refuge. Markets are held here on the last Sunday of the month. You can also visit

Sharply Vale Fruit World (☎ 4465 1325), a big fruit orchard.

The Shoalhaven and Kangaroo rivers are popular for **canoeing** and Kangaroo Valley Canoe Adventures (☎ 4465 1502) has day trips and longer journeys, usually on weekends. There's a minimum group size of six, but ring Geoff Whatmore and he might be able to fit you in with an existing group. Day trips cost $40 per person and overnight trips are $200.

In Kangaroo Valley township, *Glenmack Caravan Park* (☎ 4465 1372) is a pleasant place to pitch a tent ($12) and has cabins from $35. It also has tourist information.

The road from Kangaroo Valley to Berry is beautiful. Take the turn-off to the left just out of Kangaroo Valley township on the road to Nowra. This narrow road takes you up through thick forest to a neatly-farmed plateau, then plunges down again through the forest. Take it easy – it's about 20km of narrow, winding road and there are school buses travelling along it too.

Up here is the *Skyfarm* (call Diane Jones in Sydney for details on ☎ 9555 2522), a small, luxurious farmstay catering to one group of up to six people at a time. You have the whole farm to yourself for $330 a night midweek, $420 a night on weekends. There's a minimum stay of two nights. For a group, this is good value for a touch of luxury.

Illawarra & Wollongong

Illawarra comprises the coastal strip and the spectacular escarpment behind it which runs from Royal National Park south past the cities of Wollongong and Port Kembla.

The region was explored by Europeans in the early 19th century, but apart from timber cutting and dairy farming there was little development until the escarpment's coalfields attracted miners. By the turn of the century Wollongong was a major coal port. Steelworks were developed in the 1920s and today the region is one of the country's major industrial centres.

AROUND SYDNEY

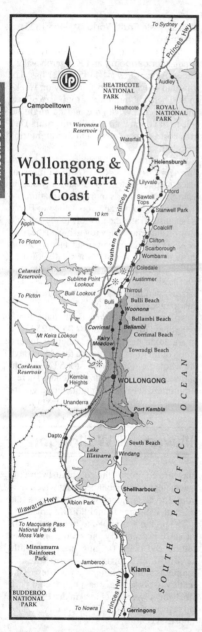

AROUND SYDNEY

Wollongong &
The Illawarra
Coast

Despite the industry, there is spectacular natural scenery and some great beaches.

WOLLONGONG & AROUND

Wollongong (population 214,000), 80km south of Sydney, is the state's third largest city and sprawls south to the biggest steelworks in Australia at Port Kembla. There are some excellent surf beaches, especially north of the centre where the Illawarra Escarpment draws closer to the coast. The hills behind provide a fine backdrop, great views over the city and coast and good walks.

Wollongong is a hard-working industrial city without the edgy weirdness of inner Sydney – a day trip to Wollongong can be a good break. It's easily reached by train from Sydney (see Getting There & Away later), an interesting ride through tunnels and the bushland of the Illawarra Escarpment. Beachside suburbs such as Bulli offer plenty of sand and waves and most have railway stations.

Orientation & Information

Crown St is the main commercial street and between Kembla and Keira Sts is a two-block pedestrian mall. Keira St is part of the Princes Highway. Through-traffic bypasses the city on the Southern Freeway.

The tourist information centre (☎ 4228 0300), on the corner of Crown and Kembla Sts, is open Monday to Friday from 9 am to 5 pm, on weekends from 10 am to 4 pm. The post office is next door.

The SpidrWeb Cafe (☎ 4225 8677), 67 Kembla St, is the Illawarra region's first Internet cafe.

Bushcraft on Stewart St has hiking and camping gear.

Things to See & Do

The fishing fleet is based in the southern part of Wollongong's harbour, **Belmore Basin**, which was cut from solid rock in 1868. There's a fish cooperative (with a fish market, cafe and the Harbour Seafood Restaurant) and an 1872 lighthouse on the point. Nearby, on the headland, is the newer Breakwater Lighthouse.

North Beach, north of the harbour, generally has better surf than the south Wollongong City Beach. The harbour itself has beaches which are good for children. Other beaches run north up the coast.

The interesting **City Gallery** (☎ 4228 7500), on the corner of Kembla and Burelli Sts, is the largest regional gallery in the country. Its collection focuses on 20th-century Australian painting and sculpture and Aboriginal paintings. It's open Tuesday to Friday from 10 am to 5 pm, on weekends from noon to 4 pm; entry is free.

The **Illawarra Museum** (☎ 4228 0158), 11 Market St, contains a reconstruction of the 1902 Mt Kembla village mining disaster and other exhibitions. It's open from Wednesday from 10 am to 1 pm, weekends from 1 to 4 pm; entry is $2 (children $1).

Wollongong Botanic Gardens, on Murphy's Ave in Keiraville, north-west of the centre, have tropical and temperate plants and a lily lake; it's open daily.

The enormous **Buddhist Temple** (☎ 4272 0600), a few km south of the city, is open to visitors.

North of the City Wollongong sprawls north, nearly to the edge of Royal National Park, but the beachside suburbs are almost individual towns. **Bulli** and **Thirroul** (where DH Lawrence lived during his time in Australia; the cottage where he wrote *Kangaroo* still stands) are both popular. In Bulli the Black Diamond District Heritage Centre (☎ 4267 4312) at the old railway station is open from Sunday from 10 am to 4 pm. At **Coalcliff** (appropriately named – coal was mined near this cliffside for most of the 19th century), the road heads up the escarpment. A short way along, near **Stanwell Park**, it enters thick forest and you drive through the Royal National Park.

Up the coast there are several excellent beaches. Those with good surf include **Sandon Point**, **Austinmer**, **Headlands** (only for experienced surfers) and **Sharkies**.

On the road to the village of **Otford** and Royal National Park, the **Lawrence Hargrave Lookout** at Bald Hill above Stanwell Park is a superb clifftop viewing-point. Hargrave, a pioneer aviator, made his first attempts at flying in the area early this century. Hang-gliders fly there today and the Sydney Hang Gliding Centre has courses; call Chris Boyce on ☎ (042) 94 9994. **Symbio Koala Gardens** (☎ 4294 1244) on Lawrence Hargrave Drive in Stanwell Tops (above Stanwell Park) has koalas, kangaroos and other animals. Near Otford, Otford Valley Farm Riding School (☎ 4294 2442) has **horseriding** for $17 an hour; there are several other outfits in the area.

South of Wollongong Just south, **Lake Illawarra** is very popular for watersports including windsurfing. South of Lake Illawarra, **Shellharbour**, a popular holiday resort, is one of the oldest towns along the coast. It was a thriving port back in 1830, but it declined after the construction of the railway lines. The name Shellharbour comes from the number of shell middens (remnants of Aboriginal feasts) that the early Europeans found here. There are good beaches on the Windang Peninsula north of the town.

In **Albion Park**, on the second Sunday of the month (every Sunday in January and all long weekends) you can ride an old tram or steam train at the **Illawarra Light Railway Museum** (☎ 4256 4627), Tongarra Rd. Admission is free and rides cost up to $2.50 ($2 children).

Illawarra Escarpment SRA, This area, which takes in land donated by the BHP company, is good for bushwalking. There's no vehicle access. The park is a number of separate sections from Bulli Pass to Bong Bong; it isn't very large but the country is spectacular. Contact the NPWS (☎ 4229 4756) for information on bush camping.

Views The most popular viewpoint in the area is the spectacular **Bulli Scenic Lookout** high on the escarpment, off the Princes Highway, with enormous views down to the coastal strip and out to sea. Nearby, **Sublime Point** and **Bald Hill Lookout** in Stanwell Tops are similarly breathtaking. **Mt Keira**

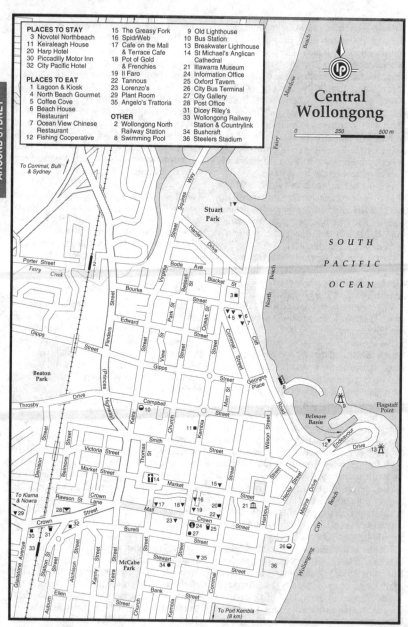

PLACES TO STAY
3 Novotel Northbeach
11 Keiraleagh House
20 Harp Hotel
30 Piccadilly Motor Inn
32 City Pacific Hotel

PLACES TO EAT
1 Lagoon & Kiosk
4 North Beach Gourmet
5 Coffee Cove
6 Beach House Restaurant
7 Ocean View Chinese Restaurant
12 Fishing Cooperative

15 The Greasy Fork
16 SpidrWeb
17 Cafe on the Mall & Terrace Cafe
18 Pot of Gold & Frenchies
19 Il Faro
22 Tannous
23 Lorenzo's
29 Plant Room
35 Angelo's Trattoria

OTHER
2 Wollongong North Railway Station
8 Swimming Pool

9 Old Lighthouse
10 Bus Station
13 Breakwater Lighthouse
14 St Michael's Anglican Cathedral
21 Illawarra Museum
24 Information Office
25 Oxford Tavern
26 City Bus Terminal
27 City Gallery
28 Post Office
31 Dicey Riley's
33 Wollongong Railway Station & Countrylink
34 Bushcraft
36 Steelers Stadium

Central Wollongong

0   250   500 m

SOUTH PACIFIC OCEAN

Summit Park, Queen Elizabeth Drive on Mt Keira, offers an even higher viewpoint.

Special Events

A big surf-lifesaving carnival is held on Australia Day.

Places to Stay

The tourist information centre books accommodation and will know of any specials.

Bottom End You have to go a little way out before you can camp. The council runs *caravan parks* on the beach at Corrimal (☎ 4285 5688), near the beach on Farrell Rd in Bulli (☎ 4285 5677) and on Fern St in Windang (☎ 4297 3166), with beach and lake frontage. From central Wollongong, Corrimal is about 6km north, Bulli 11km north and Windang 15km south, between Lake Illawarra and the sea. All charge about $15 for campsites (two people) and from $48 for vans or cabins, with prices rising sharply during school and Christmas holidays. Buses run from the railway station to within walking distance of all these.

There are quite a few privately-owned caravan parks in the area – the tourist information centre has details.

Keiraleagh House (☎ 4228 6765), 60 Kembla St north of Market St, is a large, rambling hostel catering mainly to long-term students but also to short-term visitors. It has dorms for $15 or singles for $20/25 without/with bath.

Middle & Top End Several pubs have fairly cheap accommodation, such as the central *Harp Hotel* (☎ 4229 1333), 124 Corrimal St near Crown St, which charges $40/60 for rooms with TV and bathroom (and features bands).

About the only inexpensive motel in the area is the *Cabbage Tree Motel* (☎ 4284 4000), 1 Anama St (behind the Cabbage Tree Hotel) in Fairy Meadow, off the Princes Highway 3.5km north of the city centre. Singles/doubles cost $40/45. Most buses heading north from the railway station go to Fairy Meadow.

Piccadilly Motor Inn (☎ 4226 4555), 341 Crown St near the railway station, has rooms for $55/60. The *City Pacific Hotel* (☎ 4229 7444), 112 Burelli St, has good-value budget rooms for $40/50 in the old part of the hotel; in the new section, standard rooms are $75.

Belmore Deluxe Apartments (☎ 4224 6500), 39-41 Smith St, has serviced apartments from $90 to $125. The top place to stay is *Novotel Northbeach* (☎ 4226 3555), 2-14 Cliff Rd, with standard rooms at $180 or $200 with ocean views. Call to see if there are any special deals.

Places to Eat

For good coffee, snacks, cakes and meals try *Tannous*, a Lebanese cafe on the corner of Crown and Corrimal Sts. Various shishkebabs, felafel and other takeaways are $3.50, $5.50 if you eat in. Eat-in meals come with large serves of houmous, tabouli and bread.

There are plenty of other places. *Cafe on the Mall*, on the corner of Church and Crown Sts, opens long hours for snacks and meals and has a balcony overlooking the mall. Breakfasts are $6.50. *Barnie's on Crown*, on the mall near Kembla St, is an Italian restaurant with three-course lunch specials for $9.90; it also does good cakes. Nearby in Kembla St, there's the *Pot of Gold*, a Mexican place with main courses $9.90 to $11.90 and nearby *Frenchie's Cafe* has good strong coffee and delicious snacks. Across the street is *Il Faro*, with pasta and pizza.

The Greasy Fork (☎ 4229 3651), 26 Market St, west of Corrimal St, is better than its name might suggest. Pasta mains are $11.50 to $12.50; chicken schnitzel is $14.50.

Popular with the Italian community, *Angelo's Trattoria* at the International Centre, 28 Stewart St, serves moderately-priced Italian food plus steaks and seafood. There's no sign over the door – walk along the verandah past Portofino Lounge to the back.

At Belmore Basin, *Harbourfront Seafood Restaurant* is open daily for lunch and dinner with buffets for $17.50 and $25 respectively.

More seafood is available at the *Lagoon* (☎ 4226 1766) in Stuart Park behind North Beach. Snapper fillets are $21.50.The restaurant has a great location and opens daily for lunch and dinner. The adjacent *Kiosk* is less expensive.

The *Plant Room* (☎ 4227 3030), on Crown St opposite Gladstone Ave, is up the hill from the railway station and open during the day for coffee and snacks and at night offers a $15 buffet. It has a relaxed atmosphere, a cosmopolitan menu and live music some evenings.

On Bourke St at North Beach, *Coffee Cove* and *North Beach Gourmet* are cafes serving breakfast and light meals; scrambled egg on toast at the latter is $4.

Round the corner, *Beach House Restaurant*, on Cliff Rd, serves mostly seafood; king prawns are $22.50. Next door, the *Ocean View* Chinese restaurant is cheaper; chicken dishes are around $12.

Entertainment

This is a steel town where people let their hair down on weekends. Several pubs in the centre of town usually have bands then. Your best chance of hearing an interesting young band is at the *Harp Hotel* on Corrimal St or at the *Oxford Tavern* nearby on Crown St. *Dicey Riley's*, also on Crown St, has Irish music. There are many clubs and other pubs with live entertainment.

Getting There & Away

Bus The bus station (☎ 4226 1022) is on the corner of Keira and Campbell Sts. There are several daily services to Sydney ($17) and one to Canberra ($28) which runs through Moss Vale and the Southern Highlands. Greyhound Pioneer's Sydney-to-Melbourne ($64) coastal route runs through Wollongong. Direct buses to Brisbane with Greyhound Pioneer cost $85. Pioneer Motor Service (☎ 4423 5233) – a Nowra company, not the national giant – runs through Wollongong along the south coast as far as Eden ($41.50) and also connects with buses to Canberra.

Countrylink runs buses to Moss Vale from outside the railway station.

Train Many trains run to/from Sydney (1½ hours, $6.60 one way; off-peak day return $7.80), and a fair number continue south along the coast to Kiama, Gerringong and Bomaderry (Nowra).

Saturday to Tuesday, a tourist train known as the Cockatoo Run (☎ 1800 64 3801) runs inland across the Southern Highlands from Port Kembla to Moss Vale ($11/20 one way/return) or Robertson ($10/18).

Car & Motorcycle The Princes Highway (a freeway near Wollongong) runs north to Sydney or you can follow the coast road north through Otford and Royal National Park, rejoining the highway near Sutherland. The highway also runs south to Kiama and the south coast and eventually ends in Melbourne.

The Illawarra Highway runs up the escarpment to the Southern Highlands.

Getting Around

Two local bus companies service the area: Rutty's (☎ 4271 1322) and John J Hill (☎ 4229 4911). The main stop is on Crown St, where it meets Marine Drive, next to the beach. You can reach most beaches by rail and trains are fairly frequent.

Although cycling is definitely urban in this area, bringing a bike on the train from Sydney and riding around is a good idea. A cycle path runs from the city centre north to Bulli and south to Port Kembla.

The Central Coast & Lake Macquarie

The central coast is a strange combination of the beautiful and the awful – superb surf beaches, lakes and national parks combined with huge swathes of rampant suburban housing. The central coast's population is over 200,000. There are more urban areas

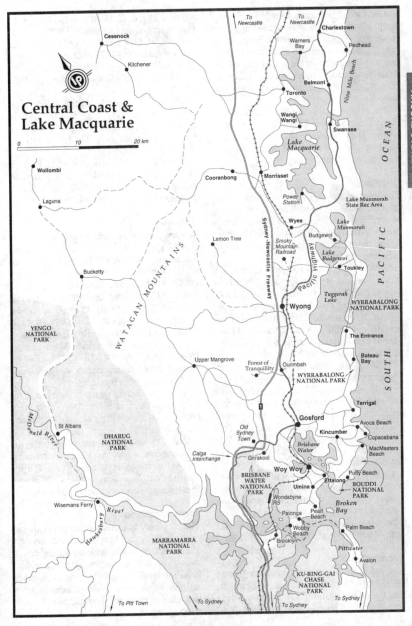

Central Coast &
Lake Macquarie

0   10   20 km

around Lake Macquarie, immediately to the north, which blend into the sprawling city of Newcastle. While you're stuck in one of the central coast's suburban-style traffic jams, you might ponder on the possibility of this situation spreading over the entire east coast of Australia. It's a depressingly likely scenario.

The central coast's symbol for tourism is the pelican and the huge birds are everywhere. They paddle around in search of a meal or glide overhead, looking about as manageable as jumbo jets.

Orientation

The central coast includes some lovely inland waterways as well as the long string of surf beaches. Broken Bay in the south is the beautiful mouth of the Hawkesbury River, with many wide bays and inlets, including Brisbane Water which runs up to Gosford. Next north is Tuggerah Lake which meets the sea at The Entrance. North of Tuggerah Lake is the smaller Lake Budgewoi near Toukley, and just north again is Lake Munmorah. These three lakes are actually contiguous. A few km north of Lake Munmorah is Lake Macquarie, which runs all the way up to outer Newcastle.

West of the lakes in the low Watagan Mountains are 13 state forests running north to the Hunter Valley. There are walking trails and camping is permitted, except in picnic areas. The old village of Cooranbong is the main access point for the Watagans. This area bore the brunt of the fires of 1994. West again you come to the vast national parks of the Blue Mountains – see that section.

Gosford is the main town in the area and blends into the surrounding urban areas. Larger beachside centres are Terrigal and The Entrance. On the eastern side of Lake Macquarie, Swansea is the start of a long strip of suburbs north to central Newcastle.

Information

Gosford City Visitors Information Centre (☎ 4385 4430, 1800 806 258), 200 Mann St, near the railway station, is open on weekdays from 9 am to 5 pm, on weekends from 9.30

am to 2.30 pm. Gosford also has large visitors information centres at Rotary Park, Terrigal (☎ 4384 6577) and Marine Parade, The Entrance (☎ 4332 9282). Information is also available from Umina (☎ 4343 2200), Toukley (☎ 4392 4666) and Wyong (☎ 4351 2277).

The Lake Macquarie Visitors Information Centre (☎ 4972 1172, 1800 802 044), in Swansea, on the Pacific Highway north of the bridge is open daily. The lake's only sea entrance is at Swansea.

There's a NPWS office (☎ 4324 4911) at 207 Albany St in Gosford. If you find an injured native animal, call the Wildlife Rescue & Care Society (☎ 4365 1121).

Activities

Watersports are the main activities, with surf right along the coast. The lakes offer excellent boating and you will be able to hire small craft in many towns. Central Coast Charters (☎ 4363 1221), 38 Mirreen Drive, Davistown, offers river cruises and fishing charters. Scuba diving is popular in the central coast waters and Pro Dive (☎ 4334 1559), 96 The Entrance Rd, The Entrance, provides guided dives and lessons. Central Coast Kayak Tours (☎ 4381 0342), 227 The Round Drive, Avoca Beach, has five-hour sea kayaking tours for $65.

Several boats will take you for a cruise on Lake Macquarie, including *Macquarie Lady* (☎ 4973 2513), which picks up from Toronto and Belmont.

Back on land, there are good walks in Brisbane Water National Park. Rock climbing and abseiling courses are provided by Central Coast Bushworks (☎ 4363 2028). Its five-hour introductory course costs $75.

Accommodation

There's plenty of accommodation in caravan parks, holiday flats and motels, but any sort of holiday or warm weather sends prices through the roof and vacancies can be scarce. Families book holidays a year in advance and you might have trouble finding even a tent site in summer. Terrigal has a backpacker hostel.

Getting There & Away
The central coast is easily accessible from Sydney, via the Sydney-Newcastle Freeway and a variety of public transport. Lake Macquarie can be reached from Sydney by car (exit the freeway at Wyong) but by public transport, access is easier from Newcastle. See the Newcastle, Getting There & Away section in the Hunter Valley chapter for more information.

Train CityRail (☎ 131500) trains running between Sydney and the Hunter Valley stop at central coast destinations, including Gosford and Wyong.

Ferry A ferry (☎ 9918 2747) runs daily from Palm Beach, a northern beachside suburb of Sydney, to Patonga in Broken Bay at 9 am, 11 am and 3.45 pm. The fare is $6 ($3 children), plus about $2 for big packs and $1 for bikes. From Patonga, Peninsula Bus Lines (☎ 4324 1255) has infrequent buses to Gosford. The 11 am ferry continues on to Bobbin Head in Ku-ring-gai Chase National Park.

From Brooklyn, you can get to Patonga on a cruise boat (☎ 9985 7566) for about $10 return or to Wobby Beach with the Dangar Island Ferry Service (☎ 9985 7605), near the trailhead, for a walking track through Brisbane Water National Park. Hawkesbury River railway station in Brooklyn is near the ferry wharf.

Getting Around
Bus Local bus services cover the main centres in the area: The Entrance Red Bus Services (☎ 4332 8655) runs between The Entrance and Gosford and Wyong. Some services connect with trains to/from Sydney. Peninsula Bus Lines (☎ 4341 1433) covers most of the rest of the Brisbane Water and Tuggerah Lake area.

Around Lake Macquarie, Busways (☎ 4368 2277) runs between Wyong and Charlestown via Swansea. Toronto Bus Service (☎ 4359 1233) runs between the Newcastle suburb of Wallsend and Wangi Wangi on Lake Macquarie, via Toronto. STA

urban buses run between Newcastle and the northern end of the lake.

Car & Motorcycle This isn't the easiest place to drive around, partly because many roads are too small for the amount of traffic they carry and partly because you have to negotiate suburban shopping centres every few km. You'll also need a detailed map (such as the NRMA's *Central Coast Holiday Map*) because the signposting gets you to Gosford and Wyong but not to many other places.

GOSFORD & AROUND
Gosford (population 129,000), the largest town in the area, is 12km inland on the shores of Brisbane Water, about 85km north of Sydney. Europeans first settled this area in the 1820s, attracted by the timber, and boat-building followed. After the construction of the railway from Sydney in the 1880s, tourism began and large guesthouses were built.

Gosford is easily accessible by train from Sydney or Newcastle and is a sensible base from which to explore the region.

Brisbane Water National Park
On the north side of the Hawkesbury River, across from Ku-ring-gai Chase National Park, Brisbane Water National Park is 9km south-west of Gosford. It extends from the Pacific Highway in the west to Brisbane Water in the east but, despite its name, the park has only a short frontage onto that body of water.

This park, which is rugged sandstone country, is known for its wildflowers in early spring and there are many walking trails. South of the township of Kariong is the turn-off for the **Bulgandry Aboriginal Engraving Site**, where there are interesting rock carvings.

The main road access is at Girrakool; travel west from Gosford or exit the Sydney-Newcastle Freeway at the Calga interchange. Wondabyne railway station, on the Sydney-Newcastle line, is inside the park near several walking trails (including part of the

Great North Walk). You must tell the guard if you want to get off at Wondabyne and travel in the rear carriage. Ferries from Palm Beach run to Patonga; ferries from Brooklyn run to Wobby Beach on a peninsula south of the park near some walking trails.

For more information contact the NPWS office (☎ 4324 4911) in Gosford.

Old Sydney Town
Off the freeway 9km south-west of Gosford, Old Sydney Town (☎ 4340 1104) is a major reconstruction of early Sydney with street theatre which retells events from the colony's early history. It's open from 10 am to 4 pm, Wednesday to Sunday, and daily during school holidays. Admission is $15.50 ($8.50 children). The Narara Dancers perform a daily corroboree in the woolshed for $15 ($5 children). Peninsula Bus Lines runs here from Gosford and several tours run from Sydney.

Other Attractions
West of Gosford, on the Pacific Highway in Somersby, the **Australian Reptile Park** (☎ 4340 1022) has native animals and birds as well as reptiles. It's open daily from 9 am to 7 pm; admission costs $9.95 ($4.50 children). Off Brisbane Water Drive in West Gosford is **Henry Kendall Cottage** (☎ 4325 2270), a small museum in the home of an early poet. It's open Wednesday and weekends and daily in school holidays from 10 am to 4 pm. Admission is $2 ($1 children). Another attraction is the **Forest of Tranquillity** (☎ 4362 1855), a private forest reserve west off the freeway at Ourimbah. It's open Wednesday to Sunday, and daily in school holidays from 10 am to 5 pm. Admission is $6 ($4 children).

As well as the area's national parks, there are several smaller reserves around Gosford with walking trails, such as **Rumbalara Reserve**. The visitors information centre has pamphlets.

The historic MV *Lady Kendall* (☎ 4323 1165) has 2½-hour cruises of Brisbane Water from Gosford Wharf at 10.15 am and 1 pm Saturday to Wednesday, daily during

school holidays. There's also parasailing and water-skiing on Brisbane Water.

South of the national park is **Patonga**, a small fishing village on Broken Bay, with camping at *Patonga Beach Caravanning & Camping Area* (☎ 4379 1287). Off the road to Patonga, **Warrah Lookout** has great views over Broken Bay.

Not far away, but screened from the housing estates of Umina and Woy Woy by a steep road over Mt Ettalong, is **Pearl Beach**, a lovely National Trust hamlet on the eastern edge of the national park. The only way to stay here is to rent a holiday house or apartment and there aren't many of them.

TERRIGAL & AROUND
Terrigal, on the ocean about 12km east of Gosford, is probably the most upmarket of the central coast's beachside towns. The big *Holiday Inn Crowne Plaza* (☎ 4384 9111) dominates the foreshore; rooms start from $230. There's also a hostel, *Terrigal Beach Backpackers* (☎ 4385 3330), a block from the beach at 10 Campbell Crescent, with dorm beds for $15, doubles for $35.

South of Terrigal is the tiny beachside town of **Copacabana**. North of Terrigal, **Bateau Bay** is adjacent to the southern section of the small **Wyrrabalong National Park** (the northern section is north of The Entrance). It's popular for surfing and the beach is patrolled. There are several caravan parks in the area.

Bouddi National Park
Bouddi National Park, 19km south-east of Gosford, extends south from MacMasters Beach to the north head of Broken Bay. It also extends out to sea in a marine reserve; fishing is prohibited in much of the park. Vehicle access is limited but there are walking trails leading to the various beaches. The park is in two sections on either side of Putty Beach which has vehicular access. The Maitland Bay Centre has information on the park but it is only open on weekends and holidays. There's camping in the park at Little, Putty and Tallow beaches but you

have to book through the NPWS office (☎ 4324 4911) in Gosford.

THE ENTRANCE & NORTH

The Entrance (the town is on the Tuggerah Lakes' sea inlet) is the only place you need to visit if you want to see the best and worst of the central coast. It's a large urban area of relentlessly cheerful cream-brick and introduced palm trees, plastic chairs on footpaths, happy urchins and beer-bellied parents – all on a supremely beautiful lake and a superb surf beach.

Daily at 3.30 pm, the **pelicans** are fed on the beachfront near the visitors information centre. The **Entrance Boathouse** (☎ 4332 2652), beside the bridge, rents bikes, canoes, rowing boats and motor boats. If you're game, Bungee 2000 (☎ 4385 5722) has bungee jumping at Forresters Beach for $75.

On the peninsula north of The Entrance is the northern section of the small **Wyrrabalong National Park**, with walking trails and diverse flora habitats. North of the park are the towns of **Toukley** and **Budgewoi**, popular bases for boating and fishing on the nearby lakes. The **Munmorah State Recreation Area (SRA)** runs up the coast for 12km. There are three *camping areas* – at Freemans, Frazer and Geebung beaches – but they're usually full at peak times; book at the office (☎ 4358 1649), off the road south of Elizabeth Bay. Day-use fees are $6.50 per car ($3 for motorbikes and pedestrians); camping costs $10 for two people plus $2 per extra person. You have to pay the day-use fee for the first night you stay.

Near Warnervale, on the west side of the lakes, **Smoky Mountain Railroad** (☎ 4392 7644) has steam-train rides on Sunday. Admission is by donation.

Places to Stay

At The Entrance on the northern side of the bridge at the end of the spit, which separates the sea from the lake, *Dunleith Caravan Park* (☎ 4332 2172) is close to the surf and has good facilities. Tent sites cost from $17

(there are no unpowered sites) and on-site vans and self-contained cabins from $45. The place is packed at peak times. Other caravan parks include *Blue Bay* (☎ 4332 1991) and *Pinehurst* (☎ 4332 2002).

The *Entrance Hotel* (☎ 4332 2001), near the waterfront, has singles/doubles for $32/66 including breakfast. Some rooms have attached bathrooms for the same price.

LAKE MACQUARIE

Lake Macquarie, Australia's largest saltwater lake, covers four times the area of Sydney Harbour and is a popular centre for sailing, water-skiing and fishing. It lies north of Munmorah Lake, separated by a narrow strip of land, and extends up to outer Newcastle. The suburban development here is a little older than that on the central coast and there's a little more room to move.

The main centres on Lake Macquarie are **Charlestown** and **Belmont**, outer suburbs of Newcastle, and **Swansea**, a long-time holiday resort for holidaymakers from Newcastle; it too is now merging into the city's sprawl. The Lake Macquarie visitors centre (☎ 4972 1172) is on the Pacific Highway just north of Swansea. Caravan parks here are cheaper than farther south.

Nine Mile Beach runs north from Swansea to **Redhead**, where there's a *caravan park* (☎ 4949 8306) near the beach. The western shores of Lake Macquarie are relatively undeveloped but they certainly aren't virgin bush.

On **Wangi Point**, on the west shore, opposite Swansea, there are walking trails through the bush and a *caravan park* (☎ 4975 1889). Also on the point is **Dobell House**, where artist William Dobell lived and worked. It's open on Sunday from 2 to 4 pm.

Vales Point power station (☎ 4352 6111) and the adjacent colliery are at the south end of the lake. Call to arrange a visit. The area's two other power stations aren't open to visitors.

The Hunter Valley

The Hunter is best known for its wines, with about 50 vineyards in the lower Hunter (mainly around Cessnock and Pokolbin) and half a dozen more in the upper Hunter (around Denman). Coal is another important commodity, Newcastle taking its name from the industrial city in England. The first export of coal sailed in 1814, in exchange for a cargo of rum. Electricity also flows out of the Hunter Valley – 75% of the state's power is generated here.

For a relatively small area, the Hunter includes some very different landscapes. West of Newcastle there's a large urban conglomeration (linked by poorly maintained roads clogged with irritating traffic); further west, beyond Cessnock, you come to the lower Hunter wineries, nestled in a pretty area of gentle hills which continues west into the upper Hunter. The Hunter River itself flows past some of the oldest towns in the country. Although there are rolling farmlands in the Hunter, there are also some stretches of rugged ranges, harbouring lush stands of temperate rainforest in the Barrington Tops National Park.

Down on the coast there are excellent surf beaches, the tranquil waterways of Myall Lakes National Park (an estuarine lakes system) and Port Stephens, a large bay which is home to dolphins – see the North Coast chapter.

History

The Hunter was settled early in the history of NSW, as it offered a large expanse of relatively flat land with coastal access. Before the Great Dividing Range was crossed such land was at a premium, attracting a growing influx of graziers, timber cutters and coal miners.

Finding a route from the Hunter to the plains beyond the mountains proved almost as difficult as crossing the Blue Mountains. For thousands of years, Aborigines had used the rocky gorges of what is now the Goul-

HUNTER VALLEY

HIGHLIGHTS

- Discovering that Newcastle isn't the grim industrial city described by Sydneysiders
- Touring the Hunter wineries – and not having to drive home!
- Drinking champagne while floating over the Hunter Valley in a hot-air balloon
- Walking through the ancient, moss-covered Antarctic beech forests of Barrington Tops National Park

burn River National Park as a route between the interior and the Hunter Valley (and thus the sea). Europeans, however, encumbered by their wagons, flocks and herds, had to settle for the long, steep climb up the Liverpool Ranges near present-day Murrurundi. The current road closely follows one of the first routes out of the Hunter.

Vines were first planted in the valley in the 1820s, and by the 1860s there were 2000 hectares under cultivation. A Hunter champagne made its way to Paris in 1855 and was favourably compared to the French product. However, most Hunter wineries gradually declined, and it wasn't until the 1960s that wine-making again became an important industry.

The Golden Grape Estate, on Oakey Creek Rd near Pokolbin, has a museum devoted to the history of wine-making in the area.

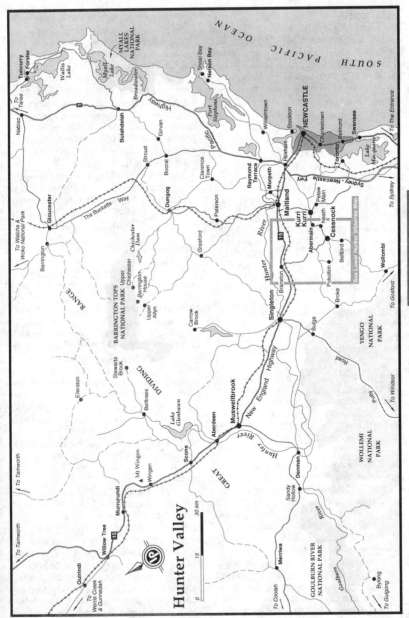

Hunter Valley

HUNTER VALLEY

Geography

The Hunter Valley cuts a triangular swathe through the Great Dividing Range, broadest on the coast and tapering as it approaches Denman. On the southern side of the valley rise the sandstone ranges of the Wollemi and Goulburn River national parks; the valley's northern side is bordered by the high, rugged ranges leading up to Barrington Tops National Park.

Getting There & Away

Air See the Newcastle and Singleton sections of this chapter for routes and fares.

Bus The major interstate lines pass through Newcastle on their Pacific Highway run up the north coast, but you're better off taking the train between Sydney and Newcastle. Kean's (☎ 1800 625 587; in Sydney book at the Sydney Coach Terminal on Eddy Ave) has at least one bus a day running from Sydney to Tamworth via the Hunter towns of Cessnock ($20 from Sydney), Singleton ($25), Muswellbrook ($29) and Scone ($35), but none to Newcastle. Greyhound Pioneer and McCafferty's run up the New England Highway between Sydney and Brisbane.

Train Trains run up the valley en route to Armidale and Moree, and north-coast trains stop at Maitland, Dungog and Gloucester. These trains don't run into central Newcastle, but trains from Sydney do – see Getting There & Away under Newcastle.

Car & Motorcycle There are several routes into the Hunter Valley from Sydney. The quickest is the Sydney-Newcastle freeway, which doesn't actually reach Newcastle but stops short near Minmi, west of the city. The alternative is to come by the slow roads of the central coast, entering Newcastle through its southern suburbs.

The road between Windsor and Singleton, known as the Putty Rd, is much longer than either of these routes, but more interesting; see Macquarie Towns in the Around Sydney chapter. There's also an interesting route (including some unsealed roads) from Wisemans Ferry, passing through Wollombi.

The Pacific Highway, the main coastal route north, branches off from the New England Highway at the big Hexham Bridge over the Hunter River, just north-west of Newcastle's outer suburbs. Heading north, the Pacific Highway runs through Raymond Terrace and Bulahdelah, but bypasses the region's coastal attractions. See North of Newcastle later in this chapter for information on the Bucketts Way, an interesting diversion from the Pacific Highway.

The New England Highway runs along the valley and climbs up to the New England tableland near Murrurundi; the other western exit from the valley is through Denman and Sandy Hollow to Merriwa.

NEWCASTLE

Newcastle (population 265,000) doesn't have much of a reputation among Sydney people – they still think of it as a dirty industrial city with little to offer. But Sydneysiders are wrong. If you must think of Newcastle as an industrial city, picture the English city of Newcastle upon Tyne (which is about the same size), then imagine it with a warm climate and superb surf beaches a stone's throw from the city centre. The old saying about working towns being friendly towns also applies here.

A few years ago, a survey judged Newcastle the best Australian city to live in, and with its good services, excellent climate, great beaches and easy access to national parks it isn't hard to see why.

History

Originally named Coal River, Newcastle was founded in 1804 as a place for the most intractable of Sydney's convicts and was known as 'the hell of New South Wales'. The breakwater out to Nobbys Head with its lighthouse was built by convicts. The Bogey Hole, a swimming pool cut into the rock on the ocean's edge below the pleasant King Edward Park, was built for Major Morriset, an early commander and strict disciplinarian. It's still a great place for a dip.

In late 1989, Newcastle suffered Australia's most destructive earthquake, with 12 people killed and a lot of property damage.

Orientation

Central Newcastle sits on the end of a peninsula separating the Hunter River from the sea, and tapers down to the long sandspit heading east to Nobbys Head. Hunter St is the 3km-long main street, and is a pedestrian mall between Newcomen and Perkins Sts. Hunter St's shops continue west for a long way, well out of the centre of town, and Hunter St eventually becomes the northbound Pacific Highway; southbound, the Pacific Highway is Stewart Ave, which meets Hunter St west of the city centre.

The railway station, long-distance bus stop, post office, banks and some fine old commercial buildings are at the northeastern end of the city centre.

King St runs parallel to Hunter St and along the bottom of steep Cook's Hill. Up on the hill you get great views of the city and the coastal lands beyond, and there are also some fine old terraces of houses up there. Church St and tree-lined Tyrrell St run along the top of the hill.

Across the railway lines (there's a footbridge beginning in Hunter Mall) is the waterfront and the Queens Wharf complex. The swimming beaches are on the other side of the peninsula, a short walk from the city centre. To get to Newcastle Beach head up Hunter St, walk across the pleasant plaza and then through the 'time tunnel' – a pedestrian underpass containing some good murals of Newcastle's beach-life history which are not *too* vandalised.

Just across the Hunter River (by now a wide estuary called Port Hunter) from Queens Wharf is Stockton, a modest town with beaches and striking views back to the city of Newcastle. It's not far from the city by ferry, but if you're travelling by road you have to wind through the docks and some dramatic industrial landscapes, a trip of about 20km.

Newcastle's sprawling suburbs and satellite towns run down to Swansea on Lake Macquarie and north to Hexham, where the big Hexham Bridge carries the Pacific Highway over the Hunter River and the New England Highway branches off for its run up the Hunter Valley. West of Newcastle are the coalfields and more large urban centres; further west are the lower Hunter vineyards and wineries.

Information

The tourist office (☎ 4929 9299) occupies the Old Stationmaster's Cottage (built 1858) at 92 Scott St, just beyond the railway station. It's open weekdays from 9 am to 5 pm, and weekends from 10 am to 3.30 pm. It sells excellent heritage walk maps.

There's a left-luggage office at the railway station, near the Watt St entrance. It's for day-use only and costs $1.50 per item.

Beaches

Surf beaches are a major attraction. Newcastle's favourite surfing son is former world champ Mark Richards, and many surfers come here to seek out the breaks where Richards cut his teeth. The main beach, **Newcastle Beach**, is just a couple of minutes' walk from the city centre. It has an ocean pool and good surf. Just north of here is **Nobbys Beach**, more sheltered from the southerlies and often open when other beaches are closed. At the northern end of Nobbys is a fast left-hander known as **the Wedge**. The most popular surfing break is about 5km south at **Bar Beach**, which is floodlit at night in summer. Nearby **Merewether Beach** has two huge pools. Bus No 207 from the Parnell Place terminus in the city runs to Merewether Beach every half-hour ($2) via Bar Beach.

Museums & Galleries

The **Newcastle Regional Museum**, 787 Hunter St in Newcastle West, opens daily except Monday (daily in school holidays) and admission is $3. It includes the Supernova hands-on science display. The **Fort Scratchley Maritime & Military Museum** opens from 10 am to 4 pm Tuesday to

HUNTER VALLEY

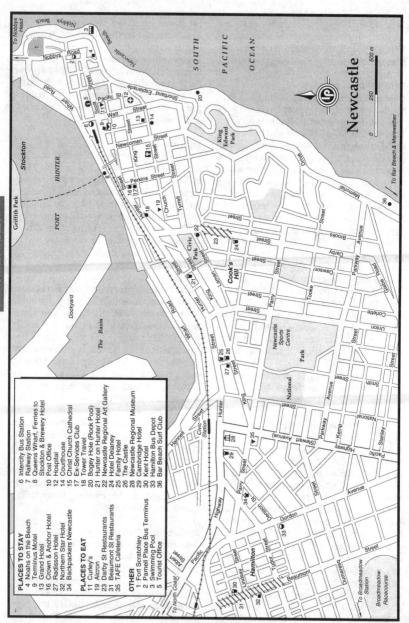

Newcastle

PLACES TO STAY
4 Noahs on the Beach
9 Terminus Motel
13 Grand Hotel
16 Crown & Anchor Hotel
27 Radisson Hotel
32 Northern Star Hotel
34 Backpackers Newcastle

PLACES TO EAT
11 Curley's
19 Alcron
23 Darby St Restaurants
31 Beaumont St Restaurants
35 TAFE Cafeteria

OTHER
1 Fort Scratchley
2 Parnell Place Bus Terminus
3 Swimming Pool
5 Tourist Office
6 Intercity Bus Station
7 Railway Station
8 Queens Wharf, Ferries to
   Stockton & Brewery Hotel
10 Post Office
12 Hospital
14 Courthouse
15 Christ Church Cathedral
17 Ex-Services Club
18 Tower Travel
20 Bogey Hole (Rock Pool)
21 Hunter on Hunter Hotel
22 Newcastle Regional Art Gallery
24 Hotel Delaney
25 Family Hotel
26 The Castle
28 Newcastle Regional Museum
29 Cambridge Hotel
30 Kent Hotel
33 Hamilton Bus Depot
36 Bar Beach Surf Club

Sunday. Admission to the museum is free, but it costs $1 to explore the tunnels under the fort, which are said to run all the way to King Edward Park. Fort Scratchley overlooks Nobbys Head.

The **Newcastle Regional Art Gallery** is on Laman St next to Civic Park. It's free and open weekdays and weekend afternoons. There are several private galleries on nearby Cook's Hill.

Blackbutt Reserve

The reserve (☎ 4952 1449) covers 182 hectares of bushland at New Lambton Heights, approximately 10km south-west of the city centre. It has bushwalks and aviaries, wildlife and fern houses, and a new koala enclosure. The reserve is open daily from 9 am to 5 pm and admission is free. Bus Nos 232 and 363 run past the upper entrance, Nos 216 and 217 past the lower; the fare is $2.

Shortlands Wetlands Centre

The wetlands are about 10km west of town on the edge of Hexham Swamp. There's lots of birdlife as well as walks and canoe trails. It's open daily from 9 am to 5 pm and admission is by a $2 donation.

Organised Tours

See the following Up the Valley section for winery tours. Several 4WD tours take you up into the rugged bush on the northern side of the valley; for example, Bush Ranging Tours (☎ 4992 1614) go to Barrington Tops and other destinations for about $70 (minimum two people).

A couple of outfits offer infrequent cruises on the harbour. *Lady Joy* departs from Queens Wharf on Thursday at 2 pm ($12), more frequently in school holidays, and *William IV*, a replica of an old steamship, leaves from near Queens Wharf at 11 am and 2 pm on the third Sunday of the month ($11).

Special Events

The Newcastle Show is held in February, and Beaumont St hosts a Jazz & Arts Festival in March. Steam engines take over several locations during the Hunter Valley Steamfest in May.

Places to Stay – bottom end

Camping Stockton is handy for Newcastle by ferry but it's 20km by road. *Stockton Beach Caravan Park* (☎ 4928 1393) is on the beach at Pitt St. Tent sites are $10 and cabins are $35, rising to $70 around Christmas/New Year. There are several caravan parks south of Newcastle, around Belmont and on the ocean at Redhead Beach.

Hostels *Backpackers Newcastle* (☎ 4969 3436) occupies a couple of fine old weatherboard houses at 42-44 Denison St, Hamilton. It's clean and friendly, and in an interesting part of town. There's backpacker accommodation at No 42, with dorm beds for $14 and doubles for $28, while No 44 is more upmarket with doubles for $36. Each house has its own communal lounge and kitchen. There are free surfboards and one of the owners is a keen surfer who can help you learn. The hostel also has lots of information about the region and can organise excursions. Hamilton is close to the city centre. Any bus heading along Hunter St can drop you at the nearby Regional Museum, or you can phone for a free pick-up from town.

Hotels The *Crown & Anchor* (☎ 4929 1027), on the corner of Hunter and Perkins Sts, has singles/doubles for $25/34.

Places to Stay – middle & top end

The *Grand Hotel* (☎ 4929 3489) is a nice old pub in the city centre on the corner of Bolton and Church Sts, across from the courthouse. The place has been well renovated and has large singles/doubles for $50/52 with bathroom.

The *Terminus Motel* (☎ 4926 3244), 107 Scott St, also known as the Harbourside Motel, has rooms for $50/55. The *Northern Star Hotel* (☎ 4961 1087), 112 Beaumont St, has motel-style rooms for $45/55. There's a string of cheaper motels along the Pacific Highway at Belmont, about 15km south of town.

HUNTER VALLEY

Noahs on the Beach (☎ 4929 5181) faces the ocean on Shortland Esplanade, and standard rates start at $90/95, but there are often specials. The *Radisson* (☎ 4926 3777), on the corner of King and Steel Sts, starts at about $100 a double, with lower stand-by and weekend rates.

Places to Eat

During term, the best deal in town is to be found at *Hunter TAFE College* on Parry St. The cafeteria operated by the college's catering and hospitality school offers main courses for $3.50 and desserts for $1.50. Opening times vary; the owners of the backpackers can tell you when it's open.

Beaumont St in Hamilton has the greatest concentration of restaurants. Once known as 'Little Italy' for its profusion of Italian eateries, Beaumont St has now taken on a more international flavour. There are literally dozens of places to choose from.

If Italian is what you're after, try *Dolomiti Gelato*, down an alleyway on the corner of Beaumont and Lindsay Sts, or the *Trieste*. The *Anatolia* Turkish restaurant at No 63 offers good value with nothing on the menu over $10. *Gandha's* Indian restaurant, upstairs at No 54, has a range of curries and tandoori dishes.

Newcastle's other main restaurant strip is closer to the city on Darby St, south of Queen St. The choices include Vietnamese *(Lan's)*, Thai *(Al-Oi)*, Malaysian *(Rumah Malaysia)* and Indian *(Taj Takeaway)*. *Natural Tucker* has a large selection of vegetarian snacks.

There are several good places for snacks and meals at the eastern end of Hunter St. *Vera's Cafe* on the corner of Pacific and Hunter Sts has footpath tables and serves breakfast for around $6. *Curley's* (the illuminated sign says Vienna Cafe), just around the corner on Pacific St, is a nice place with focaccia for $4.50 and pasta from $6.50.

If you feel like a blow-out, *Alcron* (☎ 4929 2423), 113 Church St, is perhaps the oldest restaurant in Australia. Main courses are around $20.

Entertainment

Newcastle has a busy home-grown music scene, with live bands playing somewhere in town most nights. There are gig guides in Thursday's *Newcastle Herald* or the weekly *Newcastle Post*, published on Wednesday.

One of the best rock venues to check out is the *Cambridge Hotel* on the corner of Hunter and Denison Sts, the pub where local heroes silverchair launched their career. The *Hunter on Hunter Hotel*, 417 Hunter St, is another pub that promotes local rock talent. The *Family Hotel*, on the corner of Hunter and Steel Sts, has blues, while the *Kent Hotel* and the *Northern Star Hotel*, both on Beaumont St, have jazz. The *Hotel Delaney* is a relaxed little pub on the corner of Darby and Council Sts, with music most nights. The popular *Brewery*, at the Queens Wharf complex, brews its own.

The *Castle* is a popular nightclub on King St, opposite McDonald's. It's open from Wednesday to Sunday, with live bands downstairs and a disco upstairs. Ask about free admission passes at the backpackers.

Getting There & Away

Air Aeropelican flies several times a day between Sydney ($78) and Belmont, just south of Newcastle. Eastern Australia Airlines also has daily flights to Sydney ($97), while Impulse flies between Newcastle and Port Macquarie ($154), Coffs Harbour ($195), Lismore ($256) and Brisbane ($277). Eastern and Impulse use the airport at Williamtown, north of Newcastle.

Bus Between Sydney and Newcastle you're better off taking the train, but if you're heading up the coast, buses offer a much better service. Nearly all long-distance buses stop on Watt St, near the railway station. Cheapish fares from Newcastle include: Sydney $20, Port Macquarie $34, Byron Bay $60 and Brisbane $61. Jayes Travel (☎ 4926 2000), 285 Hunter St near Darby St, handles most major bus-lines.

Sid Fogg's (☎ 1800 045 952) runs up the valley to Dubbo ($46) three times a week, and its buses go to Canberra ($45) during

school holidays. Book at Tower Travel
(☎ 4926 3199), 245 Hunter St on the corner
of Crown St, or phone the depot. Rover
Motors (☎ 4990 1699) runs to Cessnock
($7.50). Port Stephens Buses (☎ 4981 1207)
has nine buses a day to Nelson Bay and Shoal
Bay (1½ hours, $7.60).

Train CityRail runs from Sydney to Newcastle about 25 times daily, taking nearly three
hours. The one-way fare is $14; an off-peak
return is $18. Other trains heading north on
the lines to Armidale and Murwillumbah
bypass central Newcastle, stopping at suburban Broadmeadow – just west of Hamilton.
Frequent buses run from here to the city
centre. An XPT from Central Station to
Broadmeadow takes about 2¼ hours and
costs $20.

Car Rental As well as the regular places, you
can hire used cars from places such as Cheep
Heep (☎ 4961 3144), 107 Tudor St, Hamilton, from $29 a day, including insurance.

Getting Around
The Airport Port Stephens Buses (see
above) stop at Newcastle airport on the run
to Nelson Bay. The trip takes 35 minutes and
costs $4.30. Local bus Nos 348, 349, 350 and
358 stop outside Belmont airport (one hour,
$2).

Bus STA buses cover Newcastle and the
eastern side of Lake Macquarie. Fares are
time based, with a minimum fare of $2. The
ticket is valid for one hour, which is long
enough to get anywhere you want around the
city. An all-day BusTripper ticket costs $6
and is valid on STA buses and ferries. Most
services operate half-hourly. The bus information booth at the west end of the mall, on
the corner of Perkins St, has timetables. If it's
closed, see the tourist office or phone the
Travel Information Centre (☎ 4961 8933)
between 8.30 am and 4.30 pm. For sightseeing, try route No 348, 350 or 358 to Swansea
or No 306, 307 or 327 to Speers Point.

Ferry There are ferries to Stockton from

Queens Wharf approximately half-hourly
from 5.15 am to 11 pm Monday to Thursday.
On Friday and Saturday they run until midnight, and on Sunday they stop at 8.30 pm.
The ferry office on Queens Wharf has timetables.

Up the Valley

Once you leave Newcastle and the urban
centres on the south-eastern side of the
valley, the Hunter becomes a pleasant area of
vineyards, old towns and rolling pastures,
bordered by ranges.

Organised Tours
Most tours go to the lower Hunter wineries.
Hunter Vineyard Tours (☎ 4991 1659) has
daily departures from Newcastle and other
Hunter centres and charges $45 ($28 children) or $29 without lunch.
    Grapemobile (☎ 4991 2339) offers two-
day bike rides through the wineries, with a
support bus, accommodation and all meals
for $160 per person. They also have day
tours.

Getting Around
Bus Rover Motors (☎ 4990 1699) runs
between Newcastle and Cessnock ($7.50)
frequently on weekdays, less often on Saturday and not at all on Sunday. Sid Fogg's
(☎ 1800 045 952) runs up the valley on its
route from Newcastle to Dubbo. See Getting
There & Away at the start of this chapter for
Kean's service from Sydney to various
towns in the Hunter.

Car & Motorcycle The main road through
the Hunter is the New England Highway,
running north-west from Newcastle through
the old towns of Maitland, Singleton and
Muswellbrook, and climbing up to the New
England tablelands near Murrurundi. This
road carries a lot of traffic and passes through
built-up areas, so travel is quite slow. The
300km-long Hunter River comes from

HUNTER VALLEY

further west and meets the highway at Singleton.

Bicycle You can hire bicycles from Grapemobile (☎ 4998 7639), on the corner of McDonalds and Gillards Rds near Pokolbin. It charges $15/25 for a half/full day.

LOWER HUNTER WINERIES

With more than 50 vineyards concentrated in a small, pretty area, the lower Hunter wineries are a popular tourist destination, especially for weekenders from Sydney. If you can, visit midweek.

Orientation

Most lower Hunter wineries are north-west of Cessnock, the closest town to the winery area. Although it's a good base for winery visiting, Cessnock isn't especially attractive. Pokolbin Village, right among the wineries, is just a shop, motel and bistro. Nearby, Hungerford Hill Wine Village is similar but larger.

Broke is a hamlet on the north-western edge of the vineyards. Further south, getting into the ranges, is picturesque little Wollombi. A scenic but bumpy road runs between the two, and Wollombi is also accessible from both Cessnock and Sydney (via Wyong or Wisemans Ferry; either would be an interesting drive).

Information

The region's efficient information centre (☎ 4990 4477), on Wollombi Rd in Cessnock, on the way into town from Sydney, opens daily from 9 am to 5 pm. Drop in for brochures before setting out for the wineries. Plenty of free maps are available, but it's worth buying Broadbent's map of the area for around $4.

There's a tourist information radio station, FM 107.9.

Work During the grape harvest (February/March) there's usually picking work available, although it's often at very short notice. Experienced pickers are preferred.

Contact the Cessnock CES office (☎ 4991 0800).

Wineries

The major activity is visiting wineries and sampling their products. At most wineries you just drop in, but several also have tours. They include McWilliams (weekdays 11 am and 2 pm); Hunter Estate (daily 9.30 am); Tyrrells (daily 1.30 pm) and Rothbury Estate (weekends 11 am and 2 pm).

Hungerford Hill bills itself as a 'wine village'. It has a restaurant, handicrafts shop, 'farmers' market' and wine tours as well as the usual tasting and wine sales facilities – commercial but interesting. The Hunter Valley Wine Society has a pleasant bistro here and you can look round the society's display of local wines – and of course buy some if you want!

Steam Railway

The Richmond Vale Railway Museum (☎ 4936 1124), 4km south of Kurri Kurri on Mulbring Rd, operates an old steam coal train on 3.5km of track between the mines at Pelaw Main and Richmond Main. It's open on the first three Sundays of each month from 10 am to 5 pm, with departures every hour from 10.30 am. Admission is $10 ($5 children), which entitles you to ride the train as many times as you like. Other aspects of the railway are being restored, and there's a museum.

Ballooning

Balloon Aloft (☎ 1800 028 568 toll-free) has daily flights over the valley for $200 per person.

Special Events

The Hunter Vintage Walkabout in February and March attracts hordes of wine enthusiasts for wine tasting, and grape-picking and treading contests. This is a hectic time in the valley as the harvest is in full swing. Accommodation can be scarce, but with planning you can pick up some good package deals. In September there's the Wine & Food Affair.

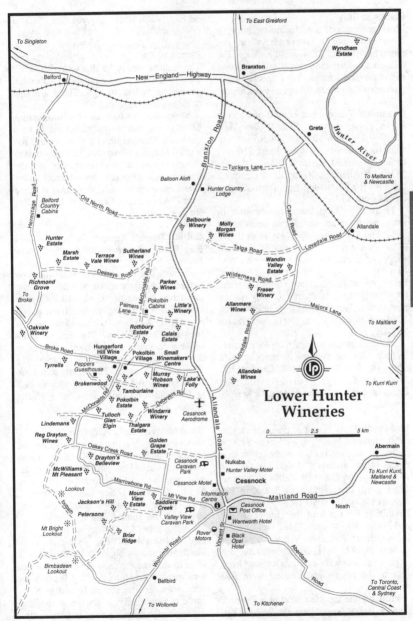

HUNTER VALLEY

To East Gresford

To Singleton

Wyndham Estate

Branxton

New England Highway

Belford

Greta

Hunter River

Branxton Road

To Maitland & Newcastle

Tuckers Lane

Balloon Aloft

Hunter Country Lodge

Allandale

Old North Road

Hermitage Road

Belford Country Cabins

Belbourie Winery

Molly Morgan Wines

Camp Road

Lovedale Road

Talga Road

Hunter Estate

Marsh Estate

Terrace Vale Wines

Sutherland Wines

Deaseys Road

Wandin Valley Estate

Wilderness Road

Richmond Grove

Parker Wines

Fraser Winery

To Broke

Palmers Lane

McDonalds Rd

Pokolbin Cabins

Little's Winery

Allanmere Wines

Majors Lane

To Maitland

Oakvale Winery

Rothbury Estate

Calais Estate

Lovedale Road

Broke Road

Hungerford Hill Wine Village

Pokolbin Village

Small Winemakers' Centre

Allandale Wines

To Kurri Kurri

Tyrrells

Peppers Guesthouse

Murray Robson Wines

Lake's Folly

Brokenwood

Tamburlaine

Debeyers Rd

McDonalds Rd

Pokolbin Estate

Windarra Winery

Cessnock Aerodrome

Allandale Road

Lower Hunter Wineries

Lindemans

Tulloch Glen Elgin

Thalgara Estate

0   2.5   5 km

Reg Drayton Wines

Oakey Creek Road

Golden Grape Estate

Abermain

McWilliams Mt Pleasant

Drayton's Belleview

Cessnock Caravan Park

Nulkaba

Hunter Valley Motel

To Kurri Kurri, Maitland & Newcastle

Lookout

Marrowbone Rd

Cessnock Motel

Cessnock

Mt View Rd

Maitland Road

Jackson's Hill

Mount View Estate

Information Centre

Cessnock Post Office

Neath

Petersons

Saddlers Creek

Valley View Caravan Park

Wentworth Hotel

Mt Bright Lookout

Rover Motors

Vincent St

Black Opal Hotel

Aberdare Road

Briar Ridge

Wollombi Road

Bimbadeen Lookout

Bellbird

To Toronto, Central Coast & Sydney

To Wollombi

To Kitchener

Places to Stay

Most accommodation, including pubs, is more expensive at weekends, when you might have to take a two-night package. The Cessnock information centre books accommodation and knows about special deals. Accommodation can fill up, so book ahead.

Cessnock There are a couple of caravan parks close to town. The *Valley View* (☎ 4990 2573) on Mount View Rd has tent sites for $10, on-site vans from $16 and cabins from $30. *Cessnock Park* (☎ 4990 5819) off Allandale Rd north of Cessnock has sites for $8, on-site vans from $20 and cabins from $30.

There's no hostel accommodation in town, but there are some good deals at the pubs. The *Black Opal Hotel* (☎ 4990 1070), at the southern end of Vincent St, the main shopping street, charges $15 per person from Monday to Thursday, $20 Friday to Sunday. Prices are identical at the *Cessnock Hotel* (☎ 4990 1002) on Wollombi Rd opposite the post office. The *Wentworth Hotel* (☎ 4990 1364), 36 Vincent St, has singles/doubles for $25/40.

Midweek prices at some Cessnock motels include $59 for doubles at the *Cessnock Motel* (☎ 4990 2699) and the *Hunter Valley Motel* (☎ 4990 1722), both on Allandale Rd. Prices at these and other motels rise steeply at weekends.

Vineyards There's a lot of places to stay in the vineyards. Most go well over $100 a night on weekends, but midweek a few places charge around $70 a double, such as *Hunter Country Lodge* (☎ 4938 1744), about 12km north of Cessnock on Branxton Rd; *Belford Country Cabins* (☎ 4991 2777), on Hermitage Rd north of the Hunter Estate; and *Potters Inn* (☎ 4998 7648), on Debeyers Rd south of Pokolbin Village. *Pokolbin Cabins* (☎ 4998 7611) on Palmers Lane is a large complex with cabins sleeping from four to 14 people and costing from $40 midweek.

Probably the top place to stay is *Peppers Hunter Valley Guesthouse* (☎ 4998 7739), on Ekerts Rd, which charges from $180 a double midweek.

Places to Eat

The dining room at the *Black Opal Hotel* in Cessnock has a good reputation, with main courses from $12 to $16. There are also cheaper counter meals.

Many wineries have cafes or restaurants, but if you're watching your budget, bring a cut lunch. Hungerford Hill Wine Village has a good *bistro*. At Pokolbin Village *Arnold's Restaurant* has a good reputation, and the upmarket *Chez Pok* at Peppers Hunter Valley Guesthouse opens daily. *Cafe Max* is in the Small Winemakers Centre on McDonalds Rd near Pokolbin.

Getting There & Away

Bus Rover Motors (☎ 4990 1699) runs between Newcastle and Cessnock ($7.50), six times a day on weekdays, three times on Saturday and not at all on Sunday. The last bus from Newcastle to Cessnock departs from Watt St on weekdays at 6.30 pm and on Saturday at 4.45 pm. There are also services between Cessnock and Maitland. Rover's office is on Vincent St in Cessnock, opposite the Black Opal Hotel. Kean's (☎ 1800 625 587) stops at Cessnock ($20) daily on the run from Sydney to Tamworth. In Sydney, book at the Sydney Coach Terminal (☎ 9281 9366) on Eddy Ave.

Car & Motorcycle Coming from Newcastle, the simplest route is to take the New England Highway and turn off to Kurri Kurri and Cessnock about 4km past Hexham Bridge. You can also get here from the Sydney to Newcastle freeway. See Getting There & Away at the start of this chapter for other routes into the Hunter Valley.

MAITLAND & AROUND

Maitland (population 47,000) has been a large town since the early days of European settlement in the Hunter Valley. It was long seen as a more desirable address than Newcastle and even had brief dreams of rivalling Sydney as the colony's most important city.

One of Maitland's most famous citizens was Les Darcy, a boxer who was a national hero before dying – perhaps under mysterious circumstances – in the USA in 1917.

Orientation & Information

Maitland's main street is High St, which follows the winding route of the original trail through the town. Part of the street is now the Heritage Mall, so driving through town is not simple. The information centre (☎ 4933 2611) is in East Maitland, on the highway on the corner of Banks St. It occupies a 100-year-old slab hut known as Hew Cottage.

Things to See & Do

The city's 19th-century wealth is reflected in the elaborate Georgian and Victorian buildings which remain. East Maitland, which was established in 1833 after floods in the original town, has its share of old buildings, and the nearby village of **Morpeth**, once the area's main riverport, is also well endowed with architectural gems, especially along Swan St.

The **City Art Gallery**, open Thursday, Friday and Saturday afternoon and from 10.30 am on Sunday, is in Brough House (1870) on Church St. The **museum of local history** is next door in Grossman House (1870) and opens on weekends. The extraordinary **Masonic Lodge** on Victoria St and the **courthouse** (1895) at the western end of High St are some of the many interesting old buildings in Maitland.

In East Maitland, have a look at the **old jail** and the nearby **courthouse** on John St, and the **Lands Department Offices** on Newcastle St.

About 15km north-west of Maitland, **Windermere**, a homestead that was built in 1821 by Captain Winder, who apparently planted the Hunter Valley's first vines. Windermere later became the home of William Wentworth, crosser of the Blue Mountains and colonial politician. Windermere and its museum are open for inspection by appointment (☎ 4930 7204). A guided tour costs $10 per person.

Action Aerobatics (☎ 4930 1009, 018 474 307), based at the Royal Newcastle Aeroclub outside Maitland, has **flights** in old biplanes. It charges $90 for 30 minutes' normal cruising, $120 for a taste of aerobatics and $150 for the works.

Special Events

Maitland Show, held in late October, is one of the biggest in the state.

Places to Stay & Eat

The *Hunter River Hotel* (☎ 4933 7244), 10 Melbourne St in East Maitland, has singles/doubles for $25/50. There's plenty of other pub and motel accommodation, much of it in East Maitland, and also a *caravan park* (☎ 4933 2950). *Cintra* (☎ 4932 8483) occupies a huge old Victorian house on Regent St in Old Maitland and charges $65/110 with cooked breakfast.

On High St east of the mall, *Pepperina Books & Coffee* is a nice place to relax after a stroll around. There are several Chinese restaurants and other eateries, but fewer interesting places to eat than you would expect in a large town near the wineries. The *Old George & Dragon Restaurant* (☎ 4933 7272), 48 Melbourne St in East Maitland, is in a restored pub dating from the 1830s and offers Anglo-French food. Allow around $50 per head. The restaurant also does dinner, bed and breakfast packages.

SINGLETON

Europeans first came to this area in 1820 and farms soon sprang up on Patricks Plains. By 1835 the village which was later to be called Singleton was established. The current population is around 12,000.

On weekends, an information kiosk opens from 10 am to 3 pm in Townhead Park, off the highway.

In the old courthouse, by shady Burdekin Park, a **museum** with displays on local history opens on weekends and admission is $1 (20c children). For other early buildings, take a stroll down George St.

The **Royal Australian Army Infantry Corps Museum** is at Singleton Army Camp.

According to the army, it's a 'top-class infantry weapons collection'. As well as the guns there are memorabilia from most wars that the Australian infantry has been involved in. The camp is 4km south of Singleton, and you can get there from the New England Highway before Singleton or from the Windsor road just out of Singleton. The museum opens from Wednesday to Sunday (but is closed in October or November) and admission is $2 ($1 children).

Singleton also claims to have the world's largest sundial.

Places to Stay
Country Acres Caravan Park (☎ 6572 2328) on Maison Dieu Rd has sites, on-site vans and cabins.

The *Caledonian Hotel* (☎ 6572 1356) on the highway near the town centre has accommodation, but things might be quieter at one of the pubs along John St, such as the *Imperial* (☎ 6572 1290). There's also a choice of motels, both on the highway and in town.

Getting There & Away
Air Yanda (book through Qantas) flies between Sydney and Singleton weekdays for $122. The airport is at Whittingham, just east of town.

UPPER HUNTER WINERIES
With far fewer wineries, the upper Hunter is less visited than the lower, but the country is pretty and the wineries are well worth seeing. The Upper Hunter Wine Weekend is the first weekend in August.

Most upper Hunter wineries are close to the small town of Denman, but don't miss Serenella Estate, tucked away in a beautiful valley near the hamlet of Sandy Hollow. Verona Winery is just north of Muswellbrook.

Denman
Denman (population 1500), the nearest town to the upper Hunter wineries, is a sleepy little place close to the forested sandstone ranges bordering the southern side of the Hunter Valley.

The information centre (☎ 6547 2731) is on the main street at the Old Carriage Restaurant, a cafe/restaurant in an old railway carriage. There's a **museum** in the old courthouse on Palace St.

Places to Stay As well as the plentiful accommodation in nearby Muswellbrook and Singleton, there are some local places. *Denman Van Village* (☎ 6547 2590) has sites for $11, on-site vans from $22 and cabins from $30. There's another *caravan park* (☎ 6547 4575) in Sandy Hollow. The *Denman Hotel* (☎ 6547 2207) has pub rooms for $15 per person, and the even more basic *Royal Hotel* (☎ 6547 2226) nearby charges just $10. The *Denman Motor Inn* (☎ 6547 2462) charges from $44/52.

Ask the information centre about B&B accommodation in the area.

Getting There & Away Sid Fogg's (☎ 1800 045 952) stops at Denman ($24) three times a week on the Newcastle-Dubbo run. The fare from Denman to Dubbo is $28.

MUSWELLBROOK
Like other towns in the Hunter Valley, Muswellbrook (population 10,100) was founded early in Australia's history and has some interesting old buildings, surrounded by spreading residential areas.

Bridge St (the New England Highway) is Muswellbrook's main shopping street. The closest thing to an information centre in Muswellbrook is the lobby of the Bridgecourt Motor Inn (☎ 6543 2170), towards the northern end of Bridge St.

The NPWS office (☎ 6543 3533) is also on Bridge St, across from the RSL Club. There's also an NPWS office (☎ 6574 5275) at Bulga on the Putty Rd and at the edge of Wollemi National Park.

The **Weidman Cottage Heritage Centre** on Bridge St near the centre of town has displays on the area's history.

St Alban's Church on Brook St dates from 1867. It's quite small and dark, which makes the stained glass blaze on sunny days.

Historic *Eatons Hotel* (☎ 6543 2403) on

the main street at the northern end of town charges $20/30 a single/double.

SCONE

Scone (which *isn't* pronounced 'skonn') is a pleasant old upper Hunter town (population 4300) known for its horse studs – there are more than 40 in the area. Like Muswellbrook, Scone is a handy jumping-off point for the upper Hunter wineries.

Just east of Scone, the Hunter River is dammed to form **Lake Glenbawn**, a popular watersports area with camping (☎ 6543 7752).

About 25km north-east of Scone, just off the interesting road across to Barrington Tops and Gloucester, **Belltrees** is an old sheep station with a beautiful and very grand homestead. The family of Patrick White, Australia's Nobel Prize-winning author, has owned the property for 150 years, and it appears as 'Kudgeri' in White's novel *The Eye of the Storm*. Belltrees isn't open to visitors, but there's a guesthouse on the property – see Places to Stay below.

Orientation & Information

Kelly St (the New England Highway) is the main shopping street. Liverpool St runs off Kelly St and becomes the road to Merriwa.

The information centre (☎ 6545 2907, 6545 1526) is off Kelly St on the north side of the town centre, near the *Mare & Foal* statue. There's a cafe and you can buy souvenirs here, starting at just 10c for a rock! Information and souvenirs are also available at the Station Gallery & Cafe at the railway station.

Horse Studs

The information centre can arrange visits to some of the area's horse studs outside the August/September foaling season. There are organised tours of some studs during Horse Week in May.

Burning Mountain

Coal seams beneath this mountain were burning when the first Europeans arrived in the area (they thought it was an active

---

Australian Stock Horses

Although it wasn't formally defined as a breed until 1971, the Australian stock horse participated in most of the major events of European-Australian history. Originally called Walers (from New South Wales), the breed served as cavalry horses in India, South Africa and during WWI. They carried the 4th Australian Light Horse regiment in the world's last cavalry charge at the taking of Beersheba in 1916.

The headquarters of the Australian Stock Horse Society (☎ 6745 1122) is in Scone. ■

---

volcano), and calculations based on the burning rate of a metre per year suggest that the fire started as long as 6000 years ago. The mountain is a nature reserve, and a 3km walking track leads through some diverse terrain up to the smoking vents. The turn-off from the New England Highway to Burning Mountain is about 20km north of Scone.

Special Events

Horse Week, with equestrian competitions and displays, is held in mid-May.

Places to Stay

Caravan Parks There are a couple of caravan parks, the *Scone* (☎ 6545 2024), with sites and cabins, and the smaller *Highway* (☎ 6545 1078), with sites and on-site vans.

Hostel The rural *Scone YHA Hostel* (☎ 6545 2072) occupies the old schoolhouse at Segenhoe, 8km east of town. Dorm beds in this historic building are $13 and doubles are $28. The owners will pick you up from Scone, or you can catch the schoolbus out at 3.20 pm.

Hotels & Motels The *Belmore Hotel* (☎ 6545 2078), on Kelly St not far from the railway station and the information centre, is a pleasant place with a fine beer garden. It has rooms for $24 per person with breakfast, rising to $30 at weekends.

HUNTER VALLEY

The *Royal Hotel* (☎ 6545 1305), on the corner of Kelly and St Aubins Sts, has pub rooms for $20/25 and motel-style rooms for around $40/50. The *Golden Fleece Hotel* (☎ 6545 1357), on the corner of Kelly and Liverpool Sts, charges $15/24, and the *Thoroughbred Hotel* (☎ 6545 1086) at the south end of Kelly St charges $15/35.

Airlie House Motor Inn (☎ 6545 1488), on the highway near the town centre, takes in a large Victorian house and charges $64/74.

Belltrees Country House (☎ 6545 1668), on Belltrees property 25km north-east of Scone, is a very comfortable guesthouse charging $190/280 for dinner, bed and breakfast. It's closed on Monday and Tuesday outside school holidays. Children are allowed during school holidays only.

Places to Eat

Le Café au Lait, at the information centre, opens daily for light meals (maximum $6) and snacks. The *Station Cafe* at the railway station has similar fare and is also open for dinner on Friday. They prefer you to book (☎ 6545 2144).

The *Summerhouse Cafe* on Kelly St across from the Civic Theatre is a pleasant place for coffee, cake and light meals during the day from Monday to Friday, and dinner on Friday and Saturday, with main courses around $12.

Further down Kelly St, across from the Village shopping centre, *Asser House* opens Monday to Saturday for snacks and light meals (up to $10, many less), and for dinner on Friday and Saturday, with main courses costing around $15. There's an outdoor area and the interesting menu is worth checking out.

The *Country Cottage* (☎ 6545 1140), 101 Liverpool St, across the railway line from Kelly St, opens for dinner on Friday and Saturday.

MURRURUNDI

This small town (population 1000) is right at the head of the Hunter Valley and from here the highway climbs steeply up the Liverpool Ranges. There's a small museum, several interesting craft shops and some fine old buildings.

MERRIWA

Although on the upper fringes of the Hunter Valley, Merriwa is very much a country town (population 1000), immune to the Hunter's creeping urbanisation. You have now entered pastoral country, a feature of this area since the 1820s.

The information centre (☎ 6548 2505) is on a side street next to the shire offices and is theoretically open daily. If no-one is there, try the shire offices.

This is a sandstone region and there are several early stone buildings here and in the surrounding area. The **Colonial Cottage Museum** on the main street is in one such building, a quite modest structure built in 1847. In the hamlet of **Cassilis**, about 45km north-west, there are a few more sandstone buildings, not worth a special trip but interesting if you're passing through.

Goulburn River National Park, 35km south-west of town, protects the upper reaches of the Goulburn River (which flows into the Hunter east of Denman). The park follows the river as it cuts its way through sandstone gorges. This was the route used by Aborigines travelling from the plains to the sea, and the area is rich in rock art and other sites. You can camp but there are no facilities. Access is from the road running south to Wollar and Bylong. The Muswellbrook NPWS office (☎ 6543 3533) has information.

Places to Stay & Eat

There's a *caravan park* (☎ 6548 2494) by the river on the western edge of town. The *Fitzroy Hotel* (☎ 6548 2235), a fine old sandstone pub, charges $17/30, and the *Royal Hotel* (☎ 6548 2285) charges $15/30 per person. Both are on the main street. *El Dorado Motel* (☎ 6548 2273) is on the main street east of the shopping centre and charges $45/53. For a mock-Spanish-American motel it's quite a nice place.

The *Merriwa Bakery* on the main street sells some of the best pies in the land.

Getting There & Away
Bus Sid Fogg's (☎ 1800 045 952) stops in Merriwa on the service between Dubbo ($25 from Merriwa) and Newcastle ($28).

Car & Motorcycle Merriwa is a modest travel crossroads, with roads leading to the upper Hunter (via Sandy Hollow and Denman), to Gulgong and Mudgee (via Cassilis), to Dubbo (via Dunedoo or Gulgong) and to Coonabarabran (via Dunedoo or Cassilis).

North of Newcastle

The inland routes running north from Newcastle and the rugged ranges on the northern side of the Hunter Valley have some attractions that are very different from the genteel vineyards.

THE BUCKETTS WAY
This old road is an alternative to the Pacific Highway as a route north, branching off the highway about 15km north of Raymond Terrace and rejoining it just south of Taree. This road is longer and narrower than the highway, but it carries much less traffic and passes through some interesting country.

Stroud
Stroud is a small village (population 600), but it's the main town in this part of the Karuah Valley. Founded by the Australian Agricultural Company in 1826, Stroud has several convict-built buildings such as **Quambi**, once a company residence and now a museum (intermittently open). Next door to Quambi is the Anglican church, and in its graveyard are some interesting old headstones, including one which pronounces, rather ominously, 'Vengeance is Mine, Saith the Lord'.

The road running past Quambi leads to **Silo Hill**, where there are some wheat silos built in the early days of the Australian Agricultural Company. These aren't your ordinary phallic silos – they are buried in the hill and you can climb down into one of

them. There isn't a lot to see down there, but the echo is weird.

Further down the main street is the old **courthouse**, which you can inspect by arrangement. Next door is **Stroud Treasure**, a local craft and secondhand shop that's several notches above the usual. It's open from Thursday to Sunday.

Special Events Stroud's annual brick-throwing contest, held in mid-July, is an international affair, linked to similar contests in the English and Canadian Strouds (female contestants throw rolling pins).

Places to Stay There's a basic but pretty *camping area* at the showgrounds, near the river. The *Central Hotel* (☎ 4994 5197) is the only hotel in town and has standard pub rooms for $20/40.

In the hamlet of Booral, 7km south of Stroud, *Gundayn House* (☎ 4994 9246) is an impressive Georgian house offering accommodation for $30/50. It's a non-smoking, non-drinking, vegetarian establishment.

The *Girvan YHA Hostel* (☎ 4997 6639) is about 15km from Stroud, on the Bulahdelah road (turn east off the Bucketts Way at Booral). See Bulahdelah in the North Coast chapter.

Getting There & Away Countrylink buses stop in Stroud on the weekday run between Newcastle and Taree. There's also a school-day-only run from Bulahdelah to Raymond Terrace and Newcastle via Stroud. This is pretty slow.

Gloucester
Gloucester is a busy country town (population 2500) on the banks of the Gloucester River. The tourist information centre (☎ 6558 1408) is in the centre of town on the corner of Church and Denison Sts.

The **museum** at the southern end of Church St opens on Thursday and Saturday, plus Tuesday during school holidays.

There are extensive **state forests** in the area offering good walks and drives, but the

---

The Australian Agricultural Company
By the 1820s the idea that NSW might be a good place to make money had filtered back to Britain. Floated in 1825, the Australian Agricultural Company raised £1,000,000 from British investors, a colossal sum, and was granted a huge tract of land from Port Stephens to the Manning River. The company also took over the Hunter coalfields and renamed the port Newcastle. A manager and workers (including convicts who were essentially slave labour) were sent out to farm sheep and cattle, and they began in the Karuah Valley around the company-built village of Stroud, named for the landscape's resemblance to the English Cotswolds.

Unfortunately, while the country is lush, well watered and beautiful, the soil lacks essential trace elements and, along with the sheep, the company failed to thrive. Just about every other form of agriculture was tried, including growing silk worms, but the land refused to turn its fertility into cash crops.

Taking up more land in the Tamworth area (which didn't look like England at all) proved to be more successful, but the company's plans for a closely settled private empire with an English social structure never materialised. Today the company still owns large properties in Queensland and the Northern Territory. ■

---

main attraction is nearby Barrington Tops National Park

The Barrington River, which rises in the Barrington Tops and flows down past Barrington, just north-west of Gloucester, is popular for **whitewater canoeing**. There are several companies offering canoe trips, including the Barrington Outdoor Adventure Centre (☎ 6558 2093) and Barrington River Lodge (☎ 6558 4316). The Barrington General Store rents canoes and can advise on the best places.

Mountain Maid gold mine (☎ 6558 4303), 1km from Copeton and 15km east of Gloucester, has **underground tours**.

Places to Stay *Gloucester Caravan Park* (☎ 6558 1720) on Denison St has sites and cabins. The *Avon Valley Inn* (☎ 6558 1016) on Church St has accommodation, and there's also *Gloucester Country Lodge* (☎ 6558 1812) near the golf course, charging from $52/60.

Getting There & Away Northbound trains stop at Gloucester, but coming in the other direction you'll have to change to a bus at Taree. The buses don't run on weekends.

Countrylink buses stop in Gloucester on the weekday run between Newcastle and Taree.

The Bucketts Way runs south to Stroud and beyond, and winds east to the Pacific Highway just south of Taree. From near Barrington, a village just west of Gloucester, you can head north on a partly sealed road to Walcha or branch off to Terrible Billy (great name!), from where a sealed road runs to Tamworth. If you keep heading west from Barrington, you'll be on a spectacular unsealed road which winds past Barrington Tops National Park, eventually reaching the New England Highway near Scone.

BARRINGTON TOPS NATIONAL PARK

Barrington Tops is a World Heritage wilderness area centred on the rugged Barrington Plateau, which rises to almost 1600 metres around Mt Barrington and Carey's Peak. The 'tops' are a series of monolithic hills known as 'bucketts', a corruption of an Aboriginal word meaning 'big rock' (hence the road called the Bucketts Way). The park also takes in the Gloucester Tops just to the north. There are good walking trails, but be prepared for snow in winter and cold snaps at any time. Drinking water must be boiled.

Vegetation in the park ranges from subtropical rainforest in the lower reaches of the park to snow-gum country on the exposed peaks. The slopes in between are dominated by ancient, moss-covered Antarctic beech forest. The park can be reached from the towns of Dungog, Gloucester and Scone.

The NPWS office (☎ 4983 1031) in Raymond Terrace has more information.

Places to Stay

The *Gloucester River Camping Area*, 31km from the Gloucester-Stroud road, is the main campsite within the park. *Barrington House* (☎ 4995 3212), 43km from Dungog on the southern edge of the park, has a spectacular setting beneath the plateau escarpment. It charges $75 per person with meals, rising to $90 in school holidays. The rates include activities like horseriding.

WOKO NATIONAL PARK

Smaller than nearby Barrington Tops National Park, Woko is similarly undeveloped and rugged, and also protects rainforests as well as other vegetation types. Access is from Gloucester, about 30km to the south-east; head for Rookhurst and take the left fork shortly after. There are *campsites* on the banks of the Manning River near the park entrance and some good swimming holes. The NPWS office (☎ 4983 1031) in Raymond Terrace has more information.

DUNGOG & AROUND

The quiet country town of Dungog (population 2500), in the steep hills to the north of the Hunter Valley, is the closest town to the southern side of Barrington Tops National Park. There are also many state forests in the area. Established in the 1830s as a military post, with the task of eradicating bushrangers (it failed), Dungog is today a service centre for the area's farms.

There are a number of small and picturesque villages in the area, such as **Clarence Town**, **Gresford** and **Paterson**, although getting to them on the winding roads can be time-consuming.

Places to Stay

There's a motel, the *Tall Timbers* (☎ 4992 1547), on Dungog's main street, and accommodation at pubs including the *Courthouse Hotel* (☎ 4992 1615) on Brown St. Along the Chichester Dam road, running north from Dungog, there are several farmstay options, such as *Bellbird Valley* (☎ 4995 9266) and *Ferndale Park Camping Reserve* (☎ 4995 9239). Camping is permitted in the area's state forests.

Getting There & Away

Train Trains on the main northern line stop at Dungog.

Car & Motorcycle Dungog is about 20km west of Stroud (the turn-off from the Bucketts Way is at Stroud Road, 7km north of Stroud), or you can get here from Singleton on the Gresford road.

The North Coast

NSW's North Coast stretches from Port Stephens right up to the Queensland border at Tweed Heads. Most places north from Coffs Harbour, especially Byron Bay, are travellers' meccas, but it's worth taking your time on a trip north from Sydney as there are excellent beaches and rugged bushland all the way. There are also some interesting places in the ranges behind the coast.

The Central Coast, between Sydney and Newcastle, is covered in the Around Sydney chapter.

Getting There & Around
Air See the Port Macquarie, Coffs Harbour, Grafton and Ballina sections for details of flights and fares.

Bus Companies running the Pacific Highway route to Brisbane include Greyhound Pioneer (☎ 132030), McCafferty's (☎ 131499) and Pioneer Motor Service (☎ 9281 2233). They call at all the resorts except Port Stephens and Forster-Tuncurry. Some typical fares from Sydney are Port Macquarie $51 (seven hours), Coffs Harbour $59 (9½ hours) and Byron Bay $70 (13 hours). The fare through to Brisbane is $75 (16 hours). Port Stephens and Forster-Tuncurry have their own services to Sydney, provided by local companies.

Bus & Train The nightly XPT from Sydney to Brisbane runs up the coast. Connecting buses at Casino run to Lismore, Ballina, Byron Bay, Mullumbimby and Tweed Heads/Coolangatta. Another XPT makes a daylight run from Sydney to Murwillumbah, from where connecting buses run to Tweed Heads/Coolangatta and Surfers Paradise.

Car & Motorcycle The Pacific Highway runs all the way up the coast. It is steadily being upgraded to cope with the ever-increasing traffic load. The long-term goal is to provide a four-lane highway all the way

HIGHLIGHTS
- Swimming with dolphins at Nelson Bay
- Visiting the koala hospital at Roto House in Port Macquarie
- Walking in Dorrigo National Park, the most accessible of Australia's World Heritage rainforests
- Seeing Grafton's magnificent jacaranda trees in full bloom in late October
- Looking down on Cape Byron from a tandem hang-glider
- Watching the sunrise from the summit of Mt Warning

from Sydney to Brisbane, but that's a long way off.

Lower North Coast

The coast from Port Stephens north to Port Macquarie is easily accessible from Sydney, but doesn't attract as much attention as the resorts further north.

PORT STEPHENS
Port Stephens is a huge sheltered bay about an hour's drive north of Newcastle. It occupies a submerged valley which stretches more than 20km inland. It's a popular

boating and fishing spot and is well known for its resident dolphins.

It's a good weekend getaway from Sydney, about three hours away by bus, and is much less developed than the Central Coast. There are also plenty of connections to nearby Newcastle.

History

Captain Cook sighted the entrance to Port Stephens in 1770, but the colony of New South Wales was seven years old before the first survey of the area was made – the first official survey, that is. Escaped convicts had made it up here five years earlier and were living with local Aborigines in what must have seemed like heaven after their time in Sydney.

Orientation & Information

Port Stephens has a long way to go before it's in the same league as the crowded Central Coast, but it's headed in the same direction, with land sales and new housing estates everywhere you look. The largest town on Port Stephens is Nelson Bay (population 7000), near the south head. The tourist office (☎ 4981 1579) at the end of the main street, near the d'Albora Marina complex, is open daily from 9 am to 5 pm.

Just east of Nelson Bay, and virtually merged with it, is Shoal Bay with its long, sheltered beach and great views across to hilly islands. It's a short walk to the surf at Zenith Beach.

Back down the Tomaree Peninsula from Shoal Bay is Anna Bay, with access to both the bay and ocean beaches. Samurai Beach, at the northern end of One Mile Beach on Anna Bay (some way east of the town of the same name), is a nude beach. One Mile Beach is one of the area's best surf beaches. On the west side of Anna Bay township, the wide Stockton Beach runs all the way back to Newcastle. Watch out for vehicles – 4WDs are allowed on the beach here. The stretch of coast between Tomaree Head (Shoal Bay) and Anna Bay is occupied by tiny Tomaree National Park.

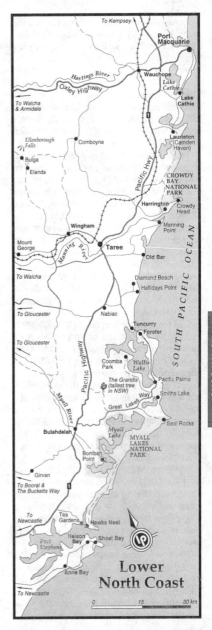

NORTH COAST

Lower
North Coast

Across the heads from Nelson Bay are the towns of Tea Gardens and Hawks Nest. See Myall Lakes National Park later for information on these.

Things to See & Do

The restored 1872 **Inner Lighthouse** at Little Beach has displays on the area's history. There's also a cafe here, with good views.

There's a huge range of **cruises** on offer, so many that the cruise boats have their own wharf and booking centre, east of the d'Albora Marina. One cruise that does leave from d'Albora Marina is Captain Mackenzie Classic Charters, which operates an old, wooden, gaff-rigged boat. Two-hour cruises are held several times a day and cost $15 per person ($7.50 children). Some boats cruise around Port Stephens, with good chances of seeing dolphins (and even swimming with them if the boat has a net; *Moonshadow* is one which does), and others head across to the Myall Lakes.

Sail Cruise Port Stephens (☎ 4982 2399) rents large **yachts** and cabin cruisers for a minimum of two days around $300.

On the beach at Shoal Bay, Fly'n'Ski has **paragliding** or you can learn to water-ski for $20 a lesson. There's also the sea sled, a sausage-like inflatable that's towed behind a speedboat. Nearby you can hire cats, canoes and sailboards. Sunseeker Sailboards on Bagnalls Beach, just west of the Nelson Bay town centre, also rents cats and sailboards.

At Nelson Bay, Pro Dive (☎ 4981 4331) at d'Albora Marina and Dive Nelson Bay (☎ 4981 2491) in Nelson Towers on Victoria Parade run **diving** courses and rent equipment. *Advance II* (☎ 018 494 386) is a long-range motor/sailing yacht which has live-on-board dive courses for up to four people – pricey but fun.

There is a large **koala colony** at Lemon Tree Passage on the Tilligerry Peninsula. A road runs to Lemon Tree Passage from the village of Salt Ash.

Tomaree Toboggan Run, near the Salamander Shopping Centre, is a one-km steel

track which you can shoot down on a toboggan for $4 (less for more rides).

Organised Tours

Horizon Safaris (☎ 018 681 600 or book at the tourist office in Nelson Bay) has various tours of the district, including a tour of Hunter Valley wineries for $35.

Places to Stay

In winter there are often good package deals at the more expensive places. Contact the tourist office to see what's available.

Caravan Parks The closest caravan parks to Nelson Bay are *Halifax* (☎ 4981 1522) at Little Beach, right on Nelson Head about two km north of town, and the council-run *Alex McDonald* (☎ 4981 1427) in Shoal Bay. Both have sites and cabins and both are expensive at peak times.

Hostels There's a YHA hostel section in the *Shoal Bay Motel* (☎ 4984 2315) on the beachfront road. Dorm beds are $15 and there are doubles for $20 per person; these rates can rise during school holidays.

Samurai Beach Bungalows (☎ 4982 1921), just east of Anna Bay on the corner of Frost Rd and Robert Connell Close, offers an opportunity for backpackers to go bush. The bungalows are dotted Asian-style around a covered communal kitchen area. It has dorm beds for $15 and doubles from $35. Host Mark is a keen surfer and angler who organises frequent outings to surrounding beaches. There's free use of surfboards and bicycles. Buses from Newcastle run past the door.

The *Seabreeze Hotel* (☎ 4981 1511), just uphill from the information centre, has beds in comfortable modern dorms for $20. Cooked breakfast is $7.

Motels Motel units at the *Shoal Bay Motel* (☎ 4981 1744) are $61/65 a single/double in the off-season, rising to $91/125 in the peak season.

There are many motels in Nelson Bay, all very expensive at peak times. In the off-season, the *Central* (☎ 4981 3393), on the corner of Government Rd and Church St, and the *Marlin* (☎ 4981 1036), east of town on Shoal Bay Rd, charge around $45/50 for singles/doubles. *Leilani Court* (☎ 4981 3304) on Gowrie Ave (the road that runs up to the Nelson Head lighthouse) has serviced apartments for $60/70 in the off-season.

Places to Eat
Good, cheap meals are available at the big *RSL Club* between Nelson Bay and Shoal Bay and at the *Bowling Club* on Stockton St.

The d'Albora Marina complex has a pleasant coffee shop and there's good seafood at the *Fisherman's Wharf Restaurant* at the Fishermen's Co-op wharf. *Waves Seafood Family Restaurant* in Nelson Square on Donald St has an all-you-can-eat deal for about $15.

Getting There & Away
Bus Port Stephens Buses (☎ 1800 045 949) has a daily service to Sydney ($22) and frequent buses to Newcastle ($7.60). If you're heading north up the coast, it's easiest to backtrack to Newcastle and catch a long-distance bus from there.

Boat Port Stephens Ferries operates between Nelson Bay and Tea Gardens three times a day (one hour, $15 return).

Car & Motorcycle If you want to drive north up the coast from Nelson Bay, you'll have to backtrack a long way to the Pacific Highway at Newcastle or Raymond Terrace, or join the highway north of Raymond Terrace by taking the partly unsealed road via Medowie.

Getting Around
It's worth hiring a bike, as there is a good network of bike paths in the area. There are a couple of bike-hire places. One is in Nelson Bay across from the tourist office, where you'll pay $4/15 an hour/day, plus $2 for a helmet. There's another in Shoal Bay, around the corner from the Shoal Bay Motel.

BULAHDELAH & AROUND
A small town on the Myall River and the Pacific Highway, Bulahdelah is the jumping-off point for Myall Lakes and, a little way north of town, the Great Lakes Way route to Seal Rocks and Forster-Tuncurry. Some interesting old towns, such as Stroud, and the spectacular Barrington Tops National Park are inland from Bulahdelah, but they're more easily reached from towns in the Hunter Valley and have been included in that chapter.

Looming over the town is **Mt Alum**, the largest above-ground deposit of alum (a salt used in various industrial processes) in the world. The mining has ceased and the mountain is now the **Bulahdelah Mountain Reserve** with some walking trails to historic sites. The entrance is a couple of blocks from the highway, on the same street as the police station. In November there's a race to the top.

The mists which often wreath Mt Alum occur all over this area and the combination of warmth and moisture is ideal for lush forests. Not far from Bulahdelah, the tallest tree in the state towers over dense rainforest. **The Grandis**, a 400-year-old flooded gum (*Eucalyptus grandis*), is an awesome sight. On a humid, misty day, with the strange calls of whip birds echoing off palm trees and tall timber, the atmosphere is almost primeval. With its immensely tall, straight trunk it's amazing that the Grandis and some of its slightly shorter cousins survived the logging which continues in this area. To get here, take the Great Lakes Way and then the signposted turn-off 12km from Bulahdelah. The Grandis is six km further on, down a bumpy all-weather road. You can also get here from the Pacific Highway, on a road that is part of a driving tour of the area's state forests.

The Forestry Commission office (☎ 4997 4206) in Bulahdelah has maps of this drive and other places of interest in the area.

On the Violet Hill road into Myall Lakes is the **Bulahdelah Logging Railway**, a re-creation of a timber train. It's open Friday and Saturday (daily except Sunday during school holidays). Pony rides and horseriding are available nearby.

NORTH COAST

Places to Stay

Bulahdelah has a *caravan park* (☎ 4997 4565) and several motels, all just highway stops. Campers are better off heading to one of the nearby beaches, at Seal Rocks or Myall Lakes National Park. Ask at the Forestry Commission office (☎ 4997 4206), near the entrance to Bulahdelah Mountain Park, for information on camping in the area's state forests.

There are two *houseboat* hire places in Bulahdelah, both on the river near the turn-off to Myall Lakes. See the Myall Lakes National Park section for details.

The simple *YHA Hostel* (☎ 4997 6639) near the tiny hamlet of Girvan, about 20km west of Bulahdelah on the winding backroad to Booral, occupies the old school and has beds for $7. There are hot showers but pit toilets. It's a pleasant, secluded spot with good walks in the surrounding forests. Great Lakes Coaches and Countrylink both go past the hostel on their Newcastle-Bulahdelah runs, weekdays only. If you're driving, look out for the YHA sign at the highway turn-off three km south of Bulahdelah. It might pay to ring before you arrive so they know you're coming – no calls after 10 pm.

Getting There & Away

Bus Great Lakes Coaches (☎ 4983 1560, 1800 043 263) services Bulahdelah on the daily run between Forster and Sydney ($30 from Bulahdelah) via Newcastle ($15). On schooldays, there are also rather slow runs to Taree and to Raymond Terrace and Newcastle via Stroud.

Car & Motorcycle The Pacific Highway runs through Bulahdelah, but if you're heading to Forster-Tuncurry take the Great Lakes Way, a scenic road that winds through state forest and passes Myall Lake, the turn-off to Seal Rocks and some other beaches, then runs between the ocean and Wallis Lake up to Forster. The Great Lakes Way leaves the highway just north of Bulahdelah. The road to Girvan and Booral (and the Bucketts Way) leaves the Pacific Highway three km south of Bulahdelah.

MYALL LAKES NATIONAL PARK

The park is one of the most popular recreation areas in the state. The large network of coastal lakes is ideal for watersports. Canoes, windsurfers and runabouts can be hired at **Bombay Point**, the park's main settlement, 11km from Bulahdelah. A car ferry links Bombah Point to the coastal regions of the park from 8 am to 6 pm. The best beaches are in the north around the hamlet of **Seal Rocks**. There are good walks through coastal rainforest at **Mungo Brush** in the south.

Places to Stay

There are several NPWS *campsites* dotted around the park, including a good one at Mungo Brush. Camping fees are $5 for two people, plus a $7.50 once-only park-use fee. Sites can be scarce at peak times. At Bombah Point, *Myall Shores* (☎ 4997 4495) has tent sites from $16 for two people, bungalows for $45 and cabins for $60. There's a shop and a restaurant. The owners can organise a minibus ride from Bulahdelah ($5).

There are caravan parks and motels in Tea Gardens and Hawks Nest. *Hawk's Nest Beach Caravan Park* (☎ 4997 0239) has just a narrow band of bush separating it from a good surf beach. Tent sites are $11 a double and cabins start at $35.

Several outfits rent houseboats to cruise the lakes. At Bulahdelah, *Myall Lake Houseboats* (☎ 4997 4221) has an ageing fleet of boats including some small two-person boats which cost from $200 to $350 for three midweek nights, depending on the season. Next door, *Luxury Houseboat & Cruiser Hire* (☎ 4997 4380) has a newer fleet of more upmarket boats. Its two to six-person boats cost from $590 to $750. It also has yachts for hire. There are a couple more places in Tea Gardens. There's a bewildering array of rates, varying with the time of week, time of year, size of boat and number of people, and there are occasional special deals. The least expensive time is midweek from about May to September; the peak time is Christmas to late January and on long weekends.

Getting There & Away

There is road access to the park from Tea Gardens in the south, from Bulahdelah on the Pacific Highway and from Forster-Tuncurry in the north. You can drive from Tea Gardens to Bulahdelah via the Bombah Point ferry. The ferry runs half-hourly from 8 am to 6 pm, shuttling between the ocean and the western sides of the park. The fare is $2.50 for cars and 50c for pedestrians. Great Lakes Coaches (☎ 1800 043 263) has a daily service from Newcastle to Tea Gardens for $12.80. There are three ferries a day between Tea Gardens and Nelson Bay.

Seal Rocks

Seal Rocks is a small hamlet on a great beach at the northern end of Myall Lakes National Park. There's a shop, a few houses and not much else. The actual Seal Rocks are some distance offshore.

Humpback **whales** swim past Seal Rocks and can sometimes be seen from the shore. In 1992 a large pod of false killer whales beached at Seal Rocks, but most were saved after a massive effort by locals and people from all over the Hunter Valley. There is good surf just south of Seal Rocks at Treachery Beach.

Places to Stay The simple *caravan park* is a bit of a walk from town but is next to an excellent beach. Sites cost $9.50 and there are on-site vans for $30. It's the sort of place you'd seriously consider staying at for a week in summer. There is a privately run *camping area* behind Treachery Beach.

Getting There & Away Seal Rocks is 11 km down a partly sealed road from the Great Lakes Way; turn off at Bungwahl, which is about 30 km from Bulahdelah and a little further from Forster-Tuncurry.

FORSTER-TUNCURRY

Forster and Tuncurry (combined population 14,000) are twin towns on either side of the sea entrance of Wallis Lake. The area boasts some great beaches, good fishing and every conceivable form of watersports, so it's hardly surprising that the place is packed with holiday-makers in summer.

Orientation & Information

Forster (pronounced 'foster'), on the southern side of the entrance, is much the larger of the twin towns. It lies at the northern tip of a narrow spit of land between Wallis Lake and the ocean. It has about two-thirds of the population and most places of importance to travellers.

The Great Lakes Way leads into town from the south, becoming first MacIntosh St then turning sharp left into Head St, which runs east to a large roundabout that marks the city centre. The helpful information centre (☎ 6554 8779), set back from the lake on Little St, just south of the roundabout, is open daily from 9 am to 5 pm. The post office is near the roundabout on the corner of Little and Wallis Sts. Head St continues east from the roundabout and crosses the long Wallis Lake bridge to become Manning St, the main street through Tuncurry.

Things to See & Do

The area has many activities, including the walking track that leads to a lookout on top of **Cape Hawke**, a few km south-east of town.

Museum The museum is on Capel St in Tuncurry (off South St, which runs off Manning St at the Tuncurry post office), and is open on Sunday afternoon and admission is $2 ($1 children).

Swimming & Surfing As well as the lake, which is great for paddling, there are some excellent sea beaches right near the town. Nine Mile Beach at Tuncurry is consistently the best for surf, but Forster Beach and Pebbly Beach can also be good. There are large swimming pools at Forster Beach and near the harbour entrance in Tuncurry. Another pool is on the lakefront near Paradise Marina on Little St.

Cruises *Amaroo II* has a daily two-hour cruise on Wallis Lake for $16 ($10 children).

There are three boats offering dolphin-watching cruises for $25/30.

Boats & Canoes Most of the marinas along Little St hire boats and other forms of water transport.

Diving There are two main outfits offering dives and courses: Action Divers (☎ 6555 4053) on the main street in Tuncurry and the Forster Dive Centre(☎ 6554 5255) at the Tikki Boatshed on Little St. Popular dives in the area include the SS *Satara*, the largest diveable wreck in Australia (this is a deep dive), and Seal Rocks, where there are grey nurse sharks.

Horseriding Clarendon Forest Retreat (☎ 6554 3162), 20 minutes inland of Forster-Tuncurry at Possum Brush, has guided rides through the Kiwarrak State Forest for $20 an hour. Bookings are essential. Eureka Trails (☎ 6554 1281), near Nabiac, is another possibility.

Organised Tours

Tobwabba Tours (☎ 6555 5411), run by the local Aboriginal land council, has tours that explain how the local people lived before European settlement. You'll need a minimum of three people.

Several outfits offer 4WD tours – the information centre has details.

Special Events

There's a market at the reserve at the bridge end of Head St in Forster on the third Sunday of the month. The annual Oyster Festival is held in early October.

Places to Stay

The place gets packed out in summer, especially the two weeks following Boxing Day.

Caravan Parks There are almost 20 caravan parks in the area. In the middle of Forster and a short walk from the lake and ocean, the council-owned *Forster Beach Caravan Park* (☎ 6554 6269) has sites for $10.50, rising to $16.50 at Christmas and during school holi-

days. On-site vans go for $24 a night ($33 with ensuite), rising to $42 ($56) at the peak. There are several places south of town along the Great Lakes Way with lake frontage. In Tuncurry the *Tuncurry Beach Caravan Park* (☎ 6554 6440) on Beach St has both lake and ocean frontages.

Hostel The YHA-affiliated *Dolphin Lodge* (☎ 6555 8155) at 43 Head St, a couple of blocks from the Forster post office, is in a renovated block of flats. Coming from the town centre it's on the left just before the road makes a right-angle turn to the right. It's very clean and airy and gets good reports. It has a surf beach pretty well at its back door, where you might be able to swim with dolphins. It has dorm beds for $13, singles for $20 and doubles/twins for $30. Boogie boards, surfboards and bikes are free.

Hotel & Motels Although there are 20 motels you'll be lucky to find a bed around Christmas, and the prices reflect this, but in the off-season there are some good deals on motel rooms, with doubles advertised for as little as $35 along the main drag.

The *Lakes & Ocean Hotel* (☎ 6554 6005), on Little St near the information centre, has a top position overlooking the lake and singles/doubles for $28/38 in the off-season. You won't get a room at Christmas unless you book months in advance, but in the off-season singles/doubles with shared bathroom are about $25/30 and that's fair value for the location, although not much cheaper than you'd pay in a motel.

Self-Catering There are a lot of holiday apartments. The cheapest go for around $100 a week in the off-season and about $350 at Christmas. You can pay an awful lot more than this. Letting agents include Hilton Mason (☎ 6554 6333), 17 Wallis St, Forster.

Places to Eat

The bistro at the *Lakes & Ocean Hotel* has pub standards for about $9 and the beer garden overlooks the lake. The plush *Ser-*

vices Club on Strand St has a coffee shop, an inexpensive bistro and a restaurant.

Veta's Fresh Pastas in the Dolphin Arcade off Manning St has eat-in, takeaway and cook-yourself (at home) pastas plus salads and bread. *Il Pozzo*, 24 Wharf St, is a pizzeria with some pasta, veal and seafood dishes.

Forster Indian Tandoori Restaurant on Little St across from the *Amaroo II* cruise jetty is open daily for dinner and most days for lunch. Tandoori main courses cost around $12 and most others are under $10; under $7 for vegetarian dishes. Down at Green Point, off the road to Pacific Palms about five km south of Forster, the *Green Point Gallery & Restaurant* (☎ 6554 5816) also has Indian food. It's open Wednesday to Sunday for lunch and dinner (bookings required for dinner).

Getting There & Away
Bus Great Lakes Coaches (☎ 4983 1560) has daily buses to Newcastle ($23) and Sydney ($38). Some services to Newcastle connect with trains to Sydney. There are also buses from Tea Gardens (on Port Stephens). Eggins Coaches (☎ 6554 8699, 6552 2700 in Taree) runs to Taree ($8.40) four times on weekdays and twice on Saturday.

In summer one of the companies running between Sydney and Brisbane usually stops here, but there isn't always a service in winter.

Car & Motorcycle Forster-Tuncurry is off the Pacific Highway, on the scenic but winding Great Lakes Way which leaves the highway at Bulahdelah and rejoins it about 20 km south of Taree.

THE MANNING VALLEY
The Manning Valley extends from the delta islands of the two mouths of the Manning River (near Old Bar and Harrington), westwards through farmland to Taree and Wingham, then through forests to the Bulga and Comboyne plateaux.

About 150km of the meandering Manning River is navigable – see the Taree section for some cruises. It's possible to canoe 60km down the Manning River from Bretti (a small town near the north side of Woko National Park, 35km north of Gloucester) to Wingham, but seek local advice about conditions. You could start 45km further upstream on the Barnard River at Corroboree Flat, although this stretch of river flows through private property and technically you need permission to land.

History
John Oxley was the first European to visit the valley (1818), although Captain Cook had sailed past in 1770 and named (renamed) mountains in the area. In 1829, Governor Darling set the Manning River as the northernmost limit of the colony, but this was ignored by the cedar cutters. A land grant to William Wynter in 1831 saw permanent European settlement on the Manning.

Taree
It's hard to get too excited about Taree (population 17,500), the largest town and service centre of the Manning Valley – although the **Big Oyster**, by the highway just north of town, surely ranks among the most bizarre of Australia's many 'big' things. It's supposed to be a tribute to the area's large oyster-farming industry.

Taree's long main street is Victoria St (the Pacific Highway); the centre of town is probably the block between Pulteney and Manning Sts, although the shops continue a long way east. The post office is in this block. A block south of Victoria St is the Manning River and the narrow **Queen Elizabeth Park** runs along the bank for the length of the city centre.

The information centre (☎ 6552 1900, 1800 801 522), on the highway north of the town centre, about three km from the post office, is open daily from 9 am to 5 pm. Next to the information centre is the town's **art gallery**, open Thursday to Sunday, noon to 4 pm.

Several boats cruise the river, including the MV *Surprise* (☎ 6552 4767) and the *Taree II* (☎ 6552 4767).

Places to Stay Taree's two caravan parks, *Taree* (☎ 6552 1751) and *Twilight* (☎ 6552 2857), on the highway north and south of town respectively, have sites, on-site vans and cabins.

The *Exchange Hotel* (☎ 6552 1160) on the corner of Victoria and Manning Sts has singles/doubles for $15/25. A block away on the corner of Pulteney and Victoria Sts, *Fotheringhams Hotel* (☎ 6552 1153), also known as Fogg's, is a bit better and a bit more expensive.

Motel fans can take their pick of the 20-odd along the highway north of town.

Manning River Holidays Afloat (☎ 6552 6271) has a range of houseboats for hire. Off-season prices start at $240 for a four-berth boat for the weekend.

Places to Eat *Only Natural*, on the south side of Victoria St between Pulteney and Manning Sts, is a large health-food cafe. It serves breakfast (muesli, free-range eggs) and throughout the day there are snacks and more substantial meals such as pasta and Thai curry for about $7. Their coffee is good. You'll find standard club grub at *Benny's Bistro* in the RSL on Pulteney St, while the *Viennaworld* restaurant beneath the Big Oyster is open 24 hours. The new *Royal Brasserie*, at the Royal Hotel on Victoria St, has been recommended and has main courses from $11 to $18. If you want to dine in a bit more style, head for *Laurent's* at the Caravilla Motor Inn, just north of the town centre on the highway.

Getting There & Away Long-distance buses stop at the Big Oyster complex on the highway. Great Lakes Coaches (☎ 4997 4287, 1800 043 263) and Countrylink both have a daily service to Newcastle ($25), which leaves from the railway station on Olympia St.

If you're driving north to Port Macquarie, consider making an inland detour through Wingham to Wauchope, passing through some interesting villages and great scenery. It would, however, mean missing out on the drive through Crowdy Bay National Park.

Wingham

Wingham (population 4900) is a quiet town serving the upper Manning Valley. It has a long association with the timber industry. The main streets surround **Central Park**, a large grassy square which was once the town's common and still hosts cricket matches. The huge brush-box log on the common is a memorial to Captain Cook, but it could equally be a memorial to the Manning Valley's vanished forests. On Farquar St, running along the south side, is the **museum** (☎ 6553 5823), open daily, 10 am to 4 pm.

Just east of the town centre, down Farquar St, is a picnic spot on a bend in the wide Manning River and **Wingham Brush**, a seven-hectare vestige of rainforest. It's a pretty place, alive with bird calls and the twitter of flying foxes.

Wingham's **market** is held on the second Saturday of the month near Wingham Hotel.

Places to Stay There are no camping areas close to town. The *Australian Hotel* (☎ 6553 4511), facing Central Park on the corner of Farquar and Bent Sts, has accommodation, as does the *Wingham Hotel* (☎ 6553 4007), across the park on the corner of Isabella and Wynter Sts. The Australian has a well-reno-vated lounge area; the Wingham is made of timber, unusual for a large hotel. There's also the *Wingham Motel* (☎ 6553 4295) on Bent St near the Australian, with singles/doubles for $42/50.

Getting There & Away Trains between Sydney and Brisbane run through Wingham. You'll find the station at the western end of Isabella St.

Mountains & Forests

Inland from Wingham there is some wild and rugged bushland, less well known than the forests of the Walcha area. Woko National Park is west of Wingham but is more easily reached from Gloucester – see the Hunter Valley chapter.

There are quite a few small communities in the area with alternative-lifestyle tendencies, especially around Elands and Bulga. There are also plenty of art and craft galleries – the Taree information centre has a brochure.

The Bulga Plateau is worth a visit to check out the spectacular **Ellenborough Falls**, which plunge 160 metres in one dramatic drop. To get here from Wingham take the Comboyne turn-off from the Oxley Highway about 10 km north of town. The falls are about 25 km west of Comboyne. In the same area you can visit **Blue Knob Lookout** and the **Wautui Falls**.

Places to Stay *Lizzard Island Lodge* (π 6550 4188) at Comboyne sounds promising. The owners have converted a collection of old timber mill buildings into a range of accommodation. For backpackers, there are dorm beds for $15 and for the more affluent there's a self-contained cabin overlooking the Thone River for $60 per night.

Near Comboyne is the *Comboyne Hideaway* (π 6550 4230), which has quality accommodation and great views. Dinner and B&B costs $115 in the homestead, or there's a choice of cottages (sleeping up to six) for $125 a day. There are various other farmstays in the area – see the Taree information centre for a complete list.

Beaches

On the coast south of the Manning's southern arm and 16km from Taree is **Old Bar**, a village with a popular surf beach. There's a *caravan park* (π 6553 7274) with sites, on-site vans and cabins. For holiday apartments contact LJ Hooker (π 6553 7650). Just south of Old Bar is **Wallabi Point**, where there's a lagoon for swimming.

Near the south side of the northern arm is **Manning Point**, a hamlet serving the oyster farms along the river. Manning Point is on a large, flat river island which supports intensive dairy farming. There are several *caravan parks* in the area. Across on the north bank of the northern arm is **Harrington**, a small village (turn off the highway at Coopernook). There's swimming in the lagoon and surf beaches nearby. Harrington

is developing into a mini-resort and there are plenty of *motels* and *caravan parks*, plus the Railway Crossing fun park.

Crowdy Head is a small fishing village four km north-east of Harrington. The views from the old lighthouse on the high head are superb, out to the limitless ocean, down to the deserted beaches and back to the apparent wilderness of the coastal plain and mountains. The only place to stay is the pleasant *Crowdy Head Motel* (π 6556 1206), which charges from $50/55 for singles/doubles.

North of Harrington and Crowdy Head, **Crowdy Bay National Park** runs up the coast, backing a long and beautiful beach sweeping north to **Diamond Head**. A rough road leads into the national park from just before Crowdy Head village. You can also enter from Laurieton at the north end of the park. There are basic, pretty *campsites* at Diamond Head and Indian Head, but you need to bring water.

North of the national park and accessible from the Pacific Highway at Kew is **Camden Haven**. This area is composed of Laurieton, North Haven and Dunbogan, villages clustering around the wide sea entrance of Queens Lake, and there are good beaches. North Brother mountain towers over Camden Haven. There are walking trails in the state forests behind Laurieton. *Beachfront Caravan Park* (π 6559 9193) in North Haven is right behind a good surf beach.

North of here the coast road runs past **Lake Cathie** (pronounced 'cat-eye'), both a town with a *caravan park* and holiday apartments and a lake with shallow water suitable for kids, and then enters the sprawling outer suburbs of Port Macquarie.

PORT MACQUARIE

Port Macquarie (population 28,000), usually called just Port, is at the southern end of the state's subtropical coast. Winters are cool but short, while summers can be sticky.

Although tourist development in Port has been gaining momentum for over 20 years, the city still has a relaxed small-town feel to it. With a series of surf beaches, the winding lower reaches of the Hastings River and its tributaries and some excellent bush in the mountains behind the coast, this is a good place to spend some time.

History
Port Macquarie was the third town to be established on the Australian mainland following John Oxley's visit to the area in 1818. Governor Macquarie established a penal settlement here in 1821, designed as punishment for convicts who found life in Sydney Cove too easy.

Orientation & Information
The city centre is at the mouth of the Hastings river, on the south side. Running south from the city centre is a long string of excellent beaches.

Horton St, the main shopping street, runs down to the water and there are views across to North Beach on the other side of the river-mouth. West of the city centre at the base of the Settlement Point peninsula is the big Settlement City shopping centre, the RSL's club and entertainment centre (with an aggressively large Australian flag) and the Port Marina.

The information centre (☎ 6583 1077, 1800 025 935), in the town centre on Clarence St, is open daily.

Bookshops There's a big Angus & Robertson on the corner of Horton and William Sts. For a good trashy paperback to read on the beach, go to Mostly Books, a secondhand place at the north end of Hay St.

Historic Buildings
Few buildings from the early days of the penal settlement still stand. Most survivors are near the city centre: **St Thomas' Church** (1828), on William St near Hay St (admission $1, 30c children); the **Garrison** (1830) on the corner of Hay and Clarence Sts, now housing a collection of cafes; the **courthouse** (1869) across the road, which is being restored; and the nearby building housing the **museum** (1830).

Museums
The **museum**, at 22 Clarence St, is open daily from 9.30 am to 4.30 pm, Sunday from 1 pm. Admission is $3 (50c children). The old pilots' cottage above Town Beach is now a **Maritime Museum**, open daily from 10 am to 4 pm. Admission is $2 ($1 children).

Observatory
The small observatory at the beach end of Lord St is open Wednesday and Sunday. You can look through the telescope from 7.30 to 9.30 pm in winter and from 8.15 to 10 pm in summer. Admission is $2 ($1 children).

Koalas
Koala habitats and new housing developments compete for space in this area, and guess which loses out? Koalas living near urban areas are at risk from traffic and domestic animals and many end up at the **Koala Hospital** (☎ 6584 1522) off Lord St, about one km south of the town centre. The convalescent koalas are in outdoor enclosures and you can visit them daily; tours of the actual hospital are by arrangement only.

The koala hospital is in the grounds of **Roto**, a historic homestead which also houses the NPWS office. Roto is open weekdays from 9 am to 4 pm, although the grounds are always open.

You can meet undamaged koalas and other animals at **Kingfisher Park** (☎ 6581 0783),

Up a gumtree: no longer the safest place for Australia's most popular marsupial, the koala

off the Oxley Highway, and at **Billabong Koala Park** (☎ 6585 1060), further out of town at the Pacific Highway interchange. Both are open daily.

Nature Reserves
The **Kooloonbung Creek Nature Reserve** is close to the town centre on the corner of Gordon and Horton Sts, but its 50 hectares of bush is home to many bird species. There are trails and boardwalks (suitable for wheelchairs). In the reserve is a cemetery dating from the earliest days of European settlement.

Five km south of the centre of Port Macquarie, between Miners Beach and Pacific Drive, **Sea Acres Rainforest Centre** (☎ 6582 3355) is a 70-odd hectare flora and fauna reserve protecting a small pocket of coastal rainforest. There's an ecology centre with displays and a 1.3-km-long elevated boardwalk, suitable for wheelchairs. Entry is $8.50 ($4.50 children). As the centre points out, the world loses an area of rainforest twice the size of Sea Acres every second of every day.

Wineries
The **Cassegrain Winery** (☎ 6583 7777) is off the Pacific Highway just north of the Port Macquarie interchange. It's open daily from 9 am to 5 pm for wine sales and tastings and there's a restaurant here as well. **Charley Brothers Wines** (☎ 6581 1332), on the Oxley Highway just east of the Pacific Highway, is open weekdays from 2.30 to 4.30 pm, weekends and holidays from 10 am to 5 pm.

Across the Hastings River
A vehicle ferry crosses the river at Settlement Point, leading to two interesting roads north. A very rough dirt road (4WD may be required) runs along the coast, past the Limeburners Creek Nature Reserve to Point Plomer (good surf) and Crescent Head, from where you can rejoin the highway at Kempsey. The second road – better and gravelled – takes a more inland route to meet the Crescent Head to Kempsey road.

Activities
Beaches The string of surf beaches running south from the town centre is backed by Pacific Drive and a lot of apartment blocks. A footpath also runs along the beachfront from Town Green on Clarence St to Lighthouse Beach, the southernmost beach in the city area.

Boat Hire A number of places help you get out onto the water, all of them on Settlement Point. At Port Marina, near the Settlement City shopping centre, Hastings River Boat Hire (☎ 6583 8811) has canoes for $5 an hour and a range of small powered craft for $16 an hour. Gypsy Boat Hire (☎ 6583 2353), 52 Settlement Point Rd, will rent you a small boat for six hours for $40 including fuel and it has a range of other craft.

Sailboarding The river is a good spot for sailboarding. Jordans Boating Centre (☎ 6583 1005), on Settlement Point Rd, rents sailboards as well as yachts and cats.

Diving The Port Macquarie Diving Centre (☎ 6583 8483) is at the Port Marina near Settlement City.

Canoeing The upper reaches of the Hastings River offer good canoeing and Port Macquarie Canoe Safaris (☎ 6581 1107) rents equipment and can arrange guided trips. There's another canoe-hire place upstream near Wauchope.

Camel Rides Port Macquarie Camel Safaris (☎ 6583 7650) has rides along Lighthouse Beach for $20.

Organised Tours
Local guide John Oakley (☎ 6584 0269) runs half-day tours of the town on Monday, Tuesday, Wednesday and Friday for $19. Port Explorer (☎ 6581 2181) has a three-hour tour of town on Tuesday for $12.50.

There are several boats offering cruises on the Hastings River and the surrounding system of creeks and wetlands upstream from Port Macquarie. The *Fanta Sea II* has

NORTH COAST

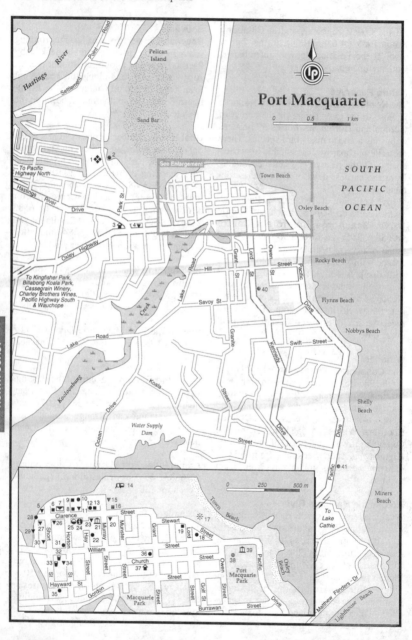

Port Macquarie

0   0.5   1 km

SOUTH

PACIFIC

OCEAN

Pelican Island

Hastings River

Settlement Road

Port Road

Sand Bar

To Pacific Highway North

Hastings River Drive

Park St

See Enlargement

Town Beach

Oxley Beach

Oxley Highway

Rocky Beach

To Kingfisher Park, Billabong Koala Park, Cassegrain Winery, Charley Brothers Wines, Pacific Highway South & Wauchope

Grant St

Lord St

Owen Street

Pacific Drive

Flynns Beach

Lake Road

Hill St

Savoy St

Granite Street

Nobbys Beach

Swift Street

Koolawnhug

Koala Drive

Kennsey Drive

Shelly Beach

Ocean Drive

Water Supply Dam

Street

Pacific Drive

Miners Beach

To Lake Cathie

14

0   250   500 m

Town Beach

5
9   10
28   6   7   8   12 13   15   Street   16
26   Clarence   Stewart   17
27   25   24   23   20   19   Lord   Street   18
29   Short   21   22   Munster   Grant   Street
30   Horton   Hay   William   Street   Street   Street   Owen   39
31   Street   36   Church   Street   38
33   32   34   Street   37   Street   Port Macquarie Park   Oxley Beach
35   Hayward   St   St   Gordon   Street   Street   Pacific Drive
Macquarie Park   Burrawan Street   Matthew Flinders Dr   Lighthouse Beach

40

41

PLACES TO STAY		11	Pancake Place	18	Observatory
3	Lindel Port Macquarie	15	Toro's Cantina	21	Museum
	Backpackers	20	Café Pacific	22	Supermarket
6	Motel Mid Pacific	23	Garrison & Cafes	24	Information Centre
8	Port Macquarie Hotel	26	Macquarie Seafoods	25	Long-Distance Bus
9	Royal Hotel	27	Cray's		Stop
13	El Paso Motel	29	Fishermen's Co-op	28	Cruise Departures
14	Sundowner Breakwall	30	Eclipse	31	Jetset Travel
	Caravan	34	Yuen Hing	32	TC's Nightclub
	Park			33	Down Under Nightclub
16	River Motel	**OTHER**		35	Port Pushbikes
19	Historic Well Motel	1	Settlement City	36	Communications Tower
37	Beachside		Shopping Centre &	38	Bowling Club
	Backpackers (YHA)		RSL	39	Maritime Museum
		2	Port Marina	40	Koala Hospital & Roto
PLACES TO EAT		7	Post Office		Homestead
4	Chiang Mai Thai	10	Mostly Books	41	Sea Acres Rainforest
	Restaurant	12	Old Courthouse		Centre
5	Chula's	17	Lookout		

two-hour cruises ($15) at 10 am and 2 pm, while the *Port Venture* has similar cruises ($15) at 10 am daily, except Wednesday, as well as longer trips. Everglades Waterbus Tours uses shallow-draught boats to explore an area known as the Everglades. It has 2½-hour cruises ($17.50) daily at 10 am and 2 pm.

All these boats leave from the riverside at the eastern end of Clarence St. Just roll up and pay as you board.

Places to Stay – bottom end

Caravan Parks The most central caravan park is the expensive *Sundowner Breakwall* (☎ 6583 2755) at 1 Munster St, near the river-mouth and Town Beach, with sites from $15 and on-site vans from $35. There are cheaper places near Flynns Beach and inland along the river.

Hostels Budget travellers are well catered for with a choice of three places. They all meet the long-distance buses.

Beachside Backpackers (☎ 6583 5512) is a YHA-associate hostel at 40 Church St, near the corner of Grant St. The telecommunications tower across the street is a landmark. This place is clean, friendly and popular, and dorm beds are $13. It's about a five-minute walk from both the town centre and the

beach. There's free use of bikes and surfboards.

Lindel Port Macquarie Backpackers (☎ 6583 1791) occupies a beautiful old house beside the Oxley Highway on the way into town, readily identifiable by the large globe standing outside. It's clean and well run, with dorm beds for $15 and doubles/ twins for $36. There's a pool and free use of bikes, boogie boards and fishing gear. The owner likes to organise regular canoeing and fishing trips if anyone shows an interest.

A relative newcomer on the scene is *Limeburners Lodge* (☎ 6583 8000), situated in the bush on the northern side of the river and reached by the Settlement Point ferry. There are lots of animals, wild and domestic, and it's a pleasant spot to rest for a few days. The owners drive into town regularly, so there are lots of opportunities to stock up on supplies. It was originally set up for school groups and has dorm beds for $10.

Places to Stay – middle

Hotels This town has grown from small beginnings, and it's an indication of the sort of people who have moved here that there are only two pubs – side by side at the north end of Horton St. The reception desk at the *Port Macquarie* (☎ 6583 1011) handles accommodation for both hotels, and has

NORTH COAST

motel-style units from $45/55 and pub rooms for $20/30 or $25/35 with bathroom. At the *Royal* there are motel-style units overlooking the water for just $32/40 and pub rooms with bathroom for $25/30. Singles aren't available at peak times and prices rise.

The pub rooms at the Port Macquarie are a bit better than those at the Royal, but at either place check the bed and listen for noise such as jukebox music wafting up from the bar, or industrial-strength air-con ducts outside the window.

Motels There might not be many pubs in town but there are plenty of motels – 31 at the last count. The cheapest, not surprisingly, are the ones furthest from the beaches. In town, the *River Motel*, 5 Clarence St near the corner of School St, has doubles for $50 and several nearby holiday apartments have similar deals. The cheaper places are along Hastings River Drive.

Places to Stay – top end

The *Motel Mid Pacific* (☎ 6583 2166) is a high-rise on the corner of Clarence and Short Sts with great views over the Hastings River. Doubles are $75, plus $10 for each extra person. There's a $20 surcharge on long weekends and around Christmas.

Further east on Clarence St, next to the old courthouse, the *El Paso Motel* (☎ 6583 1944) is an old-style motel now basking in a fashionable paint-job and renovations. (It won't be long before motels like this get National Trust listings for their unique architecture.) The experience will set you back $65/75 a single/double, plus $10 for each extra person, with a $20 surcharge at Christmas and Easter.

Midway between the centre and Settlement City, the *Country Comfort Motel* (☎ 6583 2955) is on the waterfront and charges $97 for doubles. *Sails Resort* (☎ 6583 3999, 1800 025 271 toll-free bookings) is on the waterfront near Settlement City. Rooms cost from $150; $180 with a view of the water.

Self-Catering There are a great many apartments and holiday flats. They are expensive at peak times, but in the off-season you might find a two-bedroom apartment for about $200 a week. Letting agents include Town & Country Real Estate (☎ 6584 1007) on the corner of Short and Clarence Sts.

On Clarence St, on the corner of Murray St, *Port Pacific Resort* (☎ 6583 8099) is a large block of timeshare apartments, some of which are available to let. In the low season you'll pay about $95 for two people in a single-bedroom apartment and $105 in a two-bedroom apartment, plus $12 for each extra person. Prices rise by about 15% over Christmas, Easter and other school holidays.

Places to Eat

There are dozens of restaurants and cafes around the city centre, with something to suit every budget.

The setting is perfect for seafood and you won't find it any fresher than at the Fishermen's Co-op, by the river on Wharf St. If you want your seafood cooked, *Macquarie Seafoods*, on the corner of Clarence and Short Sts, does great fish & chips for $4.20. At the top end of the market is *Cray's*, overlooking the river at the western end of Clarence St, with main courses from about $18. Fish also features prominently on the menu at the *Riverview Terrace* at the Royal Hotel. It's open for lunch and dinner Tuesday to Sunday. Main courses are in the $16 region.

Chula's is a good Thai restaurant on the corner of Short and Clarence Sts, open daily (except Monday) for lunch and Tuesday to Saturday for dinner. It's not particularly cheap, with soups and starters for around $8 and mains for $15 – but you get your money's worth. A cheaper Thai option is the *Chiang Mai* takeaway, on the way out of town at 153 Gordon St. Most dishes are priced under $9. The *Sun Hing* on William St does Chinese banquets priced from $7 to $10 per person, while the *Yuen Hing* on Horton St does lunches for as little as $3.50.

Back in the city centre, *Toro's Cantina* on Murray St is a Mexican place with main courses from $9.50. Opposite the information centre, the *Pancake Place* offers all-you-can-eat meals priced from $11.90.

For breakfast, try the *Café Pacific* on Clarence St, where cooked breakfast costs $7.50, or *Eclipse*, a small place on Short St near the corner of William St.

Margo's Cafe, in the historic Garrison building on the corner of Hay and Clarence Sts, has tables outside and is a pleasant place for coffee and a snack.

Entertainment
There are three nightclubs in town: *Lachlans*, between the Port Macquarie and Royal hotels, *TC's* on William St and *Down Under* around the corner on Short St. The *RSL Club* at Settlement City has live bands on Friday and Saturday nights.

Getting There & Away
Air Eastern Australia flies to Sydney at least three times a day for $185. Impulse flies to Sydney for the same fare, as well as to Brisbane ($234) via Coffs Harbour, Lismore and Coolangatta. The Impulse agent is Jetset Travel (☎ 6584 1411) on the corner of Horton and William Sts.

Bus Greyhound, Pioneer Motor Service and McCafferty's all stop in town and they all use the bus stop outside the information centre on Clarence St. The nearby Pioneer Motor Service office (☎ 6583 1488) also sells tickets for McCafferty's. Sample fares include Newcastle ($31), Sydney ($40), Byron Bay ($44) and Brisbane ($46). Kean's (☎ 1800 625 587) runs to Coffs Harbour ($20), Bellingen ($25), Dorrigo ($31), Armidale ($39.60) and Tamworth ($56.90). Port Macquarie Bus Service (☎ 6583 2161) runs to Wauchope several times a day for $6.40.

Train The nearest station is at Wauchope, 19 km inland. The fare from Sydney is $58. An extra $6.40 will get you into Port Macquarie on the Countrylink bus that meets the train arriving at 5.59 pm.

Car & Motorcycle The next major town on the Pacific Highway is Kempsey, about 50 km north. The Oxley Highway runs west from Port Macquarie through Wauchope and eventually reaches the New England tableland near Walcha. It's a spectacular drive.

The Settlement Point ferry operates 24 hours to the north side of the Hastings River and costs $1 per car. To get to the ferry, keep going past the RSL Club and follow the signs to Settlement Point.

Getting Around
Bike Rental Port Pushbikes on Hayward St rents ungeared bikes for $8 a half-day, $15 for a day and just $25 for a week. Graham Seers Cyclery at Port Marina near Settlement City also rents bikes.

Car Rental There are no super-cheap outfits, only the major companies. Budget (☎ 6583 5144) is on the corner of William and Short Sts.

WAUCHOPE
Wauchope (pronounced 'war hope') is a timber town of long standing. The town's main attraction is the big **Timbertown** historic park, with the emphasis on the history of the timber industry. It's one of the better theme parks and is well worth visiting. Admission is $16 for adults, $12 for YHA members and students, $8 for children and free for children below school-age. Just before Wauchope on the road from Port Macquarie is the turn-off to Lilybank Canoe Hire (☎ 6585 1600). The owner hires canoes by the hour, day or week and can advise on camping spots along the river.

Places to Stay
The YHA-associate *Rainbow Ridge Hostel* (☎ 6585 6134), 11 km west of town on the Oxley Highway, was once the only hostel between Sydney and Queensland. Times have changed! It's still an old-style hostel – quiet, friendly and definitely not the place for party animals. There are bushwalks nearby, including a six-hour climb to the top of Bago Bluff, but many people come just for the

good night's sleep they don't get in livelier places. Dorm beds are $10 or you can camp for $5 per person.

Coming from Wauchope, the hostel's driveway is on the right just before the Comboyne turn-off. Keep a look-out after you cross the Mahers Creek bridge. With prior arrangement you can probably get a lift from Wauchope, or ask around town for information on schoolbuses running out this way.

In Wauchope the *Hastings Hotel* (☎ 6585 2003), on the main street near the railway line, has accommodation and there are a couple of motels, the *Wauchope* (☎ 6585 1487) on the main street in town and the *Broad Axe* (☎ 6585 1355) on the highway near Timbertown. There's also a *caravan park* here.

Off the Oxley Highway about 60 km west of Wauchope, *Mt Seaview Resort* (☎ 6587 7144) is a large complex on the Hastings River and not far south of Werrikimbe National Park. There's horseriding and 4WD tours. It might not be everyone's cup of tea but with inexpensive camping and bunkhouse accommodation (as well as a range of rooms and suites) it might make a good base for exploring the area.

Getting There & Away
Bus Port Macquarie Bus Service (☎ 6583 2161) runs to/from Port Macquarie about four times each day for $6.40.

Train Wauchope is on the main line between Sydney ($58) and Murwillumbah or Brisbane.

Mid-North Coast

MACLEAY VALLEY
Rising in the New England tableland, the Macleay River flows east through the fertile Macleay Valley, entering the sea near South West Rocks – although until a flood in 1893 its entrance was further north near Grassy Head. The main town in the valley is Kempsey, on the Pacific Highway and about

20km inland from the nearest ocean beach at Crescent Head. There are long, uncrowded beaches north and south of Crescent Head.

Before Europeans arrived, the valley was owned by the Dangaddi people, but in 1827 the penal settlement in Port Macquarie established a camp in the valley to cut cedar and rosewood. Land grants were made in 1835 and the town of Kempsey (named because of the landscape's supposed resemblance to the Kempsey Valley in Worcestershire, England) was established by 1840. Beef cattle and dairying were early agricultural ventures and they remain the mainstay of the area, with tourism forming the third leg of a stable and prosperous economic tripod.

Kempsey
Kempsey (population 10,000) is a large rural town serving the farms of the Macleay Valley. As the main town between Port Macquarie and Coffs Harbour, it's also a handy place to stock up on supplies for a stay at the beaches east of here and the mountainous national parks to the west.

Kempsey is now the home of the Akubra hat, although this wasn't the firm's birthplace. Unfortunately, the factory isn't open to the public, but a video at the information centre shows how the hats are fashioned from rabbit-fur felt and several shops in town sell them. Another Australian icon to hail from the Macleay Valley is country singer Slim Dusty. His songs such as 'Pub with No Beer' and 'Duncan' are well known even by people who claim no knowledge of country music.

The information centre (☎ 6563 1555), off the highway at the southern entrance to town, is open daily from 9 am to 5 pm. Also here is the **museum**, open daily from 10 am to 4 pm. Admission is $2 ($1 children).

Places to Stay There are four *caravan parks*, all with sites, on-site vans and cabins. The *Pearl Perch Hotel* (☎ 6562 4586), in the town centre near the bridge, where the Armidale road splits from the Pacific Highway, sometimes advertises cheap rooms. There is other pub accommodation and 10 motels.

Getting There & Away Kempsey is on the north-coast railway line and the major bus companies stop here on the Sydney to Brisbane run. See the following Crescent Head and South West Rocks sections for information on local services.

By car, there's an interesting and largely unsealed route running west to Wollomombi (on the Dorrigo to Armidale road); head north-west to Bellbrook.

Crescent Head

This small village (population 1100), 20 km south-east of Kempsey, has both a quiet front beach and a surf-washed back beach. There's quite a lot of new holiday development, but the village is far enough off the highway to remain relaxed. South of the town is the **Limeburners Creek Nature Reserve** (☎ 6583 5866), with walking trails and campsites. North of town is Hat Head National Park (see below).

Places to Stay *Crescent Head Tourist Park* (☎ 6566 0261) is right on the beach and has sites from $12 and cabins from $40, rising to $80 in holidays.

There are plenty of holiday apartments in town and they might be cheaper than a cabin at the caravan park. In the off-season they should be available by the night, but in summer you might have to rent by the week. The cheapest one-bedroom apartments go for $30 a night, rising to $45 in school holidays. See one of the two estate agents on the main street (☎ 6566 0500 or 6566 0306).

Bush & Beach Retreat (☎ 6566 0235) is about four km north of town on Loftus Rd (turn off the main road at the Mediterranean Motel) with bushland behind and the beach not far away. It's a modern building in 'colonial' style with B&B packages starting at $50 a double. *Killuke Lodge* (☎ 6566 0077) is three km south of Crescent Head on the Point Plomer road and has accommodation in good cottages sleeping up to six

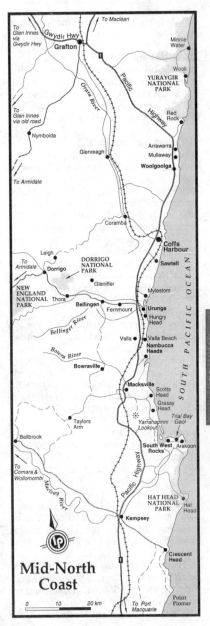

Mid-North Coast

people from $275 a week (much more in holidays).

Getting There & Away If you're driving, the turn-off to Crescent Head is near the information centre in Kemspey. King's (☎ 6562 1228) has three buses a day from Kempsey ($5.40) weekdays, two on Saturday. They leave from Belgrave St in Kempsey.

Hat Head National Park

This coastal park (6500 hectares) runs north from around Hat Head to Smoky Cape (just south of Arakoon), protecting scrubland, swamps and some excellent beaches backed by significant dune systems. Bird-life is prolific on the wetlands. Rising up from the generally flat landscape is Hungry Hill, near Hat Head and sloping Hat Head itself, where there's a walking track.

Surrounded by a national park, the village of **Hat Head** is much smaller and quieter than Crescent Head. *Hat Head Tourist Park* (☎ 6565 7501) is close to a beautiful sheltered bay. Sites cost from $12.

You can camp at Hungry Hill, five km south of Hat Head, and at Smoky Beach, but take water to the latter.

The park is accessible from the hamlet of Kinchela, on the road between Kempsey and South West Rocks. It's possible to get a lift on a schoolbus from Kempsey to Hat Head. Phone the caravan park for details.

South West Rocks

This small resort town (population 3500) lies on the coast near the mouth of the Macleay River and is popular with fishing and watersports enthusiasts. The information centre (☎ 6566 7099) shares the old Boatman's Cottage at Horseshoe Bay with a small **maritime museum**. Both are open daily from 10 am to 4 pm. The information centre has details of a **historic walk** around town.

There's good diving at **Fish Rock Cave**, south of Smoky Cape. South West Rocks Dive Centre (☎ 6566 6474) and the Fish Rock Dive Centre (☎ 6566 6614) both organise dives in the area. The Macleay enters the

sea a few km from South West Rocks at New Entrance. The boatshed here is the departure point for river trips on the *Macleay Discoverer* (☎ 6566 6863).

Places to Stay The *Horseshoe Bay Caravan Park* (☎ 6566 6370) is a small place running along the slope behind pretty little Horseshoe Bay, near the town centre. Sites cost from $14 and on-site vans from $28. Prices almost double in summer and vacancies are rare at Christmas and other major holidays.

The *Bay Motel* (☎ 6566 6909), opposite the beach on Prince of Wales Ave, has doubles for $50, rising to $85 at peak times. If you want to stay a while, Rocks Real Estate (☎ 6566 6999) has a choice of rental houses and apartments.

Getting There & Away OJ's Bus Service (☎ 6563 1776) has at least three buses a day from Kempsey (Belgrave St) on weekdays. The fare is $6.80.

Trial Bay & Arakoon SRA

Three km east of South West Rocks is Trial Bay, named after the brig *The Trial* which was stolen from Sydney by convicts in 1816 and wrecked here. The setting is dominated by **Trial Bay Gaol**, which overlooks the bay from the headland. This imposing edifice was a prison in the late 19th century and housed German internees during WWI. The jail is now a museum with wonderful views, open daily ($3.50; $1 children). **Smoky Cape Lighthouse**, a few km down the coast from the jail, can be inspected on Thursday (and Tuesday in school holidays) from 10 to 11.45 am and 1 to 2.45 pm.

The beaches on the ocean side of the peninsula are unsafe, but those on the bay side are safe and good. The sea has a habit of scouring sand from some bay beaches and dumping it on others, so if your beach doesn't have much sand, try the next one along.

On the shores of the bay behind the old jail is the *Arakoon SRA Camping Area* (☎ 6566 6168), with sites from $10. You'll pay more for waterfront sites and prices double during school holidays and in summer. During the season you can hire cats and boats on the beach here.

NAMBUCCA HEADS

This quiet resort town (population 6000) has a fine setting overlooking the mouth of the Nambucca (pronounced 'nambucka') River.

The Nambucca Valley was owned by the Gumbaynggir people when the European timber-cutters arrived in the 1840s and the name means 'many bends' in their language. There are still strong Aboriginal communities in Nambucca Heads and up the valley in Bowraville.

Orientation & Information

Nambucca can be a little difficult to get a handle on. The town is a km or so off the highway and the road in, Riverside Drive, runs alongside the wide estuary of the Nambucca River, then climbs a steep hill to Bowra St, the main shopping street. A right

turn onto Ridge St at the top of the hill leads through the old part of town to the beaches.

The information centre (☎ 6568 6954), on the Pacific Highway, just south of the Riverside Drive turn-off, is open Monday to Saturday from 9 am to 5 pm (shorter hours on Sunday).

Things to See & Do

The town's **Headland Museum** is on Liston St, opposite the turn-off to Main Beach. As well as displays on local history, the museum has 'many other interesting exhibits difficult to place into categories'! The $1 admission charge seems a small price to pay.

Among the places offering **boat hire** are Nambucca Boat Shed (☎ 6568 8138) on the waterfront at Gordon Park.

Main Beach, the patrolled surf beach, is about 1.5km east of the centre. Follow Ridge St and fork left onto Liston St when it splits. A right fork at the end of Ridge St leads along Parkes St to North Head, with stunning

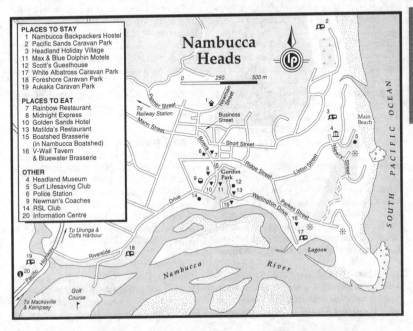

NORTH COAST

PLACES TO STAY
1 Nambucca Backpackers Hostel
2 Pacific Sands Caravan Park
3 Headland Holiday Village
11 Max & Blue Dolphin Motels
12 Scott's Guesthouse
17 White Albatross Caravan Park
18 Foreshore Caravan Park
19 Aukaka Caravan Park

PLACES TO EAT
7 Rainbow Restaurant
8 Midnight Express
10 Golden Sands Hotel
13 Matilda's Restaurant
15 Boatshed Brasserie
   (in Nambucca Boatshed)
16 V-Wall Tavern
   & Bluewater Brasserie

OTHER
4 Headland Museum
5 Surf Lifesaving Club
6 Police Station
9 Newman's Coaches
14 RSL Club
20 Information Centre

views from **Pilot Lookout**. To get to the river-mouth (where there is more good surf for experienced surfers), turn off Bowra St at the Mobil station onto Wellington Drive, which winds down past Gordon Park. This is a very scenic spot.

Places to Stay

Caravan Parks There are several caravan parks. As usual, prices rise in holidays and you might have to stay by the week at peak times. *Foreshore Caravan Park* (☎ 6568 6014) is on Riverside Drive not far from the highway and overlooking the estuary, with a beach nearby. It has sites from $11, on-site vans from $22 and cabins from $28.

The *White Albatross* (☎ 6568 6468) is near the river-mouth at the end of Wellington Drive. There's a lagoon for swimming as well as the surf beach. Sites cost from $12 (more for waterfront sites and during school holidays), on-site vans start at $22 and ensuite cabins start at $38. There's a campers' kitchen. Around near the main surf beach are *Headland Holiday Village* (☎ 6568 6547) and *Pacific Sands* (☎ 6568 6120).

There are other caravan parks further out. Near the small town of Valla Beach, off the highway 8km north of Nambucca Heads, the *Valla Beach Resort* (☎ 6569 5106) is on a lagoon not far from the surf. It has its own bar and restaurant. Outside school holidays, sites cost $12, cabins are $35 and units go for $50. They prefer families at Christmas, when they're usually booked out anyway.

Hostel *Nambucca Backpackers Hostel* (☎ 6568 6360) is a quiet hostel tucked away behind the town at Newman St. It's a one-km walk through bush to the beach. Dorm beds are $15 and doubles are $32, with discounts for longer stays. The managers meet the buses and can arrange outings in the area. They lend snorkel gear and boogie boards.

B&B *Scott's Guesthouse* (☎ 6568 6386), 4 Wellington Drive, is a stylish old weatherboard guesthouse with fabulous views of the river. It charges $40/60 for singles/doubles

with breakfast, rising to $60/80 at peak times.

Motels Sharing the view from the other side of Gordon Park are a couple of cheap (outside holiday times) motels, *Max Motel* (☎ 6568 6138) and the *Blue Dolphin Motel* (☎ 6568 700) next door. Max Motel is an old-style place with few luxury touches, but it's clean and the view is worth a lot more than the $35 it charges for a double. The Blue Dolphin is newer and costs a few dollars more. Both places are on Fraser St, the southern continuation of Bowra St.

Places to Eat

The *RSL Club* has a prime site by the river at the foot of Bowra St and turns out some of the cheapest meals in town. The *Golden Sands* has pub meals and *Midnight Express* behind the pub claims a choice of 36 burgers. The *Rainbow Restaurant* on Bowra St has some interesting Filipino dishes alongside Chinese standards.

There are some good places down by the river along Wellington Drive. The *Boatshed Brasserie* (☎ 6568 9292) turns out a three-course meal for $23.50 and has seating right by the river. Further on, the *V-Wall Tavern* is worth a visit just for the great views of the river-mouth. You can choose between pub meals at the snack bar and a multicultural menu at the *Bluewater Brasserie* (☎ 6568 6394).

Getting There & Away

Bus Most long-distance buses stop on the highway at the bus shelters just south of the Aukaka Caravan Park. Pioneer Motor Service is the only company that comes into town – occasionally. Harvey World Travel (☎ 6568 6455), on Bowra St opposite the police station, handles bookings. Fares to Sydney start at $42 and to Byron Bay it's $38.

Newman's (☎ 6568 1296) has four buses a day to Coffs Harbour ($5), Jessup's (☎ 6653 4552) has a daily bus service on the same route at 7.55 am and Joyce's (☎ 6655 6330) runs from Nambucca to Bellingen.

These local services leave from outside the police station on Bowra St and run only on weekdays.

Train The railway station is about 3km out of town: follow Bowra St then Mann St. The fare to Sydney is $65. The hostel picks up guests (for a fee); otherwise there's no transport between the station and town.

AROUND NAMBUCCA HEADS
The main roads running up the Nambucca Valley turn off from the old town of **Macksville**, on the highway about 12km south of Nambucca Heads. Taylors Arm, about 25km west of Macksville, is the home of the **Pub with No Beer**, immortalised in a song by Slim Dusty, one of the first Australian songs to sell well overseas – it stayed at the top of the Irish charts for more than two months! There's plenty of beer there now and often acoustic music at weekends. Near **Taylors Arm**, Nambucca Trails (☎ 6564 2165) at Bakers Creek Station offers horseriding through the mountains and you can also hire canoes there.

South of Macksville, off the road to the seaside village of **Scotts Head** (good surf), an unsealed road leads up through the Way Way State Forest to **Yarrahapinni Lookout**, which has great views down to the coast and back into the hinterland.

Bowraville
This small town is very different from its booming coastal neighbours. It's a close-knit community of old families, the descendants of the cedar-getters who arrived in 1842, and the Aborigines who are somewhat longer-established residents.

Along the main street you'll find several interesting craft shops and the big **Bowraville Folk Museum** (☎ 6562 7251). The museum is open during school holidays, on Sunday, Tuesday and on Wednesday morning or by request. Admission is $1 (50c children). Even if you aren't interested in the museum, have a look at the wonderful Max Hill Memorial Gates at the entrance. Just along from the museum is a building which claims to be a boarding house. It's just a facade, used in the film *The Umbrella Woman* which was shot here, and is now part of the museum.

Special Events On Saturday morning the popular Bowraville Country Market is held in a building on the main street. The market has its own tea-rooms, a great place to meet locals.

The annual Back to Bowra Festival is held over the October long weekend. Among the many events is billy-cart racing.

Places to Stay The *Bowra Hotel* (☎ 6564 7041) on High St is a nice old pub with accommodation for $15 per person. The rooms open up onto a wide verandah with views over town to the surrounding hills.

Getting There & Away The only public transport is schoolbuses. By car you can get here from Macksville and interesting backroads lead north to Bellingen and Dorrigo and south to Taylors Arm, where you can join a network of largely unsealed roads which eventually lead up to the New England tableland at Wollomombi, east of Armidale.

Urunga
The small coastal town of Urunga (population 2600), 20km north of Nambucca Heads, lies at the mouth of the Bellinger and Kalang rivers, which meet just a few hundred metres from the sea. The estuary is a popular fishing spot and there is a surf beach close by at **Hungry Head**.

There are several *caravan parks* in the area, and the *Ocean View Hotel* (☎ 6655 6221) in Urunga is a fine old pub overlooking the estuary with pub rooms for $25/35 with breakfast. The double rooms are fairly large and some have views; the smaller singles and twins are at the back. On the highway, the Honey Place (☎ 6655 6160), a nursery and craft shop with live bee displays, has tourist information.

See the Bellingen, Nambucca Heads and Coffs Harbour sections for transport information.

NORTH COAST

Mylestom

About 5km north of Urunga and just south of the big Raleigh Bridge over the Bellinger River is the turn-off for the **Raleigh Winery** (☎ 6655 4388), open for tastings and sales daily, 10 am to 5 pm. North of this bridge you come to the turn-off for Mylestom, also called **North Beach**, about five km east of the highway.

This quiet hamlet is in a great location on the north bank of the Bellinger River estuary and also has good ocean beaches.

Places to Stay & Eat *North Beach Caravan Park* (☎ 6655 4250) is close to the beach and has sites from $8 ($12 school holidays) and on-site vans from $20.

Caipera Riverside Lodge (☎ 6655 4245) is a backpacker hostel on the main street across from the river. It's the third house on the left as you enter town. Beds in two-bed 'dorms' are $13. They can help organise activities such as whitewater rafting and horseriding and there are bikes to explore the area. They can usually give you a lift from Coffs Harbour if you give a day's notice.

Beaches, also on River St, is a restaurant with snacks (minimum order $5) and main courses from around $15. Seafood features prominently on the menu here. Beaches is open for lunch Thursday to Sunday and for dinner Thursday to Saturday.

See the Bellingen, Nambucca Heads and Coffs Harbour sections for transport information.

BELLINGEN

This attractive small town (population 2600) sits on the banks of the Bellinger River, inland from the Pacific Highway just north of Urunga. It's a lively place and a centre for the sizeable artistic/alternative population living in the surrounding valleys.

History

The valley was part of the extensive territory of the Gumbaynggir people until European timber-cutters arrived in the 1840s. The first settlement here was at Fernmount, about five km east of Bellingen, but later the adminis-

trative centre of the region was moved to Bellingen. Rivercraft were able to come up here until the 1940s when dredging was discontinued. Until tourism boomed at Coffs Harbour in the 1960s, Bellingen was the most important town in this area.

Orientation & Information

The main road from the Pacific Highway to Dorrigo and beyond becomes Hyde St through town. Most things of importance are to be found here, including tourist information at Bellingen Travel (☎ 6655 2055), opposite the post office. Next to the post office, Bridge St leads across the river to North Bellingen and Gleniffer.

Things to See

The small **museum**, behind the old wooden library on Hyde St, is open daily from 2 to 4 pm and Wednesday and Friday from 10 am to noon. At other times you can phone (☎ 6655 1262) to see if there's someone available to open it for you. Admission is 50c. Talking to the volunteers who staff the museum might be as informative as looking at the exhibits. The huge old **Commercial Emporium** on Hyde St is worth a look.

A huge colony of **flying foxes** lives in a small patch of remnant rainforest on Bellingen Island, near the caravan park, during the breeding season from December to March. There are also **platypus** living in the river nearby.

There are plenty of craft shops in town and a short way out on the road east to the highway is the **Old Butter Factory** which houses several craft workshops and galleries. The old Masonic Lodge on the western edge of town has been converted into the **Lodge 241** gallery and cafe and has visiting exhibitions.

Organised Tours

Gambaarri Tours (☎ 6655 4195) can explain how the Gumbaynggir people lived in the valley and has tours to the Gleniffer area.

Special Events

The community market, held in the park on

the third Saturday of the month, is a major event, with more than 250 stalls. People from all over the valley show up and there's live music. You'll find a multicultural mix of music and performances at the annual Global Carnival in early October and a strong line-up of jazz names at the Jazz Festival in late August.

Places to Stay

Caravan Park *Bellingen Caravan Park* (☎ 6655 1338) is across the river on Dowle St (the first street on the right), right next to the island – and the bats.

Hostel *Bellingen Backpackers* (☎ 6655 1116) (also called Belfry Lodge) is a great place to hang for a few days. It occupies a beautifully renovated weatherboard house overlooking the river on Short St, behind the Federal Hotel. Dorm beds are $15, doubles $32. The owners will pick you up from Urunga by arrangement. There's free use of bikes – and the outdoor hot tub.

B&Bs *Rivendell* (☎ 6655 0060) is close to the centre of town at 10 Hyde St and charges $75 for doubles. *Jelga* (☎ 6655 2202), across the river at 1 Wheatley St, has a self-contained stone cottage overlooking the river for $80, plus $15 for each additional person. *Koompartoo Retreat* (☎ 6655 2326), on the corner of Rawson and Dudley Sts on the southern edge of Bellingen, has stylish self-contained timber cabins. Bellingen Travel has information on other places in and around town and handles bookings.

Hotel & Motel There is pub accommodation at the *Federal Hotel* (☎ 6655 1003) for about $20/30. The *Bellingen Valley Motor Inn* (☎ 6655 1599) is just west of town with singles/doubles for $68/75.

Places to Eat

Bellingen has a huge choice of restaurants for a town of its size. The *Carriageway Cafe*, in the Hammond & Wheatley building on Hyde St, is the place to head for morning coffee and a read of the newspapers. It has meals as well as good coffee and cakes.

There are several places on Church St, including the kebabs at *Kebabs & Things*, vegetarian takeaways at the *Good Food Shop* and various light meals at the *Cool Creek Cafe*. The *Bowling Club* on Bowra St has Asian food. The *Flying Fox Cafe*, on Wheatley St in North Bellingen near the roundabout, is a relaxed place and the food is innovative and excellent. Prices are reasonable, with main courses around $15, plus cheaper vegetarian options.

Getting There & Away

Bus The bus stop is on the corner of Church and Hyde Sts, diagonally opposite the courthouse. Kean's (☎ 1800 625 587) stops at Bellingen on its Port Macquarie-Tamworth run, but is not allowed to offer a service on short sectors such as Coffs Harbour to Bellingen. That route is owned by Jessup's (☎ 6653 4552), which operates one service a day – school days only. Buses leave Bellingen at 7.55 am and Coffs Harbour at 3.15 pm. Joyce's (☎ 6655 6330) has about four runs a day (fewer in school holidays), weekdays only, between Bellingen and Nambucca Heads ($6.80). There's no public transport between Bellingen and Dorrigo.

Train The nearest station is at Urunga.

Car & Motorcycle Bellingen is about 12km west of the Pacific Highway; turn off just south of the Raleigh Bridge. From Bellingen the road climbs steeply up to Dorrigo – a spectacular drive. From Dorrigo you can continue west to the Armidale to Grafton road. A network of unsealed roads leads south to Bowraville and some tiny mountain settlements.

AROUND BELLINGEN

If you have transport, there are some beautiful spots waiting to be discovered in the surrounding valleys. The most accessible of them is **Gleniffer**, 10km to the north and clearly signposted from North Bellingen. There's a good swimming hole in the **Never**

NORTH COAST

Never River behind the small Gleniffer School of Arts (hall) at the crossroads – and lots more further upstream off the **Promised Land** loop road. Half the population of Bellingen heads out here to cool off on summer weekends, so you're better off waiting for a weekday.

If you want to work up a sweat, you can tackle the **Syndicate Walking Trail**, a strenuous day-long walk of 15 km from Gleniffer up to the Dorrigo plateau, following the route of a tramline once used by timber-cutters. The starting point is signposted off Buffer's Creek Rd – coming from Bellingen, turn left at the hall.

There are a couple of good places to stay around Gleniffer. *Crystal Creek Farm Hideaway* (☎ 6655 1090), off the Promised Land road, has a self-contained cottage for $95 per day, while *Blue Gum* (☎ 6655 1592) is a stylish B&B with singles/doubles for $55/75. It's closer to town on the Bellingen road.

The **Kalang** valley, south-west of town, and the **Thora** valley, which leads off the main Bellinger valley about 10 km west of town, are also worth exploring. Alternative lifestylers represent the majority around here and there are several large communes. Bellingen Canoe Hire (☎ 6655 8510) at Thora hires canoes and equipment for $30 a half-day. There's a good chance of seeing platypus if you're out on any of the local rivers around dawn or dusk.

DORRIGO

This mountain town (population 1200), close to the edge of the Great Dividing Range's eastern escarpment, was one of the last places to be settled in the eastward push across the New England tableland. It had the usual cedar-getting pioneers and was on a railway to Glenreagh. It was (and still is) an important stop on the road between Armidale and the coast.

Today Dorrigo is a quiet country town with wide streets and a few architectural reminders of its history. As the largest town on the Dorrigo Plateau, it makes a good base for visiting the area's outstanding national parks. Dorrigo National Park is covered later in this chapter, the others in the New England chapter.

There is an information centre (☎ 6657 2486) at 36 Hickory St, open daily, 10 am to 4 pm. The proposed **Steam Railway Museum** appears no closer to opening than it was 10 years ago. There is a long line of steam engines queued up at the old railway station, just out of town on the road to North Dorrigo. A few km north of town on the road to Leigh are the picturesque **Dangar's Falls**.

Places to Stay

Dorrigo Mountain Resort (☎ 6657 2564), just out of town on the road to Bellingen, has sites for $10, on-site vans for $30 and self-contained cabins for $44.

The *Commercial Hotel/Motel* (☎ 6657 2003) is a good budget option with singles/doubles for $15/20 and motel units for $20/30. It does a hot breakfast for $5. The nearby *Dorrigo Hotel/Motel* (☎ 6657 2017) has motel units for about $40 and cheaper pub rooms.

The *Lookout Motor Inn* (☎ 6657 2511), on the Bellingen road, charges from around $55/70.

Places to Eat

People come from far and wide to eat at *Misty's* (☎ 6657 2855), downhill from the war memorial on Hickory St. It's a charming little restaurant in a renovated weatherboard house and the food is great value at around $30 for three courses from a small but innovative blackboard menu. It's open for dinner Thursday to Saturday and for lunch on Saturday and Sunday.

The *Dorrigo Hotel/Motel* does typical pub grub, with lots of meat on the menu, while vegetarians should check out the *Healthy Gourmet* on Cudgery St.

Getting There & Away

Bus The only bus service is provided by Kean's, which uses Dorrigo as a meal stop on its Port Macquarie-Tamworth run. Other ports of call are Coffs Harbour ($13.30) and Armidale ($15.90). Some regulation prevents them carrying passengers who want to travel only the Bellingen-Dorrigo sector.

Car & Motorcycle Coffs Harbour is about 60km away via Bellingen, or there's an interesting partly unsealed route via Leigh and Coramba. You can continue west to Armidale via Ebor.

DORRIGO NATIONAL PARK

This is the most accessible of Australia's World Heritage rainforests and well worth a visit. The **Rainforest Centre** (☎ 6657 2309), at the entrance, has information about the park's many walks and is open daily, 9 am to 5 pm. There's also an elevated walkway (Skywalk) over the rainforest canopy. You can see right down to the ocean on a fine day. A walking track leads to the Glade rest area, from where there's a 5.5km walk through the forest. It's well worth making the drive down to the Never Never rest area in the heart of the national park, from where you can walk to waterfalls or begin overnight walks. Walkers in this area can bush camp, but otherwise no camping is allowed. The turn-off to the park is just south of Dorrigo.

COFFS HARBOUR

With a population approaching 50,000, Coffs Harbour is the biggest town between Newcastle and the Gold Coast, and an important regional centre. It has long been one of NSW's most popular tourist destinations and boasts good restaurants, a busy nightlife and lots of things to do.

There's a string of beaches stretching north of town and it's a good base for exploring the many attractions of the hinterland.

History

Originally called Korff's Harbour, the town was settled in the 1860s. The jetty, built in 1892 to load cedar and other logs, is in disrepair and its future depends on funds being raised to restore it. Bananas were first grown in the area in the 1880s but no-one made much money from them until the railway came to town in 1918.

Banana-growing is still big business, but these days tourism is the mainstay of the local economy.

Orientation

The Pacific Highway is called Grafton St and the Woolgoolga Rd on its run north through town. The city centre is around the junction of Grafton and High Sts. East of Grafton St, High St has been transformed into a rainforest mall. High St resumes on the other side of the mall and becomes the main road to the waterfront jetty area, a couple of km east. This is where you'll find the railway station, some shops and a string of restaurants. Across the railway tracks is the harbour with its historic jetty.

High St then loops back to the highway as Orlando St. A right turn off Orlando St after the Coffs Creek bridge takes you along Ocean Parade to the Park Beach area. Towards the north end of Ocean Parade, Park Beach Rd runs back to the highway, emerging next to the giant Park Beach Plaza shopping centre. You can't turn north onto the highway here.

You have to take the highway to get to the beaches and resorts north of Coffs. Most resorts are just past the satellite suburb of Korora, 5km north of the centre. About the same distance south of Coffs is Sawtell, with more great surf beaches. Sawtell has a pleasant little main street but the rest of the town is sprawling housing developments which merge into Coffs Harbour.

Information

The information centre (☎ 6652 1522, 1800 025 650) is on the northern edge of town on the corner of Rose Ave and Marcia St. Heading north on Grafton St, take the first turning right after the Coffs Harbour Tourist Park.

The main post office is on the ground floor of the Palms Centre shopping complex on the mall. There's another post office at the jetty, opposite the Pier Hotel. The Woolworth's supermarket on Park Ave in the town centre opens until midnight on weekdays, 9 pm on Saturday, 7 pm on Sunday.

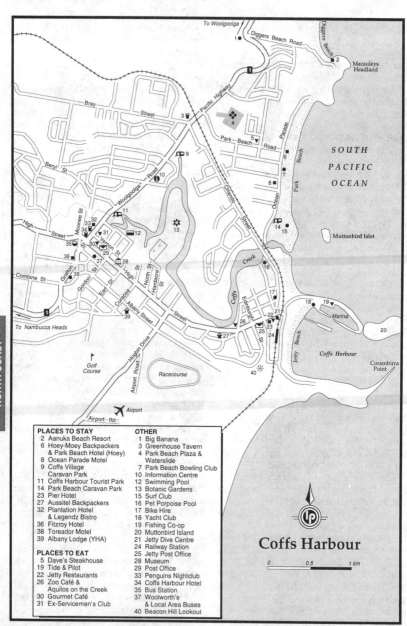

Coffs Harbour

NORTH COAST

PLACES TO STAY
2 Aanuka Beach Resort
6 Hoey-Moey Backpackers
  & Park Beach Hotel (Hoey)
8 Ocean Parade Motel
9 Coffs Village
  Caravan Park
11 Coffs Harbour Tourist Park
14 Park Beach Caravan Park
23 Pier Hotel
27 Aussitel Backpackers
32 Plantation Hotel
  & Legendz Bistro
36 Fitzroy Hotel
38 Toreador Motel
39 Albany Lodge (YHA)

PLACES TO EAT
5 Dave's Steakhouse
19 Tide & Pilot
22 Jetty Restaurants
26 Zoo Café &
  Aquilos on the Creek
30 Gourmet Café
31 Ex-Servicemen's Club

OTHER
1 Big Banana
3 Greenhouse Tavern
4 Park Beach Plaza &
  Waterslide
7 Park Beach Bowling Club
10 Information Centre
12 Swimming Pool
13 Botanic Gardens
15 Surf Club
16 Pet Porpoise Pool
17 Bike Hire
18 Yacht Club
19 Fishing Co-op
20 Muttonbird Island
21 Jetty Dive Centre
24 Railway Station
25 Jetty Post Office
28 Museum
29 Post Office
33 Penguins Nightclub
34 Coffs Harbour Hotel
35 Bus Station
37 Woolworth's
  & Local Area Buses
40 Beacon Hill Lookout

0   0.5   1 km

The Harbour

The old **jetty**, built in 1892, may be in disrepair but the rest of the harbour is very functional. The **marina**, protected by the northern breakwall, is home to a sizeable commercial fishing fleet and there are several restaurants serving excellent fish (see Places to Eat). There is a much larger fleet of leisure craft tied up outside the yacht club.

There are good views from **Beacon Hill Lookout** above the harbour up at the top of Edinburgh St and from **Corambirra Point** on the south side of the harbour.

Muttonbird Island

The harbour's northern breakwall continues out to Muttonbird Island, a nature reserve named after the 12,000-odd pairs of muttonbirds (wedge-tailed shearwaters) that call it home from late August until April. The island is dotted with their nesting burrows. The chicks emerge during December and January.

Beaches

The main town beach is **Park Beach**, which is patrolled on weekends and school holidays. If you've got wheels, you would be better off heading to beaches north of town. **Diggers Beach**, reached by turning off the highway near the Big Banana, has a nude section. Other good spots are **Moonee Beach**, about 14km north of town, and **Emerald Beach**, a further 6km. Back in town, **Jetty Beach** can be good for a swim when the surf is rough.

North Coast Botanic Gardens

The botanic gardens, at the end of Hardacre St (off High St), are well worth a visit. It's hard to believe that part of the site was once the town tip. The immaculately maintained gardens contain many endangered species and areas have been planted to re-create the region's different forest types. There's also a boardwalk out over the mangrove swamp bordering Coffs Creek, information on plants used by Aborigines and a 'sensory garden'. The gardens are open daily, 9 am to 5 pm. Admission is by donation.

Coffs Creek

The gardens can be visited as part of the popular **Coffs Creek Walk**, an easy 3.5km stroll along the creek bank that starts opposite the council chambers on Coff St and finishes near the Pet Porpoise Pool.

You can also explore the creek by boat. Promenade Leisure Hire, at the Coffs Promenade building, hires canoes and dinghies for $8 an hour, $20 for a half-day.

Coffs Harbour Historical Museum

The museum, 191 High St, is open Tuesday to Thursday and Sunday, 1.30 to 4.30 pm. Exhibits include the old 'optic' from the South Solitary Island lighthouse and displays on the Aboriginal and European history of the area. Admission is $1 (50c children).

Big Banana

This award-winning piece of kitsch was voted Australia's silliest attraction by a recent travellers' poll. It stands by the highway on the northern edge of town. You can stock up on useful household items like tinned 'skinmarks' and buttock-shaped pencil sharpeners at the nearby gift shop. Behind the banana is Horticulture World (☎ 6652 4355), a theme park which has a mini railway system. Entry to the complex is free but it costs $9 ($5 children) to take the tour. The toboggan ride is worth checking out.

Animal Acts

The **Pet Porpoise Pool** (☎ 6652 2164), next to Coffs Creek on Orlando St, has shows at 10.30 am and 2.15 pm every day for $10 ($5 children). **Coffs Harbour Zoo** (☎ 6656 1330) is on the highway at Moonee, 14km north of Coffs. The emphasis is on native animals and the koalas are 'presented' at 11 am and 3 pm daily. Admission is $9 ($4.50 children).

NORTH COAST

Activities

There's a huge range of things to get out and do – too many to list below. The Marina Booking Centre (☎ 6651 4612), at the harbour, has information about what's available. You'll find the best deals at the hostels.

Whitewater Rafting & Canoeing

The Nymboida River inland from Coffs offers some of the best whitewater rafting in Australia. There are a couple of long-established outfits that get consistently good feedback. Whitewater Rafting Professionals (☎ 6651 4066) have day trips for $125 and overnight trips for $265, fully catered. Wildwater Adventures (☎ 6653 4469) offers similar deals, plus four-day trips for $460 and more challenging rafting on the Gwydir River near Inverell in season. Be sceptical of any other outfits offering rafting on the Nymboida.

Goolang Creek, fed by the outlet from the hydro-electric scheme at Nymboida, offers world-class kayaking or you can raft down with Rapid Rafting (☎ 6652 1741) for $65.

Surfing

The Coffs Harbour surf club is at **Park Beach**. The best surfing is around Macauley's headland, between Park Beach and **Diggers**, reached by turning off the highway opposite the Big Banana. Helene Enevoldson of the East Coast Surf School (☎ 6651 5515) teaches novices to surf. She charges $20 for a two-hour lesson. Boards can be hired at Coopers Surfshop, among the jetty restaurants at 380 High St. Northside Surf in Northside Shopping Centre on Park Beach Rd has surf-skis as well.

Cruises

There's a growing band of boats offering an assortment of trips. You can go out deep-sea fishing on the *Pamela Star* (☎ 6658 4379) or the *Laura E* (☎ 6651 1434) for $50, while the *Commissioner II* (☎ 6651 3271) cruises past South Solitary Island daily for $20.

Whale Watching

Humpback whales are often sighted off Coffs Harbour during their northbound migration in June and July and during their southern migration from September to November. When there are whales around, you'll find plenty of operators willing to take you out for around $25.

Diving

There's interesting diving around the Solitary Islands, a few km up the coast. The Diver's Depot (☎ 6652 2033) does an introductory dive for $95, including equipment, and a four-day accreditation course for $250. Jetty Dive Centre (☎ 6651 1611) at 396 High St is a long-established business that also rents snorkelling gear. Up in Mullaway, north of Woolgoolga, there's also Dive Quest (☎ 6654 1930).

Horseriding

There are a number of places offering horseriding. Valery Trails (☎ 6653 4301), in the bush about 20 km south of Coffs, has two-hour rides through the adjoining Pine Creek State Forest for $30.

Skydiving

Coffs City Skydivers (☎ 66511 167) offers an introductory first-jump course for $195, captured on video to show your friends for $225.

Parasailing

Coffs Harbour Water Sports will take you aloft for 20 minutes for $48. You'll find it at Park Beach every day during summer except Tuesday. It also hires jet-skis.

Organised Tours

4WD

There are half a dozen companies running 4WD tours around the region's forests. The hostels normally have special deals.

Aboriginal Tours

Gambaarri Tours (☎ 6655 4195) has interpretative trips to a number of sites on the coast between Red Rock and Valla for $45.

Special Events

The Gold Cup, Coffs' premier horse race, is run on a Thursday in early August. It's a big day out, capping off a big week of entertainment in Coffs. Entry to the racetrack is $6.

The harbour is the finishing point of the Pittwater (Sydney) to Coffs Harbour yacht race that sets sail on 28 December. It normally attracts a few big-name boats that stuff up the start of the Sydney-Hobart.

Places to Stay

Except in the hostels, expect prices to rise by about 50% in school holidays and by as much as 100% at Christmas/New Year.

Camping The huge *Park Beach Caravan Park* (☎ 6652 3204) on Ocean Parade is right next to the beach and has tent sites from $10 a double, on-site vans from $26 and cabins from $36. There are lower weekly rates, but not at peak times. *Coffs Harbour Tourist Park* (☎ 6652 1694), on the highway a couple of blocks on from the Ex-Services Club, has sites from $10, on-site vans from $23 and cabins from $33. There are plenty of other places along the highway north and south of town.

Hostels There are three good places to choose from. They all offer free use of bikes and surfboards and they all meet the buses at the Moonee St stop.

The *Albany YHA Lodge* (☎ 6652 6462), close to the city centre at 110 Albany St, is a friendly place with dorm beds for $14 and doubles for $32. Bikes and surfboards are free and there are plans to add a pool. The hostel bus does beach runs and the owners also arrange activities and excursions – such as water-skiing on the Bellinger River at Repton.

Aussitel Backpackers Hostel (☎ 6651 1871), 312 High St, is close to the jetty restaurants and the harbour, about 1.5 km from the town centre. It's well run and has all the usual hostel facilities plus a pool. Dorm beds are $15, doubles are $30 and there are family rooms for $40. The owners have a programme of tours which includes the zoo. Coffs Creek is over the road and canoes are free.

Hoey-Moey Backpackers (☎ 6651 7966, 1800 683 322) is a new place right behind the dunes at Park Beach. The owners have spent a lot of money tidying up and converting what was once the rundown Moey

(motel) part of the Park Beach Hotel-Motel, known to locals as the Hoey-Moey. It has dorms for $14 and doubles for $35.

B&B *Illoura* (☎ 6653 1690 after 4 pm), on South Boambee road about seven km south of Coffs (get full directions when you book), has great views, wildlife and one guest suite which goes for $65/95. No children under 16 are permitted.

Hotels Many of the town's hotels have accommodation. In the off-season you're better off hunting around for a motel with deals, but pub prices tend to stay the same year-round so they can be great value in summer.

Officially on Moonee St (although it appears to be on Grafton St), the *Fitzroy Hotel* (☎ 6652 3007) is an old-style neighbourhood pub with singles/doubles for $18/25. Down near the harbour on High St, the *Pier Hotel* (☎ 6652 2110) has a few large, clean rooms for $20/36.

Motels There's a string of motels on Grafton St, on the southern approaches to town, such as *Toreador* (☎ 6652 3887) and *Golden Glow* (☎ 6652 2742). Outside school holidays, prices are around $42 a double.

There is another bunch of motels in the Park Beach area which have similar rates. You will pay around $40 a double at the *Ocean Parade Motel* (☎ 6652 6733); in the high season the rates are around $75 a double.

Self-Catering There is a huge range of holiday apartments and houses. In the off-season the cheapest of the two-bedroom apartments goes for around $50 a night (less by the week), and its $100 a night in the high season, which is not too bad between a group. Of course, there are many which are vastly more expensive. Many places are available only by the week in the high season. The tourist information centre has a free booking service (☎ 1800 025 650) and there are plenty of real estate agents.

Resorts The resorts are responsible for Coffs' upmarket image – without them it would be just another thriving coastal town. Most resorts are off the highway past Korora, about 5km north of Coffs. Most have lower weekly rates and frequently offer packages – check around.

Aanuka Beach Resort (☎ 6652 7555) is more discreet than some of the others, tucked away at Diggers Beach. It has holiday units from $75 to $320 a day. Novotel's *Opal Cove* (☎ 6651 0510), 6km north of town, is a huge development which includes a residential suburb and a par-three golf course. Rooms cost from $109. Just north of here is the long-running *Nautilus on the Beach* (☎ 6653 6699), with serviced apartments from $150 a day and motel units for $110.

Places to Eat

Some of the best cheap eats can be found in the clubs, such as the *Ex-Services Club* on the corner of Grafton and Vernon Sts and the *Catholic Club* on High St, about 1km inland from Grafton St.

City Centre The mall is full of cafes and takeaway joints that cater for the town's cruising office population at lunchtime. The *Gourmet Cafe*, in the City Boulevard Arcade off the mall, has delicious home-made pies ($1.80) and light meals from around $6. All the pubs in this area have counter meals. The best deals are at the Plantation Hotel on Grafton St, where *Legendz Bistro* has lunches for $5.50 with a free drink on weekdays.

The *Cross Roads Cafe*, opposite the giant Ex-Services Club on Vernon St, is a fun place filled with 50s memorabilia.

On Park Ave across from Woolworth's, the Chinese *Phoen Wong* has smorgasbords for $11 on Friday and Saturday nights. The ordinary menu includes quite a few vegetarian dishes for under $6. The popular *Tequila Mexican Restaurant*, just east of the mall on High St, has main courses from $9.

Jetty For choice, you can't beat the cluster of restaurants at the jetty end of High St,

where you'll find the excellent *Tahruah Thai Kitchen*, near the Pier Hotel, with filling noodle dishes for $7. Most of the neighbours are a few notches upmarket. They include *Peter's Pepermill* (French), the *Royal Viking* (grill), the *Passionfish Brasserie* (multi-cultural) and a couple of Indian restaurants. There are also pub meals and $5 breakfasts at the *Pier Hotel*.

There are a couple of promising looking places in the Coffs Promenade building, opposite Aussitel. The *Zoo Cafe* and *Aquilos on the Creek* both have outdoor seating overlooking Coffs Creek.

Harbour The harbour is the place to go for seafood. *Coffs Harbour Fishermen's Co-op* has a good takeaway section and a sushi/sashimi bar as well as fresh seafood. The nearby *Yacht Club* has $5 lunches on weekdays and *Tide & Pilot* offers fantastic views up the coast while you tuck into dishes like chilli king prawns ($19).

Park Beach There are more restaurants around the junction of Ocean Parade and Park Beach Rd. The bistro at the *Hoey-Moey* has meals from $3.50, while *Park Beach Bowling Club* also has a nightly smorgasbord for $12.

Dave's Steakhouse, 99 Park Beach Rd, has an all-you-can-eat soup, pasta and salad deal for $10.95 as well as huge steaks from $18.

Entertainment

There's something happening every night, although the pickings are fairly slim early in the week. Thursday's edition of the *Coffs Harbour Advocate* has the week's listings.

The *Plantation Hotel* on Grafton St is the main venue, with live bands from Wednesday to Sunday nights. The *Hoey-Moey* has a free band on Sunday afternoon and the *Heartbreak Hotel* at Moonee has bands on Friday night. Big-name touring bands play at the *Sawtell RSL Club*, 5km south of town, or at the *Coffs Ex-Services Club* on Vernon St. Lesser lights play at the *Greenhouse Tavern*, just off the highway at the junction with Bray St.

Nightclubs currently popular are *The Vault*, upstairs next to the newsagent on the mall, and *Penguins*, in the Bowling Centre Arcade off Grafton St.

Getting There & Away
Greyhound Pioneer (☎ 132030) has a booking office by the long-distance bus stop in Moonee St. Coffs Harbour Coaches & Travel (☎ 6652 2877), a few doors away, can fix you up with bus, air and Countrylink tickets.

Air Between them, Ansett and Eastern Australia offer at least seven flights a day to Sydney ($226). Impulse flies to Brisbane ($216) via Lismore and Coolangatta.

Bus – long-distance All long-distance services on the Sydney-Brisbane run stop at Moonee St just west of Grafton St. Fares from Coffs include: Byron Bay $33, Brisbane $41, Nambucca Heads $14, Port Macquarie $27 and Sydney $47. King's has services up to Tamworth via Armidale ($23.80) and Dorrigo ($11.80).

Bus – local area These services leave from the stop at the car park next to Woolworth's on Park Ave. Ryan's (☎ 6652 3201) runs several times daily except Sunday to Woolgoolga ($5) via beachside towns off the highway. Watson's Woolgoolga Coaches (☎ 6654 1063) has three services a day between Coffs and Grafton ($11), running via Woolgoolga and Red Rock. The afternoon service meets the 3.30 pm train from Sydney. See the Bellingen and Nambucca Heads sections for other local services.

Train The railway station (☎ 6652 2312) is near the harbour at the end of High St. The fare to Sydney is $65.

Car & Motorcycle If you're heading north, the backroad to Grafton via Coramba and Glenreagh passes through some pretty country and is a pleasant alternative to the Pacific Highway.

Boat Coffs is reportedly a good place to pick up a ride along the coast on a yacht or cruiser. Ask around or put a notice in the yacht club at the harbour. Sometimes the hostels know of boat owners who are looking for crew.

Getting Around
The Coffs District Taxi Network (☎ 6651 3944) operates a 24-hour service. There's a taxi rank on the corner of High and Gordon Sts. Bob Wallis World of Wheels (☎ 6652 5102), near the harbour on the corner of Collingwood and Orlando Sts, rents bikes.

As well as the major car-rental companies there are some local outfits offering cheaper rates, although you should compare the deals carefully. Coffs Rent-a-Wreck (☎ 6651 7933) has cars from $40 a day.

COFFS HARBOUR TO GRAFTON
Glenreagh
On the inland route which follows the railway line between Coffs Harbour and Grafton, Glenreagh is a small village (population 300) on the Orara River. Glenreagh had a gold rush in the 1880s and it was a railway junction town until the Dorrigo line closed in the 1970s. There's a **museum** in the old School of Arts, open Tuesday from 9 to 11 am.

Take the left turn from the Coffs Harbour to Glenreagh road just past Coramba, then turn right on Bushmans Range Rd and you'll come to **George's Goldmine** (☎ 6654 5355), which is actually the old Bayfield Mine. Tours of the mine are held through the day and the surrounding bush is a nice spot for a picnic. It's open Wednesday to Sunday, daily in school holidays.

Woolgoolga
The small resort town of Woolgoolga (population 4000) is notable for its fine surf beach. It has a sizeable Sikh community whose *gurdwara* (place of worship) is the impressive **Guru Nanak Temple**, overlooking the highway on the southern side of town. The Indianesque set-up further north by the roundabout is the **Raj Mahal**, a tourist-trap

that appears to be falling down faster than it went up.

Places to Stay & Eat The *Woolgoolga Beach Caravan Park* (☎ 6654 1373) is on the beach and has sites from $10, on-site vans from $24 and cabins from $34.

There are a few motels along the highway, such as the *Woolgoolga Motor Inn* (☎ 6654 1534), with rates a little cheaper than those in Coffs.

For Indian food there's the *Koh-I-Nor* restaurant at the Raj Mahal and the *Temple View Restaurant* across from the new temple.

Getting There & Away The long-distance bus-lines pass through Woolgoolga. There are local services to Coffs Harbour, Grafton and nearby beaches.

Arrawarra

This quiet seaside village one km off the highway has yet another great beach, some bushland that is noisy with birds, the inlet of a small creek and a very pleasant caravan park close to the water, *Arrawarra Holiday Park* (☎ 6649 2753). Sites cost from $10 ($17 at Christmas), on-site vans start at $25 ($40 at Christmas) and cabins are $39 ($75 at Christmas). There is free use of bikes, canoes and surfboards. A short way south is **Mullaway**, and **Corindi** is a few km north; you have to return to the highway to get to either.

Red Rock

Six km off the highway, Red Rock is a sleepy village, a little larger than Arrawarra. It's both relaxed and neat, with well-mown lawns and tidy fibro or weatherboard holiday houses. The residents reckon it's a top spot. The small Redbank River enters the sea here and there's a beautiful inlet just across from *Red Rock Caravan Park* (☎ 6649 2730), where sites cost from $10 and cottages are $35.

Yuraygir National Park

Yuraygir (20,000 hectares) is the southern-most of a chain of coastal national parks and

nature reserves which runs almost all the way north to Ballina. The beaches are outstanding and there are some stretches of forest offering bushwalks. The park is in three sections, from Red Rock to the Wooli River (turn off the highway just north of Red Rock), from the township of Wooli to the Sandon River (turn off the highway 12km south of Grafton) and from near Brooms Head to Angourie (accessible from those towns). There is no vehicle access between the sections; on foot you'd have to cross the sizeable Wooli and Sandon rivers.

Walkers can bush camp and there are basic camping areas at Station Creek in the southern section, at the Boorkoom and Illaroo rest areas in the central section and on the north bank of the Sandon River and at Red Cliff at the Brooms Head end of the northern section. These are accessible by car; there are also walk-in campsites in the northern section: Plumbago Headland, Shelly Head and Shelly Beach.

Nearby Towns There are a number of small holiday settlements surrounded by the park. **Wooli** and **Minnie Water** are reached from a road running off the highway 12km south of Grafton, or, if you're coming from the north, from Ulmarra.

Wooli is a straggling holiday hamlet, not especially attractive, but there are the usual great beaches and the very clean Wooli River, which you can apparently canoe up for 20km. Wooli's big event is the Goanna Pulling Championship held on the Queen's Birthday long weekend in June. This is not something the Royal Society for the Prevention of Cruelty to Animals need be concerned about – it's a tug-of-war between contestants with a leather strap around their heads. There is a *caravan park* (☎ 6649 7679) and cabins (☎ 6649 7519), and the pub (☎ 6649 7532) has accommodation.

Minnie Water, 12km or so north on the other side of **Lake Hiawatha**, is smaller but nicer. The *caravan park* (☎ 6649 7693) has sites from $8.50 ($11 at peak times) and cabins from $30 a double ($45). Buses run to Grafton two or three times a week and there are schoolbuses.

Brooms Head, on the coast 25km east of Maclean, remains a quiet hamlet, popular with locals. It has good beaches (lagoon and ocean), a few holiday units, a *caravan park* and proximity to Yuraygir National Park, both north and south of the town.

The Solitary Islands

This group of five islands is strung out along the coast offshore from Yuraygir National Park. It's a marine park at the meeting place of warm tropical currents and the more temperate southern currents, with some interesting varieties of fish and coral because of the unusual conditions. Cruises and dive boats from Coffs Harbour come here.

Far North Coast

As well as great beaches and a subtropical climate, rivers are a feature of this area (which is also known as the Northern Rivers district), with the mighty Clarence, Richmond and Tweed rivers sprawling through rich deltas. They are wide, deep and blue – most un-Australian.

Winters are a bit of a non-event in this part of the world. Even in June and July, daytime temperatures normally reach the mid-20s, although nights can be cool (locals think the nights are cold and shiver in woollies). By September everyone agrees that it's beach weather.

GRAFTON

Grafton is a graceful old country town (population 21,500) on the banks of the wide Clarence River. The town is famous for its fine trees, particularly the spectacular jacarandas that carpet the streets with their mauve flowers in late October. Although there isn't a lot to do or see here, this isn't a tourist town or a retirement ghetto and that makes a nice change from some of the sprawling coastal developments. The town lies at the centre of a rich agricultural district

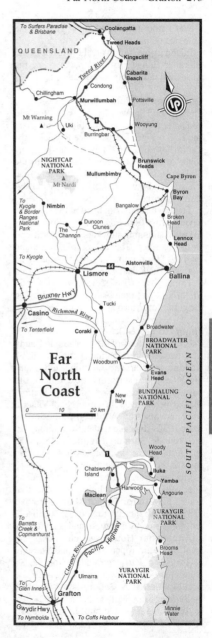

NORTH COAST

– beef cattle inland and sugar cane in the Clarence delta.

Inland from Grafton are the Washpool and Gibraltar Ranges national parks – see the New England chapter for details.

Orientation & Information

The Pacific Highway bypasses Grafton and you enter the town on a double-decker (road and rail) bridge. The Clarence River Tourist Centre (☎ 6642 4677) is on the highway south of the town, near the turn-off to the bridge. Before you cross the bridge a road leads off to South Grafton, a sleepy old riverside suburb.

The town is on a big bend in the Clarence River, across from Susan Island. Prince St is the main shopping street and runs north-east from the river. The corner of Prince and Fitzroy Sts, dominated by the sandstone National Bank, is the centre of town.

The NPWS office (☎ 6642 0613) is at 50 Victoria St and the post office is nearby on the corner of Prince and Victoria Sts.

Things to See & Do

Pick up a free copy of the Blue Guide Handy Map from the information centre, as it has a **walking tour** around Grafton's old buildings. Victoria St is worth a look, with the old post office, courthouse and police station, shaded by big trees. On the corner of Victoria and Duke Sts is the **Anglican Cathedral**, in spare 1930s style and with older buildings in the grounds. **Saraton Theatre** on Prince St is a restored movie theatre where you can still see the flicks most nights.

Fitzroy St runs off Prince St and has some interesting houses, including the one that houses the **Grafton Regional Gallery** at No 158 (open Wednesday to Sunday, 10 am to 4 pm, admission by donation) and, a bit further on, **Schaeffer House**, which houses the local **museum** (open Sunday and Tuesday to Thursday, 1 to 4 pm, admission $2, $1 children). For local art and craft, visit the **Bentleg Market & Gallery** (☎ 6643 2929) on Skinner St in South Grafton.

Across the river, the rainforest of **Susan Island** is home to the largest colony of fruit bats in the southern hemisphere. Their departure is a spectacular sight on summer evenings. Access to the island, which has a walking trail through the rainforest and picnic areas at the southern end, is by boat. You can paddle across by hiring a canoe from Acme Fibreglass (☎ 6642 4780) at 20 Bessie St in South Grafton.

About the most pleasant activity in Grafton is looking at the river, and the terrace at the Crown Hotel at the western end of Prince St is a pleasant place from which to do just that.

See the following Clarence River section for information about houseboats and river cruises.

Special Events

A Jacaranda Festival is held over a week in late October and early November, with a parade on the first Saturday in November. Grafton's July racing carnival is the richest in country Australia.

Places to Stay

Hostel *Rathgar Guesthouse* (☎ 6643 2015), next to the Caltex service station on the Pacific Highway south, is the only hostel. It occupies the old Protestant Children's Home and looks great from the outside, which is where the last renovation effort seems to have finished. The interior needs attention. Beds are $15.

Caravan Parks *Glenwood Tourist Park* (☎ 6642 3466) is on the Pacific Highway's southbound arm about 1km south of the information centre; *Sunset Caravan Park* (☎ 6642 3824) is on the Gwydir Highway about three km west of the information centre. Both have sites for around $10 and on-site vans from $30, and Glenwood has self-contained cabins from $35.

Hotels & Motels Many pubs have accommodation, including the *Crown Hotel/Motel* (☎ 6642 4000). This very pleasant place overlooks the river and has pub rooms for $20/30 a single/double or $30/40 with bathroom and motel units for $45/55. See if you

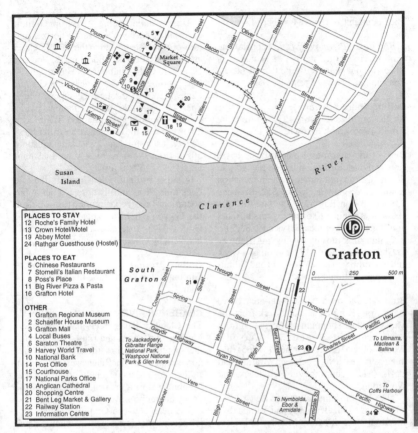

PLACES TO STAY
12 Roche's Family Hotel
13 Crown Hotel/Motel
19 Abbey Motel
24 Rathgar Guesthouse (Hostel)

PLACES TO EAT
5 Chinese Restaurants
7 Stornelli's Italian Restaurant
9 Poss's Place
11 Big River Pizza & Pasta
16 Grafton Hotel

OTHER
1 Grafton Regional Museum
2 Schaeffer House Museum
3 Grafton Mall
4 Local Buses
6 Saraton Theatre
8 Harvey World Travel
10 National Bank
14 Post Office
15 Courthouse
17 National Parks Office
18 Anglican Cathedral
20 Shopping Centre
21 Bent Leg Market & Gallery
22 Railway Station
23 Information Centre

can get a room overlooking the river. If it's one of the small pub rooms you'll have French doors opening onto a long, wide verandah. The pub beds could be newer but it's a clean and friendly place.

Another nice old pub in the same area is *Roches Family Hotel* (☎ 6644 2866) at 85 Victoria St. It has rooms from under \$24/30. Most other pubs in Grafton and South Grafton also have accommodation.

Motels near the town centre include the *Abbey* (☎ 6642 6122), on Fitzroy St behind the cathedral, which has rooms that cost from \$49/59.

Places to Eat

Dining out is not Grafton's strong suit. The town centre has the usual cafes, takeaways, clubs and pub meals. *Roches Family Hotel* has a good bistro, with most meals around \$10, and the Parkview Hotel on Prince St has Italian food at *Stornelli's*.

Poss's Place, at the far end of the Mid-City Arcade off Prince St between Fitzroy and Pound Sts, is open for lunch on weekdays and has a selection of healthy snacks, drinks and light meals. Further up Prince St, past the railway viaduct, are two Chinese restaurants, *Fountain Court* and the *New Orient*.

The Fountain Court has a few Thai dishes on the menu.

Big River Pizza & Pasta, opposite the Grafton Hotel on Fitzroy St, is mainly a takeaway but there are a couple of tables. You can get a bowl of pasta for $5.

Getting There & Away

Air Eastern flies to Sydney ($235) from the airport 10km south of town.

Bus – long-distance Long-distance buses stop at the Mobil station on the highway in South Grafton, not far from the information centre. Fares include Sydney $52, Brisbane $38 and Byron Bay $25. The fare to Coffs Harbour is about $20 on an express bus, but you'll get a slower local service for $8.50.

Countrylink runs up the Gwydir Highway to Glen Innes (about $17) four times a week and will drop you near Washpool and Gibraltar Ranges national parks.

Bus – local area Most local-area buses leave from King St, a block back from the Market Square shopping centre, not far from the corner of Pound St. Watson's Woolgoolga Coaches (☎ 6654 1063) has three services a day between Grafton and Coffs ($11), running via Red Rock and Woolgoolga.

The Grafton-Yamba Bus Service (☎ 6642 2019) runs to Maclean ($5) and Yamba ($7) several times a day from Monday to Friday, once on Saturday and twice on Sunday. Buses leave from outside the Saraton Theatre.

Train The railway station is just south of the bridge. The fare from Sydney is $70.

Car & Motorcycle The Pacific Highway runs north to Maclean and south to Coffs Harbour. Near Grafton there are several scenic routes which parallel the highway and involve ferry crossings, such as Grafton to Maclean via the north bank and the Lawrence ferry. There's also a ferry crossing between the highway and the north bank road at Ulmarra.

There's an interesting route from Grafton to Armidale via Nymboida and Ebor, passing turn-offs to Dorrigo and to the New England and Cathedral Rock national parks. You can also get to Coffs Harbour via Glenreagh.

Heading east to Glen Innes, the Gwydir Highway passes through the superb Washpool and Gibraltar Ranges national parks (see the New England chapter). It's a steep 20km climb to the tablelands, and after Jackadgery, just a store and a caravan park about 50km from Grafton, there's no fuel until Glen Innes, 130km further west.

Another route to Glen Innes is the Old Glen Innes road, mostly unsealed but in fair condition. Take the Dalmorton turn-off from the Gwydir Highway about 8km west of Grafton. This road passes through a tunnel hand-cut by convicts.

Getting Around

Grafton Radio Taxis (☎ 6642 3622) runs 24 hours.

CLARENCE RIVER VALLEY

The Clarence River rises in Queensland's McPherson Ranges and runs south through the mountains before thundering down a gorge in the Gibraltar Range west of Grafton. It then meanders serenely to the sea at Yamba, watering a beautiful and fertile valley along the way.

The delta between Grafton and the coast is a patchwork of farmland, in which the now immense and branching Clarence River forms about 100 islands, some very large. If you're driving, the profusion of small bridges and waterways makes it hard to keep track of whether you're on an island or the mainland.

This is the start of sugar-cane country and also the beginning of Queensland-style domestic architecture: wooden houses with high-pitched roofs perched on stilts to allow air circulation in the hot summers. The burning of the canefields (May to December) adds a smoky tang to the air. To arrange a visit to a cane farm contact the Clarence River Tourist Centre (☎ 6642 4677) in Grafton.

There are several outfits which can help to set you cruising on the lower Clarence, such as Captain-a-Cruiser (☎ 6645 3040) in Maclean which rents a six-berth cruiser from around $300 a weekend or $600 a week for two people, plus fuel, and Clarence Riverboats (☎ 6647 6232) at Brushgrove. There are plenty of places that rent dinghies and small boats.

Inland from Grafton

The Clarence is navigable as far upstream as the village of **Copmanhurst**, about 35 km north-west of Grafton. The *Rest Point Hotel* (☎ 6647 3125) has accommodation. Further upstream the Clarence descends rapidly from the Gibraltar Range through the rugged **Clarence River Gorge**. The gorge is a popular but potentially dangerous site for whitewater canoeing.

Private property flanks the gorge. On the south side the land is owned by the Winters family, who allow day visitors and have cabin accommodation at *Winters' Shack* (☎ 6647 2173). Access is via Copmanhurst, but you'll have to ring first to get permission and to arrange for gates to be unlocked. On the north side, *Wave Hill Station* (☎ 6647 2145) has homestead or cottage accommodation and regular 4WD or horseriding trips to the Clarence Gorge for $50 per person ($35 without lunch); you don't have to stay at Wave Hill to go along.

Ulmarra

On the Pacific Highway about 15km north of Grafton, Ulmarra (population 500) is a National Trust-classified village founded in the 1850s by early cane planters. Today the town has an abundance of craft and antiques shops. The *Commercial Hotel* (☎ 6644 5305) has limited accommodation. A vehicle ferry (not suitable for caravans) crosses the Clarence here.

Maclean

This pretty old town (population 3000) has strong Scottish roots and at Easter it holds a Highland Gathering. Maclean is at the junction of the Clarence's main and south arms,

where the river begins its lazy sprawl over the delta, and is home to a prawn-fishing fleet. It's a quiet place with excellent river views and great sunsets.

The **Bicentennial Museum** on Wharf St tells the story of the Northern Rivers area and is open Wednesday and Saturday from 2 to 5 pm. Maclean Lookout, about two km from the town centre on Wharf St, has views over the Clarence and the canefields.

The Maclean Riding School (☎ 6645 2071) on Cameron St offers horseriding.

On the second Saturday of the month a market is held in the town's main car park. There's also an agricultural show in late April and a Cane Harvest Festival in September.

Chatsworth Island

About 40 km north of Maclean the Pacific Highway crosses Chatsworth Island, bypassing the village of the same name. The village is a pretty spot, but the main attraction is the *Chatsworth Island Restaurant* (☎ 6646 4455). This is one of the state's better places to eat, with an eclectic French-based menu and the bonus of a view across the mighty Clarence. Prices are reasonable, with main courses around $18, and on Sunday from 11 am it has brunch with a variety of snacks as well as meals.

Yamba

Yamba (population 4000) is a thriving little resort town on the south head of the Clarence River's wide estuary, with beaches on three sides. There are lots of motels, holiday apartments and housing developments for retirees. It would be a pretty good place to retire to, with reputedly the warmest winters in the state.

Fishing is the favourite pastime and here you can choose between beach, rock and estuary. Oyster Channel Boat Hire (☎ 6646 0263) hires tackle as well as boats. The Yamba-Iluka ferry runs cruises up the river on Wednesday and Friday, which depart at 11 am and come back at 3 pm, for $15 ($7.50 children).

NORTH COAST

Places to Stay There are a few caravan parks, including *Easts Calypso* (☎ 6646 2468), right in town and overlooking the small harbour. Sites cost from $12, on-site vans from $28 and cabins from $30. The *Pacific Hotel* (☎ 6646 2466) at 1 Pilot St has backpacker accommodation in twin rooms for $17.50 per person. It has a great location high above Yamba Beach.

Yamba's half-dozen or so motels have relatively low rates outside peak times. The good *Aston Villa* (☎ 6646 2785) on Mulgi St (the inland continuation of Coldstream St, which crosses Yamba St) charges from $45/50.

Getting There & Away Yamba is 15km east of the Pacific Highway, turning off at the Harbord Island bridge intersection north of Maclean. The Grafton-Yamba Bus Service (☎ 6646 2019) runs to Maclean ($2.60) and Grafton ($7) several times a day from Monday to Friday, once on Saturday and twice on Sunday.

A ferry runs to Iluka, on the north bank of the Clarence, four times a day for $3 ($1.50 children). See the Lord Howe Island section for details of the ferry service between Yamba and Lord Howe.

Angourie

Five km south of Yamba, Angourie is one of the coast's top spots for experienced surfers, but beware of riptides. Also here is the Blue Pool, a quarry next to the beach filled with fresh water from a spring.

Iluka

North across the river from Yamba, Iluka (population 1800) remains something of a backwater. It's home to a small commercial fishing fleet and recreational fishing is the main activity. The town adjoins the southern end of Bundjalung National Park and a section known as the **Iluka Rainforest** has World Heritage listing. A short walking trail from the town centre to Iluka Bluff takes you through the rainforest.

To get here from Yamba it's either a short ferry ride or, if you have a car, a long drive

back to the highway, a total trip of about 40km.

BUNDJALUNG NATIONAL PARK

Stretching from Iluka north to Evans Head and covering 17,700 hectares, Bundjalung has long beaches, a river and a patch of rainforest at Woody Head, at the southern end of the park near Iluka.

Nearby is the large Woody Head *camping* area, leased from the NPWS and run privately. It has a few more facilities than most NPWS camping areas – including a kiosk and cabins – but there's no electricity, so you're spared the worst of the holiday hordes. Still, at peak times you'll need to book (☎ 6646 6134). Sites cost $10 a double and cabins start at $30. There are also simple campsites at Black Rocks, Boorooa, Jerusalem Creek and Yabbra, with pit toilets but no water.

There are three access points for the park: from near Iluka, near Evans Head and, for the middle of the park, Gap Rd, which runs off the Pacific Highway about 5km south of Woodburn.

NEW ITALY MUSEUM

This incongruous exhibition is on the highway about 10km south of Woodburn. The small museum traces the exciting events of the Marquis de Ray's plan to colonise the New Guinea island of New Ireland and how the tattered survivors of that fiasco ended up here. There's also an Italian Pavilion with a lot of information on the various provinces of Italy. The museum has a coffee shop and there's a licensed Italian restaurant nearby. Behind all this is the good **Gurrigai Aboriginal Arts & Crafts** shop, selling some local work along with pieces from the outback.

EVANS HEAD

A fishing town (population 2500) at the mouth of the Evans River, Evans Head has a pretty location and some accommodation, including an inexpensive pub. The views up the coast from **Razorback Lookout** are stunning – you can see Cape Byron on a clear day.

Evans Head is 10km east of the highway; turn off at Woodburn.

BROADWATER NATIONAL PARK

Extending from north of Evans Head to Broadwater, this small coastal park (3750 hectares) protects a 7km stretch of beach backed by coastal heath. You can drive through the park on the roads between Evans Head and Broadwater. Camping isn't allowed in the park.

BALLINA

Ballina (population 29,000) is a busy resort town at the mouth of the Richmond River, 30km south of Byron Bay. The emphasis around here is on family holidays – the bus station is called the Family Transit Centre! The main attractions are fishing and watersports.

Orientation & Information

The Pacific Highway runs into town from the south (passing the Big Prawn) and becomes River St, the long main street. The highway turns off onto Kerr St, but River St continues beside the river, crossing North Creek into East Ballina then running up the coast (to Lennox Head and Byron Bay) and changing its name a couple of times in the process.

The information centre (☎ 6686 3484) is just past the old post office, now the courthouse, at the eastern end of River St. The small **maritime museum** behind the information centre houses one of the three balsawood rafts that drifted across the Pacific from Ecuador to Australia on the Las Balsas expedition in 1973, coming ashore at Ballina after 177 days.

Beaches

The popular **Shelly Beach** is the closest patrolled beach to town. To get there, take the first turn right (coming from Ballina) after the Shaws Hotel turn-off. This road also passes **Lighthouse Beach**. The small beach

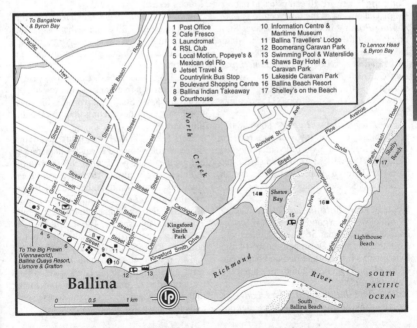

1 Post Office
2 Cafe Fresco
3 Laundromat
4 RSL Club
5 Local Motion, Popeye's & Mexican del Rio
6 Jetset Travel & Countrylink Bus Stop
7 Boulevard Shopping Centre
8 Ballina Indian Takeaway
9 Courthouse
10 Information Centre & Maritime Museum
11 Ballina Travellers' Lodge
12 Boomerang Caravan Park
13 Swimming Pool & Waterslide
14 Shaws Bay Hotel & Caravan Park
15 Lakeside Caravan Park
16 Ballina Beach Resort
17 Shelley's on the Beach

Ballina

0   0.5   1 km

curving around the **Shaws Bay Lagoon** is a safe spot for kids to swim.

Boats

The MV *Richmond Princess* (☎ 6687 1216, or book at the information centre) has two-hour cruises on Wednesday at 10 am and Thursday at 2 pm for $9.50.

The MV *Bennelong* (☎ 018 664 552, or book at the information centre) also has a variety of cruises, including a day cruise up the river to Lismore for $45 ($20 children). You can buy lunch on board. These cruises leave from near the RSL Club.

You'll find all sorts of small boats for hire at the Ballina Quays Marina (☎ 6686 4289), off the highway south of the Big Prawn.

Places to Stay

Nearly half of all visitors to Ballina stay with friends or relations. It's that sort of town. Prices at the caravan parks rise sharply during school holidays.

Camping There are 10 campsites to choose from. The closest to the town centre is *Boomerang Park* (☎ 6686 2220) on River St, a block east of the information centre, which has sites from $11 and cabins from $28. The best location is to be found at *Ballina Lakeside Caravan Park* (☎ 6686 3953), which borders on the Shaws Bay Lagoon off Fenwicke St. It has sites from $11 and cabins from $35.

Flat Rock Camping Park (☎ 6686 4848), about 5km north of town on the road to Lennox Head, is a good little camping area (tents only) just 100m from good surf. Sites are $10. There's a shop, hot showers and an ablutions block with laundry.

Hostel The *Ballina Travellers Lodge* (☎ 6686 6737) is a good, modern YHA associate at 36-38 Tamar St. They'll collect you from the bus stop. Dorm beds cost $14 and twins are $34. Bikes and boogie boards can be hired for $1 an hour and there's a pool.

Motels The *Ballina Travellers Lodge* is worth considering if you have deeper pockets, as it's also a good motel and one of the few in town which doesn't have highway noise. In the low season doubles go as low as $46, rising to around $80.

There are plenty of other motels along the highway and River St. Low-season rates get down to $35 a double at some places.

Near both Shaws Bay Lagoon and Lighthouse Beach, the *Ballina Beach Resort* (☎ 6686 8888; 1800 025 398) is well located, free of traffic noise and has good facilities. Accommodation includes doubles from $90 and family units from $125.

Houseboats *Ballina Quays Marina* (☎ 6686 4289), off the highway south of the Big Prawn, rents houseboats. Prices start at $90 for a small boat for one weeknight in the low season ($140 in the high season) for up to four people. The longer you hire, the cheaper it gets, and with over 100km of navigable river, there's plenty of space to explore.

Places to Eat

Shelley's on the Beach is the place to go for breakfast (from 7.30 am), lunch and snacks. It's a small kiosk-style cafe high above Shelly Beach with superb views of the sea and, sometimes, dolphins.

The huge modern *RSL Club* has a prime position on the riverbank on the corner of Grant and River Sts. The downstairs bistro is good value and has seating on a deck over the water.

Cafe Fresco, at the Henry Rous Tavern on the corner of Moon and River Sts, has a range of light meals and good coffee. It's open until midnight every night. There's a string of small restaurants on the other side of River St, including *Local Motion* (pasta) and *Mexican del Rio* with main courses for about $10 and cheaper snacks. The *Ballina Indian Takeaway*, diagonally opposite the courthouse on River St, has $5 curry lunches.

The restaurant at *Viennaworld*, the big service station next to the Big Prawn on the western edge of town, is reasonable for a highway stop and there are main course specials for under $10. It's open 24 hours.

Getting There & Away
Air Impulse flies to Brisbane, Ansett to Sydney.

Bus Long-distance buses stop at the Family Transit Centre at the Big Prawn, on the highway just west of town. Blanch's (☎ 6686 2144) has six buses a day to Lennox Heads ($3.60) and Byron Bay ($6.60), leaving from the Countrylink bus stop outside Jetset Travel on River St. Kirklands (☎ 6686 2992) also uses this stop for its regular buses to Lismore ($8.70).

Car & Motorcycle If you're heading to Byron Bay, take the coast road through Lennox Head. It's not only much prettier than the highway, but much shorter as well. Macadamia-nut fans might want to stick to the highway, as Macadamialand, north of Ballina, has free tastings as well as native birds and animals.

AROUND BALLINA
Inland from Ballina, the closely settled country of the north-coast hinterland begins, with winding, hilly roads running past tropical fruit farms, tiny villages and the occasional towering rainforest tree that somehow escaped the clearing of the forest which once covered the area.

Lennox Head
Lennox Head, 11km north of Ballina and 18km south of Byron Bay, is the name of both the small, pleasant town with a fine beach and the dramatic headland (a prime hang-gliding site) that overlooks it. It has some of the best surf on the coast, particularly in winter. **Lake Ainsworth**, just back from the beach, is a freshwater lake, good for swimming and windsurfing. Its dark colour is due to tea-tree oil, supposedly good for the skin and hair, seeping in from the surrounding vegetation.

Places to Stay *Lake Ainsworth Caravan Park* (☎ 6687 7249) has tent sites for $11 ($15 in high season) and cabins for $28 ($50).

Across the road is *Lennox Beach House Hostel* (☎ 6687 7636), purpose-built, very clean and very friendly. Both Lake Ainsworth and the beach are seconds away and you can use a cat and a windsurfer ($5 for as long as you stay). Boards, bikes and other sporting equipment are free. Dorm beds are $15 and there's a double for $35.

There are also a couple of motels.

Getting There & Away Pioneer Motor Service and Greyhound both call in at Lennox once a day and Blanch's stops here on the run between Ballina and Byron Bay.

BYRON BAY
Byron Bay (population 5000), one of the most popular stops on the whole east coast, is a relaxed little seaside town with superb beaches and a great climate – warm in winter, hot in summer. Despite the moans of long-time locals that tourism is over the top, the atmosphere remains very laid-back.

Byron is a meeting place of alternative cultures. It's almost a place of pilgrimage for surfers thanks to the superb surf below Cape Byron and is also close to the 'back to the land' lifestyles pursued in the beautiful far Nort! Coast hinterland. There are good music venues, wholefood and vegetarian eateries, off-beat people, distinctive craft and clothes shops, a thriving fashion and surf industry and activities ranging from didgeridoo making to trapeze lessons.

The Byron Bay market, in Butler St on the first Sunday of each month, is one of a series around the area at which the counterculture (almost establishment up here!) gets a chance to meet and sell its wares.

Orientation
Byron Bay is 9km north-east of the Pacific Highway turn-off at Bangalow, or 6km east of the turn-off further north. Jonson St, which becomes Bangalow Rd, is the main shopping street. The corner of Jonson and Lawson Sts is pretty well the town centre. South of the centre, along Tallow Beach, is the satellite development of Suffolk Park.

NORTH COAST

NORTH COAST

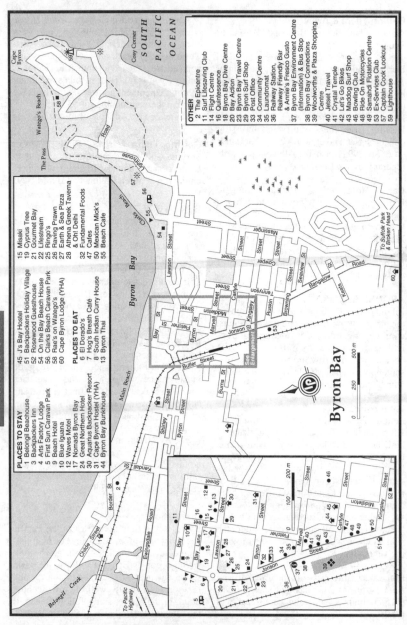

Byron Bay

PLACES TO STAY
1 Belongil Beachhouse
3 Backpackers Inn
4 Arts Factory Lodge
5 First Sun Caravan Park
9 Beach Hotel
10 Blue Iguana
12 Waves Motel
17 Nomads Byron Hotel
24 Great Northern Hotel
30 Aquarius Backpacker Resort
31 Cape Byron Hostel (YHA)
44 Byron Bay Bunkhouse
45 J's Bay Hostel
51 Backpackers Holiday Village
52 Rosewood Guesthouse
54 On the Bay Beach House
56 Clarks Beach Caravan Park
58 Rae's on Watego's
60 Cape Byron Lodge (YHA)

PLACES TO EAT
6 El Dorado's
7 Hog's Breath Café
8 South Indian Curry House
13 Byron Thai
15 Misaki
19 Cyprus Tree
21 Gourmet Bay
22 Lifestream
25 Ringo's
26 Raving Prawn
27 Earth & Sea Pizza
28 Athena Greek Taverna
     & Ohi Delhi
32 Fundamental Foods
47 Cafes
50 Mexican Mick's
55 Beach Cafe

OTHER
2 The Epicentre
11 Surf Lifesaving Club
14 Flight Centre
16 Quintessence
18 Byron Bay Dive Centre
20 Bay Action
23 Byron Bay Travel Centre
29 Byron Surf Shop
33 Post Office
34 Community Centre
35 Laundromat
36 Railway Station,
     Railway Friendly Bar
     & Annie's Fresco Gusto
37 Byron Bay Environment Centre
     (Information) & Bus Stop
38 Byron Bay Connections
39 Woolworths & Plaza Shopping
     Centre
40 Jetset Travel
41 Crystal Temple
42 Let's Go Bikes
43 Maddog Surf Shop
46 Bowling Club
48 Ride On Motorcycles
49 Samahdi Flotation Centre
53 Ex-Services Club
57 Captain Cook Lookout
59 Lighthouse

Information

The future of Byron Bay's tourist information service was the subject of heated debate at the time of research, the local council having closed its information centre on Jonson St in a cost-cutting frenzy. Tourist information was being handled by the Byron Bay Environment Centre, which has taken over from the former information centre in the old cottage outside the railway station. The situation may change. By 10 am on day one, environmentalists were already getting sick of answering questions about bus times – which you'll find posted up on the wall outside nearby Byron Bay Connections (☎ 6685 5981), along with fares and other information. You can store your bags here for $2 a day as well as buy tickets and book tours.

Read the quirky weekly *Echo* to get an idea of the way of life around here; the *Byron Shire News* mostly presents the view from the other side of the fence.

Travel Agents Travel agents include the Byron Bay Travel Centre (☎ 6685 6733) in Palm Court, opposite the Great Northern Hotel on Jonson St, Jetset Travel (☎ 6685 6554) on Marvell St near the corner of Jonson St and the Flight Centre (☎ 6685 5440) on Lawson St. The various other travel agents in town also handle most things – as with everything else in Byron Bay there's a fair degree of competition between them.

Cape Byron

Cape Byron was named by Captain Cook after the poet Byron's grandfather, who had sailed round the world in the 1760s. One spur of the cape is the most easterly point of the Australian mainland. You can drive right up to the picturesque 1901 lighthouse, one of the most powerful in the southern hemisphere. There's a 3.5km walking track right around the cape from the Captain Cook Lookout on Lighthouse Rd. It's circular, so you can leave bikes at the start (but lock them!). There's a good chance of seeing wallabies in the final rainforest stretch. A herd of feral goats, descendants of an early

lighthouse-keeper's flock, have lived here for about 80 years.

From the top you can often see schools of dolphins surfing through the waves below. During the season (best in June and July) whales swim past, sometimes quite close to shore. The area around the lighthouse (where the best lookouts are) closes at 5.30 pm.

If you were to sail due north from Cape Byron, the next landmass you'd meet would probably be eastern Siberia; heading south, the ocean rolls all the way down to Antarctica. Chile is the next stop east, but heading west it's a considerably shorter voyage – you'd probably end up on the beach in front of the Belongil Beachhouse.

Beaches

The Byron area has a glorious collection of beaches, ranging from 10km stretches of empty sand to secluded little coves. **Main Beach**, immediately in front of the town, is a good swimming beach and it sometimes has decent surf. The sand stretches 50km or more, all the way up to the Gold Coast, interrupted only by river or creek entrances and a few small headlands.

The eastern end of Main Beach, curving away towards Cape Byron, is known as **Clarks Beach** and can be good for surfing. The headland at the end of Clarks is called the Pass and the best surf is off here and at the next beach, **Watego's**. Further around is **Little Watego's**, almost at the tip of the cape. Dolphins are common, particularly in the surf off Watego's and Little Watego's.

South of Cape Byron, **Tallow Beach** stretches seven km down to a rockier stretch of shore around Broken Head, where a succession of small beaches dot the coast before opening on to **Seven Mile Beach**, which goes all the way to Lennox Head, a further 10km south.

The **Suffolk Park** area, behind Tallow Beach, is about five km south of central Byron Bay. One km further down the Byron to Lennox road is the turn-off to the Broken Head caravan park. About 200m before the caravan park, the unsealed Seven Mile Beach Rd turns off south and runs behind the rainforest of the **Broken Head Nature Reserve**. Seven Mile Beach Rd ends after five km (at the northern end of Seven Mile Beach), but several tracks lead down from it through the forest to the Broken Head beaches – **Kings Beach** (for which there's a car park 750m down Seven Mile Beach Rd) and **Whites Beach** (a foot track after about 3.25km) are just two good ones. Whites Beach is a nude beach.

A bike path runs all the way from Byron Bay to Broken Head.

Activities

There's a lot to do in and around Byron Bay. Hostels often have the best deals, but for a range of options it pays to check around a few hostels.

Surfing Most hostels have free boards for guests. Otherwise you will be up for around $20 a day to hire a board from places like the Byron Surf Shop (☎ 6685 7536), on Lawson St near Fletcher St, or Bay Action, at 14 Jonson St. You'll also find boogie boards, malibus and wetsuits. Several places offer lessons, including the Byron Surf Shop, which has three-hour lessons ($25) every day at 10 am and 2 pm. Perfect Break (☎ 6685 5980) runs three and five-day surf camps for beginners. North Coast Surfaris (☎ 1800 634 951) offers week-long surfing trips up the coast from Sydney to Byron Bay, stopping at out-of-the-way surf spots. Its bus leaves Sydney every Monday. The price of $249 includes camping and surfing gear and all meals. You'll need a sleeping bag.

Diving Divers come to Byron Bay to visit the **Julian Rocks Marine Reserve**, 3km north of Cape Byron. Cold southerly currents and warm northerly ones meet here, attracting a profusion of marine species from both. The most popular of the dives is the **Cod Hole**, known for its huge moray eels and blue groper. There's keen competition between the growing number of dive operators wanting to take you out there, so ask around to see who has the best deals. Three operators to check out are Byron Bay Dive Centre

(☎ 6685 7149), behind the Beach Hotel in Bay Lane; Sundive (☎ 6685 7755), in the Cape Byron Hostel complex on Middleton St; and Bayside Scuba (☎ 6685 8333), on the corner of Fletcher St and Lawson Sts.

Whitewater Rafting The nearest whitewater is a long way from Byron Bay. Rapid Rafting (☎ 6685 8687) has trips to Goolang Creek at Nymboida (see Coffs Harbour Activities), while Perfect Break (☎ 6685 5980) runs overnight trips to the Gwydir River at Inverell in season.

Flying The area is great for hang-gliding. Flight Zone (☎ 6685 8768) and Byron Bay Hang-gliding School (☎ (015) 257 699) both do tandem flights for $65 and offer tuition. They operate either from Cape Byron or from nearby Lennox Head – ring early to find out when and where the action is.

Trike flights (ultra-light aircraft) are run by Skylimit (☎ 6684 3711) and cost from $50 for half an hour. Skylimit also offers tandem hang-gliding. Skydive (☎ 6684 1323) has tandem skydiving; prices start at $198 for midweek jumps (minimum two people).

Kite-flying is popular and most days around 4 pm you'll see plenty on Main Beach or Tallow Beach, depending on the wind. Byron Kites (☎ 6685 5299) in the Cape Byron Hostel complex will sell you a kite or you can rent one for $20, which includes tuition and five hours flying.

Byron Air Charter (☎ 6684 2753) has joyflights as well as charters and a very short flight can work out at around $15 per person. It operates from Tyagarah airport, midway between Byron Bay and Brunswick Heads.

Whale & Dolphin Spotting Humpback whales can often be seen off Cape Byron during their northerly migration in June/July and again on their return journey between September and November. The Byron Bay Whale Centre was homeless as we went to press, following its departure from the lovely little cottage it occupied up on Cape Byron.

Dolphins are much easier to find. Byron

Bay Sea Kayaks (☎ 6685 5830) gets lots of takers for its breakfast with the dolphins off Main Beach.

Trapeze Potential circus stars can head out to the Flying Trapeze (☎ 6685 8000), west of town at the Byron Bay Beach Club. The operators offer the opportunity to make your first catch on a flying trapeze at the end of a two-hour lesson. It gets rave reports and sounds like good value at $20.

Alternative Therapies

There are at least two flotation-tank places: Samadhi (☎ 6685 6905) on Jonson St opposite Woolworth's and Relax Haven (☎ 6685 8304) at the Belongil Beachouse. These places also do massage – at Relax Haven you can get an hour in the tank and an hour-long massage for $40.

Several other places offer massage, acupuncture and alternative therapies; other outfits drift into the fuzzier edges of alternative thought. If you need your chakra realigned, contact Quintessence Healing Sanctuary (☎ 6685 5533) at 8/11 Fletcher St. It offers a wide range of services, everything from clairvoyance to sports massage!

Organised Tours

Byron Bay Bush Tours (☎ 6684 0253) and Jim's Alternative Tours (☎ 6685 7720) both run day tours of the spectacular North Coast hinterland. Jim's also has trips to The Channon markets on the second Sunday of each month and to Bangalow on the fourth Sunday.

Byron Bay Harley Tours (☎ 6685 5900) will show you the area from the back of a Harley Davidson, with rates starting at $35 for 30 minutes.

Places to Stay

There's an astonishing array of places where you can stay and more places are opening up all the time. While backpackers have long been well served, Byron now has some excellent options at the top end of the market as well.

Caravan Parks & Cabins During holidays the best sites will probably be taken and around Christmas/January and Easter you'll be lucky to find *any* kind of site. If you need camping equipment, try Byron Bay Disposals in the Plaza shopping centre on Jonson St.

The council has four caravan parks, all by beaches. *First Sun Caravan Park* (☎ 6685 6544) has a good location, on Main Beach and very close to the town centre, but there's no shade. Sites start at $10 for one person, plus $3.50 for each extra person, rising to $22 plus $7 at peak time – absurdly expensive for a tent site. There's a range of cabins, the cheapest going for $43 in the low season and $75 at the peak. *Clarks Beach Caravan Park* (☎ 6685 6496) is off Lighthouse Rd about one km east of the town centre and has plenty of trees. Prices are fractionally cheaper.

Down at Suffolk Park on Tallow Beach, *Suffolk Park Caravan Park* (☎ 6685 3353) is a friendly place with shady sites and cabins for a lot less than at First Sun.

Further south, the small council-run *Broken Head Caravan Park* (☎ 6685 3245) is behind a popular surf beach and the area is surrounded by Broken Head Nature Reserve. Sites cost from $10, rising to $15 at peak times. There are also cabins from $35. You'll need to bring supplies.

Belongil by the Sea (☎ 6685 8111) is an all-cabin place next to Belongil Beachouse hostel. The cabins are self-contained, with cooking facilities, and prices start at $45 for two people.

Hostels The moment travellers step off the bus they will be aware of fierce competition between the town's numerous hostels. Awaiting them will be a line-up of touts from all the places – 10 at the last count, with talk of more in the pipeline. While some people find the touts a bit daunting, the set-up does allow you to find out immediately where the best deals are. Not surprisingly, you'll find the cheapest rates at the places furthest from the beach – especially at quiet times. Prices peak around Christmas/January, when you should book. Most hostels offer fairly similar packages, with free use of bikes and surfboards. If you're planning a lengthy stay, check around to see which suits you best.

There are two YHA-affiliated hostels, including the new *J's Bay Hostel* (☎ 6685 8853, 1800 678 195 for reservations) on the corner of Carlyle and Middleton Sts. It's spotless and well equipped, with rooms laid out around a couple of central courtyards – one of which contains a heated swimming pool. Dorm beds are $15 and there are doubles for $40 ($42 with ensuite). The setup is very similar at the other YHA representative, the *Cape Byron Hostel* (☎ 6685 8788), 200 metres closer to the beach on Middleton St. Its rates are much the same.

A significant newcomer on the scene is *Nomads Byron Bay* (☎ 6685 8695), part of the expanding Nomads group. It has come up with a good site in the shape of the old council chambers on Lawson St, vacated by the council's move to Mullumbimby. A lot of money has been spent on the place and it shows. Many rooms are in a newer wing out the back. Dorms cost $15, doubles/twins $40.

Further east on Lawson St is the *Aquarius Backpacker Resort* (☎ 1800 028 909 tollfree), formerly the Aquarius Motel and now enjoying a new lease of life as a very well appointed hostel. The motel rooms have been converted into small dorms, each with their own ensuite bathroom, TV and fridge. Dorm beds are $16 and doubles are $45.

If you're looking for the spirit of Aquarius (the 1973 festival that brought counterculture to this region), the place to head is the amazing *Arts Factory Lodge* (☎ 6685 7709), with its permaculture gardens, clever recycled furnishings and creative energy. There's always something going on: didgeridoo making, music, yoga etc. There's a choice of accommodation from tent sites ($8) to teepees and converted double-decker buses ($14). Dorm beds are $15 and doubles start at $36. Philosophically sound food is available at the adjoining Piggery Cafe. The Arts Factory is a few minutes' walk west of

the town centre on Skinners Shoot Rd. It runs a regular shuttle bus to the beach.

It's a toss up as to which of the beach hostels is actually the closest to the sea. The *Backpackers Inn* (☎ 6685 8231), about half a km from the town centre at 29 Shirley St, is one of the contenders. To get to the beach you just walk across the lawn, cross the railway line (carefully!) and climb a sand dune. The hostel itself is a modern place with a pool and all the usual features. Rates start at $17 for dorms, $51 for doubles.

The stylish *Belongil Beachouse* (☎ 6685 7868) is a great place to stay – well run, relaxed and friendly. It's off Childe St, a quiet road adjacent to the beach. The cafe here is a big plus, with excellent healthy food served between 8 am and 10 pm. There's a nightly half-price special for guests. You can store gear here for $5 a week. Beds in small dorms are $17 and basic doubles are $38. There are also large doubles with ensuite and spa for $70 and two-bedroom cottages for $80. Rates for the better rooms rise sharply in peak season.

The *Blue Iguana Beachouse* (☎ 6685 5298), opposite the surf club on Bay St, has beds in four-person dorms for $15 during the week, rising to $20 at weekends and more at peak times.

The *Backpackers Holiday Village Hostel* (☎ 6685 8888), just past the Woolworth's complex on Jonson St, is a clean, friendly, well-equipped place with a small pool and spa. Dorm beds are $17, doubles $42 ($47 with ensuite). The *Byron Bay Bunkhouse* (☎ 6685 8311), on Carlyle St, is another new place. It lists dorms for $13 and doubles for $40. *Cape Byron Lodge* (☎ 6685 6445) is a couple of km from the town centre at 78 Bangalow Rd (the southern end of Jonson St) and likes to point out that it's only about 10 minutes' walk to Tallow Beach. There's a small pool and bikes are free. This is usually the cheapest hostel in town, with dorm beds starting at $10, doubles at $30.

Guesthouses & B&Bs There's a modest boom in guesthouses and/or B&Bs in the area. Most cater for those with deeper pockets and are discussed in the following Top End section.

Byron Bay Bed & Breakfast (☎ 6685 8230), 16 Marvell St, has singles/doubles for $28/48, rising to $58 for doubles only at peak times.

Hotels & Motels The *Great Northern Hotel* (☎ 6685 6454) on Jonson St has singles/doubles for $30/40 in low season, rising to $35/45.

Motels such as the *Wollongbar* (☎ 6685 8200) at 19 Shirley St, the *Bay Beach* (☎ 6685 6090) and *Byron Sunseeker* (☎ 6685 7369), 100 Bangalow Rd, have doubles from around $60 in the off-season. Prices skyrocket around Christmas/January and Easter and to a lesser extent during other school holidays. The *Bay Mist* (☎ 6685 6121) is a standard motel but it has a good position opposite the beach on Bay St. In the off-season you'll get a double room for $70 but around Christmas, January and Easter you'll pay $150.

Self-Catering Holiday houses and apartments start from around $350 a week in the off-season, $600 during school holidays and close to $1000 at Christmas. Letting agents include Elders (☎ 6685 6222) on Jonson St near the station, which handles bookings for the two old cottages at the lighthouse on Cape Byron. There's a two-bedroom cottage for $450 a week off-season and a three-bedroom cottage for $550. Rents rocket to $1200 and $1300 a week at Christmas.

Special Needs The *Wheel Resort* (☎ 6685 6139), just south of town on Broken Head Rd, is designed and run by wheelchair users for travellers with disabilities. Rates start at $75 for a cabin for up to three people.

Top End The latest addition to the emerging luxury market is the accommodation wing at the *Beach Hotel* (☎ 6685 6402) on Bay St. Downstairs rooms open onto lush gardens with a heated pool, while the 1st-floor rooms have ocean views. Standard rooms are priced from $155 and luxury rooms with spa start

at $205. The rates go up slightly in peak times.

The nearby *Waves Motel* (☎ 6685 5966), on the corner of Lawson and Middleton Sts, is a posh motel with units for $120 (rising to $185) and suites for $185 ($275). If you're prepared to pay this sort of money, you should check some of the B&Bs. *Rosewood House* (☎ 6685 7657) is a beautifully restored old timber house at 16 Kingsley St, near the corner of Jonson, charging $100/135 for singles/doubles, rising to $140/170 at peak times. *On the Bay Beach House* (☎ 6685 5125) has a prime position just east of town at 44 Lawson St and rooms for $160/185, rising to $185/210.

Rae's on Watego's (☎ 6685 5366) is a gleaming-white fantasy palace overlooking Watego's Beach. Room rates start at $200.

Places to Eat
People don't come to Byron Bay to spend time slaving over a hot stove. Places to eat are everywhere in the town centre and the choice verges on the overwhelming. You could dine out for months without going to the same place twice. Vegetarians are well catered for.

Breakfast Breakfast is served all over town but the place to go is the *Beach Cafe*, overlooking Clarks Beach. It isn't cheap but the views are superb. It opens at 7.30 am and stays open for lunch and dinner.

Ringo's is a cafe/secondhand bookstore on Jonson St with good coffee and bacon and eggs for $6.50.

Bottom End *Byron Bay Ex-Services Club* at the southern end of Jonson St has lunches for $2.90 every day, plus a range of specials in the evening.

The local council continues to stand firm in its resolve to keep the major junk food dealers out of town, encouraging an abundance of interesting small takeaway places. The northern end of Jonson St is the place to look. The options include a couple of kebab joints, Mexican food at *El Dorado's* and Thai noodle dishes and stir fries at the *Gourmet*

Bay. The *Cyprus Tree* on Bay Lane does souvlakis and homemade Greek dips, while *Earth 'n' Sea* on Lawson St is more imaginative than most pizza parlours with creations like 'Mullumbimby Madness' (vegetarian) and the 'Krakatoa' (enough chilli to spark an eruption).

Middle The famous *Beach Hotel* on Bay St has a wide range of snacks such as burgers from $4.50 and more substantial meals like satays ($9.50) and steaks (from $12.50). Heading down Jonson St from here, *South Indian Curry House* is a long-time favourite, with most main courses around $10. It's open nightly for dinner.

Wild at the Rails is open for lunch and dinner every day at the Railway Friendly Bar and has a mixed menu that includes Asian and Moroccan dishes. Further along Jonson St is the licensed *Mexican Mick's*, open for dinner from Tuesday to Saturday. It's an old favourite and is still reasonably priced. It often has special deals for backpackers.

Every other place on Lawson St seems to be a restaurant. They include *Oh! Delhi* (northern Indian), *Athena Taverna* (Greek) and *Byron Thai*.

Top End For a bit of a blow-out, try the excellent *Misaki Byron* on Fletcher St. Most main courses are around $18, or $23 for beautifully presented plates of sushi or sashimi.

The *Raving Prawn*, off Jonson St in the Feros Arcade, has an interesting modern menu. It specialises in seafood with most main courses around $20.

Out at Watego's Beach, *Rae's on Watego's* is a smart seafood place on Marine Parade, with great views over the beach. It's open every day for lunch and dinner.

Vegetarian Vegetarians can look forward to a choice of good restaurants. Foremost among them is *20,000 Cows*, open for dinner every day from 6 pm; it's by the Epicentre, west of town on Kendall St. You pass it on the way to the *Belongil Beachouse*, whose cafe/restaurant is also predominantly vegetarian.

Strictly Vego, in the Woolworth's complex, leaves no doubt about what it serves. It has an all-you-can-eat vegetarian smorgasbord for $9.95. It's open Monday to Saturday for lunch and dinner. Out at the Arts Factory, the *Piggery Supernatural Food Restaurant* is every bit as cosmic as the name suggests.

Other vegetarian possibilities include *Lifestream*, a large health-food cafe where you can put together a decent meal for $5. It's opposite the Great Northern Hotel on Jonson St. *Fundamental Foods*, next to the post office, has a huge range of goodies as well as organically grown fruit and vegetables. The *Byron Thai* has an unusually large vegetarian selection.

Entertainment

The busy nightlife is another of Byron Bay's major drawcards. You'll find a gig guide in the *Byron Shire News*, published on Wednesday.

The *Railway Friendly Bar* has live music most nights. The *Beach Hotel* and the *Great Northern Hotel* have live bands from Thursday to Saturday nights and sometimes on Sunday afternoons. Touring bands play at the *Ex-Services Club* at the southern end of Jonson St.

The *Pighouse Flicks* cinema, next to the Arts Factory in the old Piggery, is like no other cinema you'll have encountered. It shows an eclectic mix of cult movies, old favourites and whatever else they can lay their hands on. Call the movie hotline (☎ 6685 5828) to find out what's on.

Getting There & Away

Air The closest airport is at Ballina, but most people use the much larger airport at Coolangatta on the Gold Coast in Queensland. It has frequent direct flights from both Sydney and Melbourne, but you still have to get down to Byron.

Bus All the major bus-lines come through Byron Bay, stopping in the middle of town

RICHARD l'ANSON

JON MURRAY

JON MURRAY

North Coast
Top: Colourful shopfronts in the main street of Nimbin
Middle: Tallow Beach from Cape Byron
Bottom: Food van, Seal Rocks

Eucalypt forest with a fern understorey

Eucalypt Forest

The eucalypt tree is typically Australian but there is no typical eucalypt forest. Depending on climate and soil, you may find mountain ash (the world's tallest flowering plant), stunted alpine gum, hardy arid land ironbark or desert gum. Understorey ranges from moist ferns to dry acacias, sedges and grasses. Eucalypt-associated faunas reveal similar variety. Although there are over 600 species of eucalypt, only a handful of species in the south-east of the continent are eaten by the koala. Less particular are the common possums, the brushtail and the ringtail, who both supplement their diets of eucalypt leaves with fruits and insects. Announcing its presence with a familiar laugh, the kookaburra is a daytime hunter of lizards, snakes, frogs and small mammals. Grey kangaroos and wallabies may be seen moving into open forest in the evenings to browse shrubs and graze native grasses. Also out for a nightly forage, the common wombat, a relative of the koala, grazes its home range before returning to one of its large and conspicuous burrows.

RICHARD I'ANSON

Alpine gums are hardy enough to survive the climatic extremes
of Australia's alpine regions

RICHARD TIMBURY

Eucalypt forest covers vast expanses of Australia's landscape.
There are over 600 varieties of eucalypt, or gum tree.

Right: Despite there
being hundreds of
species of eucalypt in
Australia, the koala will
only dine on the leaves
of a select few

Far Right: The flower of
the eucalypt, showing
the distinctive cap on
the flower bud

RICHARD I'ANSON

RICHARD I'ANSON

Top: The surf at Byron Bay, north coast
Bottom Left: Terania Creek, Nightcap National Park, north coast
Bottom Right: Antarctic Beech Forest, New England National Park

on Jonson St. Typical fares are Brisbane $21, Sydney $62, Coffs Harbour $33 and Surfers Paradise $19. You can get all the way up to Cairns for $148, passing Airlie Beach ($116) on the way. Backpacker Travel, near the bus stop, sells tickets. Kirklands' Lismore-Brisbane route passes through Byron Bay and stops in other useful places such as Mullumbimby, Murwillumbah, Tweed Heads and Coolangatta airport.

Train Byron Bay is on the Sydney to Murwillumbah line, with a daily train in each direction, plus several rail/bus services. From Sydney ($79) the quickest service is the 7.05 am XPT, which reaches Byron Bay at 7.30 pm. This train continues to Murwillumbah and connects with a bus to Brisbane. The southbound train stops in town at 10 am. The fare to Coffs Harbour is $32.60.

Car & Motorcycle Rental Earth Car Rentals (☎ 6685 7472) has older cars from $35 a day (including 200 free km), more recent vehicles from $45 and new cars from $50. Jetset Travel (☎ 6685 6554) rents small current-model cars for $35 a day plus 15c per km.

Ride on Motorcyles (☎ 6685 6304), on Jonson St opposite Woolworth's, hires motorbikes from $50 a day. You need a motorbike licence, Australian or foreign.

Getting Around

Bus Blanch's (☎ 6686 2144) serves the local area with destinations such as Mullumbimby ($3.60) and Ballina ($6.60).

Bicycle The hostels lend bikes of varying quality to guests. Byron Bay Bicycles (☎ 6685 6315) in the Plaza shopping centre on Jonson St has good single-speed bikes for $12 a day, including helmet, and geared bikes for $18 a day. Let's Go Bikes (☎ 6685 6067), nearby on Jonson St, has single-speed bikes at $15 a day.

Taxi If you need a cab, call Byron Bay Taxis (☎ 6685 5008).

BRUNSWICK HEADS

Brunswick Heads (population 1700) is a small fishing town that's popular for family holidays. It's quite a pleasant place, with the Brunswick River and a good beach, but nearby Byron Bay overshadows its modest attractions.

Places to Stay & Eat

Terrace Reserve Caravan Park (☎ 6685 1233) is close to the beach and the town centre. At Christmas and Easter all accommodation, except perhaps tent sites, is booked out well in advance. Sites cost $11, rising to $15, and cabins with attached bathrooms are $38 ($70).

Heidelberg Holiday Inn (☎ 6685 1808), close to both beach and river, is the pick of three motels. Singles/doubles go for $42/48, double that at peak times.

There's good seafood at the Fins complex on the Pacific Highway. It includes the *River Thai*, which gets enthusiastic reports.

Getting There & Away

Long-distance buses on the Sydney-Brisbane runs can drop you here. The fare from Byron Bay is $6.50 with Kirklands.

THE TWEED COAST

The Pacific Highway north of Brunswick Heads curves inland to Murwillumbah (see the North Coast Hinterland section) then back to the coast at Tweed Heads. There's also a route along the Tweed Coast which is a little shorter but probably slower.

It won't be many years before the stretch of coast between Brunswick Heads and Tweed Heads is overrun by housing estates, in the all-too-familiar process whereby a superb area is ruined by tasteless developers and short-sighted local governments. Meanwhile, there are still large gaps between the cream-brick ghettoes and a series of fine beaches.

The coastal road is sealed north of **Wooyung**; the Wooyung turn-off from the highway is about 7km north of Brunswick Heads. There's a basic *camping* area at Wooyung and from here a dirt track, very rough and sandy, runs south along the coast to Golden Beach, near the big Ocean Shores residential development. Don't try this track after rain. **Wooyung Camel Farm** (☎ (015) 674 937) has 30-minute rides for $12 ($5 children), two-hour sunset rides to the beach for $30 and overnight trips for $100.

North of Wooyung, near Mooball Beach, **Pioneer Plantation** (☎ 6677 1215) is a banana plantation with a restaurant, bar and tours.

Next stop north is **Pottsville**, another residential development. After Pottsville you come to **Cabarita Beach** (also known as **Bogangar**) which has good surf and tends to have it even when other areas are quiet.

At Cabarita Beach there's a good purpose-built hostel, the *Emu Park Backpackers Resort* (☎ 6676 1190). It's one of the cleanest hostels around and the rooms are large. Dorm beds are $13 and there's a 'stay two nights, get the third night free' deal outside school holidays. Doubles cost $28 and there's an ensuite double with TV for $38. Bikes and boards are free and the beach is a minute away. The staff will drop you off at Mt Warning and pick you up after your climb for about $45 – not bad among several people. Guests can be picked up from Coolangatta.

Close to Cabarita is **Cudgen Lake**, a freshwater lake where you can hire cats and windsurfers ($15 an hour) and canoes (from $5 an hour). The hire shop is part of *Cabarita Gardens Lake Resort* (☎ 6676 2000), a motel and apartment complex with singles/doubles from $80/90. **Kingscliff** is next north and is almost an outer suburb of Tweed Heads. It's a little older and a little less raw than the beachside developments further south.

TWEED HEADS

Sharing a street with the more developed Queensland resort of Coolangatta, Tweed Heads (population 4900) marks the southern end of the Gold Coast strip. The north side of Boundary St, which runs along a short peninsula to Point Danger above the mouth of the Tweed River, is in Queensland. This end of the Gold Coast is much quieter than the resorts closer to Surfers Paradise.

Orientation

Tweed Heads sprawls south of the Tweed River, but the older town centre is quite a compact area north of the Tweed. Coming from the south, after the new bypass road branches off, the Pacific Highway crosses the river on narrow Boyds Bay Bridge and becomes Wharf St, the long main street. Wharf St ends near the Twin Towns Services Club (a large cylindrical building), with Griffith St running across the border into Coolangatta and Boundary St running east up a steep hill to the end of Point Danger.

Griffith St runs north for a few blocks then meets McLean St, which leads east to Marine Parade, Coolangatta's beachfront promenade.

Information

The Tweed Heads Visitor Centre (☎ (07) 5536 4244), at the northern end of Wharf St, just south of the giant Twin Towns Services Club, is open daily from 9 am to 5 pm. There's also an information kiosk (☎ (07) 5536 7765) in the Beach House complex on the corner of Marine Parade and McLean St in Coolangatta. It's open Monday to Friday from 8 am to 4 pm, Saturday 10 am to 4 pm. The main information centre for the Tweed region is in Murwillumbah.

Things to See & Do

The towering **Captain Cook Memorial** straddles the state border at Point Danger. The 18-metre-high monument was completed in 1970 (the bicentenary of Cook's visit) and is topped by a laser-beam lighthouse visible 35 km out to sea. The replica of the *Endeavour's* capstan is made from ballast dumped by Cook after the *Endeavour* ran aground on the Great Barrier Reef and was recovered along with the ship's cannons in 1968. Point Danger was named by Cook after he nearly ran aground there too. There are views over the Tweed Valley and the Gold Coast from the **Razorback Lookout**, three km from Tweed Heads.

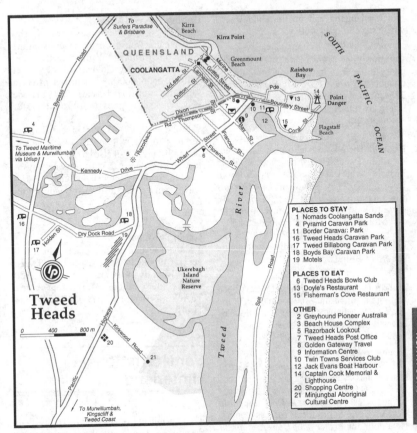

PLACES TO STAY
1 Nomads Coolangatta Sands
4 Pyramid Caravan Park
11 Border Caravan Park
16 Tweed Heads Caravan Park
17 Tweed Billabong Caravan Park
18 Boyds Bay Caravan Park
19 Motels

PLACES TO EAT
6 Tweed Heads Bowls Club
13 Doyle's Restaurant
15 Fisherman's Cove Restaurant

OTHER
2 Greyhound Pioneer Australia
3 Beach House Complex
5 Razorback Lookout
7 Tweed Heads Post Office
8 Golden Gateway Travel
9 Information Centre
10 Twin Towns Services Club
12 Jack Evans Boat Harbour
14 Captain Cook Memorial & Lighthouse
20 Shopping Centre
21 Minjungbal Aboriginal Cultural Centre

Tweed Heads

0   400   800 m

There are several good **beaches**, most in Queensland. Coolangatta's Kirra Point is famous for its surf and Rainbow Bay, on the northern side of Point Danger, is another patrolled beach.

On Kirkwood Rd in South Tweed Heads, the **Minjungbal Aboriginal Cultural Centre** (☎ (07) 5524 2109) has exhibits on the history and culture of the Minjungbal people who once owned this area. You can also buy authentic souvenirs. The nearby *bora* ground is a traditional ceremonial site. A boardwalk runs through the mangroves of adjacent Ukerebagh Island Nature Reserve. It's open

Monday to Friday from 9 am to 5 pm, weekends 9 am to 3 pm. Admission is $6.

The **Tweed Maritime Museum** on Kennedy Drive in Tweed Heads West has old photos and other bits and pieces and is open on Tuesday and Friday afternoon; admission is $1 (50c children).

Tweed Endeavour Cruises (☎ (07) 7536 8800) has a two-hour cruise for $22 ($11 children) and a four-hour cruise with a seafood buffet lunch for $48 ($24 children).

Places to Stay
Accommodation in Tweed Heads spills over

into Coolangatta and up the Gold Coast, where the choice is more varied.

Camping There are many, many caravan parks in the area. In town on Coral St is the council's *Border Caravan Park* (☎ 7536 3134). It's well located but a bit cramped. There are others south of the main centre – see the map.

Hostels There's no backpacker accommodation in Tweed Heads, but there are three hostels over the Queensland border in Coolangatta. They include the new *Nomads Coolangatta Sands* (☎ (07) 5536 3066), close to the beach on the corner of Griffith and McLean Sts. It has dorm beds for $12. There's a *YHA hostel* (☎ (07) 7536 7644) a bit further up the coast in the Coolangatta suburb of Bilinga.

Motels The motels along Wharf St have been feeling the pinch since the completion of the Tweed Heads bypass and you'll find doubles advertised for as little as $30.

Places to Eat

The *Tweed Heads Bowls Club* on Wharf St has specials such as weekday roast lunches for under $5; the other clubs are also sources of cheap eats. The smaller *Rowing & Aquatic Club* on Coral St has meals for less than $8. Next door, the *Fishermans Cove Restaurant* is known for its seafood and has main courses averaging around $16. At Rainbow Bay, on the northern side of Point Danger, *Doyle's on the Beach* has excellent seafood takeaways and a restaurant.

Entertainment

The large *Twin Towns Services Club* on the corner of Wharf St and Boundary St and *Seagulls Rugby Club* on Gollan Drive in West Tweed Heads have regular touring acts. Seagulls is open 24 hours. The *Bowling Club*, south of the Services Club on Wharf St, and the *Golf Club* south of town also have entertainment.

Getting There & Away

All long-distance buses stop at the Coolangatta Transit Centre which is on the corner of Griffith and Warner streets. Ticket sales are handled by Golden Gateway Travel (☎ (07) 5536 6600). Coachtrans offers a same-day return to Brisbane for $20, $12 one way. Kirklands goes to Byron Bay for $13.80.

Surfside (☎ (07) 5594 0055) has frequent services to Murwillumbah ($4.20) and to Kingscliff ($2.80). It also has six buses a day to Cabarita Beach ($3.50) on weekdays – three on Saturday and two on Sunday. Buses leave from outside the Tweed Heads Visitor Centre.

Getting Around

There are several car-hire places which will get you moving for $35 a day, such as Tweed Auto Rentals (☎ (07) 7536 8000), 100 metres south of the information centre. There's a 24-hour taxi service (☎ (07) 6634 1144).

Far North Coast Hinterland

The area inland from the Pacific Highway in far northern New South Wales covers some spectacular country. It's home to a high population of 'alternative lifestylers', the first of whom were attracted to the area by the Aquarius Festival at Nimbin in 1973. They have become a prominent and colourful part of the community.

The country between Lismore and the coast was once known as the Big Scrub, an incredibly inadequate description of a place that must have been close to paradise at the time of European incursion. Much of the 'scrub' was cleared for farming, after the loggers had been through and removed the prized red cedar. These days the region is marketed as Rainbow Country.

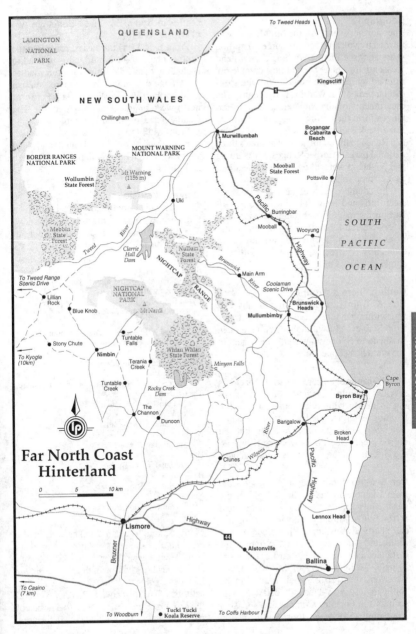

Far North Coast Hinterland

0   5   10 km

NORTH COAST

Geography

The northern part of the hinterland was formed by volcanic activity some 20 million years ago (see the Mt Warning section) and is essentially a huge bowl almost completely rimmed by mountain ranges, with the spectacular peak of Mt Warning in the centre. The escarpments of the McPherson and Tweed ranges form the north-western rim, with the Razorback Range to the west and the Nightcap Range to the south-west. The area's three national parks – Border Ranges, Mt Warning and Nightcap – are all World Heritage areas, as are some smaller nature reserves.

The country south of here is a maze of steep hills and beautiful valleys, some still harbouring magnificent stands of rainforest, others cleared for cattle-grazing and plantations – especially macadamia nuts and avocados. Coffee is a new crop that is showing a lot of promise.

Getting There & Around

Bus & Train Lismore, Mullumbimby and Murwillumbah are served by XPT trains from Sydney; Murwillumbah is on the main Brisbane to Sydney bus route and Lismore has good bus connections.

Local Transport There are some local bus services, mainly slow schoolbuses, emanating from Murwillumbah and Lismore, but hitching is an accepted way to get around. You rarely see lone women hitching, but you do see plenty of pairs of women. However, see Hitching in the Getting Around chapter.

Car & Motorcycle The area is accessible from Lismore in the south, Kyogle in the west, Murwillumbah in the north-east and Byron Bay or Mullumbimby in the east. You can nearly always approach a place by one route and leave by another. Nimbin, for instance, can be reached from Lismore, Kyogle, Mullumbimby or Murwillumbah. However, the web of small roads can be confusing, so you'll need a detailed map, such as the Forestry Commission's Casino Area map ($5) – the tourist information

centres in Byron Bay and Nimbin are two places that sell it.

From Byron Bay the easiest route into the southern half of the hinterland is to head to Bangalow then follow the Lismore road to the village of Clunes, from where you can head north to Whian Whian State Forest or north-west on the Dunoon road for The Channon and, eventually, Nimbin.

From Mullumbimby, a scenic but rough track leads north to Uki and small roads lead south-west to Whian Whian, The Channon and Lismore.

Markets & Music

The alternative community can be seen in force at the weekend markets listed below. The biggest market is at The Channon, between Lismore and Nimbin.

Brunswick Heads
    1st Saturday of the month, behind the Ampol
    service station
Byron Bay
    1st Sunday, Butler St Reserve
Lismore
    1st and 3rd Sunday, Lismore Shopping Square;
    5th Sunday, Heritage park
Murwillumbah
    1st Sunday, Sunnyside Shopping Centre
Lennox Heads
    2nd and 5th Sunday, Lake Ainsworth foreshore
The Channon
    2nd Sunday, Coronation Park
Mullumbimby
    3rd Saturday, Museum
Ballina
    3rd Sunday, Fawcett Park
Uki
    3rd Sunday, Old Buttery
Bangalow
    4th Sunday, Showground
Nimbin
    4th Sunday, Showground

Many accomplished musicians live in the area and they sometimes play at the markets or in the village pub after the market (notably at Uki). Friday's edition of the *Northern Star* includes a guide to the week's gigs and other activities. The *Brunswick Byron Echo* and the *Lismore Echo* newspapers give notice of most musical and cultural events in the area.

LISMORE

Lismore (population 41,500), 35km inland from Ballina on the Bruxner Highway to New England, is the main town of the state's far north. Once little more than a service centre for the productive surrounding district, it has developed into a cosmopolitan town with a large student population from the Northern Rivers campus of the University of New England. The local cultural agenda is strongly influenced by the alternative community which is based in the country to the north.

Orientation & Information

Lismore lies on the east bank of the Wilson River, a major tributary of the Richmond River. The Bruxner Highway becomes Ballina St as it runs through town. The main shopping street is Molesworth St.

The Information & Heritage Centre (☎ 6622 0122) is near the Wilson River on the corner of Molesworth and Ballina Sts. There's a good rainforest display here, costing $1 (50c children), but make sure you see the real thing as well. You can buy topographic maps, which are essential for

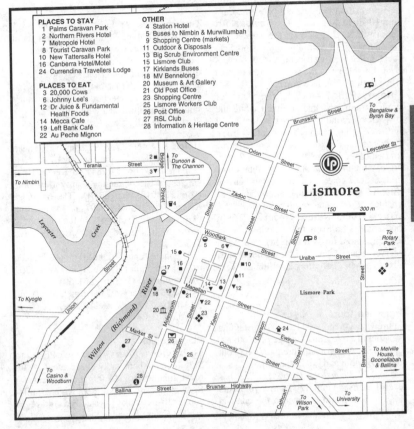

PLACES TO STAY
1 Palms Caravan Park
2 Northern Rivers Hotel
7 Metropole Hotel
8 Tourist Caravan Park
10 New Tattersalls Hotel
16 Canberra Hotel/Motel
24 Currendina Travellers Lodge

PLACES TO EAT
3 20,000 Cows
6 Johnny Lee's
12 Dr Juice & Fundamental Health Foods
14 Mecca Cafe
19 Left Bank Café
22 Au Peche Mignon

OTHER
4 Station Hotel
5 Buses to Nimbin & Murwillumbah
9 Shopping Centre (markets)
11 Outdoor & Disposals
13 Big Scrub Environment Centre
15 Lismore Club
17 Kirklands Buses
18 MV Bennelong
20 Museum & Art Gallery
21 Old Post Office
23 Shopping Centre
25 Lismore Workers Club
26 Post Office
27 RSL Club
28 Information & Heritage Centre

NORTH COAST

bushwalking and useful even if you're driving around the narrow roads in this area.

The Big Scrub Environment Centre (☎ 6621 3278) on Keen St also sells topographic maps and the volunteers who staff it might know of interesting events in the area. The district's NPWS office (☎ 6628 1177) is in Alstonville, east of Lismore on the road to Ballina.

The Outdoor 'n' Disposals shop (☎ 6621 3371) on Keen St rents camping gear.

Things to See & Do

The **Richmond River Historical Society Museum**, 165 Molesworth St (not far from the information centre), is open weekdays from 10 am to 4 pm ($2). The **Regional Art Gallery** at No 131 is open the same hours from Tuesday to Saturday, admission free. Local artists are well represented. Across from the gallery is the interesting old post office with its iron-lace dome.

Rotary Park is a six-hectare patch of remnant rainforest that survived while the town grew around it. The park is dominated by towering hoop pines and giant fig trees. It's just off the Bruxner Highway about three km east of the information centre on Rotary Drive, which is the easterly continuation of Uralba St. Access is from Rotary Drive. **Wilson Park**, off Wyrallah St on the southern edge of town, has resident koalas.

Tucki Tucki Nature Reserve, 16km south of Lismore on the Woodburn road (leave Lismore on Wyrallah St), is a koala reserve. There's an Aboriginal **bora ring** nearby, where initiation ceremonies were held.

Organised Tours

Naturewise (☎ 6621 6118), at Currendina Travellers Lodge, runs a range of ecotours. They include a permaculture tour, a day out around Nimbin and koala-spotting.

The MV *Bennelong* (☎ 6621 7729) has several cruises, ranging from two hours ($10) to a day cruise down to the coast at Ballina ($50).

Places to Stay

Caravan Parks *Palms Caravan Park* (☎ 6621 7067) by the river on Brunswick St and the small *Tourist Caravan Park* (☎ 6621 6581) on Dawson St are the closest to the town centre.

Hostel *Currendina Travellers Lodge* (☎ 6621 6118) occupies a fine old weatherboard building at 14 Ewing St. It was originally a hospital – Currendina means 'place of healing' in the language of the local Bundjalung Aborigines. It's a cosy place close to the city centre with dorms for $15, singles from $25 to $28 and doubles from $35 to $45.

Guesthouses *Melville House*, (☎ 6621 5778) 267 Ballina St, has B&B from about $40/60 or $30/45 with a shared bathroom. Further east, off Ballina St in the Goonellabah area, *Tulloona House* (☎ 6624 2897) is a National Trust-classified Victorian mansion with a huge garden. The rooms are huge and are furnished with antiques. Rates start at $50 a double.

Hotels & Motels There are some very cheap deals to be found at pubs in town. The *New Tattersalls* (☎ 6621 2284) on Keen St has singles for $15, while the nearby *Metropole* (☎ 6621 4910) charges $18. The *Northern Rivers Hotel* (☎ 6621 5797), at the junction of Terania and Bridge Sts on the road out to Nimbin, has good singles/doubles for $18/25.

The more central of the 10 motels include the *Centre Point* (☎ 6621 8877) at 202 Molesworth St (from $61/69), *Karinga* (☎ 6621 2787) at No 258 (from $49/57) and *AZA* (☎ 6621 9499) at 114 Keen St (from $50/55).

Places to Eat

The *Northern Rivers Hotel* (see Places to Stay) does unbelievably cheap meals, with roast lunches for $1.99 and dinners for $2.99. Opposite the Northern Rivers, philosophically as well as physically, is the vegan *20,000 Cows* on Bridge St.

In the town centre, *Dr Juice* on Keen St is open during the day for excellent juices and smoothies, plus vegetarian and vegan snacks. Next door is *Fundamental Health Foods*, a big health-food shop.

The large *Mecca Cafe* on Magellan St is decidedly non-vegetarian, with burgers (a Big Mec is $4.50) and other fast food. *Johnny Lee*, 75 Woodlark St, has Chinese and Vietnamese food and does smorgasbord lunch and dinner every day for $8.50.

Au Peche Mignon is a great little French patisserie on Carrington St near Magellan St. It has good coffee as well as croissants and cakes.

Entertainment
There are plenty of pubs and clubs with entertainment, such as *Powerhouse* at the Canberra Hotel on Molesworth St and the *Satellite Room* at the Commercial Tavern on Keen St. The *Station Hotel* in Union St, South Lismore, has country music on Saturday afternoon. The *Lismore Club* in Club Lane, off Molesworth St, has folk, blues and jazz on the first, second and third Thursdays of the month.

Getting There & Away
Air There are daily flights to Brisbane (Impulse) and Sydney (Hazelton).

Bus Kirklands (☎ 6622 1499) is based here and runs buses around the immediate area as well as further afield. Destinations include Byron Bay ($10.50), Mullumbimby ($11), Murwillumbah ($14.60) and Brisbane ($27.20). There's a handy service to Tenterfield in New England ($21.10) on weekdays.

Justice Bus Service (☎ 6621 6231) operates a daily bus to Nimbin ($9.90) and Murwillumbah ($13.70) weekdays only. It leaves from Woodlark St at 2 pm.

Train The XPT train from Sydney ($79) stops here.

Getting Around
Kirklands has urban-area buses and there are 24-hour taxis (☎ 6621 2618).

THE CHANNON
The Channon, a tiny village off the Nimbin to Lismore road, hosts the biggest of the region's markets on the second Sunday of each month. There is sometimes a dance in the town hall the night before the market (the *Lismore Echo* will have details) and often music at the market.

The Channon Teahouse & Craftshop is a pleasant place for a snack or a light meal and there's interesting craftwork to browse through. It's open daily, 10 am to 5 pm, with dinner on Friday and Saturday nights. The village's information centre (☎ 6688 6276) is here as well.

About 15km north up Terania Creek Rd is the rainforest of Nightcap National Park.

Places to Stay
The Channon Village Campsite (☎ 6688 6321) is basic but pretty and costs $4 per person. Out of town on the road to Terania Creek, *Terania Park Camping Ground* (☎ 6688 6121) has on-site vans and cabins as well as tent sites.

NIGHTCAP NATIONAL PARK
This park of nearly 5000 hectares is a World Heritage Area of outstanding beauty. There are three main sections.

The **Terania Creek** area, accessible from The Channon, protects a stunningly beautiful rainforest valley (some of the brush-box trees are estimated to be more than 1500 years old) and very diverse bird and animal species. From the picnic area, a 700-metre walk leads to **Protesters' Falls**, named after the environmentalists whose 1979 campaign to stop logging was a major factor in the creation of the national park. If the protesters hadn't won the battle, this area, then a state forest, would have been clear-felled!

Mt Nardi (800 metres), a steep rise 12km from Nimbin, has thick forest and good views. There are several walking trails that lead from the summit, including a 1km walk to Mt Matheson and the beautiful **Pholis Walk**, off the track to Mt Matheson. The views from **Pholis Gap** are particularly spectacular. From Mt Matheson an 8km track connects with the **Nightcap Track**, a packhorse trail which was once the main route between Lismore and Murwillumbah.

The western end of the park around **Mt Burrel** (933m) is accessible only to experienced walkers.

Place to Stay

The only *camping* area within the park is at Terania Creek (access is via The Channon). It's free but you're supposed to stay only one night. No fires are allowed.

NIMBIN

The Aquarius Festival of 1973 transformed the declining dairy town of Nimbin (population 1300), 30km north of Lismore, into a name almost synonymous with Australia's 'back to the land' counter-culture movement. It's still a very active alternative centre (even the real estate agent has a ponytail) and there are many communes ('multiple-occupancy properties') in the area. You're still likely to be asked if you want to buy some 'green' as you walk along the street.

Orientation & Information

Despite the size of its reputation, Nimbin is just a tiny village – admittedly somewhat larger than life. Cullen St is the main street through town. At the north end, near the Freemasons Hotel, a street curves away to the left, crosses a bridge and becomes Blue Knob Rd; Cullen St curves away to the right and runs past the caravan park, then climbs to the summit of Mt Nardi, 12km away.

The Nimbin Connection Ecotourist Centre (☎ 6689 1764), at the northern end of Cullen St, has tourist information. It can also arrange horseriding and trekking.

Look out for a copy of the booklet *Nimbin & Environs* for $3. It has guides to local sights and services and gives the local history. *Nimbin News*, the community newspaper, is also essential reading.

Things to See & Do

The weird and wonderful **Nimbin Museum** is on Cullen St near the Rainbow Cafe. Admission is by donation. It's worth a visit for the conversations you'll have before you get through the door.

Many people come to the area to visit **Djanbung Gardens** (☎ 6689 1755), a permaculture education centre established by Robyn Francis – a disciple of permaculture guru Bill Mollison. Contact the centre for information about courses. The centre, a five-minute walk from the town centre on Cecil St, is open for information on Thursday from 10 am to 2 pm and gives a guided tour on market days at 2 pm.

The town's biggest employer is the **Rainbow Power Company** (☎ 6689 1430). The address (No 1 Alternative Way) says a fair bit about the company. It designs and produces what it calls 'appropriate home energy systems' that use the sun, wind and water to generate electricity. These systems are sold all over the world. You can visit the complex, which is behind the caravan park.

Nimbin Explorer (☎ 6689 1557) has two-hour tours of the Nimbin area for $12 and day trips to Border Ranges National Park ($25).

Special Events

There's an annual Mardi Grass Festival at the end of April which culminates in the famous Marijuana Harvest Ball.

Nimbin holds a good market on the fourth Sunday of the month and you may catch a local band playing afterwards.

The Nimbin Show is held in late September.

Places to Stay

The council's basic *caravan park* (☎ 6689 1402) is near the bowling club – go down the road running past the pub. Sites cost $9, on-site vans $25.

Granny's Farm (☎ 6689 1333), an associate-YHA hostel, is a relaxed place surrounded by farmland, with platypus in the nearby creek. It also has a swimming pool. There's a range of accommodation, with

Nimbin People

There are a lot of different people in Nimbin and visitors try often to force them into the roles of ambassadors for their various cultural perspectives. David Hallett, in his poem *Labels of Babels*, lists, among 70 other types of people:

hippies & yuppies & greenies & junkies
smokers & tokers & dope thieves & jokers & mopers
ball-kickers & ball-hitters & ball-tearers with pit-bull terriers
drummers & dancers & dip-sticks & dobbos
yobbos & touros & musos & preggos & embryos
journos & photos & lezzos & homos
sapiens & hetero sapiens
& not-so-sapiens ■

conventional dorm beds for $13 and doubles from $30. Other options are the teepee or 'pleasure dome' (tent) for $10 per person and creekside camping for $7.50 per person. The friendly managers sometimes give rides to places of interest. To get there, go north along Cullen St and turn left just before the bridge over the creek.

Rainbow Retreat (☎ 6689 1262) is a new place just outside town with great views from its hilltop setting. The atmosphere is very laid-back. There's a good swimming hole on the creek below the guesthouse and plenty of bush to explore. Beds in dorms or doubles (if available) are $10. Phone from town for a free pick-up, or call in and see the owner, Doug, at the Nimbin Connection.

Nimbin's upmarket option is *Grey Gum Lodge* (☎ 6689 1713), a stylishly renovated weatherboard house on the road into town from Lismore. Singles/doubles are $25/40 and breakfast is available at $5 per person.

Places to Eat

The *Rainbow Cafe*, in the centre of town on Cullen St, promotes itself as the place where more than a million joints have been smoked, doubtless leading to some serious assaults on the range of delicious cakes (priced from $2.50). There are also various vegetarian snacks and meals for around $6. It also serves breakfasts, as does the nearby *Nimbin Rocks Cafe*, the closest thing you'll find to a standard country-town cafe. Across the street, *Choices* has healthy (and not so healthy) takeaways and light meals. At the northern end of Cullen St, *Nimbin Pizza & Trattoria* has pasta from $8.50 and is open daily from 5 pm.

If you have your own transport, check out

the delightful *Calurla Tea Garden* (☎ 6689 7297), 11km from town on the edge of Nightcap National Park. To get there, take Blue Knob Rd north out of Nimbin and turn onto Lillian Rock Rd after 8km. It's open daily from 10 am to 7 pm and until late on Friday and Saturday nights.

Entertainment
If there's a dance at the town hall, don't miss the opportunity to meet up with the friendly people from the country around Nimbin.

The *Freemasons Hotel* often has music and the *Bush Theatre* at the old butter factory near the bridge at the northern end of town has films on Friday and Saturday.

Getting There & Away
Bus Free Spirit Tours operates a daily service between Byron Bay and Nimbin for $12, leaving from outside Byron Bay Connections at 10 am and returning from the Nimbin Connection at 1 pm. Justice Bus Service (☎ 6679 5267) calls at Nimbin on its morning school run from Murwillumbah to Lismore and again on the afternoon return.

Car & Motorcycle The main routes to Nimbin are from Lismore to the south and off the Murwillumbah to Kyogle road 23km west of Uki.

Hitching Hitching is pretty easy in this part of the world (but see Hitching in the Getting Around chapter). Heading south, most hitch-hikers stand near the church; heading north, the bridge on Blue Knob Rd is popular.

Around Nimbin
The country around Nimbin is superb. See the earlier Nightcap National Park section for information on Mt Nardi.

The Tuntable Falls commune, one of the biggest, with its own shop and school – and some fine houses – is about nine km east of Nimbin and you can reach it by the public Tuntable Falls Rd. You can walk to the 123-metre **Tuntable Falls** themselves, 13km from Nimbin. **Nimbin Rocks**, an Aboriginal sacred site, lie about 6km south of town, well

signposted off Stony Chute (Kyogle) Rd. **Hanging Rock Creek** has falls and a good swimming hole; take the road through Stony Chute for 14km, turn right at the Barker's Vale sign, then left onto Williams Rd; the falls are nearby on the right.

The **Nimbin Rocks Gallery** (closed on Wednesday) has a large collection of local artworks. It's off the Lismore road beyond the Stony Chute turn-off.

MULLUMBIMBY
This pleasant little town (population 2700), known simply as Mullum, is in subtropical countryside five km off the Pacific Highway between Bangalow and Brunswick Heads. The distinctive cone of Mt Chincogan is just outside the town. Perhaps best known for its marijuana ('Mullumbimby Madness'), it's a centre for a long-established farming community as well as for the alternative folk from nearby areas.

Orientation & Information
Burringbar St is the main shopping street and runs off Dalley St, the main road through town.

The Lyrebird Motel (☎ 6684 1725), at the northern end of Dalley St, acts as the information centre. There are plenty of noticeboards around town; the best is probably at Santos Health Foods on Stuart St.

Things to See & Do
There's a short **walk** through rainforest by the Brunswick River.

This area is rich in artists and craftspeople and some of their work is displayed in the **Arts Gallery** (☎ 6684 1573), near the corner of Burringbar and Stuart Sts. It's open Tuesday to Friday from 10 am to 5 pm and Saturday from 10.30 am to 3 pm, daily during school holidays. The **museum**, open from 1 to 4 pm (2 to 5 pm during daylight saving), Wednesday to Friday, is off the southern end of Stuart St, in the old post office.

Although none are very grand, Mullum has some nice old buildings and their setting in this quiet town makes them seem even finer. **Cedar House**, at 140 Dalley St, has been recommended for National Trust listing. It houses an antique shop.

Special Events
A market is held at the museum on the third Saturday of the month.

The local festival is the Chincogan Fiesta, held in early September. There are bands, free camping and events such as the Chincogan Charge, a race up nearby Mt Chincogan. The agricultural show is held in mid-November.

Places to Stay
North of Mullumbimby, 12km out on Main Arm Rd, *Maca's Camping Ground* (☎ 6684 5211) is an idyllic place. On a macadamia-nut plantation, under the lee of hills lush with rainforest, it's a relaxed spot with a lot of room to move. While it's nothing like a commercial caravan park, the facilities are quite good, with a communal kitchen, hot showers and a laundry. You'll need to bring all your food supplies. It costs $6 per person ($2 children) and you can hire a tent or teepee for $6 a day. To get here, take Main Arm Rd out of Mullumbimby, go through the hamlet of Main Arm, then the sub-hamlet of Upper Main Arm and Maca's is on the right just past the school. There are blue 'Camping' signs at the intersections pointing the way.

Motels are the only option in town. *Mullumbimby Motel* (☎ 6684 2387), 121 Dalley St (the south end), has doubles for $35 outside school holidays, rising to $70. The *Lyrebird* (☎ 6684 1725), at the other end of Dalley St, is fractionally dearer.

Places to Eat
Popular Cafe on Burringbar St is Mullum's version of the country town caf and it is appropriately named. The *Pizza Hive* on Station St has vegetarian meals as well as pizza, while *Buon Appetito* on Stuart St has inexpensive pastas (from $3.50) and pizzas to eat there or take away. *Mullum House*, 103 Stuart St, is a good Chinese restaurant with main courses under $10.

The *Chincogan Tavern* and the old *Com-mercial Hotel* have inexpensive counter meals and the Tavern has live music a couple of nights a week. The *Ex-Services Club* on Dalley St and the *Bowling Club* on Jubilee Ave (the southern continuation of Dalley St) also have meals.

Getting There & Away
Bus Most Kirklands buses go through Mullum on their Lismore ($11) to Brisbane ($21.10) run. The newsagent on the corner of Burringbar and Stuart Sts is the Kirklands agent. There's no direct service to/from Byron Bay; you have to travel via Brunswick Heads.

Train Mullum is on the Sydney ($79) to Murwillumbah railway.

Car & Motorcycle The most direct route to Mullum from the Pacific Highway turns off just south of Brunswick Heads, but it's worth taking the longer but prettier Tunnel Rd route which leaves the highway north of Brunswick Heads, near the Ocean Shores turn-off. There's also the Coolaman Scenic Drive, which leaves the highway between Bangalow and the Byron Bay turn-off. For a superbly scenic drive to Uki and Mt Warning, head out to Upper Main Arm, pass Maca's Camping Ground (see Places to Stay for directions) and follow the unsealed road through the Nullum State Forest. Keep to the main road and watch for signposts at the few ambiguous intersections. It's a narrow road and steep where it crosses the range, but in dry weather it's OK if you take it easy and watch out for logging trucks. Don't try it after rain or you stand a good chance of sliding off the mountain, literally.

WHIAN WHIAN STATE FOREST
Whian Whian is west of Mullumbimby and adjoins the south-eastern side of Nightcap National Park. On the south-eastern side of the state forest, **Minyon Falls** plunge 100m into a rainforest gorge and the surrounding area is a flora reserve with several walking tracks.

Access to the reserve is on the Minyon

Drive which cuts across the south-eastern corner of the state forest. Peates Mountain Rd runs off Minyon Drive and heads north to **Peates Mountain Lookout**, with views to the coast and on to *Rummery Park*, a Forestry Commission campsite with pit toilets and cold showers. Koalas live in the nearby forest. The eastern end of the Night-cap Track walking trail emerges on the road beyond Rummery Park.

The south-western corner of Whian Whian is the **Big Scrub Flora Reserve**, the largest surviving chunk of the vegetation which once covered the Richmond Valley.

UKI

Uki (pronounced 'uke-eye') is a pretty village of 200 souls, dominated by the peak of Mt Warning. It's most famous for its big market, held at the old buttery on the third Sunday of the month. The Trading Post (☎ 6679 5351) restaurant is a helpful information centre.

Places to Stay & Eat

At *Uki Village Guesthouse* (☎ 6679 5345), next to the Trading Post in an old weather-board home, B&B costs $55 for one or two people and at weekends it's $55/75 a single/double. For $160 a double you have B&B plus a five-course seafood dinner. They will pick you up from Murwillumbah. Children aren't allowed.

The licensed *Uki Trading Post* serves light meals and Devonshire teas by day and dinner at night, seven days a week. Main courses cost $7 to $11 and vegetarians are catered for.

Around Uki There are quite a number of other places to stay in the area, mostly geared to holiday-makers. *Mt Warning Forest Hideaway* (☎ 6679 7139), 12km south-west of Uki on Byrill Creek Rd, has motel units with cooking facilities from $38/45. *Midginbil Hill Farm Resort* (☎ 6679 7158) has B&B from $46/69 and fully catered rooms for $105/169. Activities include horseriding and canoeing on the Clarrie Hall dam.

Getting There & Away

Bus Justice Bus Service (☎ 6621 6231) stops at Uki on the run between Murwillumbah and Lismore.

Car & Motorcycle Uki is on the main road between Murwillumbah and Kyogle. The turn-off to Mt Warning is four km north of Uki; the turn-off to Blue Knob and Nimbin is 23 km west of Uki.

See Getting There & Away under Mullumbimby for information on a drive through the Nullum State Forest.

MT WARNING NATIONAL PARK

The dramatic peak of Mt Warning (1157 metres) dominates the whole district. It was named by Captain Cook as a landmark for avoiding Point Danger off Tweed Heads. The mountain is the former central magma chamber of an immense volcano formed more than 20 million years ago. It once covered an area of more than 4000 sq km, stretching from Coraki in the south to Beenleigh in the north and from Kyogle in the west to an eastern rim now covered by the ocean. Erosion has since carved out the deep Tweed and Oxley valleys around Mt Warning, but sections of the flanks survive as the Nightcap Range in the south and parts of the Border Ranges to the north.

The road into the national park runs off the road between Murwillumbah and Uki. It's about six km to the car park at the base of the track to the summit. Much of the 4.5-km walk is through rainforest. The final section is steep (to put it mildly), so allow five hours for the round trip. Take water. If you're on the summit at dawn you'll be the first person on the Australian mainland to see the sun's rays that day! The trail is well marked, but you'll need a torch if you're climbing at night (to reach the summit at dawn).

Even if you don't want to climb Mt Warning it's worth visiting for the superb rainforest in this World Heritage Area. There's a short walking track near the car park.

Places to Stay

You can't camp at Mt Warning but the *Wollumbin Wildlife Refuge & Caravan Park* (☎ 6679 5120), on the Mt Warning approach road, has tent sites ($10), on-site vans (from $24) and cabins ($35). The vans and cabins cost less if you stay more than one night. There are kitchen facilities and a well-stocked kiosk – and lots of wildlife in the 120-hectare refuge, including koalas and platypus in the Tweed River. See the Uki section for more accommodation in this area.

Getting There & Away

Justice Bus Service (☎ 6621 6231) can drop you right at the base of the mountain ($3.80) on its morning school run from Murwill-umbah to Lismore. If you ask nicely, the driver will pick up on the return run at about 5 pm.

MURWILLUMBAH

Murwillumbah (population 9000) is in an area of banana and sugar-cane plantations in the broad Tweed Valley. It's also the main town in this part of the north-coast hinterland and there are several communes and 'back to the land' centres in the area, plus Hare Krishna World. You're also within reach of Mt Warning and the spectacular NSW-Queensland border ranges. You can cross into Queensland by the Numinbah Rd through the ranges between the Springbrook and Lamington areas.

Information

The tourist information centre (☎ 6672 1340) is on the Pacific Highway near the railway station. It has a good rainforest display.

Things to see & Do

The excellent **Tweed River Regional Art Gallery** is just up the road from the hostel. As well as a portrait collection and works relating to the Tweed area, there are often interesting temporary exhibitions. It's open Wednesday to Sunday from 10 am to 5 pm; admission is free. The gallery administers Australia's richest prize for traditional portraiture, the $100,000 Doug Moran Prize. Past winners are on display. The **museum** is on Queensland Rd and is open on Wednesday and Friday, from 11 am to 4 pm. Admission is $1.

The century-old **Condong Sugar Mill**

NORTH COAST

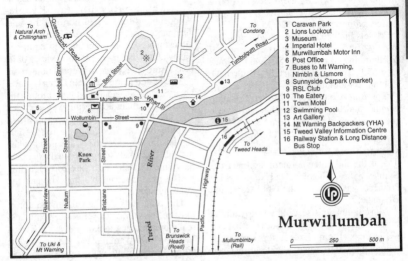

1 Caravan Park
2 Lions Lookout
3 Museum
4 Imperial Hotel
5 Murwillumbah Motor Inn
6 Post Office
7 Buses to Mt Warning, Nimbin & Lismore
8 Sunnyside Carpark (market)
9 RSL Club
10 The Eatery
11 Town Motel
12 Swimming Pool
13 Art Gallery
14 Mt Warning Backpackers (YHA)
15 Tweed Valley Information Centre
16 Railway Station & Long Distance Bus Stop

Murwillumbah

0   250   500 m

(☎ 6672 2244), 5km north of Murwill-umbah, has guided tours ($4, $2.50 children) daily during the crushing season, approximately from July to November.

Avocado Adventureland, off the highway just north of Stotts Island, might make a good break for the kids, with some rides and native animals as well as many varieties of tropical fruit and a restaurant. It's open daily.

Murwillumbah Aero Club (☎ 6672 3235) has scenic flights around Mt Warning and the surrounding ranges for $30 per person at weekends.

Places to Stay & Eat

The associate-YHA *Mt Warning Backpackers of Murwillumbah* (☎ 6672 3763) has a great location beside the Tweed River at 1 Tumbulgum Rd – you'll see it on the right as you cross the bridge into town. There are views over to Mt Warning from the verandah. Owner Tassie runs a friendly house with lots of activities, including free canoes and a rowing boat. You can hire bikes for $5 a day and Tassie has drawn up a list of rides. Dorm beds are $13, singles/twins $18/30.

Several pubs have accommodation, including the solid *Imperial Hotel* (☎ 6672 1036) on the main street across from the post office, with rooms from $20/35.

Motels include the *Murwillumbah Motor Inn* (☎ 6672 2022), on the corner of Wollumbin and Byangum Sts, and the *Town* (☎ 6672 1633) on Wharf St. Both have doubles for around $50.

The *Eatery* on Main St is open Friday to Sunday and has a mixed Asian and Aussie menu with main courses from $8 to $15.

Getting There & Away

This is the end of the northern rail line from Sydney ($85). There's a daily train which connects with a bus to the Gold Coast and Brisbane.

Murwillumbah is served by nearly all the buses on the Sydney (about $60) to Brisbane ($17) coastal run. Except for Kirklands, which goes into town, the long-distance buses stop at the railway station by the highway.

Getting Around

Justice Bus Service (☎ 6621 6231) operates a daily bus to Uki ($4.60) and Nimbin ($9.90) and, weekdays only, to Lismore ($13.70). It leaves from Knox Park in Murwillumbah at 7 am. Surfside runs to Tweed Heads ($3.80).

You can hire bikes from Jim's Cycle Centre for about $10 a day.

BORDER RANGES NATIONAL PARK

The Border Ranges National Park, a World Heritage Area of 31,500 hectares, covers the NSW side of the McPherson Range, which runs along the NSW-Queensland border, and some of its outlying spurs. The park's wetter areas protect large tracts of superb rainforest and it has been estimated that a quarter of all bird species in Australia can be found in the park.

There are three main sections. The eastern section, which includes the escarpments of the massive Mt Warning caldera, is the most easily accessible, via the Tweed Range Scenic Drive (see below). The smaller central section is accessible from the Lions Rd, which turns off the Kyogle-Woodenbong road 22km north of Kyogle. The large and rugged western section is almost inaccessible except to well-equipped bushwalkers, but there are good views of its peaks from the Kyogle to Woodenbong road.

The **Tweed Range Scenic Drive** – gravel but useable in all weather – loops through the park from Lillian Rock (midway between Uki and Kyogle) to Wiangaree (north of Kyogle on the Woodenbong road). The signposting on access roads isn't good (when in doubt take roads signposted to the national park), but it's well worth the effort of finding it. The road is unsuitable for caravans and large vehicles.

The road runs through mountain forest most of the way, with some steep hills and really breathtaking lookouts over the Tweed Valley to Mt Warning and the coast. The adrenalin-charging walk out to the crag called **the Pinnacle** – about an hour's walk from the road and back – is not for vertigo sufferers! At **Antarctic Beech** there is, not surprisingly, a forest of Antarctic beeches. Some of these trees are more than 2000 years old! From here, a walking track (about five km) leads down to **Brindle Creek**, where there is stunningly beautiful rainforest and a picnic area. The road also runs down to Brindle Creek.

From the **Sheepstation Creek** campsite a walking track connects with the Caldera Rim Walk (three or four days) in Lamington National Park, over the border in Queensland.

Mebbin State Forest is by the eastern

section of the Border Ranges National Park – this is the bush you will see if you dare to look down when you're on the Pinnacle. There's free camping at **Byrill Creek**, on the eastern side.

Places to Stay

There are a couple of NPWS *campsites*, basic but free, on the Tweed Range Scenic Drive. *Sheepstation Creek* is about 15km north of the turn-off at Wiangaree (north of Kyogle) and *Forest Tops* is 6km further on, high on the range. There are toilets but no showers. Tank water might be available but it's best to BYO.

New England

New England is the area on top of the Great Dividing Range, stretching north from around Newcastle to the Queensland border. It's a vast tableland of sheep and cattle country with many good bushwalking areas, photogenic scenery and, unlike much of Australia, four distinct seasons. If you're travelling along the eastern seaboard, it's worth taking a longer route through an inland area like New England now and then to get a glimpse of non-coastal Australia – which has a different way of life, is at least as scenic as the coast and suffers from a great deal less tourist hype.

History

Graziers first came to New England in the 1830s in search of new land. At the time, it was illegal for colonists to venture beyond the Hunter Valley and these graziers became known as squatters because they 'squatted' on land that didn't belong to them. Although they were technically outlaws, many were eventually granted long leases on huge tracts of land and became influential citizens of the colony.

New England was once called New Caledonia and that name should have stuck because of the large numbers of Scottish people involved in the area's settlement. Place names reflect this association – Armidale, Inverell and Glen Innes, which even has its own ring of Celtic-style 'standing stones'.

Geography

New England is a large, high tableland. North of Armidale the plateau rises steeply and snowfalls are common in winter. The eastern edge of the tableland ends at a steep and often densely forested escarpment, dropping down to the coastal plains below. Along this edge is a string of fine national parks, some of them World Heritage areas. Gorges and waterfalls are common features and most parks offer at least basic camping. The

HIGHLIGHTS

- People-watching at the Tamworth Country Music Festival
- Autumn colours in Armidale
- Whitewater rafting in the Nymboida River
- The Wollomombi Falls, near Armidale, especially after rain

western side of the tableland dwindles down to the plains.

Activities

Bushwalking Most of New England's national parks offer walking, some through very wild country.

Whitewater Canoeing & Rafting The Nymboida River is popular for both canoeing and whitewater rafting. Every summer, water is released from Copeton Dam (near Inverell), turning part of the Gwydir River into a challenging whitewater course.

Two companies that offer rafting in New England are Whitewater Rafting Professionals (☎ 6651 4066) and Wildwater Adventures (☎ 6653 4469), both based in Coffs Harbour.

Horseriding Steve Langley (☎ 6732 1599), based near Glen Innes, arranges 'pub crawls on horseback', lasting from three days to a

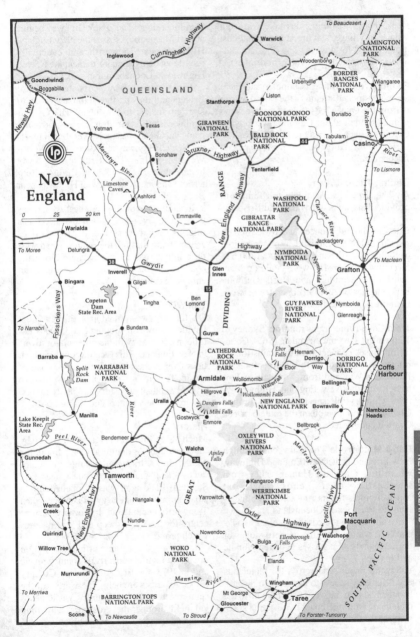

New England

0   25   50 km

QUEENSLAND

To Beaudesert
To Lismore
To Maclean
To Moree
To Narrabri
To Merriwa
To Newcastle
To Stroud
To Forster-Tuncurry

NEW ENGLAND

SOUTH PACIFIC OCEAN

week. These leisurely rides take you from village to village, staying at pubs, and cost around $900 for a week. The rides are suitable for any standard of rider (or drinker).

Fishing Trout fishing is popular and there are many stocked streams – the closed season is from the Queen's Birthday long weekend in June to the Labour Day long weekend in October. Other species are also fished. The various information centres have maps and further details.

Getting There & Away
Air The airports at Armidale and Tamworth provide daily links to Sydney and Brisbane.

Bus Greyhound Pioneer and McCafferty's run through New England from Melbourne or Sydney to Brisbane. Kean's (☎ 1800 625 587) runs between Tamworth and Port Macquarie via Armidale and Coffs Harbour. Kirklands (☎ 6622 1499) operates between Lismore and Tenterfield.

Train Countrylink trains run from Sydney to Tamworth ($58) and Armidale ($65). Countrylink buses connect with the trains for the run from Tamworth up to Inverell along the Fossickers Way and from Armidale to Tenterfield up the New England Highway. A third Countrylink service passes through Glen Innes and Inverell on the route between Grafton and Moree.

Car & Motorcycle The main route through New England is the New England Highway, which runs along the Hunter Valley from Newcastle, then heads north at Muswellbrook for its run across the tablelands to Warwick in Queensland.

An alternative route is the quieter Fossickers Way, which skirts the western slopes of the tablelands as it passes between Nundle and Inverell.

Several major roads cross the tablelands and offer easy access to the coast to the east and the plains to the west. Climbing up to the tablelands from the coast is usually a spectacular trip through the forests of the Great

Dividing Range. The Oxley Highway begins at Port Macquarie, crosses the New England Highway near Tamworth and eventually runs down onto the plains to meet the Newell Highway at Coonabarabran.

The Waterfall Way starts just north of Urunga and runs up the Bellinger Valley to Dorrigo and on to Armidale. The Gwydir Highway starts at Grafton, crosses the tablelands via Glen Innes and Inverell and meets the Newell Highway at Moree on the North-Western plains. The Bruxner Highway begins near Lismore, runs through Tenterfield and meets the Newell Highway near Boggabilla.

In addition to these major east-west roads there are many smaller, often unsealed roads offering even more spectacular forest drives as they wind through the ranges. Head west on a minor road from anywhere along the coast and you're almost guaranteed an enjoyable drive.

TAMWORTH
On the dry western slopes of the Great Divide, Tamworth (population 35,000) has little in common with the other major towns in New England. This is cattle country which ticks over to the plaintive twang of country music. The area's 'heritage' doesn't revolve around Scottish ancestors and misty moors, but around steel guitars and riding boots.

History
Much of the Tamworth area was taken up by the Australian Agricultural Company in the 1830s, after it 'traded in' its huge but unproductive land grant on the coast near Port Stephens. The area wasn't opened up to small farming until early this century, when Tamworth became an important service centre for the beef, sheep and wheat farms which provide the area's wealth.

In the 1960s, a Tamworth radio station organised regular concerts of country music and in 1973, the first Australasian Country Music Awards were held. These are now the centrepiece of the big Country Music Festival held around the Australia Day long weekend (see Special Events below).

Orientation

Tamworth lies on the northern flank of the wide Peel Valley, between the river and a range of forested hills. Behind the city centre, the older residential area runs up into these hills, with fine views back across the valley. The newer areas of West and South Tamworth are south of the centre, on the flatter land across the river.

The New England Highway is called Goonoo Goonoo Rd (pronounced 'gunna-g'noo') as it passes through the long sprawl of South Tamworth and crosses the Peel River to the city centre, where it becomes Brisbane St. Then, after a right-angled corner, it becomes Marius St, then Armidale Rd as it heads south-east on its way to Armidale (don't worry, it turns north some way out of Tamworth).

The main shopping area is bounded by Peel, Bourke, Marius and White Sts.

Information

Guitar-shaped things are all the rage, starting with the new tourist information centre (☎ 6766 9422) on the corner of Peel and Murray Sts. Pick up a map of the Heritage Walk (1½ hours), which begins at the junction of Brisbane St and Kable Ave in the city centre. You'll also find information on the longer Kamilaroi Walking Track, which begins at the Oxley Scenic Lookout, high on a hill at the northern end of White St. There are also maps of day tours around the area.

For a detailed guide to the area around Tamworth, buy a copy of Fred Hillier's *Fred's Tamworth Backtracks* ($15) at the information centre.

Country Music Paraphernalia

The **Country Collection**, on the New England Highway in South Tamworth, 4.5km south of the centre, is not hard to spot – out the front is the 12m-high Golden Guitar. Inside is a wax museum displaying effigies of 20 Aussie country music stars and, incongruously, a rock, gem and mineral display. It's open daily and admission is $4 ($2 children).

Nearby, the **Longyard Hotel** is a popular venue during the festival and presents C&W music through the year. It also holds diverse events such as cutting-horse competitions, cattle sales and highland games.

The **Heritage Hall**, opposite Tamworth Shopping World on Bridge St in West Tamworth, claims to display the largest collection of Australian country music paraphernalia ever assembled. Entry is $5 ($2 children) and it's open from 10 am to 3 pm (closed on Monday).

In town, the **Winners' Walkway** in Treloar's Arcade off Brisbane St commemorates the winners of the Golden Guitar award. Near the information centre on the corner of Kable Ave, the **Hands of Fame** are the handprints of country music luminaries. Not to be outdone, Tattersall's Hotel on Peel St has **Noses of Fame**! Other country music memorabilia around town include the collection of photos at the Good Companions Hotel, the guitar-shaped swimming pool at the Alandale Flag Inn Motel and the Hawking Brothers memorial at the Country Capital Motel on Goonoo Goonoo Rd.

Tamworth's recording studios are sometimes open to visitors – ask at the information centre.

Oxley Marsupial Park

There are friendly kangaroos and other native animals at this reserve on Endeavour Drive, the northern continuation of Brisbane St. Nearby (but accessible from the top of White St) is the **Oxley Scenic Lookout**.

Powerstation Museum

Tamworth's streets were the first in the country to be lit by electric light (in 1888) and this museum in the restored power station contains a working steam-powered generator. It's open Tuesday to Friday from 9 am to 1 pm and admission is free.

Calala Cottage

Calala Cottage, on Denison St in West Tamworth, was built in 1875 and is today part of a small cluster of reconstructed historic buildings. It's open Tuesday to Friday

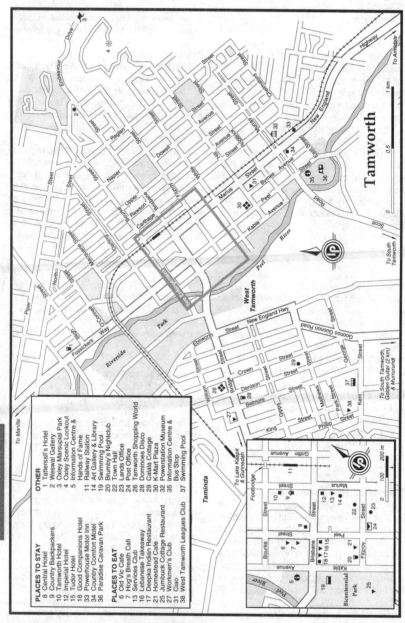

Tamworth

PLACES TO STAY
8 Central Hotel
9 Country Backpackers
10 Tamworth Hotel
12 Imperial Hotel
15 Tudor Hotel
18 Good Companions Hotel
33 Powerhouse Motor Inn
34 Country Comfort Motel
36 Paradise Caravan Park

PLACES TO EAT
6 Old Vic Cafe
7 Hog's Breath Cafi
13 Lebanese Takeaway
16 Deepika Indian Restaurant
21 Homestead Cafe
25 Jumbuck Cottage Restaurant
27 Workmen's Club
31 Ciao
38 West Tamworth Leagues Club

OTHER
1 Tattersall's Hotel
2 Weswal Gallery
3 Oxley Marsupial Park
4 Oxley Scenic Lookout
5 Information Centre &
   Hands of Fame
11 Railway Station
14 Art Gallery & Library
19 Swimming Pool
20 Brumby's Nightclub
22 Town Hall
23 Lands Office
24 Post Office
26 Tamworth Shopping World
29 Dominoes Disco
30 K-Mart Plaza
32 Powerstation Museum
35 Information Centre &
   Bus Stop
37 Swimming Pool

NEW ENGLAND

from 2 to 4 pm and on weekends from 10 am to 4 pm. Admission is $3 ($1 children).

Galleries

The **Tamworth City Gallery** has a good selection of European paintings, contemporary Australian landscapes and silverware, as well as an important collection of contemporary fibre art (tapestries, applique etc). The gallery is behind the library at 203 Marius St. Entry is free and it's open on weekdays, Saturday morning and Sunday afternoon.

The **Weswal Gallery**, at the top end of Brisbane St, is a private gallery displaying painting, pottery, jewellery and crafts, much of it for sale. It's open daily from 9 am to 5 pm.

Horseriding

There are several horseriding outfits in the area. Banyandah Equestrian Centre (☎ 6767 3006), 20 minutes north of town on Moonbi Lookout Rd, has all sorts of horsey activities and special holiday programmes. It normally has two-hour trail rides ($25) through the surrounding Moonbi Ranges at 10 am and 1 pm on weekends – bookings necessary. Echo Hills Station (see Places to Stay) can also arrange two-hour rides ($30).

Special Events

Tamworth is becoming a major convention and exhibition centre, but the biggest event by far is the annual Country Music Festival. Tamworth is the country music centre of the nation: an antipodean Nashville. Each January there's a 10-day festival, culminating in the Australia Day weekend when the Australasian Country Music Awards are handed out. Much of the music is pretty derivative of the Grand Ole Oprey, but there's also bluegrass and more Australian styles, including some good ratbag bands. With around 1000 events and performances, there's a lot to choose from. Still, this is definitely a *country* music festival, not a folk music festival. Wear your fanciest shirt.

Horse-related events fill out the calendar, including a big racing carnival and cutting horse championships for working stock-horses in summer and the Tamworth Gold Cup race and the quarter-horse championships in autumn.

Places to Stay

During the Country Music Festival in January, most of the accommodation in town has been booked out for months. The information centre maintains a 'wait-list' register of people looking for accommodation and tries to help them, but it's a long, long list. If you do manage to find something, you'll be surprised to hear that prices don't go through the roof at festival time.

Camping *Paradise Caravan Park* (☎ 6766 3120) is by the river, just beyond the tourist information centre on Peel St. Sites cost $11 and on-site vans start at $31 a double. There are other caravan parks further from the centre.

Hostels *Country Backpackers* (☎ 6761 2600) is a new hostel at 169 Marius St, opposite the railway station. It occupies a 100-year-old former boarding house and has large dorms downstairs with beds for $15 and smaller rooms upstairs with beds from $18. Prices include a light breakfast. The hostel has a kitchen and dining room as well as coin-operated laundry facilities.

B&B & Farmstay There's a simple B&B at 10 Chelmsford St (☎ 6769 4279, 6766 7276 AH), charging $40 a double. The breakfast is continental.

There are plenty of farmstays in the area; see the information centre for a complete list. *Echo Hills Station* (☎ 6769 4217, 1800 810 243), 40-odd km east of Tamworth, is a working sheep and cattle property where there's lots to do. The owners specialise in week-long courses for would-be jackaroos/jillaroos. The courses cost $349 and an extra $59 covers all meals. Backpackers are also welcome, at $30 a day with dinner and breakfast, and can join in the activities for a further $30. You can arrange to be picked up from Tamworth when the owners come to town to collect the weekly course intake (Sunday or Monday).

Hotels The *Central Hotel* (☎ 6766 2160) on the corner of Peel and Brisbane Sts in the city centre has singles/doubles with bathroom for $30/38. Other city-centre pubs include the *Good Companions* (☎ 6766 2850) on Brisbane St, the *Imperial* (☎ 6766 2613) on the corner of Brisbane and Marius Sts, the *Tamworth* (☎ 6766 2923) on Marius St and the *Tudor* (☎ 6766 2930) on Peel St.

Motels Tamworth has dozens of motels, including representatives of all the major chains. They're concentrated along the New England Highway in South Tamworth and on the way out to Armidale. Most places charge around $50/60 for singles/doubles, but when things are quiet you'll see signs along the road offering special deals.

Places to Eat

Like most country towns, the clubs are the place to go for the best meal deals. The *RSL Club*, near the information centre on Kable Ave, and the giant *Workmen's Club* (the 'Workies') on Bridge St both do $5 lunches. There's equally good value to be found at the *Tamworth Services Club* on Marius St and the *West Tamworth Leagues Club* on Phillip St. The *National 83* restaurant at the Services Club does an all-you-can-eat smorgasbord for $13.80 in the evenings.

If the clatter of poker machines is not your scene, there are plenty of cafes and small restaurants around the city centre. For breakfast, the *cafe* in K-Mart Plaza on Peel St turns out a hearty plate of bacon and eggs, fresh orange juice and two mugs of coffee for $6.95.

There's good Indian food at *Deepka* on Brisbane St and a *Lebanese takeaway* next door. Chinese restaurants include the *Empress of China* on Peel St and the *Imperial Peking* at 327 Armidale Rd (New England Highway), not far from the Powerhouse Motor Inn.

Those with a lingering cowboy/girl fantasy can head out to *Stetson's*, behind the

McDonald's on Goonoo Goonoo Rd, which offers a 'Wild West dining adventure' to go with your $15 steak.

Jumbuck Cottage (☎ 6766 1187) has good, creative modern Australian food and a pleasant setting in Bicentennial Park. It's open for lunch on weekdays and dinner daily except Sunday, with a special three-course dinner menu for $28.50 from Monday to Thursday. *Ciao* (☎ 6766 4246) is an intimate little Italian restaurant at 2 Byrnes Ave. It's open weekdays for lunch and daily except Monday for dinner.

Entertainment

There's usually something happening from Thursday to Saturday. The *Imperial Hotel* on Marius St and the *Good Companions* ('the Goodies') on Brisbane St often have bands and at the *Longyard Hotel* (behind the Golden Guitar in South Tamworth), you'll find music with a C&W flavour. There are discos at the *Workies Club* on Bridge St and the *West Tamworth Leagues Club* on Phillip St. The *RSL Club* occasionally has bands. *Dominoes Disco* on Bridge St opens from 10.30 pm, as does *Brumby's* on Fitzroy St.

Getting There & Away

The railway station on Marius St has a Countrylink Travel Centre (☎ 6766 2357).

Air Tamair (☎ 6761 5000) has five services a day between Tamworth and Sydney ($179). Eastern also operates on this route, and Impulse flies to Brisbane ($229) via Coolangatta ($214).

Bus Kean's (☎ 1800 625 587) runs down the Hunter Valley to Sydney at least once a day for $44 and other lines come through on the run from Brisbane to Sydney.

Train Tamworth is a stop on the Sydney-Moree line. You have to backtrack to Werris Creek to catch the Armidale train.

Getting Around

Bus Tamworth Bus Service buses run from Kable St in the city centre down Goonoo

Goonoo Rd to the Golden Guitar and beyond (weekdays and Saturday morning only). The information centre has timetables.

Car Rental The major companies have agencies: Avis (☎ 6765 2000), Budget (☎ 6766 7255), Hertz (☎ 6765 5344) and Thrifty (☎ 6766 9650). A local company is Keft's U Drive (☎ 6766 2323).

Taxi You can often find a taxi on Fitzroy St near the corner of Peel St. If not, phone Tamworth Radio Cabs (☎ 6766 1111).

WALCHA

Walcha is a small town (population 1700) set in pretty, rolling country on the edge of the Great Dividing Range. It lies on the Oxley Highway about 50km east of the New England Highway. The information centre (☎ 6777 1075) is in the old primary school on the highway – Fitzroy St through town.

Explorer John Oxley passed through the area in 1818 and in the 1830s, it was the first part of the tablelands to be invaded by graziers bringing their herds and flocks up from the Hunter Valley. The town dates from 1845 and the 1854 **Catholic church** on South St is one of the oldest remaining buildings. **Langford**, on the southern side of the town, is a very impressive old homestead.

Walcha is the nearest town of any size to Oxley Wild Rivers and Werrikimbe national parks. The spectacular **Apsley Falls** are 18km east of town, signposted off the Oxley Highway. Streams in the area are well stocked with trout and the season opens in October.

Places to Stay & Eat

There's a *caravan park* (☎ 6777 2501) and pub accommodation at the *Apsley Hotel* (☎ 6777 2502). The *New England Hotel/ Motel* (☎ 6777 2532) and the *Walcha Motel* (☎ 6777 2599) both charge around $40/50 a single/double. *Fenwicke House* (☎ 6777 2713) is a gallery and tea-room in an old house at 23E Fitzroy St, with accommodation for $30 per person, including cooked breakfast.

The old, atmospheric *Royal Walcha Road Hotel* (☎ 6777 5829) is about 20km west on the road to Tamworth and has rooms at $25 per person with breakfast.

There are a few farmstays in the area. Contact the information centre for details.

Getting There & Away

Bus It seems like a long way out of their way, but Kean's (☎ 1800 625 587) will come here on request on the run from Tamworth to Port Macquarie (via Armidale and Coffs Harbour). The fare to Armidale is $13.50.

Car & Motorcycle The Oxley Highway runs west to join the New England Highway at Bendemeer, from where it's 40km south to Tamworth or 70km north to Armidale. If you're heading to Armidale, there's a pretty backroad from Walcha to Uralla.

Heading east, the Oxley Highway plunges down the escarpment to Wauchope and Port Macquarie on the coast. You can also travel on small roads down to Gloucester, near the Hunter Valley.

OXLEY WILD RIVERS NATIONAL PARK

This park of scattered sections (90,270 hectares in total) east of Armidale and Walcha contains some dramatic waterfalls and gorges. **Wollomombi Falls**, 40km east of Armidale, are among the highest in Australia, with a drop of 220m; **Apsley Falls** are east of Walcha at the southern end of the park. Down at the bottom of the gorges is a wilderness area, accessible from Raspberry Rd which runs off the Wollomombi to Kempsey road. The Armidale NPWS office (☎ 6773 7211) has information.

WERRIKIMBE NATIONAL PARK

This rugged and spectacular park (35,180 hectares) has remote-area gorge walking as well as more gentle walks around the visitor areas. Access is via the Kangaroo Flat road, about 50km east of Walcha off the road to Wauchope. The Armidale NPWS office (☎ 6773 7211) has information.

URALLA

A small town (population 2300) on the New England Highway, Uralla is a good place to break the journey. The information centre (☎ 6778 4496) is on the highway and opens daily. A **market** is held here on the second Sunday of the month.

Captain Thunderbolt (the dashing name taken by young Fred Ward when he turned bushranger) roamed through much of New England in the 1860s and you'll see many sites claiming to be Thunderbolt's caves, rocks, lookouts, hideouts etc.

Thunderbolt was a popular hero and seems to have performed many acts of kindness as well as robbery. He was killed by police near Uralla in 1870, and there's a statue of him on the highway in the town centre. The bushranger's simple grave, still sometimes honoured with flowers, is in the cemetery. Whether or not Thunderbolt's body lies in the grave is another matter. There's a persistent rumour that he was spotted in Canada many years after the funeral.

The big **McCrossin's Mill Museum** has some Captain Thunderbolt artefacts (admission $2, 50c children). There's also a **foundry**, which has been operating since 1872 and has a small museum (admission $2.50, $1 children), and **Hassett's Military Museum**. Burnet's Bookshop is a large antiquarian and secondhand bookshop on the main street, open daily.

There's a **fossicking area** with a picnic spot, about 5km north-west of Uralla on the Kingstown road. Also in the area is Mt Yarrowyck, with some Aboriginal **cave paintings**. The information centre has detailed directions.

Places to Stay & Eat

There are a couple of caravan parks, pubs and three motels if you want to stay the night. The information centre has a list of local farmstays.

Expresso Caffe at the information centre opens daily and has good coffee and light meals.

GOSTWYCK

If you're beginning to wonder how New England came by its name, visit Gostwyck, a little piece of England 11km east of Uralla. This hamlet is comprised of the buildings and cottages of the Gostwyck sheep station. It's unusual for an Australian village to conform to the English pattern of the squire's house surrounded by the cottages of the labourers. There are long avenues of tall trees and a pretty chapel.

If you're heading to Armidale, you don't have to return to the highway. There's a more interesting backroad (partly unsealed) which passes turn-offs for the **Mihi Falls**, near Enmore, and **Dangars Falls**, south of Dangarsleigh.

At the Dangars Falls turn-off you'll see a refreshingly eccentric **war memorial**, which was erected by a local landowner in honour of the people of the British Empire who 'went west' during WWI. You enter through a gate labelled Nirvana. A corporal with the same surname as the landowner is listed first on the honour roll, out of alphabetical order.

ARMIDALE

The regional centre of Armidale (population 22,400) is a popular halting point. The 1000m altitude means it's pleasantly cool in summer and frosty (but often sunny) in winter. The town is famous for its autumn colours, which are at their best in late March and early April.

The town centre is attractive, with the Beardy St pedestrian mall and some well-kept old buildings. It's also a lively place, thanks to the large student population at the University of New England (UNE). Education is big business in Armidale, and there's a number of large private boarding schools. They include the Armidale School (TAS), whose imposing buildings and grounds can be seen along the road to Grafton and Dorrigo.

History

Graziers took up land in the Armidale area during the great migration up from the coast in the 1830s, and the town was established

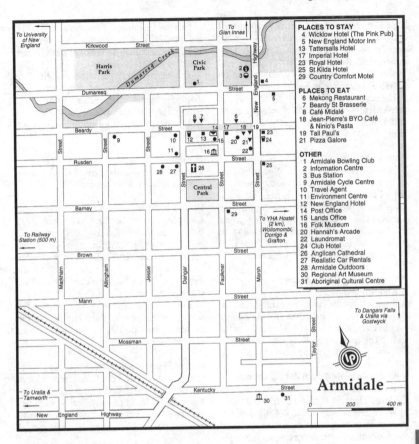

PLACES TO STAY
4 Wicklow Hotel (The Pink Pub)
5 New England Motor Inn
13 Tattersalls Hotel
17 Imperial Hotel
23 Royal Hotel
25 St Kilda Hotel
29 Country Comfort Motel

PLACES TO EAT
6 Mekong Restaurant
7 Beardy St Brasserie
8 Café Midalé
18 Jean-Pierre's BYO Café & Ninio's Pasta
19 Tall Paul's
21 Pizza Galore

OTHER
1 Armidale Bowling Club
2 Information Centre
3 Bus Station
9 Armidale Cycle Centre
10 Travel Agent
11 Environment Centre
12 New England Hotel
14 Post Office
15 Lands Office
16 Folk Museum
20 Hannah's Arcade
22 Laundromat
24 Club Hotel
26 Anglican Cathedral
27 Realistic Car Rentals
28 Armidale Outdoors
30 Regional Art Museum
31 Aboriginal Cultural Centre

Armidale

0   200   400 m

in 1839, named after Armidale castle on the Isle of Skye – the ancestral home of the Commissioner of Crown Lands, George James MacDonald.

Orientation
The New England Highway winds through the city, becoming Kentucky St, Dangar St, Barney St (briefly) and Marsh St. Barney St heads east to the national parks and then continues on to Dorrigo and Grafton. The city centre is a neat grid around the mall on Beardy St between Dangar, Faulkner and Marsh Sts.

Information
The enthusiastic information centre (☎ 6773 8527) is just north of the centre near the corner of Marsh and Dumaresq (pronounced 'Dumareck') Sts. Here you can pick up brochures detailing the Heritage Walking Tour and the Heritage Drive; just strolling down the mall is enough to whet your appetite for historic buildings, and the longer Armidale Walking Track takes you through parks to the Armidale State Forest. The information centre also sells a good range of maps covering the region's national parks.

The NPWS office (☎ 6773 7211) is in the

NEW ENGLAND

State Government building at 87 Faulkner St and the Environment Centre is on Dangar St, near the corner of Rusden St. Armidale Outdoors, 152 Rusden St, has camping and bushwalking gear. There's a laundromat on Marsh St near Beardy St.

Harvey World Travel (☎ 6772 1177) is conveniently central at the corner of Beardy and Dangar Sts at the western end of the mall.

Folk Museum

This well-presented museum is on the corner of Faulkner and Rusden Sts and opens daily from 1 to 4 pm. Admission is free, but donations are appreciated. The museum has an annexe in the village of **Hillgrove**, 30km east of Armidale, with exhibitions relating to rural industries and mining. It's open on Wednesday afternoons and weekends.

Aboriginal Cultural Centre & Keeping Place

Although there are changing exhibitions, the main purpose of the cultural centre is to preserve traditions and provide facilities for study. The centre is on Kentucky St and you can visit on weekdays; admission is $2.

New England Regional Art Museum

This excellent gallery on Kentucky St houses the large Howard Hinton collection as well as more recent acquisitions. Only a small proportion of the collection can be displayed at any one time, so there are frequent changes of exhibition, usually with interesting themes. The museum opens on weekdays and Saturday afternoon; admission is $5 ($3 students).

University of New England

UNE gained autonomy from the University of Sydney in 1938 and now has a network of campuses with branches at Lismore, Orange and Coffs Harbour.

The university's administration building is **Booloominbah**, an enormous house built by a land baron in 1888; it once housed the entire university. A large stained-glass window depicts events in the life (and death)

of General Gordon (of Khartoum fame). The building is open to visitors on weekdays. Behind Booloominbah is a **deer park**, where you'll also meet wallabies.

There are several **museums** at UNE. The Zoology Museum in the Department of Zoology opens on weekday afternoons. Admission is free, as it is at the Museum of Antiquities in the Arts Building, also open on weekdays.

Market

A market is held in the mall in Beardy St on the last Sunday of the month.

Places to Stay

Camping *Pembroke Caravan Park* (☎ 6772 6470) on Grafton Rd has sites from $12, on-site vans from $20/25 a single/double and cabins between $28/32 and $42/45. Grafton Rd is the continuation of Barney St (to the east), and the caravan park is about 2.5km from the bus station.

The *Highlander Van Village* (☎ 6772 4768), on the New England Highway north of town, has similar accommodation at similar prices.

Hostel Pembroke Caravan Park (see above) is also an associate *YHA hostel*, with a lot of bunk beds in one huge dorm, costing $13.50. There isn't a lot of privacy, but the facilities are quite good. Families might be offered an ensuite cabin at YHA rates.

B&Bs There are dozens of places to choose from in and around town. The information centre has details and handles bookings.

Hotels *Wicklow Hotel* (☎ 6772 2421), also known as the Pink Pub, is on the corner of Marsh and Dumaresq Sts, across from the information centre. It has comfortable pub rooms for $15 per person. Further south along Marsh St are the *Royal Hotel* (☎ 6772 2259), charging $20/33, and the *St Kilda Hotel* (☎ 6772 4459), charging $22/30 including breakfast. The problem with these three hotels is that semi-trailers grind past all night.

Tattersalls Hotel (☎ 6772 2247) is on the mall, so it has almost no traffic noise. Singles/doubles start at $26/36, or $35/40 with ensuite.

Motels There are more than 20 motels, and most of them are expensive. The only places with doubles under $50 are the *Rose Villa* (☎ 6772 3872) and the *Hideaway Motor Inn* (☎ 6772 5177). Both are on the New England Highway north of town.

Places to Eat
The central streets have a wide variety of eating places. The best place to start is the East Mall. *Tall Paul's*, on the corner of Marsh and Beardy Sts, has roasts ($8.20), steaks ($10) and less expensive eats such as burgers (from $2.20) and pasta (from $4). *Jean-Pierre's BYO Café*, an odd combination of a country-town café and a French restaurant, has snacks and meals. Nearby, *Ninio's Pasta* has takeaway home-made pasta (from $4) with a choice of sauces. *Café Midalé* further along Beardy St has breakfast and light meals from $5.50.

Chinese restaurants include *Mekong* on East Mall, which has weekday smorgasbord lunches for $6.50 and a smorgasbord dinner on Thursday for $8.50. *Lee's*, next to Harvey World Travel on Dangar St, has lunches for $3.90.

Beechez Restaurant at the Wicklow Hotel does a three-course meal for $12.95 in the evenings. There's similar value to be found at the *Armidale Bowling Club* and the *Ex-Services Club*, both on Dumaresq St.

Entertainment
University of New England (UNE) is Armidale's entertainment hub, with films, theatre and music. Phone the 24-hour 'what's-on' guide (☎ 6773 3100).

The *Club Hotel* on Marsh St has bands on weekends and the *New England Hotel* ('the Newie') on the mall has a dress-up disco. The *Pink Pub* sometimes has jazz on Sunday. Check the *Armidale Express* newspaper for other venues.

Getting There & Away
Air Eastern Australia and Tamair fly to Sydney ($200) and Impulse flies to Brisbane ($220).

Bus Countrylink, McCafferty's and Greyhound Pioneer service Armidale, and Kean's runs down to Coffs Harbour and Port Macquarie, via Dorrigo. Fares from Armidale include Sydney $59, Brisbane $49, Tamworth $18, Glen Innes $23 (half that with Countrylink), Dorrigo $15.90, Bellingen $22.90, Coffs Harbour $23.80 and Port Macquarie $39.60.

Train The train fare from Sydney is $65.

Car & Motorcycle The New England Highway runs north and south from Armidale, and the Waterfall Way runs east to the coast, passing through Wollomombi, Ebor and Dorrigo.

Getting Around
Taxi Phone Armidale Radio Taxis (☎ 6771 1455).

Bicycle Armidale Cycle Centre (☎ 6772 3718) at 248 Beardy St (near Allingham St) hires bikes for $4 an hour, $15 a day or $35 a week. Failes Cycleway runs past the information centre out to UNE, a ride of five km, mainly through parkland.

AROUND ARMIDALE
Saumarez Homestead
On the New England Highway between Armidale and Uralla, Saumarez is a beautiful house which still contains the effects of the rich pastoralists who built it. There are tours at 2 pm on weekdays and more on weekends. Admission is $4. One day in May a fair is held at the homestead, with hay rides and other entertainment. Saumarez is closed from June to September.

Views & Waterfalls
The Armidale area is noted for its magnificent gorges and impressive waterfalls, especially after rain. **Wollomombi Falls,**

NEW ENGLAND

39km east of Armidale off the road to Dorrigo, are among the highest in Australia, with a drop of 220m. Further along the same road, near the hamlet of Ebor, are the **Ebor Falls**. Closer to Armidale, off the road heading south to Gostwyck, are **Dangars Falls**.

NEW ENGLAND NATIONAL PARK

Right on the escarpment, New England National Park is a spectacular park of 30,000 hectares with a wide range of ecosystems. It's good for bushwalking and has 20km of walking tracks. Access is from near Ebor, and there are *campsites* with cabins near the entrance; book through the Dorrigo NPWS office (☎ 6657 2309).

Near the park and accessible from Ebor are the *Little Styx River Cabins* (☎ 6775 9166 AH), dating from the 1930s when they housed workers at a timber mill. They sleep up to 10 people and are comfortable, but basic, and have no electricity. The cabins are close to the start of some walking trails in the national park and cost about $50 a double and $5 for each additional person. You can arrange fishing and horseriding trips.

CATHEDRAL ROCK NATIONAL PARK

Cathedral Rock National park is also near Ebor, off the Ebor to Guyra road. It's a small park (6500 hectares) with photogenic granite formations.

GUY FAWKES RIVER NATIONAL PARK

Protecting the rugged gorges of the Guy Fawkes River, this park of 35,630 hectares offers canoeing as well as walking, with *camping* on the pleasant river-flats. Access (not always easy) is from Hernani, 15km north-east of Ebor, and it's 30km to the Chaelundi Rest Area, with *campsites* and water. The Dorrigo NPWS office (☎ 6657 2309) has information.

GUYRA

This small town (population 2000) is at the top of Devil's Pinch Pass, about 25km north of Armidale, and at 1320m, it gets pretty cold in winter. Guyra sits at the beginning of the

highlands of the New England tablelands, and nearby Chandlers Peak (1564m) is the highest point in the region. The C&W tear-jerker 'Little Boy Lost' tells of the desperate search for a child who went missing 'in the wild New England Ranges' near Guyra in 1960. The town was deserted during the four days it took to find him.

The **Guyra & District Historical Society Museum** has filled the old council chambers with its collection of pioneering memora-bilia. It's open only on Sunday afternoons; admission $2. **Mother of Ducks** is a waterbird sanctuary on the western edge of town. A path through the golf course leads to a viewing platform. The strange **balancing rock** can be seen by the highway 12km before Glen Innes at Stonehenge.

Places to Stay

The *Crystal Trout* (☎ 6779 1241) caravan park is on the highway south of the town, and there's pub accommodation at the *Royal Hotel* (☎ 6779 1005) and *Hotel Guyra* (☎ 6779 1018). There are also a couple of motels.

Farmstays *Wattleridge* (☎ 6779 7593), north-east of Guyra, runs sheep, cattle and angora goats, has a large wildlife refuge, a fossicking area, horseriding and accommo-dation in self-contained cabins from about $40 per person. The information centre in Armidale has details of other farmstays in the area.

GLEN INNES

This highland town (population 6200) regards itself as the Celtic capital of New England. It does have strong Scottish roots – but having bilingual (English and Gaelic) streetsigns is stretching things a bit far.

Buses stop at the new information centre (☎ 6732 2397) on the New England Highway (Church St) near the town centre. There's an NPWS office (☎ 6732 5133) on the highway at the junction with Oliver St.

Things to See & Do

This area was once known as the Land of the

Beardies because of two hirsute stockmen who lived on an early station and augmented their wages by selling advice to new settlers. The **Land of the Beardies History House** (☎ 6732 1035), in the old hospital (1875) on the corner of West Ave and Ferguson St (the Gwydir Highway), is a big folk museum open daily from 2 to 5 pm and also from 10 to 11 am on weekdays. Admission is $4.

Grey St is well worth strolling down for its almost complete Victorian and Edwardian streetscape – above shopfront level, anyway. Have a look into Mac's Mall, once the huge MacKenzies Stores, with its impressive

staircase and mezzanine levels. The Club Hotel (1906), the National Bank (1890), the town hall (1888 – see the proscenium arch in the ballroom), the courthouse (1874) and the post office (1896) stand out. The information centre has a handy guide to these buildings and a map of the longer Lands Office **town walk** which concentrates on the string of city-centre parks.

Overlooking the town from the Centennial Parklands off the eastern end of Meade St (Gwydir Highway), the **Glen Innes Standing Stones** are perhaps the first stones to be erected for 3000-odd years. Based on the

Map legend:
1 Swimming Pool
2 Land of the Beardies Museum
3 Royal Hotel
4 Courthouse
5 New England Motor Lodge
6 Imperial Hotel
7 Post Office
8 Great Central Hotel
9 Amber & Central Motels
10 Popular Cafe
11 Information Centre
12 Town Hall
13 Travel Agent
14 National Bank
15 New Tatts Hotel/Motel
16 Mac's Mall
17 Dragon Court Restaurant
18 Club Hotel
19 Hereford Restaurant
20 National Parks Office

Ring of Brodgar in the Orkneys, the 33 huge 'stones' (they weigh up to 30 tonnes) were erected in recognition of the town's Celtic roots. The traditional plan, with its astronomical/mystical orientation, is overlaid with other stones representing the Southern Cross.

The information centre has a map of fossicking areas in the district, including **Dwyers Fossicking Reserve**, where you can fossick and camp for a small fee. The information centre also sells fossicking licenses ($2.50).

Special Events
Glen Innes is big on festivals. A Celtic Festival is held on the first weekend in May and Minerama, a gem and mineral festival, is held on the first weekend in September. On the second weekend in October, the town celebrates itself in the Land of the Beardies Festival.

The Australian Bush Music Festival is held over the October long weekend and attracts about 100 artists; some are big names and an increasing number of them are Aboriginal – as the organisers point out, for an awfully long time Australian bush music was played on didgeridoos. It's a fun weekend of singing, dancing and workshops. Some years a special train runs to Glen Innes from Sydney and you can travel along with many of the performers in antique carriages. For more information contact the organisers (☎ 6732 2397).

Places to Stay
The town's five caravan parks are dotted along the highway. You'll find sites from $7, on-site vans from $22 and cabins with attached bathrooms for about $35.

The best deals are at the pubs on Grey St. The impressive *Club Hotel* (☎ 6732 3043), on the corner of Wentworth St, has singles/doubles for $25/36, or $30/48 with cooked breakfast; the *Great Central* (☎ 6732 3107) charges $23/35 with continental breakfast; the *Imperial* (☎ 6732 3103) charges $20/30 with a choice of breakfasts;

and the *Royal* (☎ 6732 3179) charges $23 per person with cooked breakfast.

Most motels are on the highway. The *Clansman* (☎ 6732 2044) is the only place with doubles for less than $50.

The *Red Lion Tavern* (☎ 6733 3271), in the village of Glencoe, 22km south of Glen Innes, is a fine old pub with loads of atmosphere and accommodation at $35/40 for a room with attached bathroom.

Places to Eat
The *Popular Cafe* is a typical old-style country cafe on Grey St with meals for around $8. All the pubs have counter meals. The bistro at the *Great Central Hotel* on the corner of Meade and Grey Sts is better than average.

The *Dragon Court*, a good Chinese restaurant on Grey St near the corner of Wentworth St, is licensed and closed on Monday. There's a cheaper Chinese place further up Grey St, opposite the Westpac bank.

The *Hereford Restaurant* at the Rest Point Motel on Church St is popular with locals for its steaks.

Getting There & Away
Air Tamair flies to Sydney at least twice daily for $209 (less with advance purchase).

Bus Long-distance buses stop near the information centre on the run between Sydney ($59) and Brisbane ($49). Countrylink (☎ 132232) buses come through on the runs from Armidale to Tenterfield and from Grafton to Inverell and Moree. Black & White (☎ 6732 3687) has a bus to Inverell ($18) from Monday to Saturday.

Car & Motorcycle If you're heading east on the Gwydir Highway to Grafton, note that Glen Innes has the last fuel for 130km. The Gwydir Highway down to Grafton is a scenic road, but to get off the beaten track take the Old Grafton Rd: it turns off the Gwydir Highway about 40km east of Glen Innes. The road, mostly unsealed but in fair condition, passes through a convict-built tunnel, and there are good camping and fishing spots along the river.

GIBRALTAR RANGE & WASHPOOL NATIONAL PARKS

Gibraltar Range and Washpool national parks – dramatic, forested and wild – lie south and north of the Gwydir Highway between Glen Innes and Grafton. Together, they form a World Heritage Area, although it's only a decade or so since Washpool was saved from logging by a protest campaign. Except for the rest areas near the entrance, most of Washpool is a wilderness of lush rainforest and river gorges offering challenging bushwalking (there's no vehicle access); Gibraltar Range is drier country and features granite outcrops.

Countrylink buses running along the Gwydir Highway between Glen Innes and Grafton stop at the Gibraltar Range visitors centre, the start of a 10km track to the Mulligans Hut rest area, and at the entrance to Washpool, from where it's about 3km to the Bellbird and Coombadhja rest areas, where you can *camp* and take a 10km walking trail. NPWS offices in Grafton (☎ 6642 0613) and Glen Innes (☎ 6732 5133) have more information.

NYMBOIDA NATIONAL PARK

The Nymboida River and its tributary, the Mann River, flow through this wilderness and offer excellent canoeing and whitewater rafting (best organised in Coffs Harbour). Although much of the park is rugged wilderness, the riverbanks are good places to camp but there are no facilities. To get there, head east from Glen Innes on the Gwydir Highway for 45km, turning off onto the Narlala road and travelling for another 35km. You can reach the eastern end of the park from Jackadgery, further east on the highway. The NPWS office in Grafton (☎ 6642 0613) has more information.

TENTERFIELD

Tenterfield is a solid country town (population 3300), with frosty winters and clear, hot summers. To the east of Tenterfield, there are forested ranges but to the west, the slopes of the tablelands descend to the plains and beef country. If you're heading north, Tenterfield is the last sizeable town before the Queensland border. Sitting at the junction of the New England and Bruxner highways, Tenterfield is also something of a travel crossroads; it's easily accessible from Lismore, so if you're staying on the far north coast, the town is worth a visit to see something of the Australia that locals call 'real'.

Tenterfield touts itself as the town where Australia's path to Federation began because of a speech made here by Sir Henry Parkes in 1889 – the claim is disputed by the Riverina town of Corowa.

Information

The information centre (☎ 6736 1082) is on the New England Highway (Rouse St) to the south of the town centre.

Things to See

The School of Arts, on the corner of Rouse and Manners Sts, is where Parkes made his famous speech. It's now a library, housing a small **museum** with exhibits relating to the politician's career.

Centenary Cottage, on the corner of High and Logan Sts, houses local history exhibits and **Petrie Cottage** next door is an early worker's cottage which has been restored. Both are open on weekends or by arrangement – see the information centre. Nearby, on High St, the old stone **Saddler's Shop** is worth visiting for a yarn with the saddler. The shop once belonged to the grandfather of Australian entertainer Peter Allen, who sang about it in the song 'Tenterfield Saddler'.

The disused **railway station**, near the western end of Manners St, is a fine building dating from 1886 and houses a collection of railway memorabilia. Other old buildings around town include **Deloraine** (1874), near the corner of High and Wood Sts, an early stone house which is open to visitors and also has a restaurant. The courthouse (1885) and post office (1881) are also worth a look.

Thunderbolt's Hideout, where bushranger Captain Thunderbolt supposedly did just that, is 11km out of town.

The New England Highway runs north from Tenterfield to the Queensland towns of Stanthorpe and Warwick. Between the state border and Stanthorpe are **Girraween National Park** and the **wineries** of the granite belt.

Organised Tours

Woollool Woollool Aboriginal Culture Tours runs tours to nearby Bald Rock and Boonoo Boonoo national parks (see below). The information centre handles bookings.

Special Events

The Autumn Colours Festival is held in the second half of April, when Tenterfield's European trees take on their autumnal hues. Events at the festival include a big bushdance at the showgrounds.

Places to Stay

Tenterfield YHA Lodge (☎ 6736 1477) is a YHA-affiliated hostel/guesthouse at the western end of Manners St, near the old railway station. It's an ex-pub and most rooms have a couple of single beds and a double bed. Shared rooms go for $15 per

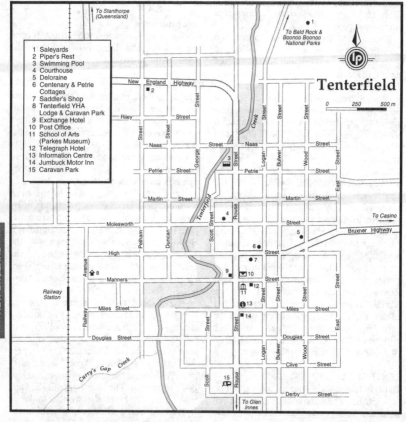

1 Saleyards
2 Piper's Rest
3 Swimming Pool
4 Courthouse
5 Deloraine
6 Centenary & Petrie
  Cottages
7 Saddler's Shop
8 Tenterfield YHA
  Lodge & Caravan Park
9 Exchange Hotel
10 Post Office
11 School of Arts
  (Parkes Museum)
12 Telegraph Hotel
13 Information Centre
14 Jumbuck Motor Inn
15 Caravan Park

Tenterfield

person, doubles are $35 and there's also a family room for $40. The hostel's kitchen and lounge are in an adjoining building, so there's no noise in the bedrooms. This place is also a small caravan park, with sites for $10, on-site vans from $24 and more expensive cabins. The managers can arrange work on fruit and vegetable farms in the area.

Several pubs have accommodation. On Manners St, the *Exchange Hotel* (☎ 6736 1054) has rooms for $12 per person and the *Telegraph Hotel* (☎ 6736 1015) charges $17/26 with light breakfast. The Telegraph also has motel units for $33/41. There's a string of motels on Rouse St, south of Manners St.

Mirrambeena Cabins (☎ 6736 2063), about 13km from Tenterfield, offers bushwalking, horseriding and accommodation.

Getting There & Away
Bus As well as the bus-lines running along the New England Highway between Sydney and Brisbane, Kirklands (☎ 6736 1074 for bookings in Tenterfield) runs to Lismore ($21.10) and from there, to the coast.

Car & Motorcycle If you've come across from the coast or up the relatively busy New England Highway, a journey west from Tenterfield is a delight – the Bruxner Highway is a wide, almost deserted road. It runs west to Boggabilla on the Newell Highway and heading east it twists and turns over the ranges to Casino, then on to Lismore.

Heading south down the New England Highway, the next major town is Glen Innes; heading north, the highway continues to Warwick in Queensland. There's an alternative route to Warwick on the unsealed road that runs past Bald Rock National Park. This is a pretty drive, but be careful: although the road is wide and smooth, it has a thick coating of fine dust which gives no traction if you have to brake or swerve.

BALD ROCK NATIONAL PARK
Bald Rock National Park (5450 hectares) is about 30km north of Tenterfield, on an unsealed road which continues into Queensland. Lying not on the escarpment but in granite country, Bald Rock is a huge monolith which has been compared to Uluru. There are several walks to the summit: an easy two-hour walk, a long seven-hour walk and a steep straight-up climb. From the top, you're rewarded with great views. There's a basic camping area near the base.

Access is from Tenterfield, off the road to Woodenbong, the unsealed route to Warwick.

BOONOO BOONOO NATIONAL PARK
Not far from Bald Rock, Boonoo Boonoo (pronounced 'bunna b'noo') is an area of pretty forest where the main feature is a 210m waterfall which waters a pocket of rainforest at the bottom. There are facilities at the rest area near the falls and basic *campsites* along the Boonoo Boonoo River.

The Fossickers Way

The Fossickers Way runs from Nundle up to Warialda, then across to Inverell. It's more or less a middle north-south route running between the Newell and New England highways. This interesting (and almost traffic-free) road begins high in the hills at Nundle, skirting the western edges of the ranges and passing through rolling cattle-country, lower and drier than the tablelands. Between Manilla and Warialda, the road runs between the foothills of the Great Dividing Range to the east and the rugged Nandewar Range to the west.

The Fossickers Way is named because of the many sites where you might discover anything from fossilised wood to diamonds. Several towns along the route have places which sell or hire the essential fossicking equipment: shovel, sieve and gold pan. You also need a licence, available from courthouses and many tourist offices for about $2.

Tamworth is on the Fossickers Way, between Nundle and Manilla, but it's also on the New England Highway and has been covered earlier in this chapter.

NUNDLE

The tiny township of Nundle (population 350) lies in the valley of the Peel River, 63km south-east of Tamworth. There was a major gold rush in the surrounding hills in the 1850s, and you can still fossick for gold, sapphires and other semi-precious stones.

The shire council (☎ 6769 3205) is open for tourist information during the week and you can pick up pamphlets at any time. The **Court House Museum** on Jenkins St opens on Sunday afternoon; admission is $1 (50c children).

The hamlet of **Hanging Rock** overlooks Nundle from the hills about 10km to the east. You can camp here by the Sheba Dams, which were built during the gold rushes.

Places to Stay

There's a *caravan park* (☎ 6769 3222) in town and good accommodation at the *Peel Inn* (☎ 6769 3377).

An alternative is to head out to the *Dag Sheep Station* (☎ 6769 3234), a new backpackers 12km south-east of town on the Crawney road. It's run by a former Oz Experience driver who figured he could have more fun showing backpackers the ropes in the bush. The Dag is a 16,000 hectare sheep and cattle grazing property, and accommodation is in the old shearers' quarters. A bed costs $16 and dinner is available for $8, breakfast for $4.

Getting There & Away

There's a sealed road from Nundle to Tamworth. A largely unsealed and hilly road runs to Walcha, passing through some lovely forest. Other minor roads head south-east to Nowendoc, then on to Taree and Gloucester, offering spectacular drives that skirt the Barrington Tops National Park. You can also head south to Scone from Nundle.

MANILLA

Manilla (population 2500) lies 45km north-west of Tamworth at the junction of the Namoi and Manilla rivers. The name is a corruption of the name of the local Aborigines, the Manellae people.

Manilla developed as a stopping-place on the main route to the grazing lands of the Namoi Valley and the north-west in the early days of European expansion.

The information centre (☎ 6785 1304) is in the council office on Manilla St, the main street. The **Royce Cottage Museum**, also on Manilla St, comprises several old buildings and opens on Monday, Wednesday and Friday from 2 to 4 pm. Admission is $1 (50c children).

Dutton's Meadery (☎ 6785 1148), on Barraba St on the northern side of town, is well worth a visit. It has a quirky shop/museum/pub where you can sample meads and melomels (meads fermented with fruit juices) and perhaps buy a bottle. The meadery opens daily and you're sure of a good chat with Mr Dutton.

Warrabah National Park, 35km north-east of Manilla, is centred on a gorge in the Namoi River and has bushwalking, climbing, canoeing and basic campsites. There's a challenging three-day canoe trip from the village of Retreat, east of the park, to Lowry Creek within the park – a 250m drop over 15km, with plenty of rapids and portages. It's for experienced canoeists only.

Places to Stay

A few km before Manilla on the road from Tamworth, you'll see a sign with the youth hostel symbol directing you to a rest area. There's no youth hostel.

Manilla St's four pubs all have accommodation and there's the *Manilla Motel* (☎ 6785 1306) on the corner of Namoi and Court Sts.

BARRABA

Barraba (population 1200) lies amid prime sheep country on the upper reaches of the Manilla River. There's an information centre (☎ 6782 1255) in a shop near the war memorial on Queen St, the main street. Ask here about having the **museum** opened for you.

Andy's Backpackers Lodge (☎ 6782 1916) is an interesting place in the middle of town on Queen St. There's a permaculture garden and a host of creative activities going on. Beds are $15, which also allows you to help yourself to breakfast, and there's normally somebody putting a meal together in the evening – contributions welcome. Barraba also has a couple of caravan parks, a motel and several pubs with accommodation.

Oz Experience comes through town four times a week or you can catch the Countrylink bus from Tamworth.

BINGARA

Bingara, on the Gwydir River, is even smaller than Barraba. Finch St, the main street, is planted with orange trees as a war memorial. The oranges are left untouched until a special ceremony in mid-June when they are picked by school children.

The council (☎ 6724 1505) on Maitland St has tourist information, as does the Fossickers Way Motel. Pick up a brochure about the fossicking sites in this geologically diverse area. Also ask about visiting the **museum** in the old Satter's Hotel in Maitland St. The Imperial Hotel has information on **canoeing** on the Gwydir (peaceful most of the year, highly exciting in late spring) and

might be able to help with canoe hire. The big **Copeton Dam SRA** is about 45km east of town.

Places to Stay

Riverside Caravan Park (☎ 6724 1209) is on Keera Rd by the bridge. The old (1879) *Imperial Hotel* (☎ 6724 1629) has good backpacker accommodation. It charges $10 for a dorm bed and $15/25 for singles/doubles, all including light breakfast. The managers can help you organise outings and activities in the district.

The *Fossickers Way Motel* (☎ 6724 1371) is on Finch St.

INVERELL

A large, pleasant country town (population 10,000) with some impressive public buildings, Inverell is at the centre of a sapphire-mining area. Other stones, such as diamonds, are also found.

Until they are cut, sapphires aren't especially impressive. There's a story, probably apocryphal, which goes that a few years ago, the council was resurfacing a stretch of road and one truckload of gravel had a bluish look to it. 'Couldn't be, there's too many of the bastards,' was the road crew's verdict, but who knows?

The Myall Creek Massacre

In 1838, not far from present-day Bingara, stockmen from the Myall Creek station rounded up 28 men, women and children, hacked them to death with knives and swords, then made a half-hearted attempt at burning the bodies.

What is unusual about the Myall Creek massacre is not that it happened but that we know about it – the stockmen were whites, their victims Aborigines. By a series of accidents, a report of the massacre reached Governor Gipps and he ordered that the stockmen be prosecuted. Amidst shocked protests from across the colony, seven of the murderers were hung. It was the first and one of the last times that whites were hung for the murder of Aborigines.

Historians assume that such massacres were routine in the 'clearing' of new grazing lands (the Myall Creek stockmen had apparently been involved in at least one other massacre), but because the new frontiers kept pushing way past the reach of the law – and because the new settlers saw Aborigines as vermin to be casually eradicated – little concrete evidence is available.

Massacres such as Myall Creek weren't just the work of semi-barbaric station workers, who were in any case usually following at least implicit orders. Myall Creek was owned by Henry Dangar, an educated Englishman who had helped set up the huge Australian Agricultural Company holdings in the Hunter Valley and through New England and the north-west. His voice was amongst the loudest protesting against the trial, and he raised money to pay for his stockmen's defence. ∎

Orientation & Information

Inverell's main shopping street is Otho St, with another shopping strip on Byron St.

The information centre (☎ 6722 1693) is in a converted water tower on Campbell St, a block back from Otho St. It's open weekdays from 9 am to 4 pm and until noon on Saturday. Pick up a map of the area's fossicking sites and if you think you've found a sapphire, any of the town's jewellers will help you evaluate it.

A supermarket on Byron St is open 24 hours during the week and long hours on the weekend. At least one of the petrol stations on Otho St opens 24 hours.

Things to See & Do

The **Inverell Pioneer Village**, opposite the racecourse on the Tingha road, is one of the better examples of this phenomenon. The village is composed mainly of old buildings, which have been gathered from the district, and it is a pleasant place to stroll around. It's open from 2 pm to 4 pm on Sunday and Monday and from 10 am to 5 pm during the rest of the week. You can fossick here and damper (bush bread) is served for afternoon tea on Sundays. Admission costs $3 ($1.50 children).

There are some interesting old buildings in town as well, such as the superb **courthouse** (1886) on Otho St and the nearby **town hall**. Around the corner in Evans St, Butler Hall now houses the **art and craft gallery**, open on weekdays and Saturday morning.

The **Goonoowigall Bushland Reserve**, about 5km south of Inverell off the Tingha road, surrounds the site of Ferndale, which is a small settlement that became derelict early this century. There are several short walking tracks and quite a lot of wildlife in the bush.

Special Events

Inverell's Sapphire City Floral Festival is held over two weeks in the middle of October. There's a wide range of events and a parade.

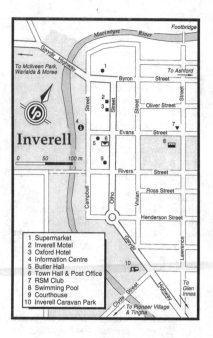

1 Supermarket
2 Inverell Motel
3 Oxford Hotel
4 Information Centre
5 Butler Hall
6 Town Hall & Post Office
7 RSM Club
8 Swimming Pool
9 Courthouse
10 Inverell Caravan Park

Places to Stay

Fossickers Rest Caravan Park (☎ 6722 2261), 2km east of town on the road to Lake Inverell, is the best of the town's five caravan parks. It has shady sites for $10 and on-site vans for $26.

In the centre of town on Otho St, the *Oxford Hotel* (☎ 6722 1101) has B&B from $26/42. Next door, the *Inverell Motel* (☎ 6722 2077) charges from $45/58. There are several other motels.

West of Inverell, near the village of Delungra, *Myall Downs* (☎ 6723 6421) has farmstays for about $80 per person with full board, less for fewer meals, and a self-catering cottage for $30 per person. They will pick you up from Inverell.

Places to Eat

The *RSM Club* on Evans St has very cheap meals in the family restaurant and you can also find more expensive meals in the Anzac Restaurant.

Getting There & Away

Air Harvey World Travel (☎ 6722 3011) at 17 Byron St (opposite the Coles supermarket) sells tickets for Tamair flights to Sydney ($209) via Tamworth; Inverell Travel (☎ 6722 2001) on Otho St is the Impulse airline agent.

Bus Buses stop at the information centre on Campbell St. Countrylink has services along the Fossickers Way to Tamworth and to Grafton via Glen Innes. Harvey World Travel and Inverell Travel both handle bus bookings. Black & White (☎ 6732 3687) runs to Armidale ($28) via Glen Innes ($18) on weekdays.

Car & Motorcycle The Gwydir Highway runs west to Moree and east to Glen Innes. Smaller roads run south to Tingha and Bundarra, from where you can head west to Barraba (a nice drive) or south-east to Uralla on the New England Highway. North from Inverell, small roads run up to Ashford and on to the Bruxner Highway.

AROUND INVERELL

The **Dejon Sapphire Centre** (☎ 6723 2222), on the Gwydir Highway 19km east of Inverell, is a working sapphire mine which offers tours twice a day at 10.30 am and 3 pm which cost $5.

The **Gilgai winery** (☎ 6723 1204), about 10km south of Inverell on the Bundarra road, was established in the late 1960s, however, wine was produced in this area as early as the 1850s. The winery is open for tastings and sales from 10 am to 6 pm Monday to Saturday and from noon on Sunday.

At the village of **Tingha**, 25km south-east of Inverell, beyond Gilgai, there was a tin-mining boom in 1870, which attracted many Chinese diggers. Large-scale mining soon took over from the small operators and it continues today. The active Nucoorilma Aboriginal Corporation on Amethyst St sells local art and craft.

Green Valley Farm (☎ 6723 3370), 10km south-east of Tingha, has children's rides, a museum (featuring grotesqueries such as an eight-legged kitten and 'Siamese' pigs) and a small zoo. Cabin accommodation is available.

Copeton Dam SRA, 40km south-west of Inverell, is a large dam popular for boating. There's a *caravan park* (☎ 6723 6269) here.

North towards the Queensland border, the **Limestone Caves** are about 30km from the village of Ashford. Main Cave is over half a km long and leads on to Great Cave, which is almost as large. About 5km north of here on the Macintyre River are the **Macintyre Falls**, with some rugged gorges, swimming holes and *campsites*.

The Central West

The Central West takes in some of the richest farmland in Australia. Although the area has an aura of being utterly typical, it is unique in NSW (and perhaps Australia) for its relatively close settlement and liberal sprinkling of fair-sized towns. The Central West is solid, respectable and, above all, rural. With some notable exceptions, such as the Western Plains Zoo in Dubbo, there isn't a lot in the way of tourist-oriented attractions – but this in itself is an attraction.

History

Much of the Central West area was owned by the Wiradjuri people before the Europeans arrived.

Soon after Blaxland, Wentworth and Lawson found a path through the Blue Mountains in 1813, the young colony began to expand onto the inland plains. A road across the mountains was built in just two years and Governor Lachlan Macquarie ordered the founding of Bathurst – Australia's first inland town (if you don't count Sydney's satellite villages) and the first to be built on a river that flowed towards the inland.

Settlement was at first restricted because the government was concerned about convicts escaping into the vast inland, and because the size and purpose of the colony was still a matter for debate – did Britain really *want* a huge colony on this continent? The government would have to administer and police new settlements, and this could be an expensive business if they spread too far. Anyway, the new road over the Blue Mountains was too rough to provide ready access to the Sydney markets. Sections were so steep that wagons had to be hauled up and down, and it wasn't until the Victoria Pass route was built in the 1830s that coaches were able to cross the mountains.

Despite these obstacles, cattle and sheep were moved into the new country, and before long Europeans were widely but thinly

HIGHLIGHTS

- Exploring the collection at the Gulgong Pioneer Museum
- The big cats at Western Plains Zoo
- Visiting the many wineries in the region
- A beer in a country pub
- Exploring the Abercrombie Caves

spread. Little is known of their adventures, as they were mainly illiterate shepherds and drovers who kept away from people who might write down their stories in official reports, but there must have been some interesting stories told in the pubs of Bathurst town.

Although most land had been taken up by squatters, the white population remained small until a string of gold rushes began at Ophir in 1851. For the next 50 years the hint of gold sent diggers pouring from one hastily built town to another, with the lucky and the disillusioned staying behind to farm or develop the township.

Geography

The area is bounded on the east by the Great Dividing Range and to the west by the vast outback plains. North of Dubbo the Liverpool Range separates the Central West from the more sparsely populated north-west of the state, and in the south the Murrumbidgee

Map: Central West

River marks the beginning of the Riverina. Geographically, the Central West is a diverse area, including some of the Great Divide's high tablelands (around Bathurst and Orange), the western slopes (all the way from Mudgee south to Cootamundra) and the flatter land further west, tailing off into the dry western plains.

The Lachlan River, rising in the Great Dividing Range near Crookwell and flowing west through Cowra, Forbes and Condobolin, runs through the heart of the area and passes through varied but always beautiful country. Like most of the state's inland rivers, it eventually enters the Murray River (via the Murrumbidgee) and reaches the sea in South Australia.

Getting There & Around

Air The Central West region is well served by air. From Dubbo ($174 from Sydney) there are flights to several places in the Central West and the far west of the state.

Bus The major bus-lines have services running through the Central West region on routes between Sydney and Broken Hill or Adelaide, and from Brisbane to Melbourne or Adelaide. Local area companies include Rendell's Coaches (☎ 6884 4199; 1800 023 328 toll-free). Sid Fogg's (☎ 1800 045 952 toll-free) runs from Newcastle as far as Dubbo.

Train Trains run from Sydney to Lithgow ($18), Bathurst ($25), Orange ($35) and Dubbo ($51). From those centres, connecting buses run to most other towns, including Cowra ($37 from Sydney), Forbes ($45), Grenfell ($42) and Mudgee ($33).

Car & Motorcycle From Sydney the main route into the Central West is the one used by the first Europeans to enter the area: west across the Blue Mountains. After Lithgow (covered in the Around Sydney chapter) you reach Bathurst, at the junction of the Mid-Western Highway, which runs south-west to Cowra and West Wyalong and meets the Sturt Highway at Hay in the Riverina, and the Mitchell Highway, which runs to Orange and Dubbo, up through Nyngan and Bourke and on into Queensland.

The Newell Highway, running from the Victorian border through the Riverina to West Wyalong, up to Dubbo and north into Queensland, is the quickest route between Melbourne and Brisbane.

The Olympic Way runs south from Bathurst to Albury, through hillier country. This was the route taken by runners carrying the Olympic torch to Melbourne for the 1956 Olympic Games.

In the west, unsealed roads lead north to the Barrier Highway and into the far west. Driving conditions here take on some of the aspects of outback travel.

BATHURST

Bathurst (population 30,670) is an old town laid out to a grand scale, and its Victorian streetscape is still relatively intact. With European trees in the streets and a cool climate, its atmosphere is different from other Australian country towns. Some of the streets in the city centre are still lit by lines of old lamps running down the middle of the road. (This is sometimes the only street lighting and it isn't very effective. Also, watch out for the metal cylinders in the centre of wide intersections, designed to keep you on the correct side of the road.)

As well as its architectural and historical interest, Bathurst hosts the annual Bathurst 1000 production car race in early October.

History

The first town west of the ranges, Bathurst was established in 1815 but remained a small administrative centre until the gold rushes of the 1850s. After the rushes it became an important service centre for the now closely settled farming and grazing lands. Cobb & Co moved the headquarters of their coach company here in 1861.

Orientation & Information

The city is laid out on a large grid of wide streets. William St between Durham and Keppel Sts is the main shopping area.

The friendly Bathurst Visitors Centre (☎ 6333 6288), 28 William St, opens daily from 9 am to 5 pm. The Land Information Centre (☎ 6332 8200), on Panorama Ave, produces many of Australia's maps and opens for map sales on weekdays. Camping supplies are available from Bathurst Camping World on Russell St.

Things to See & Do

The **courthouse** (1880), on Russell St, is the most impressive of Bathurst's many interesting old buildings. The court, the central section of the building, can be visited on weekdays from 10 am to 1 pm and 2 to 4 pm. In the east wing is the **Historical Museum** (☎ 6332 4755), open Saturday to Wednesday. Admission is $1 (50c children). **Machattie Park**, behind the courthouse, was once the site of the jail and is now a pleasant formal park, known for its begonias which flower from late summer to early autumn.

Most of the town's old buildings date from the boom following the gold rushes, but the small, brick **Old Government Cottage** (☎ 6332 4755) behind 1 George St was built soon after Bathurst was founded. It's open on Sunday from 1.30 to 3.30 pm; entry is

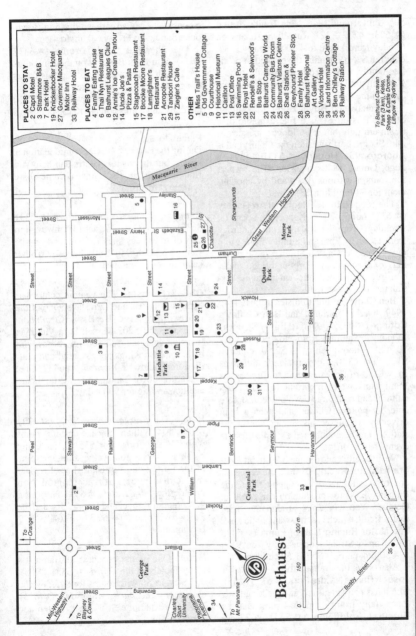

PLACES TO STAY
2 Capri Motel
3 Strathmore B&B
7 Park Hotel
19 Knickerbocker Hotel
27 Governor Macquarie
    Motor Inn
33 Railway Hotel

PLACES TO EAT
4 Family Eating House
6 Thai Nym Restaurant
8 Bathurst Leagues Club
12 Annie's Ice Cream Parlour
14 Uncle Joe's
    Pizza & Pasta
15 Stagecoach Restaurant
17 Brooke Moore Restaurant
18 Lamplighter's
    Restaurant
21 Acropole Restaurant
29 Tandoori House
31 Ziegler's Cafe

OTHER
1 Miss Traill's House
5 Old Government Cottage
9 Courthouse
10 Historical Museum
11 Carillon
13 Post Office
16 Swimming Pool
20 Royal Hotel
22 Rendell's & Selwood's
    Bus Stop
23 Bathurst Camping World
24 Community Bus Room
25 Bathurst Visitors Centre
26 Shell Station &
    Greyhound Pioneer Stop
28 Family Hotel
30 Bathurst Regional
    Art Gallery
32 Victoria Hotel
34 Land Information Centre
35 Ben Chifley's Cottage
36 Railway Station

CENTRAL WEST

50c. Built around 1845, **Miss Traill's House** (☎ 6332 4232), 321 Russell St, opens on Sunday from 11 am to 4.30 pm; entry is $4, children $2. It contains the collection of the Lee family, who lived here from the time it was built until it was donated to the National Trust in the 1970s.

The renovated **Royal Hotel**, on William St near Russell St, is a fine example of a boom-era pub, but it no longer operates as one. Six km north-west on the Ophir road is **Abercrombie House** (☎ 6331 4929), a huge, Gothic 1870s mansion. The owners run tours at various times and by appointment for $4 (children $3).

The good **Bathurst Regional Art Gallery** (☎ 6331 6066), 70-78 Keppel St, opens on weekdays from 10 am to 4 pm, Saturday from 11 am to 3 pm and Sunday from 1 to 4 pm. Grace Cossington Smith, whose paintings of the Sydney Harbour bridge under construction defined the event for many Australians, is represented.

Ben Chifley, prime minister from 1945 to 1949, lived in Bathurst and **Ben Chifley's Cottage** (☎ 6332 1444), 10 Busby St, opens Monday to Saturday from 2 to 4 pm (Sunday 10 am to noon); entry is $2.50, children $1.25. The Chifley government's initiatives in welcoming European refugees as immigrants were important to Australia's cultural and economic development. Before entering politics Chifley had been a train driver (you can see his steam train at the station), and he maintained a simple lifestyle even when in office.

Near the city centre is the 6.2-km **Mt Panorama Motor Racing Circuit**, the venue for one of Australia's most popular races, the Bathurst 1000 for production cars, held in October. You can drive around the tight, steep circuit, which is a two-way public road. The **Motor Racing Hall of Fame** (☎ 6332 1872), on Pit Straight, opens daily from 9 am to 4.30 pm; entry is $5 ($1.50 children).

Also on Mt Panorama is the 52-hectare **Sir Joseph Banks Nature Park** (☎ 6333 6285), which has native animals and walking trails (open daily from 9 am to 4 pm); and the **Bathurst Goldfields** (☎ 6332 2022), a

reconstruction of an early gold-mining town, open Sunday to Friday, 10 am to 4 pm.

The **Sheep & Cattle Drome** (☎ 6337 3634), 6km from Bathurst on the Limekilns road, is an indoor display of various facets of agriculture, including sheep-shearing and sheepdog working. The show starts at 11.30 am daily and admission is $10 ($5 children).

Places to Stay

During the Bathurst 1000 accommodation is scarce, but the visitors centre can help you find a room; it also runs a home-share scheme at that time.

Camping *Bathurst Caravan Park* (☎ 6331 8286), on the Great Western Highway 4km east of town, has sites for $10 and on-site vans for $28. During the Bathurst 1000 other camping areas are opened.

B&B & Farmstay The visitors centre has listings of B&Bs and farmstays. One of the more impressive B&Bs is *Strathmore* (☎ 6332 3252), 202 Russell St, a Victorian mansion charging $85/100 for rooms with bathroom. Bookings are essential and children aren't allowed. *Yarrabin* (☎ 6337 5712) is a farm south of Bathurst offering full board and horseriding for $90 a day.

Hotels The *Knickerbocker Hotel* (☎ 6332 4500), 134 William St, has ensuite rooms with TV and fridge for $35/50, including breakfast. This is good value, although some of the fittings and furnishings need replacing. Other pubs with accommodation include the *Park Hotel* (☎ 6331 3399), on the corner of Keppel and George Sts, and the *Railway Hotel* (☎ 6331 2964), 157 Havannah St.

Motels One of the cheapest of Bathurst's many motels is the *Capri* (☎ 6331 2966), 357 Stewart St, with rooms for $48/58. The *Governor Macquarie Motor Inn* (☎ 6331 2211), 19 Charlotte St, is well located and costs $89/99.

Places to Eat

Two large cafes-cum-restaurants face each other on the corner of William and Howick Sts, the *Stagecoach* and the *Acropole*. The menu at the Acropole is marginally more interesting, with some Greek dishes; moussaka is $7.50.

For wood-fired pizza or large servings of inexpensive pasta ($8), try *Uncle Joe's Pizza & Pasta*, opposite the post office on Howick St.

The small *Ziegler's Cafe* on Keppel St has a shaded garden and an interesting, contemporary menu of not-too-expensive dishes. There's jazz on Thursday and acoustic music on Saturday.

On George St near the corner of Russell St there's a group of eating places, including the *Thai Nyn*. It's open Wednesday to Sunday for dinner, Thursday and Friday for lunch, and has a reasonably large menu, including vegetarian dishes, with mains for around $10 to $12. Opposite you can get a sugar fix at *Annie's Ice Cream Parlour*; sundaes are $3.20 and it also serves pancakes and hot dogs.

The *Lamplighter's Restaurant* (☎ 6331 1448), in an old building at 128 William St, has a standard menu of meat and seafood dishes, but the opulent surroundings make for a good night out. Main courses are around $20, and it's closed on Sunday. Not far away, *Brooke Moore Restaurant* (☎ 6331 6470), on the corner of William and Keppel Sts, is another in an old building with period decor; it's closed on Monday.

Tandoori House, 94 Bentinck St, has a lunchtime buffet for $5.90. There are also restaurants at the *Leagues* and *RSL* clubs.

Entertainment

This is a student town and there are several music venues. The *Family Hotel* on the corner of Bentinck and Russell Sts has bands, as do the *Commercial* and *Park* hotels on George St.

Getting There & Away

The Countrylink Travel Centre (☎ 6332 3844), at the railway station, opens Monday to Friday from 8 am to 5.45 pm and Saturday from 9.45 am to 5.15 pm.

Bus Rendell's Coaches (☎ 6884 4199) runs to Sydney and Dubbo from the stop on Howick St near the corner of William St. Selwood's (☎ 6362 7963) stops here on the run between Sydney and Orange. Greyhound Pioneer stops at the Shell service station on Durham St.

Countrylink buses run from the railway station west to Orange and east to Lithgow and Sydney.

Small towns in the area have community buses into Bathurst, most only once a week or so. The Community Bus Room is in the car park under the shopping centre on Howick St. Call ☎ 6331 3322 for more information.

Train Bathurst is on the main western line, with daily trains to Sydney and Dubbo, and connections to Broken Hill and beyond. Countrylink buses connect with some suburban services from Sydney.

Car & Motorcycle The Great Western Highway from Lithgow, the Blue Mountains and Sydney enters Bathurst from the east. The Mitchell Highway heads north-west to Orange, then north to Dubbo and Bourke. The Olympic Way runs south-west from Bathurst to Cowra, eventually reaching Albury. The section to Cowra is mainly downhill, descending into the Lachlan Valley. The Mid-Western Highway (the same road as the Olympic Way until Cowra) runs south-west to West Wyalong and on to Hay.

Getting Around

Taxis (☎ 6331 1511) run 24 hours a day.

AROUND BATHURST

The high, cold tablelands around Bathurst were some of the first inland areas of Australia to be settled by Europeans, and there are some interesting old villages. The Around Orange section later in this chapter covers some villages to the north-west of Bathurst.

Blayney

Although growing fast, Blayney (population 3000), south-west of Bathurst, still has some interesting historic buildings. The Mid West Mini Market on Adelaide St has information on the town and district.

Blayney Caravan Park (☎ 6368 2799) has sites for $11. There's accommodation available at the *Exchange* (☎ 6368 2124) and *Royal* (☎ 6368 2210) hotels and the *Central Motel* (☎ 6368 3355), all on Adelaide St. At No 40, *Garthmorh* (☎ 6368 3312) has B&B for $45/65 with bathroom.

Carcoar

Sitting on the Belubula River, 52km south-west of Bathurst, this pretty village was established in 1839. It has many wonderful old buildings and has been classified by the National Trust. Enterprise Stores (☎ 6367 3085), on Belubula St, has tourist information, and **Stoke Stable Museum** is in the stables of the old Stoke Hotel. *Olde Fossickers Inne Caravan Park* (☎ 6367 3081) has sites for $10; there are pub rooms at the *Royal Hotel* (☎ 6367 3009) and B&B at the *Dalebrook Guesthouse* (☎ 6367 3149).

Rockley

Rockley is a little old village about 40km south of Bathurst, with some nice stone buildings and several craft and antique shops. There's a **museum** in the old mill and across the street is a picnic area by the mill dam.

Oberon

Thriving Oberon (population 2500), 43km south-east of Bathurst, is an elevated (1113m) rural town surrounded by farmland and extensive pine plantations. Oberon and Katoomba are the only towns in NSW other than the ski resorts to regularly receive heavy snowfalls. Oberon makes a reasonable base for visiting the Jenolan and Abercrombie caves and the Kanangra Boyd and Blue Mountains national parks.

Cobweb Craft Shop (☎ 6336 1895) on Oberon St, the main street, provides tourist information. Accommodation is available at *Oberon Plateau Caravan Park* (☎ 6336 1647), the *Royal* (☎ 6336 1011) and *Tourist* (☎ 6336 1378) hotels and several motels.

On Tuesday, Friday and Sunday, Countrylink buses run from outside Cobweb Craft Shop to Mt Victoria in the Blue Mountains, where they connect with trains to Sydney.

Abercrombie Caves

This group of about 50 caves (☎ 6368 8603) is less well known than the Jenolan Caves but is worth visiting. The Grand Arch is one of the world's largest natural tunnels and even the side tunnels are huge – in the Hall of Terpsichore you can still see the dance floor installed by miners last century. The caves are open daily from 9 am to 4 pm, and entry is $10 ($5 children). For an extra $2/1 you can go on a guided tour of the caves, held several times daily. There's swimming near the caves and fossicking at Grove Creek.

There are *campsites* ($10) and *on-site vans* (from $40). Abercrombie Caves are 15km south of Trunkey Creek (another of the area's old villages) and 70km south-west of Bathurst.

Crookwell & Around

Crookwell is the largest town (population 2100) on the high, cold plateau extending south to Goulburn. It's a pleasant place, 45km north of Goulburn and nestled in a highland valley. Crookwell Promotion Centre (☎ 4832 1988), 44 Goulburn St, the main street, has tourist information and maps. **Stephenson's Mill Museum**, in a restored flour mill (1871) on Roberts St, has exhibits on local history. Popular activities in the area include fishing (for trout) and fossicking. Crookwell's agricultural show is held in February, and over the Anzac Day long weekend in April, during the Autumn Festival, several of the town's gardens are open to the public.

Small villages dot the area around Crookwell, most founded in the early 19th century, and sheep in the surrounding paddocks produce small quantities of very fine wool, perhaps the best in the world. A network of small roads offers interesting drives. From Goulburn you can cut through this area to Bathurst or Lithgow – not a bad 'backdoor' route to the Jenolan Caves and the Blue Mountains, although some causeways flood after heavy rain. The route via Taralga involves a steep ascent from the valley where the Bummaroo Bridge crosses the Abercrombie River. The valley is a beautiful place but the road isn't suitable for caravans. You also meet semi-trailers pounding along these unsealed roads, so take care.

The nearby village of **Taralga** is an access point for the Wombeyan Caves – see the Around Sydney chapter.

Places to Stay The small, basic *Crookwell Caravan Park* (☎ 4832 1230), near the town centre on the Laggan-Taralga road, has sites for $8.50. There's accommodation at several pubs in town, including the *Criterion Hotel* (☎ 4832 1031) on Goulburn St and the *Crookwell Hotel Motel* (☎ 4832 1016), which also has motel units for $30/45. The *Uplands Pastures Motel* (☎ 4832 1999), a few hundred metres off the main street on the Taralga road, is good value with singles/doubles for $40/60.

In Taralga the *Argyle Inn* (☎ 4840 2004), on Orchard St, has rooms for $30/50 including a light breakfast.

If you're interested in staying on a farm, contact the Crookwell Promotion Centre for details.

BATHURST TO MUDGEE

The road running to Mudgee curves east to run past towns on the western edge of the huge Wollemi National Park, one of the parks which protect the Blue Mountains. The Mudgee NPWS office (☎ 6372 3122), 72 Church St, has information on this section of Wollemi.

Sofala

The village of Sofala (pronounced 'so-*fah*-la') on the fast-flowing Turon River is an old gold town, unusual because of the large

number of timber buildings which have been preserved. It was the location for Peter Weir's 1974 film *The Cars that Ate Paris*. The general store (☎ 6337 7025) has information, including the useful booklet *A Pleasant Walk Around Sofala* ($1.50). The store itself is an amazing place, thoroughly cluttered with new and ancient stock. Sofala Souvenirs houses the post office.

Places to Stay & Eat Contact the general store for information on accommodation. The *Old Miner's Cottage* has simple rooms for $10/20 and the *Old Parsonage* has rooms for $25/50 including a light breakfast. *Sofala Souvenirs* has 'Evanshire teas' for $3.50 and the *Royal Hotel* has meals. There's also the licensed *Cafe Sofala*.

Getting There & Away Sofala is on the road between Mudgee and Bathurst, but school buses and a weekly community bus offer the only public transport to Bathurst.

Hill End

In 1871 Hill End was one of the state's largest inland towns, with thousands of miners working a rich reef of gold. Deep mining required money, so, unlike other gold rushes, the Hill End rush attracted investors and speculators as well as diggers. Just two years later the gold ran out and the town declined rapidly.

Today, Hill End is almost a ghost town and most of its buildings are gone. Luckily, the town was visited by the photographer Beaufroy Merlin (see the Gulgong section), and in many empty spaces along the streets there are photos showing the vanished buildings. Hill End isn't quite deserted and the small community lives in an enviably pretty setting.

On the hill at the edge of town is the old hospital, now a museum and information centre (☎ 6337 8206), open daily from 9.30 am to 12.30 pm and 1.30 to 4.30 pm. Ask here about tours of the Bald Hill mine. In the hospital's old morgue, the *Morgue Cafe* sells 'mourning and arvo tea' for $5 and offers light meals.

Places to Stay There are three *camping* areas close to the town centre; book at the information centre. The *Royal Hotel* (☎ 6537 8261), the only surviving pub of the 28 which were once here, has singles/ doubles for $30/45. There's also the *Holiday Ranch* (☎ 6337 8224) and the *Holiday Cottage* (☎ 6337 8207).

Getting There & Away Hill End is accessible by unsealed roads from Mudgee (72km) and Bathurst (77km). The Bathurst road is a bridle path and is often suitable only for 4WD vehicles. The 2WD route from Bathurst is via Sofala. The road is narrow and winding and carries some speedy local traffic, so take care. The few remaining sections of post-and-rail fencing provide inadequate protection against the steep drops. Also watch out for horses and wandering cattle.

A weekly community bus runs to Bathurst, usually on Friday morning, returning to Hill End in the afternoon. Schoolbuses run between Hill End and Mudgee – see the Mudgee section.

Lake Windamere

This water-storage dam on the Cudgegong River, about 25km south-east of Mudgee, is accessible from the Ilford-Mudgee road (not to be confused with the Ilford-Kandos-Mudgee road). Boating and fishing are popular (but do be careful of algae) and *Tabrabucca Lodge* (☎ 6358 8414) south of the lake has accommodation. There's also a *camping* area.

Rylstone & Kandos

Rylstone is a pretty village (population 750) with some fine sandstone buildings, including the police station and St Malachi's Church. Kandos is a larger town (population 1800); it has a cement industry. Access to Wollemi National Park from these towns is on rough roads – seek local knowledge before using them. The small *Apex Caravan Park* is in Rylstone. There's also a basic *camping* area at **Dunns Swamp** (Kendells Weir), which is accessible from Rylstone, but you might have to walk in.

MUDGEE

The Mudgee area was explored by Europeans in the 1820s and a small town grew up in the 1840s, expanding rapidly with the gold rushes of the 1850s. Today Mudgee is an interesting old town (population 7500) and a thriving centre for the nearby wineries. There are some pleasant streets and interesting nooks and crannies to explore. With 22 wineries open for sales and tastings and good transport connections from Sydney, Mudgee is ideal for a rural weekend.

Orientation & Information

Mudgee is about 120km north of Bathurst and Lithgow, on the banks of the Cudgegong River. Most wineries are north of the river. The main shopping street is Church St.

The information centre (☎ 6372 5875, 1800 816 304) is on Market St, near the old police station.

Work Despite the number of wineries in the area there isn't much casual grape-picking work available, as most is done by locals and is 'pre-booked'. The four-week picking season is around February and March.

Wineries

Most of the area's wineries are small and locally owned. The harvest season is later than in the Hunter because of Mudgee's higher altitude.

Craigmoor, 4km north of Mudgee, has produced a vintage every year since 1858, making it the second oldest continually operating winery in Australia. You can see the original cellar and some antique wine-making equipment. The restaurant here is one of the area's best – see Places to Eat.

Botobolar and **Mudgee Wines** both specialise in organically produced wine.

The following is a full list of the area's wineries and their opening times.

Andreas Park Estate (☎ 6373 3763)
    By appointment
Augustine Winery (☎ 6372 3880)
    10 am to 4 pm Wednesday to Sunday
Botobolar Vineyard (☎ 6373 3840)
    10 am to 5 pm Monday to Saturday,
    closes 3 pm on Sunday
Britten's Wines (☎ 6373 5320)
    9.30 am to 4.30 pm on Saturday,
    closes 3 pm on Sunday
Burnbrae Wines (☎ 6373 3504)
    9 am to 5 pm, closed on Tuesday
Craigmoor Winery (☎ 6372 2208)
    10 am to 4.30 pm daily,
    closes 4 pm on Sunday
Huntington Estate (☎ 6373 3825)
    9 am to 5 pm weekdays, 10 am to 5 pm
    on Saturday, 10 am to 3 pm on Sunday
Knights Vines (☎ 6373 3954)
    10 am to 4 pm Sunday to Friday,
    9 am to 5 pm on Saturday
Knowland Estate (☎ 6358 4199)
    By appointment
Lawson Hill Estate (☎ 6373 3953)
    9.30 am to 5 pm daily
Macquarie Valley Vineyard (☎ 6373 5230)
    By appointment

Mansfield Wines (☎ 6373 3871)
    9 am to 5 pm Monday to Saturday, 11 am Sunday
Miramar Wines (☎ 6373 3874)
    9 am to 5 pm daily
Montrose Wines (☎ 6373 3883)
    9 am to 4.30 pm daily
Mountilford Winery (☎ 6358 8544)
    10 am to 4 pm daily (near Ilford, 50km south of
    Mudgee on the Bathurst road)
Mt Vincent Mead & Wines (☎ 6372 3184)
    10 am to 5 pm Monday to Saturday,
    closes 4 pm on Sunday
Mudgee Wines (☎ 6372 2258)
    10 am to 5 pm Thursday to Monday, by appoint-
    ment on Tuesday and Wednesday,
    10 am to 5 pm daily during school holidays
Pieter Van Gent (☎ 6373 3807)
    9 am to 5 pm Monday to Saturday,
    11 am to 4 pm on Sunday
Platts Winery (☎ 6374 1700)
    9 am to 5 pm daily
Seldom Seen Vineyard (☎ 6372 4482)
    9.30 am to 5 pm daily
Steins Wines (☎ 6373 3991)
    10 am to 4 pm daily
Thistle Hill Vineyard (☎ 6373 3546)
    9 am to 5 pm daily

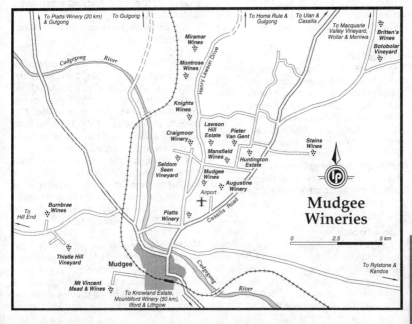

Other Attractions

You don't have to spend long in town to realise this is Henry Lawson country. The celebrated bush poet and short-story writer spent most of his childhood in and around Mudgee.

The information centre has details of a drive that takes in locations that feature in Lawson's work. They include the **Old Bark School** at Eurunderee, where he began his schooling in 1876. Eurunderee is just north of Mudgee, off Henry Lawson Drive.

The **Colonial Inn Museum** on Market St, west of the information centre, re-creates several rooms of a 19th-century pub and has a large collection of early photos. Many fittings came from the old Budgee Budgee Inn, popularly believed to be the wine shanty involved in Henry Lawson's story 'The Loaded Dog'.

Lawson Park, by the river at the top of Church St, has no especial association with the writer, and was apparently the scene of a massacre of Aborigines.

Mandurah is an interesting arts and crafts co-op, open daily at the impressive old railway station.

Special Events

The Mudgee Wine Festival, which continues through most of September, is the area's major event. Unfortunately, it occurs at the same time as another wine festival in the Hunter Valley. If you have to choose between the two events, the quality of the wine is perhaps better in the longer-established Hunter festival (many people would not agree) but the Mudgee area is much more pleasant. This is a real rural festival and it coincides with the advent of spring after a chilly winter.

Places to Stay

If you're coming to Mudgee on a weekend you should book ahead. During the September wine festival little accommodation is available, although if you do manage to find a bed you'll be pleased to learn that most prices stay the same all year.

Camping The *Cooinda* (☎ 6372 3337) and *Riverside* (☎ 6372 2531) caravan parks both have sites and cabins, and Cooinda has on-site vans as well. *Mudgee Tourist & Van Resort* (☎ 6372 1090) is a few km south-east of the centre of Mudgee on Lions Drive.

Guesthouses On the corner of Market and Douro Sts, across from Robertson Park, *Parkview Guesthouse* (☎ 6372 4477) has good doubles from $80, including breakfast. All the bedrooms have attached bathrooms and there is a guest kitchen. *Lauralla* (☎ 6372 4480), on the corner of Lewis and Mortimer Sts, is an impressive Victorian home offering B&B for $95 a double during the week.

North of town, near the wineries, *Hithergreen Lodge* (☎ 6372 1022) has motel units for $48/55. It might have special deals on weekdays – phone to check. A taxi out here costs around $4, otherwise it's a pleasant walk of about 5km. *Thistle Hill Vineyard* (☎ 6373 3546), about 10km west of Mudgee (and not in the main vineyard area), has a cottage for rent.

See the information centre for other places in the district.

Hotels There are some above-average pubs. The *Paragon Hotel* (☎ 6372 1313), on the corner of Gladstone and Perry Sts, has clean, comfortable rooms for $20 per person upstairs and $25 per person downstairs. The downstairs rooms have TVs. All rooms have washbasins and tea and coffee-making facilities. An enormous breakfast costs $8.

The *Woolpack Hotel* (☎ 6372 1908) on Market St has rooms for $15 per person. A little away from the centre is another good pub, the *Federal* (☎ 6372 1908), on Inglis St near the old railway station. It charges $17/32; $20/36 on weekends.

Motels Most motels are good but pricey. *Motel Ningara* (☎ 6372 1133), on the corner of Mortimer and Lewis Sts, charges from $52/58. Top of the range is the big *Country Comfort Inn* (☎ 6372 4500), on Cassilis Rd north of the river, charging from $94 a room.

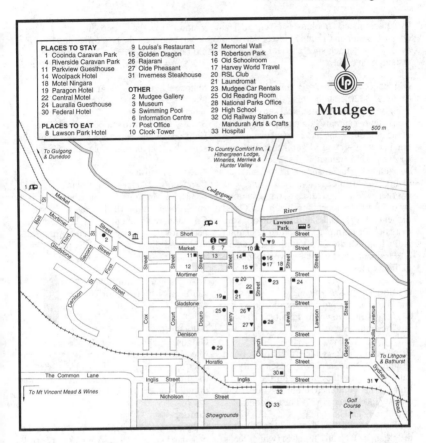

PLACES TO STAY
1 Cooinda Caravan Park
4 Riverside Caravan Park
11 Parkview Guesthouse
14 Woolpack Hotel
18 Motel Ningara
19 Paragon Hotel
22 Central Motel
24 Lauralla Guesthouse
30 Federal Hotel

PLACES TO EAT
8 Lawson Park Hotel

9 Louisa's Restaurant
15 Golden Dragon
26 Rajarani
27 Olde Pheasant
31 Inverness Steakhouse

OTHER
2 Mudgee Gallery
3 Museum
5 Swimming Pool
6 Information Centre
7 Post Office
10 Clock Tower

12 Memorial Wall
13 Robertson Park
16 Old Schoolroom
17 Harvey World Travel
20 RSL Club
21 Laundromat
23 Mudgee Car Rentals
25 Old Reading Room
28 National Parks Office
29 High School
32 Old Railway Station &
   Mandurah Arts & Crafts
33 Hospital

Mudgee

0   250   500 m

Places to Eat

The huge choice of eating places is evidence of the town's popularity as a tourist destination. As well as the usual takeaways, cafes and pubs, there are some places to eat which are a cut above the usual country-town standard.

Jumbucks, at the Woolpack Hotel on Market St, is a good bistro with most main courses under $10. The *Rajarani* Indian restaurant, on Gladstone St near the corner of Church St, does main courses from around $12 from Tuesday to Sunday. There are two Chinese restaurants on Church St, the

Golden Dragon and the plusher *Kai Sun*. *Louisa's Restaurant*, on Market St, is a fairly smart Italian place with main courses around $15.

The *Red Heifer* restaurant at the Lawson Park Hotel, on the corner of Church and Short Sts, is a popular steakhouse with good lunch specials. The licensed *Inverness Steakhouse* (☎ 6372 1701) occupies a fine old coaching inn on the edge of town at 18 Sydney Rd. It's open Wednesday to Saturday for dinner, with weekend lunches.

Lauralla guesthouse's *Grapevine Restaurant* (☎ 6372 4480) has a good reputation for its $25 set meals; booking is essential. The *Olde Pheasant* on Church St is a coffee shop by day, with lunch specials, and a licensed restaurant at night.

Out of Town The *Craigmoor Restaurant* (☎ 6372 4320), at the historic Craigmoor Winery, is one of the best places to eat in the area. The restaurant is on a mezzanine floor of the old cellars and has a varied menu, with main courses around $17 and cheaper lunch specials. Unfortunately, it's open only on weekends for lunch and on Friday and Saturday for dinner. *Augustine Winery* is another vineyard with a good restaurant (☎ 6372 6816), open for lunch daily and dinner on Friday and Saturday. Bookings are essential for both places. Neither restaurant is far from Mudgee, so taking a taxi won't cost too much and will allow you to indulge in their wines.

Getting There & Away
Air Hazelton flies to Sydney most days for $158, getting down to about $110 with advance purchase.

Bus Countrylink is the only line serving Mudgee. There are two buses daily to Lithgow, where they link with the Sydney trains. The combined train/bus fare from Sydney to Mudgee is $37. The bus continues to Gulgong and beyond.

Harvey World Travel (☎ 6372 6077), near the gigantic clock on Church St (which keeps better time than the clocks on the nearby war memorial), is the Countrylink agent. Buses depart from near the post office and from the old railway station.

If you want to visit the interesting old town of Hill End by public transport, you'll have to hope that there is room on Case's schoolbus (☎ 6372 6622), which runs from the high school on the corner of Douro and Horatio Sts and charges around $3 to the village of Hargraves. Here you connect with a smaller schoolbus to Hill End for another $3 or so.

Getting Around
Car Rental Mudgee Car Rentals (☎ 6372 6332), on Mortimer St near Church St, is a small local outfit which rents a Falcon or Commodore for about $70 a day, including petrol for the 150 free km, and other deals are possible. It's advisable to book in advance, especially on weekends.

Taxi Mudgee Radio Taxis (☎ 6372 3999) can usually be found on Mortimer St near Church St.

GULGONG
Gulgong (population 2000) was known as 'the Hub of the World' during the roaring days of gold fever. It later called itself 'the town on the ten dollar note', but since the introduction of the plastic $10 note, it isn't.

History
Gulgong was created almost overnight in the rush that began in 1870. After 1880 the rush tapered off, but it left behind a well estab-

The Holterman Collection
Rediscovered in 1951, the Holterman Collection is an extremely important record of early settlement and goldfields life, captured on thousands of photographic plates taken by Beaufroy Merlin and his assistant Charles Bayliss.

Merlin had been working as a travelling photographer for many years when he met Bernard Holterman in 1871. Holterman was a digger who had just struck it extremely rich and was interested in photography. He commissioned Merlin to produce an extensive series of photographs of NSW and Victoria, which he later used as a touring exhibition in Europe. Merlin died two years into the project, but the work was continued by Bayliss. It culminated in the building of a 25m-high tower to take panoramic shots of Sydney, using huge plates – one measured 1.5m across! The bulk of the collection is now housed in Sydney's Mitchell Library. ∎

lished town that is today classified by the National Trust.

Author Henry Lawson spent part of his early childhood in the area after his parents followed the rush to the goldfields. Not that Lawson's memories of Gulgong were rosy. It was here that he learned to dislike the squalor, meanness and brutalising hard work and poverty of the goldfields. A bitterness was instilled here which never quite faded, along with a belief in the essential worth of everyday life.

Gulgong's history is unusually well documented for a gold town, which usually came and went without much trace. As well as Henry Lawson's writings, the novel *Robbery Under Arms* (written by a Gold Commissioner under the pen name of Rolfe Boldrewood) is partly set here. British novelist Anthony Trollope dropped in and wrote about what he saw, several journalists reported the rush and there are the wonderful photos of the Holterman Collection.

Orientation & Information

The main street of modern Gulgong is Herbert St, which leads south to Mudgee. The original main street was Mayne St, a

PLACES TO STAY
5 Henry Lawson
  Van Park
6 Goldfields Motor Inn
7 The Stables
9 Centennial Hotel
10 Ten Dollar Town Motel
  & Phoebe's Restaurant
12 Commercial Hotel
24 Gulgong Motel

PLACES TO EAT
2 RSL Club
13 Saint & Sinner
15 Tea Shoppe
17 Prince of Wales Hotel

OTHER
1 Three Ways Gallery
3 Pioneer Museum
4 Church Hill
8 Henry Lawson Centre
11 Old Shopfronts
14 Old Shopfront
16 Opera House
18 Laundromat
19 Olde Books
20 Post Office
21 Town Hall
22 Information Centre
23 Wylandra Hall
25 Bus Stop

Gulgong

0   125   250 m

delightful narrow, old street that winds across town from the Wellington road. Near the junction with Herbert St is the old opera house, built during the gold rush. The information centre (☎ 6374 1202) is on Herbert St near the town hall.

Things to See

The **Gulgong Pioneer Museum** on Herbert St is one of the best country-town museums in the state. The huge collection of the important and the trivial borders on chaos, but it's all fascinating. Photographs of early Gulgong from the Holterman Collection are displayed, and there are also pin-up photos of the stars who drove the diggers wild at the local opera. The museum opens daily from 9 am to 5 pm. Admission is $4 ($2 children), and that's a bargain.

The **Henry Lawson Centre**, 147 Mayne St, houses part of the collection of the Henry Lawson Society. It also has a good selection of Lawson's works for sale. The centre opens daily from 10 am to noon or by appointment. Admission is $1.

Special Events

The second weekend in June is the time for the big Henry Lawson Festival, which celebrates the author's birthday. There is music, dramatisations of Lawson stories at the Opera House, and literary awards, some sponsored by Norwegian organisations – Lawson's father was a Norwegian immigrant. Sheepdog trials, parades and many other events make this a hectic weekend for the many people who attend.

Gulgong is also involved in Mudgee's September wine festival.

Places to Stay

Camping The *Henry Lawson Van Park* (☎ 6374 1294) is a little way out of town on the road to Wellington.

B&B The *Stables Guesthouse* (☎ 6374 1668), next to the Henry Lawson Centre on Mayne St, is a pleasant B&B in a nice old house (and converted stables). Singles/doubles are $50/70.

Hotels & Motels The two hotels on Mayne St, the *Commercial* (☎ 6374 1206) and the *Centennial* (☎ 6374 1241), both have standard pub accommodation. Across the road from the Centennial, the old Royal Hotel has been reborn as the *Ten Dollar Town Motel* (☎ 6374 1204), with units from $50/60. The *Gulgong Motel* (☎ 6374 1122) on Medley St does doubles with breakfast for $51, and the *Goldfields Motor Inn* (☎ 6374 1111) on the road to Wellington has doubles for $57.

Places to Eat

Saint & Sinner (aka *Cafe de Gulgong*) is on Mayne St, down from the corner of Herbert St. The menu is standard country-town cafe fare, but there are paintings on the wall and the local folk-music club has occasional meetings here. There are a couple of other cafes on Herbert St near the museum. *Phoebe's Restaurant*, on Medley St just north of Mayne St, has pasta for $9 and main courses from $14.

Getting There & Away

Bus The Countrylink service to Mudgee continues to Gulgong ($40 from Sydney). Olde Books on Mayne St takes bookings.

ORANGE

The city of Orange (population 35,000) is in a fertile agricultural area, but the crops grown do not include oranges – the city was named after Prince William of Orange. Cool-climate fruit and vegetables are the area's main produce.

Although it's now larger than Bathurst, Orange didn't have the administrative importance of its neighbour and lacks the grand buildings, but it is a pleasant city of wide streets and parks. The altitude (around 950m) means that there are four distinct seasons, with cold winters.

History

Land grants were made in the area in the early 1830s, but Orange didn't appear until the 1840s, and it remained a small village until the 1851 gold rush at nearby Ophir. By the 1880s, Orange was a large and prosper-

Banjo Paterson

AB Paterson remains the best-selling poet in Australia, nearly 60 years after his death. If you know 'Waltzing Matilda', you know a poem by 'the Banjo'. His popular ballads include 'The Man from Snowy River' and 'Clancy of the Overflow'.

Paterson was born near Orange in 1864 and grew up there and on stations around Yass, but was sent to an exclusive Sydney boarding school at an early age. He worked as a solicitor, but became bored and spent the rest of his life in adventurous activities such as reporting on the Boer War, breaking horses in Egypt during WWI, pearl diving at Broome and shooting crocodiles in the Northern Territory.

Paterson's cheerful doggerel is in stark contrast to the more sombre work of Henry Lawson, although they shared an obsession with bush themes. The poets were not friends and at one time engaged in a rhyming debate about which was the more 'authentic'. Paterson has a point when he complains about Lawson and his ilk:

> With their dreadful, dismal stories of the overlander's camp
> How his fire is always smoky and his boots are always damp;
> And they paint it so terrific it would fill one's soul with gloom,
> But you know they're fond of writing about 'corpses' and 'the tomb'.
> So, before they curse the bushland they should let their fancy range,
> And take something for their livers, and be cheerful for a change.

Paterson's range of experience was much wider than Lawson's, but his poetry is one-dimensional and often verges on the jingoistic. Perhaps it isn't surprising that it's Paterson who is quoted when advertisers want to add a tinge of 'the real Australia'.

> And of course there's no denying that a bushman's life is tough
> But a man can easy stand it if he's built of sterling stuff. ■

ous town shipping fruit to the Sydney markets on the new railway line. Orange was briefly considered as the site for the national capital, but Victoria didn't want the capital to be so close to Sydney and so far from Melbourne.

Orientation & Information

Suburban Orange sprawls over quite a large area, but the city centre, with its grid-pattern streets, is fairly compact and easy to get around. Summer St is the main street and the town centre begins just west of the railway line.

The big Orange Visitors Centre (☎ 6361 5226), on Byng St near the railway line,

opens Monday to Friday from 9 am to 5 pm and weekends from 9 am to 4 pm. It has a range of handy brochures, including a walking tour of the city centre and day tours around the district. It also rents gold pans and sells fossicking licences.

The post office, in a grand old building on Summer St, opens Monday to Friday from 9 am to 5 pm.

Netwit Connections (☎ 6361 0250), at Shop 20, upstairs in the Orange Arcade, offers Internet access.

Work The autumn apple-picking season lasts for about six weeks. The harvest officer at the CES office (☎ 6361 4144), on Anson St, can help you find work. Some orchards have accommodation.

Things to See

The excellent **Orange Regional Gallery** (☎ 6361 5136) in Civic Square (behind the visitors centre) has an ambitious, varied programme of exhibitions. It's open Tuesday to Saturday from 11 am to 5 pm and 2 to 5 pm on Sunday and holidays (entry is free). The **Orange Historical Museum** is on McNamara St, opposite Robertson Park.

The **Botanic Gardens** are on Clover Hill (with good views of the city), a couple of km north of the city centre on Kearneys Drive. The gardens were established in 1981 to preserve the native woodlands of the area and to grow other plants and trees suited to this cool climate, including a forest of European, North American and Asian trees. This is an interesting project, as most botanic gardens in the state were established long ago and are rigidly formal, echoing the gardens back 'home' in Britain (**Cook Park** in central Orange is a good example).

Many craftspeople live in the area and there are several outlets in town. **The Guildry** arts and craft shop in Cook Park on Summer St opens daily.

Orange has some interesting old buildings, including the old **Town Hall** (1887) and the former **Union Bank**, both on Byng St.

Poet Banjo Paterson was born on Narrambla Station near Orange in 1864. The site of the station is now **Banjo Paterson Park**, about 3km north-east of Orange on the Ophir road, with picnic facilities.

Special Events

The **Orange National Field Days**, held during the second week in November, are the largest in the state. It's your chance to catch up on the world of tractors and chemical sprays, and to see events such as sheepdog trials.

Places to Stay

As well as the accommodation listed here, the visitors centre has details of farmstays in the area.

Camping *Colour City Caravan Park* (☎ 6362 7254) is on Margaret St about 2km north-east of the city centre. It has tent sites for $7.50 and a range of other accommodation, from on-site vans for $28 a double to self-contained units for $40 a double, plus $6 for each extra person. There's also the *Canobolas Caravan Park* (☎ 6362 7279), 166 Bathurst Rd (the Mitchell Highway), south-east of the city centre, with sites for $12.

Hotels & Motels *Hotel Canobolas* (☎ 6362 2444), 248 Summer St on the corner of Lords Place, is a rarity in rural Australia: a hotel built specifically to provide accommodation. There are lifts, a ballroom and several other grand public rooms. Time has taken some toll, but the clean rooms are better than average pub rooms, most having attached bathrooms, steam heat, TV and a fridge. With singles/doubles for $26/42 or $42/62 with bathroom, it's worth a try. If you're driving, enter the car park from the bottleshop on Summer St.

Parkview Hotel (☎ 6362 1545), 281 Summer St, charges $20/30 for basic rooms, but the activity in the bars downstairs can be easily heard. The quieter *Metropolitan Hotel* (☎ 6362 1353), on the corner of Byng and Anson Sts, has rooms for $32/50 with breakfast. *Occidental Hotel/Motel* (☎ 6362 4833), on the corner of Kite St and Lords Place, charges $30/35 for pub rooms and $50/55 for motel units.

Most of the other motels are quite expensive. The central *Mid City Motor Lodge* (☎ 6362 1600), 245 Lords Place, is run by the Orange Ex-Services Club and charges $65/75.

Duntryleague Country Club (☎ 6362 3602), at the golf club on Woodward St, has singles/doubles for $60/75 and other rooms for $100. Duntryleague is an old mansion built in 1876, with the golf course constructed in its grounds in 1920.

Places to Eat

Lords Place Cafe, on Lords Place just south of the corner of Summer St, is good for

PLACES TO STAY
1   Colour City Caravan Park
7   Metropolitan Hotel
13 Mid City Motor Lodge
15 Parkview Hotel
18 Tourist Hotel
21 Occidental Hotel/Motel
22 Hotel Canobolas

PLACES TO EAT
6   Beau's on Byng
8   Union Bank Cafe
9   Cafe 48
11 Orange Ex-Services Club
12 Bad Manors
16 Loc Sing Restaurant
17 Matilda's Family Steakhouse
19 Phoenix Chinese Restaurant

23 Patmos Restaurant
24 Lords Place Cafe
26 Jurgens

OTHER
2   Orange Hospital
3   Orange Regional Gallery
4   Orange Visitors Centre
5   Civic Centre
10 Old Town Hall
14 Orange Historical Museum
20 Orange Railway Station
25 Post Office
27 Orange Arcade
28 CES Office
29 Swimming Pool
30 Indian Pacific Railway
    Station

CENTRAL WEST

breakfast, with eggs for $3. There's an interesting collection of magazines to read.

The *Union Bank Cafe*, on the corner of Sale and Byng Sts, has a varied menu and opens for lunch and dinner from Tuesday to Saturday. Not far away is *Cafe 48*, 48 Sale St, a BYO restaurant with tables outside. It's open for lunch daily, except Sunday, and for dinner Wednesday to Saturday. The menu includes the usual steak and seafood, plus curries and pasta ($10).

Open for dinner Tuesday to Saturday, *Beau's on Byng*, 123 Byng St, serves modern international cuisine; tortellini is $9, Thai seafood curry $11.50. *Patmos* is a glittery reception-centre and restaurant on Lords Place. It's licensed and the menu is chiefly steak, chicken and seafood; most mains are $12.50 to $19.50.

There are many places along Summer St. *Jurgens* Thai restaurant, next to the Orange Arcade, is a small but busy place with green curry in coconut sauce for $6.95. *Bad Manors*, although nothing like its namesake in Sydney, is a reasonable cafe with snacks and meals. Nearby is the *Loc Sing* Chinese restaurant, with another, the *Phoenix*, across the road.

The *Overlander* restaurant at the Mid City Motor Lodge on Lords Place has an Indian menu with mains from $13 to $19, as well as the usual steaks for $19.

The *Orange Ex-Services Club* on Anson St has a bistro and a restaurant.

There's a member of the small *Matilda's Family Steakhouse* chain, on the corner of Summer and McLachlan Sts, east of the centre. It's clean and has $9.95 three-course 'value meals' or steak for $14.95. Children's meals cost $5.95 or less.

Getting There & Away
You can buy bus and train tickets from the Countrylink Travel Centre (☎ 6361 9500) at the railway station near the town centre.

Air Hazelton (☎ 6361 5888) flies to Sydney ($151) daily. The airport is 13km south-east of Orange, off the Mitchell Highway near Lucknow. Shuttle buses leave from Harvey World Travel on Summer St.

Bus Rendell's Coaches (☎ 6884 4199, 1800 023 328) runs to Dubbo ($30) and Sydney ($30) daily. There's also a service to Canberra ($35) on Monday and Friday. Rendell's stops at the railway station. Selwood's Coaches (☎ 6362 7963) also runs to Sydney daily from the station. Countrylink buses run to Parkes, Forbes, Dubbo, Bathurst and Lithgow.

Train XPTs between Sydney and Dubbo stop here, as does the Indian Pacific train which has its own station some way south of the centre.

Car & Motorcycle The Mitchell Highway runs south to Bathurst, and north to Wellington and Dubbo. Smaller roads run west to meet the Newell Highway near Parkes and Forbes. There's an interesting alternative route to Wellington (see the following Molong section).

AROUND ORANGE
Mt Canobolas
Mt Canobolas (1395m) is a steep, extinct volcano 20km south-west of Orange. The views stretch a long way across the western plains, and in winter there's often snow on the peak. You can drive to the top or there are a couple of walking tracks. The road from Orange offers the choice of travelling via Towac or Pinnacle; the distances are about the same.

At the bottom of the mountain is **Lake Canobolas**, where you can see deer. There's also a *camping ground*, open from late October to the end of April, with sites for $2. Enquire at the Land Office (☎ 6362 0568), on the corner of Kite and Anson Sts, Orange.

Borenore Caves
About 17km north-west of Orange, these caves can be explored without a guide, but you'll need a torch (flashlight). You can camp nearby. For more information contact the ranger at Canobolas Regional Park Trust,

PO Box 53, Orange 2800. From Orange, take the Mitchell Highway (Woodward St) and turn off onto Forbes Rd.

Millthorpe & Around

Millthorpe is a neat village south of the highway, 29km south-east of Orange. On a grey winter's day it's somewhat reminiscent of a northern English village, with bleak hedges and dark stone houses. When the sun is shining it's a pleasant place to visit. The Old Mill Cafe (☎ 6366 3188) has tourist information; it's closed on Monday. There are several craft and antique shops, and there's B&B accommodation in the impressive old Bank of NSW building on Victoria St. It's called *Rosebank* (☎ 6366 3191) and rooms cost $75/120 a single/double, more on weekends. Children aren't allowed here but they're allowed in the adjoining cottage (the former bank manager's residence) which is more expensive. There's also pub accommodation at the *Railway Hotel* (☎ 6366 3157) and the *Commercial Hotel* (☎ 6366 3157).

Closer to Orange, **Byng** was settled by Cornish miners and retains some old buildings, notably the church (1872). The village is only accessible by dirt roads from Ophir or the Mitchell Highway near **Shadforth**, another early village. **Lucknow**, an old gold-mining village, is on the highway.

Molong is a larger town, 35km north-west of Orange, at the junction of the Mitchell Highway, which runs north to Wellington, and a smaller road running west to Parkes. Molong boasts more early buildings and craft shops. The **Molong Historical Museum** (1856), on the corner of Gidley and Riddell Sts, opens on Sunday afternoon. East of Molong, off the Orange road, is the grave of Yuranigh, an Aboriginal guide on several of Major Mitchell's explorations. You can still see carvings on several nearby trees.

Between Molong and Wellington, a slightly longer and partly unsealed route runs east of the highway, through hamlets such as **Stuart Town** (originally called Ironbark and mentioned in Banjo Paterson's poem 'The Man From Ironbark') and past the entrance to Burrendong Lake (see Around Wellington).

Ophir

The Ophir goldfield was the scene of Australia's first gold rush, and was quickly followed by other rushes in NSW and Victoria.

The Ophir field yielded nuggets rather than gold dust, so luck played as large a part as hard work. However, the easy pickings at Ophir were soon worked out, and most diggers had moved to other fields a year after

Gold!

Australia's first gold rush began at Ophir in 1851. There had been regular finds of alluvial fields before the Ophir rush, but the government had not broadcast the information, fearing the wholesale movement of population and the influx of foreigners that a gold rush would produce. Labour was needed to work the sheep stations, not to hunt for gold. Also, the idea of working people getting rich quickly went against the colony's planned social structure of an aristocracy of landowners and a peasantry of agricultural labourers.

However, in 1851 the government needed help with a stagnant economy and offered a reward to the discoverer of payable gold. Edward Hargraves, who had been on the Californian goldfields, found gold in Lewis Ponds Creek, and his associate William Tom found more nearby. Tom's father suggested the name Ophir (the biblical name for King Solomon's mines) for the field.

The government had been right to fear the consequences of a rush, as the fiercely independent 'diggers' (a word used for the first time on Ophir) from all over the world brought fresh political ideas into Australia. These democratic stirrings were to culminate in Australia's first and only popular revolt, the 1854 Eureka Rebellion on the Ballarat goldfields in Victoria.

The Ophir rush lasted only a year, but gold fever had hit NSW and wasn't about to go away. Tens of thousands of diggers moved constantly from field to field for the rest of the century. ■

the rush began. After the diggers left, deep mining was begun at Ophir and continues today at Doctors Hill. A few fossickers remain, and small finds by visitors aren't uncommon. The Orange Visitors Centre rents gold pans and sells fossicking licences. You can also buy a licence and a pan at the Gallery of Minerals in Orange (on the Mitchell Highway on the eastern side of town), and they will help you identify your finds.

Unlike those at Hill End, Ophir's diggings didn't develop into a permanent town. The rugged, bush-covered area is now a recreation reserve, with walking and fossicking the main activities. Signs of the diggers' activities remain, with mine shafts dotted all around the area (be careful – they're unmarked).

There are several walking trails and the Orange Visitors Centre has a map. Noel Rawlinson runs tours of Gunnadoo gold mine for $8, children $4; call ☎ 6366 0445 for information.

Places to Stay You can *camp* at Fitzroy Bar at the junction of Lewis Ponds and Summer Hill creeks, the site of the diggers' tent-town. There are toilets and drinking water.

Getting There & Away From Orange, head east on March St. Be careful on the access roads, as they're unsealed but carry speedy local traffic. Some sections of road within the Ophir area are steep and unsuitable for caravans. Several creek crossings are impassable after heavy rain.

Wineries
Many wineries around Orange are open for sales and tastings, including **Cargo Road Winery** (☎ 6365 6100) and **Canobolas-Smith** (☎ 6365 6113), both open weekends and holidays only and both on the road running south-west from Orange to Cargo. **Highland Heritage Estate** (☎ 6361 3612), 3km east of Orange on the Mitchell Highway, is open daily.

The Orange Visitors Centre has a map with detailed directions to the wineries.

WELLINGTON
Wellington (population 5600) was the first settlement to be established west of Bathurst and was an important stopping-place for settlers heading into the interior.

Orientation & Information
The town meanders along the east bank of the Bell River, which joins the Macquarie River just north of the town centre. Nanima Crescent, the central section of the long shopping centre, curves past the Bell River; Cameron Park runs down to the river from Nanima Crescent, and across the river is Pioneer Park.

Next to the library in Cameron Park, Wellington Travel (☎ 6845 1733) is also the information centre.

Things to See
The **Oxley Museum**, in an impressive old bank on the corner of Warne and Percy Sts, opens Sunday to Friday from 1.30 to 4.30 pm. Across the Bell River in the forested Catombal Range there's a **lookout** on Mt Arthur, about 1km west of town along Maughan St.

Special Events
The horseracing carnival in March culminates in the running of the town's answer to the Golden Slipper (Australia's premier event for two-year-olds), the Wellington Boot.

Places to Stay
There are a couple of caravan parks, the *Riverside* (☎ 6845 1370), by the highway on the north bank of the Macquarie, and the small *Wellington Valley* (☎ 6845 2778), by the highway at the southern end of town. There's also a caravan park at nearby Wellington Caves.

The *Wellington Hotel* (☎ 6845 2083) on Swift St near the railway station is probably the nicest of the pubs and charges $25/35 with breakfast. Swift St runs off Nanima Crescent at the three-way intersection near the war memorial angel in the park.

Motels in Wellington include the *Garden*

Court (☎ 6845 2288) on the highway (from $40/50) and the *Bridge* (☎ 6842 2555), by the river on Lee St (from $45/55).

Getting There & Away

Bus All long-distance buses leave from the post office. Greyhound Pioneer runs between Sydney ($45) and Wellington daily, arriving and departing in the early hours of the morning. Rendell's has a cheaper and more convenient daily service to Sydney ($40) and a service to Canberra on Monday, Wednesday and Friday ($40).

Sid Fogg's Dubbo to Newcastle run comes through Wellington on Monday, Wednesday and Friday.

Car & Motorcycle The Mitchell Highway runs north to Dubbo and south to Orange. There is a sealed road east to Gulgong via Lincoln and Goolma. To Parkes, you can take the Mitchell south to Molong and head west from there, or there's a shorter and prettier drive through the hills via the village of Yeoval.

AROUND WELLINGTON
Wellington Caves

The caves, off the highway 8km south of Wellington, are the region's main attraction. They can be seen on guided tours at 9, 10 and 11 am and 2, 3 and 4 pm. They cost $8.50 ($5 children). A growing hamlet of kitsch here has a few attractions such as the **clock museum**. There's also a *kiosk* and a *caravan park* (☎ 6845 2970).

Burrendong SRA

About 25km south-east of Wellington, Lake Burrendong is a large water-storage dam, which is popular for watersports. Entry to the SRA costs $3.50 per car ($1 for motorbikes). If you want to stay, *Burrendong Park* (☎ 6846 7435) has camping sites and on-site vans.

DUBBO

One of the larger towns in the state, Dubbo (population 38,000) is a rural centre and a transport crossroads on the farthest fringes of the Central West region. Go north or west from Dubbo and you'll find that the population density drops dramatically and the outback begins.

History

John Oxley passed though in 1817 and it was only a few years before graziers took up land in the area. The village of Dubbo appeared by 1850 and first took on its role as a highway stop in the 1860s, catering to the people rushing to the Victorian goldfields.

Orientation & Information

Dubbo's grid-pattern city centre lies just east of the Macquarie River, with parkland bordering both banks of the river.

The Mitchell and Newell highways cross at a roundabout just west of the river. The Newell becomes Whylandra St, then Erskine St as it bends east around the top end of the city centre; the Mitchell becomes Cobra St and skirts the city centre to the south. The main shopping street is Macquarie St. The main information centre (☎ 6884 1422) is at the top end of town, on the corner of Macquarie and Erskine Sts. There's another office further south on Macquarie St, next to the museum.

There's a laundromat on Brisbane St near the corner of Bultje St. Travel agents include Harvey World Travel (☎ 6881 8144) on Macquarie St.

Things to See & Do

The large **Old Dubbo Gaol** on Macquarie St is open as a museum. 'Animatronic' characters tell their stories, including that of a condemned man due for a meeting with the gallows. The gallows themselves are also on display. Admission is $3 ($1 children). Also on Macquarie St, the **Dubbo Museum** has some re-creations of old shops and displays on the area's history. Admission is $4 ($1 children).

The **Regional Art Gallery**, 165 Darling St, has a theme of animals in art – a nod towards the zoo. Admission is free.

Dubbo has a complete set of impressive old country-town buildings. The **railway** station is a fine sandstone building, and the old **pubs** along Talbragar St are suitably adorned with iron-laced verandahs. The **courthouse** on Brisbane St is an impressive neo-classical edifice. Across the street is the **Lands Department** building, which is totally different in style from the courthouse – and from any other building in town, for that matter. The information centre has maps for both the Heritage Walk and the Heritage Drive.

Dundullimal is a slab house built in 1840, about 2km beyond the Western Plains Zoo. It now houses craft displays and opens Tuesday to Sunday from 10 am to 4 pm (closed in February). Admission is $5 ($2 children).

Western Plains Zoo

The Western Plains Zoo, Dubbo's major attraction, is off the Newell Highway about 4km south-west of the town centre. The zoo is definitely worth visiting, but don't come expecting a drive-through safari park – although you can drive through, the animals are in moated enclosures. Much of the zoo's 300 hectares seems to be taken up with roads rather than space for the animals.

Of course, the animals' loss is the visitors' gain and you certainly get a good look at the inmates. The Bengal tigers and the Asiatic lions alone are worth the price of admission.

The road around the enclosures is about 6km long and if it isn't too hot it's better to walk around or hire a bike ($8 for half a day) than join the crawling cars. Better still, hire a bike in Dubbo and ride out to the zoo.

On weekends and during school holidays, keepers give talks about the various animals. A leaflet available at the main gate has details.

The zoo opens daily from 9 am to 5 pm and admission is $14.95 ($7.50 children, family tickets available).

Places to Stay

Camping There are about half a dozen caravan parks in and near Dubbo. The two closest to the centre are the small *Poplars* (☎ 6882 4067), near the river at the western end of Bultje St, and *Dubbo City* (☎ 6882 4820), also on the river but on the west bank and a fair distance by road from the centre, via Erskine or Cobra St.

Hostels *Kurrajong House* (☎ 6882 0922) is a pleasant YHA hostel at 87 Brisbane St, north of the railway line. From the bus station, head west on Erskine St. Dorm beds are $14 and there are a few twin rooms ($28) and a family room ($38). The managers, Noelene and Frank, are friendly and can advise on travel in the area and further west. Guests get a 20% discount on zoo tickets and bikes can be hired for $6 a day, which is much better value than the zoo's bikes.

A couple of doors away is the *Hub of the West* (☎ 6882 5004). There's an old house on the street but the accommodation is behind this in a large brick building with 50 rooms resembling spartan student accommodation. It's clean and perfectly adequate, but it's not the most inspiring place to stay, especially when they have school groups there, or

Slab Houses

Slab houses were the earliest form of permanent European housing in the newly settled areas of NSW – the Australian equivalent of America's log cabins. The slabs were just rough-cut tree trunks laid vertically around the frame, sometimes with mud packed into the inevitable gaps.

A slab house offered more protection than a tent but didn't require the time, tools or skills necessary for a more refined finish. Brick houses had to wait until the district was sufficiently populated to support a kiln, and stone buildings were almost exclusively the preserve of the gentry and the government.

Slab houses such as Dundullimal rarely survive, but you occasionally see more recent barns or shepherds' huts made from slabs. ■

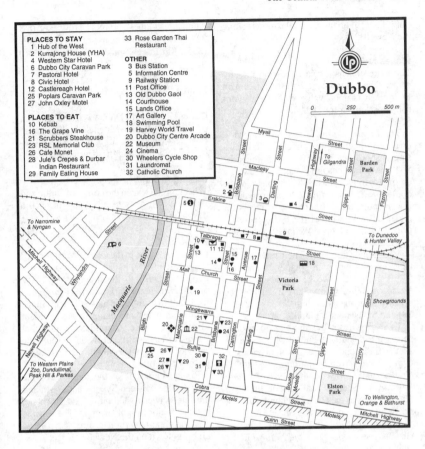

PLACES TO STAY
1 Hub of the West
2 Kurrajong House (YHA)
4 Western Star Hotel
6 Dubbo City Caravan Park
7 Pastoral Hotel
8 Civic Hotel
12 Castlereagh Hotel
25 Poplars Caravan Park
27 John Oxley Motel

PLACES TO EAT
10 Kebab
16 The Grape Vine
21 Scrubbers Steakhouse
23 RSL Memorial Club
26 Cafe Monet
28 Jule's Crepes & Durbar
    Indian Restaurant
29 Family Eating House
33 Rose Garden Thai
    Restaurant

OTHER
3 Bus Station
5 Information Centre
9 Railway Station
11 Post Office
13 Old Dubbo Gaol
14 Courthouse
15 Lands Office
17 Art Gallery
18 Swimming Pool
19 Harvey World Travel
20 Dubbo City Centre Arcade
22 Museum
24 Cinema
30 Wheelers Cycle Shop
31 Laundromat
32 Catholic Church

shearers spending their pay cheques. Singles/doubles with shared bathrooms cost $25/45.

Hotels A number of pubs have accommodation. The *Castlereagh Hotel* (☎ 6882 4877) on the corner of Talbragar and Brisbane Sts is good. As usual, you don't want a room directly above the bar and you shouldn't expect everything to work perfectly, but it's clean and friendly, and many rooms have attached bathrooms (these are allocated on a first-come first-served basis). There's a pleasant dining room and a large cooked breakfast is included in the price of a room. Singles cost $25 to $30 and doubles are $50.

The *Western Star* (☎ 6882 4644) on Erskine St is also good. The meals there have been recommended and you don't have to stay there to be able to have breakfast in the dining room.

Motels The *John Oxley Motel* (☎ 6882 4622) towards the southern end of Macquarie St is central and cheap for Dubbo ($40/45) but the rooms are pretty small. There are 30 other motels, mostly along Cobra St. On long weekends and other peak

CENTRAL WEST

times they fill up (as can all the motels along the Newell).

Places to Eat
There are dozens of places around the city centre. The 24-hour cafe at the bus station on Erskine St is good value, with an all-you-can-eat salad bar for $5.50 and hot meals for $5.95.

The *Family Eating House* on Macquarie St is recommended for big eaters. It does a smorgasbord lunch for $8.50 and dinner for $9.95. Most dishes are Asian but there is a bit of Anglo tucker as well. The bistro at the opulent *RSL Memorial Club* on Brisbane St is very popular, with a choice of meals for under $10. As well as the bistro there's a pricey restaurant, open Wednesday to Saturday nights.

Most hotels do meals. The *Castlereagh* is the pick of them, with counter lunches for $3.50 during the week. *Scrubbers Steakhouse* on Wingewarra St is a small place serving light meals during the day (around $8) and $15 steaks at night.

To escape from the mixed-grill menus, head for the southern end of Macquarie St. You'll find good coffee and light meals at *Cafe Monet*, trendy pancakes at *Jule's Crepes* and curries at the *Durbar Indian Restaurant*. There's Thai food at the *Rose Garden*, next to the Catholic church with the ski-jump spire on Brisbane St.

Vegetarians will find a good range of takeaway snacks at *Pure and Natural* in the Dubbo City Centre Arcade.

Getting There & Away
It's easiest to make bus bookings at the bus station.

Air Eastern and Hazelton fly to Dubbo. The standard fare to Sydney is $173. Hazelton also flies to Broken Hill ($276).

Bus The bus station (☎ 6884 4199) is on Erskine St, open daily from 9.30 am to 5.30 pm and 7.30 pm to 3 am.

Most major bus-lines pass through on their run along the Newell, but the local company, Rendell's (☎ 6884 4199, 1800 023 328), often has the cheapest fares to Sydney ($35). Sid Fogg's runs to Newcastle ($46) three times a week.

Train XPTs run to Sydney ($58).

Car & Motorcycle Dubbo is at the junction of the Newell and Mitchell highways, so travellers who are heading for Sydney, Adelaide, Melbourne and Brisbane pass through.

Getting Around
Wheelers Cycles, on the corner of Bultje and Brisbane Sts, rents geared bikes for $10 a day.

PARKES
Like many towns in the Central West, Parkes (population 9500) began as a gold-rush settlement. A visit to the diggings by NSW premier Sir Henry Parkes in 1871 prompted the locals to change the name of their village from Currajong and name the main street after Parkes' wife, Clarinda. It's said that Parkes influenced the decision to route the railway through the town, so this sycophancy paid off.

Today, Parkes is at the junction of the railway line between Sydney and Perth and the line between Melbourne and Brisbane, and is a major freight terminal. The town is also an important rural centre and a large highway town on the Newell.

Orientation & Information
From the south, the Newell Highway takes a twisting route through the centre of Parkes, becoming Grenfell St, Welcome St and finally joining Clarinda St, the main shopping street, to begin its run north to Dubbo. This is a three-way intersection, with Dalton St, the road running west to Condobolin, also joining Clarinda St here. South of this intersection Clarinda St curves eastwards and becomes the main route to Orange.

The Parkes information centre (☎ 6862 4365), in Kelly Reserve by the highway on the Dubbo side of the town centre, opens

Monday to Friday from 9 am to 5 pm, weekends 10 am to 4 pm.

Museums
The **Henry Parkes Historical Museum** (☎ 6862 2815), on Clarinda St, has displays on local history. It's open Monday to Saturday from 10 am to 4 pm, Sunday 10 am to 1 pm; admission is $3 ($1 children). **Pioneer Park** (☎ 6862 3732), on the Dubbo side of town, contains farm relics from around the area. It's open Tuesday, Thursday and Saturday from 2 to 4 pm; admission is $1.50 (60c children).

Vintage cars are on show Monday to Saturday from 10 am to 4 pm at **Parkes Motor Museum** (☎ 6862 1975 AH) on the corner of Bogan and Dalton Sts (just off Clarinda St near the swimming pool); admission is $2 ($1 children).

Parkes Radio Telescope
The CSIRO's Parkes Radio Telescope, built in 1961, is 6km east of the Newell Highway, about 20km north of Parkes. It has helped Australian radio-astronomers become world leaders in their science and brought pictures of the Apollo 11 moon landing. It was recently upgraded to pick up information from space 13 times further than it could before. Parkes is connected to the Australia Telescope array (the others in the array are at Siding Springs and Culgoora).

Although the telescope is off-limits, you can get close enough for a good look. There's an interesting visitors centre (☎ 6862 3677) with hands-on displays and screens which show you what the astronomers see; it's open daily from 8.30 am to 4.15 pm, and entry is free. A half-hour film is shown regularly for $3 ($2.50 children).

Special Events
The Central West Jazz Triduum is held over the Queen's Birthday long weekend in June and there's a Country Music Jamboree on the Labour Day long weekend in early October, when there's also an antique motorcycle rally. A large agricultural show takes place in late August.

Places to Stay
Camping   *Spicer Park Caravan Park* (☎ 6862 1654) is in Spicer Park on the corner of Victoria and Albert Sts. Victoria St crosses Clarinda St four blocks north of the Dalton St intersection; head east on Victoria St and the park is four blocks away. Sites are $9.50. *Currajong Caravan Park* (☎ 6862 3400) is by the Newell, just north of Kelly Park and the information centre; powered sites are $13. *Parkes Overnighter Caravans* (☎ 6862 1707), on the corner of Dalton and Bushman Sts, west of the centre, has sites for $10, as does *Parkes Highway Caravan Park* (☎ 6862 1108), on the Newell just south of town, near the railway station.

All except Spicer Park have on-site vans (between $24 and $28) and all have cabins for around $35 a double. The Spicer Park cabins are the best equipped.

Hotels & Motels   Most pubs have accommodation. The rooms at the *Parkes Hotel* (☎ 6862 2498) on Welcome St (the Newell Highway) are a bit better equipped than most and cost $18/28 a single/double. Others are the *Royal* (☎ 6862 2039), the *Cambridge* (☎ 6862 2098) and the *Commercial* (☎ 6862 1526), all on Clarinda St and charging around $20/30.

Parkes is well supplied with motels. The good value *Clarinda Motel* (☎ 6862 1655), 72 Clarinda St, south of the centre, has small but reasonable rooms at $49/54. There are several other places charging about the same, including the *Coachman* (☎ 6862 2622) on Welcome St. Of the more upmarket places, the *All Settlers Motor Inn* (☎ 6862 2022), 20 Welcome St, across from Cooke Park, is a fair example and costs $57/64.

Getting There & Away
Bus   Trans City Tours (☎ 6862 3177) has a daily service to Sydney. Countrylink runs to Cootamundra and Dubbo (both $15 one way).

Train   The Indian Pacific stops here on the run between Sydney and Perth.

Car & Motorcycle As well as the Newell Highway, smaller roads run east to Orange and west to Condobolin and into the far west.

FORBES

Smaller (population 8500) than nearby Parkes, Forbes has retained more of its 19th-century flavour and is worth a stop for a look around.

As with much of the state, John Oxley was the first European through the area, on his 1817 expedition. During the gold rush of 1861 the town boomed, shrinking rapidly a few years later when the gold ran out.

Orientation & Information

Forbes is fortunate in having a town centre that extends back from the main road; in fact there are two main roads – Dowling St (the Newell Highway) and Rankin St, parallel and a block west.

The information centre (☎ 6852 4155), in the old railway station just off the highway at the northern end of town, opens daily from 9 am to 5 pm.

Old Buildings

The **town hall** faces Victoria Park, forming a nice town square. The park is also flanked

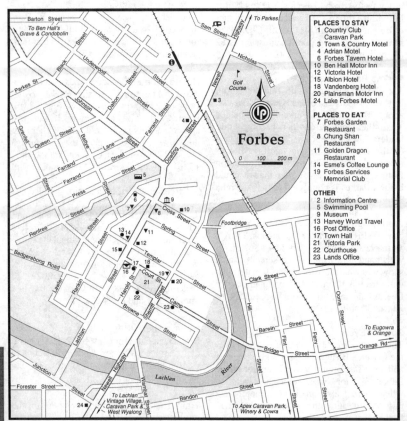

PLACES TO STAY
1 Country Club Caravan Park
3 Town & Country Motel
4 Adrian Motel
6 Forbes Tavern Hotel
10 Ben Hall Motor Inn
12 Victoria Hotel
15 Albion Hotel
18 Vandenberg Hotel
20 Plainsman Motor Inn
24 Lake Forbes Motel

PLACES TO EAT
7 Forbes Garden Restaurant
8 Chung Shan Restaurant
11 Golden Dragon Restaurant
14 Esme's Coffee Lounge
19 Forbes Services Memorial Club

OTHER
2 Information Centre
5 Swimming Pool
9 Museum
13 Harvey World Travel
16 Post Office
17 Town Hall
21 Victoria Park
22 Courthouse
23 Lands Office

Forbes

CENTRAL WEST

by the **courthouse** (1880) and the **Vandenberg Hotel**, less grandiose but better proportioned than other hotels in town, such as the three-storey **Albion Hotel** on Lachlan St. A watch was kept for Cobb & Co coaches from the tower on top of this pub. The **Lands Office** (now the state government offices) on Camp St is a fine wooden building, designed for the climate.

Osborne Hall on Cross St was the dance-hall of the Osborne Hotel and now houses the **Forbes Museum** (☎ 6852 1694) of local history, with Ben Hall relics. It's open daily October to May from 2 to 4 pm, June to September from 3 to 5 pm; admission is $2 ($1 children).

Lachlan Vintage Village

One km south, beside the Newell Highway and with some original and some re-created buildings, the village (☎ 6852 2655) is on the site of the old goldfields. It's bigger than it looks from the highway and you can pan for gold. It's open daily from 8 am to 5.30 pm; admission is $8 ($4 children).

Gum Swamp

Just off the Newell Highway about 4km south of Forbes, this wetland area is home to many species of birds. There's a hide to watch them from; sunset and sunrise are the best times.

Wineries

The **Sandhills Vineyard** (☎ 6852 1437), about 6km north-east of town, off Orange Rd (the continuation of Camp and Bridge Sts), opens for tastings on Monday and Thursday to Saturday. There's a wine museum here. **Lachlan Valley Wines** (☎ 6852 3983), on Wandary Lane, which splits from the Cowra road just after the Apex caravan park, opens daily.

Places to Stay

Camping The *Country Club Caravan Park* (☎ 6852 1957), on Sam St north of town, has sites for $11. *Forbes River Meadows Caravan Park* (☎ 6852 2694), by the Lachlan River on the Newell south-west of

town, has sites for $7 and on-site vans for $22. *Apex Caravan Park* (☎ 6852 1929), also by the Lachlan but south-east of town near the Cowra road, has sites for $9 and cabins for $25/30.

Hotels & Motels The old but clean *Vandenberg Hotel* (☎ 6852 2015), on Court St across from Victoria Park, has rooms for $20/30. On Lachlan St, the *Victoria Hotel* (☎ 6852 1269) has rooms with bath for $38; there's also accommodation at the impressive *Albion Hotel* (☎ 6852 1919).

Most motels are pricey. *Lake Forbes Motel* (☎ 6852 2922) is one of the cheapest at $43/49, but it's close to the highway, as are many others. In a quiet location near Victoria Park and the town centre, the *Plainsman Motor Inn* (☎ 6852 2466), 22 Sherriff St, is good, but not cheap at $62/70.

Places to Eat

The food options here aren't great, especially for cheap, quick meals. On Templar St, *Esme's Coffee Lounge* has toasted sandwiches for $3.

There are several Chinese places, including the *Chung Shan* which has lunch specials for $4, the *Forbes Garden* and *Golden Dragon*. The *Services Memorial Club* on the corner of Sheriff and Templar Sts has a restaurant, and there are plenty of pub meals for under $10.

At Lachlan Vintage Village the *Blackridge Restaurant* serves local wines.

Getting There & Away

Harvey World Travel (☎ 6852 2344), 6 Templar St, handles bus and air bookings.

Air Hazelton flies to Sydney twice a day.

Bus Forbes has a lot of long-distance bus traffic, including Greyhound Pioneer and McCafferty's. Countrylink buses stop at the railway station and run to Orange, Parkes and Condobolin.

Car & Motorcycle As well as the Newell Highway there are smaller roads heading

Ben Hall & Elvis

Ben Hall (1838-65) lived and died at a time when the ordinary people of Australia were beginning to see themselves as a people; a time when the concepts of democracy (in the social as well as political sense) and suspicion of authority were becoming ingrained in the national character.

However, political and economic power was still wielded by a British-oriented elite. Land and power were apportioned to people of quality (or at least wealth), and it was still expected that the British class system would take root in Australia. If ordinary colonials were not sufficiently servile it was because they were crude and uneducated. The legal system was well equipped to deal with such upstarts.

Ben Hall's parents had been convicts and he grew up with a hatred of the prevailing system and of police in particular. He lived a reasonably respectable life, working as a stockman and leasing a cattle-run, until his wife left him – for a policeman! Enraged, he joined Frank Gardiner and John Gilbert and turned to bush-ranging.

For two years they terrorised and mocked the gentry of a large area in the Central West. Their exploits smacked of larrikinism – capturing and ridiculing police, forcing respectable folk to get drunk and sing songs, stealing racehorses, giving alcohol and cigars to the poor – and above all demonstrating that it was possible to flout the conventions of society. The gang saw themselves as latter-day Robin Hoods, and to the local people they were heroes. The police were unable to capture them because no-one would inform on the gang, until 1865 when the government began to punish people who associated with Hall and his cronies.

Ben Hall was shot dead by police on 5 May 1865, but just how he was killed is uncertain. The official story is that he died while resisting arrest, but popular legend has it that he was shot while sleeping. His bullet-riddled body was displayed in Forbes as an awful warning to would-be renegades, but people openly mourned at his funeral and his status as a folk hero grew. Flowers are still sometimes placed on his grave in the Forbes cemetery.

A bitter folk-song, 'The Streets of Forbes', gives the popular version of his career and death.

In Farnell St in Forbes there's a replica of a house associated with another apparent rebel beloved of the common folk and still loudly mourned – Elvis Presley's Graceland, built, somewhat appropriately, by the local undertaker. ■

east to Canowindra and Cowra, south to Grenfell and west to Condobolin and into the far west.

Getting Around

Forbes Bus Lines (☎ 6852 1663) runs local buses. Car-rental companies Budget (☎ 6852 2245) and Hertz (☎ 6852 1755) have agents in town. Phone ☎ 6852 2222 for a taxi.

CONDOBOLIN & AROUND

Condobolin (pronounced 'con-*dough*-blin' and often called Condo for short) is a medium-sized town (population 3500) on the Lachlan River. It's the service centre for farms in the Lachlan Valley, but the dry country begins to the west and north.

There were once many Chinese living in the area and there's a restored section of Chinese graves in the town's cemetery.

The 40-hectare **Gum Bend Lake**, 3km west of Condo, is a venue for watersports. In town, Taylor's Marine, on Lachlan St, hires watersports equipment. About 8km north of Condo is **Mt Tilga**, officially the geographical centre of NSW. There's a road to the bottom and you can climb to the top of the mountain.

Places to Stay
The shaded *Riverview Caravan Park* (☎ 6895 2611), on the banks of the Lachlan south of the bridge, has sites for $8.

The pubs have accommodation and the *Condobolin Hotel* (☎ 6895 2040) has motel-style units for $40/45. Two motels, *Condobolin Motor Inn* (☎ 6895 2233) and the *Allambie* (☎ 6895 2722), are on William St.

Getting There & Away
Harvey World Travel (☎ 6895 2988), on Bathurst St, handles air and bus bookings.

Air Hazelton flies daily to/from Sydney.

Bus Countrylink buses run to Cootamundra ($42) via Lake Cargelligo, West Wyalong and Temora, and to Parkes, Forbes and Orange.

Car & Motorcycle Roads run east to the Newell Highway at Parkes or Forbes, and south to the Newell at West Wyalong. You can drive west to Lake Cargelligo and on to the Riverina and the far west. There are also some interesting routes north; see the following section.

NORTH OF CONDOBOLIN
North of Condobolin, the farmland begins to blur into the outback. If you're heading north to the Barrier Highway there are several routes from Condobolin which don't involve backtracking to the Newell Highway. These are all at least partly unsealed, so check conditions before setting out, drive carefully and take a good map.

To Cobar, the Nymagee road runs through **Bobadah** (no fuel or accommodation) and **Nymagee**, a hamlet with basic services including the *Nymagee Hotel* (☎ 6837 3854). You can also get to Cobar on the **Kidman Way**. To get to this mostly sealed route (it's due to be fully sealed by the end of 1998) you can head west to Euabalong, about 60km west of Condobolin, but for better roads head south-west through Lake Cargelligo and take the turn-off onto the Kidman Way midway between Lake Cargelligo and Hillston. **Mt Hope** consists of the *Royal Hotel* (☎ 6897 7984), a service station and a shop. It's a friendly hamlet (population 12) on the Kidman Way and used to be a large copper-mining town. If you're a motorcyclist, the annual Mt Hope Rally, held on the last weekend in May, is a good time to visit.

To get to Nyngan you can either head directly north from Condobolin (if you have a good map) or, for a better road, drive east towards Parkes and turn off to **Tullamore**, a fair-sized village about 80km north-east of Condobolin, with a pub (☎ 6892 5195), fuel and shops. Further on is **Tottenham**, a smaller but nicer place. There's a pub here as well (☎ 6892 4211). Along this route is the small town of **Trundle**, which is reputed to have Australia's widest street.

COWRA
Cowra (population 8640) developed because it was on the only easy crossing of the Lachlan River for some way. The town straggles up the side of a steep hill above the river. The main landmark in town is the one set of traffic lights, on the corner of Kendal (the Mid-Western Highway) and Brisbane Sts.

The information centre (☎ 6342 4333), on the highway west of the shopping centre across the bridge, opens daily from 9 am to 5 pm.

During WWII, the POW camp at Cowra was the scene of the Cowra breakout. The **Japanese War Cemetery** is a few km north of town on Binni Creek Rd (Brisbane St).

Japanese Garden
Built as a token of Cowra's connection with Japanese POWs (but with no overt mention of the war or the breakout), the garden and the attached cultural centre are worth visiting. The large garden, serene and beautifully maintained, was a gift from the Japanese government. The cultural centre is a peaceful place with displays of modern Japanese art,

CENTRAL WEST

The Cowra Breakout

During WWII the large prisoner-of-war (POW) camp at Cowra held mainly Italian and Japanese prisoners. In the early hours of 5 August 1944 the Japanese prisoners overran their section of the camp and nearly 400 went over the wire in an escape attempt that never had a chance of succeeding. Of the 230 Japanese who died, many had committed suicide.

The official report of the Cowra breakout (available at the information centre for $2.50) makes interesting reading. It's strange that amid the racist propaganda of WWII, the inquiry into the breakout was concerned about how much force was used on the escapees and whether the Japanese dead were treated with respect. Soldiers hunting the escapees were armed only with bayonets until one was killed.

The book *Die Like the Carp* (available at the information centre) tells the story of the breakout. ■

some modern Japanese kitsch and some antiques. There's a collection of Ukiyo-e paintings, depicting everyday events in the lives of ordinary people in pre-industrial Japan.

The garden opens daily from 8.30 am to 5 pm; admission is $6 ($4 children).

The garden is at the top of Bellevue Hill, a steep km or so north up Brisbane St. Also on the hilltop is the **Bellevue Hill Flora & Fauna Reserve**, a complete contrast to its formal neighbour.

Steam Museum

Cowra Steam Museum (☎ 6341 1052), on Campbell St, opens on weekends and holidays from 9.30 am to 4.30 pm; entry is $5. From here, the Lachlan Valley Railway Society runs steam trains two or three days a month to Blayney and Canowindra.

Special Events

The agricultural show and Sakura Matsuri, the Cherry Blossom Festival, are held in October.

Places to Stay

Camping *Cowravan Park* (☎ 6342 1058), by the river on Lachlan St, south of Kendal St, has sites for $10 and cabins for $40.

Hotels & Motels Most hotels have accommodation, including the big *Imperial Hotel* (☎ 6342 1588) at the western end of Kendal St, with basic rooms for $20/30.

Motels include the *Cowra Motor Inn*

(☎ 6342 2799), 3 Macquarie St, with rooms for $36/46 and the *Aalana* (☎ 6341 1177), 161 Kendal St ($63/70); the *Vineyard* (☎ 6342 3641), a small place about 4km south-west of town on Chardonnay Rd, away from highway noise, has rooms for $70/75.

Places to Eat

Most eateries are on Kendal St. The pies at *Royce's Bakery* regularly score well in the Great Aussie Meat Pie competition. The *Garden of Roses* cafe has sandwiches for $2, burgers for $2.90 and pizza. Nearby, the *Hoang Hing* Chinese restaurant opens daily for lunch and dinner.

Ilfracombe (☎ 6341 1511), 127 Kendal St, east of the traffic lights, is a historic cottage housing an excellent restaurant with a cafe in its next-door extension. The restaurant, open for dinner Wednesday to Saturday, has a French-based menu using local produce and serves local wines. Mains are $15 to $18. The cafe opens Tuesday to Saturday for lunch and dinner, with mains from $10 to $15. On Saturday night you can have dinner in the cafe and get a movie ticket for $18.

Getting There & Away

Bus Rendell's Coaches runs daily to Orange ($25) and Canberra ($30) from the information centre. Greyhound Pioneer stops at the Mobil station, near the information centre, on its run between Melbourne and Brisbane. Countrylink runs between Bathurst and Cootamundra, and stops on Macquarie St near the corner of Kendal St.

Lachlan Travel (☎ 6342 4000), 61 Kendal St, sells tickets and is the Countrylink agent.

Car & Motorcycle Cowra is on the Mid-Western Highway, which runs west through Grenfell to the Newell Highway north of West Wyalong and north-east to Bathurst. The Olympic Way runs south-west to Young and Wagga Wagga. Smaller roads run south to the Hume Highway at Yass, south-east to Crookwell and Goulburn (also on the Hume), north to Canowindra and north-west to Forbes.

AROUND COWRA
To the west of Cowra the Lachlan River flows through picturesque, fertile farmland. The road to Forbes (turn off the Mid-Western Highway about 5km south of Cowra) runs along the south bank of the Lachlan and is a nice drive. At Paynters Bridge, about 45km on from the turn-off, cross the Lachlan to visit **Eugowra**, a rambling village in the shadow of bush-clad hills. Eugowra was held up by Ben Hall in 1863, and there is a re-enactment every October. Granite quarried here was used to build the new Parliament House in Canberra. You can also get here (and to Forbes) via Canowindra, via a road along the Lachlan's north side.

Canowindra
The sprawling town of Canowindra (population 1720), about 30km north of Cowra, is a service centre for the surrounding rich farmlands. It has a number of old buildings, and curving Gaskill St, the main street, follows the route of a bullock-cart track. In 1863 bushranger Ben Hall held up the town for three days.

Schneider's Bakery, on Gaskill St, has limited tourist information and good pies; it's open daily. Nearby, a library window displays some finds from a rich fossil-bed discovered in the area. More fossils are in the **Age of Fishes Museum** (☎ 6344 1008), whose temporary home is in the old courthouse on Gaskill St, while a new museum is being built. It's open weekends from 11 am to 3 pm; entry is $5 ($3 children), which includes a tour and talk. It also arranges visits to the fossil sites.

Canowindra's main attraction is **ballooning**. Several outfits offer flights; Balloon Aloft (☎ 6344 1852, 1800 028 568) charges $130 for a flight and champagne breakfast.

Places to Stay *Canowindra Caravan Park* (☎ 6344 1272), by the river near the top of Gaskill St, has powered sites for $12. *Canowindra Hotel* (☎ 6344 1407), on Gaskill St near the park, has singles/doubles for $20/35. *Blue Jacket Motel* (☎ 6344 1002), on the Cowra road a couple of km from the village centre, charges $45/54.

Getting There & Away Countrylink buses stop on the corner of Gaskill and Blatchford Sts at the northern end of town.

Wyangala Waters SRA
Taking in Wyangala Dam south-east of Cowra, the SRA (☎ 6345 0877) is popular for watersports such as windsurfing, swimming, canoeing and sailing. Accommodation includes tent sites, a caravan park, cottages and cabins. There's also a *houseboat* sleeping seven or eight for $160 per night Sunday to Thursday, $300 per night on Friday and Saturday. It costs more in the peak season when there's also a two-night minimum.

Conimbla National Park
This small park (7590 hectares) is in two sections, only one of which has ready access. There's some pleasant forest and, in the spring, wildflowers.

There's camping within the park along Barryrennie Rd, the main access road. *Barryrennie Camping Ground* (☎ 6342 9239), at the south-eastern end of the park, is a simple place geared to bushwalkers and with basic facilities. The owners are friendly and can help with information on the park. Sites cost $7 per person.

The park can be reached from Gooloogong to the north (on the Cowra-Forbes road) or from Cowra – head west towards Grenfell for 9km and turn right at the signposted turn-off.

Nangar National Park

Even smaller, this park (4000 hectares) is 15km east of Eugowra on the road to Cudal and Orange. Despite its size there is a range of vegetation and it offers some tough bushwalking. There are no facilities and only foot access. The Bathurst NPWS office (☎ 6331 9777) has more information.

Grenfell

Grenfell (population 2300) is a quiet country town today, but in 1867 there were 10,000 diggers here searching for gold. Main St curves through the town centre and has some beautiful old buildings, notably the banks. Running parallel is tiny George St, the original (and even more curved) main street where a couple of the original buildings still stand.

Tourist information is available from the Wool & Craft Centre on Main St; it's open daily from 10 am to 4 pm.

The town's main claim to fame is that Henry Lawson was born here in 1867, although he and his family left for the goldfields near Gulgong when he was an infant. A memorial marking Lawson's birthplace is off the highway at the eastern edge of town; turn off just before the railway crossing. The annual **Henry Lawson Arts Festival** is held around the writer's birthday on 17 June.

For something completely different, Grenfell hosts the **National Guinea Pig Races** in June.

Places to Stay The *Exchange Hotel* (☎ 6343 1034), on Main St, has rooms for $20 per person including breakfast, while the equally impressive *Railway Hotel* at the bottom of Main St charges $15 per person. The *Grenfell Motel* (☎ 6343 1333), also on Main St, charges $41/50 a single/double.

Weddin Mountains National Park

Nineteen km south-west of Grenfell, Weddin isn't large (8361 hectares) but it's a rugged place with lots of wildlife, Aboriginal sites and some good walking trails. *Holy Camp* in the north-west and *Seatons Camp* in the north-east are camping areas; both have road

access and you can walk between them. The NPWS office (☎ 6331 9777) in Bathurst has more information.

WEST WYALONG & AROUND

West Wyalong, a middling town (population 3800) on the Newell and Mid-Western highways, is a rare example of stubbornness winning out over bureaucracy. A settlement grew up here during a gold rush late last century, but the government decided that Wyalong, a few km east, was to be the town. A grid of streets was laid out, official buildings were erected and the government waited for the population of West Wyalong to get the message and move. They didn't. West Wyalong is still the larger town and its Main St follows the same curving path it did when it was a bullock track.

The information centre (☎ 6972 3645) is in an old railway carriage in McCann Park, on the Mid-Western Highway at the eastern end of Main St.

Things to See & Do

The Bland District (West Wyalong is part of this unfortunately named shire) **museum**, at the eastern end of Main St, has a collection of photos of the goldfields and the town's development. It's open daily from 2.30 to 5 pm; entry is $3/50c.

The local Aboriginal Land Council has a craft and artefact shop at 76 Main St, towards the eastern end.

In **Barmedman**, 35km south, there's a huge mineral-water swimming pool. (See Temora in The Riverina chapter.)

When it's full, **Lake Cowal** is the largest freshwater lake in the state. The area is an animal sanctuary and the lake supports plenty of bird-life, but getting to see it isn't simple. The lake is surrounded by farmland and even the usually accurate NRMA map has problems with the tangle of backroads and farm tracks around the lake. Don't travel on them after heavy rain. A road leading in the general direction of the lake leaves the Newell Highway about 15km north of Marsden, a hamlet at the junction of the Mid-Western Highway. Good luck.

Places to Stay

There are two caravan parks, the *Ace* (☎ 6972 3061), on the corner of the Newell and Mid-Western highways, and the *West Wyalong* (☎ 6972 3133) on Main St. Both have sites for $10 as well as cabins and on-site vans.

Tattersalls Hotel (☎ 6972 2030), on the corner of Main and Monash Sts, is a friendly place with pub rooms for $25/35 including breakfast. Across the road, the *Post Office Hotel* (☎ 6972 2118), which is a fair way from the post office, also has accommodation.

There are about a dozen motels, many on the Mid-Western Highway between West Wyalong and Wyalong. The *Acacia Golden Way Motel* (☎ 6972 2155), 45 Main St, is good value at $46/56 for large rooms. The *Central* (☎ 6972 2777) at the eastern end of town is cheaper ($34/40).

Places to Eat

The *New Paragon Cafe* is West Wyalong's main-street eatery, with steak sandwiches for $3.50. *Rowie's Diner*, near McCann Park, has sausage and eggs for $6.50.

The pubs on Main St have counter meals. *Tattersalls Hotel* has specials for $5. There's also the *Jan Wah* Chinese restaurant on Main St, and the *Services & Citizens Club* on Monash St.

In Wyalong you can buy meals at a 24-hour service station.

Getting There & Away

Countrylink buses run to Cootamundra and Condobolin. The stop is on Church St off Main St, around the corner from the post office. Harvey World Travel (☎ 6972 2744), next to the post office, takes bookings.

YOUNG

Young (population 12,000), Australia's 'cherry capital', is on the edge of the western slopes of the Great Divide. East of here is rolling country; to the west the plains of the Riverina begin.

Cherries were first planted here in around 1860 by Nicole Jasprizza, who arrived during one of the Central West's many gold rushes. His orchard was an immediate success and expanded rapidly.

Today there are about 130 orchards producing a large proportion of Australia's crop and earning Young its 'cherry capital' tag. Prunes are also an important local industry, but 'prune capital' doesn't have quite the same ring.

The notorious 'White Australia policy' of Australia's early years had its origins near Young – goldfield riots at Lambing Flat in 1861 led to the government restriction on Chinese immigration, a classic example of blaming the victim.

Information

The tourist information centre (☎ 6382 5433), near the creek on Short St (the Olympic Way as it enters town from the south), opens Monday to Friday from 9 am to 5 pm, weekends 9.30 am to 4 pm.

Work The cherry harvest is in November and December. In January other stone fruits are harvested and in February the prune harvest begins. The CES office (☎ 6382 3366), 187 Boorowa St, if it still exists, can help you find fruit-picking work.

Wineries

This area produced wine grapes from the 1880s until the 1930s, when the more profitable cherry orchards took over. In the 1970s the Barwang vineyard was established, and there are now about 15 small vineyards in the area, with a couple you can visit for tastings and sales. **Woodonga Hill** (☎ 6389 2972), north-east of Young on the Cowra road, opens daily; **Demondrille Vineyards** (☎ 6384 4272), south on the Prunevale road near Kingsvale, opens Friday to Sunday.

Other Attractions

The **Lambing Flat Folk Museum** (☎ 6382 2248), on Campbell St, displays many artefacts from the goldfields. It's open daily from 10 am to 4 pm; entry is $2/50c.

The information centre can tell you about

orchards open for inspection and where you can pick your own fruit.

The **Millard's Building** is on Boorowa St, the main street, opposite the town hall with its memorial tower. It was once a huge department store, built by Edward Millard who started out as a 'carpenter, joiner and undertaker'.

Special Events
The Cherry Festival is held over several weeks in late November and early December – but if you want to see the trees in blossom, come in early October, when there's a Cherry Blossom Festival.

The Young Show is held in late September. The Young-Burragong Picnic Races are held in May, and this is one of the largest picnic race meetings in the state.

Places to Stay & Eat
Young Caravan Park (☎ 6382 2190), on Zouch St (the Olympic Way) across the railway line north of the town centre, has tent sites for $10, on-site vans from $25 to $27 and self-contained units from $38.

A number of pubs have accommodation, the cheapest being the *Empire* (☎ 6382 1665) on Lovell St at $15/25. Most others charge about $20/35. The *Great Eastern Hotel Motel* (☎ 6382 2411) on Boorowa St charges $20/30 in the hotel section, $35/40 in the motel. Other motels, including the *Cherry Blossom* (☎ 6382 1699), the *Colonial* (☎ 6382 2822) and the *Goldrush* (☎ 6382 3444), are in the $50/60 bracket.

The information centre has details of B&Bs and farmstays in the area.

Gabriella's Place, on the corner of Zouch and Lovell Sts (a block north of Boorowa St), serves pasta for $6 to $9 from 5.30 pm. Next door, *PJ's* is a popular daytime fast-food stop.

Getting There & Away
Bus Buses stop at the old railway station on Lovell St. Countrylink buses run to Cootamundra and Bathurst, Greyhound Pioneer to Melbourne and Brisbane. Lachlan

Travel (☎ 6382 4340), 12 Boorowa St, sells tickets.

Car & Motorcycle The Olympic Way runs north-east from Young to Cowra and south to Cootamundra. Smaller roads run north to Grenfell, west to Temora and south-east to Yass.

COOTAMUNDRA
Cootamundra (population 8240), by the Cootamundry Creek and with the smaller Muttama Creek flowing through town, is the service centre for the surrounding fertile farmland and is also an important railway junction. The town was founded in around 1860 and was known as Cootamundry. It wasn't until the 1950s that the current name was officially recognised.

The town is some way from the main through-routes and retains a coherence lacking in highway towns. Its neat grid of streets contains many fine examples of houses built in the Federation style, and there are also a few earlier Victorian gems.

Cootamundra is in the foothills of the Great Dividing Range and the town is cold in winter, sometimes receiving snowfalls.

Orientation & Information
Parker St is the main shopping street, and its intersection with Wallendoon St, where you'll find the impressive post office, town hall and several banks, is the centre of town. At the railway station on Hovell St, there's a tourist office (☎ 6942 4212), open daily from 10 am to 4 pm.

Things to See & Do
Donald Bradman, Australia's greatest cricketer, was born here in 1908, and his family's home, a modest weatherboard house at 89 Adams St (the north-east end of Adams St), is now a **museum** (☎ 6942 2744). It's open daily 8.30 am to 4.30 pm; entry is $2, children free. The Bradmans moved to Bowral when he was still very young, and it's there that The Don learned his craft.

The climate means that European trees flourish (the elms along Cooper St are over

100 years old) and there are several quite formal parks. **Albert Park** is on Hovell St near the railway station and **Jubilee Park**, on the other side of the city centre, has an Olympic-size swimming pool dating from 1935. Just south of town, across the Cootamundry Creek, **Pioneer Park** is a nature reserve taking in some hilly bushland with picnic places, good views and a short walking trail.

The town of Cootamundra is best known for the **Cootamundra wattle** *(Acacia baileyana)*; its profuse yellow flowers are a sign that winter is nearly over. Although native to this area, Cootamundra wattle has been planted throughout the cooler areas of southern Australia. The Wattle Time Festival is held in August.

Places to Stay & Eat

Cootamundra Caravan Park (☎ 6942 1080) is well sited in pretty Jubilee Park, beside the Muttama Creek, just west of the town centre. It has sites for $13 and on-site caravans for $25.

The *Globe* (☎ 6942 1446) and *Albion* (☎ 6942 1177) hotels, on the corner of Parker and Wallendoon Sts, have pub rooms for $25/35. There are several motels, including the *Wattle Tree* (☎ 6942 2688) on Wallendoon St, not far from the railway station, which charges from $39/49.

There aren't many places to eat in Cootamundra. *Country Cuisine* on Parker St has coffee and light meals, such as chicken for $5. Next door, the *Chatterie* is a BYO restaurant; quiche is $8. *Cootamundra Country Club*, on Hurley St, and the pubs also have meals.

Getting There & Away

There's a Countrylink Travel Centre (☎ 6942 0446) at the railway station.

Bus Countrylink buses meet the train and run to Bathurst ($30 one way) via Cowra, Dubbo via Forbes and Parkes, Condobolin via West Wyalong and Lake Cargelligo, and Balranald via Griffith.

Train XPTs running between Sydney and Melbourne stop here twice daily.

Car & Motorbike The Olympic Way runs north-east to Young and south-west to Junee and Wagga Wagga. Smaller roads run north-west to Temora and south to the Hume Highway; you can also meet the Hume by heading south-east to Yass.

The North-West

This wedge of NSW, between New England and the Mitchell Highway, is flat, dry but largely fertile country, especially in the broad valley of the Namoi River. Cattle and cotton are the main industries.

Many of the towns in the area are small, relaxed places, still conscious of the hard work that went into their establishment, and aware that their status as outposts of settlement gives them an importance greater than their size. It's only since WWII that good roads have linked many towns, and even today they can be isolated by floods.

Except for visitors to the Warrumbungle National Park and the steady stream of traffic on the Newell Highway, the north-west doesn't see many tourists.

Geography
Unlike other regions west of the Great Dividing Range, there are few significant foothills in the north-west. The Warrumbungle and Nandewar ranges straddle the fertile Namoi Valley, whose river meanders west onto the plains to join the Barwon River, which becomes the Darling River – which eventually joins the Murray and flows to South Australia.

Much of the area is a vast artesian basin, and there are hot artesian baths in Moree and Lightning Ridge. Bore water is often too salty for human consumption, and even potable water can taste strongly of sulphur – if you let it stand for a while, the gases dissipate and the taste fades.

Getting There & Away
Air Yanda (book through Qantas), Hazelton (book through Ansett) and Eastern Australia (book through Qantas) are among the airlines serving the north-west.

Bus Towns on the Newell Highway are served by Brisbane to Melbourne or Adelaide buses. Countrylink connects most other towns in the area with Sydney, usually with

HIGHLIGHTS

- Bushwalking in the Warrumbungle Range in spring
- The view from the summit of Mt Kaputar
- Soaking in the hot spa baths at Moree after a long day's drive
- Meeting up with some of the characters who mine for opal at Lightning Ridge

a train/bus combination via Dubbo, Tamworth or Moree.

Train Explorer trains from Sydney run north as far as Moree ($70).

Car & Motorcycle The Newell Highway, running through the north-west, is a good road that provides the quickest route between Melbourne and Brisbane. The Castlereagh Highway, forking off the Newell at Gilgandra, runs more or less directly north into the rugged opal country towards the Queensland border. The Mitchell Highway heads west through Nyngan, and the Gwydir Highway runs east from Collarenebri through to New England.

GUNNEDAH
Gunnedah is a large country town (population 10,000) on the Oxley Highway and the edge of the Namoi Valley's plains. Back in

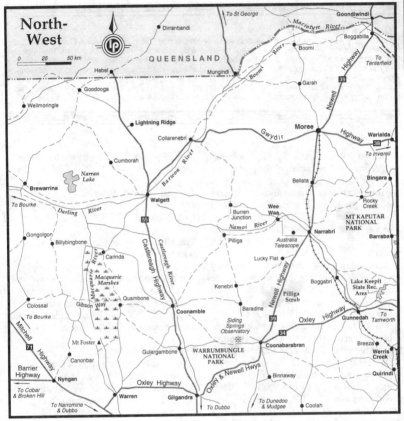

North-West

QUEENSLAND

0   25   50 km

To St George
Dirranbandi
Goondiwindi
Macintyre River
Boomi
Boggabilla
Hebel
Mungindi
To Tenterfield
Garah
Newell Highway
39
Goodooga
Weilmoringle
Lightning Ridge
Collarenebri
Moree
Warialda
Gwydir
Highway
38
To Inverell
Cumborah
Barwon River
Narran Lake
Bellata
Bingara
Brewarrina
Rocky Creek
To Bourke
Darling River
Walgett
55
Wee Waa
Burren Junction
MT KAPUTAR NATIONAL PARK
Namoi River
Barraba
Gongolgon
Pilliga
Narrabri
Billybingbone
Australia Telescope
Carinda
Castlereagh Highway
Lucky Flat
Macquarie River
Macquarie Marshes
Castlereagh River
Kenebri
Boggabri
Lake Keepit State Rec. Area
Colossal
Gibson Way
Quambone
Pilliga Scrub
Newell Highway
To Bourke
Coonamble
Baradine
Oxley Highway
Gunnedah
To Tamworth
Mitchell Highway
71
Mt Foster
Siding Springs Observatory
39
34
Breeza
Gulargambone
WARRUMBUNGLE NATIONAL PARK
Coonabarabran
Werris Creek
Barrier Highway
Canonbar
Oxley & Newell Hwys
Quirindi
Nyngan
Oxley Highway
Binnaway
To Cobar & Broken Hill
Warren
Gilgandra
To Dubbo
To Dunedoo & Mudgee
Coolah
To Narromine & Dubbo

the hills to the north-east is Lake Keepit, a big dam on the Namoi which provides water for irrigating the region's cotton crops.

There's also coal in the area, and in a few decades production might rival that of the Hunter Valley.

Information
The Gunnedah Visitors Centre (☎ 6742 4300) is in Anzac Park, just south of the railway lines from the town centre.

Things to See & Do
Just uphill from the visitors centre is the

Water Tower Museum, open from 2 to 5 pm on Saturday, while opposite is a memorial to poet **Dorothea Mackellar**. Her poem 'My Country' contains arguably the most famous stanza in Australian poetry:

I love a sunburnt country,
A land of sweeping plains,
Of ragged mountain ranges,
Of droughts and flooding rains.

You can listen to a recording of Mackellar reading her poem on local radio 88 FM. It's a very short-range transmitter – you have to

Ode to a New Country

While many Australians know the second verse of 'My Country', the one that begins 'I love a sunburnt country', not many know the whole poem, which is a declaration of independence from 'The love of field and coppice/Of green and shaded lanes'. These sentiments weren't very remarkable in Australia in the early 1900s, when writers and painters had already staked Australia's claim to an individual identity. However, Dorothea Mackellar came from a wealthy, landed family, the sort of people who looked to England as 'home'. That she wrote poetry not just extolling the Australian landscape but comparing it more than favourably to England was a sign that the new nation had found its feet. ■

be within 100m of the statue. The information centre has free copies of the poem.

At the visitors centre, pick up a copy of the **town tour** map. There are also brochures detailing the Lands Department's **Bindeah Walking Track**, which leads from the visitors centre to Porcupine Lookout. On the way you might see some kangaroos and koalas.

Gunnedah Rural Museum on the Oxley Highway to the west of the town boasts 'the largest gun display in northern NSW' as well as antique farm equipment. It's open daily and admission is $3 ($1.50 children).

On the corner of Abbott and Little Conadilly Sts, across from the police station, is the **grave-site of Cumbo Gunnerah**, an 18th-century Aboriginal leader known as Red Kangaroo. His burial place is marked by a bronze cast of the carved tree which once stood over the site. It's rare to have any physical reminder of individual Aborigines who lived before European contact. The events of Cumbo Gunnerah's life are related in *The Red Chief* by Ian Idriss.

Lake Keepit, 35 km north-east of Gunnedah, is a popular holiday centre, with boating and other activities. The large *Easts Van Park* (☎ 6769 7620) has sites from $8 and on-site vans and tents.

The village of **Breeza**, 57 km south-east of Gunnedah, is the disputed birthplace of bushranger Ben Hall, and a mural here shows the events of Ben's last years.

Places to Stay

There's camping at the *Tourist Caravan Park* (☎ 6742 1372), pub accommodation at the *Regal Hotel* (☎ 6742 2355) and a number of motels.

Getting There & Away

Air Yanda flies between Sydney and Gunnedah for $176.

Train Trains stop in Gunnedah ($58) on the way from Sydney to Moree.

Car & Motorcycle The Oxley Highway runs east to Tamworth and south-west to Coonabarabran. Smaller roads run north to Boggabri and Narrabri, and south to Coolah and the upper end of the Hunter Valley.

BOGGABRI & AROUND

Boggabri, 40km north-west of Gunnedah on the road to Narrabri, is a sleepy little town which still manages to support three old pubs. There's a small **museum**.

Gin's Leap, about 6km north of Boggabri, is a sheer rockface with great views from the top. (There are probably as many gins' leaps in Australia as there are bushrangers' caves – many cliffs seem to have presented themselves as suicide places for Aboriginal women, at least in white imaginations, just as any hole in the ground is obviously the hide-out of some desperado.)

About 35km from Boggabri and 85km south-east of Narrabri, **Dripping Rock** is a 50m waterfall that's spectacular after rain and never quite dries up. To get there, take the Manilla road turn-off just north of Boggabri and turn left at the Maules Creek sign after 8km. Three km later, take the right-hand turn and travel for 16km. You'll pass through a couple of gates before you arrive at the car park, from where it's a short walk to the falls. This is a dry-weather road.

The **Wean Picnic Races** are held on the first Monday in May and attract large crowds. The racetrack is about 80km south-east of Narrabri, 22km east of Boggabri.

Up the Newell

GILGANDRA

Gilgandra is a sizeable town (population 2700) on the Castlereagh River, at the junction of the Newell, Castlereagh and Oxley highways.

The visitors centre (☎ 6847 2045) and a small **museum** (admission $2) are in Coo-ee March Memorial Park on the Newell Highway south of the town centre. During WWI, Gilgandra was the starting point for the Coo-ee March, when 26 volunteers set off for Sydney to enlist. Along the way they attracted 237 others, and all of them were duly shipped to the trenches.

The privately-run **Gilgandra Observatory** (☎ 6847 2646), on Willie St, has a 31cm telescope. It's open every evening except Sunday from 7 to 10 pm (from 8.30 pm during daylight saving). It also has an audio-visual display of the moon landings and other space flights. Admission is $8 ($5 children).

The **Australia Collection** is a large private exhibit of Aboriginal artefacts. It's on the northern edge of town by the Castlereagh Van Park, admission $2.

For some reason, Gilgandra is well supplied with antique and secondhand shops.

Places to Stay

There are three caravan parks, including the *Rotary Caravan Park* (☎ 6847 2423) by the river across the bridge from town. Tent sites cost $7 and cabins start at $30.

On the main street, the *Golden West Hotel* (☎ 6847 2109) has singles/doubles for $15/24. Nearby, and marginally better, the

Royal Hotel (☎ 6847 2004) charges $15/25 and has a guest kitchen.

As Gilgandra is a junction town, there are plenty of motels, most charging around $45 for doubles.

Getting There & Away

Bus The major lines stop here on their Newell Highway services. Countrylink buses run to Lightning Ridge and Dubbo.

Car & Motorcycle The Newell Highway runs north-east to Coonabarabran (this section of it doubles as the Oxley) and south to Dubbo; the Castlereagh Highway runs north to Coonamble; and the Oxley Highway runs west to Warren and Nyngan (and north-east to Coonabarabran). A smaller road runs south-east to Dunedoo and Mudgee.

COONABARABRAN

Coonabarabran (pronounced 'coona-*barra*-brn') is a small country town (population 3000) which has retained its shady main street (John St), despite the street being both the Newell and Oxley highways.

As well as serving as a base for visits to the Warrumbungle National Park, Coonabarabran is a handy stop on the Newell, being roughly halfway between Brisbane and Melbourne (although motels tend to be cheaper further south in Gilgandra). It's about 450km from Sydney, a fairly easy day's drive.

The town's name comes from Cooleburbarun, a squatting lease which was taken up in 1839, 20 years after John Oxley's party made the first European foray into the homelands of the Kamilario people.

Information

The information centre (☎ 6842 1441), on John St a few blocks south of the clocktower, opens daily from 9 am to 5 pm. There's also an NPWS office (☎ 6842 1311) on Cassilis St. Harvey World Travel (☎ 6842 1566) is on Dalgarno St.

The Ryder Brothers sports store on John St sells everything you've forgotten to bring for your camping trip to the Warrumbungles. It's a pleasantly chaotic old shop.

Things to See & Do
The area's main attraction is the nearby national park (see following section). Mike Caruana (☎ 6842 1560) offers **scenic flights** over the Warrumbungle Range for $40 per person (minimum two people). **Miniland**, 9km from town on the Warrumbungles road, has animated dinosaurs and children's activities.

Places to Stay
There's an associate *YHA hostel* on the road to Warrumbungle National Park – see the following section.

John Oxley Caravan Park (☎ 6842 1635) is a good park just north of the town centre. There's another caravan park, the *Wayfarer* (☎ 6842 1773), a few km south of town.

The *Imperial Hotel* (☎ 6842 1023), across from the clocktower, is a well-maintained, family-run pub with singles/doubles for $26/40, including breakfast. Rooms with attached bathroom go for $36/49. Other pubs in town also have accommodation. The town's 10 motels occasionally indulge in price wars.

Places to Eat
There's the usual country-town cafes, pub meals and motel dining rooms, such as the *Gunyah Restaurant* at the Country Gardens Motel (main courses about $17). The big *Golden Sea Dragon* Chinese restaurant has a $10.50 two-course deal, and there's a steakhouse at the northern end of John St. *Jolly Cauli* is a cafe serving salads and snacks. The smoothies ($3) are large and refreshing.

Getting There & Away
Air Yanda flies between Sydney and Coonabarabran ($190).

Bus The major bus-lines stop here on their Newell Highway services. Countrylink buses meet some trains at Lithgow and run to Coonabarabran via Mudgee from Sunday to Friday.

Car & Motorcycle The Newell Highway runs north to Narrabri and south to Gilgandra, and the Oxley Highway runs north-east to Gunnedah. Smaller roads run west to Warrumbungle National Park and on to the Castlereagh Highway at Gulargambone, and north to Baradine and Pilliga.

WARRUMBUNGLE NATIONAL PARK
The Warrumbungle Range makes an abrupt appearance in the midst of the region's gentle slopes. It was formed by volcanic activity 13 million years ago, and has been eroded into a strikingly rugged mountain range. In 1818, John Oxley described the Warrumbungles as:

...lofty hills arising from the midst of lesser elevations, their summits crowned with perpendicular rocks, in every variety of shape and form that the wildest imagination could paint...

The national park (20,900 hectares) is popular with sightseers, bushwalkers and rock climbers. There are many walking trails, both short and long. You need to see the rangers at the informative visitors centre (☎ 6825 4364), open daily, before undertaking the longer walks or rock climbing.

Entry fees are $7.50 for cars and $3 per person for hikers, motorcyclists etc.

There's a great range of flora and fauna, with spectacular displays of wildflowers in the spring. (Wildflowers aren't the only plants to thrive in the area – the national park grew by 620 hectares in 1993, when land confiscated from a marijuana-grower was added to it.)

Summers can be hot but it usually cools down at night, and while winter days are often sunny, there can be heavy frosts at night. The best time to visit is spring or autumn.

For more information on the park, *Warrumbungle National Park* by Peter Fox is an excellent guide to the park put out by the NPWS. Lonely Planet's *Bushwalking in*

Australia ($24.95) details the Grand High Tops walk.

Observatories
The elevation, remoteness and clear skies of the Warrumbungles make them a perfect place for stargazing, which is why the Australian and British governments chose to locate one of the world's most precise large telescopes here. The Anglo-Australian Telescope, with its 3.9m mirror, is one of eight telescopes dotting the hilltops at **Siding Springs Observatory**, 23km west of Coonabarabran on the road to the national park. There's a visitors centre, open daily from 9.30 am to 4 pm, where you can see the 'Exploring the Universe' exhibition of hands-on displays and videos. Admission to the exhibition is $5 ($3 children, $12 families). You can ride the lift to a viewing gallery inside the Australia telescope building (free), but there are no public viewing facilities.

If you want to view the stars, call in at the new **Skywatch Observatory**, 2km from Coonabarabran on the Warrumbungles road. It has a planetarium and astronomy exhibition for day visitors, open daily from 9 am, and astronomy sessions after dark. Day admission is $6, or $10 including an astronomy session.

Places to Stay
In the Park There are sites with electricity for $15 for two people, plus $3 for each extra person, and unpowered sites for $10 for two people, plus $2 for each extra person. Most of the park's camping areas are accessible by car. Hikers are charged $1 per night for bush camping. The *Woolshed* is a bunkhouse designed for groups, costing $4.50 per person and a minimum charge of $25.

Nearby The *Warrumbungles Mountain Motel* (☎ 6842 1832), 9km west of Coonabarabran on the road to the national park, doubles as an associate YHA hostel with a few rooms set aside as dorms. It charges $15 per person.

Tibuc (☎ 6842 1740, evenings best) is an organic farm on the boundary of the park,

with accommodation in a range of mud-brick buildings. The facilities range from no electricity at all to a solar system or full mains power. Each building sleeps up to six people. Rates start at $72 for one night, and much less for longer stays. Catering facilities are provided, or you can pay $25 for a three-course meal. There are also campsites for $5 per person or a caravan for $15. The turn-off to the farm is 16 km from Coonabarabran on the road to the park. Tibuc is popular and books out during school holidays.

On the western side of the park, *Gumin-Gumin* (☎ 6825 4368) is a beautiful old 1870s homestead with self-contained accommodation for $25 per person, less if you bring your own bedding.

Getting There & Away
The park entrance is 33km west of Coonabarabran, and most people come via that town, but you can also get here on smaller roads from Gulargambone or Coonamble, both on the Castlereagh Highway to the west of the park.

THE PILLIGA SCRUB
This 400,000-hectare forest between Coonabarabran and Narrabri has an interesting history which you can read about in Eric Rolls' outstanding book *A Million Wild Acres*. Rolls says that the current dense forest, a beautiful place with some interesting little roads winding through it, is a recent phenomenon. The early settlers cleared the land and wiped out the small marsupials which would have eaten many of the tree seedlings. After the farms failed because of unsuitable soils, the new forest exploded into life.

Baradine, north-west of Coonabarabran, is the main town in this part of the world, and roads running into the Pilliga Scrub run east from here and from Kenebri, 20km further north. The Forestry Office in Baradine has maps of drives through the Scrub. The hamlet of **Pilliga** itself, 50km north of Kenebri, remains much as it ever was. **Yarrie Lake**, near the Narrabri end of the Scrub and

NORTH-WEST

a few km south of the Australia Telescope, has prolific bird-life.

NARRABRI

As in so many other areas of the north-west, Major Mitchell made the first European foray and was quickly followed by others who took up land as squatters. Mitchell's visit was perhaps inevitable, but it was sparked by the capture of George Clark, a runaway convict who had lived with Aborigines for six years. The unfortunate Clark was sent off to Norfolk Island, but before leaving he told of rich lands and a big river flowing to an inland sea.

Split by the Namoi River and the Narrabri Creek, this old town (population 7300) is today in danger of becoming just another highway stop on the busy Newell. There are good places for picnics in the riverside parks.

The visitors centre (☎ 6792 3583) on the Newell Highway near the town centre has maps of drives and walks around town. It's open weekdays from 8.30 am to 5 pm and weekends from 9 am to 1 pm. There's an NPWS office (☎ 6792 4724) at 165 Maitland St.

There's good fossicking, especially for

Major Thomas Mitchell, the first European to explore many parts of the north-west

agates, near the township of **Bellata**, 40km north of Narrabri off the Newell Highway.

Places to Stay

There are several caravan parks in town. The *Council Caravan Park* (☎ 6792 1294), a block back from the highway, has a camping area by the river. The *Narrabri Motel* (☎ 6792 2593), on the highway south of the town centre, is the cheapest of the many motels. Ask at the visitors centre about the several farmstays in the area.

Getting There & Away

Air Eastern Australia flies between Sydney and Narrabri ($218) at least once a day.

Bus The major lines stop here on their Newell Highway services. McPhersons Coaches runs to Tamworth via Boggabri several times a week; buy tickets at the Ampol station (☎ 6743 4327) on the highway. Countrylink buses run to Wee Waa and other small towns.

Train The train running between Sydney and Moree stops here.

Car & Motorcycle The Newell Highway runs north to Moree and south to Coonabarabran. Smaller roads run south-east to Gunnedah, west to Wee Waa and on to Walgett, and north-east to Mt Kaputar National Park.

AUSTRALIA TELESCOPE

The Australia Telescope, 25km west of Narrabri, is an array of eight radio telescopes which form the Paul Wild Observatory. Six of them are here: five are lined up on a stretch of 'railway' track and the sixth is a few km away. There's another receiver near Siding Springs in the Warrumbungles and the last is a long way south, near Parkes. When all the receivers operate together, the effective diameter of the telescope is 320km!

This array, which began operating in 1990, helps keep Australia at the forefront of radio astronomy. One of the many wonderful facts about radio astronomy: all the radio telescopes in the world have collected less energy than is released by a raindrop falling to earth.

The visitors centre (☎ 6790 4070), with hands-on displays and videos, is near the railway track and one of the receivers is usually nearby. The centre is open daily from 8 am to 4 pm, and is staffed on weekdays.

MT KAPUTAR NATIONAL PARK

A rugged park on the westernmost spur of the Nandewar Range, Mt Kaputar National Park (36,800 hectares) is popular for bushwalking, rock climbing and, between August and October, wildflowers. Mt Kaputar itself rises to 1524m and snow has been known to fall on its peak. A road (unsuitable for caravans) runs close to the summit. From the Doug-Sky Lookout you can see 10% of NSW.

There are two established campsites with good facilities, *Dawsons Springs* and *Bark Hut*, both accessible from the road up the mountain. There are also cabins at Dawsons Springs – you have to book through the NPWS office (☎ 6792 4724) in Narrabri and there's a minimum stay of two days. The park visitors centre (☎ 6792 1147) at Dawsons Springs isn't always staffed. The road to Mt Kaputar runs north-east from Narrabri.

Sawn Rocks, at the northern end of the park, is a spectacular 40metre cliff-face formed of octagonal columns of basalt. The site is signposted off the Bingara road about 40 km north-east of Narrabri (turn off the highway about 3km north of Narrabri). A 900-metre walking trail leads through bush from the car park.

WEE WAA

Wee Waa is a quiet little town (population 2300) today but it was the first settlement to be established in the Namoi Valley. The 'waa' in Wee Waa is pronounced 'wor' – we're lucky that the early cartographers didn't spell it 'waugh'. The grand Imperial Hotel was the first three-storey building erected in the north-west.

Cotton was planted near Wee Waa in the 1960s and its success sparked the widespread planting of cotton throughout the area. Cotton is planted from late September to the end of October, the bolls begin to open in late February and the picking season is April and May. The **Namoi Cotton Co-op** (☎ 6790 3000) in Wee Waa arranges guided tours of farms and gins (processing plants) at 10.30 am and 2.30 pm during the picking season.

Cubbaroo (☎ 6796 1741), 45km west of Wee Waa, is the area's only winery and is open Wednesday to Sunday 10 am to 8pm.

Yanda flies between Sydney and Wee Waa ($175).

MOREE

Moree (population 10,000) was first settled in the 1840s and is the largest town on the north-west plains. It is the centre of a cotton and grain-growing district. The lush gardens of Moree's residential districts are in striking contrast to the bare surrounding plains.

The information centre (☎ 6752 7480) is west of the highway on Alice St, south of the first bridge.

Things to See & Do

Moree's **Spa Baths** (☎ 6752 7480) on Anne St claim some fairly unlikely successes in the miracle-cure line, but they certainly are a good way to get the cricks out of your back after a long day in a bus or car. The baths are hot (41°C) artesian water which pours out of a bore at the rate of 13 million litres a day. The spa is open weekdays from 6.30 am to 8.30 pm, weekends 7 am to 7 pm. Admission is $3.50.

The new **Moree Plains Gallery**, in an impressive old building on the corner of Frome and Heber Sts, specialises in Aboriginal art. The gallery is open from 10 am to 5 pm on weekdays, noon to 4 pm on Saturday and 1 to 4 pm on Sunday. The **Yurundiali Aboriginal Corporation** at 3 Endeavour Lane produces clothing using traditional and contemporary designs.

There are several other interesting buildings near the art gallery. These include the

Lands Department Office on Frome St and the nearby **courthouse**.

Places to Stay

Camping Caravan parks include the *Mehi* (☎ 6752 7188) on the river at the eastern end of Alice St. There are sites, on-site vans and cabins.

Hotels & Motels The *Victoria Hotel* (☎ 6752 5177), on Gosport St, and the *Moree* (☎ 6752 1644), on Alice St, both have singles/doubles for $20/25. There are no fewer than 18 motels to choose from, mostly on the Newell Highway (Frome St) and Warialda St on the southern side of town.

Getting There & Away

Bus The major lines stop here on their Newell Highway services. Most buses leave from Wadwell's travel agency (☎ 6752 4677) on Heber St, across from the art gallery, and you can buy most tickets here (but not Countrylink – go to the railway station). Countrylink has a daily service heading east along the Gwydir Highway to New England and on to Grafton, while Taylor's (☎ 6752 3250) goes to Tamworth ($34.50) on Monday and Friday.

Train Moree is the terminus of the passenger line from Sydney.

Car & Motorcycle The Newell Highway runs north to the Queensland border at Boggabilla and south to Narrabri. The Gwydir Highway runs east to Warialda and Inverell. Heading west on the Gwydir to Collarenebri you pass through 140-odd km of flat scrubland, beautiful in the spring with lush growth and wildflowers. There's no petrol available between Moree and Collarenebri, and there are several unsealed sections. Heading north, small roads run to Boomi near the state border or, branching off at Garah, to Mungindi.

BOGGABILLA & GOONDIWINDI

Boggabill is overshadowed by the more substantial town of Goondiwindi, 10 km across the Queensland border. Goondiwindi is a pleasant town and has quite a few accommodation options – you'll find a list with phone numbers and approximate prices on the door of the information centre in the old water tower, just off the main street. The impressive wooden *Victoria Hotel* seems a good place to stay. The giant *New Bridge Garage* on the Goondiwindi bypass is reputed to be the busiest truck stop in the southern hemisphere and offers fuel, meals and showers to truckies – and anyone else.

The Castlereagh Highway & Westwards

The large slice of country between the Castlereagh and Mitchell highways is a flat artesian basin. In spring this is a beautiful area, with the vast, steamy plains bursting into life. Much of the area is black-soil country, with the dry outback beginning as you approach the Mitchell Highway.

WARREN

This small town on the Macquarie River takes its name from an old meaning of the word: a park noted for wildlife. It must have once been an attractive town, but unfortunately the old buildings along the main streets have been stripped of their verandahs and balconies. The visitor information centre (☎ 6847 3181), on the main road next to the post office, is open on weekdays from 10 am to 4 pm and Saturday until noon.

The Macquarie Marshes once extended south to near Warren, but dams and irrigation projects are shrinking these huge wetlands. **Tiger Bay Wildlife Park**, off the Oxley Highway 1km north-east of Warren, has been created to provide birds and other wildlife with a refuge. There's a hide from which many species can be seen.

In town, pleasant **Macquarie Park** runs along the river and there's a walk, starting near the bridge, which takes you to a 500-year-old river red-gum. **Warren Weir**, 5km to the south, is a good spot for a picnic, and you can camp here.

Places to Stay
There are two motels, the *Macquarie Motor Lodge* (☎ 6847 4396) and the *Warren Motor Inn* (☎ 6847 4404), and pub accommodation at the *Club House Hotel* (☎ 6847 4923). There are also a couple of caravan parks. Ask at the information centre about camping on the district's many stock routes.

THE MACQUARIE MARSHES
This huge wetlands area was thought by Captain Oxley to be the beginning of the inland sea that he had been sent down the Macquarie River to find in 1818. Captain Sturt came the same way in 1828, but it was a drought year and the dry marshes clearly were not part of a sea. To avoid the marshes Sturt headed north and came upon the Darling River, which he realised joined the Murray (and thus flowed into the ocean), and so ended the whitefellas' inland-sea dreaming.

Bird-life on the marshes is varied and prolific, with native and migratory species breeding here. In the 1930s one casual observer reckoned that 3000 birds flew overhead in an hour. The wetlands have suffered from the damming of rivers and are receding, but while the skies are no longer dark with birds there are still plenty to be seen. The best time to visit is during the breeding season, generally in spring but varying according to the water level.

The main nature reserve on the marshes is on the west side, about 100 km north of Warren and off the sealed road from Warren to Carinda. From here the unsealed Gibson Way runs east to Quambone and it's along here that you're most likely to see birds. A sealed road runs from Quambone back to Warren, so you can make a round trip. The Gibson Way floods in a good season, but usually doesn't close just because of rain. Other unsealed roads in this area should be treated with caution as this is black-soil country and you can easily get bogged.

COONAMBLE
The first Europeans into this area arrived in 1817, just three years after the Blue Mountains were crossed, but the town wasn't established until 1855. You're well into the north-west when you get to Coonamble, and there's a relaxed feel to things. There isn't much to see but it's a pleasant place to wander around.

The Castlereagh Highway runs through town and the town centre is between the Castlereagh River and the Warrena Creek. The local roadhouse sells all the necessities of life: 'Fuel, Food, Ammo'.

The **museum** on Aberford St is in the old police station and is open weekdays from 10 am to 1 pm and 2 to 4 pm. **St Barnabas** is a big, wooden Anglican church on the corner of Aberford and Namoi Sts. The **Ellimatta Centre** is run by the Aboriginal community and sells arts and crafts. It's opposite the police station on Aberford St.

Places to Stay
The *Riverside Caravan Park* (☎ 6822 1926) on the highway south of the centre has sites only.

The impressive *Sons of the Soil Hotel* (☎ 6822 1009) on Castlereagh St, the main street, has single/double rooms for $20/30, including breakfast. A block back from Castlereagh St on the corner of Taloon and Namoi Sts, the quieter *Club House Hotel* (☎ 6821 1663) charges $15/20. The *Coonamble Motel* (☎ 6822 1400) is on the highway just south of the town centre and charges $36/46. There are a couple of other motels a little further out.

Getting There & Away
Bus Countrylink buses stop here on the run between Dubbo and Lightning Ridge.

Car & Motorcycle The Castlereagh Highway runs north to Lightning Ridge and south to Gilgandra. Smaller roads run south-east to the Warrumbungle National Park and Coonabarabran. See the earlier Macquarie Marshes section for routes west from Coonamble.

WALGETT

The small town of Walgett is near the junction of the Namoi and Barwon (a tributary of the Darling) rivers. Walgett and the Barwon feature in Banjo Paterson's poem 'Been There Before'. Other than this, there isn't a lot of interest in this rundown little town. Steel shutters on shop windows (but, surprisingly, not on the bank windows) indicate that alcohol-induced disturbances are a problem. Despite this, it's a friendly place and far enough from anywhere for people to be interested in telling you about local sights. There's an information centre (☎ 6828 1399) in the council chambers on Fox St (the Castlereagh Highway).

History

Charles Sturt's 1829 expedition up the Castlereagh River brought the first Europeans to this area. Squatters followed quickly and Walgett takes its name from Walchate, a cattle station established here in the 1830s. Covering 13,000 hectares, it could support only 300 head of cattle! At this time the area was a centre for Aboriginal corroborees, but the coming of the squatters soon put an end to that. Even running 0.02 of a cow per hectare was a good enough excuse to drive the Aborigines from their lands.

By the 1880s, paddle steamers were travelling up the Darling to Walgett, bringing in supplies and taking wool downstream.

Mechanical shears were invented on Euroka Station near Walgett in the 1870s, and Australia's first artesian bore was sunk in the area at around the same time.

Places to Stay & Eat

Two Rivers Caravan Park (☎ 6828 1381) is on Pitt St near the Namoi River. The *Oasis Hotel* (☎ 6828 1394), on Fox St, has singles for $15. Motel options include the *Walgett Motel* (☎ 6828 1355) with singles/doubles for $40/50.

The *RSL Club* on Fox St has a dining room, various pubs and motels have meals, and there's a Chinese restaurant and the odd cafe and takeaway.

Getting There & Away

Air Hazelton flies to Sydney most days ($253) via Dubbo. Azevedo's Gift Inn (☎ 6828 1433) on Fox St is the local agent.

Bus Countrylink buses stop here on the run between Dubbo and Lightning Ridge. Book at the Duncan & Duncan garage (☎ 6828 1781) on Fox St.

Car & Motorcycle The Castlereagh Highway runs north to Lightning Ridge and Queensland, while the Gwydir Highway goes north-east to Collarenebri and Moree. No petrol is available along the 143km of scrub country between Collarenebri and Moree.

Sections of the road west to Brewarrina are unsealed and impassable in wet weather.

AROUND WALGETT

If you think Walgett is a small place, check out some of the other towns in the shire! This is not a densely populated area.

As well as the opal fields around Lightning Ridge, there are the smaller **Grawin**, **Glengarry** and **Sheepyard** opal fields, west of Cumborah, a hamlet 47km north-west of Walgett on the road to Goodooga. You can have a drink with the opal miners at the Glengarry Hilton, or at the Club in the Scrub at Grawin.

West of these fields is **Narran Lake**, virtually inaccessible but home to a rich variety of bird-life in good seasons. If you want to visit, phone the landowner (☎ 6874 4957) for permission and directions. The best route is off the Brewarrina to Goodooga road.

Collarenebri, the second-largest town in the area, is 75km north-east of Walgett on the Moree road and is also on the Barwon River. Its name is an Aboriginal word meaning 'place of many flowers', and in spring that is very appropriate. The weir near town is supposed to be one of the best fishing holes in the state. There are gravel pits suitable for fossicking 10km out of town on the Lightning Ridge road. The Great Raft Race is held on the river in the first week in March. *Tattersalls Hotel-Motel* (☎ 6756 2205) has accommodation, and *camping* is permitted at several sites along the river.

Tiny **Burren Junction**, 93km east of Walgett on the road to Wee Waa, has artesian baths and hosts a gyrocopter and ultra-light air show at Easter.

BREWARRINA

Brewarrina (known locally as Bree) is a pleasant little town (population 1500) with some pride in its history, both Aboriginal and European. The town is bright with coral-tree blossom from July to September.

The shire council offices (☎ 6839 2106) on Bathurst St (the main street) have a couple of pamphlets and can help with local information.

One of the most important Aboriginal sites in the country is the **Brewarrina Fisheries** *(Ngunnhu)*, a series of rock traps on the Darling River where, perhaps for thousands of years, the Ngemba people caught fish to feed the huge inter-tribal gatherings which they hosted. Adjacent to the fisheries is the **Aboriginal Cultural Museum**, an excellent place which is open Monday to Friday, admission $6.

For white history, visit the **Settlers Museum** behind the well-maintained courthouse on Bathurst St. It's open on Friday afternoon from 2 to 3 pm, or you can arrange to have it opened. Admission is $2.

Places to Stay & Eat

The council *caravan park* (☎ 6839 2330) is by the swimming pool on Church St. There's another camping place on the river 6.5 km upstream from Bree. The *Hotel Brewarrina* (☎ 6839 2019) has accommodation and pub meals. The *Swan Crest Motel* (☎ 6839 2397), opposite the fish traps on the corner of Sandon and Doyle Sts, has rooms for $40/48.

The *De-Luxe Cafe* on Bathurst St is a great old country-town cafe, with lots of the original shop-fittings, including a sign boasting 'Iced Fountain Drinks. We Excel in Sundaes, Cleanliness & Civility'.

Getting There & Away

Air Hazelton connects Brewarrina with Dubbo and Sydney.

Bus Countrylink buses run between Dubbo and Brewarrina.

Car & Motorcycle You can reach Brewarrina from Bourke, from the Mitchell Highway at Coolabah or Byrock (both routes run via Gongolgon) and from Walgett. The Walgett road includes some long unsealed sections of black soil – great when it's dry, impassable in the wet. The track north to Goodooga also has a long unsealed section. Tracks through the Macquarie Marshes area also lead here, but you'll need a good map and local advice.

LIGHTNING RIDGE

Like Coober Pedy in South Australia, Lightning Ridge is a scruffy little town, entirely dependent on opal mining and the tourism which has followed. 'The Ridge' doesn't have the sense of other-worldly desolation that marks Coober Pedy, but it's a hot, unwelcoming stretch of landscape nevertheless. Although the entire town is geared towards relieving you of some cash, Lightning Ridge is no slick tourist trap. It has a decidedly eccentric feel to it and there are some interesting characters to meet.

Opal mining is still the domain of the 'battler', the little bloke (or sheila) whose hard work and tenacity pays off – sometimes. For those who don't make it, an existence of scraping a living among rusting car bodies and extremely basic huts is not considered socially demeaning. Towns like Lightning Ridge (and there aren't many) are the last refuge of 'the bushie', usually down on his/her luck but infinitely resourceful and just as wary of authority. These true-blue types sell their finds to visiting opal buyers who set up shop in motel rooms, and the meeting of these two very different worlds is an odd contrast. Some buyers come all the way from Hong Kong to buy black opals, the speciality of the area.

Most claims are 50sq metres and no-one can hold more than two claims.

Orientation & Information

Bill O'Brien's Way, the road in from the highway, becomes Morilla St, which is the main street. The corner of Morilla and Opal Sts is pretty much the town centre. The official tourist information centre (☎ 6829 1462) is next to the Lightning Ridge Mining Centre, on the left on the way into town from the highway, but you can get tourist information from practically anyone in town.

Things to See & Do

On the north and west sides, the town is surrounded by intensively mined opal fields. Be careful walking around the diggings, as they're riddled with deep, unmarked holes. Young children are especially at risk. Dropping anything down a hole won't make you popular if someone is working at the bottom.

The **Bush Museum** (or Moozeum) is worth a visit. It's an eccentric collection of memorabilia, some genuinely historic, the rest interesting junk. There's also a large underground area in an old mine, with more displays, including cartoons from the extremely sexist but strangely innocent magazines which provided entertainment for lonely miners (and which still grace small-town barber shops). Admission is $4 ($1 children). The museum is down a dirt track off Black Prince Drive, which runs off

Pandora St near the swimming pool. Look for the boat in the tree.

The **Walk-In Mine**, north of town off Gem St, is open daily and you can see a video on opal mining; admission is $4. Nearby **Spectrum Mine** also has a video (hourly from 10 am to 4 pm) and it's free. Off the track into the Walk-In Mine is **Bevan's Black Opal & Cactus Nursery**, the many species of cactus including some very old plants. In the same area but a km further out of town is the **Drive-In Mine**. **The Big Opal**, off Bill O'Brien's Way, has a daily mine tour at 10 am. The **Bottle House** on Opal St is built from bottles and contains mining memorabilia as well as souvenirs and opals.

If you need to relax, the 42°C **hot artesian baths** at the northern edge of town on Pandora St are free and open 24 hours. As well as miners and jewellers, Lightning Ridge is home to many artists and craftspeople. John Murray's engaging paintings and limited-edition prints of outback life are displayed at his **gallery** on Opal St near the corner of Morilla St, as well as some B&W photos. There are more paintings at the **Motor Village** complex further south on Morilla St – the punning sculpture *Emus on the Plane* is out the front.

Opals

The main business in town is selling opals and there are outlets everywhere, ranging from The Local Guy who has a sidewalk

---

Buying Opals

There are various grades and types of opals. Top of the heap are black opals, which are solid opals (called stones) consisting of a black 'potch' overlaid by 'colour'. (The best quality are more expensive than diamonds.) Grey and white opals are the same, but the potch is grey or white. Solid crystals are clear or opaque opals without any potch.

Prices can be astronomical – up to $2000 a carat or $3000 for a black opal – but you can pay as little as $50 for a stone of lower quality. The price depends on flaws and the brilliance of the colour. The variation in shades of colour is enormous, and if you're lucky, the one you like won't be one of the most expensive.

Much less expensive are non-solid opals. Doublets are precious opals stuck (by a jeweller, not by nature) to a potch of non-precious opal. Domed doublets are worth more than flat doublets because the section of precious opal is thicker. Triplets are flat doublets with a dome of glass or quartz crystal stuck on top, protecting and magnifying the opal. ■

stand on Morilla St selling bottles of opal chips for a couple of dollars, to showrooms where you can see $5000 opals on display. If you want to buy something, take your time and look at as many places as you can.

Organised Tours
Black Opal Tours (☎ 6829 0368) and Victor's Opal Mining Tours (☎ 6829 0287) have tours of the town and area.

Special Events
The Great Goat Race is held at Easter, along with horse races.

The Opal Festival is held during the school holidays in late September/early October, culminating in horse races, a parade and entertainment over the October long weekend.

Places to Stay
The *Tram-o-Tel* (☎ 6829 0448), on Morilla St, has self-contained accommodation in old trams and in caravans for $20/30 ($120/150 per week). The trams seem to have been carefully chosen – one is a St Kilda Beach tram, a long way from Melbourne, and an old Bondi tram contains an opal shop.

There are two motels, the *Black Opal* (☎ 6829 0518), on the corner of Morilla and Opal Sts, and the *Wallangulla* (☎ 6829 0542) on the corner of Morilla and Agate Sts. Both charge around $50/60 and neither is very luxurious. The big *Motor Village* (☎ 6829 0304) on Morilla St has cabins from $35 and units for $59/69.

Places to Eat
The best deals in town are to be found at the huge *Bowling Club* on Morilla St, where the bistro has a selection of meals for $6.95. The *Bus Stop Cafe* on Opal St has Thai food as well as standard takeaways. If you strike it rich, the smartest restaurant in town is *Nobby's* in the Motor Village complex.

Getting There & Away
Air Hazelton flies to Sydney ($270) via Dubbo. Buy tickets at the Lightning Ridge News office (☎ 6829 1182), on Morilla St next to the post office.

Bus Buses run north and south along the Castlereagh Highway including Countrylink to Dubbo ($45). Book at the Log Cabin Opal Shoppe (☎ 6829 0277) on Morilla St opposite the post office. Grahams Coaches run from Lightning Ridge to Toowoomba ($79) in Queensland on Monday and Friday, travelling via St George ($26) and Dalby ($60). They leave from Pip's Place, in the industrial estate opposite the tourist office.

Car & Motorcycle The Castlereagh Highway runs south to Walgett and on to Dubbo. North of Lightning Ridge the road leads eventually to the Queensland town of St George.

The Far West

The far west of NSW is the state's 'empty quarter', but this vast expanse of dry country is one of the most interesting areas in the state and is much more diverse than it first appears.

South of the Darling River, much of the land is taken up by precarious cattle and sheep stations and saltbush scrub, and the horizons are vast. Elsewhere there's a surprising amount of bush, with low, tenacious trees surviving in the harsh climate. Towards the north-western corner, the long ridges of sand dunes that make up so much of central Australia begin, but even these support vegetation can be quite beautiful.

The outback is sparsely populated but the people you meet are often much larger than life – they have room to grow, sometimes in pretty quirky ways.

Geography & Climate
Nearly all of the far west is the Murray-Darling Basin, red and black-soil plains riddled with usually dry waterways and clay-pans. In the north-west corner the sandy plains of outback Australia begin.

From November to February this area, especially the north, is almost impossibly hot. By 9 am the thermometer is nudging 100°F in the shade and by 10 am the Celsius landmark, 40°C, is passed. That leaves another 10 hours of daylight for the current record, 51.7°C, to be broken. Air-conditioning helps to make this season more tolerable. Winter nights can be chilly, with frosts, but the days are usually warm and sunny.

Getting There & Away
Air Broken Hill is the main centre for air traffic in the region, but small charter planes serve much of the area. There are also a few scheduled feeder services.

Bus Major bus-lines run along the Barrier Highway, and Countrylink runs up the Mitchell Highway.

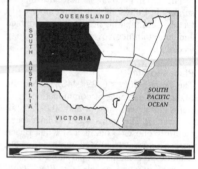

HIGHLIGHTS

- Outback landscapes, especially at sunset
- Camping under the red gums on the bank of the Darling River in Kinchega National Park
- Bushwalking in Mootwingee National Park
- Underground accommodation at White Cliffs
- The extraordinary archaeological record at Lake Mungo National Park

Train The Indian Pacific stops at Broken Hill en route from Sydney to Adelaide and Perth.

Car & Motorcycle Two long, sealed roads skirt the edge of this area: the Barrier Highway, running from Cobar west to Broken Hill and on to South Australia; and the Mitchell Highway, beginning in Dubbo and running through Nyngan to Bourke, then straight up into Queensland, through Cunnamulla to Charleville.

You'll see a lot more of the outback if you venture off the sealed roads. As long as conditions are dry (which is the usual state of affairs out here) you won't get into too much trouble on the main roads if you have good maps, drive carefully and are prepared for minor breakdowns. See the Getting Around chapter for more information on outback driving.

Inside the map:

QUEENSLAND

To Innamincka | To Eulo | To Cunnamulla

Cameron's Corner | Warri Warri Gate | Hungerford | Barringun

STURT NATIONAL PARK | Tibooburra | Yantabulla | Enngonia | Collerina | To Goodooga

Milparinka | Wanaaring | Fords Bridge | To Walgett

Urisino Station | Brewarrina

Far West | Bourke

0   50   100 km | Golgolgon | Bogan River

Packsaddle Roadhouse | Louth | Byrock | Coolabah

White Cliffs | Tilpa | 71

SOUTH AUSTRALIA | MOOTWINGEE NATIONAL PARK | Mt Grenfell | Cobar | Hermidale | Nyngan

Wilcannia | 32 | Barrier Highway | Mt Boppy | To Dubbo

Silverton | Barrier Highway | Nymagee

Broken Hill | Yelta Station

To Peterborough & Adelaide | 79 | Menindee

KINCHEGA NATIONAL PARK | Ivanhoe | Mt Hope

Silver City Highway | 75 | WILLANDRA NATIONAL PARK | Euabalong | To Condobolin

Mossgiel | Lake Cargelligo

Pooncarie | MUNGO NATIONAL PARK | Hillston | West Wyalong

Merriwagga | 24

Darling River | Booligal | Mid Western Hwy

Wentworth | Lachlan River | Griffith

Murray River | Gol Gol & Buronga | Mildura | Murrumbidgee River | Hay | To Deniliquin | Leeton

Renmark | VICTORIA | To Ouyen & Melbourne | To Balranald | To Narrandera

Berri

Box text: Just because a road is shown on this map doesn't mean it will always be safe to use. There are many more outback tracks in the far west than are shown on this map, but you need detailed maps and local knowledge before heading off the major roads.

BOURKE

Nearly 800km north-west of Sydney, Bourke (population 3400) is on the edge of the outback; 'back of Bourke' is synonymous with the outback, the back of beyond. A glance at the map will show just how outback the area beyond Bourke is – settlements of any sort are few and far between and the country is flat and featureless as far as the eye can see. Its very remoteness attracts a steady stream of visitors. Bourke is a surprisingly pretty town and the surrounding country can be beautiful – the sheer space is exhilarating.

History

The Ngemba people lived in a large area, centred on the Brewarrina Fisheries and including Bourke and Louth. Other peoples in the area were the Barranbinja, Kula, Valaria, Kamilaroi and Wiradjuri. Early European explorers observed that local Aborigines lived in permanent structures.

The first Europeans to see this area were the members of Captain Sturt's party of 1828. Sturt didn't think much of the country and Major Mitchell's party of 1835 didn't manage to explore much of the area. Still, by 1860 there were enough graziers in the area for a paddle-wheeler to risk the difficult journey up to Bourke. By the 1880s, many of the Darling River's 200 paddle-steamers were calling at Bourke to take wool down to the river ports at Echuca (for Melbourne) and Morgan (for Adelaide). It was possible for wool to be in London just six weeks after leaving Bourke – somewhat quicker than a sea-mail parcel today!

Bourke is still a major wool-producing area, but droughts and low prices have forced farmers to look to other products, such as cotton and rockmelons. There's even a vine-yard.

Quite a few famous Australians have passed through Bourke at one time or another. Henry Lawson lived at the Carriers Arms Hotel in 1892 while painting the Great Western Hotel. Fred Hollows, the ophthalmic surgeon whose philanthropic work in third-world countries made him a national hero, chose to be buried here.

Orientation & Information

The Mitchell Highway winds through town then heads out to North Bourke (just a pub) 6km away, across the old bridge. The shopping centre is on Oxley St between Sturt St and Richard St (the highway). The courthouse is on the corner. At North Bourke the highway turns right to begin its run to the Queensland border; keep going straight ahead for Wanaaring and Tibooburra.

The information centre (☎ 6872 2280) is at the bus depot (the old railway station) on Anson St. It's open Monday to Saturday from 9 am to 5 pm and Sunday from 12.30 to 5 pm (closed on Sunday from November to March). Pick up a leaflet called *Bourke Mud Map Tours*, detailing a town walk and drives to places in the district.

Lachlan Travel (☎ 6872 2092) on Oxley St is the agent for Countrylink and the regional Hazelton airline.

Work Limited seasonal work is available in the Bourke area: picking onions (around October), picking rockmelons (November or December) and cotton chipping (weeding, November or December). Contact the CES

(☎ 6872 2511) near the Post Office Hotel on Oxley St for details. You'll notice that all these activities take place around summer and it can be *hot*!

Things to See & Do

Although the river can no longer accommodate the big paddle-wheelers, there are plenty of reminders of the time when they were the town's lifeline. The impressive three-tiered **wharf** at the northern end of Sturt St is a faithful reconstruction of the original, which was built in 1897.

Just north of town, the **North Bourke Bridge** (1883) once lifted to let the steamboats through. It also obligingly bends to avoid the pub on the north bank. One of the reasons that boats can no longer navigate the river is the concrete weir built downstream from the town in the 1940s. It replaced a wooden weir which tilted to allow the boats through.

Many old buildings in town are reminders of Bourke's important past. The **courthouse** (1900) on the corner of Oxley and Richard Sts has a shady courtyard and is topped by a spire with a crown on it – signifying that it can hear maritime cases! Next door is an older courthouse, very similar in design to the court at Brewarrina. Across the road is the **old police station**. The **London Chartered Bank** (1888) is a very impressive old building, but the bank went bust just a few years after it was built. The State Offices, once the **Lands Office** (1900), is an elegant but simple structure of wood and corrugated iron.

The only big old **pubs** left are the Post Office Hotel on downtown Oxley St and the Central Australian Hotel on the corner of Richard and Anson Sts. A small old pub, the Carriers Arms on the corner of Mitchell and Wilson Sts, was a watering hole of the writer Henry Lawson. The North Bourke Hotel is a good place to go to meet the locals. The Old Royal Hotel on Mitchell St is comparatively sedate.

Watch out for information about **bush dances**, such as the ones held at Urisino

FAR WEST

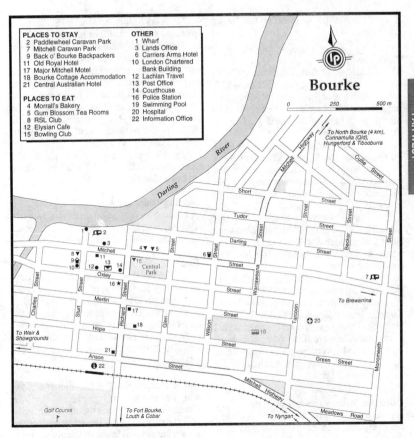

Bourke

PLACES TO STAY
2 Paddlewheel Caravan Park
7 Mitchell Caravan Park
9 Back o' Bourke Backpackers
11 Old Royal Hotel
17 Major Mitchell Motel
18 Bourke Cottage Accommodation
21 Central Australian Hotel

PLACES TO EAT
4 Morrall's Bakery
5 Gum Blossom Tea Rooms
8 RSL Club
12 Elysian Cafe
15 Bowling Club

OTHER
1 Wharf
3 Lands Office
6 Carriers Arms Hotel
10 London Chartered Bank Building
12 Lachlan Travel
13 Post Office
14 Courthouse
16 Police Station
19 Swimming Pool
20 Hospital
22 Information Office

Station – a long way to go, but that's why everyone has a good time.

Cotton is picked in March and April. From about May to August you can see the cotton gin in action by phoning Clyde Agriculture (☎ 6872 2528), or ask at the tourist office about tours of the plantations and gins.

Organised Tours
Mateship Country Tours offers town and surrounding area tours at 10 am weekdays if there are enough takers. Longer tours can also be arranged. Contact the information office for more details.

Special Events
The Agricultural Show is held in April, with important ram and bull sales as well as a sideshow alley. At Easter there's a fishing competition with other events such as wool-bale rolling, egg-and-spoon races and other village-green activities.

The Mateship Festival, held in late September, is a recent innovation and the dates haven't yet been settled on, but late September seems to be about the time. The new festival's name derives from Henry Lawson's literary theme of male bonding in the bush, a powerful strain in Aussie culture.

Events are similar to those at the Easter festivities.

Places to Stay

The *Paddlewheel Caravan Park* (☎ 6872 2277) has tent sites for $10, vans from $26, cabins from $30 and old-style self-contained units from $35. There's a free *camping area* on the north bank of the Darling a few km upstream from town.

Back o' Bourke Backpackers (☎ 6872 3009), beside the London Chartered Bank building on Sturt St, has beds in two-bed dorms for $12. Unfortunately, the place was in serious need of repair at the time of research.

The best of Bourke's hotels is the *Old Royal* (☎ 6872 2544) on Mitchell St between Sturt and Richard Sts. The rooms are good value at $25/35 for singles/doubles. The motels are an uninspiring lot. The smartest of them is the *Major Mitchell* (☎ 6872 2311) on Mertin St, which charges $59/69.

A nicer option than any of these is *Bourke Cottage Accommodation* (☎ 6872 2837), 51 Hope St. There is a choice of two renovated cottages in the middle of town, both equipped with everything you could need. Rates are $50 for one person, plus $10 for each additional person.

Outback Accommodation There are several places to stay on stations in the (very large) Bourke area. Of particular interest is the historic *Urisino Station*, which has camel treks. Cruising on the Darling River from Louth in a *houseboat* is also an option.

See the following Around Bourke, Down the Darling and Bourke to Tibooburra sections for details on these and other places or contact the information centre, which makes bookings.

Places to Eat

There are several cafes, such as the pleasant *Gum Blossom Tea Rooms* on Mitchell St in the Towers Drug Co building (1890) and the *Elysian Cafe*, Bourke's country-town cafe on Oxley St.

Morrall's Bakery, on Mitchell St, has great pies and a good choice of breads.

The best place for dinner is the *Old Royal Hotel Dining Room* on Mitchell St. It's a much better restaurant than you would expect to find in such a small and remote town. As well as the usual steaks and pastas there are some interesting dishes on the changing menu. Main courses are around $15. The dining room opens Tuesday to Saturday from 7.30 to 9 pm.

There's typical club grub at the nearby *RSL Club* and the *Bowling Club* on Richard St has a Chinese restaurant.

Getting There & Away

Air Hazelton flies several times a week to Dubbo, where it connects with another service to Sydney ($284 one way).

Bus The only bus is the Countrylink service to Dubbo ($43) which connects with a train to Sydney. It *might* be possible to go along on the bi-weekly mail runs to Wanaaring and Brewarrina. These tend to head out to the town in the afternoon, then make deliveries to stations the next day. The post office (☎ 6872 2017) can put you in touch with the contractors.

Car & Motorcycle The Mitchell Highway, which runs south to Nyngan and north to Cunnamulla in Queensland, is the only sealed road in the area. The other roads in the region are covered in the following sections.

AROUND BOURKE

Somewhere that is 'around Bourke' can be as far away as the old Urisino Post Office, more than 200km west on a dirt road. The Mud Map Tours brochure details some trips. If you don't already have a roadmap, pick one up from the NRMA office on Oxley St near the Post Office Hotel.

If the roads are dry, all the places mentioned in the following sections can be visited in a normal car. *Wherever* you're going, however, check current conditions with locals, preferably the police, and carry plenty of water. If you're heading off a main route, let someone know what you're doing and take spare parts.

Closer to Town
The climb up **Mt Oxley**, 30km south-east of Bourke off the Brewarrina road, is worth the effort for the views you can enjoy from the summit, especially at sunset. There are more good views and abundant flora at **Mt Gundabooka**, about 70km to the south-west off the Cobar road. The rock pools here almost always have water in them and the mountain is thought to have been of religious significance to Aborigines, whose cave paintings can still be seen. Before heading to either of these two mountains, visit the tourist office in Bourke to pick up a key for Mt Oxley or to pay the Mt Gundabooka entry fee of $5 ($3.50 children) and the camping fee ($15).

Fords Bridge, about 60km north-west on the road to Hungerford, is apparently a top spot for yabbying. You'll find meals and accommodation at the *Warrego Hotel*

(☎ 6874 7540), an unusual mudbrick hotel built in 1912.

On the highway, 70-odd km south of Bourke, is the hamlet of **Byrock**, with a pub, the *Mulga Creek Hotel-Motel* (☎ 6874 7311), which has accommodation and campsites. In early October, Byrock hosts the Outback Arts Festival and the Bog-Eye Races.

The **Cornerstone Community**, between Bourke and Wanaaring, is a sort of a Christian kibbutz on a cotton farm. This is the site of the Pera Bore, the first artesian water supply in the area. Visitors are welcome; the tourist office has more details.

Myandetta Station (☎ 6872 3029) is on the north bank of the Darling River, accessible from the Wanaaring road. Phone for detailed directions. There's accommodation in shearers' quarters here and at *Glenvilla*, owned by the same people and 16km further downstream.

See the North-West chapter for information on Brewarrina.

Shinglebacks

Shingleback lizards are those slow-moving stumpy critters that love to lie on the road, and are so ugly that they're cute. Locals call them bog-eyes, or stumpies, depending where you are. When approached, a shingleback will open that big mouth wide and show its blue tongue and crimson gullet. If you poke a finger too close to one, it might just chomp onto it.

Shinglebacks aren't poisonous, but they have a very strong grip. Locals kill the lizards to get them off, but the NPWS advises resting your hand on the ground and hoping that the lizard will eventually get bored and let go. It can take a while... ∎

Further Out

The hamlet of **Enngonia** is 95km north of Bourke on the Mitchell Highway and has accommodation at the *Oasis Hotel/Motel* (☎ 6874 7577). The sandhills around here are covered with flowers in spring, and you'll see lots of bird-life if there's any water in the surrounding swamps. On the first weekend in September, up to 2000 people arrive for the annual races.

Further north, almost on the Queensland border, **Barringun** is a hamlet with a pub (once frequented by Breaker Morant), a roadhouse and not much else.

Henry Lawson walked from Bourke to **Hungerford** in 1892 and he wasn't all that impressed with what he saw there. Read about it in his story *Hungerford*. The population today is about 10, but the beautiful old *Royal Mail Hotel* (☎ (07) 7655 4093) is still going strong. It has doubles for $40 and good food. The Hungerford Field Day in July attracts thousands of visitors and the Sports Day in October is also popular. Hungerford straddles the Queensland border, and just over the border is the small **Currawinya National Park**, where large lakes provide a habitat for many birds.

DOWN THE DARLING

The Darling River first takes its name just north-east of Bourke, after the Barwon is joined by the Culgoa and Bogan rivers. It flows south-west across NSW and meets the Murray River at Wentworth. Although it passes through some of the driest country in the state, the Darling usually has at least some water in it and its banks are lined with massive river red-gums. With the Murray, the Darling forms one of the world's longest exotic rivers – that is, one that for much of its length flows through country from which it receives no water.

The road that runs along the south bank of the Darling is the main route downstream from Bourke. It's possible to drive all the way down the Darling to Wentworth, although the road is unsealed and impassable after rain. Apart from kangaroos and emus, you won't encounter much along the way.

Fort Bourke, signposted off the Louth road about 15km south-west of Bourke, is a replica of the crude stockade built by Major Mitchell in 1835 to guard his stores while he took a boat down the Darling. The area is also a wildlife refuge with lots of water birds.

The tiny town of **Louth**, about 100km from Bourke, hosts up to 4000 people during the annual race-meeting on the first or second Saturday in August. The landing strip is crowded with planes, racehorses outnumber the town's usual population and a score of bookmakers turn over hundreds of thousands of dollars.

Shindy's Inn, the local pub, doesn't have accommodation, but *Louth Cabin Park* (☎ 6874 7416) has a choice of cabins (singles only) for $30 or a cottage for $40. The *Hollyanna* (☎ 6874 7443) is a houseboat based at Louth. It hasn't done much travelling in recent years because the river has been so low, but it's still available for rent when conditions permit.

Another 90-odd km further downstream is **Tilpa**, where the *Tilpa Hotel* (☎ 6837 3928) has meals, fuel, accommodation and, of course, beer. On the north bank, 12km upstream from Tilpa, Kallara Station has self-contained accommodation right on the river bank at *Coolabah Lodge* (☎ 6837 3963), originally built to house irrigation workers. They prefer groups or families and charge $35/45 for singles/doubles, an extra $10 for children sharing with parents.

From Tilpa, the Darling flows down to **Wilcannia**, then down to a system of lakes at **Menindee**, surrounded by **Kinchega National Park**. These places are accessible by sealed road from Broken Hill and are covered in the following Barrier Highway section.

Beyond Menindee, another 125km of dirt road brings you to **Pooncarie**, a pretty hamlet with a pleasant pub, the Telegraph Hotel, and a jumping-off point for Mungo National Park. From Pooncarie, a sealed road runs to **Wentworth**, not far from the city of Mildura across the border in Victoria. See the Riverina chapter for information on Wentworth.

RICHARD I'ANSON

JON MURRAY

Top: The Bread Knife, Grand High Tops, Warrumbungle National Park, north-west
Bottom: Hill End, central west

The red sand of the central deserts of Australia – the reason why a
large portion of inner Australia is known as 'the red centre'

Central Desert

In the arid centre of Australia life is most conspicuous in shaded gorges and along dry river
courses where river red gums, home to colourful and noisy parrots, are able to tap deep
reserves of water. On this ancient, eroded landscape, sparse vegetation and red sandy
soils are infrequently and temporarily transformed by rain into a carpet of wildflowers.
Tell-tale tracks in the sand lead to clumps of spinifex grass and burrows. Small marsupials
and mice are mostly nocturnal; the rare and endangered bilby was once common to much
of Australia but is now only found in the deserts of central Australia. A few of the lizards,
such as the thorny devil, will venture out into the heat of the day for a feed of ants. Among
the scattered mulga and desert oak, mobs of kangaroos, the males brick-red and over two
metres tall, seek shelter from the sun; but seemingly impervious to the heat, emus, with an
insulating double layer of feathers, continue the search for seeds and fruit. In the evenings
rock-wallabies emerge from rocky outcrops to browse on nearby vegetation. Most animals
breed in the cooler winter – their eggs and young attracting the attention of dingoes, eagles
and perenties.

Flora and fauna of the central deserts – emus, Sturt's desert pea
and kangaroos

Left: River red gums line a dry creek bed
Right: Major Mitchell cockatoos

Thousands of years ago, as the climate changed and lakes dried up,
animals like the thorny devil adapted to life in the arid desert

BERNARD NAPTHINE

BERNARD NAPTHINE

BERNARD NAPTHINE

BERNARD NAPTHINE

JON MURRAY

A	
B	C	D
E	

The Far West
A: Peter Browne's studio, Silverton
B: Dingo Fence, Sturt National Park
C: Windmill, corner country

D: Desert, Sturt National Park
E: Outback road

BOURKE TO TIBOOBURRA

The lonely road running west from Bourke to Tibooburra is an adventurous drive.

Wanaaring, about 190km west of Bourke, may well be tiny but it's the largest settlement for a long way. There's accommodation at the *Outback Inn* (☎ 6874 7758) and you can buy fuel and provisions at Cooper's Corner. Paroo Sports Day is held during the September–October school holidays.

About 35km west from Wanaaring and 2km south of the main road, you can see the remains of the old mudbrick **Urisino Post Office**. Next to the post office is *Urisino Homestead* (☎ 6874 7639), a large mudbrick homestead dating from the early 1900s, with even older date palms perhaps planted by the Afghan cameleers. The property was part of Sir Sidney Kidman's cattle empire and the homestead is surprisingly comfortable, with marble fireplaces. Urisino Station once covered 500,000 hectares but today is a mere 32,000 hectares.

The homestead is worth seeing and passers-by are encouraged to drop in for morning or arvo tea and a look around. There's also accommodation, either in good rooms in the homestead ($45 per person for dinner, bed and breakfast or $72 including all meals and activities) or in backpacker accommodation in old mudbrick cottages ($20 per person). Swags are available if you want to camp. There's a bar and there will be air-con at the homestead when mains electricity is connected.

The young people running the homestead spent a couple of years travelling on camels and they offer camel rides and canoe trips on the Paroo River by arrangement. If you don't have transport, it might be possible to arrange a lift on the mail run or phone Urisino to see if someone is making a trip to Bourke. Keep an eye out for leaflets advertising dances at the station.

West of Urisino, the scrub thins and there are some large claypans that fill with birds after rain. After you pass the turn-off to Milparinka, the country changes and you drive past the small mesas of the eastern half of **Sturt National Park**. The mesas aren't very high but they look like mountain ranges after the flat country further east.

CORNER COUNTRY

The far western corner of the state is a semi-desert of red plains, heat, dust and flies. To quote Henry Lawson (1893), 'There are no 'mountains' out west, only ridges on the floor of hell'. But it's worth seeing for its interesting physical features and prolific wildlife. As well as kangaroos and emus, watch out for goannas and other lizards on the road and even big wedge-tailed eagles, which take a long time to get airborne. Running along the Queensland border is the dingo-proof fence, patrolled every day by boundary riders who each look after a 40km section.

Tibooburra

Tiny Tibooburra, 335km north of Broken Hill and the hottest town in the state, boasts two fine sandstone pubs, a couple of petrol stations, a small shop or two, a police station, a bush hospital and even a tiny outdoor cinema. Tibooburra is the closest town to Sturt National Park and there's a large and helpful NPWS office (☎ 8091 3308) in town, open daily from 8.30 am to 5 pm.

Tibooburra used to be called The Granites, after the granite outcrops nearby, which are good to visit on a sunset walk.

Places to Stay & Eat There's camping in the national park just north of town at *Dead Horse Gully*. There's a camping fee of $5 for two people, plus a park entry fee of $7.50. In town, *The Granites Caravan Park* (☎ 8091 3305) has sites for $10, on-site vans for $24, cabins for $34 and motel units from $40/50.

Both the pubs, the *Family Hotel* (☎ 8091 3314) and the *Tibooburra Hotel* (☎ 8091 3310) (known as 'the two-storey'), have accommodation. The Family has singles/doubles for $20/35, while the Tibooburra charges $25/30. Both bars are worth a beer: the Family has a bacchanalian mural by Clifton Pugh, while the two-storey has more than 60 impressively well-worn hats on the wall, left behind when their owners bought new headgear at the pub.

The pubs have good counter meals and tables outside where you can sit and watch the occasional 4WD pass by.

Milparinka

Milparinka is very nearly a ghost town. Not much remains of the gold town which once had a population of 3000, except the pub, the courthouse, and a few occupied houses. The courthouse is a fine sandstone building with a very solid sandstone dunny out the back.

Members of Charles Sturt's expedition from Adelaide, searching for an inland sea, were forced to camp near here for six months in 1845. The temperatures were extreme, the conditions terrible and their supplies inadequate. Ask at the pub for directions to the grave of James Poole, Sturt's second-in-command, who is buried about 14km north-west of the settlement. Poole died of scurvy.

The only fuel between Milparinka and Broken Hill is at the Packsaddle roadhouse, about halfway along the Silver City Highway – largely unsealed despite the name.

Sturt National Park

Taking in both gibber plains and the edge of the great Strzelecki Desert, this huge park (310,650 hectares) was once a pastoral lease. The park has 300km of driveable tracks, camping areas and walks, on the Jump Up Loop drive and to the top of Mt Wood. It's recommended that you inform the ranger at Tibooburra before venturing into the park. The entry fee is $7.50 per car.

At **Camerons Corner** there's a post to mark the place where Queensland, South Australia and NSW meet. It's a favourite goal for visitors and a 4WD is not always necessary to get there. In the Queensland corner, the *Corner Store* (!) does good sandwiches, homemade pies and even ice cream. Everybody coming by the Corner stops here and they have good advice on road conditions. You can also buy fuel here.

The Barrier Highway

The Barrier Highway, running from Nyngan west through Cobar, Wilcannia and Broken Hill, is the far west's main road and is the main route to Adelaide. Several of the state's more remote places are some way south of the highway and are included in this section.

NYNGAN

Nyngan (population 2500) is at the junction of the Barrier and Mitchell highways and is also close to the centre of NSW; a cairn marks the exact spot 72km south of the town. Tourist information is available from Burns Video & Gifts (☎ 6832 1155) on the main street.

Major Mitchell's party passed through in 1835, but the town didn't begin to grow until the 1880s. The great flood of 1990, when the Bogan River overwhelmed the town and the entire population was evacuated by helicopter, still looms large in local memory. You can see photos of the flood at Arnold's Cafe on the main street.

Nyngan's dusty main street isn't very interesting, but on Cobar St, parallel and a block south, there are three public buildings in very different styles: the solid **courthouse**, the Corinthian **town hall** and the more modest **post office**, which is closer in style to the town's domestic architecture.

Places to Stay & Eat

There are a couple of caravan parks: the *Nyngan* (☎ 6832 1705) east of town and the *Riverside* (☎ 6832 1729) west of town.

Barrett's Hotel (☎ 6832 1028), a big old place across the railway line from the main street, has pub accommodation, as does the more modern *Canoba* (☎ 6832 1559) on the main street, which also has motel units. The *Alamo Motel* (☎ 6832 1324) is on the Cobar side of the town centre and is the cheapest of the motels at $41/51.

Arnold's Cafe is a takeaway place on the main street with tables and a limited menu.

Getting There & Away

Bus Countrylink buses run to Dubbo, Broken Hill, Brewarrina and Bourke.

Car & Motorcycle As well as the highways, an unsealed but fairly well-travelled road runs south through Tottenham to Bogan Gate, on the road between Parkes and Condobolin. See North of Condobolin in the Central West chapter for more information on routes in this area.

COBAR

On the edge of the outback, beyond the fences but before the low bush tails off into saltbush, Cobar (population 5500) is at the start of the Barrier Highway, which runs west to Broken Hill, 455km away. Semi-arid woodland is the main vegetation in the area and there's a quiet beauty to the rolling sea of tough little trees. Sheep manage to eke out an existence on the clearer sections, in competition with destructive feral goats and pigs.

After rain, the flood plains of the usually dry creeks come alive with flowers.

History

Like Broken Hill, Cobar is a mining town, but here copper is the mainstay. Rich copper ore was discovered in 1871 and for the next 40 years the town grew steadily. In the 1920s, the two biggest mines, Great Cobar and the Cornish, Scottish & Australian (CSA), closed down, and Cobar began to decline. The CSA was reopened in the 60s and is now 1km deep. The new Elura mine, 47km west of Cobar, is exploiting a rich plug of zinc, lead and silver. Gold is also mined in the area. Cobar has alluvial gold but there was no gold rush because of the lack of water, which is essential for gold panning!

Information

The information centre (☎ 6836 2448) is at the eastern end of town in the same building

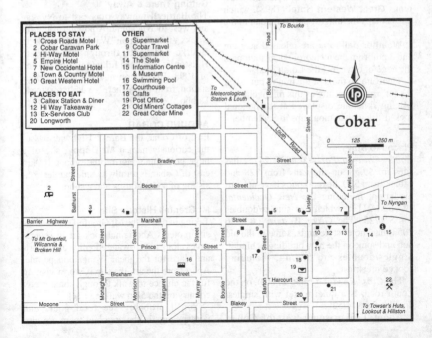

PLACES TO STAY
1 Cross Roads Motel
2 Cobar Caravan Park
4 Hi-Way Motel
5 Empire Hotel
7 New Occidental Hotel
8 Town & Country Motel
10 Great Western Hotel

PLACES TO EAT
3 Caltex Station & Diner
12 Hi Way Takeaway
13 Ex-Services Club
20 Longworth

OTHER
6 Supermarket
9 Cobar Travel
11 Supermarket
14 The Stele
15 Information Centre & Museum
16 Swimming Pool
17 Courthouse
18 Crafts
19 Post Office
21 Old Miners' Cottages
22 Great Cobar Mine

Cobar

FAR WEST

as the museum. There's a NPWS office (☎ 6836 2692) at 45B Marshall St.

Things to See

The excellent **Cobar Regional Museum**, open daily, is well worth the $3 admission ($2 children). It's housed in the former head office of the Great Cobar Copper Mining Company and many of the displays reflect this association. There are also good displays on the environment, local Aboriginal life and the early Europeans. Don't miss it.

Next to the museum is the **Stele monument** dedicated to the town and its mining past. Egyptian motifs are combined with the names of the three men who found copper here and the occupation (*bagal*, Cornish for someone who grades copper ore) of the woman who identified it.

Pick up a walking-tour map of the town from the information centre. There are a surprising number of interesting buildings, most fairly modest. An exception is the enormous **Great Western Hotel** (1898), which has perhaps the longest pub verandah in the state.

Weather balloons are released at 9 am and 3 pm from the meteorological station on the edge of town, off the Louth road.

There are no tours of the mines, but ask at the information centre as this might change. Mining skills are displayed at the national rock-drilling championships in September.

Places to Stay

Cobar Caravan Park (☎ 6836 2425) has sites for $9.50, on-site vans from $28 and cabins from $30. Several pubs have accommodation, including the *New Occidental* (☎ 6836 2111), which has singles/doubles for $15/25. The *Great Western* (☎ 6836 2053) has motel-style units, some in the old pub and some in the new building behind it. Singles/doubles are $34/44, including cooked breakfast.

The *Cross Roads* (☎ 6836 27110), on the Louth road, is a quiet motel with singles/doubles for $44/52.

About 130km south-west of Cobar,

Keewong Station (☎ 6837 3756) offers outback accommodation.

Places to Eat

The 24-hour Mobil and Caltex *service stations* have grills and snacks. Truckies seem to prefer the Caltex. The New Occidental Hotel has a *Chinese restaurant* and there are restaurants at the *Barrier, Copper City* and *Town & Country* motels. Under the Great Western Hotel, *The Hi Way Takeaway* has pizzas and some pretty greasy takeaways. There are a couple of other cafes along the main street. The better is the *Country Kitchen*, 32 Linsley St, with coffee and light meals such as quiche and lasagna. It is also a craft and souvenir shop. The *Golf Club* and the *Ex-Services Club* have meals.

The best place to eat is *Longworth*, 55 Linsley St, a licensed restaurant in a beautiful old house. It's open for dinner Tuesday to Saturday.

Getting There & Away

The Barrier Highway runs east to Nyngan and west to Wilcannia. A popular route for trucks, the Kidman Way runs north to Bourke and south through Mt Hope to Hillston; it should be fully sealed by the end of 1998. Buses stop at the Caltex service station, from where there's a daily service to Dubbo.

AROUND COBAR

East of Cobar, the Barrier Highway passes the curiously named **Mt Boppy**, site of a huge gold mine. **Hermidale**, about 100km east of Cobar, is a railway-side hamlet consisting of a few houses and a shop.

Mt Grenfell Historic Site

Taking in part of the Mt Grenfell station, this site protects Aboriginal rock art in several caves along a well-watered gully, an important place for the local Wongaibon people. Apart from the art, the site is worth visiting for the chance to walk through some pretty country on the 5km walking track.

You'll probably see feral goats and perhaps pigs in the area and there are also plenty of kangaroos and emus. From about July onwards, you'll see father emus herding their broods of chicks. If a couple of males are travelling together, they can have quite a kindergarten to look after.

To get here, travel west from Cobar on the Barrier Highway and turn off after 40km. The site is another 32km away on a good dirt road. There's water at the site but camping is not allowed.

WILCANNIA
Today, the small town of Wilcannia (population 900), on the banks of the Darling River 195km east of Broken Hill, is little more than a refuelling stop on the Barrier Highway. It's hard to imagine that back in the 1880s, the boom years on the Darling River, Wilcannia was the third-busiest port in Australia – dubbed the 'Queen City of the West'.

There isn't much commerce here today but some of the old buildings remain, such as part of the old wharf, the impressive sandstone police station and courthouse on Reid St (turn left just after the bridge if you're coming from Cobar) and the Athenaeum Chambers, also on Reid St but on the other side of the highway, which house the local **museum**.

Places to Stay & Eat
The choice rests between two motels, *Grahams* (☎ 8091 5040) and the *Wilcannia* (☎ 8091 5802), both charging around $50/60. For food, try the basic cafe at the service station. You're not advised to visit the pubs here.

Getting There & Away
From Wilcannia you can take the Barrier Highway east to Cobar or west to Broken Hill. There's a good road (mostly sealed) north to White Cliffs, and the Cobb Highway (see below) leads south.

THE COBB HIGHWAY
The Cobb Highway runs south from Wilcannia through Ivanhoe, Hay and Deniliquin to Moama (and Echuca) on the Victorian border. It's a handy route.

The 190km of road between Wilcannia and Ivanhoe is mostly unsealed and passes through some of the emptiest country in the state, although there are a few stations off the road. *Yelta* (☎ 8091 9467) is a sheep station 11km off the Cobb Highway about 70km south of Wilcannia. It offers accommodation (homestead, camping or shearers' quarters) and the chance to participate in station activities. They can collect you from Wilcannia or Ivanhoe (where the Indian Pacific train stops).

Tiny **Ivanhoe** is the largest town for a very long way. It's built on the railway line (there's even a 'suburb' called Railtown) rather than on a river, and it isn't especially interesting – but, with a pub (with accommodation), a friendly club (with meals), a petrol station (an NRMA affiliate), a caravan park ($4 for a tent site), a bush hospital and a few shops, it can be very useful.

South of Ivanhoe, the Cobb is sealed for the 50km run to **Mossgiel**, just a pub on the corner of the road running east to Willandra National Park and Hillston – this road closes at a hint of rain. The Cobb is again unsealed from Mossgiel to **Booligal**, a tiny town on the Lachlan River with a pub and some basic services. The historic **One Tree Hotel**, on the highway 38km north of Hay, is now a private home.

See the Riverina chapter for information on Hay.

WHITE CLIFFS
There can be few stranger places in Australia than the tiny opal-mining town of White Cliffs (population 150), 97km north-west of Wilcannia. The town is surrounded by some of the harshest country the outback has to offer and many of the residents have gone underground to escape the heat. Although the town is still a major opal producer, it's a fair bet that tourism brings in almost as much money these days.

The town centre, such as it is, is on flat land south of the main digging area. There's a pub, a post office and a corner store selling fuel and provisions. At the digging area, there are thousands of holes in the ground and miners' camps surrounded by car grave-yards (which seem to be a necessary part of opal mining). The two bare hills, Turley's Hill (with the radio-telephone mast on top) and Smith's Hill (south of the centre), are relatively densely populated and command the plains like diminutive city-states.

You can fossick for opals around the old diggings, but keep a close eye on kids around those deep, unfenced holes. There are a number of opal showrooms and under-ground homes open for inspection. **Jock's Place** on Turley's Hill is worth seeing. Jock has a jumble of relics from the area and what he doesn't know about opal mining isn't worth knowing.

In the centre of town is the **solar power-station** (it drives a steam-turbine) where emus often graze out the front. The station is open for inspection daily at 2 pm and is worth a visit if only to see the guide in action. Bill Finney goes through a lot of shirts! Until recently the solar station supplied White Cliffs' electricity needs but when the town grew beyond its capacities, a diesel generator was installed. This seems to be a rotten idea, given that the solar dishes use 2L of distilled water a day while the generator chugs through who-knows-how-much diesel fuel. Also, as everyone gets billed for the genera-tor, there isn't much incentive to keep the numerous wind generators in action.

Places to Stay & Eat
There's a very uninspiring little *camping area* (☎ 8091 6627) next to the swimming pool on the road to Mootwingee. Sites cost $3 per person and showers are $1.

The *White Cliffs Hotel* (☎ 8091 6606) has basic rooms, but they have air-con and are reasonable value at $20/30 for singles/doubles. A cooked breakfast is $8. The man-agement is friendly and other meals are available (although pricey).

The most interesting place to stay is *PJ's Underground* (☎ 8091 6626) on Turley's Hill. Energetic owners Peter and Joanne Pedler have performed miracles in convert-ing their old mine workings into a cool sanctuary with whitewashed walls, beautiful

stone floors and elegant furnishings. Rates are $55/66 for singles/doubles, including breakfast. Self-caterers can pay $2 to use the barbecue in the evening; others can pay $20 for a three-course meal. PJ's has only three guest rooms, so bookings are advisable.

The other underground option is the *White Cliffs Underground Motel* (☎ 8091 6677, 1800 021 154 bookings), which is popular with tour groups. Custom-built with a tun-nelling machine, the place is quite a maze (you get a map when you check in) but it's surprisingly bright, comfortable and not at all claustrophobia-inducing. The rooms are simple, with no TV, but they are well-fur-nished and very quiet, with several metres of rock separating guests from their neigh-bours. There are separate bathrooms ('off-suites'). Singles/doubles are $45/70. Meals cost $6 for a continental breakfast, $12 for a cooked breakfast and $21 for a set-menu dinner.

Getting There & Away
The emergence of White Cliffs as a tourist destination has led to an upgrading of the road south to Wilcannia. Most of the 97km was sealed at the time of research. All other roads out of White Cliffs are unsealed. Infor-mation on road conditions is posted outside the general store.

MOOTWINGEE NATIONAL PARK
Mootwingee lies in the rugged Bynguano Ranges, 131km north-east of Broken Hill. The area teems with wildlife and is a place of exceptional rough beauty. In spring the roads can be like country lanes, flanked by 'hedges' of blue and white flowers. Entry to the park costs $7.50 per car.

The reliable water supply in the range was vital to Aborigines in the area and there are important **rock carvings** and **cave paint-ings**. Some cave paintings have been badly damaged by vandals and the major site is now controlled by the Aboriginal commu-nity and is off-limits to visitors except on ranger-escorted tours on Wednesday and Saturday morning ($4). The NPWS office (☎ 8088 5933) in Broken Hill has details.

There are walks through the crumbling sandstone hills to rock pools, which often have enough water for swimming, and rock paintings can be seen in the areas that are not off-limits.

There's a *camping area* ($10 for two people) at Homestead Creek, with toilets, showers and gas barbecues. Water for drinking may not always be available; fuel and food are not available in the park. You should collect firewood from the signposted areas near the park entrance. Book sites, especially during school holidays.

Getting There & Away
Car & Motorcycle There are no sealed roads to Mootwingee, which means the park is inaccessible in wet weather. Most people head out to Mootwingee from Broken Hill. The turn-off is 56km north of town along the Silver City Highway and then it's a further 68km to the park entrance along a good unsealed road. The back road to White Cliffs is also good but tends to stay muddy longer after rain and has a number of creek crossings – these are usually dry but fill quickly after rain, and, even when the water has gone, deep drifts of mud remain.

BROKEN HILL
Out in the far west, Broken Hill (population 27,000) is an oasis in the wilderness. It's a fascinating town, not only for its comfortable existence in an extremely unwelcoming environment, but also for the fact that it was once a one-company town which spawned one equally strong union. Some of the state's best national parks are in the area, plus some interesting near-ghost towns.

Elements of traditional Australian culture that are disappearing in other cities can still be found in Broken Hill: hard physical work, hard drinking and the sensibilities which come with easy access to a huge, unpopulated landscape. The less-attractive aspects of this culture (forcefully expressed in the novel and film *Wake in Fright*) have been considerably mellowed by the city becoming a major centre for naive artists, most of them

local. This is a surprising but delightful development.

History
The Broken Hill Proprietary Company (BHP), after which the town was named, was formed in 1885 after a boundary rider, Charles Rasp, discovered a silver lode. Miners working on other finds in the area had failed to notice the real wealth. Other mining claims were staked, but BHP was always the 'big mine' and dominated the town. Charles Rasp went on to amass a personal fortune and BHP, which later diversified into steel production, became Australia's largest company.

Early conditions in the mine were appalling. Hundreds of miners died and many more suffered from lead poisoning and lung disease. This gave rise to the other great force in Broken Hill, the unions. Many miners were immigrants – from Ireland, Germany, Italy and Malta – but all were united in their efforts to improve mining conditions.

The first 35 years of Broken Hill saw a militancy rarely matched in Australian industrial relations. Many campaigns were fought, police were called in to break strikes and though there was a gradual improvement in conditions, the miners lost many confrontations. The turning point was the Big Strike of 1919–20, which lasted for over 18 months. The miners won a great victory, achieving a 35-hour week and the end of dry drilling, which was responsible for the dust that afflicted so many miners.

The concept of 'one big union', which had helped to win the strike, was formalised in 1923 with the formation of the Barrier Industrial Council, which still largely runs the town.

Today the richest silver, lead and zinc deposit in the world is still being worked, but lead and zinc have assumed a greater importance in the Silver City, as Broken Hill is known. There's enough ore left to ensure at least another 20 years of mining, but new technology has greatly reduced the number of jobs in the mines.

FAR WEST

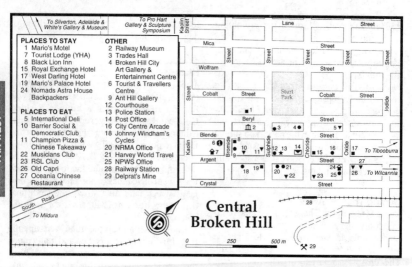

Central
Broken Hill

Orientation

The city is laid out in a straightforward grid pattern and the central area is easy to get around on foot. Argent St is the main shopping street and the blocks between Bromide and Iodide Sts make up downtown Broken Hill.

Information

The big Tourist & Travellers Centre (☎ 8087 6077) on the corner of Blende and Bromide Sts opens daily from 8.30 am to 5 pm. This is where the buses arrive and there's a bus booking agency on the premises, as well as a cafeteria and a car rental desk (Hertz). Also here is the Broken Hill Interpretive Centre, with displays on all aspects of Broken Hill and the area, and information on walks around the city. The Heritage Trails Map is a good buy at $2.

The NPWS office (☎ 8088 5933) is at 5 Oxide St. The Royal Automobile Association of South Australia (☎ 8088 4999), at 261 Argent St, provides reciprocal service to members of other auto clubs. If you're venturing into the outback areas of South Australia you'll need a Desert Parks Pass, which is sold here.

There's a laundromat on Argent St just east of the West Darling Hotel.

If you find injured wildlife, contact Rescue & Rehabilitation of Australian Native Animals (RRANA; ☎ 8087 7753) at the veterinary clinic on Rakow St.

Time Broken Hill operates on South Australian time (Central Standard), which is half an hour behind the time in the rest of the state. Towns near Broken Hill *don't* follow the Silver City's lead, keeping NSW time instead.

Mines

There's an excellent underground tour at **Delprat's Mine** (☎ 8088 1604) Monday to Saturday, where you don miners' gear and descend 130m for a tour lasting nearly two hours. It costs $18 ($15 students). Nobody under eight years of age is allowed. To get there, go up Iodide St, cross the railway tracks and follow the signs – it's about a five-minute drive.

Day Dream Mine, established in 1881, is 33km from Broken Hill, off the Silverton road. A one-hour tour costs $10 ($5 children, all ages allowed) and sturdy footwear is essential. Contact the tourist centre for bookings.

At **White's Mineral Art Gallery & Mining Museum**, 1 Allendale St, you can walk into a mining stope and see mining memorabilia and minerals. It has a craft shop and sells crushed mineral collages. Follow Galena St out to the north-west for 2km or so. Whites now incorporates the Gladstone Mining Museum and is well worth visiting. It's open daily until at least 6 pm and admission is $4.

Royal Flying Doctor Service
You can visit the Royal Flying Doctor Service at the airport. Bookings must be made through the tourist information centre. The tour includes a film about the service, and you inspect the headquarters, aircraft and the radio room that handles calls from remote towns and stations. Tour times are Monday to Friday, 10.30 am and 3.30 pm, and weekends at 10.30 am. The cost is $2 (children free).

School of the Air
You can sit in on School of the Air broadcasts to kids in isolated homesteads on weekdays at 8.30 am sharp. The one-hour session costs $2 (children free); book through the information centre. You can visit even when school is out, as a tape-recording is played for visitors during vacations.

Artists
Broken Hill seems to inspire artists and there's a plethora of galleries, including the **Pro Hart Gallery**, 108 Wyman St, and **Jack Absalom's Gallery**, 638 Chapple St. Wyman and Chapple Sts run parallel to Mica St to the north-west of the town centre.

Pro Hart, a former miner, is Broken Hill's best-known artist and a local personality: there's even a Pro Hart gym! Apart from his own work, his gallery displays minor works of major artists (such as Picasso, Dali, Rouault), but his collection of Australian art is superb. It's one of the largest private collections in the country and is displayed in a very relaxed manner. You can also see his collection of antique baby rattles. He charges admission ($2), but many others don't.

The **Ant Hill Gallery**, opposite the tourist Centre on Bromide St, features local and major Australian artists.

FAR WEST

The Flying Doctor
The flying doctor service was founded by John Flynn ('of the inland') in 1927. He envisioned a 'mantle of safety' for isolated properties in outback Australia, and with the development of simple, inexpensive short-wave radios – at first pedal-powered – much of the country suddenly had access to emergency health care in a matter of hours, instead of days of hard travelling.

Today, the service doesn't just respond to emergencies, it holds regular clinics, complete with specialists, in even the tiniest and remotest towns – and it's all free. That's why you should drop a few coins into a Royal Flying Doctor Service donation box.

One of the longest-running soap operas on Australian TV was *The Flying Doctors*; one of the shortest was its supposedly more realistic replacement, *RFDS*. It seems that audiences weren't ready for themes such as bitchiness, greed and racism sullying one of the few remaining icons of 'the real Australia'. ■

John Flynn, founder of the Royal Flying Doctor Service

In the **Broken Hill City Art Gallery** (in the Entertainment Centre on the corner of Blende and Chloride Sts), you can see *Silver Tree*, an intricate silver sculpture which was commissioned by Charles Rasp. One room of the gallery is devoted to the artists of Broken Hill. The art gallery is open weekdays from 10 am to 5 pm and weekends from 1 pm to 5 pm. Admission is $2 ($1 children). There are more galleries out at Silverton.

Make sure you have a look inside the residential entrance of Mario's Palace Hotel on the corner of Argent and Sulphide Sts.

Sculpture Symposium

In 1993, 12 sculptors from around the world were invited to record their impressions of Broken Hill and the surrounding country at a hill-top site 4km north-west of town. After seeing all those paintings by local 'brushmen of the bush', it's interesting to see how foreign artists responded to this limitless landscape. They certainly don't see it full of cuddly marsupials and laconic stockmen! To get here, follow Kaolin St out of town on to Nine Mile Rd and the sculptures are signposted to the right after a couple of km. From here it's a steep 20-minute climb to the sculpture site. Bring water in summer. You can also drive up the hill from further along Nine Mile Rd and there's wheelchair access to the sculptures from the car park. You need to get the keys to a gate on the road from the tourist centre.

Apart from the sculptures, there are excellent views over the plains and this is a good place to watch one of Broken Hill's famous sunsets.

Historic Buildings

The **Afghani Mosque** is a simple old corrugated-iron building dating from 1891. Afghani cameleers helped to open up the outback and the mosque was built on the site of a camel camp. It's on the corner of William and Buck Sts in North Broken Hill and opens Sunday from 2.30 to 4.30 pm. It no longer functions as a mosque.

The **Trades Hall** on the corner of Sulphide and Blende Sts is a wedding-cake of a building, totally incongruous both in its setting and in relation to its function.

Even apart from the dreadful working conditions in the mines, the early settlers here lived tough lives. Miners' cottages were made of galvanised iron and must have literally been like ovens in the 40°C summers. Some corrugated-iron houses remain, especially in South Broken Hill.

Other Attractions

The **Sulphide St Station Railway & Historical Museum** is in the Silverton Tramway Company's old station on Sulphide St. The tramway was a private railway running between Cockburn (South Australia) and Broken Hill via Silverton until 1970. Also in the complex is a mineral display and a hospital museum. It's open daily from 10 am to 3 pm and admission is $2.

The Mint, on Beryl St near Chloride St, opens daily (only until 1 pm on weekends) and admission is free.

Organised Tours

There are two-hour guided walks of Broken Hill from the tourist centre at 10 am on Monday, Wednesday, Friday and Saturday. Plenty of companies offer tours of the town and nearby attractions, some going further out to White Cliffs, Mootwingee and other outback destinations. You'll pay about $25 for a tour of Broken Hill or Silverton and $75 for a trip to Mootwingee or Kinchega national parks. The tourist centre has information and takes bookings.

Several outfits have longer 4WD tours of the area. Goanna Safaris (☎ 8087 6057) has 4WD outback tours which get good reports from travellers. Corner Country Adventure Tours specialises in trips to the area around Tibooburra and Sturt National Park.

An interesting way to see some of the country beyond Broken Hill is to go on an outback mail run. Contact Crittenden Air (☎ 8088 5702), as far in advance as possible. The mail run departs at 6.30 am on Saturday and calls at about 14 outback stations, stopping in White Cliffs for a tour and lunch. The cost is $210. They also do various air tours and if you're in a group of four, these can work out cheaper than the mail run.

Special Events
There's a country music festival in early October. It features a rodeo and camel races as well as country music.

Places to Stay
Camping *Broken Hill Caravan Park* (☎ 8087 3841) on Rakow St (the Barrier Highway) north-west of the centre has sites for $10, cabins from $30 and on-site vans from $23; *Lake View Caravan Park* (☎ 8088 2250) on Argent St (the Barrier Highway) to the east has sites for $8 and cabins from $30.

Hostels There are two excellent hostels. *Tourist Lodge* (☎ 802086), very close to the tourist centre at 100 Argent St, is a well-appointed associate YHA hostel with a large kitchen/common room, a games room and a small swimming pool. It has dorms for $15, singles for $18 and doubles for $30. It also has air-con singles/doubles for $22/36.

Nomads Astra House (☎ 8087 7788), in the centre of town on the corner of Argent and Oxide Sts, is a good backpacker hostel in a former pub. There's still a bit of renovating to be done, but it's a friendly place with huge verandahs and clean rooms. There are bikes for hire ($5 a day) and twice a week there's a free meal for backpackers. Dorm beds are $12, singles (when available) are $15, doubles $28.

Hotels High ceilings, wide corridors and long verandahs are standard in pubs in this hot city. All the places mentioned here have air-con. As Broken Hill is the only large town for a very long way, its pubs are in the business of offering accommodation; their welcome isn't grudging.

The elegant old *Royal Exchange Hotel* (☎ 8087 2308), on the corner of Argent and Chloride Sts, has singles/doubles for $24/40 or $34/50 with attached bathroom, fridge and TV. All rooms have tea and coffee-making facilities. The price drops by about 10% if you stay more than a couple of days.

Further west on Argent St, *Mario's Palace Hotel* (☎ 8088 1699) is an impressive old pub (1888) in its own right, but its coating of murals makes it extraordinary. All rooms have ceiling fan (as well as air-con), fridge, TV and tea- and coffee-making facilities. Some have a phone. There's a lift (elevator). Singles/doubles cost $28/38 or $38/48 with attached bathroom. There are also some family rooms, one completely covered in murals. You might want to check out your room before taking it, as some have very thin walls.

Offering more standard pub accommodation is the *West Darling Hotel* (☎ 8087 2691) on the corner of Argent and Oxide Sts. This is yet another fine old pub (1883), but the rooms are in more original condition (perfectly reasonable, but you might want to check the bed). There's a variety of rooms, including some interconnecting family rooms. A few rooms have attached bathrooms and go for $36 a single or double. There's also a family unit for $45. Rooms with shared bathroom (some have a shower attached but no toilet) are $23/36.

The *Black Lion Inn* (☎ 8087 4801), across from the tourist centre, has reasonable rooms for $18/28 (no air-con in the single rooms).

Motels It's hard to understand why anyone would opt for a motel in a town with so many interesting places to stay. Still, there are 14 to choose from and the tourist centre has a list of places and prices.

Cottages There are some beautiful cottages for rent around town. *Broken Hill Historic Cottages* (☎ 8087 5305) and *Sue Spicer's Holiday Cottages* (☎ 8087 8488) are both worth checking out. The cottages come complete with just about everything you could need and sleep up to six people. Rates start at around $65 per night, or $350 per week.

Places to Eat
Broken Hill is a club town if ever there was one. They welcome visitors – you just sign the book at the front door and walk in. The *Barrier Social & Democratic Club* ('the

Demo'), 218 Argent St, starts early with breakfast from 6 am (7 am at weekends). The *Musicians Club* at 267 Crystal St is slightly cheaper, while the *RSL Club* is a bit more upmarket.

There are lots of pubs too – this is a mining town – like the *Black Lion Inn* across from the tourist centre, which has a $5 counter lunch and main courses in the evening for around $10. Many other pubs also have counter meals.

The *Champion Pizza & Chinese Takeaway*, behind Pizza Hut on Sulphide St, does an all-you-can-eat Chinese buffet for $6 after 6 pm. There's a cluster of places at the eastern end of Argent St. The *Oceania Chinese Restaurant* is popular, with $6.50 lunch specials and main courses from around $7.50 and the *Old Capri* is a small Italian place offering home-made pasta.

Vegetarians need not despair. *Jhoolas*, in the City Centre Arcade on Argent St, has an assortment of curries and tofu meals from $6, as well as takeaway snacks and smoothies.

If you spend too long in the pub and forget all about dinner, you can pick up a late-night pie from the *Camp Oven Pie Cart*, usually parked on Oxide St opposite Nomads Astra House. Also good for late-night supplies is the *International Deli* on Oxide St near Beryl St, open until midnight all week. It has a good range of cheeses and smallgoods, plus takeaway salads.

Entertainment

Maybe it's because this is a mining town that plays hard or maybe it's because there are so many nights here when it's too hot to sleep, but Broken Hill stays up late. There isn't a great deal of formal entertainment, but you can find pubs doing a roaring trade almost until dawn on Thursday, Friday and Saturday.

The *Theatre Royale* on Argent St has a disco. *The Demo* often has music and sometimes good bands. The *Black Lion*, across from the tourist centre, has been recommended as a good pub for a drink. They have a three-page cocktail list and two-for-one deals some nights. If you're after country

music, try the *Newtown Hotel* on weekends. It's a small pub north-east of the centre on the corner of Buck and Lane Sts.

Two-up (gambling on the fall of two coins, illegal until recently) is played at Burke Ward Hall on Wills St near the corner of Gypsum St, west of the centre, on Friday and Saturday nights. Broken Hill claims to have retained all the atmosphere of a real two-up 'school', unlike the sanitised versions played in casinos.

Getting There & Away

Air Standard one-way fares from Broken Hill include $173 to Adelaide with Kendell (Ansett), $218 to Melbourne with Southern Australia (Qantas) and $354 to Sydney, via Dubbo, with Hazelton.

Bus Greyhound Pioneer runs daily to Adelaide for $56, to Mildura for $37.50 and to Sydney for $99. Buses depart from the tourist centre, where you can book seats.

A Victorian government V/Line bus runs to Mildura ($37.50) on Wednesday and Friday. Book at the railway station.

Train The Indian Pacific passes through Broken Hill on its way between Sydney and Perth. It leaves Broken Hill at 3.20 pm on Sunday and Wednesday and arrives in Sydney at 9.15 am the next day. The economy fare is $86. It leaves for Adelaide ($44) and Perth (from $214) at 8.20 am on Tuesday and Friday.

There's a slightly faster and marginally cheaper daily service to Sydney called Laser. This is a Countrylink bus departing Broken Hill daily at 4 am (groan) and connecting with a train at Dubbo, arriving in Sydney at 8.45 pm.

The Countrylink booking office at the railway station (☎ 132 232) opens weekdays. Travel agents, such as Silver City Tours & Travel (☎ 8087 3310) on Argent St near the corner of Chloride St, make Countrylink bookings.

Car & Motorcycle The Barrier Highway runs east to Wilcannia and Cobar and west into South Australia. The Silver City Highway runs south to Wentworth and, mostly unsealed, north to Tibooburra.

Getting Around

The Legion, Sturt, RSL and Musicians clubs have a free bus to drive you home after a night's drinking. It leaves hourly between 6 pm and midnight. Phone (☎ 8088 0093) to arrange a pick-up.

Car Rental Hertz (☎ 8087 2719) has an office at the tourist centre, which is open daily. Other companies include Avis (☎ 8087 7532), 22 Bonanza St; Budget (☎ 8088 2160), 73 Oxide St; SCV (☎ 8087 3266), 320 Beryl St; Thrifty (☎ 8088 1928), 190 Argent St; and Broken Hill 4WD (☎ 8088 4265), 2 William St.

Taxi Phone numbers which will get you a taxi include (☎ 8088 1144) and (☎ 8087 2222). There's a taxi office on Chloride St near Argent St.

SILVERTON

Silverton, 25km north-west of Broken Hill, is an old silver-mining town. Its fortunes peaked in 1885, when it had a population of 3000 and public buildings designed to last for centuries, but in 1889 the mines closed and the population (and many of the houses) moved to the new boom-town at Broken Hill.

Today it's an interesting little ghost town, used as a setting in films such as *Mad Max II* and *A Town Like Alice*. A number of buildings still stand, including the old jail (now the museum) and the Silverton Hotel. The hotel is still operating and displays photographs taken on the film sets. There are also a couple of art galleries. The information centre, in the old school, has a walking-tour map. Several artists, including Peter Browne, have studios here.

Bill Canard (☎ 8088 5316) runs a variety of **camel tours** from Silverton. The camels are often hitched up near the hotel or the information centre. You can take a 15-minute tour of the town for $5, a one-hour ride for

$20 or a two-hour sunset ride for $40 ($20 children). There are also overnight treks for $150 ($75 children) and there is a five-day journey through the Barrier Ranges.

There's accommodation at *Penrose Park* (☎ 8088 5307), signposted to the right as you approach town from Broken Hill. Campsites cost $2.50 per person or you can bed down in a choice of 'bunkhouses' – $20 with kitchen, $15 without. There are coin-operated showers and there is water for washing, but bring or boil drinking water.

The road beyond Silverton becomes bleak and lonely almost immediately, but the **Umberumberka Reservoir**, 13km from Silverton, is a popular picnic spot.

MENINDEE

This small town (population 500) on the Darling River is 112km south-east of Broken Hill on a good sealed road. It's right by the big Menindee Lakes and Kinchega National Park, which surrounds one of the lakes.

Burke and Wills stayed at Maidens Hotel on their ill-fated trip north in 1860. The hotel was built in 1854 and has been with the same family for about 100 years. There's a courtyard, which is a nice spot for a drink on a hot day.

The town has a small but reasonably well-stocked supermarket, so you don't need to bring too many supplies.

The **Menindee Lakes** are natural lakes on the meandering Darling River, but they have been dammed to ensure year-round water. They offer the parched folk of Broken Hill a chance for watersports and this area can be crowded on summer weekends. The Broken Hill Yacht Club is not far out of Menindee. Its pennant has a camel on it, appropriate for these ships (well, yachts) of the desert.

Places to Stay

Menindee has pub accommodation at the historic *Maidens Hotel* (☎ 8091 4208) and at the *Albermarle Hotel* (☎ 8091 4212). Just across from the Maidens is *Burke & Wills Motel* (☎ 8091 4313), charging $43/53.

There are caravan parks and cabins out of town by the lakes. There's also camping in

Kinchega National Park with some excellent sites among the red gums along the banks of the Darling.

Getting There & Away

Train Menindee is on the main railway line between Sydney and Adelaide, so you can catch the Indian Pacific here.

Car & Motorcycle A good road runs to Broken Hill, and unsealed roads on both sides of the river run south to Pooncarie and Wentworth. The road on the east bank is usually a bit better than the west-bank road but if there has been rain, ask for advice on the best route. Another unsealed road follows the river upstream to Wilcannia.

KINCHEGA NATIONAL PARK

Kinchega National Park is close to Menindee and includes the Darling River and several of the lakes in the Menindee system. These are a haven for bird life. The visitor centre is at the site of the old Kinchega homestead, about 16km from the park entrance, and the shearing shed has been preserved. There's accommodation at the shearers' quarters (book at the Broken Hill NPWS office) for $15 and plenty of campsites ($5) along the river. Entry to the park costs $7.50.

MUNGO NATIONAL PARK

Mungo National Park (27,850 hectares), part of the Willandra Lakes World Heritage Area, is remote, beautiful and a most important

place, full of great significance for the human species. The echoes of over 400 centuries of continuous human habitation are almost tangible.

The story of both Australia and its oldest inhabitants is told in the dunes of Mungo. At least 40,000 years ago, Aborigines settled on the banks of the fertile lakes, living on the plentiful fish, mussels, birds and animals. Some of the animals were much larger than their modern relatives. After 25,000 years the climate changed, the lakes dried up and the Aborigines adapted to life in a harsh semi-desert, with only periodic floods filling the lakes. The constant westerly wind drifted sand from the lake bed up onto the dunes, gradually burying old campsites.

The people maintained their culture for another 15,000 years, but it was destroyed when Europeans arrived with their sheep in the early 19th century. Along with the remains of incredibly ancient animals and people, the dunes hold tracks of the Cobb & Co coaches which cut across the lake last century.

The park includes the dry lake bed (it sometimes fills after heavy rain) and the spectacular 'lunette', a semi-circular range of sand dunes which line the eastern side. Some of the compressed sand has weathered into shimmering white cliffs known as the **Walls of China**. This weathering process began last century after sheep destabilised the dunes, which are now moving slowly eastwards under the constant west wind,

Mungo Dreaming

Under these dunes that sing to the perpetual west wind lie the bones and debris of a civilisation which is unlikely to be matched by the brief and sooty flicker of our materialist culture. The Mungo lunette is thick with spirits. Spirits from the 25,000 years of Eden, when the lakes were full and the land was fat. Spirits from the 15,000 years after the lakes dried up and new skills were perfected.

Mungo is a good place for dreaming.

Dream of our cultural ancestors, the Greeks, and their strange urge to build and to shape the world, and how this led to our experiment with industrialisation and urban life.

The Mungo people had already been here for 35,000 years when the Parthenon was new. Humanity's earliest known funerals were conducted here.

The dream became a nightmare of syphilis, smallpox, guns and Christians, and this unimaginably old civilisation was wiped out in a generation. ∎

leaving exposed immensely important archaeological evidence.

There's a visitor centre (not always staffed) where you can see some of the archaeological finds. Near the visitor centre is the old woolshed from the sheep station which was established here last century. During school holidays there are organised activities, such as walks and even bush dances. The NPWS office (☎ (03) 5023 1278) at Buronga near Mildura has information.

A 60km drive circles the lunette and there are various stopping places with informative noticeboards. There are a couple of short walks, the **Grassland Nature Trail** (1km), beginning near Main Camp, and the **Mallee Walk** (500m), off the road on the east side of the lunette. You can get onto the lunette from the Walls of China and there are good dune walks from Vigars Wells on the north-east side of the lunette.

In summer, be sure to carry water with you when you go walking on the dunes.

Organised Tours

Mallee Outback Exploration (☎ (03) 5021 1621) and Junction Tours (☎ (03) 5027 4309) are two Mildura-based companies offering tours.

Places to Stay

Accommodation fills up during school holidays. There are two campsites in the park: Main Camp is 2km from the visitor centre and Belah Camp is in bushland on the eastern side of the lunette, a few km away. On this side of the lunette you're sheltered from the west wind, but you can hear it singing eerily along the dunes.

Camping costs $5 a night (plus the $7.50 entry fee). There's also shared accommodation in the old shearers' quarters, costing $15 per person or $25 for a room to yourself. There are cooking facilities. Accommodation in the shearers' quarters must be booked through the NPWS office (☎ (03) 5023 1278) in Buronga near Mildura.

On the Mildura road, about 4km from the visitor centre, is *Mungo Lodge* (☎ (03) 5029 7297). Singles/doubles go for $58/68 and there's a self-contained cottage which can sleep up to six ($78 for two people and $10 for each extra person). There's also a restaurant.

Getting There & Away

Air Mungo Lodge has an airstrip where charter flights can land.

Car & Motorcycle No fuel is available in the park or along the roads leading to it. The unsealed roads into Mungo are well maintained, but they can be closed by rain. Even after a light shower, sections are treacherous. Also, watch out for deep drifts of sand or soft dirt. These appear without warning and if you hit one at speed, you'll have no control over the steering until you reach the end, hopefully still pointing in the right direction. Kangaroos and emus are another hazard – or rather, you are a hazard for these locals.

Mungo is 110km from Mildura and 150km from Balranald. When you're adding up the km to make sure you have enough fuel to get to Mungo and back, don't forget the 60-odd km you'll probably drive within the park.

Coming from Balranald, you can take the signposted turn-off about 15km north of town. This is Burke & Wills Rd; it's an interesting drive, but a little rough. If you want to travel on tar as far as possible, keep heading north to another signposted turn-off, 53km from Balranald.

The Riverina

The Riverina takes in much of southern NSW, specifically the mighty Murray and Murrumbidgee rivers and the plains created by these waterways as they changed their courses over the millennia. Away from the rivers, which are popular for fishing holidays, much of this region sees few visitors. This is part of the Riverina's attraction – you can meet locals whose daily life isn't geared to extracting dollars from your wallet.

History

The rivers of the Riverina provided an idyllic home for the Aborigines, and before Europeans arrived the area around Deniliquin was probably the most densely populated part of the continent. John Oxley, the first European to visit the area, wasn't impressed:

There's a uniformity in the barren desolation of this country which wearies one more than I am able to express...I am the first white man to see it and I think I will undoubtedly be the last.
John Oxley, expedition of 1817

A century later, after graziers had established sheep stations on the plains, Europeans were coming to terms with the environment:

The monotonous variety of this interminable scrub...so grave, subdued, self-centred...bespeaks an ungauged, unconfined potentiality...
Joseph Furphy, *Such is Life*, 1903

Not long after, the great irrigation schemes of the Murrumbidgee Irrigation Area (MIA) were begun and parts of the plains bloomed into fertile farmland.

Oddly, the name 'Riverina' isn't the recent brainchild of a tourism committee but was widely used last century. The old-timers' Riverina was much larger than today's region. For them, the Riverina included the vast griddle of plains south of the Darling River.

To get an idea of the terrain and conditions of the Riverina, drive south along the Cobb

HIGHLIGHTS

- The Botanic Gardens in Wagga Wagga
- A pub crawl in Junee
- Visiting the region's wineries, especially around Griffith
- Willandra National Park
- Hot-air ballooning along the Murray River near Corowa

Highway from Wilcannia to Hay. This isn't a trip to take lightly, as much of the 400km is unsealed and there are few services along the way. Imagine how the trip would have been in a bullock wagon hauling eight tonnes of wool at a rate of less than 20km a day!

Geography & Climate

To the east, the landscape is broken up by the last hills of the western slopes of the Great Dividing Range. Much of the region, however, is a huge, flat space, usually with a line of river red-gums straggling along a creek on the horizon, native pines clustered on a sandy ridge overlooking grazing country or, in the west and north, expanses of saltbush or mulga.

Nor is the country far above sea level. The Murray River descends only 100 metres or so between Corowa and its mouth in South Australia. The inland rivers meander lazily, often changing course and often breaking

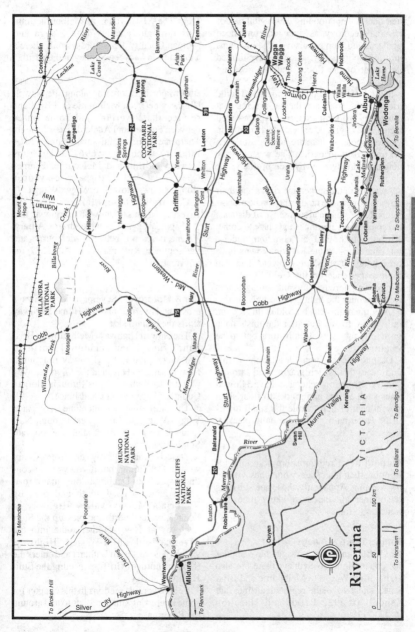

RIVERINA

Riverina

their banks. This flooding was a vital part of the area's ecology, as river red-gums need regular inundation to survive. The big dams built for the irrigation schemes have limited the extent of the floods and the trees are suffering.

In the west the fences disappear and cattle grids on the road are the only signs that you're in working country. Wedge-tailed eagles waft overhead or perch awkwardly on telegraph poles – there are no peaks or even tall trees for their eyries. The western grey kangaroos are dwarfed by their brothers, the big reds.

Away from the serpentine rivers and their red-gum forests the landscape can be monotonous, but if you're after a sense of distance and space, the Riverina is the place to come. Flat horizons of 360° are common, under a hot, blue sky – some Riverina towns have more hours of sunshine per year than you might experience on the Gold Coast. The shimmering horizon blurs into mirages, and even in winter the light is blindingly strong.

Autumn nights can be cold in this region, with heavy frosts, but after the mists have burnt off, the days usually turn out to be beautiful.

Despite the apparent desolation of this landscape, this is rich grazing and farming country. Irrigation schemes have allowed crops such as rice and grapes to flourish in several centres here, while the small towns of the Riverina region are usually pleasant oases.

Warning River red-gums are notorious for dropping their huge, heavy branches without any warning. Apparently, those hot, still days in summer are the most likely times for branches to fall.

Getting There & Away
Air Griffith and Wagga Wagga have regular passenger flights to Sydney; there are also flights from Wagga to Melbourne and Brisbane. The two main regional airlines are Kendell (☎ 6922 0100) and Hazelton (☎ 131713).

Train The XPT Sydney to Melbourne train runs through Junee, Wagga Wagga and Morgan Country. On Saturdays only there's a direct train between Sydney and Griffith.

Bus Major lines running along the Newell Highway between Melbourne and Brisbane service the Riverina, and some buses between Sydney and Adelaide pass through. There are some useful smaller lines. MIA Intercity Coaches (☎ 6962 3419) runs between Griffith and Melbourne. Fearnes Coaches (☎ 6921 2316) services various Hume Highway towns to Wagga Wagga.

Countrylink buses links most of the Riverina region's towns with the railway line at Wagga Wagga, Cootamundra or Albury. V/Line buses run between Melbourne and the southern Riverina. Call ☎ 132232 for information.

Car & Motorcycle Several major highways cross the Riverina, and the Hume Highway skirts the eastern side.

The Newell Highway (Melbourne to Brisbane) runs from Tocumwal north to Narrandera, the Cobb Highway runs north from Moama to Hay, and the Olympic Way (Albury to Bathurst) runs through Morgan Country, Wagga Wagga and Junee.

The Sturt Highway enters the Riverina at Wagga Wagga and runs west through Narrandera, Hay and Balranald, and on into South Australia.

The Riverina Highway runs from Albury west to Deniliquin, but if you want to continue west from Deniliquin on a major road you'll have to head south and pick up Victoria's Murray Valley Highway at Echuca, or head north and pick up the Sturt Highway at Hay. Another route into the Riverina is the Mid-Western Highway, which runs west from Bathurst and enters the Riverina north of Griffith, meeting the Sturt Highway at Hay.

See the various sections in this chapter for some interesting smaller roads to and around the Riverina.

Down the Murrumbidgee

The Murrumbidgee rises in the Snowy Mountains and by the time it reaches Wagga Wagga, not far from the foothills, it's already a broad river. Further downstream its waters form part of the big MIA around Griffith, then it flows though harsher country and meets the Murray downstream from Balranald.

WAGGA WAGGA

Wagga Wagga (population 59,000), usually just called Wagga, is the state's largest inland city. Despite this, it's a relaxed country town, with a little diversity added by the nearby Charles Sturt University.

The largest Aboriginal tribe in NSW, the Wiradjuri, lived in this area. Charles Sturt's 1829 expedition saw the beginning of European encroachment and by 1849 the town of Wagga Wagga was established. The name derives from Aboriginal words meaning 'place of many crows'.

Orientation & Information

The town centre sits on the west bank of the Murrumbidgee River. Baylis St and its northern extension Fitzmaurice St form the two-km spine of central Wagga and run from the railway station to the Hampden and New bridges over the river.

Wagga Wagga Visitors Centre (☎ 6923 5402), on Tarcutta St, opens daily from 9 am to 5 pm. Pick up a driving-tour map of the town from here. The post office, on Morrow St, opens weekdays 8.30 am to 5 pm.

Two camping supplies shops, Camping World and True Blue Camping, are near the corner of Baylis and Tompson Sts.

Things to See & Do

The excellent **Botanic Gardens**, open daily, are south of the centre; turn south off Edward St onto Edmondson St (which becomes Mitchelmore St), then follow the signs. The entrance is on the right just before the archway telling you that you're entering Lord Baden Powell Drive – which leads up to a good lookout and the scenic **Captain Cook Drive**. In the gardens is a small **zoo**. Geese and peacocks roam free and there's a free-flight aviary containing some colourful native birds, although others are crowded into small cages. You can ride a model train on the first and third Sundays of the month.

The **Wiradjuri Walking Track** begins at the visitors centre and eventually returns there after a 30km tour of the area, including some good lookouts. There's a shorter 10km loop past the Wollundry Lagoon. The walks can be done in stages and the visitors centre has maps. From the **beach** near the Tourist Caravan Park you can go swimming and fishing.

The **City Art Gallery** (☎ 6923 5419), opposite the Ngungilanna Culture Centre at 40 Gurwood St, is home to the National Art Glass collection; it's open Tuesday to Friday 11 am to 5 pm, Saturday 10 am to 5 pm, Sunday 2 to 5 pm. **Riverina Galleries** (☎ 6921 5274), The Esplanade, has interesting programmes of exhibitions by Australian artists.

Wagga Wagga is a major centre for **livestock sales**, although the computerised bidding and indoor ring at the Livestock Marketing Centre in Bomen don't have quite the same atmosphere as a smaller town's outdoor saleyards.

Wagga Wagga Winery (☎ 6922 1221), midway between Wagga and Oura on the Gundagai road, opens daily from 11 am for tastings and sales; meals are available for $10. **Charles Sturt University** is north of town, off the Olympic Way. The campus is huge, although there aren't yet many buildings. It has a **winery** (☎ 6933 2435), open weekdays 10 am to 4 pm, weekends from 11 am. The winery is reached through the Agriculture Research Unit, off the Olympic Way about 3km north of Wagga.

Aurora Clydesdale Stud & Pioneer Farm (☎ 6928 2215) is a working farm where you can see magnificent Clydesdales. Aurora is south of the Sturt Highway west of Wagga, about 9km west of Collingullie. The

RIVERINA

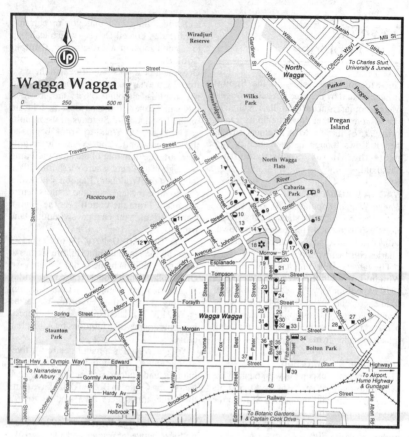

stud opens Friday to Wednesday 9 am to 4 pm; admission is $3 ($1 children).

Special Events

The Wagga Wagga Show, held in late September or early October, is rural NSW's largest agricultural show. The Festival of Wagga Wagga is also a biggie, and is held in October.

Places to Stay

Camping Of the several caravan parks in the area, the *Tourist Caravan Park* (☎ 6921 2540) has the best location. It's on the river

next to a swimming beach, and only a couple of blocks from the town centre. You could walk here from the railway station and the bus terminal. Tent sites are $10 for two people, on-site vans cost $30 and cabins are $38 to $44 with TV and bathroom. Add $5 for each extra person.

Hotels Several pubs have accommodation, including *Romano's Hotel* (☎ 6921 2013) on Fitzmaurice St, with good rooms for $30/38, some with attached bathrooms. Also on Fitzmaurice St there's the *Duke of Kent* (☎ 6921 3231), and the *Tourist Hotel*

PLACES TO STAY		5	No 96		OTHER	
3	Duke of Kent Hotel	12	RSL Club		6	Ngungilanna Culture
4	Tourist Hotel	13	Firenze			Centre
7	Romano's Hotel	14	Cafe Europa		9	Courthouse
8	Tourist Caravan Park &	23	Indian Tavern		10	Wagga Wagga Coach
	Swimming Beach	24	Emma Chissett's &			Terminal
11	Crepe Myrtle		Cafe Tuscany		15	Riverina Playhouse
	Guesthouse	25	Union Club Hotel		16	Wagga Wagga Visitors
19	The Manor Guesthouse	29	Nahiba's Kitchen			Centre
26	Charles Sturt Motor Inn	32	Montezuma's Mexican		17	Civic Theatre
27	Garden City Motor Inn		Restaurant		18	Memorial Gardens
28	Old Wagga Inn	35	Victoria Hotel & Tira		20	Post Office
33	Club Motel		Thai		21	True Blue Camping
37	William Farrer Hotel	36	Aussie Cafe, Family		22	Camping World
			Eating House,		30	Choices & The
PLACES TO EAT			Saigon Restaurant			Broadway
1	Kebab Place		& Bianca's Place		31	NRMA
2	Pavilion Garden	38	Il Corso Pizza		34	Swimming Pool
	Restaurant		Restaurant		39	Red Lion Hotel
					40	Railway Station

RIVERINA

(π 6921 2264), with modest rooms for $20/30. The *William Farrer* (π 6921 3631), not far from the railway station on the corner of Peter and Edward Sts, isn't in the same league but it's good for pub accommodation and costs $28/40 to $35/50 for B&B.

Motels There are many to choose from. The *Palm & Pawn Motor Inn* (π 6921 6688), on the Olympic Way 2km north of town is among the least expensive at $45/55. More expensive places include *Charles Sturt* (π 6921 8088), 82 Tarcutta St, with rooms for $64/72 and the huge *Old Wagga Inn* (π 6921 6444), on the corner of Morgan and Tarcutta Sts, at $80/90.

B&Bs *The Manor* (π 6921 5962) is a small, well-restored guesthouse (furnished with antiques) opposite the Memorial Gardens on Morrow St, just west of Baylis St. Singles/doubles cost $45/60 including breakfast. Another B&B in a restored house, this one much older, is the interesting *Crepe Myrtle* (π 6921 4757), 102 Kincaid St, where rooms cost $70/90.

Places to Eat
Along Fitzmaurice and Baylis Sts there's a diverse range of good places to eat. A culi-

nary stroll beginning near the top of Fitzmaurice St might include the following.

Kebab Place, a Lebanese restaurant and takeaway, has gained good reviews from food writers. It's closed on Monday. A little further down is *No 96*, a trendy bar where you can eat and drink if you aren't wearing runners (sneakers). It's open 6 pm to 3 am Monday to Saturday and for lunch on Friday; pasta is $8.50 to $11.

Cafe Europa is on Johnston St just west of Baylis/Fitzmaurice Sts. It's open for lunch and dinner daily and has pasta ($9.50) and pizzas (from $7.50). Further west on the corner of Johnston and Trail Sts is the upmarket *Firenze*. Wagga Wagga Writers Writers, a local literary group, sometimes holds readings here.

Back on Baylis/Fitzmaurice St, *Scribbles* is a light-hearted cafe serving focaccia, coffee and light meals during the day and into the evening from Thursday to Saturday. Nachos will set you back $8. *Indian Tavern* ($\pi$ 6921 3121), in D'Hudson arcade at 176 Baylis St, has a tandoori oven and opens for dinner daily and for lunch Wednesday to Friday. Main courses range from $7.50 to $16. It also does takeaways.

Across the street is a cluster of places. *Emma Chissett's* ('emma chissett' is Strine for 'could you please tell me the price of this article?') serves coffee, snacks and light meals during the day. Nearby but upstairs is *Cafe Tuscany*, an airy place with a small balcony overlooking the street. It serves some interesting, moderately priced dishes. Lunch specials are $7.50, ratatouille $7.

In Neslo Arcade is *Nabiha's Kitchen*, a small Lebanese takeaway (with tables) where everything is cooked in front of you. The mostly vegetarian menu of simple, inexpensive dishes includes some Indian items. They grow their own vegetables and use free-range eggs. Felafel is $4.80, Lebanese coffee $3. It's open Monday to Saturday and well worth checking out.

The *Union Club Hotel* has counter meals starting at $6.

For something completely unauthentic try *Montezuma's Mexican Restaurant*, where *comidas* (meals) cost $11 to $12 and other mains $13. It's open from 6 pm Tuesday to Sunday and for lunch Wednesday to Friday.

The *Baylis St Bistro* at the Victoria Hotel has a good reputation, a large menu (steak costs $11.50), and dress regulations – no thongs (flip-flops), singlets or work clothes. In the Baylis Centre next door is the popular *Tira Thai Restaurant*, a large, plush place which has a $5 lunchtime buffet and main courses in the $9 to $12 range.

Dick Eyle's *Aussie Cafe* on Baylis St is good and opens for breakfast. Bacon and eggs are a bit pricey at $8.30, but they come with chips. A few doors down is the *Family Eating House*, a huge smorgasbord place where you can eat as much as you like for $8.30 at lunch (11 am to 2.30 pm) and $9.30 at dinner (5.30 to 9.30 pm). The mainly Asian menu is changed weekly.

Farther down, the small *Saigon Restaurant*, with most dishes for $7.60 to $10.50, stays open until at least 9.30 pm. *Bianca's Place* is a coffee-shop serving breakfast, snacks and light meals; quiche is $6. Across the road, *Il Corso Pizza Restaurant* has pasta dishes for $9.50, pizza from $8 and other mains for $12.50 to $14.50.

The *RSL Club* on Kincaid St has $6 lunches and $12 smorgasbord dinners; the *Pavilion Garden Restaurant*, 22-30 Kincaid St (in an extravagantly designed motel) has fish for $18, filet mignon $19. *Bernie's* at the Tourist Hotel is a good vegetarian restaurant.

Entertainment

The *Riverina Playhouse* (☎ 6921 6861) and the *Civic Theatre* (☎ 6923 5405) have regular stage performances.

This is a student town, of sorts, and a few of the pubs have bands, including the *Duke of Kent* and the *Tourist* hotels on Fitzmaurice St. The *Red Lion Hotel*, on Edward St near the railway station, has live music Friday nights. Two nightclubs on Baylis St, *Choices* and *The Broadway*, sometimes have live big-name bands and stay open until late most days of the week.

Other popular watering-holes are the *Union Club Hotel*, on Baylis St, and *Romano's Hotel* on Fitzmaurice St.

Getting There & Away

Air Kendell (☎ 6922 0100) and Hazelton (☎ 131713) have services connecting Wagga with Sydney, Melbourne, Brisbane and a number of regional centres in NSW. The standard economy one-way/return fare to Sydney is $175/350.

Train Wagga is on the main line between Sydney and Melbourne. The one-way economy fare to both is $62. The Countrylink Travel Centre (☎ 6922 0448), at the railway station, opens Monday to Friday 8.30 am to 5 pm, Saturday 9 am to 1 pm.

Bus Countrylink buses meet some trains and run daily to Griffith ($17) via Narrandera and Leeton, and to Echuca (Victoria) via Jerilderie, Finley, Deniliquin and Moama. Countrylink leaves from the railway station. Other long-distance services leave from the coach terminal (☎ 6921 1977) at the corner of Gurwood and Trail Sts; it's open Monday to Friday 8.30 am to 7 pm, Saturday 8.30 am to noon. You can book here or at a travel agent along Baylis St. Fearnes Coaches (☎ 6921 2316) runs to Sydney ($39) via the Hume Highway, stopping at most major towns, such as Gundagai, Goulburn and Mittagong.

Glass Buslines (☎ 6924 1633) runs a local service to Junee ($7) on weekdays and picks up along Baylis St.

Car & Motorcycle Wagga is at the junction of the Sturt Highway, which runs east to the Hume Highway and west to Narrandera, and the Olympic Way, which runs north-east to Cootamundra and south to Albury. Smaller roads, often interesting drives, link Wagga with the small towns of this area.

Car Rental Avis (☎ 6921 1077) is near the railway station at the corner of Edward and Fitzhardinge Sts.

AROUND WAGGA WAGGA
The Rock & Around
On the Olympic Way about 25km south-west of Wagga, The Rock is a small village near a large, craggy hill rising out of the flat plain. The town was called Hanging Rock until the boulder balanced on top of the hill fell off late last century.

Heckenberg's (☎ 6920 2218) is an interesting antique room and also provides tourist information.

The hill is in **The Rock Nature Reserve**; there's a walking trail to the summit and the return journey takes about three hours. Near the top, the going is steep and you have to be careful of falling rocks.

Three km north of **Yerong Creek**, 15km south of The Rock off the Olympic Way, *Hanericka Farmstay* (☎ 6920 3709) is a 1600-hectare complex geared mostly to overseas visitors. Accommodation costs $55/90 a single/double, including meals and farm activities. For something simpler you could try the impressive *Yerong Creek Hotel* (☎ 6920 3515).

Galore Scenic Reserve
Henry Osborne walked from Wollongong to Adelaide in 1840 and on the way he climbed this sudden hill, exclaiming at the top, 'There's land and galore'. Now a scenic reserve, Galore Hill is worth a visit for its

bush (and the plantings near the base of the hill) and for the 360° views from the platform at the top. There are toilets and fireplaces near the platform but you can't camp here. This reserve is refreshingly free of the ravages of beer parties and trail-bike vandals.

Galore Hill is 14km south of the Sturt Highway, down a turn-off about 60km west of Wagga, and it's also accessible from Lockhart.

Lockhart
This little town of 1000 people is known for its verandahs – both sides of Green St, the main street, are lined with them. The gates to the showground, where there's an old pavilion, are concrete wool bales. The small Greens Gunyah Museum & Craft Shop opens at various times on Wednesday and Friday to Sunday and has tourist information. Entry to the museum is $2 (50c children).

Accommodation can be found in the small *Lockhart Caravan Park* (☎ 6920 5119), pubs such as the *New Gunyah Hotel* (☎ 6920 5449), and the *Lockhart Motel* (☎ 6920 5357).

Ganmain
Ganmain is a sleepy village on the interesting road between Junee and Narrandera, and is accessible from Wagga via Junee or more directly via **Coolamon**, a larger, prettier place. North of Coolamon, 4km out on the Temora road, you can stay in an old railway carriage or in a self-contained cottage at *Avondale Farm* (☎ 6927 3055) for $35 per person.

Apart from its somnolent charm, Ganmain is notable for its hay industry. The farms have been producing high-quality wheaten hay and chaff (about 20,000 tonnes a year) since the last century. The area is special because the hay is still often bound into sheaves which are stooked by hand and carted in horse-drawn wagons to be stacked into 'real' haystacks, which you can see sitting in the stubbled paddocks. There's a roadside display centre in Ganmain where you can see a video on hay production and even activate one of the old binders. The hay-cutting season is October and November.

Ganmain's other claim to fame is its meat pies, which are highly regarded in the district.

MORGAN COUNTRY

The area known as Morgan Country is a rough circle of pretty country south of Wagga Wagga, west of Holbrook and north of Albury, containing some interesting little towns, including Henty, Culcairn and Jindera.

This was once the stamping-ground of bushranger Mad Dog Morgan. Unlike Ned Kelly, Morgan was a bushranger no-one respected. He began his career in Victoria in the 1850s but was captured and spent six years on a prison hulk in Port Phillip Bay (probably enough to turn anyone into a mad dog). On receiving parole he escaped and moved into NSW, where for two years he killed and looted in this small area. Declared an outlaw, he fled to Victoria (where he was still wanted) in 1865, resolving to 'take the flashness out of the Victorian people and police'. He didn't get very far. At Peechelba station, just south of the Murray near Corowa, he was shot dead. His head was cut off and it's said that his scrotum became a tobacco pouch.

Information

For tourist information on the area, see the post office on Balfour St in Culcairn; it's open weekdays 8 am to 5.30 pm, Saturday 8 am to 5 pm, Sunday 10 am to 5 pm, or phone Gaynor McLeish (☎ 6029 6136) who works in the post office.

Culcairn

Culcairn was once a major overnight stop for people travelling by train between Sydney and Melbourne, and the town's main feature, the **Culcairn Hotel** (1891), reflects this status. It's a grand old hotel, the largest between the two cities until the 1930s, with a beer garden that deserves a more lavish name – there's even a fountain! Next to the

pub is Sholz's Building, a long terrace of shops, and these two structures form the bulk of the town.

Across the tracks from the pub, the old stationmaster's residence is being restored as a **museum**. There are several other historic buildings in this little town, with half the main street classified by the National Trust. On Gordon St is the artesian pumping station, first used to supply Culcairn's water in 1926.

Three km east of Culcairn on the Holbrook road is **Round Hill Station** (☎ 6029 6136), featuring an enormous, old woolshed. The functions held here are sometimes open to the public (bush dances, for example).

At **Premier Yabbies** (☎ 6029 8351), about 6km south-west from Culcairn off the Walla Walla road, you can see an interesting display on yabbies. Admission is $5 ($2.50 children) and refreshments, including yabbie sandwiches, are available. You can also catch your own. The farm opens Monday and Wednesday to Saturday 10 am to 5 pm, Sunday noon to 5 pm; it's closed Tuesday and throughout August.

Places to Stay & Eat The small *Culcairn Caravan Park* (☎ 6029 8248), by the creek, has sites for $8 and on-site vans for $20.

The *Morgan Country Motel* (☎ 6029 8233) is good and has rooms for $54/67, but it's hard to resist a night at the *Culcairn Hotel* (☎ 6029 8501), at $28/38 including a serve-yourself breakfast. The rooms are standard pub accommodation with shared bathrooms, and the decor steers an uneasy course between genuine antiques and gaudy kitsch, but the pub is big enough to take it. Tour groups stay here, so it's advisable to book.

As well as a couple of simple cafes, there's a *bistro* at the hotel and Devonshire teas and Chinese meals at the *Collector's Haven* antiques store.

Morgan's Lookout

A low hill with a cluster of huge boulders on top, this would have made a superb lookout for any bushranger. You can climb up for great views and there are gas barbecues. The lookout is about 18km south-west of Culcairn on the sealed road to Walla Walla, just past the Walbundrie turn-off. The pub in **Walbundrie** makes the modest claim of having 'the best and only beer in town'.

Walla Walla

This little town (population 700) was settled in 1869 by Germans from South Australia's Barossa Valley. Today there's a large Lutheran Church and a boarding school. On the second Sunday of each month a **craft market** is held in the old blacksmith's shop on Main St; German food is available.

About 5km north of town there's a wetland area, **Walla Walla Tank Wildlife Refuge**, with a stand of river red-gum forest. It's home to many local and migrating birds.

Walla Walla has camping and motel accommodation.

Henty

The Taylor Header, which revolutionised grain harvesting around the world, was invented in Henty in 1913 by Headlie Taylor. There's a display commemorating this claim to fame in Henty Memorial Park.

Each year the **Henty Machinery Field Days** are held on Tuesday, Wednesday and Thursday of the third week in September. If you're interested in farm equipment (or are interested in the people who are) this is the place to come. About 50,000 people turn up for this event, perhaps the best of its type in Australia.

Doodle Cooma Swamp is a wetlands area, 2km west of town on the Pleasant Hills road.

The *Doodle Cooma Arms* (☎ 6929 3013), beside the railway lines, and the more conservatively named *Central Hotel* (☎ 6929 3149), on the main street, have meals and pub accommodation.

Jindera

Jindera was also settled by German immigrants, and the early days are remembered in the outstanding **Jindera Museum** (☎ 6026 3622). The museum centres around

Wagners store, an old-style country store that was left as it was when it closed in 1958 – although it must have been an old-fashioned store even then. The many exhibits include some buggies and wagons, including one which carried the area's first German settlers across from Adelaide. Check out the enormous builder's wagon, too. Interior scenes from the film *Mad Dan Morgan* were shot here.

The museum opens Tuesday to Sunday from 10 am to 3 pm; admission is $5 (50c children).

Getting There & Away

Bus Greyhound Pioneer stops in Culcairn, Henty and The Rock on its Melbourne-Brisbane run.

Train Sydney to Melbourne XTP trains stop at Culcairn, Henty and The Rock.

Car & Motorcycle The Olympic Way (Albury to Bathurst) runs through this area, which is also accessible from the Hume Highway at Holbrook.

JUNEE

Junee, a small friendly country town (population 5000) with a disproportionate number of impressive buildings, is well worth a stop. Tourist information is available from the service station on Main St and from the Crossing Motel.

Monte Cristo

The mansion of Monte Cristo (1884) was the home of Christopher Crawley, a shrewd land-owner who predicted the railway's arrival in Junee and the subsequent boom in land prices. Actually, it's suspected that he was a little more than shrewd, as the railway was supposed to go through Old Junee, some way distant, but somehow ended up running through Crawley's land.

Monte Cristo isn't especially large but it's full of superb antiques collected by the owners during their 30-year restoration of the property. It had nearly been destroyed by weather and vandals, who weren't deterred

RIVERINA

by the house's reputation for supernatural goings-on.

The mansion (☎ 6924 1637) opens daily 10 am to 4 pm, and the admission price of $7 ($3.50 children) includes an informative guided tour. You can also wander through the outbuildings which contain other exhibits, including a large display of old carriages and buggies. On some nights ghost tours are held from 9 pm onwards for $15, which includes refreshments.

Monte Cristo sits on a hill on the west side of town, near the impressive St Joseph's Catholic Church; access is from John Potts Drive.

Old Buildings

If you like pubs, central Junee is like a glimpse of heaven, with two magnificent old pubs, their massive verandahs dripping with iron lace, standing cheek by jowl. Across the tracks looms another enormous old hotel. Each pub deserves at least one beer, and there are another three in town if you want to make a day of it.

The **Commercial Hotel** has a busy bar crowded with after-work drinkers. The **Loftus** is the town's grandest hotel, with a frontage running for an entire block. Don't miss the residential entrance and the staircase.

Across the tracks, the **Junee** is at least as big as the Loftus and was built by Christopher Crawley, owner of the Monte Cristo mansion on the hill behind. The pub hasn't had a lot done to it over the years, but that just means that the original fittings are still intact. On Broadway St, the **Broadway** is another fair-sized pub, a bit the worse for wear but with green-tiled walls that deserve a look. The **Locomotive** on Hill St is just a country pub, a little out of its league in this company, but it's popular. The single-storey **Red Cow** hides away on Junction St from its mammoth brethren.

As well as the pubs a number of other old buildings are worth a look, including the **railway buildings** on the small square in the centre of town. In complete contrast, next to Memorial Park, is the humble building

which contains the **Junee Historical Museum**, open Wednesday and weekends from 2.30 to 5 pm.

Places to Stay & Eat

Willow Caravan Park (☎ 6924 1316), at the northern end of Broadway St on the outskirts of town, is small but pleasant and charges just $6 for a tent site.

There are motels, but this is a town where you should try a pub. The *Commercial* (☎ 6924 1023) is a friendly, popular place with good rooms for just $15/30. There's a large guests' lounge and kitchen facilities. In the bistro, standard counter-meal dishes cost $6 to $10. Next door, the *Loftus* (☎ 6924 1511) has some simple motel-style units, but you should consider taking one of the hotel rooms which cost $25/40 (including a light breakfast) and look out onto that fabulous verandah. Despite its more upmarket feel, counter meals at the Loftus are slightly cheaper than at the Commercial. There's also a Chinese restaurant in the old dining room at the back.

Across the railway lines, the *Junee* (☎ 6924 1124) has clean but more original rooms (complete with old iron bedsteads) for $15/30.

The *Junee Motor Inn* (☎ 6924 1266) has rooms for $50/54; at *The Crossing* (☎ 6924 3255), they're $65/72.

Getting There & Away

Bus Greyhound Pioneer runs through Junee on the run between Melbourne and Brisbane. Junee Travel (☎ 6924 2399) on Railway Square sells tickets. Junee Buses (☎ 6924 2244), on Main St near the railway level crossing, runs weekday services to Wagga Wagga ($7 one way).

Train Junee is on the main Sydney to Melbourne line. You can get tickets at Junee Travel.

Car & Motorcycle The Olympic Way runs north to Young and south to Wagga Wagga. The road from Junee west to Narrandera is interesting (see Around Wagga Wagga) and there's a good drive south-east to the Hume Highway at Gundagai, some of it alongside the Murrumbidgee River.

TEMORA & AROUND

On the edge of the Riverina, and almost part of the central west, Temora (population 4600) is a pleasant place, with a classic country-town main street and an air of solidity. Late last century there were over 20,000 diggers here searching for gold, but today sheep and wheat keep the town going.

The tourist office (☎ 6978 0585), on Hoskins St, the main street, opens Monday to Friday 9 am to 4 pm, weekends 10 am to 2 pm.

Things to See & Do

A number of **old buildings** reflect the prosperity of the area and its social distinctions. On one corner in the town centre is the stolid Anglican church, backed by banks and the post office and next to the courthouse and police residence. Diagonally opposite this display of the established powers of church and state is the large Catholic church, with a school behind it, a gorgeous presbytery beside it and a pretty little park next door to that.

Taking the most prominent corner in town is a life-size statue of **Paleface Adios**, a local horse which won 108 harness races. Temora is in harness-racing territory and there are several studs in the area.

The interesting **Temora Rural Museum**, on the Junee-Wagga road across the railway line and south of the town centre, displays implements and historical items relating to the district. It's open daily 2 to 5 pm; entry is $3 ($1 children).

Temora's airport is one of the most reliably fog-free in the state and there's quite a lot of activity there, including **skydiving**. Instruction and tandem dives are available from Skydive Temora (☎ 6978 0137).

If you haven't had your fill of small Riverina villages, drop into sleepy **Ariah Park**, 35km west of Temora on the road to Griffith. It's just a hamlet in flat, red-soil country, but it has an atmosphere of times fast vanishing. Yarning on the bench outside the post office, beating the heat with a cold beer at the verandahed pub and smelling the peppercorn trees in the middle of the main street – these are essential Aussie activities which the theme parks and tourist towns can't quite match. Three km out of Ariah Park toward West Wyalong, **Lake Centenary** has swimming, fishing and water skiing. In town there's a basic but free *camping area* at the recreation ground; call ☎ 6977 1099.

In **Bardeman**, 30km north on the West Wyalong road, there's a huge mineral-water swimming pool. Whether it has therapeutic properties is debatable, but it's a good place for a swim.

Special Events

The Trotting Club holds harness races at the showgrounds track from October to April, with the prestigious Temora Pacers' Cup run at the first meeting in February.

If you are here in late September you can attend the Temora Show.

Places to Stay & Eat

Temora Caravan Park (☎ 6977 1712), near the rural museum on the Junee-Wagga road, has tent sites from $8.

The *Shamrock Hotel* (☎ 6978 0400), on Hoskins St, has pub rooms and motel units, the latter for $40/50 including breakfast. The good *Goldtera Motel* (☎ 6977 2433), on the corner of Baker and Loftus Sts, charges $55/64. The other motels, the *Temora* (☎ 6977 1866) and the *Aromet* (☎ 6977 1877), are cheaper.

There are several cafes on Hoskins St. Opposite Fossey's store, the *Waratah Cafe* serves hamburgers for $2.60 and other snacks. The pubs have counter meals, and in winter the *Federal Hotel* bakes its famous Federal Pies. There's an *Ex-Services Club* on Loftus St.

Getting There & Away

Countrylink buses stop at Temora on the run between Balranald and Cootamundra via

Griffith and Hay. Lynch's travel agency (☎ 6977 1296), 194 Hoskins St, sells tickets.

NARRANDERA

Charles Sturt passed through here on his 1829 journey down the Murrumbidgee and many other people have done so since, as Narrandera (population 5000) straddles the Sturt and Newell highways, with good connections to Sydney, Melbourne, Adelaide and Brisbane. Despite the amount of through traffic, Narrandera remains a friendly country town with good services and accommodation.

Orientation & Information

The Newell Highway runs through town as Cadell St; the Sturt passes just south of it. East St is the commercial centre. The Tourist Information Centre (☎ 6959 1766), in Narrandera Park on the Newell Highway, opens weekdays 9 am to 5 pm, weekends 10 am to 4 pm. Here you'll find 'the world's largest playable guitar', although you wouldn't get much of a tune out of it. The centre has a walking-tour map of the town which takes you past many old buildings.

Things to See & Do

Behind the information centre there's a lovely **cricket ground**, complete with a small wooden grandstand. In another corner of the park is the **Mini Zoo**, consisting mainly of birds and some bored animals. There's also a **ceramic fountain**, Royal Doulton no less, perhaps one of only two in the world.

Parkside Cottage Museum is across from the park on the corner of Twynam St. The extremely diverse collection, from '1000 years of monarchy' to skis from Scott's Antarctic expedition, is in the best tradition of small-town museums. It's open Monday and Tuesday 2 to 5 pm, the rest of the week from 11 am. Admission is $2 (50c children).

Lake Talbot is a watersports reserve, partly a long artificial lake and partly a swimming pool complex with some good waterslides. For 30c you can ride a wooden toboggan down a slide, shooting out across

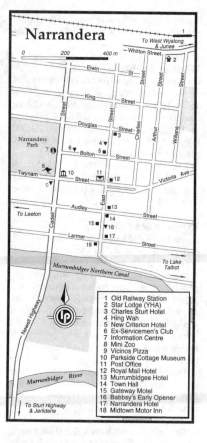

Narrandera

To West Wyalong & Junee
To Leeton
To Lake Talbot
To Sturt Highway & Jerilderie

Murrumbidgee Northern Canal

Murrumbidgee River

1 Old Railway Station
2 Star Lodge (YHA)
3 Charles Sturt Hotel
4 Hing Wah
5 New Criterion Hotel
6 Ex-Servicemen's Club
7 Information Centre
8 Mini Zoo
9 Vicinos Pizza
10 Parkside Cottage Museum
11 Post Office
12 Royal Mail Hotel
13 Murrumbidgee Hotel
14 Town Hall
15 Gateway Motel
16 Babbsy's Early Opener
17 Narrandera Hotel
18 Midtown Motor Inn

the pool like a skipped stone. A great way to relieve highway tensions!

Bush (including a koala regeneration area) surrounds the lake and a number of trails make up the **Bundidgerry Walking Track**. The information centre has a map and brochure. The complex can be reached from the top of Larmer St, where there's a good view down the Murrumbidgee before you take the steep road down to the lake. This is also the trackhead for the trails.

The **John Lake Centre** at the Inland Fisheries Research Station (☎ 6959 1488) opens weekdays 9 am to 4 pm and has guided tours (on which you can see a huge Murray cod) at 10.30 am. Tours cost $5 ($2.50 children). The turn-off to the centre is on the Sturt Highway 4km south-east of Narrandera.

Near Painters Siding, 9km north of Narrandera, **Craigtop Deer Farm** (☎ 6959 1915) has pet deer 'available for public interaction'. It's open daily 9 am to 6 pm and admission is $3.

Special Events
In early January, water-skiing championships take place on Lake Talbot; in late January there's a rodeo. March sees the Country Music Festival, which explains that guitar at the information centre. In early September the town has its agricultural show. In October there's the Murrumbidgee Sheepdog Trials, the Tree-mendous Celebration (centred around Narrandera's trees but including a home-brewing competition) and the National Guinea Pig Show.

Places to Stay
The information centre takes bookings for the various farmstays in the area.

Camping *Lake Talbot Caravan Park* (☎ 6959 1302) is on a hill overlooking Lake Talbot and the dense red-gum forest stretching to the horizon. It has a good tent area ($12 for a site) as well as on-site vans ($27) and self-contained units (from $41). It's some way from the town centre at the eastern end of Larmer St. *Narrandera Caravan Park* (☎ 6959 2955) is slightly cheaper, but it's across the river south of town.

Hostel/B&B Narrandera's impressive *Star Lodge* (☎ 6959 1768), in a fine old hotel complete with verandahs and iron lace, is a B&B that also offers dorm accommodation to YHA members. Dorm beds cost $14 ($10 children) and breakfast is extra. Other rooms cost $30/55 with breakfast. One room has an attached bathroom (narrow because it's built into the old chimney niche!) and costs $65. This is a clean, pleasant place and is handy for long-distance buses to stop at, being opposite the old railway station.

Hotels Most of the pubs along East St have accommodation. The cheapest ($10/20) is the *Royal Mail* (☎ 6959 2007) on the corner of Twynam St; the most expensive ($20/30) is the *Murrumbidgee* (☎ 6959 2011) on the corner of Audley St.

Motels Narrandera has many motels. The *Midtown Motor Inn* (☎ 6959 2122), on the corner of East and Larmer Sts, is in a quiet but central location. Singles/doubles cost from $43/59, more at peak times.

Places to Eat
Babbsy's Early Opener, 173 East St, serves takeaway snacks from 5 am to 2.30 pm and claims to have the lowest prices in town. The *Railway Refreshment Rooms* cafe at the disused station is full of bric-a-brac and open daily 6.30 am to 9 pm. There are snacks and some good-value meals from around $3.50. The owner is a good source of local information.

Vicinos Pizza, south of the information centre, has a wide variety of dishes, including Sunday roast lunches for $7. There are two Chinese restaurants: *Treasure Court* in the Royal Mail Hotel and *Hing Wah*, 96 East St. The *Ex-Servicemen's Club* on Bolton St has a bistro and a dining room. The pubs have the usual counter meals.

Getting There & Away
Bus McCafferty's stops daily at the old railway station on its Melbourne to Brisbane and Sydney to Adelaide runs. Greyhound Pioneer stops here between Sydney and Adelaide. Countrylink runs to Wagga Wagga (where there are trains to Sydney and Melbourne) and Griffith.

Car & Motorcycle As well as the highways linking Narrandera with four capital cities, smaller roads run north-west to Leeton and Griffith and east to the Olympic Way at Junee.

LEETON & AROUND
Leeton (population 6500) is the MIA's oldest town and its headquarters. Although it

Lawson in Leeton
One early resident of Leeton was Henry Lawson, who came here in 1916 in an attempt to break the cycle of poverty and drunkenness which dogged his later years. Things seemed promising: Lawson had a grant from the NSW government, he was 'dry', and he ran into an old mate he'd known in Bourke, when his star was on the rise. Lawson began a new series of works (the *Previous Convictions* stories), but he returned to Sydney after a year and died a few years later. ■

doesn't have the range of services of Griffith, it makes a pleasant base for exploring the area. Seeds from the agricultural college were used to plant the numerous palm trees that line the roads.

Leeton was founded as an MIA town in 1913; there was no settlement here before the water came. It was the first of the Walter Burley Griffin-designed MIA towns, and it works better than nearby Griffith, partly because until relatively recently limits were placed on development. Now that restrictions have been lifted, a highway sprawl is developing.

Rice-growing began near Leeton in 1924, and today the Riverina's Ricegrowers' Co-operative exports 85% of its 1.2 million-tonne crop each year.

Orientation & Information
Leeton Visitors Centre (☎ 6953 2832), 8-10 Yanco Ave, in the former manager's residence of the MIA, opens weekdays 9 am to 5 pm, weekends 9.30 am to 12.30 pm. It has a presentation area and historical display. Most streets are named after trees or products in the area, with the main street being called Pine Ave from the Murray pine, a native species. The visitors centre has several walking-tour maps.

Things to See & Do
A number of food-processing plants have guided tours or presentations. The **SunRice Country Visitors Centre** (☎ 6953 0596),

Calrose St, opens weekdays 9 am to 5 pm and has presentations at 9.30 am and 2.45 pm. The **Sunburst Juice Factory** (☎ 6953 3144), 37 Brady Way, has guided tours on weekdays at 10.45 am. You must wear shoes for these tours.

Lillypilly Estate (☎ 6953 4069) and Toorak Wines (☎ 6953 2333) are two **wineries** near Leeton, open Monday to Saturday for tastings and for tours on weekdays – 11.30 am at Toorak Wines, 4 pm at Lillypilly Estate.

There are daily tours of the restored **Historic Hydro Motor Inn** daily at 11.30 am; there's also a historical display and local artists' gallery.

In **Yanco**, a village that's virtually a suburb of Leeton, the Powerhouse Museum is being developed but progress is slow due to lack of funds; a model railway may be built soon. Yanco was the original railhead for the MIA and the powerhouse once supplied all the area's electricity.

A few km west of Yanco (the signposted turn-off is south of the town) is **Yanco Agricultural High School**. Visitors are welcome to drive through and during school hours you can wander around the buildings. If you keep going down the road that leads to the school entrance, you'll come to an old bridge across the Murrumbidgee, where there's a fireplace and a potential camping spot. This road leads on to Euroley and the Sturt Highway west of Narrandera.

Also out of Yanco on the Narrandera road is the **Yanco Agricultural College**, opened in 1908 as an experimental farm for the new irrigation scheme. Today the college has educational programmes and offers an advisory service to farmers in the area. You can drive through, but there isn't a lot to see.

Whitton, 25km west of Leeton, was here before the MIA started, and there's a museum in the old courthouse and jail.

The north bank of the Murrumbidgee near Leeton has several beaches and picnic areas. Ask the visitors centre for a map.

Special Events
The SunRice Country Festival is held over

Easter in even-numbered years; the Murrumbidgee Farm Fair is held at Yanco's Agricultural College in May; and the Leeton Agricultural Show is held on the second Friday and Saturday in October. The Leeton Eisteddfod is held over three weeks in August, culminating in a big concert.

Places to Stay

Several properties in the Leeton area offer farmstays. The Leeton Visitors Centre makes bookings.

Camping *Leeton Caravan Park* (☎ 6953 3323), 2km south of town on Yanco Ave, has sites for $9, on-site vans for $26 and cabins for $36. The smaller *Gilgal Family Holiday Centre* (☎ 6953 3882), east on Corbie Hill Rd (off Yanco Ave), has similar rates.

Hotels & Motels The *Leeton Hotel* (☎ 6953 2027), 71 Pine Ave, charges $20 per person for bed and breakfast and the nearby *Wade Hotel* (☎ 6953 3266) at 42 Pine Ave also has accommodation.

The well-positioned *Historic Hydro Motor Inn* (☎ 6953 2355) is a huge old guesthouse with a National Trust listing. Motel-style units are $40/50 to $50/60 a single/double, including a cooked breakfast. There are also rooms with shared bathroom. Despite its restoration, the Hydro is somewhat faded. If it doesn't appeal try the *Bygalorie Motor Inn* (☎ 6953 4100), 439 Yanco Ave, or *Motel Riverina* (☎ 6953 2955), 1 Yanco Ave.

Places to Eat

Leeton doesn't have the range of eateries that nearby Griffith has. On Pine Ave there are a few cafes and coffee shops; *Penny's Pantry*, at No 117, has salmon patties for $6. There are also a couple of Chinese places, *Lee's* and *Chan's Hong Kong*. Other than that, there are counter meals and bistros in the hotels, in the motel dining rooms and in the *Leeton Soldier's Club* and the *Yanco All-Servicemen's Club*.

Getting There & Away

Countrylink buses stop daily at the visitors centre on the runs between Griffith and Cootamundra or Wagga Wagga and connect with the trains in those towns.

On Saturday only there's a Sydney to Griffith train that stops in Leeton.

GRIFFITH

Griffith (population 22,000) is a small but relatively sophisticated city and the main centre of the MIA, although it is some way north of the river. The city styles itself the wine and food capital of the Riverina, and it certainly has reason to do that. There are vineyards which you can visit and Griffith's cafes and restaurants offer a variety and quality unmatched for a very long way. West of here you're definitely into 'steak-and-lots-of-it' country.

Griffith lies on the edge of the last hills of the Great Divide's western slopes. West of here the country becomes very flat; due west is the beginning of the outback, and southwest is the Riverina heartland.

Like nearby Leeton, Griffith was designed by Walter Burley Griffin, the American architect who designed Canberra. Griffith does have something of Canberra's openness about it, and Griffin had similar climate and country to work with. Leafy suburbs rise up the steep hills behind the flat town centre, and Banna Ave, beginning at the circular roads of the administrative centre, is a wide boulevard. It's also a very long boulevard – a country town's shopping street magnified several times and too long to conveniently walk. As the railway line and canal interrupt the flow of cross-traffic, Banna Ave can be slow driving.

Information

The Griffith Visitors Centre (☎ 6962 4145), on the corner of Banna and Jondaryan Aves, opens weekdays 9 am to 5 pm, Saturday until 3 pm, Sunday 10 am to 2 pm; beside it is a Fairey Firefly plane perched on a pole. The district office of the NPWS (☎ 6962 7755) is on Banna Ave.

RIVERINA

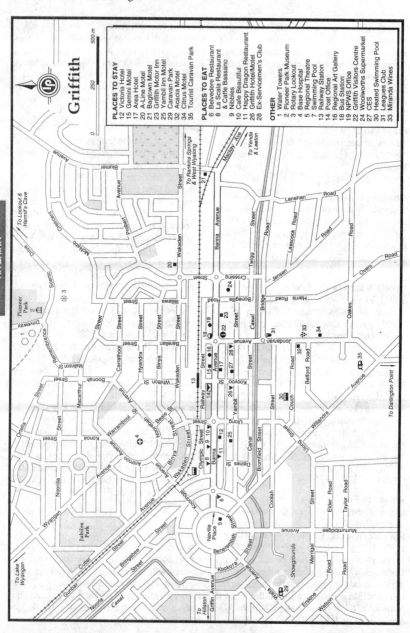

Griffith

PLACES TO STAY
12 Victoria Hotel
15 Gemini Motel
17 Area Hotel
20 A-Line Motel
21 Bagtown Motel
23 Griffin Motor Inn
25 Yambil Inn Motel
29 Caravan Park
32 Acacia Motel
34 Citrus Motel
35 Tourist Caravan Park

PLACES TO EAT
6 Belvedere Restaurant
8 La Scala Restaurant
 & Caffe Bassano
9 Nibble
10 Cafe Beautiful
11 Happy Dragon Restaurant
26 Griffin Hotel/Motel
28 Ex-Servicemen's Club

OTHER
1 Water Towers
2 Pioneer Park Museum
3 Rotary Lookout
4 Base Hospital
5 Regional Theatre
7 Swimming Pool
13 Railway Station
14 Post Office
16 Regional Art Gallery
18 Bus Station
19 NPWS Office
22 Griffith Visitors Centre
24 Woolworths Supermarket
27 CES
30 Heated Swimming Pool
31 Leagues Club
33 Miranda Wines

Work Many people come to Griffith to work on the grape harvest, which usually begins around mid-February and lasts about six to eight weeks. The citrus harvest begins in November and runs through to about March, and other crops are harvested during the year. The Griffith CES office (☎ 6969 1100) on Yambil St will help you find harvest work.

Fewer than half the vineyards and almost none of the properties have accommodation or even space to camp, so you'll probably have to stay in Griffith, which means that you'll need your own transport.

Things to See & Do

High on a hill north of the town centre, **Pioneer Park Museum** (☎ 6962 4196) is a re-creation of an early Riverina village which is worth seeing. There are about 40 displays, and unlike at some other village re-creations many of the old buildings are original, having been relocated here. A friendly wallaby might follow you around. Admission is $5 ($2 children) and the park opens daily 9 am to 5 pm. To get there from Banna Ave take Crossing St or Ulong St, then Beale Ave.

Not far from Pioneer Park is the **Rotary Lookout**, with great views of the town and the surrounding farmland. Also up here on Scenic Hill are three **walking tracks**, Trates Loop (2km), Barinji Loop (5km) and Narinari Loop (6.5km). There's another lookout at **Sir Dudley's Chair**, 1.5km east of Pioneer Park. Just below this lookout is the **hermit's cave**, home of an Italian recluse for many years – until he was interned during WWII on suspicion of being a spy.

The Art Deco **Griffith Regional Art Gallery** (☎ 6962 5991), on Banna Ave, opens Wednesday to Saturday 10.30 am to 4.30 pm. Exhibitions change monthly and there's also a permanent collection of Australian jewellery.

The **Griffith Regional Theatre** (☎ 6962 7466), Neville Place, has a huge, community-produced soft-sculpture curtain depicting the region and its activities. You can see it weekdays at 11 am and 2.30 pm,

and on Saturday at 10 am, providing there are no productions under way.

Lake Wyangan, north of the city, is home to a lot of noisy water transport – there's a jet sprint-boat course.

On Sunday mornings, a **market** is held in Verona Place on Banna Ave; another is held in Woodside Hall at the showgrounds on the second and fourth Saturday of each month.

Wineries Although the Hunter Valley is the best-known wine-producing area in NSW, the Griffith area produces 80% of the state's wine and some of it's very good. The first winery was McWilliams (1913), with others following soon after. Today there are about 16 wineries, with 11 open to visitors. Most don't open on Sunday and some don't open on Saturday. The visitors centre has the latest times. Tours are held at McWilliams (2 pm Friday), Miranda (2.15 pm Wednesday) and De Bortoli (2 pm Tuesday).

Special Events

The four-day Festival of Griffith is held over Easter. It's a major occasion, with events ranging from grape-treading competitions to chariot races and a Mardi Gras.

Griffith's big agricultural show is held in early October.

Places to Stay

There are several B&Bs and farmstays in the area, charging from $30/40. The information centre makes bookings. On Saturday rooms fill up quickly, especially if there's a big Italian wedding on.

Camping There are several caravan parks. The two most convenient for the town centre are the small *Tourist Caravan Park* (☎ 6962 4537) on Willandra Ave and the more basic *camping area* at the showgrounds, off Murrumbidgee Ave. The Tourist Caravan Park has tent sites for $14 with power, on-site vans for $36 and units for $38. At the showgrounds you'll pay $12 per person ($50 per week) for a site. Before setting up your tent check in at the office (☎ 6962 3148) in Woodside Hall, fronting the main arena.

RIVERINA

Hostel Up on the hill overlooking the town, *Pioneer Park* (☎ 6962 4196) has shared accommodation in an old tin building once used as shearers' quarters. It costs $10 per person ($60 a week). The rooms are quite small and basic – this is a historic building – but there's a good communal kitchen and lounge. Despite appearances, this is not purely a backpacker hostel and during the grape and fruit harvest it can fill up. The problem with staying here is that it's a steep walk from the town centre and there's no public transport.

Hotels & Motels The *Area Hotel* (☎ 6962 1322) on Banna Ave near the corner of Kooyoo St is a popular pub and has rooms for $40 with breakfast. The *Victoria Hotel* (☎ 6962 1299) a couple of blocks west also has rooms, but the pub music is loud.

Cheaper motels include the friendly *A-Line* (☎ 6962 1922) on Wakaden St ($48/60) and the *Citrus* (☎ 6962 6233) on Jondaryan Ave (from $50/60). Other motels include the *Acacia* (☎ 6962 4422) on Jondaryan Ave (from $55/61) and *Yambil Inn* (☎ 6964 1233) on Yambil St (from $60/65). The central *Gemini Motel* (☎ 6962 3833), 201-227 Banna Ave, has a popular bar and rooms for $77/87.

Places to Eat
The district's pioneers included Italians, and Griffith still has a large Italian community. As a result, several places serve Italian food.

For good coffee and cake or some delicious pasta, try *Caffe Bassano*, 453 Banna Ave. It's also open daily for breakfast. Nearby, down some sloping steps, the Vico family's *La Scala* (☎ 6962 4322) is perhaps the best of the Italian restaurants. The menu includes a good range of classic dishes and there's an extensive wine list. Minestrone is $6.50, pasta and gnocchi dishes are $9 to $11, and main courses $16.50 to $23. La Scala opens from 6 pm Tuesday to Sunday.

Not far away, on the corner of Banna Ave and Kookora St, is the *Belvedere Restaurant*. This has more of a cafe atmosphere and it's also a busy takeaway pizzeria, but the food

is good. The prices are a little lower than La Scala's and there's a delivery service (☎ 6962 1488).

There are a few Chinese places in the same area. The *Cafe Beautiful* on the corner of Banna Ave and Ulong St is a large, pleasant place with an extensive menu (including non-Asian dishes) and a bar. There's a buffet lunch special for $10, and at dinner most main courses are around $10. It's closed Monday. Across the street, the *Happy Dragon* is cheaper and has some good specials: beef chow mein is $5.

The *Griffith Hotel/Motel* on Yambil St has reasonable pub grub; calamari is $6.50. The *Ex-Servicemen's Club* on Jondaryan Ave has a restaurant and a bistro, and meals are also available at many of Griffith's other clubs, but often only on weekends.

If you just want a hamburger, there's *Nibbles* on Banna Ave, where good old-fashioned hamburgers ($4 with the lot) can be taken away or eaten at old-fashioned partitioned tables.

Entertainment
Most of the entertainment is in clubs such as the *Ex-Servicemen's* on Jondaryan Ave, the *Leagues Club* on the corner of Jondaryan Ave and Bridge Rd and, probably the most lively, the *Yoogali Club* on Leeton Rd. The *Area Hotel* and the *Gemini Motel* are popular watering holes.

Getting There & Away
Air Hazelton (☎ 131713) flies daily to Sydney; the standard one-way economy fare is $218.

Bus The long-distance bus stop is at the Griffith Travel & Transit Centre (☎ 6962 7199), 121 Banna Ave in the Mobil service station opposite the visitors centre. You can make bookings here daily.

Greyhound Pioneer runs to Sydney ($40), Adelaide ($60) and Canberra ($39). McCafferty's also runs daily to those cities and is a little cheaper.

Countrylink runs to Balranald via Hay,

Wagga ($45) via Leeton and Narrandera, and Cootamundra ($21) via Temora.

A local company, MIA Intercity Coaches (☎ 6962 3419), runs to and from Melbourne on Monday, Wednesday and Friday ($60, 6½ hours). This service is a handy way of getting around the MIA, with stops including Tocumwal ($35 from Griffith) and Jerilderie ($35). The service also stops in Leeton ($6).

Train On Saturday only there's a direct Countrylink train from Sydney to Griffith (8¼ hours, $70).

Getting Around
Taxi Griffith has a taxi service (☎ 6964 1444).

Car Rental Avis (☎ 6962 6266) is at 83 Banna Ave, Budget (☎ 6962 7473) is at 7 Wyangan Ave and Hertz (☎ 6964 1233) is at the Yambil Inn Motel on Yambil St.

AROUND GRIFFITH
Cocoparra National Park
Cocoparra (8350 hectares) takes in one of the fingers of low ranges that make up the westernmost edge of hills in the state. Heading west, the country is very flat, but the whole area is pretty. **Rankins Springs**, on the Mid-Western Highway just north of the park, is a tiny town with a pub and a motel set in a beautiful horseshoe valley. See the Central West chapter for more information on towns north and east of Cocoparra.

The park isn't large but its hills and gullies provide some contrasts and there's a fair amount of wildlife and birds. At Spring Hill picnic area, in the southern section of the park, there's a walking trail to Falcon Falls (dry unless there has been rain). From the **Binya State Forest**, adjoining the south-western end of the park, there's a walking track which leads you to the top of Mt Brogden.

The camping area is on Woolshed Flat in the north of the park, not far from Woolshed Falls. Day-use of the park costs $7.50 and camping is another $5. Bush camping is permitted away from the roads. Bring your own water.

Access is from the unsealed (and sometimes impassable) Whitton Stock Route, which runs along the park's western edge. The stock route meets the Yenda to Ardlethan road just east of Yenda. You can also get here from the Mid-Western Highway via a turnoff to Griffith about 15km west of Rankins Springs.

Darlington Point
Due south of Griffith and on the Murrumbidgee, Darlington Point (population 650) was an important riverport last century. It has dwindled to a quiet, picturesque town with good swimming beaches and red-gum forest. *Riverside Caravan Park* (☎ 6968 4237) has sites for $10 and vans for $25.

West of here, either via the Sturt Highway or along a dirt road that follows the north bank of the Murrumbidgee, **Carrathool** is another old port quietly dying in a pretty location. Each February a picnic race-meeting brings in a lot of visitors.

Coleambally
About 30km south of Darlington Point and in a huge triangle of almost uninhabited plains lying between Narrandera, Jerilderie and Hay, Coleambally (population 600) is the centre of a new irrigation area. The town is also new and dates from 1968, in complete contrast to old Darlington Point. There are a couple of motels and a caravan park.

The Black Stump
Between Griffith and Hillston there is a roadside hamlet, **Merriwagga**, which claims to be the home of the Black Stump. The Black Stump is a useful Australian geographical indicator – places 'beyond the Black Stump' are a long way from anywhere. However, as a plaque in Merriwagga will tell you, there's no actual stump because the name is a grisly reference to the death by burning of one Barbara Blain in the 1880s.

RIVERINA

LAKE CARGELLIGO

Midway between Condobolin and Hillston, Lake Cargelligo (the first 'g' is soft, the second hard; the town is known locally as 'the Lake') is both a town (population 1300) and the adjacent lake. The town was founded in 1879 when gold was found in the region.

Some tourist information is available from the craft shop (☎ 6898 1501) at the lake end of Foster St, the main street.

The lake is home to numerous species of birds, including swans and black cockatoos, and is popular for watersports. Next to Lake View Caravan Park is a large collection of rusty old farm machinery, part of the **museum**.

Places to Stay

The council-run *Lake View Caravan Park* (☎ 6898 1077) is near the sportsground, which is by the lake. From Foster St, turn right at the lake. Tent sites cost $8, cabins $33.

The *Royal Mail Hotel* (☎ 6898 1006) is a solid pub with a big verandah, on the main street near the lake. Single/double rooms are $15/30, including breakfast. There are a couple of motels, the *Lake Cargelligo* (☎ 6898 1303) on Canada St and the more expensive *Lachlan Way* (☎ 6898 1201) on Foster St with rooms for $45/55.

Getting There & Away

Bus Countrylink buses stop here daily on the run between Condobolin and Cootamundra via West Wyalong.

Car & Motorcycle There are some interesting routes to and from the lake, but as far as major roads go it's quite isolated. A sealed road runs south-east to West Wyalong and partly sealed roads run east to Condobolin and west to Hillston. See the Hillston section for a route to Cobar.

HILLSTON

This is a pretty little town (population 1050) on the Lachlan River and the edge of nowhere. The local **museum** (☎ 6967 2283), open on Sunday, is a few blocks from the town centre, on the Lake Cargelligo road. No longer in use, the Real Cafe on the main street is long past its glory days but it still has its high, pressed tin ceilings and leadlight windows. The Golden Gate milk bar opposite the Club House Hotel isn't as grand but is in better nick.

Places to Stay & Eat

Hillston Caravan Park (☎ 6967 2575) is at the northern end of the main street. Nearby is the *Kidman Way Motor Inn* (☎ 6967 2151), and there's also the *Hillston Motel* (☎ 6967 2573) at the southern entrance to town. The *Ex-Servicemen's & Citizens Club* and the pubs have meals.

Getting There & Away

Hillston is on the Kidman Way (the semi-official name for the partly unsealed road running to Cobar and on to Bourke). The turn-off for the Kidman Way is on the Lake Cargelligo road 35km east of Hillston; the road heading directly north from Hillston isn't as good. See the North of Condobolin section in the Central West chapter for information on towns on and near this road.

An unsealed road heads west for about 40km to the Willandra National Park turn-off, and continues on, narrower and rougher, for another 55km to Mossgiel on the Cobb Highway. A largely unsealed road runs east to Lake Cargelligo, a nice drive through well-treed country around the Lachlan River and past the Lachlan Range.

Except for the sealed road running south to the Mid-Western Highway, all the roads out of Hillston can be cut off by rain.

WILLANDRA NATIONAL PARK

Like Mungo National Park, Willandra is part of a huge sheep station on a system of dry lakes. The lakes here tend to become temporary wetlands more often than Mungo's ancient basins, especially Hall's Lake, and birdlife is abundant. The plains in this area are home to many emus, and kangaroos are plentiful, even during the day. You'll see both western greys and big reds; the latter can grow taller than two metres.

The historical interest of Willandra centres around the wool industry, although there were certainly Aboriginal civilisations in the area, probably of the same antiquity as those at Lake Mungo. The Willandra area was first grazed in the 1840s, then in 1868 some enterprising Melbourne grocers acquired several runs and formed the sheep station **Big Willandra** – the national park (about 19,400 hectares) is less than 10% of Big Willandra.

The old shearing shed, with its latitude and longitude painted on the roof to assist pilots in this featureless landscape, is still occasionally used and you can watch the shearing if you're here at the right time. The park manager has details. The nearby old shearers' quarters are not used, partly because they don't meet current union standards (which must be higher than the standards in some hostels).

A discreet distance away from the shearers' quarters is the restored homestead, the third to be built on the increasingly busy station. This homestead was built in 1918, using a then revolutionary material, fibro-cement. It's a large building, with rooms for visiting wool-buyers as well as the manager's family and staff, but it's by no means palatial. Life here, with the gardens, tennis courts and a nearby weir on the creek for swimming, would have been pleasant but not easy.

The thatched ram shed, where the real kings of the station lived, is near the homestead.

There are several walking tracks in the park, none of them very long, and the Merton Motor Trail which takes you on a loop around the eastern half of the park. The western half, beyond the stock route, has no vehicular access but you can walk here – if you're *very* sure of what you're doing.

Places to Stay

You can *camp* at the site near the homestead ($5) or, with permission, anywhere else in the park. Shared accommodation is available in the *old station's men's quarters* for $10 a night. During school holidays all accommodation, including campsites, can be booked out.

Getting There & Away

The turn-off to Willandra is on the Hillston to Mossgiel road, about 40km west of Hillston. If you're coming from Mossgiel you can take the Trida turn-off, about 10km west of the main turn-off. The unsealed Hillston to Mossgiel road is quite good between Hillston and the park turn-off, but deteriorates between the turn-off and Mossgiel. Slow down to cross cattle-grids on this section. The roads into Willandra are definitely dry-weather only; it takes less than 10 mm of rain to close them. You should phone the park manager (☎ 6967 8159) to check on conditions before you arrive, and bring in enough supplies to tide you over if you are stuck – there's no shop here. The NPWS office (☎ 6962 7755) in Griffith also has information on Willandra.

HAY

Hay is a substantial town (population 3800) for this part of the world, and its position at the junction of the Sturt and Cobb highways makes it an important transit point.

It's very much a rural service-centre and on Saturday morning the main street is full of utes (utility vans). Station hands from the big merino properties in the area make good use of the half-dozen pubs on weekends.

The Tourist & Amenities Centre (☎ 6993 1003), 407 Moppett St, just off Lachlan St (the main street), opens weekdays from 9 am to 5 pm, weekends 9 am to noon. You can pick up a drive-tour map of the town here, although if you have time it's nicer to walk around.

Things to See & Do

There are several impressive old buildings in town, including the **Department of Lands & Water Conservation** on Lachlan St and, around the corner in Moppett St, the **courthouse**.

Bishop's Lodge, off the highway east of the roundabout at the entrance to Hay, is a mansion built entirely of corrugated iron as a residence for the Anglican bishop. From the highway it doesn't look especially inviting, but the building faces the other way, towards the river, and there's a garden at the front. Bishop's Lodge opens on Saturday from 2 to 4 pm; admission is $2. The tourist office can arrange to open it at other times. The old, renovated **railway station** on Murray St is home to Hay's community radio station and a youth employment project.

The **Old Hay Gaol**, on Church St east of Lachlan St, is well worth the $1 entry fee. The jail itself is small and surrounded by a wall with almost toy-like guard towers. The museum, in the old cells, consists of a fairly random collection of the district's memorabilia and detritus. It's like a good junk shop. One cell is set up as it was when the jail was a detention centre for wayward girls, its last incarnation before it closed in 1973. Perhaps more appalling than the dim, spartan cubicle is the fact that the cells were called cabins! Still, the place was run by the Child *Welfare* Department, perhaps another inappropriate euphemism...

Ruberto's Winery, on the highway near Bishop's Lodge, opens daily for tastings of the local product.

A short way north-west of town, off Thelangerin Rd, is a **wetlands area** being developed as a bird sanctuary.

The **sunset viewing area**, 16km north of Hay on the Cobb Highway, is a good place to watch the sun go down over the flat horizon.

Special Events
On Australia Day, Hay holds a fun 'Surf Carnival' at Sandy Point beach on the Murrumbidgee (a good place for a swim at any time).

Places to Stay & Eat
Hay There are several caravan parks, with *Riverina X-Roads* (☎ 6993 1875) on Nailor St being the closest to the town centre; the *Hay Caravan Park* (☎ 6993 1415), on the highway (and close to the river), is not far east.

Most of the pubs advertise accommoda-

tion. The big *Commercial Hotel* (☎ 6993 1504) on the corner of Lachlan and Leonard Sts singles/doubles for $15/25. *Hay Motel* (☎ 6993 1804), by the roundabout, and the *New Crown Hotel/Motel* (☎ 6993 1600) on Lachlan St are the least expensive motels, with rooms at $35/45. *Bishop's Lodge Motel* (☎ 6993 3003), on the Sturt Highway, is similar in design to the original Bishop's Lodge nearby and costs $72/79.

On Lachlan St, *Paragon Cafe* is a standard country-town cafe, and there's also *Our Coffee Shop*, opposite the post office and open on weekdays. *Hay Fish Shop* has some good salads, and fish and chips costs $4. *Bishop's Lodge* motel has a dining room, as do the *Bowling Club* and *Ex-Services Club*.

Around Hay Off the Sturt Highway 11km east of Hay, *Bidgee Beach Camping Ground* (☎ 6993 1180) is a simple campsite on the banks of the Murrumbidgee. There are toilets and showers, and tent sites are $10, van sites $15. In the hamlet of Booroorban, on the Cobb Highway about 45km south of Hay and 70km north of Deniliquin, the historic *Royal Mail Hotel* (☎ 6993 0694) has single/double rooms for $25/40 or $50 for a double with attached bathroom. This place is worth a look even if you don't stay here.

Getting There & Away
Bus Long-distance buses stop on Moppett St near the tourist office and the old Cobb & Co coach, *Sunbeam*, which once made the tough run between Deniliquin and Wilcannia.

Greyhound Pioneer and McCafferty's come through on the run between Adelaide and Brisbane or Sydney. Countrylink's Balranald to Cootamundra run also stops here. There are no direct services to Melbourne. The nearest town on the Melbourne run is Deniliquin.

Traveland (☎ 6993 1974), 181 Lachlan St, handles bookings.

Car & Motorcycle The Sturt Highway runs west to Balranald and east to Narrandera; the Mid-Western Highway runs north-east to West Wyalong; and the Cobb Highway runs south to Deniliquin. See the Far West chapter for information on the Cobb Highway north to Wilcannia.

BALRANALD

On the Sturt Highway west of Hay, Balranald is a sleepy little town (population 1400) today, but it was once a bustling riverport. Most of the town is new and not especially inspiring but there's a definite sense that you're on the brink of a vast emptiness. North of here the water dries up and the farms are enormous, barely viable stations. Balranald makes a good jumping-off point for Mungo National Park.

The information centre (☎ (03) 5020 1599), on the main street, opens weekdays 9 am to 4 pm, Saturday 9 am to 2 pm. Check here for road conditions before venturing into Mungo National Park, although the NPWS office (☎ (03) 5023 1278) in Buronga (near Mildura) has better information.

There's a swimming and picnic area on the banks of the Murrumbidgee at the end of the oddly named We St (turn off the highway at the fire station). There are other picnic sites at Yanga Lake, 8km east along the Sturt Highway, and the Low Level Weir, 6km west of town.

Places to Stay & Eat

The *Balranald Caravan Park* (☎ (03) 5020 1321), on a sharp bend in the Murrumbidgee, close to the bridge, has tent sites for $9 and on-site vans from $26.

There are a few motels in town. *Sturt Motel* (☎ (03) 5020 1309) on River St and the *Shamrock Hotel/Motel* (☎ (03) 5020 1107) on Mayall St are far enough off the Sturt Highway (Market St) to avoid the rumble of semis running past.

The *Shamrock* has counter meals and a dining room with lasagne for $5. *Rafferty's Coffee House* nearby on Market St opens during the day for snacks and light meals. The *Ex-Servicemen's Memorial Club* on Market St has reasonably priced meals.

Getting There & Away

V/Line buses stop twice weekly on the run between Melbourne and Mildura. Countrylink runs here daily, and McCafferty's and Greyhound Pioneer also stop here.

The Southern Riverina

Albury, the largest town on the Murray River, is covered in the South-East chapter.

If you plan to do some fishing for Murray cod, note that there's a closed season between 1 September and 30 November, and at other times you're only allowed to catch two a day and have in your possession a maximum of four. You'll also have to learn to distinguish between Murray cod and Murray trout, as the latter is totally protected.

COROWA

This sizeable river town (population 5200) is one of the few instances of a town on the NSW side of the border which is larger than its twin (Wahgunyah) across the river in Victoria. However, Rutherglen, the main town in Victoria's best-known wine region, is only 10km further away.

History

The Bangerang people were living in this area when the first Europeans arrived in the 1830s. The first town to be established was Wahgunyah, then a private town on John Foord's Wahgunyah station. North Wahgunyah, today's Corowa, was also founded by Foord, but the influx of people on their way to the Beechworth goldfields, and the trade and river traffic that followed, saw Corowa become an official town.

As in many towns, the proclamation of the Colony of Victoria in 1850 and the ensuing customs hassles across the Murray caused many people in the area to push for Federation of the colonies. In 1893 a conference was held in Corowa which began the process of Federation, achieved in 1901. There had been previous conferences, but Corowa's was the first to capture the public's attention and was the first at which the vague democratic leanings of the Federationists were put into practice.

Another lasting product from Corowa is the famous Tom Roberts painting *Shearing the Rams*, which was researched in the woolshed of Brocklesby station.

Orientation & Information

The main street, where you'll find most of the pubs and shops, is Sanger St. It leads down to the Foord Bridge across the Murray to the small town of Wahgunyah on the Victorian side. Federation Ave is a leafy street cutting through town to the Mulwala road. The information centre (☎ 6033 3221), in the old railway station on John St, opens Monday to Saturday from 9.45 am to 4.30 pm.

Things to See & Do

The **Federation Museum** (☎ 6033 1107), in an old music hall on Queen St, opposite the neat Ellerslie Gardens, opens on Tuesday from 10 am to noon, weekends 2 to 5 pm. Admission is $1.50. It's worth a look for the display on the history of Federation and to see some of Tommy McCrae's sketches. McCrae was a member of the Bangerang people at the time of first contact with Europeans. The sketches are among the few concrete records of an indigenous people's reaction to European invasion.

Murray Bank Yabby Farm (☎ 6033 2922), next to the Corowa Caravan Park on the road to Mulwala, charges $10 per family for a visit. You can catch your own yabbies and cook them there. The farm opens daily 11 am to 4 pm.

There are about a dozen **wineries** in Victoria's Rutherglen area which are open for tastings.

Corowa is a centre for **gliding** and **hot-air ballooning**. The National Parachute School (☎ 6033 2435) offers gliding as well as parachute jumps. Zauril Aviation (☎ 6040 4950), based in Albury, has balloon flights along the Riverina here; ask at the information centre for details.

Beneath the Star Hotel is an arcade of shops, built there for summer coolness; ask at the bar about tours.

Special Events

From the weekend before the Australia Day weekend in January, Corowa holds the week-long Federation Festival, with parades, marching bands and general merriment.

The Rutherglen Winery Walkabout in June is the premier event on the Victorian wine-buff's calendar, and Corowa is a good place to base yourself.

Places to Stay

Camping There are several caravan parks in the area, including *Rivergum Caravan Park* (☎ 6033 1990) on the road in from Albury, *Corowa Caravan Park* (☎ 6033 1944) on the road out to Mulwala and *Ball Park Caravan Park* (☎ 6033 1426) on Bridge Rd. They're by the river and all have sites ($10 to $16) and cabins ($30 to $55 a double). The Corowa and Ball Park have on-site vans too.

Hotels & Motels Most of the pubs have accommodation, ranging upwards from $15 per person (including light breakfast) at the *Star Hotel* (☎ 6033 1145) on Sanger St.

There are lots of motels and their prices rise in summer and around holidays. The cluster on the Mulwala road (Federation Ave) are in hot competition and most singles/doubles are in the $45/55 region.

Places to Eat

The pubs along Sanger St compete for your meal-time dollars and there are some counter-meal bargains, from $5 for steak and mushroom pie or lasagne at the *Star Hotel*. Check the blackboards. The *Sanger St Deli* has light meals during the day and the various clubs (including the *Bowling Club*, which has 54 rinks and seven greens) have restaurants.

Getting There & Away

Bus Countrylink stops here daily on its run between Albury and Echuca (Victoria), via

Cobram (Victoria), Tocumwal, Finley and Deniliquin.

Car & Motorcycle The Riverina Highway runs east to Albury and north-west to Deniliquin. A smaller road runs west along the river to Mulwala and Tocumwal.

Getting Around
There's a 24-hour taxi service (☎ 6033 1634).

MULWALA
This small town (population 1500) on Lake Mulwala was the base for several big rock concerts in the 1970s, Australia's answer to Woodstock. Today it's a quiet place, over-shadowed by Yarrawonga, a resort and retirement centre across the river in Victoria. Lake Mulwala, an irrigation dam on the Murray, is a popular spot for fishing and power-boating.

There are several lakeside caravan parks, many motels and the old *Royal Mail Hotel*, (☎ (03) 5744 3121) which charges $20/30 including breakfast.

TOCUMWAL
Tocumwal is a small, pleasant town (population 1750) along the Newell Highway and on a big bend in the Murray River. The nearest Victorian town is Cobram, but the two don't have the usual Siamese-twin relationship of river towns because they're separated by a wide red-gum forest growing on the meanderings and billabongs of the Murray.

The Tocumwal Tourist Centre (☎ (03) 5874 2131), in the middle of town, opens daily from 9 am to 5 pm.

Things to See & Do
A huge statue of a Murray cod stands next to the information centre; in the bar of Tattersalls Hotel across the road you'll see some stuffed Murray cod almost as big. There are riverboat cruises on the *Matilda* for $12 ($8 children); book at the tourist office.

The **Murray River Heritage Centre** (☎ (03) 5874 2151), about 3km out of town on the Finley road, is in the process of being

built and the main centre has been completed: a homestead-style building in local timber and mud-brick.

Across the river at the Time Out complex, there's **horseriding** for about $12 an hour for guided rides.

Tocumwal is a centre for **gliding** and you can also get your ultra-light pilot's licence here. The Sportavia centre (☎ (03) 5874 2063) at the aerodrome (a very large airbase during WWII) has package deals including flights, tuition and accommodation. For $60 you can try a glider flight.

Just out of **Barooga**, a small town 20km east of Tocumwal (and across the river from Victoria's Cobram), are Seppelts vineyards and the Kranmer Cellars, open daily and weekend afternoons.

Places to Stay
Camping There are several basic *campsites* by the river, such as Mulberry and Pebbly beaches, but most are across the river from town and quite a distance away on winding tracks.

There are a couple of caravan parks in town. They're nice enough, but semis roll through Tocumwal at night and things can be noisy. You might have a better night's sleep at *Bushlands on the Murray* (☎ (03) 5874 2752), not far east of town as the cod swims but about 3km by road. Tent sites cost $10 to $12, units $36 to $42; prices are for two people.

Further out, in the red-gum forest (part of Tocumwal Regional Park, administered by the Victorian Department of Conservation & Natural Resources) and by the river, is *Time Out* (☎ (03) 5874 2031), a large caravan park. Take the signposted turn-off just after the first bridge on the road to Victoria and it's about 3km along a dirt road. Watch out for stray cattle. Tent sites cost $5 per person ($2 children) all year and on-site vans are $40 a double, rising to $50 in January and at Easter. There's a fairly well-stocked shop out here. Free camping is allowed in the regional park, but you can't use Time Out's facilities unless you stay there.

RIVERINA

Hotel & Motels The *Tocumwal Hotel* (☎ (03) 5874 2025), a nice place but with an air of importance out of proportion to the modest town, has motel-style units at $30/40 with breakfast. There are several other motels, all more expensive.

Places to Eat

The interesting *Central Store Antiques* near the information centre has tea-rooms. The *Lime Tree Coffee Lounge* nearby on the main street serves Devonshire tea for $4. The *River Garden* Chinese restaurant does $6.50 lunch specials. *Tokumwal Cafe* on the Melbourne side of the town centre opens for breakfast. The pubs have counter meals; steaks are $10.50. The *Bowling Club* and the *Golf Club* have restaurants.

The nice old *Terminus Hotel*, near the roundabout on the Mathoura road, has a shaded beer-garden.

Getting There & Away

Bus Countrylink buses pass through Tocumwal three times weekly between Echuca and Albury. Victoria's V/Line runs daily to Tocumwal from Melbourne via Seymour and Barooga. MIA Intercity Coaches stop in Tocumwal on runs between Griffith and Melbourne.

Greyhound Pioneer stops here on its run between Brisbane and Melbourne.

The bus stop is near the tourist office and you can book buses at Tezza's Gear (☎ (03) 5874 2604), 30 Deniliquin St.

Car & Motorcycle The Newell Highway runs north to Finley and Jerilderie, south to Melbourne. A smaller road runs east along the river to Corowa and Albury. Heading west, minor roads run to the Cobb Highway at Mathoura, passing through a state forest full of river red-gums, and indirectly to Deniliquin.

JERILDERIE

Jerilderie (population 1100) is a highway town on the Newell, a welcome oasis in this baking landscape.

The Kelly Gang held up Jerilderie for three days in 1879, earning themselves an Australia-wide reputation for brazenness. The speech Ned Kelly made to his captives in the Royal Hotel (still operating as a pub) and the letter he wrote complaining of his treatment at the hands of the authorities aroused the suspicion that young Ned might be a latent political activist. Holding up the town sealed Kelly's fate, for the NSW government declared him an outlaw (anyone could kill him without penalty) and the colony was no longer a safe haven – he was already outlawed in Victoria.

The Willows (1878), an old house by the Billabong Creek, is part museum and part souvenir shop; it serves drinks and snacks daily. On the lawns of the house is a unique Jerilderie red tree, a cross between a kurrajong and an Illawarra flame tree. Nearby in Luke Park beside Jerilderie Lake is **Steel Wings**, a massive windmill dating from 1910.

Places to Stay & Eat

Jerilderie Caravan Lodge (☎ (03) 5886 1366), on the highway beside the pretty Billabong Creek, has sites for $12, on-site vans for $24. The three pubs have accommodation and there are three or four motels, including the *Jerilderie Budget* (☎ (03) 5886 1301), a couple of km south of the town centre, with rooms for $35/40.

The *New Riverina Hotel* serves schnitzel for $7.

A few km out of Jerilderie, *Pittfour Homestead Restaurant* (☎ (03) 5886 1271) is a restaurant on a sheep station on Billabong Creek. There's also a cottage where you can stay. Bookings are essential.

Getting There & Away

Bus MIA Intercity Coaches stop here on the run between Griffith and Melbourne. Countrylink stops here on its run between Wagga Wagga and Echuca (Victoria). McCafferty's and Greyhound Pioneer stop on their runs between Brisbane and Melbourne.

Car & Motorcycle The Newell Highway runs north to Narrandera and south to Finley and Tocumwal. A smaller road runs west along the Billabong Creek to Conargo then south to Deniliquin, and a network of minor roads run to small villages.

DENILIQUIN

Deniliquin (population 8200) is a pretty, bustling town on a wide bend of the Edward River. It's big enough to offer most services but small enough to retain an easy-going rural feel. Summing up the sense of prosperity, continuity and conservatism is the local Holden-dealer's ad: 'Where did your father buy his first Holden? Probably the same place you did and your son will in years to come'.

History

Before the white invasion, the Deniliquin area was the most densely populated part of Australia. The flood plains and their networks of creeks and billabongs provided plenty of food, although stone for tools was hard to come by in this vast expanse of rich soil.

The Edward River was missed by Hume's 1838 expedition; a party sent by the enterprising Ben Boyd found the river in 1842 and established a station called Deniliquin ('sand hills'), along with a pub. Boyd's shaky empire fell apart soon after (see the South Coast chapter) but a town was growing and by 1849 it was officially recognised. It initially prospered because it was at the end of major droving routes leading down from Queensland, but later wool-growing and sheep-breeding became important.

Orientation & Information

Deniliquin is in the crook of a bend in the Edward River. Although the town covers quite a wide area, its centre, the blocks around Napier and Cressy Sts, is compact.

The Visitors Information Centre (☎ (03) 5881 4150), part of the Peppin Heritage Centre on George St, opens daily and the manager is a good source of information.

Things to See & Do

Deniliquin is an interesting old town and a detailed **historical town walk** is available from the information centre.

The pleasant **Waring Gardens** run beside Cressy St, and an old church and hall have been converted into an arts centre here. An example of riverine wetlands is not far away, at the **Island Sanctuary**, bushland on a big island in the river. There's a walking track through the sanctuary and along the river. If you want to feed the birds (there are about 80 species), you can get birdseed at the information centre. The over-friendly emus are kept out of the picnic hut by iron bars!

The **Peppin Heritage Centre** (☎ (03) 5881 4150) on George St is an interesting museum largely devoted to the wool industry. It's housed in an old school, with a classroom set up as it was at the turn of the century. It's frighteningly realistic!

Medium wools are the backbone of the Australian wool industry and the Peppin merinos which grow them were developed in the district by the Peppin family from 1862. As interesting as the historical displays are the photos of 'Riverina Ram of the Year' winners and their owners. Sheepdog displays and other events are sometimes held in the old schoolyard, where there's also an old ram shed, still smelling strongly of its pampered inhabitants. The centre opens 9 am to 4 pm on weekdays, weekends 11 am to 2 pm. Admission is $3 ($1 children).

The **SunRice Mill** is the largest rice mill in the southern hemisphere. Its visitors centre is due to move to the Peppin Heritage Centre.

The Graeco-Roman style **courthouse** (1883) on Poictiers St is an extremely imposing building. Cases resulting from pioneering drinking habits probably formed the bulk of its work in early years. Near the courthouse is **Deniliquin Parish Church**, which seems to have far too many little spires for its size.

Pioneer Gardens (☎ (03) 5881 5066), on Hay Rd (the Cobb Highway), is an odd collection: a nursery, a motel and caravan park with offices in an old pub, a display of old petrol pumps and steam engines, a gallery and a craft shop.

RIVERINA

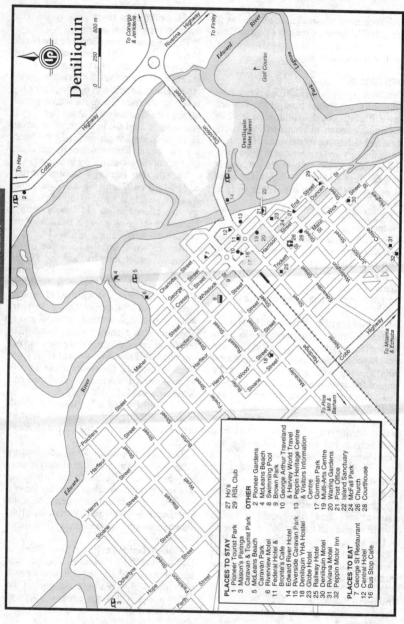

Deniliquin

To Conargo & Jerilderie

To Finley

To Hay

Riverina Highway

Cobb Highway

Davidson Street

Edward River

Mossom Park

Golf Course

Deniliquin State Forest

Charlotte Street

George Street

Cressy Street

Whitelock St

Russell Street

Poictiers Street

Harfleur Street

Henry Street

Butler Street

Wood Street

Sloane Street

Fowler Street

Maher Street

Harrison Street

Trickett Street

End Street

Duncan St

Wick St

Mann St

Jean St

Wellington Street

Edwardes Street

Hardinge Street

Macauley St

Napier Street

Crispe

Hopbush

Cobb Highway

To Rice Mill & Barham

To Moama & Echuca

Edward River

Poictiers Street

Harfleur Street

Henry Street

Sloane Street

Wyatt Street

Blackwell Street

Buron Street

Perth Street

Hope Street

Ochertyre Street

Davidson Street

0   250   500 m

PLACES TO STAY

1   Pioneer Tourist Park
3   Mason's Paringa
    Caravan & Tourist Park
5   McLeans Beach
    Caravan Park
6   Riverview Motel
11 Federal Hotel &
    Bronte's Cafe
14 Edward River Hotel
15 Riverside Caravan Park
18 Deniliquin YHA Hostel
23 Globe Hotel
25 Railway Hotel
30 Deniliquin Motel
31 Riviana Motel
32 Peppin Motor Inn

PLACES TO EAT

7   George St Restaurant
12 Central Hotel
16 Bus Stop Cafe

27 Ho's
29 RSL Club

OTHER

2   Pioneer Gardens
4   McLeans Beach
8   Swimming Pool
9   Brown Park
10 George Arthur Traveland
    & Harvey World Travel
13 Peppin Heritage Centre
    & Visitors Information
    Centre
17 Gorman Park
19 Multi-Arts Centre
20 Waring Gardens
21 Post Office
22 Island Sanctuary
24 McFall Park
26 Church
28 Courthouse

For river swimming, **McLeans Beach**, said to be the finest riverside beach in Australia, is popular. There are picnic facilities and a walking track.

Special Events

If you want to see some champion sheep and the squatters' descendants who own them, try the Deniliquin Show (first weekend in March) or attend one of the Riverina Merino Field Days, held in various centres in mid-March.

Places to Stay

Camping Close to the town centre and by the swimming beach, *McLeans Beach Caravan Park* (☎ (03) 5881 2448) is shady and pleasant. There's also the *Riverside Caravan Park* (☎ (03) 5881 1284), a little closer to the centre at 20 Davidson St, just north of the bridge. Tent sites are $10, cabins $35/45.

Some way from the centre, *Mason's Paringa Caravan & Tourist Park* (☎ (03) 5881 1131) is by the river, off the western end of Ochertyre St. It's a large place with sites for $10 and cabins for $40.

About 4km north of town is *Pioneer Tourist Park* (☎ (03) 5881 0566) with tent sites for $9, caravan sites for $15 and motel-style cabins for $42.

Hostel & Hotels The *Deniliquin YHA Hostel* (☎ (03) 5881 5025), on the corner of Wood and Macauley Sts south-west of the town centre, is pretty basic but clean. YHA members (only) can stay here for $7 ($3.50 children). The manager, Des Lutton, lives behind the hostel in Macauley St.

The hotels have accommodation. The *Globe Hotel* (☎ (03) 5881 2030) on Cressy St is good value, with rooms at $20 per person including a breakfast cooked by Shirley. At the other pubs you're left to make your own. The *Federal Hotel* (☎ (03) 5881 1260) on the corner of Cressy and Napier Sts has clean rooms for $25/40 a single/double. The *Railway Hotel* (☎ (03) 5881 1498), on Napier St a few blocks south-west of the

centre, has some rooms with attached bathroom for just $18/32.

The *Edward River Hotel* (☎ (03) 5881 2065), on Davidson St, has five singles and one double room at $15 per person, including breakfast.

Motels Among Deniliquin's many motels, the *Riverview Motel* (☎ (03) 5881 2311) at the top end of Charlotte St probably has the best position, overlooking the river and some blocks from the highway and those midnight semi-trailers. Rooms are $45/55. The *Peppin* (☎ (03) 5881 2722) and the *Riviana* (☎ (03) 5881 2033) on Crispe St have similar rates. At the *Deniliquin* (☎ (03) 5881 1820), on the corner of Crispe and Wick Sts, the rates are $48/56.

Centrepoint Motel (☎ (03) 5881 3544), 399 Cressy St, has a saltwater pool, free laundry and rooms for $50/60.

Places to Eat

Next to the Federal Hotel on Napier St is *Bronte's Cafe*, with light meals and coffees during the day. Around the corner is the *Bus Stop Cafe*. The *George St Restaurant*, 369 George St, serves home-made meals and snacks and has a courtyard at the back.

The *Federal Hotel* has mixed grills for $10 and $6 counter-meal specials. The *Central Hotel*, further north-east on Napier St, has a comfortable bistro and counter lunches from $4.

There's a large Chinese restaurant, *Ho's* (☎ (03) 5881 2089), on the corner of Wellington and End Sts, open for lunch and dinner Tuesday to Sunday.

The RSL Club has the *Club Grill*, with seafood for $11, as well as the more upmarket *Ambassador Chinese Restaurant*.

Entertainment

The *Edward River Hotel*, *Railway Hotel* and the *RSL Club* sometimes have bands on weekends. Try the *Central Hotel* for events such as horizontal bungee-jumping or mock-Sumo wrestling.

RIVERINA

Getting There & Away
Bus Long-distances buses stop outside the Bus Stop Cafe, on Whitelock St near the corner of Napier St. If you walk through the arcade near here you'll emerge on Cressy St near the two travel agents, George Arthur Traveland (☎ (03) 5885 2060) and Harvey World Travel (☎ (03) 5881 1544).

Countrylink stops here four times weekly on the run between Wagga Wagga and Echuca (Victoria). McCafferty's stops daily on the run between Melbourne and Brisbane. Victoria's V/Line runs daily to Melbourne via several other Riverina towns.

On the second Tuesday of the month, a community bus runs to Shepparton in Victoria ($12 return) via Finley ($10 return) and Tocumwal ($8 return), departing Deniliquin at 8 am. Harvey World Travel is the booking agent.

Car & Motorcycle The Cobb Highway runs south to Echuca (Victoria) and north to Hay. The Riverina Highway runs south-east to Albury. Smaller roads run south-west to Barham and north-west to Balranald.

Getting Around
Bus Harvey World Travel (☎ (03) 5881 1544) operates a local bus service.

Taxi There are two taxi companies, Black & White Bonds (☎ (03) 5881 2129) and Taits (☎ (03) 5881 1373).

AROUND DENILIQUIN
Outside **Wanganella station**, on the Newell Highway 40km north of Deniliquin, is a memorial to the Peppin family's merino breeding.

Finley
On the Riverina Highway 50km east of Deniliquin, Finley is a quiet rural town. The Mary Lawson Rest Centre is a roadside stop at the southern end of the main street with a small log-cabin museum and craft shop, where you can buy tea and coffee. The *Lakeside Caravan Park* (☎ (03) 5883 1170) is at the other end of town. A Japanese company has established the world's first commercial liquorice farm 14km north of Finley (liquorice is usually harvested from wild plants, but the supply is dwindling).

Mathoura
On the road south of Deniliquin, heading to Moama and Echuca, Mathoura is a tidy hamlet with a couple of small *caravan parks*. The nearby **Moira State Forest** is the largest remaining stand of river red-gum anywhere, even if it is mostly regrowth. You can drive through it all the way to Tocumwal (partly on dirt roads) or take one of the scenic drives.

At **Picnic Point**, in the forest about 11km east of Mathoura, there's a swimming beach on the banks of the Murray and several accommodation options, including the *Picnic Point Caravan Park* (☎ (03) 5884 3375), where a tent site costs $10 and on-site vans are from $20 a double. They hire canoes for $6 an hour and some fairly ordinary bikes for $3 an hour, both less for longer hires. Nearby, *Tarragon Lodge* (☎ (03) 5884 3387) has accommodation for $18 per person and offers canoe trips, cycling and horseriding. It mainly caters to groups, so phone first to see if there's a free place.

Picnic Point is a popular holiday spot and the sound of power boats could make it less than idyllic at peak times. A courtesy bus (☎ (03) 5884 3290) takes people between Picnic Point and Mathoura Bowling Club daily, so you might be able to get a lift.

Moama & Echuca
Moama, the poor relation of the big Victorian town of Echuca, still lures gamblers across the bridge into NSW despite Victoria's legalisation of poker machines. Over the river in Echuca there's a lot to do and see, including the restored Port of Echuca, and plenty of accommodation, including the *Echuca YHA Hostel* (☎ (03) 5480 6522), 103 Mitchell St.

Plenty of transport passes through Echuca/Moama, with Countrylink running four times weekly to Albury and Wagga, and V/Line daily to Adelaide, Albury and Melbourne. Book on ☎ (03) 5482 5308. Dyson's

☎ (03) 5482 2576) also runs daily from Melbourne to Moama.

BARHAM & AROUND

Barham is a small town without many attractions of its own to offer, but it's on the river and is popular for fishing holidays. Tourist information is available from the community centre. The Barham & District Memorial Services Club has regular entertainment, including movies; there are dress restrictions. There's plenty of accommodation in and near the town, most of it fairly expensive at weekends.

Barham is the last sizeable settlement on the NSW side of the Murray River until Wentworth. The skeins of creeks and rivers downstream from here also mean that the roads are indirect, so if you want to keep following the Murray you'll be better off crossing over to Victoria and taking the Murray Valley Highway through Swan Hill to Euston/Robinvale, where you meet the Sturt Highway.

Wakool is just a hamlet with a pub, a club and a store in a Nissen-hut-style building. Just north of here on the road to Moulamein is a big red sandhill planted with rows of European trees. Both the hill and the trees are incongruous in this landscape.

Moulamein feels much larger than Wakool, although its population is only 500. The town is on the Edward River and has a couple of pubs. There's accommodation (motel-style) at *Tattersalls Hotel* (☎ (03) 5887 5017) for $34/50 with breakfast. The *Moulamein Caravan Park* (☎ (03) 5887 5206) is on the edge of town by the lake; it's an inviting place but home to power boats.

North of Moulamein the country rises a little and the plains give way to red soil, mulga and native pines.

Getting There & Away

The road from Barham east to Moama runs parallel to the Murray, with several access points to the state forests along the river. It's a reasonable road, although narrow, but there's a 25km unsealed section which is slippery after rain and also has some sand patches. The other roads through this river-riddled part of the world are similar. The unsealed section between Moulamein and Balranald is a little rocky but should be OK in the wet.

WENTWORTH

This old riverport (population 1300) is overshadowed by nearby Mildura in Victoria, but it's a quiet, pleasant place to contemplate the impressive merging of the Murray and Darling rivers. Wentworth was originally known as The Junction, because of its location at the meeting of the rivers, and the town was shortlisted to become the new nation's capital.

Information is available at Cameo Antiques & Giftware (☎ (03) 5027 3714) on Adams St.

You can see some local history in the **Old Wentworth Gaol** (admission $4.50, $2.50 children) and across the road in the **Pioneer World Folk Museum** (admission $3.50, $1 children), which has a large collection of photos of the paddle steamers which once made this a major port. Both open daily 10 am to 5 pm. The old paddle-steamer *Ruby* is on display near the Darling River bridge in **Fotherby Park**, where there's a statue of Possum, one of the river's last swaggies.

The **confluence** of the Murray and Darling is an impressive sight. The two rivers are often different colours, depending on whether one has had rain somewhere upstream. Six km out of town, off the road to Broken Hill, the big, startlingly orange **Perry Dunes** present the drier side of the outback.

The MV *Loyalty* (☎ (03) 5027 3330), built in 1914, has two-hour cruises to the confluence and Lock 10 from Sunday to Friday, leaving the Wentworth & District Services Memorial Club at 1.45 pm. The fare is $12 ($4 children). There's no need to book.

Places to Stay

Camping *Willow Bend Caravan Park* (☎ (03) 5027 3213), on Darling St, has sites ($9), on-site vans ($23) and cabins ($36).

RIVERINA

Motels There are motels in town and more out on the road to Broken Hill. Most cost in the region of $45/55. The *Royal Hotel/Motel* (☎ (03) 5027 3005), 41 Darling St, is a bit cheaper at $36/48.

Houseboats Staying on a houseboat is popular here. There are a number of places you could try, including *Sunshine River Houseboats* (☎ (03) 5027 3237), *Drifter Houseboats* (☎ (03) 5027 3325) and *Riverside Houseboats* (☎ (03) 5027 3633). The boats accommodate from six to eight people. Rates vary depending on the time of year, and you usually have to stay a minimum number of nights. At peak times you can expect to pay around $560 for five nights on a six-berth boat.

Farmstay *Avoca Station* (☎ (03) 5027 3020), a grand homestead on the Darling dating from 1868, has accommodation in self-contained cabins from $250 a week for two people. It also does B&B for $60/80 a night. It's about 26km north-east of Wentworth – get detailed directions when you book (essential).

Getting There & Away
Many more long-distance buses run through Mildura than through Wentworth. Greyhound Pioneer has a run between Mildura and Broken Hill which stops in Wentworth, and the Victorian V/Line bus running between Melbourne and Broken Hill also stops here.

Coomealla Bus Lines (☎ (03) 5027 4704) runs three times daily to Mildura ($3.50).

The South-East

This chapter covers the rugged south-eastern corner of NSW – the high country bounded to the north and west by the Hume Highway. There are three main sections: the Monaro Tableland, including the Snowy Mountains and Kosciuszko National Park; the area west of the Snowies, between Kosciuszko National Park and the Hume Highway; and the Hume itself, from Goulburn to Albury.

The south coast and the ACT have their own chapters, while the chain of national parks in the Great Dividing Range, stretching from Nowra down to the Victorian border, is covered in the South Coast chapter.

The Monaro Tableland

The tableland is just that – undulating, but largely flat (cyclists might not agree) and, in places, bare of trees. It can be a bit lunar at times. Monaro is pronounced 'mon-*air*-ro' (although Holden's popular muscle-car of the 70s is pronounced 'mon-*ah*-ro').

History

The Ngarigo people lived on the high plains at the time of the first white encroachment. Other people came up here during the annual bogong moth harvest – a big event for many people.

Explorer John Ovens passed through in 1823 and graziers soon followed. In the 1860s there was a goldrush at Kiandra and, despite the inhospitable climate, thousands of diggers flocked to the area. Bushrangers, who had earlier preyed on the graziers and their herds, now became endemic. They were extremely hard to catch as they knew the area well and were superb riders.

After the gold fizzled out, the area settled back into its pastoral activities. It was again disturbed when the ACT was carved from the Monaro in 1908 and when the huge Snowy Mountains Hydro-Electric Scheme was constructed in the 1950s and 60s. The disturbance continues every winter when skiers flock to the mountains.

Although the Monaro is rich in history, little of it is obvious. The goldminers established no large towns, the graziers were too few to leave much of a mark (although their cattle certainly left their mark on the ecology) and the towns that grew around their industry mainly did so on the lower slopes of the winter pastures. Several of the small towns that were established up on the Monaro were drowned in the dams of the Snowy Mountains Hydro-Electric Scheme.

Geography

The Monaro is one of the string of tablelands along the Great Dividing Range, running south from around Goulburn to the Victorian border. On the south-western side, the

433

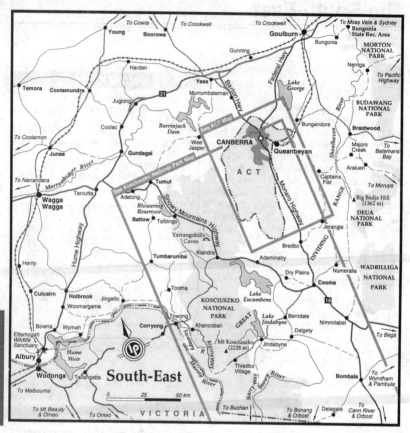

Snowy Mountains rise above the tablelands; on the eastern side the range drops to the coastal strip.

Activities

Although snow sports are the obvious and most popular activities in this area it is also well worth visiting outside winter.

A couple of major operators hire equipment and organise activities. Talk to these people to get an idea of what's available. In Jindabyne see Paddy Pallin (☎ 6456 2922) at the Thredbo turn-off and in Tumut see Adventure Sports (☎ 6947 1531). There are

plenty of other operators – see the various sections in this chapter. Thredbo Village has an extensive activities programme in summer.

Snow Sports See the following Skiing & Resorts section for details. Ski hire is available on the slopes and in many towns in the nearby area. Outfits such as Paddy Pallin in Jindabyne can arrange cross-country skiing.

Bushwalking Summer bushwalking is popular in Kosciusko National Park and other areas. Remember that conditions can change rapidly and snow can fall at any time of year. Be prepared and don't walk alone. See if you can find a copy of *Snowy Mountains Bushwalks*, which is published by the Geehi Bushwalking Club (about $15). On the west side of the mountains, the Hume & Hovell Walking Track runs from near Yass to near Albury and trackheads include those close to Wee Jasper, Tumut, Holbrook and Tumbarumba.

Horseriding When the weather warms up the Monaro is a popular place for horseriding and there are many outfits offering day rides and longer treks.

Watersports Because of the big dams, watersports are popular. It's strange to be in an area where some cars have ski-racks and others are towing power boats. Jindabyne, on the doorstep of the ski-fields, even has sailing boats and seagulls!

There's also the Murray River, which rises at the Pilot, a peak in the Pilot Wilderness Area of Kosciuszko National Park. Upper Murray White-Water Rafting (☎ 6076 9566) has trips from near Tom Groggin Station, off the Alpine Way, to near Khancoban. Parts of the ride offer genuine white-water excitement, but in other stretches you get a chance to take in some excellent scenery. A day-trip costs $110. There's also more sedate rafting on the Swampy Plains River near Khancoban.

Other outfits offering rafting on the upper Murray include Paddy Pallin (☎ 6456 2922), Wilderness Sports (☎ 6456 2966) and Alpine River Adventures (☎ 6456 1199) – which are all in Jindabyne – and Rapid Descents (☎ 6072 5212) in Khancoban.

Canoeing is also popular and in summer you'll find many outfits like Paddy Pallin and Wilderness Sports offering one-day and longer trips.

The Goobarragandra and Tumut rivers to the north of this area also offer rafting and canoeing. Adventure Sports (☎ 6947 1531) in Tumut can organise trips and rent equipment.

Cycling Summer cycling in this area can be superb, if hilly. The summit of Mt Kosciuszko was first conquered by bicycle last century! Taking your bike on the Skitube up to Perisher cuts out some of the uphill work. You can hire mountain bikes at the nearby Novotel Lake Crackenback Resort.

Getting There & Away
Air There are regular flights with Impulse (☎ 131381) from Sydney and Melbourne to Cooma.

Bus The ski-fields are well served by buses in winter, but there are fewer in summer. Cooma is the main transport hub; buses from Melbourne, Sydney and Canberra run there.

Car & Motorcycle The Monaro is easily accessible from Canberra, Sydney and the south coast, and by some interesting routes from the south and west.

From Canberra, the Monaro Highway runs down to Cooma. It's a good road, although not especially wide for the amount of traffic it carries.

The quickest route from Sydney is to take the Hume Highway to Goulburn and the Federal Highway to Canberra. A longer alternative is to take the Princes Highway then climb up onto the tableland from Wollongong, Batemans Bay or Bega.

The Snowy Mountains Highway runs from Bega to Cooma (the road between Cooma and Bombala is both the Monaro Highway and the Snowy Mountains Highway), then north-west through Kosciuszko National Park to Tumut, meeting the Hume Highway at Gundagai.

From Cooma, the Monaro Highway heads south to Bombala and the Victorian border, where it becomes the Cann Valley Highway and meets the Princes Highway in Cann River. From the small town of Delegate, near Bombala, the unsealed Bonang Highway runs south to meet the Princes Highway in Orbost (Victoria).

The Barry Way is a largely unsealed, narrow and winding mountain road running from near Jindabyne to Buchan in Victoria.

SOUTH-EAST

It's a spectacular route through national parks, but it can be difficult when wet. Caravans can't use this route, but logging trucks do, so be careful. Fuel isn't available anywhere along this road.

The Alpine Way, a spectacular mountain road, runs from Khancoban past the southern end of the ski-fields, passing close to Mt Kosciuszko, Thredbo and Jindabyne. Caravans aren't permitted on parts of the Alpine Way, which climbs 1000m in the 18km between Tom Groggin and Dead Horse Gap near Thredbo Village.

The Alpine Way is the most direct route from Albury to the ski-fields and the Monaro, but it can be closed by snow in winter. If so, you'll have to take the Elliott Way to the Snowy Mountains Highway near Kiandra or, if the Elliott Way is closed, you might head up to Tumut and take the Snowy Mountains Highway.

BRAIDWOOD & AROUND

Braidwood (population 1100), on the road between Canberra and Batemans Bay about 85km south of Goulburn, is near the eastern edge of the Monaro Tableland. A well-planned, well-preserved town, it's classified by the National Trust. Most historic buildings date from the 1850s when it was the main town in the southern goldfields. Today, Braidwood is a centre for visiting the spectacular national parks in the ranges tumbling down to the south coast.

It also has a thriving arts and crafts community. Poet Judith Wright is one of many artists and writers living in the area.

Information

Braidwood Information Centre (☎ 4842 2310) is in the museum on Wallace St (the main street), north of the courthouse and park. It has a good range of information, including a walking-tour map of the town (free) and maps and books on scenic drives and bushwalks in the nearby national parks. It's open Thursday to Monday from 9.30 am to 4.30 pm. Many businesses in Braidwood close Tuesday and Wednesday – the weekend for this visitor-oriented town.

Things to See

A stroll along Wallace St is an experience, especially if you've just arrived from the rough-and-ready towns of the Monaro Tableland or the ugly strip-development of the coast.

Braidwood Museum, on Wallace St, has displays on gold mining and Koori history; it's open the same hours as the information centre and entry costs $2 (50c children).

There are quite a few galleries and studios. Don't miss the Italianate **Studio Altenburg** (☎ 4842 2384) in one of the more impressive buildings on Wallace St, an old bank built in 1888. The gallery displays a wide range of goods by local artists and craftspeople, and some from further afield. It's open Monday to Thursday from 10 am to 5 pm and Friday to Sunday until 9 pm; entry is free.

St Andrews Church, on Elrington St, has a restored pipe organ inside and a fine collection of gargoyles leering from the tower.

Bedervale (☎ 4842 2421), an impressive homestead reached from Monkittee St, was built in 1836 to the design of John Verge, architect of Elizabeth Bay House in Sydney. It was owned by the same family for generations and their accumulated furnishings and knick-knacks provide a good overview of the taste of more affluent Australians over 130 years. It's still a working farm but opens to the public the first Sunday of the month from September to April ($5, $1.50 children) or by appointment at other times (though it requires a minimum number of 25 people).

The **Old Rectory** on Wilson St is a nursery which has a cottage garden worth seeing. Several private **gardens** are open to the public at certain times of the year, including Open Gardens Day in November. The information centre has details.

The superb bushwalking country of **Budawang National Park** and the southern end of **Morton National Park** is accessible from Braidwood. There are also state forests nearby which have some interesting walks and drives. The alternative routes to Cooma and the coast at Moruya skirt **Deua National Park**; see the Getting There & Away entry below.

Special Events

The Braidwood Show, an annual event since 1872, is held in late February or early March. There are several horse-racing meetings each year, including the Braidwood Cup in early February. The Braidwood Heritage Festival takes place in early April culminating in a dinner and cabaret in Torpy's Restaurant.

Places to Stay

The impressive *Royal Mail Hotel* (☎ 4842 2488), on Wallace St, used in the *Ned Kelly* film starring Mick Jagger, has rooms for $30/50 a single/double, including breakfast.

Torpy's Motel (☎ 4842 2395), at 202 Wallace St, is a pleasant place with a good restaurant. The motel units are well-designed and look out onto a shady lawn. During the week singles/doubles go for $45/55 with a light breakfast. There's also a restored cottage (once the postmaster's residence) where you can stay in very pleasant rooms for $90, including breakfast.

There are a couple of other motels. *Braidwood Cedar Lodge* (☎ 4842 2244), back from the main street on Duncan St, and *Braidwood Colonial Motel* (☎ 4842 2027), at the north end of Wallace St, both charge about $40/55 a single/double.

The *Doncaster Inn* guesthouse (☎ 4842 2356), at 1 Wilson St, has an impressive garden and restored rooms. It's a large building (once a pub and a convent) across the park from the courthouse. Bed and breakfast costs $60/90.

Places to Eat

In the courtyard of Studio Altenburg, *Cafe Altenburg* is a pleasant, relaxing place for a snack or a meal and has healthy food at reasonable prices. Main courses cost $7 to $11 and the servings are large.

Diagonally opposite Studio Altenburg is *Cafe Cornucopia*, a whole-food store selling takeaways and some meals to eat there. It's the place with the giant carrot hanging over the footpath.

The good *Torpy's Restaurant* is in an old house at Torpy's Motel. The *Ex-Servicemen's Club* on Victory St (at the west end of Wilson or Duncan St) has a Chinese restaurant.

Getting There & Away

Bus Murrays stops daily in each direction on its run between Canberra and Batemans Bay. The information centre has details of school bus routes which take you (eventually) to some of the smaller places in the area.

Car & Motorcycle Braidwood is on the road between Canberra and Batemans Bay. About 20km east of Braidwood the road enters thick forest then drops over the edge of an escarpment to begin the winding drive to the coast. The first few kilometres are extremely steep and winding; the rest of the way is less steep, but this is one of those roads where you should take the speed recommendations on the corners seriously!

An alternative route to the south coast at Moruya runs through Araluen and some

---

A Small Triumph for Innocence

On the road between Braidwood and Batemans Bay, just after you begin the steep descent, there's a sharp corner signposted Pooh Corner. In the apex of the corner is a tiny cave with the nameboard Mr Sanders. Inside, people leave notes, flowers and 'hunny' – messages and gifts for Pooh. Despite the slick sign-writing and the Disney-Pooh figure, this is a spontaneous and touching place, a rarity on Australia's commercialised and vandalised roadsides. When Pooh's house was to be demolished by the local council during road upgrading, there was so much public outcry that the council not only left the site alone but widened the road at the inside, at greater expense, and paid for the new sign!

In India, journeys are often broken by *puja* stops at roadside shrines. Perhaps here you should stop for *pu*. ■

beautiful country on the northern edge of Deua National Park. The road is sealed as far as Araluen, but after that it isn't suitable for caravans. Another unsealed route heads north-east to the coast near Nowra, via Nerriga, passing through the southern end of Morton National Park. Only 4WDs should use this road when it's wet. Check with the Braidwood Information Centre about conditions.

If you're heading to Cooma, consider taking the scenic, partly-sealed road via Numeralla. It follows the Shoalhaven River to its source, Big Badja Hill (also called Badja Mountain). Several sections of this road can be cut by floods, so if it has been raining be prepared to change your plans. There are also a couple of unexpected one-lane bridges on the sealed section. This route is shorter (although maybe not any faster) than taking the main road to the Monaro Highway and following the highway south.

Goulburn and the Hume Highway are about 95km north on a good road.

LAKE EUCUMBENE AREA

Lake Eucumbene is a massive dam, built as part of the Snowy Mountains Hydro-Electric Scheme, and is adjacent to the central section of Kosciuszko National Park. Some of the lake's forested arms and inlets are scenic, although much of the area has been cleared of trees. The lake is popular for fishing in summer and there are several small communities on the shores with camping and other accommodation.

Adaminaby

Adaminaby is a tiny town (population 300) on the Snowy Mountains Highway, built to replace the old town now lying beneath Lake Eucumbene 10km away. Still, it's the largest town for some way and there is a good range of services. The town might be small, but the trout in front of it is big.

Adaminaby is the closest town to the **Mt Selwyn ski-fields** (a day-use resort) and the Adaminaby Bus Service (☎ 6454 2318) runs there and to Cooma. You can hire ski gear at

Adaminaby Ski Hire (☎ 6454 2455) on Baker St (the main street).

Places to Stay & Eat The *Alpine Tourist Park* (☎ 6454 2438), on the corner of the highway and Lett St, has sites for $12, on-site vans from $29 and a range of cabins from $29 to $75. *Tanderra Lodge* (☎ 6454 2470), on Denison St, charges from $30/45 for singles/doubles, including breakfast. The *Snow Goose Hotel/Motel* (☎ 6454 2202), on Baker St, has hotel rooms for $10 per person and motel rooms for $35 a double.

Further up the scale, the *Adaminaby Country Club* (☎ 6454 2380), on the highway, charges from $40/50 a single/double. All these places charge more in winter and might be booked out by groups on ski packages.

On Baker St, there are counter and bistro meals at the *Snow Goose* (one of the few places open in the evening), while several cafes serve fish and chips and the like. The *Bullwheel Steakhouse* has been recommended.

Around the Lake

The area's brief gold-rush of the 1860s saw the construction of 14 pubs in Adaminaby, all of which closed soon after as the diggers rushed on to the richer Lambing Flat. The town all but disappeared beneath Lake Eucumbene, but a sizeable replacement for it is growing on the lake's shores – **Old Adaminaby** is probably newer than 'new' Adaminaby. A few buildings escaped the flood, including the school (now the office of the caravan park) and a small church which was once on a hill above the town, but is now on the lake's shore.

Anglers Reach is a modern development on a pretty, forested arm of Lake Eucumbene, about 18km from Adaminaby. The caravan park and Lakeside Village (see Places to Stay below) rent boats for $48 a day, plus fuel. They also have ski hire.

Other settlements by the lake are **Buckenderra**, where there's horseriding (☎ 6453 7242) most of the year, **Eucumbene**, **Braemar Bay** and **Frying Pan Creek**.

The Snowy Mountains Hydro-Electric Scheme

In 1946 the government decided to embark on one of the largest and most challenging engineering projects the world had seen. In 1947 work began in mountainous country that had barely been explored, much less settled. Workers from around the world flocked to the project, 17 large dams were built (Lake Eucumbene alone could hold the water of eight Sydney Harbours), rivers were diverted and all sorts of tunnelling and building records were smashed.

The project was completed in 1974 and today provides electricity to Canberra, NSW and Victoria. Water from the diverted rivers irrigates the inland. It's estimated that if the electricity produced by the scheme were produced by coal-fired turbines, five million tonnes of carbon dioxide would be released into the atmosphere each year!

Although little account was taken of the environmental impact of diverting the waters of the Eucumbene, Murrumbidgee, Murray, Snowy, Tooma and Tumut rivers, the project did have an unexpected social benefit. Australia in the 50s was a parochial island and the post-war turmoil in Europe and Asia didn't do much to change that. With workers from 30 countries vital to a project that was a source of immense national pride, attitudes to 'reffos' (refugees) changed and Australia's multiculturalism began.

Also, the sheer size of the project meant a government commitment previously unheard of in this country and perhaps indirectly led to acceptance of later 'socialist' programmes such as universal health care. ∎

Places to Stay At Old Adaminaby is the rather pleasant *Rainbow Pines Tourist Caravan Park* (☎ 6454 2317) with sites from $12 and basic on-site vans for $30 a double.

At Anglers Reach, the *Anglers Reach Caravan Park* (☎ 6454 2223) has tent sites for $11 and four-berth cabins for $50. The nearby *Lakeside Village* (☎ 6454 2276) has cabins for $50/55 a double/triple (but much more in winter).

Farmstays

Reynella (☎ 6454 2386) is a working sheep and cattle property which offers accommodation and horse riding. You can stay in two to six-person cabins for $120 for adults, $75 for those aged 15 to 18 and $60 for children under 15; this includes all meals and horseriding. In the ski season there are cheaper rates ($86 for adults), that don't include riding, and they also have skiing packages. Reynella specialises in horseriding holidays; day rides are available, as well as treks of up to five days through the north of Kosciuszko National Park. A four-day ride costs about $690 per person. The Reynella turn-off from the Snowy Mountains Highway is about 8km south of Adaminaby.

Other places offering farmstays are *San Michel* (☎ 6454 2229), off the highway between Adaminaby and Cooma, and *Old Yaouk* (☎ 6454 2421), 21km north of Adaminaby, near the ACT border.

COOMA & AROUND

Cooma is the largest town on the Monaro. Although its present population is 8000, in the 1950s and 60s during the construction of the Snowy Mountains Hydro-Electric Scheme (for which it was the headquarters), 16,000 people crowded into the town. Today, each winter it's a base for many skiers who, despite the town's distance from the ski fields, stay here because of the cheaper accommodation.

Orientation & Information

The Monaro and the Snowy Mountains highways meet in central Cooma. The main shopping street is Sharp St, which becomes the Snowy Mountains Highway to the west of town and the Monaro Highway to the east.

The Cooma Visitors Centre (☎ 1800 636 525), at 119 Sharp St next to Centennial Park, opens daily from 9 am to 5 pm and has a lot of information on the area. It makes accommodation bookings and may know of special deals. The post office is at 25 Vale St.

SOUTH-EAST

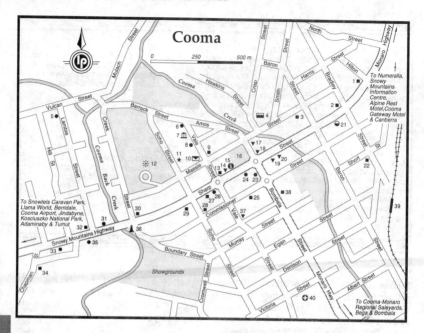

Cooma

0   250   500 m

At Snowstop Village, on Sharp St a few blocks north-east of the main shopping centre, there's a restaurant and you can hire ski gear. Most long-distance buses stop here.

For film and camera equipment go to Schoo's Studio (☎ 6452 1282), at 27 Bombala St near the corner of Sharp St. Blue Star Laundrette is at 63 Sharp St, while Snowy Camping World, at 98 Sharp St, sells outdoor gear.

Things to See & Do

Next to the visitors centre in **Centennial Park** is a series of mosaic scenes from the history of the Monaro. In the park are the flags of the 28 nations represented in the Snowy Mountains Scheme workforce. There's also a relief map of the mountains cast in metal, which is handy for orienting yourself to the ups and downs of the area.

The **Snowy Mountains Information Centre** (☎ 6453 2003, 1800 623 776) is in the Snowy Mountains Hydro-Electric

Authority headquarters, off the Monaro Highway a couple of kilometres north of the town centre. It's concerned with the hydro-electric scheme and has models of the tunnels and power stations, a large 3D map and a video about the project. The centre is open on weekdays from 8 am to 5 pm and weekends from 8 am to 1 pm. Three **power stations** are open daily to visitors, but none is very close to Cooma. Murray 1 station near Khancoban (tours at 10, 11 am, noon, 1 and 2 pm) and Tumut 3 station near Talbingo (tours at 10, 11 am, noon, 1 and 2 pm) are free. Tumut 2 station near Cabramurra (tours hourly from 11 am to 3 pm, September to April) costs $6 (children $4).

The **Southern Cloud Memorial**, by the Cooma Back Creek bridge, incorporates some of the wreckage of the *Southern Cloud* – an aircraft which crashed in the Snowies in 1931, but wasn't discovered until 1958.

Cooma Gaol Museum (☎ 6450 1357), on Vale St, is open on weekdays from 9 am

PLACES TO STAY		PLACES TO EAT		11	Police Station
1	Kinross Inn	14	Pizza House & Cafe	12	Nanny Goat Hill
2	Sovereign Motor Inn		Upstairs		Lookout
3	Family Motel & Swiss	17	Cooma Chinatown	15	Cooma Visitor Centre
	Motel		Restaurant	16	Centennial Park
9	Cooma Hotel	18	Alpine Cafe	21	Snowstop Village,
13	Australian Hotel	19	Khai's Chinese		Grand Court
22	Coffey's Hotel		Restaurant		Restaurant & Bus
25	Dodds Hotel	20	East End Cafe		Stop
27	Alpine Hotel	37	RSL Club	23	Schoo's Studio
28	Bunkhouse Motel			24	Snowliner Travel
29	Hawaii Motel	**OTHER**		26	Blue Star Laundrette
30	Alkira Motel	4	Swimming Pool	31	Top Cherry Organic
32	Royal Hotel	5	Lord Raglan Inn (Art		Supermarket
33	White Manor Motel		Gallery)	35	Hain Centre & Little
34	High Country Motel	6	Cooma Correction		Gallery
38	Nebula Motel		Centre	36	Southern Cloud
		7	Cooma Gaol Museum		Memorial
		8	Cooma Courthouse	39	Old Railway Station
		10	Post Office	40	Hospital

to 4 pm and on weekends at varied hours. Entry is free. The actual museum is in a modern house near the old jail, which still functions as a jail though now it's called a 'correctional facility'. Inmates' work is sold at the museum. Nearby is the imposing granite **Cooma Courthouse**.

On **Lambie St**, Cooma's oldest street, are a number of historic buildings classified by the National Trust. Lord Raglan Inn was built in 1855 and is now a gallery (☎ 6452 6145) for Monaro artists. It has a small museum and is open Wednesday to Sunday from 10 am to 4 pm. Other local work is shown at the nearby **Little Gallery** (☎ 6452 2576) in the Hain Centre. It's open Tuesday to Friday, Monday afternoon and Saturday morning.

Llama World (☎ 6452 4593), off the Snowy Mountains Highway 19km west of Cooma, is the place to visit if you want to meet llamas. You can tour the farm, see a video and perhaps buy llama wool and products made from it. You can also go on a half-day (or longer) walk with a llama carrying your lunch. The farm opens on Friday, weekends and holidays from 10 am to 4 pm. The farm tour costs $10 (children $5).

Cooma is a major centre for **cattle sales** and a big sale is worth seeing. The Cooma-Monaro Regional Saleyards are just south-east of town on the Monaro Highway.

There are several **horseriding** outfits in the area, including Reynella (see the previous Lake Eucumbene Area section); the Magellan Riding School (☎ 6452 1110), 6km east of Cooma on the road to Numeralla; and Yarramba (☎ 6453 7204), near Dry Plains, midway between Adaminaby and Cooma on a small road east of the highway. Magellan is mainly for day rides and Yarramba has both short rides and one-and two-day treks along the upper Murrumbidgee for $75 a day. All offer tuition for novices.

The hamlet of **Numeralla** is 22km east of Cooma at the end of the sealed road. It's the starting-point for partly sealed routes to Braidwood to the north and Nimmitabel in the south. It has several craft shops.

Places to Stay – bottom

Camping *Snowtels Caravan & Camping Area* (☎ 6452 1828) is a big place on the Snowy Mountains Highway (Sharp St) 1.5km west of town. It has sites from $12, on-site vans for $29 (you can hire doonas and linen) and self-contained flats sleeping six for $53 a double.

Hostels Two motels provide backpacker accommodation. The friendly *Bunkhouse Motel* (☎ 6452 2983), which is on the corner

SOUTH-EAST

of Commissioner and Soho Sts, has dorm beds for $15. The *Family Motel* (☎ 6452 1414), at 32 Massie St, has shared rooms for $12 per person ($60 weekly). The Bunkhouse has been dealing with backpackers longer.

Pubs Cooma's six pubs all have accommodation and charge around $20/30 a single/double. They include the big *Alpine Hotel* (☎ 6452 1466) and the *Australian Hotel* (☎ 6452 1844) which are both on Sharp St. At *Coffey's Hotel* (☎ 6452 2064) on Short St, singles/doubles are only $15/25. At the beautiful old sandstone *Royal Hotel* (☎ 6452 2132), at the corner of Sharp and Lambie Sts, you might get a room leading onto that wonderful verandah; rates are $20 per person.

Motels Expect prices to rise in winter. The *Bunkhouse Motel* (☎ 6452 2983), on the corner of Commissioner and Soho Sts, has small singles for $25 and better rooms for $35. This is a large place with a somewhat institutional feel to it, although it's clean and comfortable enough. Outside the ski season you might do better by shopping around the mid-range motels.

The *Family Motel* (☎ 6452 1414), at 32 Massie St, charges $25/30. A few kilometres north-east of the centre, on Polo Flat Rd near the Monaro Highway, the Christian-run *Alpine Rest Motel* (☎ 6452 1085) charges $20 per person. The *Cooma Gateway Motel* (☎ 6452 1592), at No 14, has rooms for $25 a double plus self-contained units with kitchens.

Places to Stay – middle & top end

See the visitors centre for a full listing of motels and current prices, which can vary according to the season.

There are plenty of mid-range motels, charging around $30 to $40 for singles and $45 for doubles. These include the *Swiss Motel* (☎ 6452 1950) at 34 Massie St and the *High Country Motel* (☎ 6452 1277) at 12 Chapman St – both part of the Budget chain – and the *Hawaii Motel* (☎ 6452 1211) at 192

Sharp St. A notch higher up the scale is the *White Manor Motel* (☎ 6452 1152), at 252 Sharp St, with rooms for $50.

The *Alkira Motel* (☎ 6452 3633), at 213 Sharp St, is one of the better of Cooma's 20-odd motels, with bed and breakfast for $50/62. Other highly-rated places include *Kinross Inn* (☎ 6452 4133), at 15 Sharp St, with a heated pool and neatly manicured lawn; the *Sovereign Motor Inn* (☎ 6452 1366), at 35 Sharp St; and the *Nebula Motel* (☎ 6452 4133), at 42 Bombala St. The Kinross is the cheapest of the three, with singles/doubles for $52/55.

Places to Eat

If you're self-catering, there's a supermarket in the Hain Centre on Sharp St, about 1km south-west of the visitor centre; it's open daily from 7 am to 9 pm. Across the street is *Top Cherry*, a supermarket selling organic fruit and vegies.

Sharp St has a lot of places to eat, although they're mainly cafes. There's a cluster around the corner of Bombala and Sharp Sts. Right on the corner, the *Alpine Cafe* has breakfasts from $6 and spaghetti for $8. Across the road in Sharp St, *Khai's* serves Vietnamese and Chinese food without MSG. Singapore noodles costs $9.20. Around the corner on Bombala St opposite Centennial Park is another Chinese place, *Cooma Chinatown*, which is bigger and more upmarket. It's open for lunch and dinner daily and has main courses for $9 to $15. The *Grand Court* Chinese restaurant is in the Snowstop Village on Sharp St.

Near Khai's, the *East End Cafe* opens for breakfast from 7 am; a hamburger with the lot is $4.50.

Most pubs do counter meals. The *Australian Hotel*, on Sharp St, has a bistro with lunchtime roasts for $5. The *Royal Hotel*, on the corner of Sharp and Lambie Sts, does a mixed grill for $11 and the *Cooma Hotel*, an impressive old structure, has a steakhouse.

Upstairs in the arcade next to the visitor centre, the licensed *Cafe Upstairs* is open from noon to around 2 am. You can get cocktails (and fruit 'mocktails') and there's a big menu, with hamburgers from $4, pancakes for $6 and many other dishes.

The big *RSL Club* on Vale St has both a bistro and a restaurant (Friday to Sunday) and claims to have the cheapest beer in the mountains.

Getting There & Away
Air Impulse (☎ 131381) flies from Sydney for $175. From Melbourne, Kendell (☎ 131300) flies via Sydney. The airport is about 10km southwest of Cooma on the Snowy Mountains Highway.

Bus Cooma is about 6½ hours from Sydney and under two hours from Canberra. Snowliner Travel (☎ 6452 1422), on Sharp St opposite the visitors centre, handles bus bookings. All buses except V/Line (which stops near the visitors centre) stop at the Snowstop Village.

Greyhound Pioneer runs to Cooma from Canberra ($16) and Sydney ($44). In winter most of their services continue to the Skitube terminal and ski resorts, or connect with the resort shuttle service at Jindabyne. Outside the ski season there's a daily service from Sydney and Canberra to Cooma.

Countrylink runs between Canberra and Eden on the far south coast, via Cooma, Bombala and Merimbula.

Victoria's V/Line runs twice weekly between Melbourne and Canberra via Cooma on a service taking you by train to Sale and connecting with a bus running up the Cann Valley/Monaro Highway to Cooma and Canberra. Going the other way the entire trip is by bus. Melbourne to Cooma takes 9½ hours. This would be an interesting trip.

Adaminaby Bus Service (☎ 6454 2318) runs between Cooma and Mt Selwyn daily.

Car & Motorcycle The Snowy Mountains Highway runs north-west to Tumut and south-east to Bega; the Monaro Highway runs north to Canberra and south to Bombala. Other roads run west to Jindabyne and the Snowy Mountains.

If you wish to get from Cooma to Batemans Bay, you can travel via Numeralla

to Braidwood on a partly-sealed road skirting Deua National Park. At Braidwood you can continue south-east to Batemans Bay on a major road or take another beautiful road through Araluen to Moruya. This section, largely unsealed, isn't suitable for caravans.

NIMMITABEL
Nimmitabel is a pretty little place (population 250) on the highway 35km south of Cooma, with flowers in the gardens and a slow pace to life. It's a good place to break your trip, although its only real 'attraction' is the impressive old **windmill**. A German immigrant spent seven years building the mill last century, but when it was finished he was told he couldn't use it because the spinning sails would frighten horses! There are several antique shops along the main street and one junk shop where you could find anything.

Places to Stay & Eat
The *Caravan & Camp Park* (☎ 6454 6225) is small, but neat and clean. There are hot showers. It's in the recreation area near the northern edge of town. Tent sites cost from $5.

The *Royal Arms* (☎ 6454 6422) is a handsome restored hotel which is now a guesthouse and cafe. Rooms cost $38/70 single/double. In the cafe, coffee and muffins costs $4.60.

The *Tudor Inn* (☎ 6454 6204) is a cosy pub with accommodation for $18/30 a single/double with breakfast. The small *Nimmitabel Motel* (☎ 6454 6387) has rooms for $38/48.

The *Bakery & Cafe*, opposite the Royal Arms, does breakfast and other meals and has a good range of breads and cakes. The Nimmity Emporium claims to have the largest range of lollies in NSW.

BOMBALA
The sign at the outskirts announces that Bombala (population 1500) is a timber town, but it's also the centre of a prime cattle district. It's a good base from which to explore the new South-East Forests National

Park. Maybe St is the tentatively named main street. Tourist information is available from the Mobil service station. The NPWS office (☎ 6458 4080) is in a restored building on Maybe St.

Endeavour Reserve, on a hill overlooking the town, is a good place for picnics. The Bombala Agricultural Show, an annual event since 1878, is held in late March.

Places to Stay & Eat

The small *Bombala Park Caravan Reserve* (☎ 6458 3270) is pleasantly situated by the river on the northern edge of town. It has sites for $9 and a few on-site vans for $28.

On Maybe St, all three pubs – the *Globe* (☎ 6458 3077), the *Imperial* (☎ 6458 3211) and the *Bombala* (☎ 6458 3155) – have accommodation. In the Globe, rooms cost $25/45 with breakfast.

The *Mail Coach Inn* (☎ 6458 3721), on the corner of Maybe and Young Sts, is a good guesthouse in the renovated old post office. Bed and breakfast costs $50/60 in the two rooms with en suite bathrooms, or $24 per person in the room which uses a nice old bathroom across the hall. This is good value. *Maneroo Motel* (☎ 6458 3878) on Maybe St is fairly spartan, but it has recently been taken over by the couple who run the guesthouse, so it will probably improve. Single/double rooms go for $40/48.

Cafes and takeaways along Maybe St include *Top Cafe*, open until at least 9 pm, and *Magic Munchies* which is open daily. The pubs offer inexpensive counter meals. The big *Ex-Servicemen's Club*, in an old building on the corner of Maybe and Caveat Sts, has Chinese meals Tuesday to Sunday. The *Mail Coach Inn* has good lunches and dinners Monday to Saturday, with main courses for about $15.

Getting There & Away

Bus Countrylink runs to Cooma, where you can connect with a bus to Canberra. V/Line stops here on the run between Cooma and Melbourne. The bus stop is opposite the Bombala Hotel.

Car & Motorcycle The Monaro Highway runs north to Cooma and south to the Victorian border, where it becomes the Cann Valley Highway and meets the Princes Highway at Cann River. The road running south-west from Bombala through the hamlet of Delegate crosses the border and becomes the Bonang Highway, running through Bonang and meeting the Princes Highway at Orbost.

A road runs east from Bombala to the Princes Highway near Merimbula, and a road off the Monaro Highway south of Bombala runs east through the national park to the Princes Highway near Eden.

SOUTH-EAST FORESTS NATIONAL PARK

This newly established national park (90,000 hectares), combining state forests and former smaller national parks, extends south from Nimmitabel to the Victorian border. The creation of the park came after a long battle between loggers and environmentalists. The Monaro Highway runs down the western side and Imlay Rd cuts through the southern section between the Monaro and Princes highways. Contact the NPWS office (☎ 6458 4080) in Bombala for more information.

JINDABYNE

Jindabyne (population 2000) is the closest town to the major ski-resorts. It's a sizeable place, with a lot of new development happening. In winter, when the scores of apartments and motels fill up, the town sleeps more than 20,000 visitors!

Orientation & Information

As with so many other towns on the Monaro, today's Jindabyne is a modern incarnation of an original settlement which is now below the surface of a hydro-electric dam – in this case Lake Jindabyne.

The magnificent new Snowy Region Visitor Centre (☎ 6450 5600) is on Kosciuszko Rd – the main road in from Cooma – on the left as the road curves around. It's operated by the NPWS, but has information on the whole region. There are display areas, a theatre and a cafe. It's open daily 8 am to 6 pm.

Nugget's Crossing, further around Kosciuszko Rd, is a handy shopping centre with a supermarket, banks and places to eat. It's named after a local pioneer and horseman.

Ski 'n' Save (☎ 6456 2687), in Snowy Mountains Plaza on Kosciuszko Rd before the visitor centre, is an excellent source of information and can organise accommodation, activities and transport.

Summer Activities

Many people come to this town at the foot of Australia's largest ski-fields to sail on Lake Jindabyne. Alpine Sailing (☎ 018 484 062), at Snowline Caravan Park, rents Hobie cats, sailboards and canoes. You can go for a cruise on the lake on MV *Kalinga*; book at the visitor centre.

Several places rent out bikes including Ski 'n' Save (☎ 6456 2687) which rents mountain bikes for $30 a day. They're also available from Paddy Pallin (☎ 6456 2922) and Snowy Mountains Sports (☎ 6456 2530).

Horseriding is popular and is provided by a number of outfits. Jindabyne Trail Rides (☎ 6456 2421) has 90-minute rides for $20 and can organise accommodation. Snowy River Horseback Adventures (☎ 6453 7260) has half-day rides for $50 and longer ones with overnight stops.

Paddy Pallin (☎ 6456 2922), at the Thredbo turn-off, rents tents and other walking equipment. A sleeping bag costs $20 for one day's hire (lower rates for longer hires). They also package guided walks. These range from leisurely one-day walks for $59, up to seven-day walks in the Grey Mare mountains for $739. Wilderness Sports (☎ 6456 2966) in Nugget's Crossing also has organised walks.

Places to Stay

Winter sees a huge influx of visitors to Jindabyne. Prices soar, overnight accommodation all but disappears and many places book out months in advance. Prices also rise

on Friday and Saturday nights throughout the year. If you're coming to ski, plan well ahead and check out the various packages offered by the resorts and lodges. Travel agents throughout Australia have information on these, and they can be good value. With a group of four to six people sharing, costs come down to a more realistic level.

Overnight Accommodation At *Jindabyne Holiday Park* (☎ 6456 2249), in town by the lake, powered sites cost $15.50 and on-site vans $45 (two-berth). Units sleeping up to five people cost $75.

Snowline Caravan Park (☎ 6452 2099), east of town at the intersection of the Alpine Way and Kosciuszko Rd, is better equipped, with a restaurant, heated amenities block and bar. You can hire boats and fishing tackle. Tent sites cost $11.50 for two, plus $4.50 per extra person; five-berth cabins with TV and bathroom cost $75.

There's a fair range of motel-style places, with some of them converting to long-term accommodation in winter and most offering bed and breakfast. *Aspen Hotel/Motel* (☎ 6456 2372), at 1 Kosciuszko Rd, has doubles from $64 in summer and $100 in the peak season. *Lakeview Plaza Motel* (☎ 6456 2134), on Snowy River Ave (behind Nugget's Crossing), charges $70 a double in summer and up to $98 in winter. These rates are pretty cheap for this town. *Lake Jindabyne Hotel/Motel* (☎ 6456 2203), a big place by the lake in the centre of town, has conference facilities and a gym. Singles/doubles can cost as little as $50/60 in summer, but rocket up to $125 in winter.

A guesthouse with moderate summer prices is *Sonnblick Lodge* (☎ 6456 2472), at 49 Gippsland St, which offers bed and breakfast for $30/60 a single/double.

Flats, Apartments & Lodges There are many places offering accommodation to skiers, but they can fill up. If possible you should book months in advance (some places don't refund your hefty deposit if you give less than 60 days' notice of cancellation). There are many letting agents, some of

SOUTH-EAST

which have glossy brochures showing the properties on their books, including Jindabyne Real Estate (☎ 6456 2216, 1800 020 657).

There are five pricing seasons: low winter (late May to early July and mid-September to mid-October), high winter (early July to early September), shoulder (early to mid September), low summer (mid-September to mid-December and early February to late May) and high summer (mid-December to early February, plus Easter and the April school holidays). Cheaper, fully equipped apartments which sleep six people cost from approximately $300 a week in low summer to $600 a week in high winter. You can pay a hell of a lot more.

Farmstay *Eagles Range* (☎ 6456 2728), 12km south-east of Jindabyne off the road to Dalgety, has purpose-built accommodation, with breakfast from about $45/50 in summer. It has a variety of packages available in winter.

Places to Eat

There are several cafes and takeaway places on Snowy Mountains Plaza, but the best place to read through the brochures you've picked up from the visitor centre is *Walita's Coffee Shop*, which has good views, coffee and a range of cakes and pastries.

In Nugget's Crossing, *Bacco's* is a good Italian restaurant; spaghetti carbonara is $11. It also does takeaway pizzas. *Lake Jindabyne Hotel* has a Thai restaurant and several of the lodges have restaurants.

Getting There & Away

Air Cooma is the nearest airport for passenger flights. Contact Ski 'n' Save (☎ 6456 2687) in Snowy Mountains Plaza, or Snowy River Travel (☎ 6456 2184) behind Nugget's Crossing.

Bus Ski 'n' Save (☎ 6456 2687) and Snowy River Travel (☎ 6456 2184) handle bus bookings.

Greyhound Pioneer runs from Sydney ($58, about 7½ hours) and Canberra ($38, about three hours) to Jindabyne and the ski-fields, as well as shuttle services from Jindabyne to the resorts in winter.

To the Ski-Fields The Skitube terminal at Bullock Flat is less than half an hour from Jindabyne by car.

Greyhound Pioneer's shuttle service operates in winter only and makes about six runs a day to and from the Crackenback Resort, Bullocks Flat and Thredbo, and at least three runs a day to and from Sawpit Creek, Smiggin Holes and Perisher. From Jindabyne to Smiggin Holes costs $10 one way (including the national-park entry fee), Perisher $15, Thredbo $14 and Bullocks Flat $10. The trip to Perisher takes 45 minutes; to Thredbo it's about an hour.

Jindabyne Coaches (☎ 6457 2117) runs buses to Thredbo in winter.

Jindabyne Taxi Service (☎ 6456 2644) takes up to five people to the ski-fields from Jindabyne. The one-way fare to Thredbo or Perisher is about $50 and to Bullocks Flat (the Skitube terminal) about $30. You can buy a return ticket for $120 which includes a week's car-parking in Jindabyne. These prices don't include the national-park entry fee. Taxis run all night on Fridays in the ski season, when you're advised to book ahead. Another taxi service operates from the Sawpit Creek garage (☎ 6456 2321).

Car & Motorcycle At the intersection west of Jindabyne you can head south on the Alpine Way to Bullocks Flat, Thredbo and Khancoban. The right-hand road is Kosciuszko Rd which runs to Sawpit Creek (the visitor centre for Kosciuszko National Park) and on to Perisher and Charlotte Pass. You have to carry chains if you're venturing into the ski-fields in winter – there's a big fine if you don't.

The Barry Way (unsealed and unsuitable for caravans) runs south into Victoria; other roads run north-east to Berridale and Cooma, and south-east to Dalgety and the Monaro Highway near Bombala.

AROUND JINDABYNE
Berridale
You'll know you're approaching the ski-fields when you get to Berridale (population 900), north-east of Jindabyne. It's a small village with a lot of accommodation and ski-hire places. In the off-season the accommodation can be great value, but you're advised to book in winter as they get a lot of coach tours.

You can visit the **Snowy River Winery** (☎ 6456 5041), south of Berridale off the road to Dalgety which is open daily from 10 am to 5 pm.

Places to Stay Motels include *Snowy Mountains Coach & Motor Inn* (☎ 6456 3283), a quiet place charging $35/48 October to May. It becomes lively in winter with a disco and games room but prices triple. There's a heated indoor pool.

Getting There & Away Greyhound Pioneer between Sydney/Canberra and Thredbo stops here, so it's a feasible base for skiing if you don't have transport. Berridale to Sydney costs $48 (seven hours), Canberra $27 (two hours), Jindabyne $24 (30 minutes) and Thredbo $24 (45 minutes).

Dalgety
Dalgety is a hamlet which stands practically in the shadow of Mt Kosciuszko, but it's a rural centre rather than a ski-resort town. A few kilometres west is the **Ag Barn** (☎ 6456 5102), where you can see hour-long demonstrations of sheep and goat shearing, milking and other such agricultural pastimes. It's a working angora stud, but has moved into tourism in a big way. General entry is $2, but the demonstrations, held daily at 2 pm, cost $8 ($6 children).

KOSCIUSZKO NATIONAL PARK
The state's largest national park (647,100 hectares) includes caves, glacial lakes, forest and all of the state's ski-resorts, as well as the highest mountain (2228m) in Australia. Mt Kosciuszko (pronounced 'kozzyosko') was named by the Polish explorer Paul Edmund Strzelecki after a Polish hero of the American War of Independence.

Most famous for its snow, the national park is also popular in summer when there are excellent bushwalks and marvellous alpine wildflowers. Outside the snow season you can drive to within 8km of the top of Mt Kosciuszko via the Kosciuszko Rd from Jindabyne to Charlotte Pass.

Orientation & Information
Mt Kosciuszko and the main ski resorts are in the south-central area of this large national park. From Jindabyne, Kosciuszko Rd leads to the NPWS visitor centre (☎ 6456 2102) which is about 15km north-west at Sawpit Creek. The road then heads to the resorts of Smiggin Holes, Perisher Valley (33km) and Charlotte Pass, with a turn-off before Perisher Valley to Guthega and Mt Blue Cow. The Alpine Way also runs from Jindabyne, to Bullocks Flat and Thredbo (35km from Jindabyne) and then continues on to Khancoban on the south-west side of the mountains.

The Mt Selwyn resort is in the north of the park, off the Snowy Mountains Highway west of Kiandra.

There's another NPWS visitor centre at Yarrangobilly Caves (☎ 6454 9597) in the north of the park and there are park-ranger stations at Perisher (☎ 6457 5214) and Thredbo (☎ 6457 6255).

Entry to the national park (including all ski resorts) costs $12 per car, *per day*. Motorbikes pay $3.50 and bus passengers $4 ($2 children; this is usually included in the bus fare). A car parked anywhere in the park without a permit is liable for a $200 fine. There are toll booths on the Alpine Way and the road up to Charlotte Pass and you can also buy permits at Sawpit Creek and in Thredbo Village. Think about buying the $60 annual permit which gives you unlimited access to every national park in NSW, although no other park costs as much to enter as Kosciuszko.

The CMA's useful *Snowy Kosciuszko* map ($4.95) includes maps of the resorts.

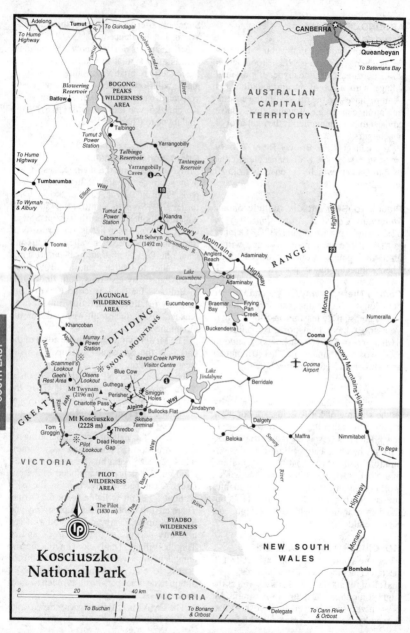

Kosciuszko
National Park

SOUTH-EAST

PAUL STEEL

JON MURRAY

BERNARD NAPTHINE

The Riverina
Top: Wheat harvesting
Bottom Left: Grain silos, Deniliquin
Bottom Right: Wentworth – where the Murray and Darling Rivers meet

MARK KIRBY

JON MURRAY

The South-East
Top: Charlotte Pass, Mt Kosciuszko National Park
Bottom: The Ettamogah Pub, north of Albury

Flora & Fauna

There's a surprising amount of birdlife in the park, with stately eagles sweeping the sky, bright parrots, noisy kookaburras and the haunting warble of magpies. Marsupials abound and they can be pretty tame.

If you come across a baby animal in need of help, contact either the NPWS or LAOKO – Looking After Kosciuszko's Orphans (☎ 6456 1313). They'll give you some advice.

Accommodation

Bush camping is permitted in most of the national park, but not in ecologically fragile areas. Some picnic areas, where you can camp, have fireplaces and pit toilets. The only formal camping area is near Sawpit Creek. Many resorts have good deals on accommodation in summer.

Winter Accommodation In winter, the cheapest (and most fun) way to get to the slopes is to gather a bunch of friends and rent an apartment. If your budget is tight you could stay in Jindabyne or further afield, although there's a YHA hostel at Thredbo. Bring food and drink, as supplies in the resorts are expensive.

For the ski season, begin making enquiries as early as February. Costs vary enormously, but can be within the bounds of reason. As rough examples, a two-bedroom apartment in Thredbo costs from about $2500 for a week during the peak ski season (roughly mid-July to early September) and a double room in a lodge costs over $1000, including some meals. There are midweek and weekend deals, but it's unlikely that you'll find overnight accommodation on the mountain in season.

If you investigate the various packages and have a group of at least four people, there's a good chance that you'll pay considerably less. Many agents (including most travel agents) book accommodation and packages on the ski-fields. Specialists include the Snowy Mountains Reservation Centre (☎ 6456 2633, 1800 020 622) aka Ski 'n' Save, Perisher Blue Snow Holidays (☎ 6456 1084, 1800 066 177) and the Thredbo Resort Centre (☎ 6459 4294, 1800 02 0589). Travel agents, including the NSW Travel Centre (☎ 132077) in Sydney and other capital cities, also make bookings.

Sawpit Creek

This has the main NPWS visitor centre (☎ 6456 2102) in Kosciuszko National Park.

Up the road from the Sawpit Creek visitor centre, *Kosciuszko Mountain Retreat* (☎ 6456 2224) is a pleasant place in bushland. It has tent sites for $19 for two (plus $7 per person) and cabins at $62 a double, plus $7 per person. There are no one-night stays in the ski season or around Christmas. The lawns are kept short by friendly kangaroos and in the evenings you'll probably be visited by amiable possums looking for some tucker. Several walking tracks lead into the surrounding bush.

Yarrangobilly Caves

Although they aren't as well known as some other caves in NSW, the Yarrangobilly Caves (☎ 6454 9597) are among the most interesting. You can visit the Glory Hole by yourself between 10 am and 4 pm for $6 ($4 children), and there are guided tours of other caves on weekdays at 1 pm and weekends at 11 am, 1 and 3 pm for $10 ($7 children).

There's a good NPWS visitor centre (☎ 6454 9597) and there are some short walks in the area and a thermal pool where you can swim in 27°C water.

You don't have to pay the park fee if you're only visiting the caves – provided you pay the caves entry fee.

Kiandra

Kiandra was a gold-rush town in the 1860s, but little remains today. In winter you can pay the national park entry fee here. The **Gold Seekers Walking Track**, a two-hour return walk, leaves Elliott Way east of the Mt Selwyn turn-off.

Bushwalking

See the Sawpit Creek NPWS visitor centre

SOUTH-EAST

for information on the many walks – some short, some long – in the park.

From Charlotte Pass you can walk to the summit of Mt Kosciuszko (16km return); you can also walk to the summit from Thredbo (12km return). There are other walking trails from Charlotte Pass, including the 20km lakes walk which includes Blue, Albina and Club lakes.

Skiing & Resorts

Snow skiing in Australia can be a marginal activity. The season is short (July, August and early September) and good snow isn't always likely, although the increased use of snow-making machines is making it more so. Nor are the mountains ideal for downhill skiing – their gently rounded shapes mean that most long runs are relatively easy and the harder runs short and sharp. Worse, the short seasons mean operators have to get their returns quickly, so costs are high.

The good news is that when the snow's there and the sun's shining, the skiing can be great. You'll find all the fun (not to mention heart-in-mouth fear) you could ask for.

The open slopes are a ski-tourer's paradise – nordic (cross-country or langlauf) skiing is popular and most resorts offer lessons and hire equipment. The national park includes some of the most famous trails – Kiandra to Kosciuszko, the Grey Mare Range, Thredbo or Charlotte Pass to Kosciuszko's summit and the Jagungal wilderness. The possibilities are endless; often old cattle-herders' huts

are the only form of accommodation apart from your tent.

There's also cross-country racing (classic or skating) in the Perisher Valley. On the steep slopes of the Main Range near Twynam and Carruthers the cross-country downhill (XCD) fanatics get their adrenaline rushes. In winter, the cliffs near Blue Lake become a practice ground for alpine climbers.

Lift charges vary – see the following information on the various resorts. Group lessons including a lift ticket cost about $60 a day or less per day for five days. Boots, skis and stocks can be hired for around $35 a day. It will cost less for longer periods or if you hire them away from the mountain. It's a trade-off whether to hire in the city and risk adjustment problems or hire at the resort and pay more. There are hire places in towns close to the resorts and many garages hire ski equipment, as well as chains. Snow chains must be carried during winter even if there's no snow – heavy penalties apply if you don't.

Australian ski resorts are short of the frenetic nightlife of European resorts, but compensate with lots of partying between the lodges. There's also a variety of alternative activities, including snowboarding and toboggan runs. Weekends are crowded because the resorts are so convenient, particularly to Canberra.

For snow and road reports ring the various visitor centres. Thredbo has its own number (☎ 0055 34320).

Bullocks Flat Bullocks Flat, on the Alpine Way between Jindabyne and Thredbo, is the site of the Skitube terminal. The Skitube train (☎ 6456 2010) runs from here mostly underground to Perisher and Mt Blue Cow. The return fare is $19 ($13 children).

There's a free, pretty but basic campsite near the Skitube, called *Thredbo Diggings*. Nearby, at the other end of the price-scale, is *Novotel Lake Crackenback Resort* (☎ 6456 2960), a superb complex below the main snowline, but within walking distance of the Skitube terminal. There are four pricing seasons, the highest being early July to early September and the lowest the months either

---

Skiing's Early Days

The first people to ski in Australia were the fur hunters of Tasmania in the 1830s, using three-foot (about 1m) boards. Norwegians at the Kiandra goldfields introduced skiing in the 1860s and the world's first ski races were held there. The skis in those days were home-made, crude objects; the method of braking was a pole held between the two skis. Early in the 20th century the development of the sport began, with lodges like the one at Charlotte Pass and the importing of European skis. ■

side of this. Costs range from $156 a double to $218 a double, with lower rates for longer stays or for up to four people sharing a room. There are also winter packages which include accommodation, some meals and lift tickets. In summer, activities include white-water canoeing and horse-riding.

Thredbo Thredbo (1370m) has the longest runs (the longest is over 3km through 670m of vertical drop) and the best and most expensive skiing in Australia. A day ticket costs $58, a five-day pass $250 and a five-day lift and lesson package costs $305. In summer Thredbo is still a good place to visit, unlike the other resorts which become ghost towns. It's a popular bushwalking centre with excellent, scenic tracks.

Although Thredbo Village covers only a small area, streets wind around the steep valley side and it's tightly packed with lodges. There are two turn-offs for Thredbo from the Alpine Way, one directing you to the lodges and the other to the commercial centre. Both will get you to the village, but if you take the lodges' turn-off it's a good idea to know where you're going. Pick up a map of the village at the Thredbo Centre in Jindabyne before you arrive. If you've arrived by bus, there's a map in the bus-shelter showing the location of the lodges. There's an information centre in the Valley Terminal – walk there on the wooden foot-bridge near the bus shelter.

The chairlift to the top of Mt Crackenback runs right through the summer for $16.50 return ($8.50 children). From the top it's a 2km walk or cross-country ski to a good lookout point over Mt Kosciuszko, or 7km to the top of the mountain itself. Other walks, longer and shorter, leave from the top of the lift. Maps are available at the Sports Centre. Remember to carry adequate clothing and be prepared for all conditions, even in summer.

The Thredbo Centre (☎ 6459 4100/4151) organises all sorts of activities including hiking, mountain biking, canoeing, white-water rafting, abseiling and horse-riding.

The Thredbo World Music Festival is held in mid-March and the Jazz Festival towards the end of April.

Places to Stay Accommodation at Thredbo is in commercial lodges or privately owned apartments.

Thredbo YHA Lodge (☎ 6457 6376) costs just $15 a night ($18 per person twin-share) outside the ski season and $38 a night ($55 Saturday night) and $225 a week in the ski season. Not surprisingly there's stiff competition for beds in winter. A ballot is held for winter places and you have to enter by April. Most people get the nights they want and, even if you aren't in the ballot, it's worth checking to see if there are cancellations. In June and at the end of September, when snow might be scanty, there's less pressure on places. There's plenty of room in the off-season. The YHA Travel Centre (☎ 9261 1111) in Sydney is the best place to start making enquiries.

Several Thredbo lodges, such as the *Snow Goose* (☎ 6457 6415) and *House of Ullr* (☎ 6457 6210), have reasonable deals outside the ski season. The House of Ullr has doubles for $69 or $79, depending on the view.

Perisher Blue In 1995 the resorts of Perisher Valley, Smiggin Holes, Mt Blue Cow and Guthega combined to become Perisher Blue (☎ 6456 1084, 1800 066 177). The mega-resort provides skiing on seven peaks across 1250 hectares, with 50 lifts and one ticketing system. For a snow report call ☎ 0055 26664.

Perisher Valley has a good selection of intermediate runs. Smiggin Holes (1680m) is just down the road from Perisher. Guthega (1630m) is mainly a day resort which is best suited to intermediate and, to a lesser extent, beginner skiers. It's smaller and less crowded than other places; from here, cross-country skiers head to the Main Range or Rolling Ground. Mt Blue Cow (1640m), between Perisher Valley and Guthega in the Perisher Range, has beginner to intermediate skiing. Mt Blue Cow is a day resort (no accommodation) accessible via the Skitube, but there are accommodation packages which include shuttles and Skitube tickets.

Day tickets for lifts cost $58 ($30 children); a one-day combined lesson and lift ticket costs $75 ($50 children). Add an extra $8 ($6 children) for use of the Skitube. One-day lift tickets and lessons for beginners cost $62 ($42 children). There are various deals available if you take more days.

Places to Stay Most accommodation is in Perisher Valley and Smiggin Holes. Contact Perisher Blue direct or travel agents like Ski 'n' Save (☎ 6456 2687) in Jindabyne.

In Perisher Valley the *Sundeck Hotel* (☎ 6457 5222) has nightly rates of $165 with breakfast in the peak season. Peak winter rates at *The Lodge* (☎ 6457 5012) at Smiggin Holes, are around $160 including ski hire, dinner and light breakfast.

In Guthega, *Guthega Lodge* (☎ 6457 5383) is the only commercial accommodation.

Charlotte Pass At the base of Mt Kosciuszko, this is one of the highest (1780m), oldest and most isolated resorts in Australia. In winter you have to snowcat the last 8km from Perisher Valley (about $30, although this is often included in the price of a package). Five lifts service rather short, but uncrowded, runs and this is good ski-touring country.

There are a number of lodges, including *Kosciuszko Chalet* (☎ 6457 5245, 1800 026 369), a grand old place dating from the 1930s. In summer, packages with dinner, bed and breakfast cost $100/190. The chalet also offers good winter packages. Other lodges at Charlotte Pass include *Stillwell Lodge* (☎ 6457 5073) which is also open in summer.

Mt Selwyn Mt Selwyn (1492m) is the only ski resort (☎ 6489 4485) in the north of the park, halfway between Tumut and Cooma. It has 12 lifts and is ideal for beginners. One-day lift tickets are $28 ($16 children) and packages including five days plus lessons are $225 ($165 children). It's another day resort

– most accommodation is in the Adaminaby area. Adaminaby Bus Service (☎ 6454 2318) runs between Cooma and Mt Selwyn.

To commemorate the early skiers on the Kiandra goldfields, Mt Selwyn hosts the Kiandra Goldrush in July, a race in period costume and equipment.

Getting There & Around
Bus Greyhound Pioneer (☎ 132323) is the main carrier in this area. There are plenty of services from Sydney and Canberra to Cooma and Jindabyne, from where shuttles run to the resorts in winter. From Jindabyne to Smiggin Holes it costs $10 (30 minutes), Perisher $15 (45 minutes) and Thredbo $14 (one hour). In summer, buses run to Thredbo ($38 from Canberra), but not always daily.

Car & Motorcycle In winter you can normally drive as far as Perisher Valley, but snow chains must be carried and fitted where directed. There are sometimes parking restrictions in the park in winter. The simplest, safest way to get to Perisher and Smiggin Holes in winter is to take the Skitube, a tunnel railway up to Perisher Valley and Blue Cow from below the snowline at Bullocks Flat (see that entry earlier in this chapter) on the Alpine Way. You can hire skis and equipment at Bullocks Flat, while luggage lockers and overnight parking are available. The Skitube runs to a reduced timetable in summer.

See the following West of the Snowies section for western routes into the national park.

Taxi See the Getting There & Away entry under Jindabyne.

THE ALPINE WAY
From Khancoban, this spectacular route runs through dense forest, around the southern end of Kosciuszko National Park to Thredbo Village and onto Jindabyne. Sections can be closed during winter and caravans and trailers aren't permitted on the section between Tom Groggin and the Pilot Lookout at any

time. There's no fuel available between Khancoban and Thredbo.

Murray 1 Power Station (☎ 6076 9463), off the Alpine Way 8km south of Khancoban, has free daily tours on the hour from 10 am to 2 pm.

Another 7km further south is **Scammel's Lookout**, offering superb views. There are toilets and picnic tables here. You can camp at **Geehi**, a National Parks rest area, and the facilities are currently being upgraded.

At **Tom Groggin**, home of the original Man From Snowy River, the road skirts the Murray River, which is good for a swim on a hot day. You can camp here and there's another site about 10km further on. Also near Tom Groggin is **Tom Groggin Station** (☎ 6076 9455), from where there are two to seven-day horserides. After Tom Groggin there's an unsealed section as the road climbs 800m to the **Pilot Lookout** (1300m), with views across a wilderness area to the Pilot (1830m), the source of the Murray River. There's another climb to **Dead Horse Gap** (1580m), named after some brumbies which froze here, then a descent to Thredbo Village (1400m), the Skitube terminal at Bullocks Flat, and Jindabyne.

West of the Snowies

The western slopes of the Snowy Mountains are steeper than on the east, and the area is more intensively farmed, although there's still plenty of bush. South of Khancoban on the Alpine Way is some of the most spectacular scenery in the whole region. The farms and small towns in the area blaze with colour in the autumn when poplars and fruit trees prepare to shed their leaves. This is a rural area, totally different in atmosphere from the resort-minded Monaro.

Getting There & Around

Bus A Countrylink bus runs from Cootamundra and Gundagai to Tumut, Adelong, Batlow and Tumbarumba.

Car & Motorcycle There are several approaches to the Snowies from the west, all of which are accessible from the Hume Highway. The main route, the Snowy Mountains Highway, leaves the Hume about 30km south of Gundagai and takes you to Tumut, Kiandra, Adaminaby and Cooma. A smaller road also leads to Tumut from the Hume Highway near Gundagai.

From Albury you can travel on Victoria's Murray Valley Highway to Corryong, then head across the river to Khancoban for the Alpine Way or north to other roads crossing the mountains. The Murray Valley Highway exit from the Hume Highway is about 10km south of Albury.

Another road in Victoria parallels the Murray Valley Highway, but follows closely the south bank of the Murray. This road leaves the Hume Highway just north of Albury and crosses back into Victoria at the big Hume Weir. This route is longer, but perhaps more interesting, than the Murray Valley Highway and offers a choice of places to cross the Murray. You can drive all the way around to Towong, the crossing near Corryong and Khancoban; you can cross near Jingellic and take the partly unsealed road to Tumbarumba; or you can cross on the vehicle ferry near Wymah and take the dirt road following the north bank of the Murray to Jingellic. The Wymah ferry runs on demand September to April from 6 am to 9 pm and May to August between 7 am and 8 pm, with breaks for the crew's breakfast (7.15 to 8 am), lunch (11.45 am to 1 pm) and dinner (5.15 to 6.30 pm).

The dirt road along the north bank of the Murray, which is narrow and winding, but in good condition, is also accessible from the Hume Highway at Bowna and Woomargama.

From Holbrook on the Hume Highway, a sealed road runs through to Jingellic, while another sealed road runs from the Hume to Tumbarumba.

The road down the western side of the range – from Tumut to Khancoban and the Alpine Way – passes through Batlow and Tumbarumba. It's a hilly, scenic drive. From

Tumbarumba you can cross the mountains on the Elliott Way to get to Mt Selwyn and the Snowy Mountains Highway at Kiandra. This crossing is also accessible via several roads near Towong if you're coming from Corryong but the crossing sometimes closes in winter.

There's another crossing to Mt Selwyn and Kiandra just north of Khancoban, but snow ploughs don't clear sections of it in winter, and you're advised to leave the area as soon as snow begins to fall. Caravans can't use this road.

TUMUT

A mountain town in the pretty Tumut Valley, Tumut (population 6300) is the closest centre to the northern end of Kosciuszko National Park. In the area there are many pine plantations (second only to the great swathe of pines in South Australia's south-east) and orchards, which mainly grow apples.

The explorers Hume and Hovell were the first Europeans to see the Tumut Valley. Farmers and graziers followed, but development of the town was slow. One of the area's most famous early residents was author Miles Franklin (her best known book is *My Brilliant Career*), who was born at Talbingo.

Information

Tumut Visitors Centre (☎ 6947 1849) on Fitzroy St opens daily from 9 am to 5 pm.

Things to See & Do

The **Rotary Lookout**, at the top of Wynyard St, gives a good view of the town and the Tumut Valley.

The **Old Butter Factory** on the Adelong road (Snowy Mountains Highway), just in front of the dilapidated old railway station, has closed for refurbishment, but when it opens will have information on national parks. Opposite is the **Tumut Broom Factory** (☎ 6947 2804) where brooms are still made from millet; it's open weekdays from 9 am to 4 pm (closed 12.30 to 1.30 pm).

The rather small **Tumut & District Historical Museum** (no phone), at the corner of Capper and Merivale Sts, has a room devoted

to Miles Franklin. The museum is open Monday, Wednesday, Friday, Saturday and school holidays from 2 to 4 pm; entry is $2 (children 50c).

Adventure Sports (☎ 6947 1531), behind the old butter factory, is a friendly, knowledgeable outfit which can organise just about any outdoor activity – canoeing, rafting, abseiling, mountain biking or bushwalking – for groups or individuals. It also hires out skis in winter.

You can take a short flight over the Tumut Valley for $30 per person (minimum two people). Contact the visitors centre, or phone the airport (☎ 6947 1148).

Special Events

The Tumut Agricultural Show and rodeo are held in early March and the Festival of the Falling Leaf is held in late April and early May.

Places to Stay

The closest caravan park to town is the shady *Riverglade Caravan Park* (☎ 6947 2528) on the highway a few blocks from the centre on the Tumut River. Sites cost $12 and cabins $40. You'll need to book ahead at Christmas and Easter. *Blowering Holiday Park* (☎ 6947 1383), 5km south, has sites for $10 and on-site vans for $34.

The *Oriental Hotel* (☎ 6947 1174), on the corner of Fitzroy and Wynyard Sts, has rooms for $20/40. It's a nice old pub and the rooms look onto that big balcony. Across the street is the *Woolpack Hotel* (☎ 6947 1027).

The *Royal Hotel* (☎ 6947 1129) and the *Commercial Hotel* (☎ 6947 1040) have motel-style units for $40/55.

There are also several motels, including the *Tumut Motor Inn* (☎ 6947 4523) on Fitzroy St, with rooms for $56, and the *Ashton* (☎ 6947 1999) at 124 Wynyard St, with rooms for $60.

Places to Eat

There are several bakeries and cake shops on or near Wynyard St. *Sugar 'n' Spice*, opposite the RSL Club on Russell St, has tables on the footpath. *Chit Chat Coffee Shoppe*, off

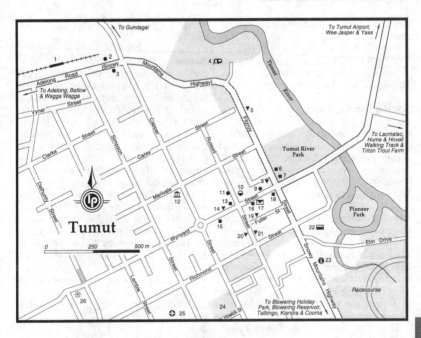

PLACES TO STAY
4   Riverglade Caravan
    Park
6   Tumut Motor Inn
7   Oriental Hotel
13 Commercial Hotel
15 Ashton Motel
16 Royal Hotel
18 Woolpack Hotel

PLACES TO EAT
5   Brooklyn on Fitzroy
8   Huang's

14 Chit Chat Coffee
    Shoppe & Bernie's
    Family Restaurant
19 Tirami-Su
20 RSL Club
21 Sugar 'n' Spice

OTHER
1   Old Railway Station
2   Old Butter Factory &
    Adventure Sports
3   Broom Factory

9   The Hub & Courtyard
    Restaurant
10 Bus Stop
11 Supermarket
12 Tumut & District
    Historical Museum
17 Post Office
22 Swimming Pool
23 Tumut Visitors Centre
24 TAFE College & CES
    Office
25 Hospital
26 Rotary Lookout

Wynyard St is open during the day and has
sandwiches for $3 to $4 and snacks $5 to $6.
The pubs all have counter meals (from $6 at
the *Royal Hotel* on Wynyard St). Behind the
Royal, off Fuller St, *Tirami-Su* (☎ 6947
4285) has Italian food which is pricey at $15
to $17 for main course pastas.

There are several Chinese places, including the BYO *Huang's* (☎ 6947 1508) at 47

Fitzroy St. It's open daily for lunch and
dinner and the food is MSG-free.

In The Hub, a small complex on Wynyard
St near the corner of Fitzroy St, *The Courtyard* (☎ 6947 1472) is a pleasant licensed
restaurant and cocktail bar with main courses
which cost around $14. *Bernie's Family Res-
taurant* (☎ 6947 1802), upstairs on Wynyard
St, is fully licensed although it doesn't feel

especially 'family'. A steak will set you back about $12.

Tumut's best restaurant is *Brooklyn on Fitzroy* (☎ 6947 4022) at 10 Fitzroy St in an impressive, renovated house. It's open Tuesday to Saturday for dinner only.

Getting There & Away

Bus Countrylink buses, which connect with Cootamundra, Adelong, Gundagai, Batlow and Tumbarumba, stop Sunday to Friday outside the National Bank on the corner of Russell and Wynyard Sts. Harvey World Travel (☎ 6947 3055), in The Hub centre on Wynyard St, sells tickets.

Car & Motorcycle The Snowy Mountains Highway runs north-west to the Hume Highway and south-east through Kosciuszko National Park to Adaminaby and Cooma. Another smaller road runs to the Hume near Gundagai. From the Snowy Mountains Highway at Adelong, 22km west of Tumut, you can drive south to Batlow, Tumbarumba and Khancoban.

There's an interesting road from Tumut north to Wee Jasper, from where you can get to Yass. It's reasonable, but in wet weather you might need a 4WD.

AROUND TUMUT

The Thomas Boyd Trackhead of the **Hume & Hovell Walking Track** is 23km south-east of Tumut and it has camping facilities. Tumut Visitors Centre sells route maps. On the way here, 19km from Tumut on the Lacmalac road, you could catch your own dinner at the **Triton Trout Farm** (☎ 6947 5759). It's open Wednesday to Monday from 9.30 am to 5 pm. You can hire rod and tackle for $2 and you pay by the kilogram for the fish that you catch.

Blowering Reservoir, nearly 20km long, is part of the Snowy Mountains Hydro-Electric Scheme. There are walks along the forested shores and the lake is popular for watersports. Hundreds of kangaroos appear at dusk; drive carefully. The small town of **Talbingo** is nearby. South of Talbingo, **Tumut 3 Power Station**, on Murray Jackson

Drive, has free tours daily between 10 am and 2.30 pm.

Batlow

Batlow (population 1250) clusters around one side of a bowl-shaped valley, in the middle of the apple orchards which are the town's main reason for existing. The orchards blossom in October and the harvest starts around mid-March. Picking work is usually available. A part-time CES office (☎ 6947 2077) in the TAFE college on Capper St in Tumut can help with enquiries, or contact the Wagga Wagga CES (☎ 6938 3444), at 25 Tompson St. Tourist information for the area can be found at Springfield Orchard (☎ 6949 1021), just north of town.

Batlow Caravan Park (☎ 6949 1444), on the Tumut road down by the shady creek off Kurrajong Ave, has sites for $9 ($11 with power). *Diggers Rest Motel* (☎ 6949 1342), opposite the post office, has singles/doubles for $48/56.

Countrylink buses stop in town Monday to Friday.

Adelong

This neat village (population 900) was the centre of a goldrush in the 1850s and 60s, and several buildings in the main street, notably the Old Bank, reflect this status. The Old Bank has tourist information.

The **Adelong Falls**, 1.5km from the town centre, are worth seeing. Head up the main street, take the right turn towards Gundagai then the turn-off to the falls on the right, just after the stockyards. More interesting are the nearby extensive remains of the ingenious **Reefer Battery**. They look like the foundations of an ancient city and this curiosity was entirely powered by waterwheels.

The small, friendly *Golden Gully Caravan Park* (☎ 6946 2282), across the river near the swimming pool, has powered sites for $12. *Adelong Hotel* (☎ 6946 2009) also has accommodation and the *Old Bank* (☎ 6946 2408) is a combination of an antique shop, tea rooms and bed and breakfast, charging $65 a single or double. *Miner's Plate* at the Adelong Services & Citizens'

Club (☎ 6946 2163) serves Chinese and Australian food.

TUMBARUMBA

Tumbarumba (usually called just Tumba) is a large town for this part of the world (population 2000) and there are some nice old buildings, such as the courthouse and the council chambers opposite. The area was first settled by graziers, who wintered their cattle here when the snows came to the high plains, and a small gold rush in the 1860s boosted the population. Today, forestry is the major industry, along with orchards growing cool-climate fruits. There are also some wineries, while sheep and cattle are farmed on the lower hills to the west.

Orientation & Information

The main street through town is Tumbarumba Parade, which is usually just called The Parade.

The interesting Mountain Gum Antiques shop (☎ 6948 3055), at 36 The Parade, has tourist information (☎ 6948 3444) and is open daily from 9 am to 5 pm. The Wool & Craft shop (☎ 6948 4805), at the corner of Bridge St and The Parade, also has some tourist information. The Forestry Commission office on Winton St has details of the area's forests and can give advice on the numerous tracks winding through the state forests. The newsagency sells topographic maps of the area.

Things to See & Do

The **Bicentennial Gardens** on Tumbarumba Creek is a good place for a picnic lunch; it's on the Khancoban road, a couple of blocks from the town centre. The town's **library** is here, housed in an A-frame building which was once a prison chapel. A small walking track in the **Old Police Paddock Arboretum**, near the Girl Guides' hall up behind the town, leads into 16 hectares of bush.

Some of the district's many **orchards**, growing nuts, cherries and apples, welcome visitors. Ask at Mountain Gum Antiques for opening times and directions. Also ask about the several nearby **wineries**.

Special Events

The Tumbarumba rodeo is held in early January and the annual show takes place during the fortnight before Easter. There is also a polocrosse carnival held around April/May.

Places to Stay & Eat

There's camping available at the *Henry Angel Flat Trackhead* (see the Around Tumbarumba entry below). The small *Tumbarumba Creek Caravan Park* (☎ 6948 3330), just off The Parade beside the creek near the showground, has sites for $6 and cabins for $30. You can also camp at the small *Tumbarumba Motel* (☎ 6948 2494) on Albury St which has single/double rooms for $44/58.

The *Tumbarumba Hotel* (☎ 6948 2562), on The Parade, charges $25/40 including a light breakfast; the *Union Hotel* (☎ 6948 2013) also has rooms.

The Parade has a bakery (open daily) and a couple of coffee shops. The *Old Times Coffee Shop* has sandwiches for $2, lasagne for $6 and good coffee. The pubs serve counter meals and the *Tumbarumba Motel* has an upmarket restaurant. The *golf club*, on the northern edge of town, and the *bowling club*, on Winton St, also serve meals.

The antiques shop sells home-made 'fruit leather' – rolls of pressed dried fruit, a bit like beef jerky for fruitarians – for $2.

Getting There & Away

Countrylink buses stop in town and you can buy tickets at the newsagency. From Tumbarumba, roads run west to the Hume Highway, north to Tumut, east to Mt Selwyn and the Snowy Mountains Highway, and south to Khancoban, the Alpine Way and Corryong (in Victoria).

The ski slopes at Mt Selwyn are about an hour away on the Elliott Way. You'll need chains in winter.

SOUTH-EAST

AROUND TUMBARUMBA

The **Pioneer Women's Hut** (☎ 6921 6565) is in the **Glenroy Heritage Reserve**, 8km west of Tumbarumba on the road to Rosewood (known as the Wagga road). The hut has historical displays on rural women's lives, crafts and a tea room. The reserve opens Wednesdays, weekends and public holidays from 11 am to 4 pm.

The Henry Angel Flat Trackhead, 7km south-east of town on the Khancoban road, provides access to a 6km trail along Burra Creek and to the **Hume & Hovell Walking Track**. The information office in Tumba sells tracknotes. Another 5km farther on there's a turn-off for **Paddy's River Falls**, 2km down a steep but sealed road. There are toilets, water, picnic tables and a walking trail to the base of the falls.

Two areas in the Bago State Forest north of Tumbarumba are popular for **fossicking** for gold and sapphires. You'll need to buy a fossicking licence ($2.50, or $5 for a family) from the courthouse or Mountain Gum Antiques (which also has maps).

Jingellic is a pretty hamlet with a store, a petrol station and a pub – and lots of big deciduous trees. This is a pleasant place to break the journey into the Snowies. You can camp for no charge at the basic, but attractive, camping ground by Horse Creek on the eastern edge of town, next to the pub (the Bridge Hotel).

Just across the border from Jingellic on the Corryong road, Upper Murray Resort (☎ 6037 1226) runs canoe and mountain-bike tours. Equipment and accommodation are provided. A one-day paddle costs $55. You can rent one of the self-catering cottages without taking part in a tour.

The road from Jingellic to Tumbarumba isn't all sealed; some of it is gravel. Watch out for logging trucks.

KHANCOBAN

Khancoban (pronounced can-*co*-bn) is a small town (population 520) built by the Snowy Mountains Authority. Towns built by public authorities are often bureaucratic monstrosities, but Khancoban is a beautiful exception. With Kosciuszko National Park 5km away and good road connections to Victoria and Albury, it's an ideal base for exploring the Snowies and the upper Murray River. At an altitude of 300m, Khancoban's climate is relatively mild, but just 70km on you're crossing the 1580m Dead Horse Gap.

If you're heading along the Alpine Way, there's a NPWS office (☎ 6076 9393) where you must buy your park visitor's permit ($12 per car per day or a $60 pass that gets you into every park in NSW for a year). It has a good range of information and publications and opens daily from 8.30 am to 4 pm (but closes for lunch). Khancoban Roadhouse (☎ 6076 9400) has some tourist information and sells permits when the NPWS office is closed.

Upper Murray Accommodation & Tours (☎ 6076 9222) is a local travel agency that can book activities, as well as accommodation and tours.

Activities

Upper Murray White-Water Rafting (☎ 6076 9566) based in Jindabyne has trips from near Tom Groggin Station, off the Alpine Way, to near Khancoban. See the Activities section at the start of this chapter.

Khancoban Trail Rides (☎ 6076 9566) offers horse-borne adventures between October and April, from a half-day to a week. You can go rock-climbing or abseiling in Kosciuszko with Alternative Adventures (☎ 6076 9350) who offer day trips for $90.

The caravan park hires boats and fishing tackle.

Places to Stay & Eat

Khancobal Lake Caravan Park (☎ 6076 9488), by the Khancoban Dam, has tent sites for $12, on-site vans for $25 and good cabins from $40.

Khancoban Backpackers & Fisherman's Lodge has share accommodation for $12 and single/double rooms for $17/25. Each extra person (up to six) costs $6. You need to supply your own bedding and cooking utensils. Book and check in at the nearby Khancoban Alpine Inn. There's also backpacker accommodation at *Snowgum Lodge* (☎ 6076 9522), on Mitchell Ave, for $15. Twin rooms cost $20 per person and have fridge and TV.

Khancoban Alpine Inn (☎ 6076 9471), is a pleasant hotel/motel with rooms from about $47/58 a single/double. The *Pickled Parrot Restaurant* here is open for breakfast, lunch and dinner daily.

Alpine Hideaway Village (☎ 6076 9498), across the valley from the town – the road crosses the dam's spillway – has great views of the Snowies. It's a nice place, offering good accommodation in fully equipped, self-catering lodges and with a good value restaurant. There's a variety of packages with overnight rates at $50/55 a single/double. It closes during June and July.

Up the hill from the Hideaway is *Lyrebird Lodge* (☎ 6076 9566), a smaller place offering bed and breakfast for $40/55. This is a base for Khancoban Trail Rides which operates from Tom Groggin Station.

The *Country Club* has a good à la carte restaurant.

Getting There & Away

There's no public transport to Khancoban, but the Straycat bus stops here on route between Sydney and Melbourne.

From Corryong, over the border, RS Wilkinson (☎ 6076 1418) runs taxis and taxi-minibuses into Kosciuszko National Park.

The Hume Highway

The Hume is the busiest road in Australia, running nearly 900km from Sydney down to Melbourne, Australia's second-largest city. See the Around Sydney chapter for towns between Sydney and Goulburn.

From Sydney to south-west of Goulburn, the Hume is a freeway, but up to the border with Victoria there are long stretches of narrow, two-lane road carrying a lot of traffic with tired drivers behind the wheel. Drive carefully!

The highway is named after Hamilton Hume, who followed roughly this route when he walked from Parramatta to Port Phillip, later the site of Melbourne, with William Hovell in 1824. Hume was a native-born Australian, while Hovell was an upper-crust Englishman, and their association was not entirely happy. Their return journey became a race to be the first in Sydney with news of new lands. Despite chicanery on Hovell's part, they both arrived at the same time.

GOULBURN & AROUND

Surrounded by sheep country, Goulburn is a big town (population 24,000) that has many fine 19th-century buildings. It makes a good break between Sydney and Melbourne.

John Oxley was the first European to visit the site of Goulburn, in 1820. The town developed to serve the grazing communities on the region's high pastures and was proclaimed in 1833.

Orientation & Information

After the Hume Highway bypassed Goulburn in 1992, the town discovered that this didn't mean the death-knell for retail activity and the interesting old city centre is recovering from the traffic. The town's main shopping street is Auburn St.

Goulburn Visitors Centre (☎ 4823 0492), at 6 Montague St (off Auburn St) across from Belmore Park, is open Monday to Friday from 9 am to 5 pm and on weekends from 9.30 am to 5 pm. Pick up its 'two foot' walking-tour map. The post office is at 165 Auburn St.

Things to See & Do

The old house of **St Clair** (☎ 4821 4442), at 318 Sloane St, dates from 1843 and contains a small museum. It's open Thursday to Sunday from 1 to 4 pm; entry is $2. Of all the impressive country courthouses in NSW, Goulburn's **courthouse** (☎ 4821 9522), on Montague St and built in 1887, must be the most imposing. The **old courthouse**, which did a lot of business in sentencing the bushrangers who plagued the highlands, is around the corner on Sloane St. Other interesting old buildings in the town centre include the **post office** (1881) on the corner of Auburn and Montague Sts, the Catholic **SS Peter & Paul Cathedral** (1886), on the corner of Bourke and Verner Sts, and the Anglican **St Saviours Cathedral** (1844) nearby on the corner of Montague and Bourke Sts.

A three-storey-high **Big Merino**, stands on the corner of Cowper St (the old highway) and Mary St beside a service station, about 1.5km south-east of the centre. It looks truly diabolical with its green eyes glowing at night. By day you can climb up inside and check out the view from those eyes, passing through an interesting display on the Australian wool industry on the way. A visit to the display is free – the big souvenir shop no doubt provides the profits.

The **Old Goulburn Brewery** (☎ 4821 6071), a large complex down on the riverflats off Bungonia Rd, dates from 1836. As well as the brewery, you can see a cooper in action, the maltings, tobacco curing and a steam-powered flour mill. And, of course, you can try the traditional ale. There's a restaurant (sometimes a theatre restaurant) and accommodation. The complex is open daily from 11 am and there are tours by appointment.

Riversdale (☎ 4821 4741), on Maude St at the north side of town by the Wollondilly River, began its career in 1840 as a coaching inn. It's now a National Trust property with very fine gardens and a collection of colonial furniture, arts and crafts. It's open Friday, Saturday and Sunday from 10.30 am to 4.30 pm and entry is $2.

Pelican Sheep Station (☎ 4821 4668) is a working property that is heavily into tourism. The various tours are by appointment and mainly for groups, but individuals are catered for. The basic tour takes 1¼ hours and looks at types of sheep, sheep shearing and working sheep dogs.

About 40km south-east of Goulburn and abutting Morton National Park **Bungonia SRA** (☎ 4848 4277) has a dramatic forested gorge and some deep caves. Bushwalking

and canoeing are popular. There's a camping ground near the main entrance with showers, but no powered sites.

Just off the highway between Goulburn and Yass, **Gunning** is a small town with restored buildings and a number of antique and craft shops.

See also the **Yurt Farm** under Places to Stay.

Special Events

The Australian Blues Music Festival takes place at the end of January and the Lilac City Festival is held over the Labour Day long weekend in early October.

Places to Stay

Camping   *Governors Hill Carapark* (☎ 4821 7373), on the old highway north of town, has sites for $13 and on-site vans for $30. *Goulburn South Caravan Park* (☎ 4821 3233), on the old highway south of town, has sites for $11 and cabins from $26 for two.

Hotels & Motels A number of pubs on Sloane St (the street parallel to the railway line) have accommodation, including the *Carlton* (☎ 4821 3820) with rooms for $30/35 and the *Coolavin* (☎ 4821 2498) with rooms for $20/30. The *Exchange Hotel* (☎ 4821 1566), at 9 Bradley St, charges $28/46/54 for a single/double/triple with breakfast.

There are plenty of motels. Some close to the city centre include the *Alpine Lodge Motel* (☎ 4821 2930), at 248 Sloane St not far from the railway station and the visitors centre (from $35/45 a single/double), and *Goulburn Central Motor Lodge* (☎ 4821 1655) on the corner of Auburn and Verner Sts ($45/55).

Other Accommodation The rustic *Old Goulburn Brewery* (☎ 4821 6071) has good accommodation in the renovated mews for $35 per person, including breakfast.

The *Yurt Farm* (☎ 4829 2114) is 20km north of Goulburn on the Grabben Gullen road (the continuation of Clinton St). It includes an activities camp for school children, with the emphasis on learning to live simply. There are many signs and notices around the 'yurt village', but almost none of them say 'Do Not...'. Like-minded travellers are welcome to stay in the yurt village for $10 a night if there's room; if not, you can stay in the farmhouse for $10 and do a few hours' work in exchange for meals. You'll need to have a sleeping-bag. It's interesting, friendly and a great place to stay. Phone first to see if there's room. If you ring a few days in advance they might be able to arrange a lift out from Goulburn or even from Sydney.

Ask at the visitors centre about farmstays in the area.

Places to Eat

As a legacy of the days when the Hume Highway ran through town, there are several cafes on Auburn St. The *Paragon Cafe* opposite the post office is the most impressive. It's licensed and has a large menu, including seafood from $8.50 and pasta dishes for $7. *Coolavin Hotel* is a pub with a reasonably priced bistro.

The Big Merino is at a service station complex which includes the bland but good (for a truck-stop cafe) *Billabong Restaurant*, where fish & chips are $5.50.

Stonegate Restaurant (☎ 4821 4833), at 19 Market St, is on the ground floor of the Goulburn Club, across Belmore Park from the courthouse. The small menu changes often and emphasises fresh local produce, and it's licensed. Gaspacho is $6.50 and chicken, ham and egg pie is $15.50.

Out at the *Old Goulburn Brewery* you can have a three-course dinner for around $35.

Getting There & Away

Bus Buses travelling the Hume Highway between Sydney and Melbourne stop in Goulburn. Some stop outside the Big Merino, others outside the Paragon Cafe. The visitors centre takes bus bookings.

Train Trains between Sydney and Melbourne stop here daily. The Countrylink Travel Centre (☎ 4827 1485), at the railway station, is open weekdays from 7.15 am to 5

pm and on weekends from 6.15 to 11 am and 12.10 to 3.15 pm.

Car & Motorcycle The Hume Highway runs north-east to Mittagong and west to Yass. The Federal Highway to Canberra branches off the Hume about 10km west of Goulburn. Smaller roads run south to Braidwood, south-east to Bungonia SRA and north into the country around Crookwell (see the Central West chapter). The Wombeyan Caves (see the Around Sydney chapter) are 60km north of Goulburn, via Taralga.

YASS

The Ngunawal people owned the area when Europeans arrived in the 1820s. Among the first to pass through were the explorers Hume and Hovell. Graziers soon followed and, by the time Hume returned to settle in the area in 1830, a town was growing on the banks of the Yass River. Yass was considered as a site for the national capital but was passed over and remains a busy rural centre. Some of the finest wool in the world is grown on the sheep in the surrounding paddocks.

The town is now bypassed by the Hume Highway and the main street, Comur St, has been spruced up, shops have replaced their long-lost verandahs and applied liberal coats of paint in 'heritage' colours.

Yass has a fearsome reputation as a place for stranding hitch-hikers midway between Sydney and Melbourne. It always seems to be cold, wet and dark when you're dropped here.

Yass Tourist Information Centre (☎ 6226 2557), in Coronation Park on Comur St on the Sydney side of town, is open daily from 9 am to 5 pm.

Things to See

The **Yass Railway Museum** (☎ 6226 2169), on Lead St off Comur St, tells the story of Yass' trains and trams. It's open Sunday from noon to 4 pm; entry is $2 (children $1).

Next to the information centre, the **Hamilton Hume Museum** (☎ 6226 2557) has a model reconstruction of the town in the 1890s. It is open on weekends from 10 am to

SOUTH-EAST

4 pm; entry is $4 (children $2). Hume's house, **Cooma Cottage** (☎ 6226 1470), is off the highway across from the Barton Highway turn-off on the Sydney side of Yass. The original timber cottage was built in 1835 and other buildings here date from later in the 19th century. The National Trust has restored the buildings and you can visit Wednesday to Monday from 10 am to 4 pm.

The Sheep's Back (☎ 6226 3072) is an art and craft gallery in the impressive old State Bank building on Comur St. It's open daily.

Places to Stay

Camping *Yass Caravan Park* (☎ 6226 1173) takes up one corner of pretty Victoria Park, on the Gundagai (and Melbourne) side of town. There are sites for $10 and cabins with en suites for $40.

Hotels & Motels Several hotels on Comur St have accommodation. The *Australian Hotel* (☎ 6226 1744), at No 180, has motel-style rooms for $35/40.

Most motels are pricey, but the completion of the highway bypass has kept rates stable. The *Hamilton Hume* (☎ 6226 1722), on the old highway south of the centre, has singles/doubles for $40/48 and a licensed restaurant. The *Thunderbird* (☎ 6226 1158), Comur St, has rooms for $58/65.

Getting There & Away

Bus Long-distance buses heading to Melbourne stop near the information centre; heading to Sydney they stop at the NRMA garage across the road.

Transborder Buses (☎ 6226 1378) has several daily services between Yass and Canberra ($10). They leave from Rossi St, the first cross street on the town side of the river.

Train Trains between Sydney and Melbourne stop at Yass Junction, 2km north of town.

Car & Motorcycle The Hume Highway runs east to Goulburn and south-west to Gundagai. The Barton Highway, branching

off the Hume 4km on the Sydney side of Yass, runs to Canberra. Smaller roads run south to Wee Jasper and on to Tumut (after rain, ask advice before attempting this section). Other small roads run north-east into the country around Crookwell – see the Central West chapter.

AROUND YASS
Burrinjuck SRA

Burrinjuck Dam, about 57km south-west of Yass, supplies water to the Murrumbidgee Irrigation Area and its long arms wind among steep valleys. It's popular for watersports, including water skiing and fishing, and there's wildlife in the surrounding bush. There are cruises on the dam on the *Lady BJ* (☎ 6227 7270). Several well-equipped caravan parks are by the lake, including *Lake Burrinjuck Leisure Resort* (☎ 6227 7271) with sites for $10 and cabins with en suites for $50; you can also hire boats. The Hume & Hovell Walking Track passes the south-eastern end of the dam and offers simpler camping at *Careys Reserve* (☎ 6227 9626) near Wee Jasper.

Wee Jasper

About 60km south-west of Yass, Wee Jasper is a small village in a beautiful valley. You can join the **Hume & Hovell Walking Track** here and there are limestone caves to visit on weekend afternoons. There's a store and a pub and fuel is available.

There's bush camping at five reserves in the area which have been developed by the DCLM; for information call the ranger on (☎ 6227 9626). In old shearers' quarters, *Wee Jasper Station* (☎ 6227 9642) has shared accommodation geared to groups, but might have room for individuals.

The road from Yass has a 10km unsealed section and you should check conditions after rain. Continuing south-west to Tumut the road deteriorates for the climb out of the valley, but it's OK when dry.

Wineries

Around **Murrumbateman**, on the Barton Highway south-east toward Canberra, you'll find a number of cool-climate wineries. Most are open for sales and tastings on weekends and some during the week. Ask at the Yass information centre for directions.

GUNDAGAI

Gundagai (population 2400), on the Murrumbidgee River 398km from Sydney, is one of the more interesting small towns along the Hume.

Information

The tourist office (☎ 6944 1341), on Sheridan St (the main street) a little before the shopping centre, is open Monday to Friday from 8 am to 5 pm, and on weekends from 9 am to noon and from 1 to 5 pm.

Things to See

The long, wooden **Prince Alfred Bridge** (closed to traffic, but you can walk it) crosses the flood plain of the Murrumbidgee River.

It's a reminder that in 1852 Gundagai suffered Australia's worst flood disaster; 78 deaths were recorded, but probably over 100 people drowned. There's a disused railway bridge (built 1901) here too.

Goldrushes and bushrangers were part of Gundagai's colourful early history and the notorious Captain Moonlight was tried in Gundagai's 1859 **courthouse**.

Gundagai Historical Museum (☎ 6944 1995), on Homer St, is in a modern building with an impressive old sandstone portico. It's open Monday to Saturday from 9 am to 2 pm; admission is $3 ($1 children). Other places of interest include the **Gabriel Gallery** (☎ 6944 1722) of historic photos, on Sheridan St next to the Westpac Bank, and, at the tourist office, **Rusconi's Marble Masterpiece**, a 21,000-piece cathedral model. Is it art? Is it lunacy? Is it worth the $1 entry fee? Probably. You at least get to hear a snatch of *Along the Road to Gundagai*. It was Frank

---

The Dog on the Tuckerbox

Gundagai features in a number of famous songs, including *Along the Road to Gundagai*, *My Mabel Waits for Me* and *When a Boy from Alabama Meets a Girl from Gundagai*. Its most famous monument is eight km east of town just off the Hume Highway. There, still sitting on his tuckerbox, is the Dog on the Tuckerbox memorial (made by Frank Rusconi). It's a sculpture of the dog who in a 19th-century bush ballad (and a more recent, perhaps even better known, poem by Jack Moses) refused to help its master get his bullock team out of a bog. The original poem goes:

As I was coming down Conroys Gap
I heard a maiden cry,
'There goes Bill the bullocky,
He's bound for Gundagai.
A better poor old bastard
Never earned an honest crust,
A better poor old bugger
Never drug a whip through dust'.

His team got bogged at Five Mile Creek,
Bill lashed and swore and cried,
'If Nobby don't get me out of this
I'll tattoo his bloody hide'.

But Nobby strained and broke his yoke
And poked out the leader's eye,
Then the dog sat on the tuckerbox
Five miles from Gundagai.

A popular tale has it that the dog was even less helpful because in the original version it apparently shat, rather than sat, on the tuckerbox! ∎

Rusconi who made the Dog on the Tucker-box memorial.

Places to Stay

Camping *Gundagai River Caravan Park* (☎ 6944 1702) is by the river near the south end of the Prince Alfred Bridge (take Homer St from town), with sites for $8. In town, *Gundagai Caravan Village* (☎ 6944 1057), on Junee Rd, has sites for $12 and on-site vans for $29.

Hotels & Motels On Sheridan St the *Criterion Hotel* (☎ 6944 1048) and the *Royal Hotel* (☎ 6944 1024) have accommodation for $20/35 a single/double. Motels include the *Gundagai* (☎ 6944 1066) on Sheridan St (from $42/50) and the *Poets Recall* (☎ 6944 1777) on the corner of Punch and West Sts (for $47/57).

Places to Eat

The 1902 *Niagara Cafe* has an illustrious history (prime minister John Curtin once visited) and is something of a gem among country town cafes, although the menu doesn't differ much from standard snacks and grills. Sandwiches are $2 and steak meals $10.50.

One Chinese place on Sheridan St is the *Chan Kong*, while the pubs have counter meals. Hamburger and chips at the *Criterion Hotel* cost $5.

Getting There & Away

The tourist office sells bus tickets for the services which stop outside, including those running on the Hume Highway between Sydney and Melbourne. Countrylink runs north to Cootamundra and south to Tumut and Tumbarumba. V/Line buses stop here between Melbourne and Canberra.

HOLBROOK & AROUND

This small town (population 1420) is worth a look around and it's the best place to turn off the highway for a drive through Morgan Country to the west (see the Riverina chapter). To the east a road runs through the pretty Wontagong Valley and past a track-head of the **Hume & Hovell Walking Track** at Lankey's Creek (a nice picnic spot), to Jingellic and then on to Tumbarumba or Khancoban – the gateway towns for the mountains.

Holbrook's good **Woolpack Inn Museum** (☎ 6036 2131), on Albury St (the name of the highway in town), is open daily from 9.30 am to 4.30 pm; admission is $3 ($1 children, $1.50 students). The museum is also the information centre for the area. There's an impressive dining room which seats 16, and you can book five-course meals including wine served by people in period costume. If there are 16 of you it costs about $30 a head.

Near the museum is a short walking track, the **Ian Geddes Bushwalk**, along the banks of Ten Mile Creek, which is a nice break from the rigours of the Hume.

Kincardin Ostriches (☎ 6023 2463), north of town along Bath St, is an ostrich

---

Holbrook & Submarines

The town, founded in 1858, was called Germanton until WWI, when it was thought politic to display some patriotism.

British naval commander, Douglas Holbrook, and his crew earned the first Victoria Crosses (VCs) of the war when their submarine sank a Turkish ship near the Dardanelles. Germanton decided to adopt Holbrook's name. A 9m model of the vessel was acquired and is displayed in town. The town forged enduring links with the Australian navy's submarine corps and Holbrook's wife, who has been over from Britain a number of times. The navy has donated to the town a decommissioned submarine, the top part of which is on display near the model. Occasional visits by official parties of sailors have seen some riotous times in the pubs.

All this in a town more than 250km from the sea! ■

farm offering guided tours (by appointment) for $4.50 (children $2).

Places to Stay & Eat

There are a couple of pubs, including the *Holbrook Hotel* (☎ 6036 2099) with single/doubles for $20/30. The *Jolly Swagman Leisure Inn* (☎ 6036 3131) is a motel with rooms for $60, including breakfast, and has its own squash court. Several coffee shops line Albury St, including the *Holbrook Bakery*, and they are open daily. The pubs have counter meals from $5 and the motels have licensed bistros. There are also meals at the *Returned Servicemen's Club* in Bowler St.

In the surrounding area are several farms with accommodation. *Glenfalloch* (☎ 6036 7203) – about 9km east of the Hume, down a signposted turn-off 19km north of Holbrook – is a long-established sheep station. It's a beautiful place with big elms and 200 hectares of bush, through which there are walking trails. The accommodation is in bunkrooms ($10 per person) and there's a good kitchen and common room. You're advised to book ahead. Other rural accommodation includes *Giles Creek* (☎ 6036 8140) and *Oxton* (☎ 6036 4125).

Getting There & Away

V/Line coaches between Canberra and Wodonga stop outside the Westpac Bank on Albury St. If you're heading to Jingellic you might be able to get a lift in the mail car, which runs daily. Ask at the post office.

ALBURY

Albury (population 42,500) is on the Murray River, just below the big Hume Weir. The city makes a good base for trips into a wide variety of country: downstream to the Riverina and the Victorian wineries around Rutherglen; upstream to the Snowy Mountains; and across to the Victorian high country.

In summer bring the insect repellent as there are lots of mosquitoes.

History

Aboriginal tribes once gathered near Albury to plan their annual expeditions into the mountains to gather Bogong moths. Europeans were attracted to the area because the Murray was fordable here. The explorers Hume and Hovell were the first Europeans to cross the river, which they named the Hume. Well, *Hume* named it the Hume – Hovell probably disagreed with such presumption. He contented himself with carving his name into a tree on the riverbank and a plaque marks his tree which still stands in Noreuil Park. The river was renamed by Charles Sturt when he explored the area further downstream.

A town grew up and became an important stop-over on the route between Sydney and Melbourne (and remains so today). In the 1850s paddle-steamers began carrying the area's wool clip down to South Australia.

Orientation & Information

The long Lincoln Causeway over the Murray's flood plain links Albury with Wodonga, its large twin on the Victorian side of the river. Downtown Albury consists of the blocks bounded by Wodonga Place, Swift St, Young St and Hume St. Dean St, where you'll find the post office, is the main shopping street. From the north, the Hume Highway runs down Young St, turns onto Hume St then onto Wodonga Place which runs south onto the Lincoln Causeway.

The large Gateway Information Centre (☎ 6041 3875), with information on both NSW and Victoria, is on the highway in Wodonga. It's open daily 9 am to 5 pm. Tourist information is broadcast on 88 FM.

The post office, 570 Dean St, opens Monday to Friday 9 am to 5 pm.

Work Some seasonal fruit-picking is available in the area; see the CES (☎ 6021 3400) at 488 Swift St. Albury Backpackers hostel can also help you find work.

Things to See & Do

The **Albury Regional Museum** (☎ 6021 4550), on Wodonga Place in Noreuil Park, is

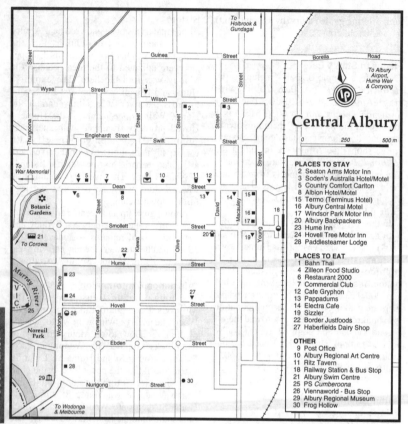

Central Albury

0   250   500 m

PLACES TO STAY
2 Seaton Arms Motor Inn
3 Soden's Australia Hotel/Motel
5 Country Comfort Carlton
8 Albion Hotel/Motel
15 Termo (Terminus Hotel)
16 Albury Central Motel
17 Windsor Park Motor Inn
20 Albury Backpackers
23 Hume Inn
24 Hovell Tree Motor Inn
28 Paddlesteamer Lodge

PLACES TO EAT
1 Bahn Thai
4 Zilleon Food Studio
6 Restaurant 2000
7 Commercial Club
12 Cafe Gryphon
13 Pappadums
14 Electra Cafe
19 Sizzler
22 Border Justfoods
27 Haberfields Dairy Shop

OTHER
9 Post Office
10 Albury Regional Art Centre
11 Ritz Tavern
18 Railway Station & Bus Stop
21 Albury Swim Centre
25 PS Cumberoona
26 Viennaworld - Bus Stop
29 Albury Regional Museum
30 Frog Hollow

open daily from 10.30 am to 4.30 pm and contains material on migration, transport and Aboriginal culture. Admission is free.

Albury Regional Art Centre (☎ 6023 8187), at 546 Dean St, has a good collection of Australian paintings, with works by Russell Drysdale and Fred Williams, and contemporary photography. The centre is open Monday to Friday from 10.30 am to 5 pm and weekends until 4 pm. Admission is free.

The **Botanic Gardens**, beside the north end of Wodonga Place, are old, formal and beautiful.

The steamboat *Cumberoona* (☎ 6021 1113), moored on the river behind Noreuil Park, isn't the original boat, which lies at the bottom of the Darling River. It's a replica built as a community project to celebrate Australia's Bicentenary. It runs September to March, when its relatively deep draught can find enough water, and costs $8 (children $4.50) for one hour.

In summer there's **river swimming** from Noreuil Park behind the Albury Regional Museum. Albury Backpackers (see Places to Stay) has popular, two-day canoe trips on the Murray River for $35.

Frog Hollow (☎ 6041 1117), at the east end of Nurigong St, is an amusement park with a maze, lawn snooker (based on croquet), mini golf and sometimes entertainment in the Courtyard Theatre. Snacks are available. It's open Wednesday to Monday from 9 am to 6 pm, or 9 pm during summer school holidays. Admission to the maze is $3 (children $2), to the golf is $4; a combined ticket is $6 (children $5).

The **Nail Can Hill Walking Track** rambles over the steep, bush-covered ridges on the eastern side of town. There are sometimes views across to the Victorian alps. You can start from Noreuil Park or head up Dean St to the war memorial and pick up the trail there. The information centre has a map.

You can take a **scenic flight** from the Air Centre (☎ 6021 2929) at Albury Airport from $45 for 20 minutes; the fee is for up to three passengers. Zauril Aviation (☎ 6040 4950), also at the airport, has balloon flights along the Riverina.

In 1934 the citizens of Albury turned out to light the runway with their car headlights so a lost plane taking part in an air race from London to Sydney could land.

Organised Tours

Mylon Motorways (☎ 6056 3100), at 153 High St in Wodonga, has a number of day tours in and around Albury; some go south to the historic areas of the Victorian high country. It has a two-hour tour of Albury for $19.50 or a five-hour one for $22.50.

Places to Stay

Accommodation Albury Wodonga (☎ 1800 806 939) books most places to stay.

Camping The closest is *Albury Central Caravan Park* (☎ 6021 8420), a couple of kilometres north of the centre on North St. It has tent sites for $10 and cabins from $38. There are a few other caravan parks on the highway further north.

Hostels *Albury Backpackers* (☎ 6041 1822), at 459 David St, is a good backpacker hostel with dorm beds at $14 for the first

night ($13 thereafter) and doubles for $30; rates include breakfast. This is a friendly place which takes care of its guests. It hires out bikes, organises adventure activities and helps you find farm work.

At the YHA *Albury Motor Village* (☎ 6040 2999), at 372 Wagga Rd (Hume Highway), about 4.5km north of the centre, a dorm bed costs $14.

Hotels *Soden's Australia Hotel* (☎ 6021 2400), on the corner of Wilson and David Sts, has some interesting leadlighting on its verandah. Pub rooms go for $22/36 single/double and claustrophobia-inducing motel-style units cost $38/45. The *Termo* (☎ 6024 1777), the Terminus Hotel on the corner of Young and Dean Sts, has rooms for $30/40. The *Albion Hotel/Motel* (☎ 6021 3377), at 593 Dean St, has pub rooms for $25/38.

Motels With 40 motels, Albury isn't short of rooms. Finding one which costs less than $60/70 isn't easy and you might have to head out to the northern suburb of Lavington, where there's a string of them along the highway. There are other motels across the border in Wodonga. However, when things are slow, many offer special rates.

Some cheaper, central motels include the *Albion Hotel/Motel* (☎ 6021 3377), at 593 Dean St at $38/48 a single/double; the *Windsor Park Motor Inn* (☎ 6021 8800) at 424 Smollett St near the railway station, with rooms for $52; and the *Hume Inn* (☎ 6021 2733) at 406 Wodonga Place for $65.

The *Seaton Arms Motor Inn* (☎ 6021 5999), on the corner of Olive and Wilson Sts, has good ground-floor rooms and more average upper-storey rooms for $66/75.

Top places to stay include the *Country Comfort Carlton* (☎ 6021 5366), the tall semicircular landmark on the corner of Dean and Elizabeth Sts, from $90 a single or double. *Paddlesteamer Lodge* (☎ 6041 1711), for $79, and *Hovell Tree Motor Inn* (☎ 6041 2666), for $109, are both on Wodonga Place near the Albury Regional Museum.

SOUTH-EAST

Places to Eat

Dean St is a long strip of takeaways, cafes and restaurants, while many pubs have counter meals for about $3 to $7.

Cafe Gryphon does good coffee and serves light meals for around $10 until late. *Electra Cafe*, on the corner of Dean and Macauley Sts, is a trendy place with a varied menu; prawn laksa is $13.50.

The large *Restaurant 2000*, at 639 Dean St, has all-you-can-eat smorgasbords daily for $7.90 at lunch and $12.50 at dinner. Similar is *Sizzler*, part of the 'family restaurant' chain on the corner of Young and Smollett Sts, with lunch specials for $5. The *Commercial Club*, at 618 Dean St, has fairly stiff dress regulations, but also a reputation for good food. As well as the dining room, where most mains are $15 to $18, there's a cheaper bistro where a mixed grill is $10.

Pappadums, at No 465, is good for Indian food; mains are $13 to $14. Next to the Country Comfort Carlton, the modern *Zilleon Food Studio*, is a restaurant and bar serving Atlantic salmon or roast lamb for $20. *Bahn Thai*, at 592 Kiewa St in a beautiful Victorian house, is a good Thai restaurant open nightly.

Haberfields is a large dairy which manufactures an interesting range of cheeses. You can buy them at *Haberfields Dairy Shop* on Hovell St, between David and Olive Sts. You might encounter some oddities there, as the shop is used to test customer reaction to new products. Organic produce is sold from *Border Justfoods* next to the big Barbecues Galore store on Hume St.

Entertainment

Albury's nightlife is mainly in pubs and clubs. Check the local paper for details. The *Termo* (the Terminus Hotel), on the corner of Young and Dean Sts, has bands (sometimes quite big acts) mainly on weekends. The *Ritz Tavern*, at 480 Dean St, has a nightclub on weekends. *Soden's* is a popular watering hole with young people.

The *Commercial Club*, on Dean St, has a bar and a large area with poker machines.

If you have a chance to see the *Flying Fruit-Fly Circus*, a wonderful project teaching circus skills to local kids, take it. Despite the turnover of performers (members hand in their leotards when they leave school), the circus is excellent and performs around the country and overseas.

Getting There & Away

Air Ansett Express (☎ 131300), Kendell (☎ 6922 0100) and Hazelton (☎ 131713) all fly from Albury to Sydney, Melbourne and Wagga Wagga. Air Facilities (☎ 6041 1210) flies daily to Canberra.

Splitters Creek Airlines (☎ 6021 1136) has suspended flights in historic DC3 planes to Mungo National Park because it has no operational aircraft, but plans to start them again as soon as it does have one.

Bus Long-distance lines running on the Hume between Sydney and Melbourne stop at the railway station. Most also stop at Viennaworld (a service station/diner) on the highway on the corner of Hovell St, across from Noreuil Park. You can book buses at the Countrylink Travel Centre (☎ 6041 9555) at the railway station; the centre is open weekdays from 8.30 am to 5 pm and weekends from 9.30 am to 4.30 pm.

Countrylink runs to Echuca, on the Murray River in Victoria, via several towns in the southern Riverina. The one-way fare to Canberra is $25. V/Line runs to Mildura ($19.10) along the Murray.

Mylon Motorways (☎ 6056 3100) has a daylight service to Adelaide, which goes via Bendigo and western Victoria.

Train XPTs running between Sydney and Melbourne stop here. If you're travelling between the two capital cities, it's much cheaper to stop over in Albury on a through ticket than to buy two separate tickets. From Albury the one-way fare to Melbourne is $36.40 and to Sydney it's $70.

AROUND ALBURY

See the Riverina chapter for the interesting towns in Morgan Country, not far north of Albury.

Ettamogah Wildlife Sanctuary, 11km north on the Hume Highway is open daily from 9 am to late ($5, children $2.50) and has a collection of Aussie fauna. Most animals arrive sick or injured, so this is a genuine sanctuary. Choice's tourist information centre (☎ 6040 2114, 1800 640 699) is also here.

About 4km north, the grotesque **Ettamogah Pub** looms up near the highway. It's a real-life recreation of a famous Aussie cartoon pub and proof that life (of a sort) follows art, not vice versa. **Ettamogah Winery** is over 100 years old; it was formerly Cooper's Winery, but has been taken over by its tacky neighbour.

About 15km further north is **Bowna**, a town that has shrunk to a couple of buildings, including Jeff Leury's boomerang factory (☎ 6002 3240) – and the boomerangs fly well. At Bowna there's a turn-off to the *Great Aussie Camping Resort* (☎ 6020 3236) on the banks of the Hume Reservoir. This is a well-equipped place with fairly pricey sites ($14), on-site tents ($34), on-site vans ($41) and rather elaborate cabins ($71). This road leads to **Wymah**, which is also accessible by vehicle ferry from the Murray Valley Highway on the other side of the river. See the West of the Snowies section earlier in this chapter for information on this route to the snowfields.

SOUTH-EAST

The South Coast

Although it doesn't attract anywhere near as much attention as the north coast, the south coast is well worth visiting – partly for that reason and partly for the excellent beaches.

The Princes Highway runs along the south coast from Sydney to the Victorian border and beyond. Although this is a longer, slower route between Sydney and Melbourne than the Hume Highway, it's infinitely more interesting.

This chapter covers the coast from Kiama down to the Victorian border. The coast between Sydney and Wollongong is covered in the Around Sydney chapter.

Geography & Climate

Like the north coast, this area is a coastal strip of good beaches backed by the mountains of the Great Dividing Range. South of Nowra the sandstone of the Sydney area gives way to granite and good soils, and the forests start to soar.

The south coast's climate is pretty good for most of the year – Batemans Bay is on the equivalent latitude to the French Riviera. You're unlikely to want to swim in winter, but summers are as hot as on the north coast and winter has its share of pleasant days.

Getting There & Around

Bus Greyhound Pioneer travels along the Princes Highway daily between Sydney and Melbourne. Typical fares from Sydney include Batemans Bay $34, Narooma $42 and Bega $49. Greyhound also has a Princes Pass ($86), that is valid for six months and which allows you to stop off anywhere along the highway between Sydney and Melbourne.

A local company, Pioneer Motor Service, offers more comprehensive services between Eden and Sydney and its sector fares are cheaper. The company's head office (☎ 4421 7722) is in Nowra and most towns along the south coast have ticket agents.

Various companies have services running inland to Mittagong, Canberra, Cooma and Bombala.

Car & Motorcycle The Princes Highway starts at Sydney's George St and continues all the way to Adelaide via Melbourne. It's known as the coastal route, but don't expect too many ocean views (although there are some beauties); most of the way the highway runs a little way inland. All the way along this route there are turn-offs to some interesting places, both on the coast and up in the Great Dividing Range where there's an almost unbroken chain of superb national parks and state forests.

For more information on routes from the coast up to the Snowy Mountains and the Monaro tablelands, see the South-East chapter.

Kiama to Ulladulla

Shoalhaven is a large municipality stretching from north of Nowra almost as far south as Batemans Bay. It takes in some great beaches, state forests and, in the ranges to the west, the big Morton National Park (see the Around Sydney chapter). The Shoalhaven River, which winds through the area, was named by explorer George Bass in 1797 when his boat encountered shoals at the river-mouth.

This is a popular family holiday destination. In fact, in terms of beds and caravan park sites occupied, it's the most popular municipality in the state. There's also a lot of new residential development. However, the area isn't yet as crowded as parts of the north coast.

There are regional tourist information centres in Bomaderry (across the Shoalhaven River north of Nowra) and Ulladulla. There's also a 24-hour toll-free information phone number (☎ 1800 024 261).

Take care driving through this area, as the narrow highway is crowded and there are lots of unexpected turn-offs to quite large residential areas.

If you come across sick or injured native animals, contact the Native Animal Network Association (NANA; ☎ 4443 5110).

KIAMA

Kiama (population 11,000) is a pretty town with some old buildings and a sense of community. The Kiama Area Visitors Centre (☎ 4232 3322), on Blowhole Point, is open daily from 9 am to 5 pm. It's near the town's major attraction, the **Blowhole**, which has drawn visitors for a century and is now floodlit at night. Beside the visitors centre is the **Pilot's Cottage Museum**, open Friday to Monday from 11 am to 2 pm; admission is $2 ($1 children).

Inland from Kiama, the old village of **Jamberoo** is near the eastern edge of **Budderoo National Park** (☎ 4423 9800) where the **Minnamurra Rainforest Park**

(☎ 4236 0469) has a visitor centre and a 1.6km elevated boardwalk through the rainforest. Admission is $7.50 per car.

Places to Stay
Blowhole Point Caravan Park (☎ 4232 2707) is terrific if it's not too windy. It has sites from $11, on-site vans for $35. Several pubs have accommodation, including the basic *Grand Hotel* (☎ 4232 1037) on the corner of Manning and Bong Bong Sts with rooms for $25/35. The *Kiama Inn Hotel* (☎ 4232 1166), 50 Terralong St, has the same rates.

Near the Grand and the surf beach is *The Pines* motel (☎ 4232 1000), 10 Bong Bong St, with colour TV, phone, bathroom etc and rooms for $49.

Gerringong, 10km south of Kiama and also on the railway line, isn't as attractive as Kiama but it does have *Nestor House* (☎ 4234 1249), an associate YHA hostel. It's on Fern St, a five-minute walk up the hill from Werri Beach. Beds are $13 for YHA members.

Getting There & Away
Train Frequent CityRail trains run north to Wollongong and Sydney ($10.60) and south to Gerringong and Bomaderry/Nowra.

Bus Long-distance buses stop in Kiama (but only if there's a booking) outside the Group Seven Leagues Club on Terralong St, the main street.

Car & Motorcycle The Princes Highway runs north to Wollongong and south to Berry. Smaller roads run west to Jamberoo and through Budderoo National Park to the Illawarra Highway near Robertson.

BERRY
Inland and about 20km north of Nowra is the pretty little town of Berry. Founded in the 1820s, it remained a private town on the Coolangatta estate (see Around Nowra) until 1912. Berry's short main street is worth a stroll for its National Trust-classified buildings and interesting shops.

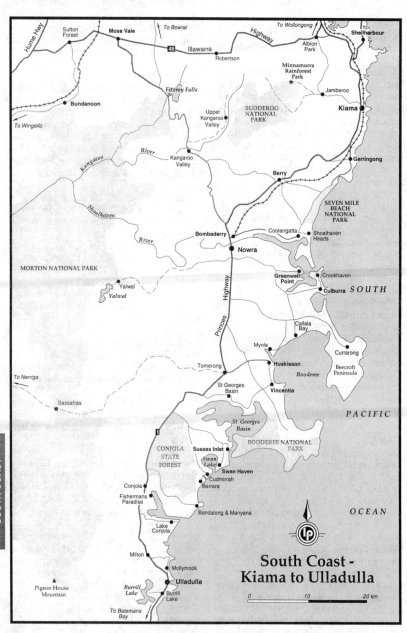

SOUTH COAST

South Coast -
Kiama to Ulladulla

Pottering Around (☎ 4464 2177) in the Berry Stores complex on the main street has some tourist information.

Berry Stores, a large old building, contains several craft shops. The nearby **museum** is in an interesting old building but it's only open Saturday from 11 am to 2 pm, Sunday to 3 pm, and holidays. Among the several **antiques shops**, Berry Antiques stands out for its attractive shopfront and its fascinating stock: largely old machinery and scientific instruments.

The popular **Berry Country Fair** is held on the first Sunday of the month at the showgrounds.

Off the highway south of Berry is **Jasper Valley Winery** (☎ 4464 1596), open Monday to Saturday for tastings and lunches.

Places to Stay

The *Hotel Berry* (☎ 4464 1011) is a rarity – a country pub that caters to weekending city-slickers without totally losing its status as a local watering hole. This has been achieved largely by sensible management, by undertaking quality renovations and by providing a coffee shop and restaurant, which gives patrons an alternative to a bar-room atmosphere. Accommodation costs $40/50, with weekend packages available. You'll probably have to book on weekends. The rooms are standard pub bedrooms, but large and well presented. Why can't more pubs be like this?

The excellent *Bunyip Inn Guesthouse* (☎ 4464 2064) is next to the hotel and in one of the town's more impressive buildings, an old bank. It has 10 rooms from $70/100 only some of which have attached bathrooms.

The *Great Southern Hotel* (☎ 4464 1009), a new place built in an old style, has motel units for $30/50, more on weekends.

Places to Eat

On the main street, next to Berry Antiques, *For Love of Country* is a simply decorated restaurant serving interesting Italian-inspired and other dishes, including game,

from around $13 to $21. It's open for dinner Tuesday to Sunday.

There are several cafes, including the *Postmasters Coffee Shop*, which has an outdoor seating area. It is next to the museum. On the other side of the museum, inside the Berry Community Activities Centre, is *Geoff's Gallery Cafe*, with good coffee and snacks for around $5. The coffee shop at the *Hotel Berry* serves light meals, and for $14 you can get a huge breakfast.

Getting There & Away

The Princes Highway runs north-east to Kiama, south-west to Bomaderry/Nowra. The main road to Kangaroo Valley and to Mittagong leaves the highway south of Berry, but there's also a scenic route to Kangaroo Valley from Berry via the hamlets of Woodhill and Wattamolla.

NOWRA

The largest town in the Shoalhaven area (population 22,000), Nowra is a centre for the area's dairy farms and its increasing tourism and retirement development.

Orientation & Information

Central Nowra is south of the Shoalhaven River and west of the highway. The main shopping streets are Kinghorne and Junction Sts. Junction St continues west up the hill to the showgrounds, which you enter through impressive memorial gates.

The useful Shoalhaven Tourist Centre (☎ 4421 0778, 1800 024 261) is in Bomaderry, on the highway north of the bridge about 4km from central Nowra.

There's a NPWS office (☎ 4423 9800) at 55 Graham St.

Things to See & Do

The 6.5 hectare **Nowra Animal Park** (☎ 4421 3949), on the north bank of the Shoalhaven, upstream from Nowra, is a pleasant place to meet some Australian animals. It's open daily from 9 am to 5 pm and costs $6 ($3 children). Head north from Nowra, cross the bridge and immediately turn left, then branch left onto McMahons Rd

SOUTH COAST

at the roundabout; turn left again at Rockhill Rd. The park is about 4km from the bridge.

Shoalhaven Historical Museum (☎ 4421 2021) at the corner of Kinghorne and Plunkett Sts is open on weekends from 1 to 4 pm. **Meroogal**, on the corner of West and Worrigee Sts, is a historic house containing the artefacts accumulated by its generations of owners. It's open on Saturday from 1 to 5 pm, Sunday from 10 am to 4 pm; admission is $5 ($3 children).

Walks The tourist centre produces a handy compilation of walks in the area. The Nowra Lands Office's 5.5km **Bomaderry Creek Walking Track** runs through sandstone gorges, from a trackhead at the end of Narang Rd, off the highway about 500m north of the tourist centre. This walk can connect with **Bens Walk**, which starts at the bridge and runs along the south bank of the Shoalhaven River in Nowra and up Nowra Creek.

Cruises Shoalhaven River Tours (☎ 4423 1844), 1 Scenic Drive, on the river west of the bridge, will take you up the beautiful river for $15.

Horseriding Valhalla Trail Rides (☎ 4447 8320) near Falls Creek, 13km south of Nowra, charges $20 for an hour of horseriding, less per hour for longer rides.

Swimming Nowra is a handy centre but it isn't on the sea. The nearest beach is at Shoalhaven Heads and just north of the heads is **Seven Mile Beach National Park**. If you don't have your own transport the most accessible beach is south of Kiama, a 20-minute train trip from Bomaderry. Get off at Kiama.

Places to Stay
Camping The small *Easts Van Park The Willows* (☎ 4421 2977) is off the highway close to the bridge (and thus noisy); it has sites for $13 and on-site vans for $33. *Shoalhaven Caravan Village* (☎ 4423 0770), Terrara Rd, on the river a kilometre or so east

of the town, has a lot of permanents, but there's a good camping area. There's no shop, so buy your supplies before you come. The *Nowra Animal Park* (☎ 4421 3949) has tent sites in bushland for $9, rising to $11 at peak times.

Hostel The associate-YHA *Coach House* (☎ 4421 2084), part of Armstrong's White House at 30 Junction St, has dorm beds for $13. It also hires out bikes.

Guesthouses, Hotels & Motels *Armstrong's White House* (☎ 4421 2084), 30 Junction St is reasonably priced at $25/35. The *Empire Hotel* (☎ 4421 2433) is an ugly cream-brick building at the corner of Kinghorne and Moss North Sts with single/double rooms for $25/35.

The *City Centre Motel* (☎ 4421 3455), 16 Kinghorne St, is beginning to show its age but it's centrally located and quiet and a good deal at $40/45 (more in summer). The *George Bass Motor Inn* (☎ 4421 6388) is on leafy Bridge Rd, the northern continuation of Berry St. Rooms cost from $52/58. There are plenty of more-expensive motels.

Places to Eat
The *Wholemeal Tea & Coffee Inn* is a cosy place in an alley running into Stewart Place from Junction St near the corner of Berry St. It's open during the day on weekdays and sometimes on Thursday, Friday and Saturday evenings. You can buy snacks, Mexican and Lebanese dishes (felafels are $5.50), as well as cakes and good tea and coffee. *Ted's Milk Bar* is an old-style grills and hamburger cafe facing Stewart Place, behind Kinghorne St.

One of the best places to eat in Nowra, for snacks or meals, is *Adam & Eve's Garden of Eatin'* on the Junction St mall just east of Kinghorne St. The healthy, interesting food is mostly vegetarian, but there's meat too. It's a cafe on weekdays, with focaccia, salads, cakes and light meals, and a BYO restaurant on Thursday, Friday and Saturday nights. Lunchtime pasta with mushrooms and shallots in a cream sauce is $5.

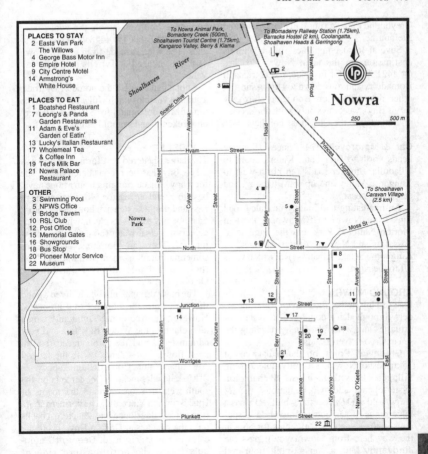

PLACES TO STAY
2 Easts Van Park
   The Willows
4 George Bass Motor Inn
8 Empire Hotel
9 City Centre Motel
14 Armstrong's
   White House

PLACES TO EAT
1 Boatshed Restaurant
7 Leong's & Panda
   Garden Restaurants
11 Adam & Eve's
   Garden of Eatin'
13 Lucky's Italian Restaurant
17 Wholemeal Tea
   & Coffee Inn
19 Ted's Milk Bar
21 Nowra Palace
   Restaurant

OTHER
3 Swimming Pool
5 NPWS Office
6 Bridge Tavern
10 RSL Club
12 Post Office
15 Memorial Gates
16 Showgrounds
18 Bus Stop
20 Pioneer Motor Service
22 Museum

To Nowra Animal Park,
Bomaderry Creek (500m),
Shoalhaven Tourist Centre (1.75km),
Kangaroo Valley, Berry & Kiama

To Bomaderry Railway Station (1.75km),
Barracks Hostel (2 km), Coolangatta,
Shoalhaven Heads & Gerringong

Nowra

0   250   500 m

To Shoalhaven
Caravan Village
(2.5 km)

Lucky's Restaurant is an Italian pasta and pizza place in the old fire station on Junction St west of Berry St.

On North St, near the intersection of Kinghorne St, there are a couple of Chinese restaurants. *Leong's* has an Australian and Chinese menu and *Panda Garden* has Singaporean and Chinese food. Both are open daily and both are licensed. The large *Nowra Palace*, on the corner of Berry and Worrigee Sts, serves Malaysian and Chinese food, with lunch specials for $5.

For meals with a view, try the upmarket *Boatshed Restaurant*, overlooking the river just next to the bridge. It has a bar and a cafe and is open daily from 11 am to 1 am.

Getting There & Away
Train The nearest station is across the river at Bomaderry (☎ 4421 2022). Frequent CityRail trains run up the coast to Sydney taking 2½ to three hours and costing $12.40 one way.

Bus Pioneer Motor Service's head office (☎ 4423 5233) is in Stewart Place; it runs services north to Sydney and south to Eden.

Greyhound Pioneer runs daily to Sydney and Melbourne.

Several local companies run to various destinations in the area. Nowra Coaches (☎ 4421 2855), for instance, meets trains in Bomaderry and runs down to Huskisson and other destinations on Booderee (formerly Jervis Bay), weekdays only, with one service on Saturday in the Christmas holidays.

Car & Motorcycle The Princes Highway heads north to Berry and Kiama, south to Ulladulla. Smaller roads run north-west to Kangaroo Valley and up to Mittagong, and east to the coast.

An interesting and mainly unsealed road runs from Nowra to Braidwood, through Morton National Park and the hamlets of Sassafras and Nerriga. At the south end of Kinghorne St take Albatross Rd, which veers off to the right.

AROUND NOWRA
East of Nowra the Shoalhaven River meanders through dairy country in a system of estuaries and wetlands, finally reaching the sea at Crookhaven Heads.

Greenwell Point, on the estuary about 15km east of Nowra, is a pretty, quiet fishing village. The village boasts a champion oyster-opener and 'world famous' fish & chips, sold at *DJ's* near the wharf. DJ's has a huge range of seafood and good daily specials such as snapper with chips for $6. On the way here from Nowra you'll pass the **Jindyandy Mill**, a convict-built flour-mill that is now a craft centre.

On the north side of the estuary is **Shoalhaven Heads**, where the river once reached the sea but is now blocked by sandbars.

Just before you get to the town of Shoalhaven Heads, which is partly a dormitory suburb of Nowra and partly a holiday resort, you pass through **Coolangatta**, the site of the earliest European settlement on the south coast. The **Coolangatta Historic Village Resort** (☎ 4448 7131) has craft shops and expensive accommodation ($78/85 single/double) in convict-built buildings. You can sample the wines from Coolangatta Estate (☎ 4448 7131) on weekends. The wine is made from grapes grown here but vintaged at Tyrrells in the Hunter Valley.

Coolangatta is also the home of **Bigfoot**, a strange vehicle which will carry you to the top of Mt Coolangatta for $10 ($5 children) on weekends and school holidays.

BOODEREE
This large, sheltered bay, formerly known as Jervis Bay, has been considered as the site for many projects, ranging from a huge naval base to a nuclear reactor. None has come to pass and despite extensive housing development the bay retains its clean, white beaches and crystal-clear water (no large rivers flow into it). There are dolphins, and whales sometimes drop in when swimming past on their annual migrations from June to October.

The bay's original inhabitants lived a good life here until the coming of Europeans. However, the Aboriginal community won a land claim in the Wreck Bay area and now administers Booderee (pronounced 'bud' – as in flower bud – 'aree') with the federal Australian Nature Conservation Agency.

Most development in Booderee is on the south-western shore, around the towns of Huskisson and Vincentia. The northern shore is much less developed and state forest backs onto the beaches at **Callala Bay**. There are caravan parks near here. **Beecroft Peninsula** forms the north-eastern side of Booderee. Most of the peninsula is navy land which is off-limits to civilians, but **Currarong**, at the end of the peninsula near Beecroft Head, is a small town with camping at *Currarong Tourist Park* (☎ 4448 3027). This area is largely cleared.

Huskisson
With much of this area turning into a vast urban sprawl, it's surprising that Huskisson, the oldest town on Booderee, remains a small fishing port (population 1000) with a sense of community.

The *Lady Denman*, a ferry dating from

1912, is the centrepiece of the **Lady Denman Heritage Complex**, by the bay on the Nowra side of Huskisson. Also here is Timbey's Aboriginal Arts & Crafts, which has work produced by the local Aboriginal community. There's also a boardwalk through wetlands. The museum in the complex is open Tuesday to Friday from 1 to 4 pm, weekends and holidays from 10 am to 4 pm; admission is $3 ($1.50 children); the rest of the complex is open daily from 9 am to 5 pm.

Cruises Dolphin Watch Cruises (☎ 4441 6311) has several cruises on offer, starting at $25 ($17.50 children) for two hours.

Diving Booderee is popular with divers and at least two places in Huskisson offer diving and courses. Pro Dive (☎ 4441 5255) 34 Owen St (the main street) charges $35 for a boat dive or $55 for two dives, plus equipment hire (about $15 for a full set). Sea Sports (☎ 4441 5598), also on Owen St, has similar rates and also runs cruises.

Places to Stay The Shoalhaven Council's *Holiday Haven Huskisson Beach Resort* (☎ 4441 5142) is a good place to stay. It's a little way out of Huskisson, on the road to Vincentia, and there are other caravan parks in the area. Huskisson has several motels including the two-storey *Huskisson Beach Motel* (☎ 4441 6387), 9 Hawke St, overlooking the beach. Room rates start at $55; it's a good idea to book on weekends.

Booderee National Park

The national park takes up the south-eastern spit of land on Booderee. It's an interesting park offering good swimming, surfing and diving on bay and ocean beaches. Much of it is heathland, with some forest, including small pockets of rainforest. It's administered by the federal government (it's in federal territory) so you won't read about it in NPWS brochures.

There's a good visitor centre (☎ 4443 0977) at the park entrance. Inside the park is the **Booderee Botanic Gardens**, open daily

from 8.30 am to 5 pm, and the **Royal Australian Naval College**, with a museum which is sometimes open to the public.

Be careful on the clifftops as apparently people fall off regularly. Cliff bottoms on the ocean side can be dangerous too – watch out for waves. After walking in the park check for ticks, which are common.

Entry to the park costs $5 per car and is valid for a week. There are campsites at Green Patch and Bristol Point and a more basic camping area at Caves Beach ($8 to $10). You have to book and sites might not be available at peak times.

BOODEREE TO ULLADULLA

Booderee's southern peninsula encircles **St George's Basin**, a large body of water which has access to the sea through narrow Sussex Inlet. The north shore of the basin has succumbed to housing developments that are reminiscent of the suburban sprawl on the Central Coast.

On the southern side of **Sussex Inlet** is a fair-sized town of the same name, in an area a little less developed than that on the northern side of the basin. You can hire houseboats at Sussex Inlet House Boats (☎ 4441 1850).

Further south is **Swan Lake**, which connects with the ocean via a narrow inlet. The small towns of **Swan Haven**, **Berrara** and **Cudmirrah** lie between the lake and the sea beaches. The beach south of Berrara is backed by the **Conjola State Forest.**

South of the state forest are **North Bendalong** and **Bendalong**, small towns with caravan parks on nice beaches, and further south is **Manyana**. These places are about 15km east of the highway and are quieter than the towns further north. There's a fair amount of bush in the area.

The next inlet and lake is pretty **Lake Conjola**, with a quiet town of holiday shacks and a couple of caravan parks; the *Lake Conjola Entrance Tourist Park* (☎ 4456 1141) is the closest to the ocean. Lake Conjola township isn't far south of Manyana but it's across the inlet, so travelling by road between the two involves a trip back to the highway and over 30km. Lake Conjola (the

SOUTH COAST

lake, not the township) extends west almost to the highway and near this end there's the holiday hamlet of **Fishermans Paradise**.

Milton, on the highway 6km north of Ulladulla, is this area's original town, built to serve the nearby farming communities. Like so many early towns in this coastal region, Milton was built several km inland – tastes have changed. *Pilgrim's Wholefood* has healthy lunches and coffee.

ULLADULLA

Ulladulla (population 10,000) isn't an especially attractive town but it has excellent beaches and is close to the Pigeon House Mountain in the far south of Morton National Park, and to Budawang National Park. It's also the largest town on the highway between Nowra and Batemans Bay and it has a good range of services and accommodation.

The town's sonorous name is perhaps a corruption of 'holey dollar', the punched-out coin that was an early Australian currency. 'Holy dollar' wouldn't be an appropriate substitute; this is still a fishing port and surfers' hangout rather than a tacky sprawl of housing estates.

Orientation & Information

Ulladulla itself is on rocky Warden Head, but a short walk north of Ulladulla harbour is Mollymook, a suburb on a lovely surf beach. A little further north is Narrawallee, another residential area with surf beaches and a quieter inlet.

Burrill Lake, a few kilometres south of Ulladulla, is a small town on the inlet to the lake of the same name. Kings Point is a residential area inland, on the lake's north shore. The lake is pretty, but there are few facilities for visitors and lots of powerboats.

Ulladulla's information centre (☎ 4455 1269, 1800 024 261), in the Civic Centre at the bottom of the main-street hill, is open weekdays from 9 am to 5 pm, weekends from 10 am to 5 pm.

Activities

Murramarang Wildtrails (☎ 4457 1421)

organises **walks** in Murramarang National Park as well as biking trips. Bike tours start at $40 for a three-hour, 15km forest loop.

The **Coomie Nulunga Cultural Trail** is a walking trail in town that has been established by the local Aboriginal Land Council (☎ 4455 5883). It begins near the Lighthouse Oval (take Deering St east of the highway) and follows the headland through native bush to the beach.

Climbing the **Pigeon House** Mountain (1400m) in the far south of Morton National Park is a popular activity. A road runs close to the summit, from where it's a walk of four hours to the top and back. The first hour's walk from the car park is a steady climb, but after that it levels out a little. The main access road to the Pigeon House leaves the highway about 8km south of Ulladulla; from the highway it's 26km to the car park. You can also get there from Milton and Termeil.

Around Ulladulla, **watersports** are popular. The Dive Shop (☎ 4455 5303), on Wason St (the street leading down to the fishing wharf), has four-hour diving trips for $45. Surfit (☎ 4455 3063), 56 Princes Highway in Milton, provides surf coaching.

Special Events

At Easter there is a Blessing of the Fleet ceremony and other non-marine celebrations such as a rodeo. In late August there's a Food & Wine Fair. In nearby Milton, the Settlers Fair is held on the first holiday Monday in early October.

Places to Stay

Camping The *Ulladulla Tourist Park* (☎ 4455 2457), one of those in the Shoalhaven Council's well-run chain, is on the headland a few blocks from the town centre (at the end of South St) but a bit of a walk from the beach. There are more caravan parks off the highway south of town.

Hostel *South Coast Backpackers* (☎ 4454 0500), 67 Princes Highway, is near the top of the hill, north of the shopping centre. Coming from the north, look for it on your right as you turn the corner just before descending the hill. It's a small, clean place with spacious five-bed dorms and all the usual facilities. Dorm beds cost $15, and there are double rooms for $32. If you're staying here the staff will take you to Murramarang National Park or the Pigeon House for $15, to Booderee for $4.50.

Motels Ulladulla has plenty of motels. *Top View Motel* (☎ 4455 1514), 72 South St, is a clean, friendly motel. Most rooms, which start at $40/48, have a small balcony with views of the bay.

Mollymook, 2km north of Ulladulla, is a nicer place to stay. Most motels are pricey during holiday periods but reasonable at other times. Less-expensive places include *Surfside* (☎ 4455 1966) on Golf Ave (the beachfront road), costing from $45/49.

Following the beachfront road north through Mollymook you rise up onto the headland and come to *Bannisters Point Lodge* (☎ 4455 3044), 191 Mitchell Parade, a motel with superb views of the coast and ocean. Rates start at $49/54. There's a licensed restaurant here.

Places to Eat

There are plenty of coffee shops and pasta places on Ulladulla's main street and in the arcades running off it. *Just Good Food*, in Rowen's Arcade towards the bottom of the hill, opposite the supermarket, has snacks, quiche ($6) and felafel ($4). *Rudolf's Pasta & Pizza*, across from the Marlin Hotel, has pizzas from $6.

The best views are at the *Harbourside Terrace* where there's a restaurant selling the catch of the day for $17.50 and other steak and seafood dishes, and a cheaper cafe. Breakfast costs about $8.50.

At the fishing wharf on Wason St you can buy fresh fish. Across the road is *Tony's Seafood Restaurant* where seafood specials go for $13. It's licensed and there are good views. Downstairs is a takeaway section selling fresh fish and chips.

For meals which are really good value you can't beat the *Milton-Ulladulla Bowling Club*, near the tourist office, where lunches cost as little as $2.

Getting There & Away

Bus Fares with Pioneer Motor Service include Sydney, $23; Nowra, $11; Merry Beach (at the north end of Murramarang National Park), $6.40; the North Durras turn-off (about 10km to Pebbly Beach in Murramarang National Park), $7.80; Batemans Bay, $8.80; and Eden, $29.40. Ticket agents are Traveland (☎ 4455 1588) on the main street and Harvey World Travel (☎ 4455 5122) in Powers Arcade.

Car & Motorcycle The Princes Highway runs north to Nowra and south to Batemans Bay, passing Murramarang National Park. The small towns at the north end of the park are reached from Termeil, on the highway 20km south of Ulladulla.

Getting Around

Bus Ulladulla Bus Lines (☎ 4455 1674) services the local area, mainly between Milton, Mollymook, Ulladulla and Burrill Lake. There are two services a day, Monday to Friday only.

BUDAWANG NATIONAL PARK

South of Morton National Park, Budawang isn't large (16,100 hectares) but it offers rugged scenery and wilderness walking. There are no roads through the park, nor are there any facilities in it. The easiest access is from the hamlet of Mongalowe, 14km east of Braidwood.

For more information contact the NPWS office (☎ 4423 9800) in Nowra.

The Far South Coast

The far south coast is the least developed stretch of coast in the state and it has some of the best beaches and forests. The population triples during holiday times, especially in the Eurobodalla area (from Batemans Bay to Narooma), and prices rise accordingly. As

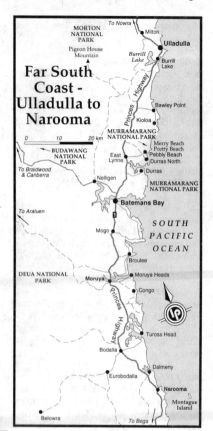

Far South Coast - Ulladulla to Narooma

To Nowra
MORTON NATIONAL PARK
Milton
Ulladulla
Pigeon House Mountain
Burrill Lake
Burrill Lake
Bawley Point
Kioloa
MURRAMARANG NATIONAL PARK
0   10   20 km
BUDAWANG NATIONAL PARK
East Lynne
Merry Beach
Pretty Beach
Pebbly Beach
Durras North
Durras
To Braidwood & Canberra
Nelligen
MURRAMARANG NATIONAL PARK
To Araluen
Batemans Bay
SOUTH PACIFIC OCEAN
Mogo
Broulee
DEUA NATIONAL PARK
Moruya
Moruya Heads
Congo
Tuross Head
Bodalla
Dalmeny
Eurobodalla
Narooma
Montague Island
Belowra
To Bega

well as the beaches and inlets, with swimming, surfing and fishing, there are good walks in the national parks.

The visitor centres in Batemans Bay and Narooma sell topographic maps and copies of Graham Barrow's book *Walking on the South Coast*, which details mainly short walks between Nowra and Eden.

MURRAMARANG NATIONAL PARK

This beautiful coastal park begins about 20km south of Ulladulla and stretches almost all the way south to Batemans Bay. The park is in two sections, with a break in the middle around Durras Lake.

The park includes some thick forest with big old trees. (There are state forests west of the park where you can see how logging has deprived them of the age and diversity of trees that the national park enjoys.)

Depot, Pebbly and Merry beaches are all popular with surfers, as is Wasp Head south of Durras.

Places to Stay

In the Park The national park's campsite (☎ 4478 6006) is at lovely Pebbly Beach. It costs $10 a double, plus the park entry fee of $7.50 per car. Tent sites are scarce during school holidays so you should book. A kiosk operates during the holidays. The kangaroos are incredibly friendly here. Don't feed them bread (it's bad for them), but unless you keep your food locked away they'll probably find it anyway. To get here, turn off the highway south of East Lynne. Caravans can't be taken on the last section of the road to Pebbly Beach.

Nearby Settlements There are small towns on the borders of the park and one or two on old leases within the park itself. If campsites in the park are booked out you could try these places.

Turn off the highway at Termeil to get to **Bawley Point** and **Kioloa**, near the north end of the park. There are caravan parks in these small towns and just south of Kioloa are caravan parks at **Merry Beach** and **Pretty Beach**, both privately run but within the boundary of the national park. They're reasonable places and the beaches are, as usual, excellent, but they lack the steep and forested slopes behind the beaches that you'll find farther south. There's a shopping centre on the road between Bawley Point and Kioloa.

Take the East Lynne turn-off from the highway to get to **Depot Beach** and **North Durras** and to the NPWS camping area at Pebbly Beach. Any of these places is worth spending time in because of the great beaches and beautiful bushland.

The basic *Moore's Caravan Park* at Depot

MARK KIRBY

MARK KIRBY

MARK KIRBY

JON MURRAY

MARK KIRBY

A	C
	D
B	E

The South Coast

A: St Georges Basin, Booderee
B: Kangaroos at Murramarang National Park
C: Fishing from Tathra wharf, Bega

D: Kianga lake, Narooma
E: Dusk on the beach, Booderee

RICHARD I'ANSON

RICHARD I'ANSON

TONY WHEELER

Australian Capital Territory
Top: War Memorial & Parliament Houses from Mt Ainslie, Canberra
Bottom Left: Parliament House & mosaic, Canberra
Bottom Right: National Gallery of Australia, Canberra

Beach (☎ 4478 6010), has tent sites for $10 and cabins for $45 a night. There's no shop but a truck selling essentials calls in most mornings.

Nearby, North Durras is on the inlet to Durras Lake. It has a small shop and several large caravan parks but little else except a superb beach. *Durras Lake North Caravan Park* (☎ 4478 6072) has a cabin or an on-site van set aside for backpackers and charges $10 a bed. Ask at the shop. The tent sites here are good, as you can camp in the bush and may meet some bandicoots.

At the south of the park (turn off the highway at Bendanderah), **Durras** is a quiet village of substantial holiday houses. The great beaches are backed by thick bush. At the south end of the town is *Murramarang Resort* (☎ 4478 6355). It's a big place with sites (from $11), on-site vans (from $34) and cabins (from $48). Prices rise considerably during holidays. It also has lots of activities and even 'floor-show' entertainment! That a complex like this, on the edge of one of the world's more beautiful national parks, should win tourism awards says something about Australian taste.

One or two km north of Durras is South Durras (yes – it's south of North Durras on the other side of Durras Lake), on a spit of land between the ocean and the lake. This is a fibro-cement town and the two caravan parks don't aspire to the heights of their competitor.

Getting There & Away
The Princes Highway runs parallel to Murramarang but it's about 10km from the highway to the beach or the small settlements in and near the park. Pioneer Motor Service runs to Merry Beach and will drop you on the highway at the North Durras turn-off. Staff at the backpacker hostel in Ulladulla will drive guests to Pebbly Beach for $15.

BATEMANS BAY
Batemans Bay (population 8300) is a fishing port which has boomed to become one of the south coast's largest holiday centres, partly because of its good beaches and beautiful

estuary and partly because it's the closest coastal town to land-locked Canberra.

Orientation & Information
Batemans Bay is on the neck of the beautiful Clyde River estuary. The estuary winds up to near Nelligen, about 10km inland on the road to Canberra. The actual bay is the flaring of the estuary as it enters the sea. Small islands, including Tollgate Island, dot the estuary mouth.

Batemans Bay township is a small, pleasant place with a mixture of tourism and commercial fishing activity. There's a long strip of tourist development merging into housing estates as you follow Beach Rd (which becomes George Bass Drive) south from the town centre through the suburbs of Batehaven, Denhams Beach and Surf Beach. Further south the development dwindles and the forest takes over. The small satellite suburb of Broulee marks the southern end of Batemans Bay's sphere of influence.

The large visitor centre (☎ 4472 6900, 1800 802 528), on the Princes Highway near the town centre, is open Monday to Saturday from 9 am to 5 pm, to 4 pm on Sunday.

Things to See & Do
Corrigans Beach is the closest beach to the town centre. South of Corrigans is a series of small beaches nibbled into the rocky shore. There are longer beaches along the coast north of the bridge, leading into Murramarang National Park.

Surfers flock to Surf Beach, Malua Bay, the small McKenzies Beach (just south of Malua) and Broulee, which has a small wave when everywhere else is flat. For the experienced, the best surfing in the area is at Pink Rocks (near Broulee) when a north swell is running, sometimes producing 6m waves.

On the north side of the estuary just across the bridge (if you're driving you'll have to keep going to the Canberra turn-off and take the first left) Oyster Shed Boat Hire (☎ 4472 6771) hires out **paddleboats** (when the tide is right) for $10 an hour and outboards from $40 for two hours. **Sailing boats** are hired out on Corrigans Beach in summer.

SOUTH COAST

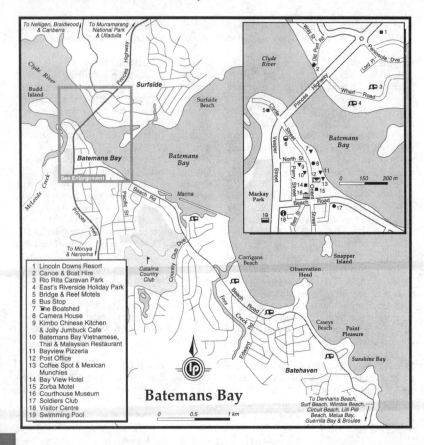

Batemans Bay

1 Lincoln Downs Resort
2 Canoe & Boat Hire
3 Rio Rita Caravan Park
4 East's Riverside Holiday Park
5 Bridge & Reef Motels
6 Bus Stop
7 The Boatshed
8 Camera House
9 Kimbo Chinese Kitchen
& Jolly Jumbuck Cafe
10 Batemans Bay Vietnamese,
Thai & Malaysian Restaurant
11 Bayview Pizzeria
12 Post Office
13 Coffee Spot & Mexican
Munchies
14 Bay View Hotel
15 Zorba Motel
16 Courthouse Museum
17 Soldiers Club
18 Visitor Centre
19 Swimming Pool

Several outfits offer **cruises** up the Clyde estuary; the visitor centre can supply you with details. Some cruises can be combined with 4WD expeditions into the bush with Tangletours (☎ 4472 5859). Some of these are good value. Tangletours (run, as you would expect, by a Mr Tangles) offers other interesting day trips. There are also sea cruises, during which you might see penguins on the islands of Tollgate Islands Nature Reserve in the bay. The visitor centre has details.

The small **Old Courthouse Museum** (☎ 4472 8993), on the corner of Orient and Beach Sts, has displays relating to local history. It's open Thursday and Saturday from 1 to 4 pm; admission is $2 ($1 children).

Birdland Animal Park (☎ 4472 5364) on Beach Rd near Batehaven is open daily from 9.30 am to 4 pm. Admission is $8 ($5 children).

The **Corn Trail** in the Buckenbowra State Forest, about 30km north-west of Bateman's Bay off Kings Highway, is a 13km walking trail down the Buckenbowra River from Clyde Mountain. Contact the visitor centre for more information.

Special Events
The Neptune Festival is held over the second weekend in November and there's a game fishing tournament in February. Up in Nelligen, a Country Music Festival twangs over the first weekend in January. The Moruya Rodeo is held on Easter Sunday and Eurobodalla Shire's agricultural show is held here on the Australia Day weekend in late January.

Places to Stay
Camping As with other accommodation, you might have to book for a minimum period or pay a surcharge for sites at peak periods. Coming from the north on the Princes Highway, turn left just before the bridge to get to the big *East's Riverside Holiday Park* (☎ 4472 4048), with sites from $14.50, and the much smaller and simpler *Rio Rita Caravan Park* (☎ 4472 5741).

Other caravan parks include *Coachhouse Tourist Van Park* (☎ 4472 4392), off Beach Rd at the beginning of Corrigans Beach. Sites cost $14 and on-site vans from $25 a double. Cabins with ensuites start at $40 a double. There's a kitchen for campers.

Hotel & Motels The *Bay View Hotel* (☎ 4472 4522), in the town centre on Orient St, has rooms for $20/30.

There are many motels. The *Bridge Motel* (☎ 4472 6344) is a good mid-range place. It's on Clyde St; turn right immediately after crossing the bridge if you're coming from the north. Off-season rates are about $50/58. Next door, the *Reef Motor Inn* (☎ 4477 6000) is a good example of an upper-range place, with a range of accommodation from $72/82; more than double that at Christmas and Easter.

Off-season prices at the resorts are worth checking out. For example, the well-equipped *Surf Beach Country Resort* (☎ 4471 1671), a little way inland from Surf Beach, has B&B for $85 a double.

Self-Catering There are many holiday apartments which do good business in summer. Out of season you might be able to rent one for less than a week. Letting agents include Real Estate Professionals (☎ 4472 4444) and David Burdett (☎ 4472 5722).

Houseboats *Bay River Houseboats* (☎ 4472 5649) on Wray St, west along the estuary on the north side, hires eight- and 10-berth houseboats. From May to August an eight-berth boat costs $500 for four nights (Monday to Friday) and $550 for the weekend. This almost doubles in December and January. Shared between a few people this could be good value and a great way to get around. *Clyde River Boat Hire* (☎ 4472 6369) also on Wray St, hires houseboats for about the same rates.

Places to Eat
The Boatshed is on the foreshore by the fishing wharf and sells seafood straight off the boats. They'll also cook you sit-down or takeaway meals; the menu depends on the catch. Whiting costs $5.

Mexican Munchies, upstairs at the back of the building south of the post office, is licensed, opens at 6 pm and has main courses from $12 to $14. The food and service are pretty good. Downstairs, on the foreshore walk, the *Coffee Spot* has outdoor tables and serves breakfast, meals (main courses around $11) and snacks. The breakfasts are a little pricey at $8.50 for bacon and eggs, but you may see a dolphin swim past while you're eating. To the north, also on the foreshore walk, is *Bayview Pizzeria*, with pasta for $7.50 as well as pizzas.

Across from the post office, the *Batemans Bay Vietnamese, Thai & Malaysian Restaurant*, a small place with a long name, has lunchtime specials at $5 and main courses for $8. It's a neat, spartan place which would look right at home on Melbourne's Victoria St strip of Vietnamese restaurants.

On North St, near the corner of Orient St, the *Jolly Jumbuck Cafe* is a little more upmarket than the name suggests. Fish and chips with salad is $8. Next door, *Kimbo Chinese Kitchen* is a small restaurant that sells mostly takeaway food; Mongolian beef is $5.50.

Taliva (☎ 4472 4278), 236 Beach Rd in Batehaven, is a highly rated French restaurant with game and seafood featuring on the menu. Most mains are $19 to $22; the garlic and chilli prawns starter is $11. Also in Batehaven, the licensed *Stockyard* is a family-oriented place with steak and salad dinners from $10, Wednesday to Monday.

Many of the motels have restaurants, including the *Reef* at the Reef Motel, with main courses from $15 to $20. *Briars Restaurant*, at the upmarket Lincoln Downs Resort north of the bridge, has a menu featuring game and terrines.

Entertainment

Beachies Nightspot on Beach Rd in Batehaven stays open late most nights in the summer, but you have to arrive by 11.45 pm, in neat clothes. The *Bowling Club*, the *Soldiers Club* and the *Catalina Country Club* have music of some sort on weekends. Check the local paper for details. *Mexican Munchies* has live guitar music some nights.

Getting There & Away

Bus Harvey World Travel (☎ 4472 5086) on Orient St handles bus bookings and has timetables in the window. The bus stop is outside the newsagent on Clyde St.

Greyhound Pioneer stops here on the run between Sydney ($34) and Melbourne ($64).

Pioneer Motor Service (☎ 4421 7722 in Nowra) runs between Eden ($24.90 from Batemans Bay) and Sydney ($29) via Batemans Bay at least daily. Some services connect with trains at Bomaderry.

Murrays (☎ 6295 3611 in Canberra) runs between Narooma ($12 from Batemans Bay) and Canberra ($21.75) at least daily. The Sapphire Coast Express (☎ 4473 5517) runs between Batemans Bay and Melbourne ($61) twice a week.

Car & Motorcycle The Princes Highway runs north to Ulladulla and south to Moruya and Narooma. You can follow the beachfront road south as far as the north shore of the

Deua (Moruya) River and rejoin the highway at Moruya. A scenic road runs inland to Nelligen, Braidwood and Canberra from the highway just north of Batemans Bay.

Getting Around

Priors Bus Service (☎ 4472 4040) runs regular but infrequent services to Moruya via Batehaven and Broulee. There are even fewer services north of the bridge, to Surfside, Longbeach and Maloney's Beach.

There is also a taxi service (☎ 4471 1444).

DEUA NATIONAL PARK

Inland from Moruya, Deua National Park (81,800 hectares) is a mountainous wilderness area with swift-running rivers (good for canoeing) and some challenging walking. There are also many caves. There are simple camping areas off the scenic road running between Araluen and Moruya and off the road between Braidwood and Numeralla, plus a couple more on tracks within the park.

See the NPWS office (☎ 4476 2888) in Narooma for more information.

BATEMANS BAY TO NAROOMA

This stretch of coast is known as the Eurobodalla Coast, a reference to the many lakes, bays and inlets along it. Eurobodalla is an Aboriginal word meaning 'place of many waters'.

Mogo

This strip of old wooden shops and houses is almost entirely devoted to Devonshire teas, crafts and antiques. Half a kilometre back from the highway is **Old Mogo Town** (☎ 4472 4040), a re-creation of a small pioneer village, open Friday, Saturday, Sunday and holidays. Admission is $6 ($3 children). Two km east off the highway from Mogo is Mogo Zoo (☎ 4474 4930), open daily from 9 am to 5 pm. Admission is $6 ($3 children). There's a fair range of animals here but some of the more exotic ones are stuffed. Two km further down this road, about halfway between Mogo and the sea, is **Mogo Goldfields** (☎ 4471 7381), another small historic park. There's also a caravan park here.

Broulee

Almost an outer suburb of Batemans Bay, Broulee (pronounced *brow*-lee) is on a good beach and there are holiday houses as well as the *Broulee Beach Van Park* (☎ 4471 62 47) with sites from $14 and cabins from $45 a double. There are several other large resort-style parks between here and Batemans Bay.

Priors buses run as far south as Broulee. See the Batemans Bay Getting Around section.

Moruya

Moruya, 25km south of Batemans Bay and about 5km inland, is on the estuary of the Deua River (also called the Moruya). This small town is more a rural service centre than a tourist haven and it's the administrative centre of Eurobodalla Shire. The river's banks turn into wetlands as it sprawls down to the sea at **Moruya Heads**, the hamlet on the south head, where there's a good surf beach and views from Taragy Point.

In town there are a couple of motels and a caravan park by the river, but you're better off going to Moruya Heads, 7km east. The large and pleasant *Dolphin Beach Caravan Park* (☎ 4474 2728) charges about $12 for tent sites and from $35 a double for on-site vans. Prices jump during the Christmas week and at Easter. Priors buses run from Batemans Bay to Moruya and you might be able to get a lift to Moruya Heads on a school bus. Over on the north head (you have to return to Moruya to get there) is the big *River Breeze Caravan Park* (☎ 4474 2370) where sites cost from $11.

Congo

South of Moruya Heads, Congo, in **Eurobodalla National Park**, is a small cluster of houses on an estuary and a long surf beach. It's very pretty and peaceful. Volunteers are helping to repair damage to the dunes here and they welcome assistance. There's a basic camping area where sites cost $8 or $10 in summer, $5 other times. You'll need to bring in all your food and bring or boil drinking water.

A dirt road to Congo runs off the road between Moruya and Moruya Heads; another partly sealed road to Congo leaves the highway about 10km south of Moruya. The latter also leads to **Meringo**, another tiny place on the coast.

Tuross Head

This big development of suburban houses is at the end of a peninsula that separates Coila Lake and Tuross Lake, both large inlets. **Tuross Lake** is attractive, although most of the country around it has been cleared, but the town could be part of any suburb in the country.

There's a small caravan park on the good ocean beach and another on Tuross Lake, several kilometres away from the town and the sea. The *Tuross Hotel* (☎ 4473 8112) in town has motel units.

South of Tuross Head, on the other side of Tuross Lake, is **Potato Point**, where there's another good beach.

NAROOMA

Narooma (population 5000) is a seaside holiday town that isn't as developed as Batemans Bay to the north or Merimbula to the south. The town is on a strip of land between the ocean and beautiful Wagonga Inlet.

The town should be called Noorooma, an Aboriginal word meaning 'clear blue water', but a clerical error produced today's spelling. Late last century the town was a timber-milling and ship-building centre, as well as a service centre for the dairy farms in the district.

Part of the town is on a point between two sections of the inlet but many of the facilities and residential streets are south of here, up a steep hill. To get to the surf beach turn off the highway down Fuller St, near the information centre, and follow it around.

The good information centre (☎ 4476 2881) on the beachfront is open daily from 9 am to 5 pm. Here you will also find the small **Lighthouse Museum**. You can buy CMA

SOUTH COAST

maps and Forestry Commission maps which detail walking trails in the nearby state forests. Narooma is also an access point for both Deua and Wadbilliga national parks, and there's a NPWS information office (☎ 4476 2888), on the highway on the corner of Field St, north of the information centre.

Things to See & Do
About 10km offshore from Narooma is **Montague Island**, once an important source of food for local Aborigines (who called it Barunguba) and now a nature reserve. Fairy penguins nest here and although you'll see some all year round, there are many thousands in late winter and spring. Many other seabirds, along with hundreds of seals, make their homes on the island. There's also a historic lighthouse. A boat trip to Montague Island and a tour conducted by a NPWS ranger costs $50 ($35 children). The boat leaves at 3.30 pm on Monday, Wednesday and Friday (in time to see the penguins waddle up the beach at dusk), with extra trips in summer.

The clear waters around the island are good for **diving** especially from February to June; you can snorkel with the seals.

You can **cruise** up the Wagonga River on the *Wagonga Princess*, a nice old boat. A three-hour cruise, including a stop for a walk through the bush and some billy tea, costs $15 ($12 children). Book at the information centre. There are several boat-hire places along Riverside Drive, running off the highway near the bridge, so you can go boating on Wagonga Inlet under your own steam.

A good rainy-day weekend activity is to see a film at the **Narooma Kinema**, a picture palace that began showing flicks in 1928 and hasn't changed much since.

For **surfing**, Mystery Bay, between Cape Dromedary and Corunna Point, is rocky but good, as is Handkerchief Beach, especially at the north end. Narooma's Bar Beach is best when a south-easterly is blowing. Potato Point is another popular hang-out. These beaches are for experienced surfers only.

Special Events
The Lighthouse Festival and the Surfboat Marathon are held in November.

Places to Stay
Narooma Real Estate (☎ 4476 2169) handles holiday letting.

Camping There are several caravan parks, with two members of the Easts chain (☎ 4476 2161, 4476 2046) on the highway near the information centre and the smaller, cheaper, quieter *Surf Beach Caravan Park* (☎ 4476 2275) around by the surf beach.

Hostel The YHA's *Bluewater Lodge* (☎ 4476 4440), 11-13 Riverside Drive, is a popular, recommended hostel. It has dorm beds for $15, twins and doubles for $18 per person.

Hotel & Motels *Lynch's Hotel* (☎ 4476 2001), up on the hill on the highway at the south end of town, has basic singles/doubles for $20/30.

There are plenty of motels, most of which charge around $45 a single in the off-season but much more in summer. Cheaper places include *Vintage Motor Inn* (☎ 4476 2256), on the corner of Tilba St and the highway, with rooms for $40/45. *Whale Motor Inn* (☎ 4476 2411), on the hill, has large, clean rooms for $50/60 and a restaurant.

Places to Eat
Casey's Cafe, diagonally opposite Lynch's, has the best coffee in town and serves beautifully presented meals; Thai chicken salad is $8. It's open for breakfast too.

Quarterdeck Marine on Riverside Drive has a bistro overlooking the lake and fresh takeaway seafood; grilled fish is $6.50. *Rockwell Restaurant*, 107 Campbell St, is a licensed restaurant featuring local wines.

The *Ex-Servicemen's Club* has snacks at lunchtime and meals from 6 pm. The *Bowling Club* serves good, cheap meals.

Getting There & Away
Bus Bus bookings are handled by Traveland

(☎ 4476 2688), near the post office on the hill. Buses stop nearby.

Greyhound Pioneer stops here on the run between Sydney and Melbourne; Murrays stops on the run between Narooma and Canberra via Batemans Bay; and Sapphire Coast Express stops on its run between Batemans Bay and Melbourne.

Car & Motorcycle The Princes Highway runs north to Batemans Bay and south to Bega. South of Narooma a scenic route loops inland to Central Tilba, rejoining the highway near Tilba Tilba. The northern turn-off for Wallaga Lake and Bermagui is also near Tilba Tilba.

AROUND NAROOMA
Dalmeny
A suburb of Narooma, 5km south, Dalmeny is a quiet residential area on Mummaga Lake, yet another of the Eurobodalla Coast's pretty inlets. There's a council *camping area* (☎ 4476 7180).

Mystery Bay
Near Dromedary Head, about 12km south of Narooma, this little settlement of new houses has a fine rocky beach (there are sandy beaches nearby) and a big but basic *camping area* (☎ 4473 7242) in a forest of spotted gums. Sites cost $7 and $10 in summer. Mystery Bay is so named because the boat of a surveying party which vanished in 1880 was found here.

Central Tilba & Around
Central Tilba is a tiny town, built in wood, that has remained almost unchanged since it was built last century – except that now the main street is jammed with visitors' cars. You can get a good guide to the town from the store at the start of the main street. There are several working craft shops and the **ABC Cheese Factory** (☎ 4473 7387), is open daily from 9 am to 5 pm.

Not far from Central Tilba are **Tilba Valley Wines** (☎ 4473 7308) and **Brooklands Deer Farm** (☎ 4473 7330).

The **Tilba Festival**, with lots of music and entertainment, is held at Easter; it's hard to imagine how this small town can cope with the 8000-plus visitors.

Central Tilba perches on the side of **Mt Dromedary** (800m), one of the highest mountains on the south coast and renamed by Captain Cook in 1770 (the original name is Gulaga). There's lush forest on the mountain, which is a flora reserve, and great views from the top. Beginning at the **Tilba Tilba** store (where you can buy lunch for the walk) you can walk up, following an old packhorse trail. The return walk of 11km takes about five hours. There is often rain and mist on the mountain, so come prepared. You could also ride up with Mt Dromedary Trail Rides (☎ 4476 3376).

From Tilba Tilba the highway swings inland to **Cobargo**, another small town that has changed little since it was built, and where there are craft shops, a pub and motels. There's also a tantalisingly named antique shop, No Wife, No Horse, No Moustache.

Places to Stay & Eat *Dromedary Hotel* (☎ 4473 7223) in Central Tilba has a couple of basic rooms for $30/50 including a cooked breakfast. If you've come to stay in an original town it perhaps makes sense to stay in an original pub, but you won't pay much more for considerably more comfort at *Wirrina Guesthouse* (☎ 4473 7279), which charges $60 a double for B&B. A few kilometres away near Tilba Tilba is *Green Gables* guesthouse (☎ 4473 7435) with B&B doubles for $65.

In Central Tilba, *Tilba Teapot* has snacks and meals. You can also get reasonable snacks at the Tilba Tilba store.

Getting There & Away Pioneer Motor Service comes through both Central Tilba and Tilba Tilba on its daily run between Sydney and Eden.

By car, you can reach Central Tilba from the turn-off near Tilba Tilba, but if you're coming from Narooma you can also take a signposted scenic diversion of about 15km.

If you're heading for Bermagui or if you just want an interesting drive, leave the

SOUTH COAST

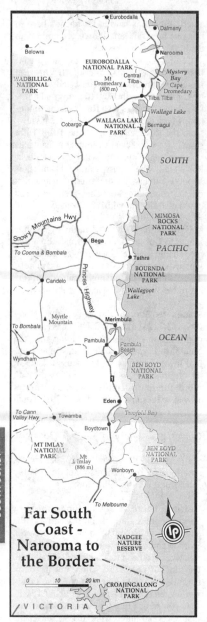

Far South
Coast -
Narooma to
the Border

highway at Tilba Tilba and take the sealed road that follows the coast through Wallaga Lake National Park to Bermagui.

WADBILLIGA NATIONAL PARK

A rugged wilderness area of 79,000 hectares, Wadbilliga offers good walking for experienced bushwalkers. One popular walk is along the 5km Tuross River Gorge to the Tuross Falls. There's a camping area on the north-western side of the park, near the walk to the falls. Access is off the road running from Countegany (east of Numeralla) south to Tuross.

For more information, contact the NPWS office (☎ 4476 2888) in Narooma.

Wadbilliga Wilderness Canoes (☎ 6492 7328) offers canoeing trips through the park for $35.

WALLAGA LAKE NATIONAL PARK

This small park takes in most of the western shore of Wallaga Lake, a beautiful tidal lake at the mouth of several creeks. There's also another chunk of the park off the highway west of here. The shores of the lake are forested (mainly regeneration after logging) and its many tiny bays and twisting shoreline invite leisurely exploration by boat. Birdlife is prolific and you'll probably meet animals in the bush.

There's no road access into the park, but the little towns of **Beauty Point** and **Regatta Point** are on the lake and you can hire boats there. Merriman Island, in the lake off Regatta Point, is off-limits because of its significance to the Aboriginal community. Similarly, sites (such as middens, the remains of shellfish feasts) and relics you might come across in the park are protected.

Umbarra Cultural Tours (☎ 4473 7232, 4473 7414 AH), run by the Yuin people from Wallaga Lake Koori community, has a tour of the lake and other places of historical and cultural importance. It's actually more than a tour since you get to share in their culture and take part in a traditional ceremony. The cost is $30.

Places to Stay

There are several caravan parks in and near Regatta Point and Beauty Point, small neighbouring towns on a peninsula separating the lake from the ocean. The lake is a popular place in summer – prices can double and there might be minimum stays around Christmas and Easter.

Perhaps the nicest caravan park is the big *Ocean Lake Caravan park* (☎ 6493 4055) with sites for $10 and on-site vans from $25 a double. Nearby, *Uncle Tom's Tourist Park* (☎ 6493 4253) is a bit cheaper and also has self-contained units costing from $32 a double. Both places are on the lake and are a bit of a walk to the ocean beach. Closest to the ocean is *Wallaga Lake Park* (☎ 6493 4655), off the main road between Bermagui and Narooma, just south of Beauty Point. Sites cost $10.50, vans $30.

BERMAGUI

Bermagui is a small fishing community (population 1560) centred on pretty Horseshoe Bay. Many visitors come here, mainly to fish, and there are six big-game tournaments a year. It's a handy base for visits to both Wallaga Lake and Mimosa Rocks national parks, and for Wadbilliga National Park, inland in the ranges.

American western novelist Zane Grey once visited Bermagui and included his experiences in a book.

The main information centre (☎ 6493 4174) is on Cutajo St south of the bridge.

Places to Stay & Eat

Zane Grey Park (☎ 6493 4382), in the town centre, overlooks Horseshoe Bay and has sites for $12, on-site vans for $35. Prices rise considerably at peak times.

Blue Pacific (☎ 6493 4921), 77 Murrah St, has backpacker accommodation for $15 and a double room for $34. Blue Pacific is a friendly, clean place, and worth considering for non-hostel accommodation as well. Self-contained flats sleeping six cost $600 a week around January and Easter, dropping to $250 in winter, when they also offer doubles for $200 a week. Overnight stays cost $45 a double all year, although there's unlikely to be a vacancy in the peak season. Blue Pacific is up a hill off the road running along the beach north of the town centre. The turn-off is signposted, just north of the fishing-boat wharf. Joe, one of the owners, will pick you up from the highway for a small fee.

There are many other holiday houses and apartments. Letting agents include Town & Country (☎ 6493 4124).

The *Horseshoe Bay Hotel/Motel* (☎ 6493 4206) has units from about $30/40. Other motels are more expensive, very much so in summer.

Bermagui Fishermen's Cooperative at the wharf has very fresh fish & chips. Nearby, *Roly's Wharf Restaurant* (☎ 6493 4328) serves seafood in the evenings; mains are $14.50 to $19. *Arnold's Sea Grill*, 4 Bunga St, has good-value meals from $6.

Getting There & Away

Bus Bermagui is off the highway, so transport can be a little complicated. Bega Valley Coaches (☎ 6492 2418) has a weekday service between Bermagui and Bega ($11) and a feeder service connects with Pioneer Motor Service's bus north to Nowra.

Car & Motorcycle Heading north, the quickest way back to the highway is to go north past Wallaga Lake National Park, and this is also a pretty drive. Heading south, the quickest way is to go west and join the highway at Cobargo, but if you have time you could drive south on the unsealed road that runs alongside Mimosa Rocks National Park to Tathra, from where you can rejoin the highway at Bega. Watch out for lyrebirds.

MIMOSA ROCKS NATIONAL PARK

Running along 17km of beautiful coastline, Mimosa Rocks (5180 hectares) is a wonderful coastal park with dense and varied bush and great beaches. There are basic campsites at Aragunnu Beach, Picnic Point and Middle Beach, and a camping area with no facilities at Gillards Beach. Camping costs $5 plus the $7.50 park entry fee. These camping areas and the picnic areas are accessible from the road running between Bermagui and Tathra.

Contact the NPWS office (☎ 6476 2888) in Narooma.

TATHRA

This small town is popular with people from the Bega area in summer. The town is on a long beach and continues up on the headland. Here, up the steep road, you'll find the post office and the pub, as well as access to the historic wharf where there is some tourist information.

Tathra wharf is the last remaining coastal steamship wharf in the state and a popular place for fishing. The wharf storehouse now houses a small **Maritime Museum** (admission $2) as well as a tackle shop and small cafe.

Cliff Place, a narrow street that runs off the headland road next to the road down to the wharf, has great views. You can walk up on a path that begins near the surf club.

Diving is popular in the waters off Tathra at Snapper Reef and other places; dives are organised by Sea Trek (☎ 6494 1799).

Places to Stay

Prices for accommodation in Tathra rise considerably in summer.

There are three caravan parks. *Tathra Beach Tourist Park* (☎ 6494 1302), on the beach in the centre of town, has sites for $9, on-site vans for $28. There could be a bit of road noise here. *Seabreeze Holiday Park* (☎ 6494 1350) is across the road and has sites for $13, on-site vans for $25 and cabins for $60. *Tathra Beach Motor Village* (☎ 6494 1577), north of the centre, is less cramped than the other two. It has sites from $14 and cabins from $28.

Tathra Hotel (☎ 6494 1101) is a popular eating, drinking and dancing place up on the headland. There's motel accommodation in adequate but not especially nice units for $35/45, rising to $95 in summer. The pub has entertainment on weekends (which means noise for the motel units) and in summer they host big touring acts.

LJ Hooker (☎ 6494 1077) is one of the real estate agents handling holiday letting.

Places to Eat

The *Tathra Hotel* has counter meals and a bistro. Also on the headland, next to the road going down to the beach, the *Harbourmaster Restaurant* is a pleasant place in an old house, with three-course meals for $20. *Ocean Paradise* is a Chinese restaurant in the Bowling Club. On the beach next to the surf-lifesaving club, the *Tathra Beach Eatery* is a good BYO restaurant; lasagne costs $7 at lunchtime. There's also a takeaway kiosk here.

Getting There & Away

Bus Buses to Bega depart at 8.20 am (schooldays only), 10.20 am and 2.30 pm on weekdays. See the Bega Getting There & Away section for more details.

Car & Motorcycle Tathra is 18 winding km from the Princes Highway at Bega. If you're heading north, consider the unsealed road through to Bermagui which runs through forest and by Mimosa Rocks National Park. Heading south to Merimbula you can turn off the road to Bega 5km out of Tathra onto Sapphire Coast Drive, which runs past Bournda National Park.

BEGA

Bega (population 4500) is a centre for the rich dairy and cattle country of the southern Monaro. Most of Canberra's milk comes from the valleys around here.

Orientation & Information

The information centre (☎ 6492 2045), in Gipps St (Princes Highway) near the corner of Carp St, is open weekdays from 10 am to 5 pm, Saturday from 10 am to 2 pm. It sometimes opens on Sunday as well in the summer.

In Church St, running north off Carp St, the Environmental Network has information about environment-related events and campaigns in the area. You can buy health food here and more in Candelo Bulk Foods next

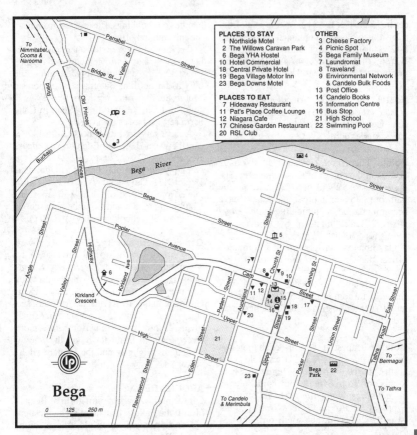

PLACES TO STAY
1 Northside Motel
2 The Willows Caravan Park
6 Bega YHA Hostel
10 Hotel Commercial
18 Central Private Hotel
19 Bega Village Motor Inn
23 Bega Downs Motel

PLACES TO EAT
7 Hideaway Restaurant
11 Pat's Place Coffee Lounge
12 Niagara Cafe
17 Chinese Garden Restaurant
20 RSL Club

OTHER
3 Cheese Factory
4 Picnic Spot
5 Bega Family Museum
7 Laundromat
8 Traveland
9 Environmental Network
  & Candelo Bulk Foods
13 Post Office
14 Candelo Books
15 Information Centre
16 Bus Stop
21 High School
22 Swimming Pool

Bega

door. Sportscene, on the corner of Carp and Auckland Sts, sells camping gear. Candelo Books is on the pedestrian mall south of Carp St. There's a laundromat on Auckland St.

Things to See & Do

There are a number of mildly interesting old buildings. The information centre has a walking-tour map.

The **Bega Family Museum** (☎ 6492 1453, on Bega St near Auckland St, is open weekdays from 10.30 am to 4 pm, Saturday from 10 am to noon. Admission is $2 (20c children). You can visit the **Bega Cheese Factory**, across the river, weekdays from 9 am to 5 pm, weekends from 10 am to 4 pm. **Grevillea Estate Winery** is open to visitors daily and has a restaurant. It's about 2km from the town centre – follow the highway across the river and take the first left after the bridge.

Numbugga Trail Rides (☎ 6492 8436), Desert Creek Rd, has one and three-hour trail rides in the area and offers riding lessons.

Places to Stay

Camping *Bega Caravan Park* (☎ 6492 2303), on the Princes Highway south of the centre, has sites for $12, on-site vans from $25. It also has self-contained units costing $42 a double, much more in summer. *Willows Caravan Park* (☎ 6492 2106) is just north of the bridge near the cheese factory.

Hostel The modern, friendly *Bega YHA Hostel* (☎ 6492 3103), on Kirkland Crescent, is made of mud-brick. Dorm beds cost $13, double rooms $34.

Hotels The *Hotel Commercial* (☎ 6492 1011), on the corner of Gipps and Carp Sts, has rooms for $20/40, or $30/50 with ensuite bathroom. Several other pubs also have accommodation, including the *Grand Hotel* (☎ 6492 1122), on Carp St, with ensuite rooms for $30/40.

On Gipps St, across from the information office, the *Central Private Hotel* (☎ 6492 1263) is a big, slightly musty place with some permanent residents. A room with shared bathroom costs $25/40 and there's a motel section costing $35/50. It has good breakfasts.

Motels Cheapest of the half-dozen motels is the *Northside* (☎ 6492 1911), a couple of km north of the centre on the old highway, where rooms cost from $45/50. Others include the *Bega Village Motor Inn* (☎ 6492 2466) on Gipps St ($55/65) and *Bega Downs Motel* (☎ 6492 2944) further south on Gipps St ($65/75).

Places to Eat
Niagara Cafe on Carp St is your standard, large country-town cafe, selling meals and takeaways. On Auckland St, south of Carp St, there's *Pat's Place Coffee Lounge*. On Carp St, just east of Gipps St, *Chinese Garden* has MSG-free meals with main courses about $7. The *RSL Club* has meals.

The recreation reserve by the river at the north end of Auckland St is a good place for a picnic.

Getting There & Away
Bus Traveland (☎ 6492 3599), 163 Carp St,

handles bus bookings. Buses leave from near the information office.

Greyhound Pioneer stops here on the run between Sydney and Melbourne. Sapphire Coast Express also runs to Melbourne but only as far north as Batemans Bay. Pioneer Motor Service runs north to Sydney and south to Eden. Countrylink's Eden to Canberra service passes through Bega.

A local service, Edwards (☎ 6496 1422), runs between Bega and Eden on weekdays. Bega Valley Coaches (☎ 6492 2418) has a weekday service between Bermagui and Bega ($11). On weekdays, buses to Tathra leave from the post office at 9.30 am, from Church St at 2 pm and from the high school on Upper St (schooldays only) at 3.30 pm.

Car & Motorcycle The Princes Highway runs north to Narooma and south to Merimbula and Eden. The Snowy Mountains Highway branches off the Princes Highway 5km north of Bega and runs to Cooma. Smaller roads run east to Tathra and south-west to Candelo and on to other small towns, eventually reaching Bombala. A more direct route to Bombala is via the Snowy Mountains Highway and the Monaro Highway.

AROUND BEGA
Off the highway about 5km north of Bega is **Mumballa Falls**, where there's a picnic area.

Candelo is a pleasant old village southeast of Bega, straggling along both sides of a steep valley and split by the large, sandy Candelo Creek. The nearby country is cleared, but it's still pretty. There are several craft galleries, including the Old Hospital Gallery on the hillside high above town. To get there follow the road on the Bega side of the creek and turn left near the end and follow Queen St up past the police station. West of Candelo is **Kameruka Estate**, a National Trust homestead, open daily, and further on is the **Bimbaya Moozeum** in an old butter factory. The *Candelo Hotel* (☎ 6493 2214) has accommodation.

From Candelo you can drive back to the Princes Highway via Toothdale, or continue south to the Bombala road. This route takes you over **Myrtle Mountain** where there's a picnic area with good views, and drives in the state forest. The Bombala road leads you west to **Wyndham**, a small village just after the intersection with the Candelo road, or east to Pambula and Merimbula.

MERIMBULA

Merimbula (population 4250) is a holiday and retirement mecca, and motels and apartments have mushroomed on the hillsides surrounding the impressive lake (which is actually an inlet). If this sounds like a recipe for tackiness you're partly right, but there's still some charm about the town's setting and the lake is big enough to dwarf the development. Nearby Pambula Beach is much quieter but is close enough to take advantage of Merimbula's services.

Orientation & Information

The road enters Merimbula from the west, runs south through the town centre and crosses Merimbula Lake to the spit of land that forms the southern head of the lake's sea entrance. It then runs south to Pambula. There are lakeside beaches and surf beaches on the ocean sides of the peninsulas that form the north and south sides of the lake entrance.

The tourist information centre (π 6495 1250), on the waterfront at the bottom of Market St, the main shopping street, is open daily from 9 am to 5 pm. There's a NPWS office (π 6495 4130) on the corner of Merimbula and Sapphire Coast Drives.

Camping World, on Merimbula Drive near the post office, has camping equipment.

Things to See & Do

At the wharf on the eastern point is the small **Merimbula Aquarium** (π 6495 3227), open daily from 9 am to 5 pm; admission is $6 ($4 children). There are good views across the lake from near here.

Diving is popular, with plenty of fish and several wrecks in the area, including two tugs sunk in 1987. Merimbula Divers Lodge (π 6495 3611) offers basic instruction and

one shallow dive for $60. They also do PADI-certificate courses.

Various outfits offer **cruises**, which you can book at the information centre.

There are two **boat-hire** places, Bottom Lake, on the jetty near the information centre, and Top Lake, on the north shore west of the bridge, at the end of Lakewood Drive. They have various types of power boats, little trimaran yachts, canoes and rowing boats. Cycle 'n' Surf (π 6495 2171), on Marine Parade (near South Haven Caravan Park south of the bridge), hires bikes, body boards and surf-skis as well as fishing tackle. Sapphire Coast Canoes (book at the information centre) has day trips on various inland waterways in the area.

Magic Mountain on Sapphire Coast Drive is an amusement park with waterslides, go-karts and the like.

Places to Stay

Camping *South Haven Caravan Park* (π 6495 1304) and the smaller *Tween Waters Tourist Park* (π 6495 1530) are south of the bridge with access to surf and lake beaches. Both have sites from about $16 and cabins from $30 to $35. East of the town centre but right on the surf beach on the north side of the lake entrance, *Merimbula Caravan Park* (π 6495 1269) has sites from $14, on-site vans from $27 and cabins from $38. Access is from Cliff St, which branches off the road that runs around the north side of the lake.

Other Accommodation *Wandarrah YHA Lodge* (π 6495 3503), 8 Marine Parade near the surf beach, has dorm beds for $15 and double rooms for $34. It also provides some organised tours and activities.

Merimbula Divers Lodge (π 6495 3611), 15 Park St, offers backpackers shared accommodation in a self-contained unit for $20 per person – a bargain. Whole units are also available. To get here from Market St cut through the Centrepoint Mall (really an arcade) then head across the car park. Park St is on your right and the lodge is only a few doors up.

In quiet times you can find motel rooms

from around $40/50, but in summer prices go through the roof. Your best chance of finding an affordable room is at one of the motels on the highway west of the town centre.

Letting agents for the area include Fisk & Nagle (☎ 6495 1301), in Centrepoint near the information centre, and LJ Hooker (☎ 6495 1026), nearby at 35 Market St. One of the many apartment places deserves a special mention: *Gracelands* (☎ 6495 2005), at the corner of Cameron St and Munn Sts, is in the style of that well-known monument to excess and has a guitar-shaped swimming pool with a portrait of you-know-who on the bottom!

Places to Eat
Merimbula offers quite a wide range of eateries. The *Waterfront Cafe*, next to the information centre, is a good place to have a coffee or snack while looking out over the busy Merimbula Lake. Burger and chips cost $7.90. Next door, without the views but with tables outside, is the *Panda Garden Chinese Restaurant* with three-course dinners for only $7.80. Diagonally across from these, on the corner of Alice St, *Poppy's Courtyard Cafe* has breakfasts for around $7 and a wide range of sandwiches and snacks.

There's a cluster of restaurants at the bottom of Market St, including *Thai Noodle House* where chicken satay is $7; it also does takeaways. Toward the top of Market St, *Monty's* is a mid-range bar and restaurant serving grilled fish for $13.

There are many other places, and all the clubs, including the *Bowling Club* and the *RSL Club*, have bistros and restaurants.

Getting There & Away
Air Kendell flies to Melbourne ($185) and Hazelton flies to Sydney ($213).

Bus Bus bookings can be made at Harvey World Travel (☎ 6495 1205) on Merimbula Drive, or Summerland Travel (☎ 6495 1008), 16 Market St. Buses stop outside the Centrepoint Mall on Market St.

Greyhound Pioneer Australia stops here on the run between Sydney and Melbourne. Pioneer Motor Service runs up the coast between Eden and Sydney. Countrylink stops here on the run between Eden and Canberra.

Edwards (☎ 6496 1422) is a local bus company which runs between Bega and Eden; it also does tours.

Car & Motorcycle The Princes Highway runs north to Bega and south to Eden. Ten km south of Merimbula, just south of Pambula, a minor road runs west to Bombala.

Getting Around
You can contact the local taxi service on ☎ 6495 2103.

AROUND MERIMBULA
Bournda National Park
Taking in most of the coast from Merimbula north to Tathra, Bournda (2350 hectares) has some good beaches and several walking trails which can get pretty crowded at peak times. Camping is permitted at Hobart Beach, on the southern shore of the big Wallagoot Lagoon, where there are toilets and hot showers. During the Christmas and Easter holidays, sites are usually booked out. Contact the NPWS office (☎ 6494 1209) in the park for more information.

Woodbine Park (☎ 6495 9333) borders Bournda and is 1km from the beach. It's a friendly place with six-person self-contained cabins from $200 a week for a double, extra for more people, in the lowest season (May to September, other than school holidays) and up to $760 in January. Head north from Merimbula on Sapphire Coast Drive and take the signposted turn-off after about 7km.

Pambula
Just south of Merimbula, Pambula is a small town that has largely avoided the development of its glitzy neighbour. At Pambula Beach, 4km east, there's *Holiday Hub* caravan park (☎ 6495 6363) with some very friendly wildlife. Keep your food hidden!

The northern section of Ben Boyd

National Park begins just south of Pambula Beach, across the inlet.

In Pambula, *McKell's* has roast dinners every night for $12.50 and also offers B&B.

NALBAUGH NATIONAL PARK

This small park (4100 hectares) is a rugged wilderness area with no facilities. Access is difficult, with just a 4WD track running off the Cann Valley Highway south of Bombala. Contact the NPWS office (☎ 6496 1434) in Merimbula.

EDEN & AROUND

Eden (population 3270) remains very much a fishing port, with one of the largest fleets in the state. It's also a timber town. The town's population doubled when a woodchip mill opened in the 70s, so you won't meet many people voicing anti-woodchipping sentiments.

Eden Tourist Centre (☎ 6496 1953) on Imlay St (the Princes Highway) is open weekdays from 9 am to 5 pm, weekends from 9 am to noon.

Things to See and Do

The interesting **Killer Whale Museum** (☎ 6496 2094), at the bottom end of Imlay St, was established in 1931, mainly to pre-serve the skeleton of Old Tom, a killer whale (orca). Old Tom led a pack of killer whales which rounded up other whales so they could be killed by Eden's whalers. The killer whales ate only the tongues of their prey, so it was a good working relationship. After Old Tom died, the pack lost interest in the hunt and this contributed to the demise of whaling here.

If you've ever read *Moby Dick*, this is your chance to see a real whale boat with all those arcane pieces of equipment described by Melville. The museum is open weekdays from 10.15 am to 3.45 pm, weekends from 11.15 am to 3.45 pm. Admission is $4 ($1 children).

Whales still swim along the coast in October and November, no doubt singing dark songs about the terrible days of Old Tom. Cat Balou Cruises (☎ 6496 2027) has

whale-spotting cruises for $45 ($30 children). These and other boat and canoe day-trips can be booked at Eden Tourist Centre.

Boydtown, off the highway 10km south of Eden, has relics of Ben Boyd's stillborn empire. The ruins of a church can be seen, and the impressive Seahorse Inn still oper-ates (see below).

If you have time, there's the five-hour **Wallagaraugh Forest Drive** through Nadgee State Forest (not to be confused with the better preserved Nadgee Nature Reserve east of here) that leaves the highway 27km south of Eden and rejoins it near the Victor-ian border. There are great views from Mallacoota Lookout.

Places to Stay & Eat

The *Garden of Eden Caravan Park* (☎ 6496 1172) and the *Fountain Caravan Park* (☎ 6496 1798) are by the highway north of town. On Aslings Beach is *Eden Tourist Park* (☎ 6496 1139) with sites from $11, on-site vans from $28. From Eden Tourist Centre head north-east on Mitchell St, which becomes Aslings Beach Rd. The caravan park is on a spit separating Aslings beach from Lake Curalo.

The *Australasia Hotel* (☎ 6496 1600) on Imlay St has backpacker beds for $15, hotel rooms for $25 and motel-style units for $35. The *Great Southern Inn* (☎ 6496 1515), 158 Imlay St, has $20 singles with bathroom.

Motels include the *Centre Town* (☎ 6496 1475) on Imlay St between Mitchell and Bass Sts ($38/40), the *Halfway* (☎ 6496 1178) on the corner of Imlay and Mitchell Sts ($46/54) and the *Twofold Bay* (☎ 6496 3111) on Imlay St between Chandos and Cocora Sts (from $58/62). Prices rise in summer.

The interesting *Seahorse Inn* (☎ 6496 1361), at Boydtown overlooking Twofold Bay, is a solid old building, built by Ben Boyd as a guesthouse in 1843. Rooms cost $85, less in the low season. You could just visit for a meal at *Benjamin's Restaurant*. There's also a *camping ground* here, with sites for $10.

SOUTH COAST

Down at Snug Cove, Eden's fishing harbour, *Neptune's Kitchen* has seafood to take away or eat there. For more upmarket seafood try the *Wheelhouse Restaurant* around the corner; king dory fillets are $14. Back on Imlay St, *Eden Fishermen's Club* has a dining room and a cafe/bar.

Getting There & Away

Bus Bookings can be made at Traveland (☎ 6496 1314), on the corner of Bass and Imlay Sts.

BEN BOYD NATIONAL PARK

Protecting some relics of Ben Boyd's operations, this national park (9450 hectares) has dramatic coastline, bush and some walks. The main access road to the park is the sealed Edrom Rd, which leaves the Princes Highway about 25km south of Eden. Edrom Rd runs to the big woodchip mill on the south shore of Twofold Bay (and along the road you can see the dense but regimented and unvaried plantings that have replaced the bush, which has been turned into paper).

Before the mill there's a turn-off to the left which leads to the old **Davidson Whaling Station** on **Twofold Bay**, now a historic site. Further along Edrom Rd is the turn-off for **Boyd's Tower**, an impressive structure built with sandstone brought from Sydney. It was intended to be a lighthouse but the government wouldn't give Boyd permission to operate it.

Off Edrom Rd, closer to the highway, is Green Cape Rd, which runs right down to Green Cape, from where there are some good views. Running off Green Cape Rd are smaller roads which lead to **Saltwater Creek** and **Bittangabee Bay**. There are campsites at both places and a 9km walk between the two. You should book sites for Christmas and Easter at the NPWS office (☎ 6495 4130) in Merimbula.

The northern section of Ben Boyd National Park runs up the coast from Eden; access is from the Princes Highway north of the town. From Haycock Point, where there are good views, a walking trail leads to a headland overlooking the Pambula River.

The Rise & Fall of Benjamin Boyd

Benjamin Boyd was a strange person, part empire-builder, part capitalist and part adventurer, mixed with a large dash of incompetence. He never really completed anything he set out to do and he was unsuccessful in a big way.

Boyd was a stockbroker in London who decided that the colony of New South Wales offered scope for the large amounts of money he could raise. His plans were vague and included a half-baked idea for a private colony in the South Pacific.

He founded the Royal Bank, which quickly attracted £1,000,000 in investments, then set out for Sydney in his racing yacht *Wanderer*, arriving in 1842. Boyd, who so far had accomplished nothing except the acquisition of a great deal of other people's money, was greeted with much official and public enthusiasm in Sydney.

He began a coastal steamship service, but the boat was damaged and withdrawn in its first year of operations. Boyd nevertheless convinced the governor that he was a fit person to be granted vast landholdings, second only in size to the Crown's.

Boyd decided to set up headquarters at Twofold Bay and an extensive building programme began. Money ran short, although the investors were assured that their golden reward was just around the corner, and Boyd issued his own banknotes.

Things went from bad to worse and the Royal Bank (nominally the owner of Boyd's empire) sacked him. By 1849 the bank decided that it was easier simply to collapse than to untangle Boyd's complex financial wheelings and dealings.

The entrepreneur smiled amid the ruins of his speculations, decided New South Wales wasn't really the right place for his ventures after all and set sail in *Wanderer* for the Californian goldfields.

Things didn't quite work out there either, and in 1851 Boyd sailed back into the Pacific. One morning, while moored at Guadalcanal in the Solomon Islands, he left his yacht to go shooting and disappeared without trace. ■

NADGEE NATURE RESERVE

Nadgee continues down the coast from Ben Boyd National Park but it's much less accessible. A large part of this pristine reserve is an official Wilderness Area and vehicle access is only allowed as far as the ranger station near the Merrica River. From the ranger station it's a 7km walk to Newton's Beach. In the north of the reserve a road is being built to allow vehicle access to Wonboyn Beach.

On Wonboyn Lake at the north end of the reserve, the small settlement of **Wonboyn** has a store selling petrol and basic supplies. Wonboyn is near access roads into Nadgee, including one down to Wonboyn Beach. To get to the beach at Disaster Bay you'll need a 4WD or a boat (available from the caravan park) – or legs.

Places to Stay

At *Wonboyn Cabins & Caravan Park* (☎ 6496 9131), where you'll meet some friendly rainbow lorikeets, tent sites cost from $12, on-site vans $27, cabins $45.

Across the lake from Wonboyn, but with access from Green Cape Rd in Ben Boyd National Park, is *Wonboyn Lake Resort* (☎ 6496 9162), which has self-contained cabins from $55 for four people. As usual, in-season prices are higher. Canoes and boats can be hired.

MT IMLAY NATIONAL PARK

This small national park (3808 hectares), 32km south-west of Eden, surrounds **Mt Imlay** (886m) and you can walk to the top. The tough, 3km **Mt Imlay Walking Track** from the car park to the summit is steep, and the last 500m follows an extremely narrow ridge. There are no facilities in the park.

The road to the start of the track runs west from the Princes Highway just south of the turn-off into Ben Boyd National Park. A little farther south, past the turn-off to Wonboyn, Imlay Rd leads west to meet the Monaro–Cann River Highway near the Victorian border. It passes to the south of Mt Imlay National Park and there's a picnic area beside the Imlay River.

SOUTH COAST

Australian Capital Territory

When the separate colonies of Australia were federated in 1901 and became states, the decision to build a national capital was part of the constitution. The site was selected in 1908, diplomatically situated between arch-rivals Sydney and Melbourne, and an international competition to design the city was won by the American architect Walter Burley Griffin. In 1911 the Commonwealth government bought land for the Australian Capital Territory (ACT) and in 1913 decided to call the capital Canberra, believed to be an Aboriginal term for 'meeting place'.

Development of the site was slow and until 1927, when parliament first convened here, Melbourne was the seat of the national government. The Depression virtually halted development and things really only got under way after WWII. In 1960 the population topped 50,000, reaching 100,000 by 1967. Today the ACT has around 300,000 people.

Canberra

Canberra (population 298,000) is well worth visiting. The first things you'll notice are the space and how green it is. Some of the best architecture and exhibitions in Australia are here and the whole city is fascinating because it's totally planned and orderly, although you'll soon appreciate that living here without a car might not be such fun. If you do have wheels you'll enjoy some of the best urban driving or cycling conditions anywhere.

The city also has a beautiful setting, surrounded by hills and close to good skiing and bushwalking country.

Canberra is a place of government with few local industries and it has that unique, stimulating atmosphere that's only to be found in national capitals. It also has the furnishings of a true centre of national life –

like the exciting National Gallery of Australia, the new and splendid Parliament House and the excellent Australian National Botanic Gardens. What's more, Canberra has quite a young population, including a lot of students, and entertainment is livelier than we're usually led to expect. Finally, this is the only city in Australia where it's really possible to bump into kangaroos – they've been spotted grazing in the grounds of Parliament House.

Orientation

The city is arranged around the natural-looking, but artificial, Lake Burley Griffin. On the north side is Canberra's city centre, known as Civic. Nearby is most of the short-term accommodation, the Australian National University and a number of the

ACT

498

suburbs which are the basic unit of Canberra's urban structure.

The huge Vernon Circle on the north side of the lake is the centre of Civic. Surrounding the circle is the hexagonal London Circuit. The mirror-image Sydney and Melbourne buildings (slightly reminiscent of Connaught Place in New Delhi) flank the beginning of Northbourne Ave. The Sydney building is on the west side and the Melbourne building is on the east side. Northbourne Ave is the main artery north of the lake and leads to the nearby suburbs of Braddon, Lyneham, Downer and Dickson. At the Jolimont Centre in Northbourne Ave is the long-distance bus terminal, Countrylink Travel Centre, airline offices and luggage lockers.

The main shopping and restaurant area is in the Sydney building and the nearby pedestrian malls – Garema Place, City Walk and Petrie Plaza. The merry-go-round here began life in 1914 on Melbourne's St Kilda Beach and now operates daily except Sunday in summer ($1.50). The big Canberra Centre is Civic's largest shopping centre and City Market, on the ground floor of the car park behind it, is another shopping centre.

South of Vernon Circle, Northbourne Ave becomes Commonwealth Ave which runs over Lake Burley Griffin to Capital Circle. Capital Circle surrounds the new Parliament House on Capital Hill and is the apex of Walter Burley Griffin's parliamentary triangle, formed by Commonwealth Ave, Kings Ave (crossing the lake on the north-east side) and the lake. Many important buildings are concentrated within this triangle, including the National Library of Australia, the High Court, the National Gallery of Australia and the old Parliament House.

The suburbs surrounding Capital Circle are Parkes, Barton, Forrest, Deakin and Yarralumla. South-east of Capital Hill is Kingston, where you'll find the railway station, and Manuka, where there is another large shopping centre.

As well as the city centre and its surrounding suburbs, Canberra includes the 'towns' of Belconnen, Woden, Weston Creek, Tuggeranong and Gungahlin, each with its own collection of suburbs.

Maps The NRMA (☎ 132132), at 92 Northbourne Ave, has an excellent map of Canberra; the Visitor Information Centre has a black-and-white version. If you plan to do a lot of driving, Gregory's and UBD publish useful street directories.

For topographic maps of the ACT try the Visitor Information Centre (see below), or the ACT Government City Shop, on the corner of Mort and Bunda Sts , near the Civic bus interchange. The Travellers Maps & Guides (☎ 6249 6006) shop in the Jolimont Centre has a wide range of maps.

Information

Tourist Information The Visitor Information Centre (☎ 6205 0044, 1800 026 166) is on Northbourne Ave near the corner of Morphett St, Dickson, about 2km north of Vernon Circle (see Canberra Suburbs map). It's currently being completely rebuilt, but should be open by the time you read this. Its opening times were 9 am to 5 pm daily (from 8.30 am on weekends). The friendly Travellers Maps & Guides (☎ 6249 6006), in the Jolimont Centre, is an excellent source of information on Canberra (as well as being a travel agent and selling maps and guides).

The Canberra Reservation & Information Centre has an office (☎ 9233 3666) in Sydney, at suite 611A, Wingello House, Angel Place.

Post & Communications Have your mail addressed to poste restante at the Canberra City Post Office, 53-73 Alinga St, Civic, ACT 2601. It's open Monday to Friday 8.30 am to 5.30 pm.

There are payphones and credit card phones outside the GPO and in the nearby Jolimont Centre (and elsewhere). Canberra's STD telephone area code is 02.

Foreign Embassies There are about 60 embassies and high commissions in Canberra. Embassy-spotting enthusiasts can buy

ACT

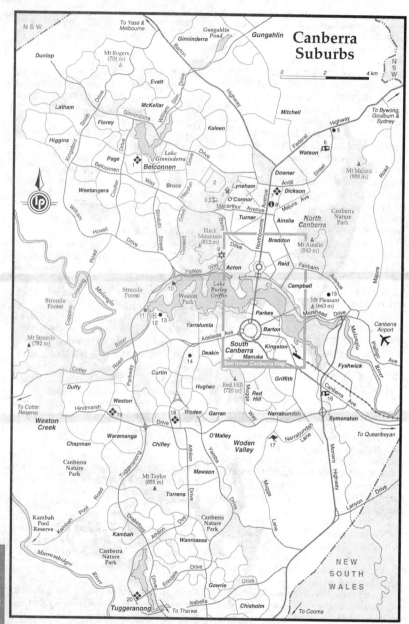

Canberra Suburbs

NSW

To Yass & Melbourne

Gungahlin Pond

Ginninderra

Gungahlin

NSW

Dunlop

Mt Rogers (704 m)

Evatt

McKellar

Mitchell

Latham

Florey

Ginninderra Drive

Kaleen

To Bywong, Goulburn & Sydney

Higgins

Page

Lake Ginninderra

Belconnen

1

Watson

6

5

Federal Highway

Mt Majura (888 m)

Weetangera

Bruce

Haydon Drive

2

Lyneham

O'Connor

Downer

Antill

Dickson

7

8

Majura Ave

Canberra Nature Park

Hovell Drive

Coulter Drive

Belconnen Way

3

Macarthur Avenue

Turner

Ainslie

North Canberra

William

Bindubi Street

Caswell Drive

Black Mountain (812 m)

Berry

9

Northbourne Avenue

Braddon

Mt Ainslie (843 m)

Reid

Fairbairn

Stromlo Forest

Parkes Way

Acton

Lake Burley Griffin

10

Weston Park

Campbell

15

Mt Pleasant (663 m)

Morshead Drive

Canberra Airport

Coppins Crossing

Molonglo River

11

12

13

Yarralumla

Parkes

Barton

Pialligo Ave

Molonglo River

Mt Stromlo (782 m)

Adelaide Ave

South Canberra

Manuka

Kingston

See Inner Canberra Map

Fyshwick

Canberra Ave

Cotter Road

Deakin

14

Curtin

Hughes

Red Hill (720 m)

Mugga Way

Red Hill

Griffith

To Cotter Reserve

Hindmarsh

Weston

18

Woden

Garran

Narrabundah

Symonston

16

Weston Creek

Waramanga

Chifley

Drive

Athllon Drive

O'Malley

Woden Valley

Narrabundah Lane

17

Monaro Highway

To Queanbeyan

Chapman

Tuggeranong

Mt Taylor (855 m)

Mawson

Yamba Drive

Canberra Nature Park

Kambah Pool Road

Torrens

Mugga Lane

Lanyon Drive

Kambah Pool Reserve

Kambah

Drakeford Drive

Athllon Drive

Canberra Nature Park

Wanniassa

NEW SOUTH WALES

Murrumbidgee River

20

Gowrie

Chisholm

To Cooma

Tuggeranong

Isabella Drive

To Tharwa

Erindale Drive

ACT

0   2   4 km

1 Belconnen Mall
2 Australian Institute of Sport
3 Canberra Motor Village
4 Youth Hostel
5 Australian Heritage Village
6 Canberra Lakes Carotel
7 Dickson Shopping Centre
8 Visitor Information Centre
9 Australian National Botanic Gardens
10 National Museum of Australia Visitor
    Centre
11 National Aquarium
12 Scrivener Dam Lookout
13 Government House
14 Royal Australian Mint
15 Royal Military College, Duntroon
16 Canberra South Motor Park
17 Mugga Lane Zoo
18 Woden Plaza
19 Weston Creek Centre
20 Tuggeranong Hyperdome

Canberra's Embassies by Graeme Barrow (Australian National University Press). A few are worth looking at although many operate from rather nondescript suburban houses. Most are in Yarralumla, the area south of the lake, and west and north of Parliament House. Some have an open day when the public can visit; check with the Visitor Information Centre to see if any are scheduled.

The US Embassy is a facsimile of a mansion in the style of those in Williamsburg, Virginia, which in turn owe much to the English Georgian style. The Thai Embassy, with its pointed, orange-tiled roof, is in a style similar to that of temples in Bangkok. The Indonesian Embassy is no architectural jewel but beside the dull embassy building itself there's a small display centre exhibiting examples of Indonesia's colourful culture. It's open weekdays from 9.30 am to 12.30 pm and 2 to 4 pm. Papua New Guinea's High Commission looks like a *haus tambaran* spirit-house from the Sepik River region of PNG. There's a display room with colour photographs and artefacts; it's open weekdays from 10 am to 12.30 pm and 2 to 4.30 pm.

Embassies and high commissions in the Australia capital include:

Austria
  12 Talbot St, Forrest (☎ 6295 1533)
Canada
  Commonwealth Ave, Yarralumla (☎ 6273 3844)
France
  6 Perth Ave, Yarralumla (☎ 6270 3800)
Germany
  119 Empire Court, Yarralumla (☎ 6270 1911)
India
  35 Moonah Place, Yarralumla (☎ 6273 3999)
Indonesia
  8 Darwin Ave, Yarralumla (☎ 6250 8600)
Ireland
  20 Arkana St, Yarralumla (☎ 6273 3022)
Japan
  112 Empire Circuit, Yarralumla (☎ 6273 3244)
Malaysia
  7 Perth Ave, Yarralumla (☎ 6273 1543)
Netherlands
  120 Empire Circuit, Yarralumla (☎ 6273 3111)
New Zealand
  Commonwealth Ave, Yarralumla (☎ 6270 4211)
Norway
  17 Hunter St, Yarralumla (☎ 6273 3444)
Papua New Guinea
  39-41 Forster Crescent, Yarralumla (☎ 6273 3322)
Singapore
  17 Forster Crescent, Yarralumla (☎ 6273 3944)
Sweden
  5 Turrana St, Yarralumla (☎ 6273 3033)
Switzerland
  7 Melbourne Ave, Forrest (☎ 6273 3977)
Thailand
  111 Empire Circuit, Yarralumla (☎ 6273 1149)
UK
  Commonwealth Ave, Yarralumla (☎ 6270 6666)
USA
  21 Moonah Place, Yarralumla (☎ 6270 5000)

Bookshops Canberra has many good bookshops. Dalton's (☎ 6249 1844), at 54 Marcus Clarke St in Civic, specialises in computer, business and limited edition titles. The Commonwealth Government Bookshop (☎ 6247 7211) at 10 Mort St has useful publications, plus some glossy ones that make good souvenirs. Smith's Bookshop (☎ 6247 4459), at 76 Alinga St on the north side of the Melbourne building, is a good general bookshop.

Electric Shadows (☎ 6249 8352), on City Walk near the cinema of the same name, has books on theatre, films and the arts. It's open daily.

Book Lore (☎ 6247 6450), at 94 Wattle St near Tilley Devine's bar in the Lyneham

ACT

shopping centre, is an excellent second-hand bookshop.

Medical Services The Travellers' Medical & Vaccination Centre (☎ 6257 7154/7156), upstairs in the City Walk Arcade near the city bus interchange, is open Monday to Friday from 9 am to 5 pm. Treatment is by appointment only and it doesn't bulk-bill. Several other clinics are nearby.

Emergency Emergency phone numbers are ☎ 000 for ambulance, fire and police; ☎ 131114 for Lifeline and ☎ 1800 424 017 for the Rape Crisis Centre.

Lookouts

There are fine views of Canberra from the surrounding hills. West of Civic, **Black Mountain** rises to 812m and is topped by the 195m **Telstra Tower** (☎ 6248 1911), complete with a revolving restaurant. There is also a display on telecommunications history. The tower is open daily from 9 am to 10 pm; admission is $3 ($1 children). There are also splendid vistas from nearby lookouts and from the approach road. Bus No 904 runs to the tower or you can walk up on a 2km trail through the bush, starting on Frith Rd. Other good bushwalks, accessible from Belconnen Way and Caswell Drive, wander round the back of the Canberra mountain. The information centre has a brochure with a map.

Other lookouts, all with road access, are **Mt Taylor** (855m), **Mt Ainslie** (843m), **Red Hill** (720m) and **Mt Pleasant** (663m). Mt Ainslie is close to the city on the north-east side and has particularly fine views across the city and out over the airport. From the top you'll also appreciate how green and full of parks Canberra is. The view is excellent at night. There are foot trails up Mt Ainslie from behind the War Memorial and out behind Mt Ainslie to Mt Majura (888m) 4km away. You may see a kangaroo or two on the hike up.

Lake Burley Griffin

The lake was named after Canberra's designer but was not finally created until the Molonglo River was dammed in 1963. Swimming in the lake isn't recommended, but you can go boating (beware of strong winds which can blow up suddenly from nowhere). You can hire boats, bikes and in-line skates (rollerblades) near the Acton Park ferry terminal, on the northern side of the lake.

There are a number of places of interest around the 35km shore. The most visible is the **Captain Cook Memorial Water Jet** which flings a six-tonne column of water 147m into the air and gives you a free shower if the wind is blowing from the right direction (despite an automatic switch-off if wind speeds get too high). The jet, built in 1970 to commemorate the bicentenary of Captain Cook's visit to Australia, operates from 10 am to noon and 2 to 4 pm daily (plus 7 to 9 pm during daylight-saving time). At **Regatta Point**, nearby on the northern shore, is a skeleton globe with Cook's three great voyages traced on it.

The **National Capital Exhibition**, also at Regatta Point, is open daily from 9 am to 6 pm and has displays on the growth of the capital. It's free and interesting. Farther around the lake, to the east, is **Blundell's Farmhouse** (1860). The simple stone and slab cottage containing period furnishings and fittings is a reminder of the area's early farming history; it's open Tuesday to Sunday 10 am to 4 pm ($2).

A little further around the lake, at the far end of Commonwealth Park, which stretches east from the Commonwealth Ave Bridge, is the **Carillon**, on Aspen Island. The 53-bell tower was a gift from Britain in 1963 to commemorate Canberra's 50th anniversary. The Carillon was completed in 1970 and the bells weigh from 7kg to six tonnes. There are recitals Wednesday from 12.45 to 1.30 pm and on weekends and public holidays from 2.45 to 3.30 pm.

West of the bridge, still on the north side of the lake, are the Acton and Black Mountain peninsulas. The southern shore of the lake, along which are the impressive National Gallery of Australia and the High

Court, forms the base of the parliamentary triangle.

Parliament House

South of the lake at the end of Commonwealth Ave, the four-legged flagpole on top of Capital Hill marks the new Parliament House. This, the most recent aspect of Walter Burley Griffin's vision to become a reality, sits at the apex of the parliamentary triangle. Opened in 1988, it cost $1.1 billion, took eight years to build and replaced old Parliament House lower down the hill on King George Terrace, which served 11 years longer than its intended 50-year life. The new Parliament House was designed by the US-based Italian Romaldo Giurgola, who won a competition entered by more than 300 architects.

It's built into the hill and the roof has been grassed over to preserve the shape of the original hilltop. The interior design and decoration is splendid. A different combination of Australian timbers is used in each of its principal sections. Seventy new art and craft works were commissioned from Australian artists and a further 3000 were bought.

The building's main axis runs north-east to south-west in a direct line from the old Parliament House, the War Memorial across the lake and Mt Ainslie. On either side of this axis, two high, granite-faced walls curve out from the centre to the corners of the site – on a plan these walls look like back-to-back boomerangs. The House of Representatives is to the east of the walls and the Senate to the west. They're linked to the centre by covered walkways.

Extensive areas of Parliament House are open daily to the public from 9 am to 5 pm. You enter through the white marble **Great Verandah** at the north-east end of the main axis, where Nelson Tjakamarra's *Meeting Place* mosaic, within the pool, represents a gathering of Aboriginal tribes. Inside, the grey-green marble columns of the foyer symbolise a forest, while marquetry panels on the walls depict Australian flora. From the 1st floor you look down on the **Great Hall**, with its 20m-long Arthur Boyd tapestry. A public gallery above the Great Hall has a 16m-long embroidery, created by 500 people.

Beyond the Great Hall you reach the gallery above the Members' Hall – the central 'crossroads' of the building – with the flagpole above it and passages to the debating chambers on each side. One of only four existing originals of the **Magna Carta** is on display here. South of the Members' Hall are the committee rooms and ministers' offices. The public can view the committee rooms and attend some of their proceedings.

You can also wander over the grassy top of the building.

If you want to make sure of a place in the **House of Representatives'** gallery, book by phone (☎ 6277 4890) or write to the Principal Attendant, House of Representatives, Parliament House, Canberra. Some seats are left unbooked but on sitting days you'd have to queue early to get one. Seats in the **Senate** gallery are almost always available. Senate debates are much tamer affairs than those in the House of Representatives where the prime minister and leader of the opposition slug it out.

On non-sitting days there are free **guided tours** every half-hour; on sitting days there's a talk on the building in the Great Hall gallery every half-hour.

Bus Nos 231, 234, 235 and 901 run from the city to Parliament House.

Old Parliament House

On King George Terrace, halfway between the new Parliament House and the lake, this building was the seat of Australia's federal government from 1927 to 1988.

The end of its parliamentary days was marked in style. As the corridors of power echoed to the defence minister's favourite Rolling Stones records the prime minister and the leader of the opposition joined together in song, arm-in-arm. Bodies were seen dragging themselves away well after dawn the next morning – and that's just what got into print!

The views from the grounds are good and there are tours of the building and displays

ACT

Federal Politics Since 1901

With less than a century of federal government, Australian political history is much more accessible than that of older nations. The virtues, failings and foibles of the 20-odd prime ministers are remembered and form part of the country's folk history.

The Early Years In the first decade or so, questions of trade (free or protected) dominated the governments, and the notorious White Australia policy was established. Although it was blatantly racist, the alternative might have been worse, as the policy stopped the importing of people from Pacific islands to work the Queensland canefields. This was practically slavery and many of the labourers had been tricked into coming to Australia; some were even kidnapped.

During WWI the Labor Party won office and in 1915 Billy Hughes ('the little digger') became prime minister. Hughes decided that conscription was necessary to bolster Australia's contribution to the European war, but his party disagreed, as did the Australian people who narrowly rejected conscription in an acrimonious referendum. Hughes was sacked as leader of the Labor Party, but he joined with conservatives to form a new government and remained prime minister. Another referendum on conscription was lost in 1917, but Hughes established himself as a world figure during the post-war peace conferences at Versailles and remained prime minister until 1923.

Stanley Bruce, the epitome of a conservative prime minister, took over from Hughes and led the government until 1929 when Labor won the general election. Internal squabbling saw Joe Lyons leave the party and join the conservatives to form the United Australia Party (UAP), which won government in 1931.

The Menzies Era In 1939 Robert Menzies became leader of the UAP, and thus prime minister. Like Stanley Bruce, he was very proper and very conservative. The Labor Party ousted Menzies in the 1941 election and John Curtin steered the country through WWII. Curtin died just before the war ended and Joe Chifley, a train-driver from Bathurst, became the Labor prime minister.

Chifley's policies of welcoming refugees from Europe, building universities and instituting large projects such as the Snowy Mountains Hydro-Electric Scheme shaped postwar Australia.

In 1949 the conservatives won office, again under Robert Menzies, now leader of the new Liberal Party (which is *not* a liberal party, except in the economic sense). He was to rule until 1966, when he retired. After a bout of McCarthy-style repression of Communists, the Menzies years passed like a long, long dream where old values comfortably enveloped and smothered new ideas.

Menzies was besotted with the British royal family, but saw that alliance with the USA had become essential and he led the country into the Vietnam disaster. After his retirement, subsequent Liberal prime ministers continued conscripting 18-year-olds (who were too young to vote) to fight in Vietnam.

from the collections of the National Museum and the Australian Archives. The building is also home to the **National Portrait Gallery** (☎ 6273 4723).

Old Parliament House is open daily from 9 am to 4 pm; admission is $2 ($1 children).

National Gallery of Australia

This excellent art gallery (☎ 6240 6411/6502) is on Parkes Place beside the High Court and the south bank of Lake Burley Griffin.

The Australian collection ranges from traditional Aboriginal art through to 20th-century works by Arthur Boyd, Sidney Nolan and Albert Tucker. Aboriginal works include bark paintings from Arnhem Land, *pukumani* burial poles from the Tiwi people of Melville and Bathurst Islands off Darwin, printed fabrics by the women of Utopia and Ernabella in central Australia, and paintings from Yuendumu, also in central Australia. There are often temporary exhibitions from the Kimberley and other areas where Aboriginal art is flourishing.

In addition to works from the early decades of European settlement and the 19th-century romantics, there are examples of the early nationalistic artistic statements of Charles Conder, Arthur Streeton and Tom Roberts. The collection is not confined to paintings: sculptures, prints, drawings, photographs, furniture, ceramics, fashion, textiles and silverware are all on display. The

'All the way with LBJ', simpered Prime Minister Harold Holt. Massive protests against the war helped the Labor Party under Gough Whitlam to win power in the 1972 elections.

Whitlam & the Dismissal The Whitlam government irrevocably changed Australia. In the government's three hectic years many things now taken for granted were instituted: free health care, free tertiary education (now disappearing), land rights for Aborigines, equal pay for women, no-fault divorce, legal aid and much more.

However, the pace of change stirred up strong opposition and the government became embroiled in a series of scandals. On 11 November 1975, Governor General John Kerr dismissed the government. (Coincidentally, 11 November is also the date of the WWI armistice and the day Ned Kelly was hung – the Armistice Day minute of silence has varied meanings in this country.)

The proclamation dismissing Whitlam and installing Liberal leader Malcolm Fraser as prime minister ended with the phrase 'God save the Queen'. Whitlam's fiery response concluded 'Well may you say God save the Queen, because *nothing* will save the Governor General'. Until then most Australians had considered the governor general as a quaint piece of decoration, a hangover from the days when the country was a British colony. To find that the Queen, via the governor general, could dismiss an elected government came as a rude shock, but Whitlam nevertheless lost the subsequent elections.

Malcolm Fraser then spent six years dismantling Whitlam's reforms. It seemed that another Menzies era was beginning, but Bob Hawke, leader of the powerful Council of Trade Unions, was hurried into parliament and manoeuvred into leadership of the Labor Party in time to win the 1983 elections. The Labor leader whom Hawke replaced was Bill Hayden, a left-winger with republican leanings who later became governor general. After the Whitlam debacle the Labor Party decided not to rock the boat, with the result that Hawke's years at the helm seemed comparatively bland.

Politics in the '90s In 1991 Hawke was ousted as party leader by his treasurer, Paul Keating, who thus became prime minister. Keating earned his spurs by winning the apparently unwinnable elections of 1993 and, despite a penchant for Italian suits and antique clocks, his rough-house debating style earned him a reputation as a tough Labor leader of the old school.

Keating was a politician who liked to lead from the front and pushed for closer ties with Asia and for Australia to become a republic. Maybe he pushed too fast, maybe it was his perceived arrogance, maybe after 13 years of Labor rule people wanted a change, but whatever the reason, in 1996 the conservative Liberal-National Party coalition was returned to power. Liberal leader, John Howard, became prime minister and National leader, Tim Fischer, became his deputy. One of Howard's first acts as PM was to hang a picture of the Queen in his office.

Waiting in the wings for the top job is the treasurer, Peter Costello. And the politician he most admires? Paul Keating. ∎

Sculpture Garden, which is always open, has a variety of striking works. The garden is a great place to listen to Carillon recitals.

The gallery is open daily from 10 am to 5 pm. Admission is $3 (free for children and full-time students). There are tours at 11 am and 2 pm daily. Every Thursday and Sunday at 11 am there's a free tour focusing on Aboriginal art. The gallery often provides free lectures relating to its exhibitions and presents films on Fridays at 12.45 pm. Phone the gallery for details or check Saturday's *Canberra Times*.

High Court

The High Court building (☎ 6270 6811), on King Edward Terrace by the lake next to the National Gallery, is open daily from 9.45 am to 4.30 pm (admission free). Opened in 1980, its grandiose magnificence caused it to be dubbed 'Gar's Mahal', a reference to Sir Garfield Barwick, Chief Justice during the construction of the building. High Court sittings are open to the public (call to find out the times) and, because of the good acoustics, music is often played in the lobby on weekends.

Questacon – National Science & Technology Centre

This is a 'hands on' science museum (☎ 6270 2800) in the snappy white building on King Edward Terrace between the High Court and the National Library of Australia. There are

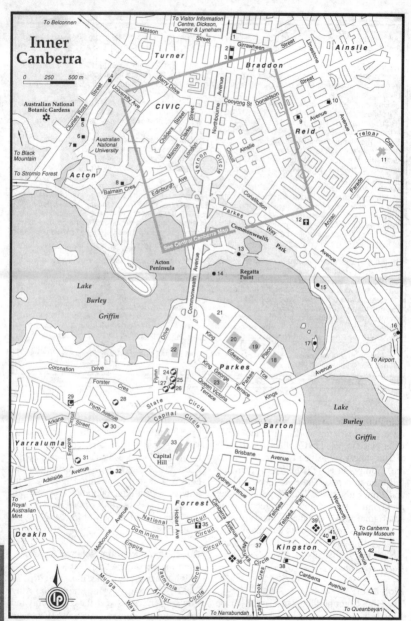

Inner Canberra

To Belconnen

Masson Street

To Visitor Information
Centre, Dickson,
Downer & Lyneham

Girrawheen Street

Limestone

Ainslie

0   250   500 m

Clunies Ross Street

University Ave

Barry Drive

Turner

Braddon

Street

2
3

Cooyong St

Donaldson

10

Australian National
Botanic Gardens

5

CIVIC

Childers Street

Clarke Street

London Circuit

Northbourne Avenue

Ainslie

9

Reid

Street

Avenue

To Black
Mountain

6
7

Australian
National
University

Marcus Clarke Street

11

Treloar Cres

To Stromlo Forest

Acton

Balmain Cres

8

Edinburgh Ave

Vernon Circle

Constitution

Parkes

Parade

Anzac

12

To
Parkes
Way

See Central Canberra Map

Commonwealth Park

Avenue

Acton
Peninsula

Commonwealth Avenue

13

Lake

14

Regatta
Point

Burley

15

Griffin

16

21

King Edward

20   19

17

22

18

Place

Coronation   Drive

Parkes Tce

Forster Cres

Flynn

24

25

27   26

Parkes

King George Terrace

23

Queen Victoria
Terrace

Parkes Terrace

Kings

Avenue

To Airport

29

Perth Avenue

28

State

Circle

Capital   Circle

Lake

Arkana

Empire Circuit

30

Burley

Yarralumla

Street

Barton

Griffin

31

Brisbane   Avenue

33

Adelaide   Avenue

32

Capital
Hill

Sydney Avenue

34

To
Royal
Australian
Mint

Forrest

National   Circuit

Melbourne Avenue

Dominion Circuit

Hobart Ave

Canberra Avenue

35

Deakin

Empire   Circuit

Tasmania Circle

Mugga   Way

Arthur   Circle

36

37

38

Kings

Telopea Park

Telopea Park

Wentworth

39

40   41

Kingston

42

Canberra   Avenue

Capt. Cook Cres

To Canberra
Railway Museum

Avenue

To Narrabundah

To Queanbeyan

ACT

PLACES TO STAY		OTHER			
1	Capital Executive Apartments	11	Australian War Memorial	24	UK High Commission
2	Country Comfort Hotel	12	Church of St John the Baptist	25	NZ High Commission
3	Kythera Motel	13	National Capital Exhibition	26	Canadian High Commission
4	Bruce Hall	14	Captain Cook Memorial Water Jet	27	PNG High Commission
5	Burton & Garran Hall	15	Blundell's Farmhouse	28	Indonesian Embassy
6	Ursula College	16	Australian-American Memorial	29	Canberra Mosque
7	Burgmann College	17	Carillon	30	US Embassy
8	University House	18	National Gallery of Australia	31	Thai Embassy
9	Acacia Motor Lodge	19	High Court	32	The Lodge
10	Olim's Canberra Hotel	20	National Science & Technology Centre	33	Parliament House
22	Hyatt Hotel Canberra	21	National Library of Australia	35	Serbian Orthodox Church
34	Macquarie Private Hotel	23	Old Parliament House	36	Manuka Shopping Centre
38	Kingston Hotel			37	Manuka Swimming Pool
40	Motel Monaro			39	Kingston Shopping Centre
41	Victor Lodge			42	Railway Station

over 200 'devices' in the centre's five galleries plus outdoor areas where you can use 'props' to get a feeling for a scientific concept and then see its application to an everyday situation. Displays include the earthquake experience, the 'thongaphone' and the exhibit which gives you the chance to be a judge of Olympic diving. It might be educational, but it's also great fun.

It's open daily from 10 am to 5 pm. Entry is $8 ($4 children, concessions $5).

National Library of Australia
Also on Parkes Place beside the lake is the National Library of Australia (☎ 6262 1111), one of the most elegant buildings in Canberra. The visitor information desk is staffed Monday to Friday from 9 am to 5 pm.

The library has more than five million books and among its displays are rare books, paintings, early manuscripts and maps, Captain Cook's *Endeavour* journal, a fine model of the ship itself and special exhibitions. There are guided tours (☎ 6262 1699) Tuesday to Thursday at 2 pm and free films (☎ 6262 1475) are shown on Thursday night at 7 pm. You can access the Internet at a terminal in the foyer and in the Brindabella Bistro on the 4th floor.

The library is open from 9 am to 9 pm

Monday to Thursday, from 9 am to 5 pm Friday and Saturday and from 1.30 to 5 pm on Sunday.

Royal Australian Mint
The mint (☎ 6202 6999), south of the lake on Denison St in Deakin, produces all Australia's coins. Through plate-glass windows (to keep you at arm's length) you can see the whole process, from raw materials to finished coins. There's also a collection of rare coins in the foyer. The mint is open weekdays from 9 am to 4 pm and weekends from 10 am to 3 pm; admission is free. Bus Nos 230, 231 and 267 run past it.

Australian War Memorial
The massive war memorial, north of the lake and at the foot of Mt Ainslie, looks along Anzac Parade to the old Parliament House across the lake. It was conceived in 1925 and finally opened in 1941, not long after WWII broke out in the Pacific. It houses an amazing collection of pictures, dioramas, relics and exhibitions, including a fine collection of old aircraft. For anyone with an interest in toy soldiers, the miniature battle scenes are absorbing.

For the less military-minded, the memorial has an excellent **art collection**.

ACT

The **Hall of Memory** is the focus of the memorial. It features a beautiful interior, some superb stained-glass windows and a dome made of six million Italian mosaic pieces. Entombed here is the Unknown Australian Soldier whose remains were brought here from a WWI battlefield in 1993. Leading to the hall is the reflecting pool.

The War Memorial is open daily from 10 am to 5 pm (when the *Last Post* is played) and admission is free. Several free tours are held each day – some focusing on the artworks. Phone ☎ 6243 4268 for times. Bus Nos 233, 302, 303, 362, 363, 436 and 901 run nearby.

Several specific conflicts and campaigns also have memorials along Anzac Parade, including the impressive **Australia Hellenic memorial** and the **Vietnam memorial** further towards the lake. A new one is to be built commemorating those who served and died in the Korean War.

Australian National University (ANU)
The ANU's attractive grounds take up most of the area between Civic and Black Mountain and are pleasant to wander around. University House (☎ 6249 2229) on Balmain Crescent is open weekdays. The University Union on University Ave offers a variety of shops, cheap eats and entertainment. On Kingsley St near the junction with Hutton St is the **Drill Hall Gallery** (☎ 6249 5832), an offshoot of the National Gallery of Australia, with changing exhibitions of contemporary art. It's open Wednesday to Sunday from noon to 5 pm. Admission is free.

National Film & Sound Archive
The archive (☎ 6209 3111) is housed in an Art Deco building on McCoy Circuit at the south-eastern edge of the university area. Interesting exhibitions (some interactive) from the archive's collections are on show. The archive is open daily from 9 am to 5 pm; admission is free.

Over the road is the **Australian Academy of Science** (not open to the public), known locally as the Martian Embassy – it looks like a misplaced flying saucer.

Australian National Botanic Gardens
On the lower slopes of Black Mountain, behind the ANU, the beautiful 50-hectare botanical gardens are devoted to Australia's unique native flora. There are educational walks, including one among plants used by

---

Life in Canberra
Thus did people live who had such an income; and in a land where each man's pay, age and position are printed in a book, that all may read, it is hardly worth while to play at pretences in word or deed.
Rudyard Kipling, 1898

Kipling's observation about the British Raj in India is less applicable to Canberra than it once was, as private enterprise is booming. However, the various strata of public service jobs are still the major social indicators in the city. Add to that the fact that the average wage in Canberra is about $100 a week higher than in the rest of the country and you have a city very different from the Australian mainstream.

Rules and regulations spill over from the public service into other areas of life and the city has strict planning regulations. Just finding a corner store can mean a major trek through the curving streets of the neighbourhoods, and you won't find petrol stations on prime sites. (Neon-light junkies can get a hit on Lonsdale St, where there are several service stations and a junkfood outlet in full regalia.)

Not surprisingly, there's a bit of a 'barrack-room lawyer' tendency and people lodge appeals about neighbours building houses a centimetre or so higher than the rules allow.

Life in Canberra isn't as secure as it once was. There has been a large reduction in the number of jobs as the federal public service 'downsizes'. And people must question the significance of a prime minister choosing to live in Kirribilli House in Sydney, rather than in the Lodge, the PM's official residence in Canberra. ■

Aborigines. A highlight is **Rainforest Gully**, achieved in this dry climate by a 'misting' system. The **eucalypt lawn** has 600 species of this ubiquitous Australian tree, while the **Mallee section** displays the typical vegetation of semi-desert country.

There are **guided walks** from Monday to Friday at 11 am and on weekends at 11 am and 2 pm. The information centre (☎ 6250 9540), open 9.30 am to 4.30 pm daily, has an introductory video about the gardens and the **Botanical Bookshop** has an excellent range of books, cards and posters. Near where the walks start and finish is the *Kookaburra Cafe* with a pleasant outdoor section.

The gardens open daily from 9 am to 5 pm and are reached from Clunies Ross St (take bus No 904).

Australian Institute of Sport (AIS)
Founded in 1981 as part of an effort to improve Australia's performance at events like the Olympics, the AIS (☎ 6252 1111) is on Leverrier Crescent, in the northern suburb of Bruce, not far from the YHA hostel. It provides training facilities for the country's top athletes who lead hour-long **tours** of the institute daily at 11 am and 2 pm for $7 ($3 children). The tennis courts and swimming pools are open to visitors; phone ☎ 6252 1281 for bookings.

Bus No 431 runs to the AIS from the city centre.

National Aquarium & Australian Wildlife Sanctuary
The impressive aquarium (☎ 6287 1211) is about 6km south-west of the centre on Lady Denman Drive near Scrivener Dam, at the west end of Lake Burley Griffin. It also includes a wildlife sanctuary of native fauna. It's open daily from 9 am to 5.30 pm and admission is $10 (children $6). Take bus No 904 from the Civic bus interchange in the city centre.

National Museum of Australia
A site for the long-awaited museum has finally been found on Acton Peninsula, west of the Commonwealth Ave Bridge. It is due to open on 1 January 2001. Meanwhile, the visitor centre (☎ 6256 1126) on Lady Denman Drive, north of Yarralumla, is open weekdays from 10 am to 4 pm and weekends from 1 to 4 pm. It displays items from the museum's collection, including the heart of Phar Lap, Australia's wonder racehorse of the 1930s who died in suspicious circumstances in California. The rest of him is in the National Museum of Victoria in Melbourne.

Mugga Lane Zoo
About 7km south of the city centre, the zoo (☎ 6295 3610), on Mugga Lane in Red Hill, has over 100 species of native and exotic animals and birds. It's open daily from 9 am to 5 pm but 4 pm is the latest you can get in. Admission is $7.50 (children $3.50).

Take bus No 238 to the Mugga Lane intersection along Hindmarsh Drive; the zoo is about half a kilometre south.

Other Attractions
You can do no more than drive by and peek through the gates of the prime minister's official Canberra residence, **The Lodge**, on Adelaide Ave, Deakin – Australia's version of 10 Downing St. The same is true of **Government House**, the residence of the governor general, which is on the south-west corner of Lake Burley Griffin, but there's a lookout beside Scrivener Dam at the western end of the lake giving a good view of the building. The governor general is the representative of the Australian monarch – who lives in London and also happens to be the British monarch.

The **Australian-American Memorial**, at the eastern end of Kings Ave, is a 79m-high pillar topped by an eagle which commemorates US support of Australia during WWII.

The **Church of St John the Baptist**, in Reid just east of Civic, was built between 1841 and 1845 and thus predates the capital. The stained glass windows show pioneering families of the region. The adjoining **St John's Schoolhouse Museum** (☎ 6249 6839) has some early relics and is open on Wednesday from 10 am to noon, weekends from 2 to 4 pm and more often during school

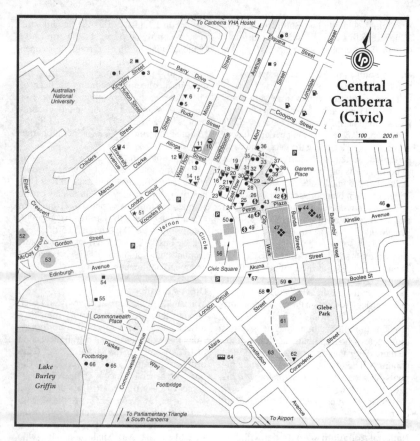

Central
Canberra
(Civic)

To Canberra YHA Hostel

Australian
National
University

Lake
Burley
Griffin

Civic Square

Garema
Place

Glebe
Park

Commonwealth
Place

To Parliamentary Triangle
& South Canberra

To Airport

holidays ($1.50). The **Serbian Orthodox Church** on National Circuit in Forrest has its walls and ceiling painted with a series of biblical murals.

The **Royal Military College, Duntroon** was once a homestead, with parts dating from the 1830s. From April until October, tours of the grounds start at the sign in Starkey Park, Jubilee Ave, on Tuesdays and Thursdays at 2.30 pm (except public holidays). Bookings are advised (☎ 6275 9408).

The enterprising **Tradesmen's Union Club** (☎ 6248 0999), at 2 Badham St off Antill St in Dickson, has a large collection of

'old and unusual bicycles' in its Bicycle Museum. It's good for kids and there's a BMX track next door which hires out bikes.

The club also runs the **Downer Club** (☎ 6248 5333) nearby on Hawdon St, home to 'the world's largest beer collection', although it has been put in storage indefinitely. The club also has an Antarctic igloo on display. Not interested? Well, what about an observatory with an astronomer on duty nightly from 7.15 pm? A new planetarium is being built. Admission to all this is free.

Near the railway station on Geijera Place (off Cunningham St) in Kingston, you'll find

PLACES TO STAY
2   Toad Hall
9   Downtown Spero's
     Motel
31 City Walk Hotel
54 Rydges Canberra
     Hotel & Bobby
     McGee's
55 Capital Tower
60 Capital Parkroyal

PLACES TO EAT
6   Fringe Benefits
7   Psychedeli
14 Charcoal Restaurant
15 Lemon Grass
16 Waffles Piano Bar
18 Waffles Patisserie &
     Bakery
20 Pancake Parlour
21 Thai Lotus & Canberra
     Vietnamese
24 Bailey's Corner,
     Tosolini & Australian
     Pizza Kitchen
25 Antigo Cafe
33 Mama's Cafe & Bar
37 Sammy's Kitchen &
     Gus' Cafe
38 Ali Baba & Heaven
     Nite Club
40 Noshes Cafe
41 Red Sea Restaurant,
     Club Asmara &
     Tutu Tango

44 Sizzle City
57 Anarkali Pakistani
     Restaurant
62 Food Hall

OTHER
1   Drill Hall Gallery
3   Environment Centre
4   Canberra Worker's
     Club
5   Dalton's Bookshop
8   NRMA
10 Jolimont Centre
     (Countrylink,
     Airlines, Bus Station)
11 GPO
12 Wig & Pen
13 Smith's Bookshop
17 Private Bin
19 Pandora's
22 Moosehead's Pub
23 Asylum & Phoenix
26 ANZ Bank
27 Commonwealth
     Government
     Bookshop
28 ACT Government City
     Shopfront
29 Police Kiosk
30 Civic Bus Interchange
32 Travellers' Medical &
     Vaccination Centre
34 Center Cinema
35 Civic Cinemas 3

36 ACT Government City
     Shop
39 Wilderness Society
42 Commonwealth Bank
43 Merry-go-round
45 City Market &
     Supermarket
46 Gorman House
     Community Arts
     Centre & Cafe Luna
47 Canberra Centre
48 Westpac Bank
49 National Australia Bank
50 Women's Information &
     Referral Centre
51 Canberra City Police
     Station
52 National Film & Sound
     Archive
53 Academy of Science
56 Canberra Theatre
     Centre
58 Electric Shadows
     Cinema & Bookshop
59 Canberra Blade Centre
61 Casino Canberra
63 National Convention
     Centre
64 Olympic Swimming
     Pool
65 Bike Hire
66 Acton Park Ferry
     Terminal & Boat Hire

Australia's oldest steam locomotive, at the **Canberra Railway Museum** (☎ 6239 6707). It's open Saturday and Sunday 1 to 4 pm. Admission is $4 ($2 children).

About 7km north of the centre on the corner of Anthill St and the Federal Highway, the **Australian Heritage Village** (☎ 018 481 643) is a collection of craft shops, galleries and tea-rooms housed in some substantial old-style buildings. It's actually quite a pleasant place.

Canberra's **mosque** is in Yarralumla, the embassy area, on the corner of Hunter St and Empire Circuit. Kids might enjoy a visit to **Weston Park** in Yarralumla beside the lake. There's a maze and a miniature railway which operate on weekends and during school holidays, as well as treehouses and other entertainments.

Activities
Bushwalking Tidbinbilla Nature Reserve has marked trails; for this and other places see the Around Canberra section. Contact the Canberra Bushwalking Club through the Environment Centre (☎ 6247 3064) on Kingsley St in the ANU campus. Here you can buy *Above the Cotter*, which details walks and drives in the area. Graeme Barrow's *Exploring Namadgi National Park and Tidbinbilla Nature Reserve* is also useful. There are also some good rockclimbing areas in Namadgi National Park.

Bushwalking information is also available from the ACT Government City Shop, on the corner of Mort and Bunda Sts.

Watersports Dobel Boat Hire (☎ 6249 6861) at the Acton Park ferry terminal on

ACT

Lake Burley Griffin rents out canoes at $12 an hour and catamarans at $35 an hour, plus paddle boats, sailboards and surf skis. However, private power boats are not allowed on the lake. Canoeing in the Murrumbidgee River, about 20km west of Canberra city centre at its closest point, is also popular.

Swimming pools around the city include the Olympic Pool on Allara St, Civic, and the Manuka Swimming Pool on Currie St. Swimming in Lake Burley Griffin is not recommended.

River Runners (☎ 6288 5610) offers a 5½-hour white water rafting trip on the Shoalhaven River, 1½ hours from Canberra, for $115 – or less if you can meet them there.

Cycling Canberra has a great series of bicycle tracks – probably the best in Australia. See Getting Around for more information.

In-Line Skating Several places hire out in-line skates. Mr Spokes Bike Hire (☎ 6257 1188), near the Acton Park ferry terminal, charges $15 for the first hour and $5 for subsequent hours. Canberra Blade Centre (☎ 6257 7233), at 38 Akuna St in the city, charges $15 for the first *two* hours and $5 for subsequent hours. Fees at both include all safety gear.

Organised Tours

The visitor information centre has details of the many tours of the city and the ACT. Half-day city tours start at around $30 and there is a variety of day trips to places like the Snowy Mountains, nature reserves, the satellite tracking station, sheep stations, horse studs and fossicking areas around the ACT. Canberra Region Tours (☎ 6247 7281), at 57 Macleay St in Turner, offers day tours of the ACT for $49 (children $30); this includes lunch and admission fees.

Canberra Cruises (☎ 6295 3544) has 1½-hour cruises daily at 10.30 am and 12.30 pm on Lake Burley Griffin for $12 (children $6).

Umbrella Tours (☎ 6285 2605), at 1 Bailey Place in Yarralumla, has 1½-hour walking and cycling tours of the city.

The Environment Centre on the ANU campus offers tours looking at nature and ecology in Canberra and beyond; call ☎ 6249 1560 for information and bookings.

Taking a flight is a good way of seeing the grand scale of the city's plan and several outfits offer aeroplane flights. The Canberra Flight Training Centre (☎ 6248 6766), based at the airport, has 40-minute scenic flights for $80 (minimum two people).

Special Events

The Canberra Festival takes place over 10 days each March and celebrates the city's birthday with music, food, Mardi Gras, displays, an exciting raft race, a birdman and birdwoman rally, and a big parade. Many of the events are held in Commonwealth Park, which is the site of a carnival. A popular event is the Royal Military College band playing the *1812 Overture*, complete with cannon!

After the sort of winter they get here on the Monaro Tableland, spring is something to celebrate and Canberra does it with verve through its Floriade Festival in September and October. It concentrates on Canberra's spectacular spring flowers, but there are many related events and activities.

Out of character with Canberra's image as a somewhat staid centre of government, the Street Machine Summernats (basically a big hot-rod show) is held in late December at Exhibition Park in Mitchell.

Places to Stay

Large numbers of public servants arrived in Canberra before residential areas were developed, so the government established hostels to house them. Many of these are now privately run as guesthouses, private hotels and even motels. They can be perfectly all right but some retain a rather institutional feel.

Camping *Canberra Motor Village* (☎ 6247 5466), 3km north-west of the centre on Kunzea St, O'Connor, has a bush setting and charges $18 for sites, $39 a double for on-site vans and from $65 to $79 a double in cabins. There's a restaurant, kitchen, tennis court and swimming pool. *Canberra Lakes Carotel* (☎ 6241 1377) off the Federal Highway in Watson, 6km north of the centre, has sites from $10, on-site vans for $33 for two people and more expensive motel-style cabins.

Canberra South Motor Park (☎ 6280 6176) is 8km south-east of the city in Fyshwick, on Canberra Ave, the main road to Queanbeyan. A tent site costs $12 or $15 with power; cabins with bathroom are $55.

More-rural camping – cheaper too – can be found out of the city at places like Cotter Dam. See the Around Canberra section.

Hostels In the centre of Canberra, the *City Walk Motel* (☎ 6257 0124), at 2 Mort St on the corner of City Walk, has dorm beds for $16 and single/doubles from $37/42. Most rooms share bathrooms but it's a reasonable option with a spacious TV lounge and kitchen facilities.

Canberra YHA Hostel (☎ 6248 9155) on Dryandra St in O'Connor, about 6km north-west of Civic, was recently named the second most popular YHA hostel worldwide. It's purpose-built and well designed and equipped. There's a travel desk (☎ 6248 0177) which handles domestic and international travel. Dorm beds cost $16; twin rooms with attached bathrooms cost $22 a person or $20 with shared bathroom. (Add $3 if you aren't a YHA member.) The office is open from 7 am to 10.30 pm but you can check in up until midnight if you give advance warning.

Bus No 304 runs regularly from the Civic bus interchange to the Scrivener St stop on Miller St, O'Connor. From there, follow the signs. From the Jolimont Centre, take bus Nos 307 or 308 to the corner of Scrivener and Brigalow St, head north-east up Scrivener St to Dryandra St and turn right. Driving, turn west off Northbourne Ave onto Macarthur Ave and after about 2km turn right onto Dryandra St. You can hire bicycles at the hostel.

Kingston Hotel (☎ 6295 0123) is a large, popular pub on the corner of Canberra Ave and Giles St in Manuka, a couple of kilometres from Parliament House. It offers shared accommodation for $12 with optional linen hire ($4). There are cooking facilities and counter meals are available. Bus No 238 from the city runs past.

Colleges The Australian National University (ANU), in Acton just west of Civic, is a pleasant place to stay. A selection of residential colleges rents rooms during vacations at the Easter (one week), June or July, (two weeks), September (two weeks) and late-November to late-February.

Toad Hall (☎ 6267 4999), on Kingsley St near the corner of Barry Drive, is the closest to town and has basic rooms for $16.50/98 a day/week. There are two bathrooms per residential block, with 10 people in each block.

Most other colleges are along Daley Rd at the western end of the campus near Clunies Ross St. At *Burgmann College* (☎ 6267 5222) rates for students/nonstudents are $30/40 with breakfast or $38/48 for full board. *Bruce Hall* and *Burton & Garran Hall* (☎ 6267 4333) have rooms for $30 a night for the first two nights and less per night if you stay longer. The weekly rate is $105 and $17 a night thereafter. *Ursula College* (☎ 6279 4300) charges students/nonstudents $35/45 per night; if you stay a week you're only charged for six nights. Rates include breakfast and other meals are available.

Fenner Hall (☎ 6279 9000) has basic rooms for $25/110 a day/week.

Guesthouses & Private Hotels *Victor Lodge* (☎ 6295 7777) is a clean, friendly place at 29 Dawes St in Kingston, half a kilometre from the railway station and a couple of kilometres south-east of Parliament House. Rooms with shared bathrooms are $35/44 a single/double or you can share a four-bunk room for $16, including a light breakfast. It has a barbecue and offers bike rental. From the city take bus No 238 to the

ACT

nearby Kingston shops, or phone to see if they can pick you up.

Also south of the lake, *Macquarie Hotel* (☎ 6273 2325), at 18 National Circuit at the corner of Bourke St, is a large, fairly modern place with over 500 rooms, all of which have shared bathrooms. Singles cost $30 to $40 ($120 to $160 weekly) and doubles $50 ($200 weekly). Bus No 310 from the city stops at the front door.

Entering Canberra from the north you pass a cluster of guesthouses on the east side of Northbourne Ave in Downer, south of where the Barton Highway from Yass meets the Federal Highway from Goulburn. All are clean, straightforward and comfortable. It's worth checking to see if there are any special deals. It's 4km or so into town, but buses run past and Dickson shopping centre isn't far away.

At No 524, the *Blue & White Lodge* (☎ 6248 0498), which also runs the similarly priced *Blue Sky* at No 528, has singles/doubles from $40/50 to $55/65. Prices include a cooked breakfast and rooms have TV and a fridge, but most bathrooms are shared. Rooms with attached bathroom go for $60 a single or double. They can probably pick you up from the bus station. *Chelsea Lodge* (☎ 6248 0655) at No 526 also does pick-ups and charges $60/75 with private bathroom; rates include breakfast. *Northbourne Lodge* (☎ 6257 2599) at No 522 is a pleasant place that's a little more expensive. Rooms, including breakfast, cost $58/68 or $68/70 with bathroom.

Motels Most motels are quite expensive. You might do better than the prices listed here if you book at the visitor information centre, as it often has special rates.

Not far from the city centre, *Acacia Motor Lodge* (☎ 6249 6955) at 65 Ainslie Ave charges $68/74, including light breakfast. As usual for Canberra, this doesn't much resemble the popular idea of a motel and the rooms are fairly small.

Downtown Spero's Motel (☎ 6249 1388), at 82 Northbourne Ave close to the city centre, has standard rooms for $80 or deluxe

ones for $100. Rooms have TV, telephone, fridge and tea/coffee-making facilities. A little further out, *Kythera Motel* (☎ 6248 7611), at No 98, charges $65 for a room.

South of the centre in Kingston next to Victor Lodge, *Motel Monaro* (☎ 6295 2111), at 27 Dawes St, has singles/doubles for $76/79.

Other places are scattered through the suburbs, with a concentration of mid-range motels about 8km south of the city in Narrabundah, mostly on Jerrabomberra Ave. *Crestwood Gardens* (☎ 6295 2099), at No 39, has rooms with full facilities for $55/65. *Sundown Village* (☎ 6239 0333), on Jerrabomberra Ave south of Hindmarsh Drive, is quite attractive with self-contained 'villas' (with kitchenettes) costing $75 to $86, plus $10 for an extra person.

Some caravan parks also have motel-type accommodation: *Canberra Lakes Carotel* (☎ 6241 1377), off the Federal Highway in Watson has 'chalets' with cooking facilities, TVs and bathrooms for $45 to $65. Bedding is provided and there's a pool and a cafeteria. *Red Cedars Motel* (☎ 6241 3222), on the corner of Stirling Ave and Aspinall St in Watson, has units from $49/59/69 a single/double/triple. There's a pool and rooms have TVs.

Apartments *Canberrawide Budget Apartments* (☎ 6257 7637), at 8 Ijong St in Braddon, has a range of apartments around the city. These are usually let by the week at $525 for a one-bedroom apartment and $700 for a two-bedroom apartment, but it also offers overnight stays for $75/130.

University House (☎ 6249 5211), on Balmain Crescent at the ANU campus, has one-bedroom/two-bedroom apartments for $99/140 (it also has cheaper standard motel rooms $81/90 a single/double).

Capital Executive Apartments (☎ 6295 1111), at 108 Northbourne Ave, has studio apartments for $112 per night and larger single-bedroom apartments with spa for $145. *Capital Tower* (☎ 6276 3444), at 2 Marcus Clarke St, has serviced apartments from $145 to $190.

Top-End Hotels Rates at top-end places can vary depending on the package; ring around or ask at the visitor information centre.

At the old but pleasant *Olim's Canberra Hotel* (☎ 6248 5511), at the corner of Ainslie and Limestone Aves in Braddon, rooms cost from $130 a single or double.

Northbourne Ave has several hotels in this category. The 156-room, four-star *Canberra Rex Hotel* (☎ 6248 5311), at No 150, has singles/doubles for $100/110. Closer to the centre, the *Country Comfort Hotel* (☎ 6249 1411, 1800 065 064), at No 102, has rooms for $132, or $120 if you're a member of the NRMA or its equivalent. *Canberra International Hotel* (☎ 6247 6966, 1800 026 305), at No 242 near the corner of Wakefield Ave, has standard rooms for $115, or apartments with spa for $145.

The rack rate at the *Capital Parkroyal* (☎ 6247 8999), at 1 Binara St near the casino, is $225 but it has package deals for $165 including breakfast.

The 15-storey *Rydges Canberra Hotel* (☎ 6247 6244), at 1 London Circuit southwest of Vernon Circle, has singles/doubles with full facilities including breakfast for $156/263.

Canberra's only five-star hotel is the *Hyatt Hotel Canberra* (☎ 6270 1234) on Commonwealth Ave in Yarralumla. This is the old Hotel Canberra, a venerable institution. Rooms cost $290 to $350, with suites starting at $650.

Places to Eat

Canberra's fine eating scene is continually improving. Most places are around Civic with an upmarket selection in Manuka, an Asian strip in Dickson and other possibilities scattered around the suburbs. Smoking isn't allowed in Canberra's eateries, one reason why you see so many people sitting at outside tables.

City Centre There's a food hall in the *Canberra Centre* where you can fill up on burgers, pasta, croissants and more for $4 to $7. There's a smaller food hall on the ground floor in *City Market* on Bunda St where the excellent *Sizzle City* has cheap Japanese lunch packs. Another food hall is in *Glebe Park* beside the National Convention Centre.

Upstairs in the Sydney building at 21 East Row, the *Canberra Vietnamese Restaurant* (☎ 6247 4840) has main courses for less than $10. Nearby, upstairs at No 27, one of the best places to eat is the *Thai Lotus* (☎ 6249 6507), open nightly for dinner and for lunch from Tuesday to Friday. The food is excellent and prices reasonable – most meat mains are $12.50 and vegetable mains $9.50.

Bailey's Corner, on the corner of East Row and London Circuit, has a couple of places with outdoor tables. *Tosolini's* (☎ 6247 4317) is an Italian-based bistro which is good for a drink or a meal, including breakfast. Lunchtime specials cost from $10 and in the evening pasta dishes are $9 and mains $14. Downstairs, *Australian Pizza Kitchen* (☎ 6257 2727) has wood-fired pizzas for $8 to $12; it also brews its own beer. Around the corner on Petrie Plaza, *Antigo* (☎ 6249 8080) is a cafe and bar open daily until late. The diverse menu includes seafood barbecue for $15.90 and pasta for $12.90; during its 'happy hour', daily from 3 to 7 pm, mains cost $11.90.

Waffles Piano Bar (☎ 6247 2913), on the Northbourne Ave side of the Sydney building, offers a variety of food including pasta ($13), burgers ($10.50) and burritos ($11). Around the corner on Alinga St, *Waffles Patisserie & Bakery* (☎ 6257 7077) at No 102 has good ice creams, as well as cakes. A few doors east on the corner of East Row, *Pancake Parlour* (☎ 6247 2982), open 24 hours daily, has a three-course special for $12 on Saturday night.

On the south end of the Melbourne building, *Lemon Grass* (☎ 6247 2779) is a Thai restaurant with seafood mains for $14 and a good vegetarian selection for $11. Nearby, the *Charcoal Restaurant* (☎ 6248 8015) offers good steaks and seafood for $15.50 to $21. Beside the Westpac Bank on the corner of London Circuit and Akuna St, the *Anarkali Pakistani Restaurant* (☎ 6247 6135) has lunch specials for $15, dinner specials for $19.

The excellent *Fringe Benefits* (☎ 6247 4042), at 54 Marcus Clarke St, is a brasserie which has regularly won national wine and food awards and has main courses around $20. Nearby at No 60, *Psychedeli* (☎ 6247 0018) has good coffee, focaccia and pizza.

The *Brindabella Buffet* at the Capital Parkroyal, at 1 Binara St, has an all-you-can-eat hot breakfast buffet from 6.30 am for $19.95 and a lunch buffet for $24.95.

Garema Place Garema Place, just northeast of London Circuit, is full of restaurants and cafes, many with outside tables.

Noshes Cafe has breakfast all day for $4. *Happy's* (☎ 6249 7015) is a popular, reasonably priced Chinese restaurant with noodle dishes for $7.50 to $9.50. Nearby, *Mama's Cafe & Bar* (☎ 6248 0936) does home-made pasta for $9 and other meals for around $12.

Around the corner on Bunda St, *Gus's Cafe* (☎ 6248 8118) has outdoor tables and serves reasonable food with soup for $6 and pastas $8.50. It's open until midnight during the week and later on weekends. Not far away, *Sammy's Kitchen* (☎ 6247 1464) is a Chinese/Malaysian place with a good reputation and many dishes between $7 and $11. *Ali Baba* (☎ 6257 2538), on the corner of Bunda St and Garema Place's southern arm, does Lebanese takeaways, with shwarmas and felafels for around $4, meals for $9 to $10.50.

Red Sea Restaurant (☎ 6257 6633), at Club Asmara, at 121 Bunda St, has interesting decor and main courses, some African, from $13 to $15. It's closed Sundays. *Tutu Tango* (☎ 6257 7100), at No 124, is a cafe and bar with a varied menu: pizzas are $12 and vegetarian tostados $15.50.

Manuka South of the lake, not far from Capital Hill, is the Manuka shopping centre which services the diplomatic corps and well-heeled bureaucrats from surrounding suburbs. There are plenty of cafes and restaurants on Franklin, Fourneaux and Bougainville Sts and Flinders Way.

Several bars-cum-cafes stay open late. *On Fourneaux* (☎ 6295 6086), at 2 Furneaux St on the corner of Franklin St, has pizzas for $12.90 and burgers for $13.90; it also serves good gelati. Further south on Franklin St, the stylish *La Grange* (☎ 6295 8866) bar and brasserie has main courses for around $16 and live music on weekends.

Across Franklin St is *My Cafe* (☎ 6295 6632), with bagels and focaccia for $4.50 and main courses for between $8.50 and $10.50. Upstairs in the nearby Style Arcade, *Alanya* (☎ 6295 9678) is a good Turkish restaurant with starters for $8 to $10 and mains between $10 and $15. Also here is *Chez Daniel* (☎ 6295 7122), one of Canberra's better restaurants, serving French and Moroccan food. Main courses usually cost around $20, but it has a lunchtime three-course special for $27.90. *Timmy's Kitchen* (☎ 6295 6537) on Furneaux St is a popular Malaysian/Chinese place with main courses from $7.50 to $12.70. It has a good vegetarian selection.

Dickson The Dickson shopping area, a few kilometres north of Civic, is also a busy restaurant district and is sometimes called Little China because of its many Asian restaurants.

Dickson Asian Noodle House (☎ 6247 6380), at 19 Woolley St, is a popular Lao and Thai cafe with dishes for around $9. The Japanese *Sakura* (☎ 6247 1455), at No 51 opposite the BP service station, has lunch specials for under $10. The Malaysian *Rasa Sayang* (☎ 6249 7284), at No 43, is reasonably priced with noodles for $8.80 and a good vegetarian selection.

Pho Phu Quoc (☎ 6249 6662), at 4-6 Cape St, is a good Vietnamese restaurant with wonton soup for $2.50 and beef and rice noodles for $6. *La Lupa* (☎ 6247 7763) is a popular cafe with outside tables and jazz on Sunday mornings.

Elsewhere There's cheap food at the student union *Refectory*, on University Ave, at the ANU.

In Lyneham, *Tilley Devine's* (☎ 6249 1543), at 96 Wattle St on the corner of Brigelow St, is a well known cafe and bar.

The food is healthy (if you don't count the great cakes) and the clientele is diverse. Burgers are $6.90 and salads $9.80.

Cafe Luna (☎ 6249 6050), in the Gorman House Arts Centre on Ainslie Ave, a few minutes' walk from Civic, serves bagels for $6.50 and pasta for $7.50. It's closed Sunday.

A popular place for Sunday breakfast is *Cornucopia Bakery* (☎ 6249 1494)0, at 40 Mort St in Braddon, north of the city centre. *Delicateating* (☎ 6247 1314), on Macpherson St in O'Connor, is a good place for Sunday lunch when there's live jazz. Soup is $5.50 and pasta $11.

Entertainment

Canberra is more lively than its reputation suggests. Liberal licensing laws allow hotels unlimited opening hours and there are some 24-hour bars. Under-age drinking is strictly policed; if you don't have ID proving you're over 18, forget it. The 'Good Times' section in Thursday's *Canberra Times* has entertainment listings, while the free monthly *BMA* magazine lists bands and other events.

Also check with the foreign cultural organisations like the British Council (☎ 6326 2365) and the Goethe Institute (☎ 6247 4472) to find out what's on.

If you'd like a change from Australian leagues clubs and workers' clubs, phone one of the clubs which cater to Australians of foreign descent and ask if you can visit – see the yellow pages under 'Clubs, Social & General'.

Performing Arts *Canberra Theatre Centre* (☎ 6257 1077, 1800 802 025), on Civic Square, has several theatres with a varied range of events from rock bands and drama to ballet, opera and classical concerts. *Gorman House Arts Centre* (☎ 6249 7377), Ainslie Ave, Braddon, is home to several theatre and dance companies which put on occasional performances and exhibitions.

Music, Dancing & Drinking Friday night is the big drinking night in Canberra when everyone winds down after a hard week.

There's live music two or three nights a week during term at the *ANU union bar*, a good place for a drink even when there's no entertainment. Big touring acts often play at the *Refectory* as well as at the *Theatre Royal* ☎ 2574095) in the National Convention Centre, 31 Constitution Ave and *Bruce Outdoor Stadium*, (☎ 253 2111), Battye St, Bruce, part of the AIS complex.

In Civic, the Sydney building has a number of venues including the popular *Moosehead's Pub*, on the south side at 105 London Circuit. Around the corner, *Private Bin*, at 50 Northbourne Ave, is a big bar and nightclub that's popular with younger dancers. *The Phoenix* (☎ 6247 1606), at 21 East Row, has poetry and quiz nights. *Asylum*, upstairs at No 23, has live music most nights; entry costs $4 to $8, depending on who's playing. Not far away, *Pandora's* (☎ 6248 7405), on the corner of Alinga and Mort Sts, has a bar downstairs and a dance club upstairs.

Heaven Nite Club (☎ 6257 6180), on Garema Place, is popular with gays. *Club Asmara* (☎ 6257 6633), at 128 Bunda St near Garema Place, is home to the Red Sea Restaurant. The musical emphasis is on African, Latin and reggae rhythms. After about 9 pm you can listen to the music, sometimes live, without ordering a meal; on Friday and Saturday, however, there's a $5 cover charge.

The *Wig & Pen* (☎ 6248 0171), on the corner of West Row and Alinga St, is a British-style pub serving real ale.

Bobby McGee's (☎ 6257 7999) at Rydges Canberra Hotel, on London Circuit, is a popular dining/drinking/dancing complex. *Olim's Canberra Hotel* (☎ 6248 5511), in Braddon, has a piano bar with free jazz on a Thursday night and a popular beer garden.

In Kingston at the Green Square shopping area, *Filthy McFadden's* (☎ 6239 5303), at 62 Jardine St, is an Irish pub with music most nights. Nearby, the *Durham Castle Arms* (☎ 6295 1769) occasionally has live bands performing jazz and blues.

In Lyneham, *Tilley Devine's* (☎ 6249 1543), at 96 Wattle St on the corner of Brigelow St, has live music (usually a cut

ACT

above pub bands) on weekend nights. It also has poetry nights and talks by guest writers.

Canberra Southern Cross Club (☎ 6283 7200), on the corner of Corinna St and Hindmarsh Drive in Phillip south-west of the city, has local bands on Friday night and sometimes good jazz.

Other places that occasionally have bands include *Canberra Workers' Club* (☎ 6248 0399), on Childers St in Civic, the *Tradesmen's Union Club* (☎ 6248 0999), at 2 Badham St in Dickson, and *Canberra Labor Club* (☎ 6251 5522), on Chandler St in Belconnen.

Cinemas In Civic, *Center Cinema* (☎ 6249 7979), on Bunda St near the corner of Mort St, and *Civic Cinemas 3* (☎ 6247 5522), at 6 Mort St, show mainstream films, as does *Capitol Cinema* (☎ 6295 9042) on Franklin St in Manuka. *Electric Shadows* (☎ 6247 5060) is an art-house cinema on City Walk near Akuna St; entry is $12.

The *National Library of Australia* (☎ 6262 1475) shows free films Thursday night at 7 pm. The *National Gallery of Australia* (☎ 6240 6502) has screenings on art-related topics on Friday at 12.45 pm.

Casino The *Casino Canberra* (☎ 6257 7074, 1800 806 833), at 21 Binara St near the National Convention Centre, is open daily from noon to 6 am. It's a fairly casual place: before 7 pm T-shirts, jeans and sports shoes are OK but after 7 pm men have to wear a shirt with a collar and no-one can wear sports shoes.

Things to Buy
Artwares Gift Gallery at Gorman House Arts Centre (☎ 6249 7377), on Ainslie Ave, sells craftwork by local and international artisans. There's also an interesting craft market at the centre on Sundays.

The Old Bus Depot Market, on Wentworth Ave in Kingston, is on every Sunday selling art and craft with a New Age slant, as well as food from around the world.

The Wilderness Society Shop (☎ 6249 8011), on Garema Place, and the Bogong

Environment Shop, in the Environment Centre (☎ 6247 3064) on Kingsley St, sell ecologically related books, gifts and other products.

Getting There & Away
Air Canberra's isn't an international airport. Sydney is about half an hour away and the standard one-way fare with the two major airlines is $158; the flight to Melbourne is about an hour and costs $222. Direct flights to Adelaide cost $327 and to Brisbane $329. These prices drop dramatically when you book in advance and other special deals are often available. Ansett Express offers a night flight to Sydney for $178 return.

Qantas (☎ 131313) and Ansett (☎ 131300) are both in the Jolimont Centre on Northbourne Ave.

Fares on Eastern Australia Airlines (☎ 131313) and Ansett Express are the same as the regular flights although these fly more frequently. Other smaller airlines fly to NSW country destinations. Air Facilities (☎ 6041 1210) flies daily to Albury.

Bus Several bus lines have booking offices and their main terminal at the Jolimont Centre.

Greyhound Pioneer (☎ 132030) has the most frequent Sydney service ($32), which takes four to five hours. It also runs to Adelaide ($99) and Melbourne ($50). Services to Cooma ($16) and to Thredbo in the NSW snowfields ($38, including park entry fees) are frequent in winter and less so at other times.

Murrays (☎ 6295 3611) has daily express buses to Sydney (under four hours) for $28 and to the NSW coast at Batemans Bay ($21.75) and connects with buses to Nowra ($38.75). Capital Coachlines (☎ 6292 9412) runs to Bathurst ($36), Orange ($36) and Dubbo ($45); book through the Countrylink Travel Centre (see Bus & Train below).

McCafferty's (☎ 6249 6006) has buses to Sydney ($28), Melbourne ($45) and Adelaide ($96); you can book through the Travellers Maps & Guides shop next to Murrays.

Transborder Express (☎ 6226 1378) runs to Yass for $10 one way; a same-day return is $12. Sid Fogg's (☎ 4928 1088) runs between Newcastle and Canberra on Monday, Wednesday and Friday for $45 one way.

Bus & Train Canberra's railway station (☎ 6239 7039) is south of Lake Burley Griffin, on Wentworth Ave in Kingston. You can make bookings for trains and connecting buses at the Countrylink Travel Centre (☎ 6257 1576, 132232) in the Jolimont Centre. To Sydney ($40) there are two trains daily, taking about four hours.

There's no direct train to Melbourne. The daily V/Line Canberra Link service involves a train between Melbourne and Wodonga and a connecting bus to Canberra ($44, about nine hours). A longer, more interesting bus/train service to Melbourne is the V/Line Capital Link. It runs three times weekly via Cooma and Bombala and the superb mountain forests of Victoria's East Gippsland, then down the Princes Highway to Sale where you catch a train. This takes just over 11 hours and costs $47.

Car & Motorcycle The Hume Highway, connecting Sydney and Melbourne, passes about 50km to the north of Canberra. The Federal Highway runs north to the Hume near Goulburn, while the Barton Highway meets it near Yass. To the south, the Monaro Highway connects Canberra with Cooma.

Car Rental Major companies with offices in the city are:

Avis
   17 Lonsdale St, Braddon (☎ 6249 6088)
Budget
   Corner of Mort and Girroween Sts, Braddon (☎ 6257 1305, 132727)
Hertz
   32 Mort St, Braddon (☎ 6257 4877, 133030)
Thrifty
   29 Lonsdale St, Braddon (☎ 6247 7422)

These companies also have desks at the airport.

Cheaper outfits include Rumbles (☎ 6280 7444), at 157 Gladstone St in Fyshwick, and Rent a Dent (☎ 6257 5947), at 8 Ijong St in Braddon, who'll pick you up from the Jolimont Centre. Expect to pay from $35 or $40 a day including 200k free, with better deals on longer rentals.

Getting Around
The Airport Canberra airport is 7km southeast of the city centre. The only airport bus service is ACT Minibuses (☎ 6291 4592) which charges $8 and picks up from the Jolimont Centre, various hotels and the YHA. You have to book.

The taxi fare from the airport to Civic is around $10.

Bus Buses operated by the Australian Capital Territory Internal Omnibus Network (ACTION; ☎ 6207 7611) run fairly frequently.

The T-shaped main interchange is along Alinga St east of Northbourne Ave, plus East Row and Mort St in Civic. The information kiosk, at the corner of Alinga St and East Row, is open daily until about 11.30 pmthough it only sells tickets until about 5.30 pm. If you'll be using buses a lot it's worth buying the *ACTION Bus Book* ($2) here, though it isn't exactly pocket sized.

The flat 'one route' fare is $2 and if you pay cash you should have the exact change. Commuter express buses – the No 700 series – cost $4. You can save money with pre-purchase tickets, available from newsagents and elsewhere, but not on buses. A book of 10 FareGo tickets costs $14; a weekly ticket is $24. Daily tickets are great value as they offer unlimited travel for $6.

Special Services The free Downtowner service is a bus disguised as a tram which runs around the Civic shopping centre, stopping at designated stops.

Sightseeing bus No 901 runs to the War Memorial, Regatta Point, Questacon, the National Gallery of Australia, Parliament House and several embassies in Yarralumla. Bus No 904 goes to the Australian National

ACT

Travel for People with Disabilities in the ACT

Access in Canberra's central business district (Civic) and the main suburban shopping precincts of Manuka, Woden and Belconnen is good, with several dedicated parking spaces allocated near ramped crossovers to footpaths. Civic is the shopping, meeting, cafe and restaurant precinct where air conditioned shopping centres provide plenty of parking (for a fee) and accessible toilets. The pedestrian malls City Walk, Garema Place and Petrie Plaza contain outdoor cafes, several banks, the post office (with a short but quite steep ramp) and lots of shops, many with ramps or a small step in.

NICAN (Freecall 1800 806 769 or TTY (02) 6285 3713), PO Box 407 Curtin ACT 2605, should be your first stop for information on access and has a database of recreation, sport, the arts and tourism for people with a disability. In conjunction with Qantas, NICAN has developed a Carer Concession Card where a carer may travel for half price.

The ACROD Access Committee (☎ (02) 6286 934) can be found at 29 Hawker Street, Torrens, ACT 2607 and the Independent Living Centre (☎ (02) 6205 1900) can provide you with equipment hire options.

Accessible attractions include Parliament House (☎ (02) 6277 5023), which publishes *Visitors Guide, a Brochure for People with Disabilities*; the National Gallery (☎ (02) 6240 6411), Australian War Memorial (☎ (02) 6243 4211), Telstra Tower (☎ (02) 6248 1911) at the summit of Black Mountain, and Questacon, the Science & Technology Centre (☎ (02 6270 2800). There are no specialist tour operators in the ACT.

Cheap accessible accommodation is scarce; Fenner Hall (☎ (02) 6279 9101), part of ANU, has two rooms with large wheel-in showers but small bedroom areas, and is available during holiday periods.

Countrylink trains (☎ (02) 6257 1576 or Freecall 13 2232) have at least one carriage per train which is wheelchair accessible and has an accessible toilet.

Aerial Cabs (☎ (02) 6285 9222) has six accessible cabs, but book at least an hour in advance.

Useful publications are *Canberra Access: A Guide for People with Disabilities & for the Elderly* (1988), available from ACROD (☎ (02) 6282 4333), 33 Thesiger Court, Deakin, and *Access Guide to Hotels/Motels & Conference Venues* (1994), also available from ACROD at the above address.

For more information for disabled travellers in NSW, see the aside in the Facts for the Visitor chapter.

Bruce Cameron

Botanic Gardens, National Museum of Australia, National Aquarium and to Telstra Tower. Both services depart hourly from the Civic interchange: bus No 901 between 9.35 am and 4.05 pm, and bus No 904 between 10.20 am and 3.20 pm. You'll need a Daily Ticket ($6) to ride these services.

Murray's Canberra Explorer (☎ 132251) runs a 25km route around 19 points of interest; you can get on and off wherever you like. It departs hourly from the Jolimont Centre each day from 10.15 am to 4.15 pm and tickets ($18, $8 children) are sold on the bus. If you want to make one circuit without getting off – a good way to orient yourself – buy a one-hour tour ticket ($7, $5 children).

Car & Motorcycle Canberra's wide, relatively uncluttered main roads make driving a joy, although once you enter the maze of curving roads in the residential areas things become more difficult. Take a map. Speeding on the main roads is common (if illegal as well as dangerous for the newcomer because of unexpected roundabouts and exits), but *everyone* observes the 40km/h limit in school areas.

You could also spend some time looking for a petrol station. By design, most are off the main roads – look for signs.

Taxi Call Aerial Taxi Cabs (☎ 6285 9222).

Bicycle Canberra is a cyclist's paradise, with bike paths making it possible to ride around the city while hardly touching a road. One popular track is a circuit of the lake; there are also peaceful stretches of bushland along some suburban routes. Get a copy of the *Canberra Cycleways* map ($6.40) from bookshops or the information centre.

Mr Spokes Bike Hire (☎ 6257 1188), near

the Acton Park ferry terminal, charges $8 an hour and $7 for subsequent hours. Another company is Dial a Bicycle (☎ 6286 5463) which delivers and picks up the bike. It hires out 10-speed mountain bikes including helmet and chain for $25 for one day, $40 for two days or $80 for a week.

Around Canberra

The ACT is about 88km from north to south and about 30km wide. There's plenty of unspoiled bush just outside the urban area and a network of paved roads into it. The NRMA's *Canberra & District* map and the tourist bureau's *Canberra Sightseeing Guide with Tourist Drives* are helpful.

The plains and isolated hills around Canberra rise to rugged ranges in the south and west of the ACT. The Murrumbidgee River flows across the territory from south-east to north-west. Namadgi National Park in the south covers 40% of the ACT and adjoins Kosciuszko National Park.

Picnic & Walking Areas

Picnic and barbecue spots, many with gas barbecues, are scattered through and around Canberra. There's no public transport to most of them.

Black Mountain, west of the city, is convenient for picnics and there are good swimming spots along the Murrumbidgee and Cotter rivers. Other riverside areas include **Uriarra Crossing**, 24km north-west of Civic, on the Murrumbidgee near its meeting with the Molonglo River; **Casuarina Sands**, 19km west at the meeting of the Murrumbidgee and Cotter Rivers; **Kambah Pool**, about 14km farther upstream (south) on the Murrumbidgee; the **Cotter Dam** (☎ 6207 2204), 23km west of town on the Cotter, which also has a camping area ($10); **Pine Island** and **Point Hut Crossing**, on the Murrumbidgee, upstream of Kambah Pool; and **Gibraltar Falls**, 45km south-west, which also has a camping area.

There are good walking tracks along the

Murrumbidgee from Kambah Pool to Pine Island (7km), or to Casuarina Sands (about 14km).

The spectacular **Ginninderra Falls** (☎ 6257 6633), at Parkwood, north-west of Canberra across the NSW border, are open daily; there are gorges, a nature trail, canoeing and camping. Admission is $5.

Tidbinbilla Nature Reserve (☎ 6237 5120), 45km south-west of the city in the hills beyond the Tidbinbilla tracking station, has bushwalking tracks – some leading to interesting rock formations. The reserve is open from 9 am to 6 pm (later during daylight-saving time) and the visitor centre is open weekdays from 11 am to 3 pm and weekends from 9 am to 6 pm. South-west of here in the **Corin Forest** (☎ 6247 225), there's a 1km-long metal 'bobsled' run on weekends and during school holidays; you can get three rides for $15. There's also a flying fox.

Other good walking areas include **Mt Ainslie**, on the north-east side of the city, and **Mt Majura** behind it. These are part of the **Canberra Nature Park** which incorporates at least a dozen parks throughout Canberra.

Namadgi National Park, occupying the south-west of the ACT and partly bordering mountainous Kosciuszko National Park in NSW's Snowy Mountains, has seven peaks over 1600m and offers challenging bushwalking. Booroomba Rocks in the park are popular with rockclimbers and there is sometimes enough snow for cross-country skiing. The partly-surfaced Boboyan Rd crosses the park, going south from **Tharwa** in the ACT to **Adaminaby** on the eastern edge of the Snowy Mountains in NSW.

The park visitor information centre (☎ 6237 5222) is on this road, 2km south of Tharwa, but you can get brochures and maps at Canberra visitor information centre. There are several picnic areas but the only formal **campsites** are at the Orroral River crossing and Mt Clear, both accessible from Boboyan Rd. Wildthing Tours (☎ 6254 6303) and MudMaps Australia (☎ 6257 4796) have tours into the park; you can also book through the travel agency at the YHA hostel.

ACT

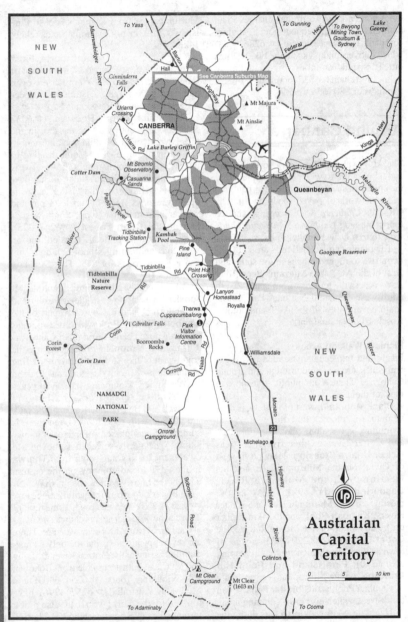

Australian Capital Territory

0   5   10 km

Observatories & Tracking Stations

The ANU's **Mt Stromlo Observatory** (☎ 6249 0230), 16km south-west of Canberra, has a 188cm telescope plus a visitors' annexe open daily from 9.30 am to 4 pm. A joint US-Australian deep-space tracking station, the **Canberra Deep Space Communication Complex** (☎ 6201 7800), also called the Tidbinbilla Tracking Station, is 40km south-west of Canberra. The visitor centre has displays of spacecraft and tracking technology. It's open daily from 9 am to 5 pm (to 8 pm during daylight-saving time); admission is free. The area is popular for bushwalks and barbecues.

Ginninderra

Near the Barton Highway about 11km north-west of the city, Ginninderra has a number of attractions. Hard to resist is the **National Dinosaur Museum** (☎ 6230 2655). This is a private collection with replica skeletons of 10 dinosaurs and many real bones and fossils. It's open daily from 10 am to 5 pm (from 9 am during school holidays); admission is $8 ($5 children).

Ginninderra Village, on the corner of the Barton Highway and Gold Creek Rd, is a collection of craft workshops and galleries; it's open daily from 10 am to 5 pm and admission is free. Next door, ·**Cockington Green** (☎ 6230 2273) is a miniature replica of an English village, open daily from 9.30 am to 4 pm; admission is $7.95 ($3.95 children).

Other Attractions

About 25km north-east of Canberra, **Bywong Mining Town** (☎ 6236 9183), on Millyn Rd off the Federal Highway, is a re-creation of a mining settlement. It's open daily from 10 am to 4 pm and there are tours at 10.30 am, 12.30 and 2 pm. Admission is $7 ($4.50 children). Bring a picnic if you intend to spend a bit of time here.

The beautifully restored **Lanyon Homestead** (☎ 6237 5136), on Tharwa Drive off the Monaro Highway beside the river near Tharwa, is about 30km south of Canberra's city centre. The early stone cottage on the site was built by convicts and the grand homestead was completed in 1859. This National Trust homestead, which documents the life of the region before Canberra existed, is open Tuesday to Sunday from 10 am to 4 pm. The **Nolan Gallery** (☎ 6237 5192), containing a collection of Sidney Nolan paintings, is a major attraction.

Cuppacumbalong (☎ 6237 5116), on Naas Rd near Tharwa, is another old homestead, although not as grand as Lanyon. It's now a craft studio and gallery open Wednesday to Sunday from 11 am to 5 pm.

Day Trips

A popular drive is east into NSW, past Bungendore, to **Braidwood** (see the South-East chapter). **Bungendore** is a small country town which has craft galleries and some old buildings.

Another good route takes in **Tharwa** and the nearby old homesteads (see Other Attractions above) in hilly grazing lands. From there, the route goes north-west to Gibraltar Falls and Tidbinbilla Nature Reserve (see Picnic & Walking Areas above). The Canberra Deep Space Communication Complex (see Observatories & Tracking Stations above) is on the way back into town along a slow, winding, scenic road.

QUEANBEYAN

Across the NSW border, about 12km south-east of central Canberra, is Queanbeyan (population 27,000), now virtually a suburb of the capital it predates. It's obvious that Canberra's planning regulations don't apply here. Most of its historic buildings date from around 1838 when it was proclaimed a township. The Queanbeyan Information & Tourist Centre (☎ 1800 026 192) is at 1 Farrer Place.

There's a **museum** with displays on the town's history and good lookouts on **Jerrabomberra Hill** (5km west of the town centre) and **Bungendore Hill** (4km east).

Motel accommodation is slightly cheaper than in Canberra.

ACT

Eastern Islands

Lord Howe Island

Beautiful Lord Howe is a tiny subtropical island 500km east of Port Macquarie and 770km north-east of Sydney. It's the largest of a cluster of 28 islands and outcrops that are the eroded remnants of a huge shield volcano which emerged from the ocean about seven million years ago. The island is dominated by the towering peaks of Mt Lidgbird (807m) and Mt Gower (875m), visible from almost 100km out to sea. Tourism is the island's main industry, but it's not a budget destination. You're not allowed on the island without an accommodation booking – which is why everyone takes a flight and accommodation package.

The island has some beautiful beaches and a wide lagoon sheltered by a coral reef, but the main attraction is walking in the World Heritage-listed rainforest that covers the southern two-thirds of the island. The forests are home to some 70-odd plant species that occur naturally only on Lord Howe. They include the hardy kentia palm *(Howea forsteriana)*, prized by gardeners all over the world.

History

The first Europeans to set eyes on Lord Howe Island were the crew of the ship HMS *Supply*, which sailed past on 17 February 1788, on its way from the newly founded Port Jackson (Sydney) to Norfolk Island under the command of Lieutenant Henry Lidgbird Ball.

From a distance, Ball thought he had discovered two islands. He named the larger one Lord Howe, after the first lord of the admiralty, and named the lesser one Lidgbird Island, after himself. Upon closer inspection, the 'islands' turned out to be two mountains rising from the one landmass. Tactfully, he chose to run with Lord Howe's name for the

HIGHLIGHTS

- Bushwalking in the World Heritage listed forests of Lord Howe Island
- The historic convict settlement of Kingston on Norfolk Island

island, while his 'island' became Mt Lidgbird.

The first settlers didn't arrive until 1834, when a whaling supply station was established at Old Settlement Beach. The islanders have dabbled in various activities over the years in search of an income. For a long time there was good money to be made selling seed from the kentia palm. The first tourists arrived at around the turn of the century, and today the island is almost entirely dependent on tourism.

The island is a dependency of NSW, with local government in the hands of the Lord Howe Island Board.

Orientation & Information

The island measures just 11km by 2km, and is shaped like a small boomerang surrounding a shallow lagoon to the west. There's nothing large enough to call a town, but most people live in the small area of flatter land just north of the airport. You'll find a general store and a post office (Commonwealth Bank) on the road between Old Settlement Beach and Ned's Beach. Most of the accommodation is around here and facing the lagoon south of Old Settlement Beach. Your accommodation owner will be able to supply you with a map and any information you need.

Travel Agents Pacific International Travel (☎ 9262 6555, 1800 221 713) and the NSW Travel Centre (☎ 132077) are two Sydney travel agents that specialise in holidays to

Lord Howe. They can supply information of a glossy nature, as can Jetset Travel (☎ 6584 1411) in Port Macquarie.

Bushwalking
Bushwalking is very popular and there's a good network of walking tracks. The mountains are obvious targets. **Mt Eliza**, on the north-western tip of the island, is a comfortable walk starting from beyond the Milky Way Apartments. Only serious walkers should attempt the arduous all-day hike to the summit of **Mt Gower**, while **Mt Lidgbird** is a challenge for mountaineers, not walkers.

Other Activities
The best snorkelling is off **Ned's Beach** in the north. **Blinky Beach**, just west of the airport, occasionally has decent surf. The nine-hole **golf course** is as picturesque as you could hope to find.

Organised Tours
Ron and Sam's Nature Walks offer a range of short walks around the island, while Jim Dorman does boat trips around North Bay. Both can be booked at the Lagoon Store (☎ 6563 2019).

Places to Stay
Camping isn't permitted on the island. There's plenty of accommodation in lodges and self-contained apartments, but the only way to get a decent deal is to buy a package. In winter, you'll pay around $780 for five nights at cheaper places like the *Broken Banyan*, rising to $1150 in summer.

Getting There & Away
Air Eastern Australia has daily flights from Sydney for $812 return ($698 with seven-day Apex), while Sunstate flies from Brisbane on Sunday for $792 return. Kentia Link operates charters from Coffs Harbour and Port Macquarie.

Boat The *Island Trader* sails out to Lord Howe every second Thursday from the northern NSW port of Yamba. Primarily a cargo vessel, it has only four passenger berths. The trip takes about 40 hours, and the fare is $400 return. The boat normally spends a couple of days at Lord Howe before returning to Yamba. The operators can organise accommodation on the island. Call ☎ 6646 0238 for information and bookings.

Getting Around
There are motorbikes and a few rental cars on the island but a bike is all you need. They can be hired from Wilson's Bike Hire (☎ 6563 2010). There's a 25-km/h speed limit throughout the island.

Norfolk Island

Norfolk Island is a green speck in the middle of the Pacific Ocean, 1600km north-east of Sydney and 1000km north-west of the New Zealand capital, Auckland. It's the largest of a cluster of three islands emerging from the Norfolk Ridge, which stretches from New Zealand to New Caledonia – the closest landfall, almost 700km to the north.

Norfolk is a popular tourist spot, particularly with older Australians and New Zealanders, and tourism is by far the biggest contributor to the local economy. The cost of airfares means it's not a cheap destination, and there's no budget accommodation.

Many visitors enjoy Norfolk Island's lush vegetation. The rich volcanic soil and mild subtropical climate provide perfect growing conditions. There are 40-odd plant species that are unique to the island, including the handsome Norfolk Island pine *(Araucaria heterophylla)* which grows everywhere.

History
Little is known about the island before it was sighted by Captain Cook on 10 October 1774 and named after the wife of the ninth Duke of Norfolk. Fifteen convicts were among the first settlers to reach the island on 6 March 1788, founding a penal colony that survived until 1814. The island was abandoned for 11 years before colonial authorities decided to try again. Governor Darling planned this

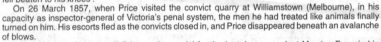

John Giles Price

The exploits of John Giles Price as commandant of Norfolk Island are vividly recorded in Robert Hughes' study of the Australian convict era, *The Fatal Shore*. Hughes paints a picture of a demented sadist who ran the island like a torture chamber. The evidence of Price's excesses was provided by two visiting clergymen who were appalled by what they saw. Their reports eventually led to his recall and the closure of the penal colony.

While Price's predecessors had contented themselves with flogging their charges into submission, Price devised new ways to make their lives a misery. A mere flogging was reserved for trivial offences such as losing a shoelace. More serious offenders would be flogged, put in a straitjacket and strapped to a bed frame for a week or two while their wounds festered. Others were reportedly transformed into living corpses by being left strapped to a bed for up to six weeks.

Price was also a larger-than-life character in the flesh. He was a tall, powerfully built man with a withering stare, yet he dressed like a dandy – complete with a monocle in his left eye. While he was a bully, he was no coward. Hughes relates how Price 'once stared down a convict who snatched a pistol from his belt, taunting the man as a coward and a dog until the prisoner handed back the weapon and fell beaten to his knees'.

On 26 March 1857, when Price visited the convict quarry at Williamstown (Melbourne), in his capacity as inspector-general of Victoria's penal system, the men he had treated like animals finally turned on him. His escorts fled as the convicts closed in, and Price disappeared beneath an avalanche of blows.

Author Marcus Clarke used Price as the model for the brutal commandant Maurice Frere in his convict novel *For The Term of His Natural Life*. ∎

second penal settlement as 'a place of the extremest punishment short of death'. Under such notorious sadists as commandant John Giles Price, Norfolk became known as 'hell in the Pacific'.

The penal colony lasted until 1855, when the prisoners were shipped off to Van Diemen's Land (Tasmania) and the island was handed over to the descendants of the mutineers from the HMS *Bounty*, who had outgrown their adopted Pitcairn Island. About a third of the present population of 2000 are descended from the 194 Pitcairners who arrived on 8 June 1856.

Orientation & Information

The island measures only 8km by 5km. Vertical cliffs surround much of the coastline, apart from a small area of coastal plain (for-

merly swamp) around the historic settlement of Kingston. The only settlement of any consequence is the service town of Burnt Pine, at the centre of the island and near the airport. Most of the northern part of the island is taken up by Norfolk Island National Park.

The Norfolk Islander Visitors Information Centre (☎ 22 147) is next to the post office on the main street in Burnt Pine. The Communications Centre (Norfolk Telstra) is at the edge of town on New Cascade Rd. If you're addressing mail to the island from Australia, the postcode is 2899.

The Commonwealth Bank and Westpac have branches in Burnt Pine.

Communications If calling from outside the island, use the international telephone code 6723 before dialling the local number.

Visas The island is a self-governing external territory of Australia; this has important ramifications in terms of passports and visas. Travelling to Norfolk Island from Australia means you will pay departure tax, get an exit stamp in your passport and board an international flight. (The same applies from New Zealand.) To return to Australia you will need a re-entry visa, or a valid Australian passport. On arrival at Norfolk Island, you will get a 30-day visa on presentation of a valid passport.

Kingston

The historic settlement of Kingston, built by convicts of the second penal colony, is the island's main attraction. Several of the buildings have been turned into small **museums**. The finest buildings are those of the colonial administrators along **Quality Row**, as the settlement's main road is called. The sandstone used for the buildings was quarried from nearby Nepean Island. One place that should not be missed is the **convict cemetery**, next to the ocean at the far (eastern) end of Quality Row. There are some very poignant epitaphs on the headstones, such as that of James Saye, who was killed in 1842 during an abortive mutiny:

Stop Christian, stop and meditate
On this man's sad and awful fate
On earth no more he breathes again
He lived in hope but died in pain.

Other Attractions

Just south of Kingston is **Emily Bay**, a good sheltered beach, and there are several operators who will take you out in glass-bottom boats to view the corals in the bay.

St Barnabas Chapel, west of Burnt Pine along Douglas Drive, is a magnificent chapel built by the (Anglican) Melanesian Mission, which was based on the island from 1866 to 1920.

There are various walking tracks in **Norfolk Island National Park**, and good views from Mt Pitt (320m) and Mt Bates (321m). Mt Pitt was the higher of the two

before the top was levelled to build a radio transmitter.

Organised Tours

Pinetree Tours (☎ 22 424), in the middle of Burnt Pine, runs a busy schedule of tours around the island. The half-day introductory tour ($18) takes in all the major points of interest.

Places to Stay

Accommodation is expensive, but the cost is often disguised as most visitors come on package deals. There are lots of places to choose from, but few that make the most of the island's natural attributes. Modern motel-style units predominate, priced from $79 a double.

Highlands Lodge (☎ 22 741) is a good place nestled on the hillside below the national park, with doubles for $105. *Channer's Corner* (☎ 22 532), on the edge of Burnt Pine, has stylish apartments at $95 for two people.

Places to Eat

There are dozens of restaurants, offering everything from humble fish & chips to upmarket à la carte. Competition is stiff and prices are quite reasonable, although groceries are expensive by Australian standards.

The *Bowling Club* in Burnt Pine has roasts for $8, and the *Workers Club* opposite is equally good value. The *Bounty Inn*, right outside the airport, brews its own beer.

Getting There & Away

Ansett flies four times a week from Sydney ($619 Apex return) and three times a week from Brisbane ($579 Apex return). Air New Zealand flies twice a week from Auckland (from NZ$599 return).

There's a departure tax of $25.

Getting Around

Car hire can be organised at the airport for as little as $9 a day, plus insurance ($3). Petrol is expensive, but you'll struggle to use much. Cows have right of way on the island's roads, and there's a $300 fine for hitting one.

Index

PLANET TALK

Lonely Planet's FREE quarterly newsletter

We love hearing from you and think you'd like to hear from us.

When...is the right time to see reindeer in Finland?
Where...can you hear the best palm-wine music in Ghana?
How...do you get from Asunción to Areguá by steam train?
What...is the best way to see India?

For the answer to these and many other questions read PLANET TALK.

Every issue is packed with up-to-date travel news and advice including:

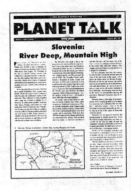

* a letter from Lonely Planet co-founders Tony and Maureen Wheeler
* go behind the scenes on the road with a Lonely Planet author
* feature article on an important and topical travel issue
* a selection of recent letters from travellers
* details on forthcoming Lonely Planet promotions
* complete list of Lonely Planet products

To join our mailing list contact any Lonely Planet office.

Also available: Lonely Planet T-shirts. 100% heavyweight cotton.

LONELY PLANET ONLINE

Get the latest travel information before you leave or while you're on the road

Whether you've just begun planning your next trip, or you're chasing down specific info on currency regulations or visa requirements, check out Lonely Planet Online for up-to-the minute travel information.

As well as travel profiles of your favourite destinations (including maps and photos), you'll find current reports from our researchers and other travellers, updates on health and visas, travel advisories, and discussion of the ecological and political issues you need to be aware of as you travel.

There's also an online travellers' forum where you can share your experience of life on the road, meet travel companions and ask other travellers for their recommendations and advice. We also have plenty of links to other online sites useful to independent travellers.

And of course we have a complete and up-to-date list of all Lonely Planet travel products including guides, phrasebooks, atlases, Journeys and videos and a simple online ordering facility if you can't find the book you want elsewhere.

www.lonelyplanet.com
or
AOL keyword: lp

LONELY PLANET PRODUCTS

Lonely Planet is known worldwide for publishing practical, reliable and no-nonsense travel information in our guides and on our web site. The Lonely Planet list covers just about every accessible part of the world. Currently there are eight series: *travel guides, shoestring guides, walking guides, city guides, phrasebooks, audio packs, travel atlases* and *Journeys* – a unique collection of travel writing.

EUROPE

Amsterdam • Austria • Baltic States phrasebook • Britain • Central Europe on a shoestring • Central Europe phrasebook • Czech & Slovak Republics • Denmark • Dublin • Eastern Europe on a shoestring • Eastern Europe phrasebook • Estonia, Latvia & Lithuania • Finland • France • French phrasebook • German phrasebook • Greece • Greek phrasebook • Hungary • Iceland, Greenland & the Faroe Islands • Ireland • Italian phrasebook • Italy • Mediterranean Europe on a shoestring • Mediterranean Europe phrasebook • Paris • Poland • Portugal • Portugal travel atlas • Prague • Russia, Ukraine & Belarus • Russian phrasebook • Scandinavian & Baltic Europe on a shoestring • Scandinavian Europe phrasebook • Slovenia • Spain • Spanish phrasebook • St Petersburg • Switzerland • Trekking in Greece • Trekking in Spain • Ukrainian phrasebook • Vienna • Walking in Britain • Walking in Switzerland • Western Europe on a shoestring • Western Europe phrasebook

Travel Literature: The Olive Grove: Travels in Greece

NORTH AMERICA

Alaska • Backpacking in Alaska • Baja California • California & Nevada • Canada • Florida • Hawaii • Honolulu • Los Angeles • Mexico • Miami • New England • New Orleans • New York City • New York, New Jersey & Pennsylvania • Pacific Northwest USA • Rocky Mountain States • San Francisco • Southwest USA • USA phrasebook • Washington, DC & the Capital Region

CENTRAL AMERICA & THE CARIBBEAN

Bermuda • Central America on a shoestring • Costa Rica • Cuba • Eastern Caribbean • Guatemala, Belize & Yucatán: La Ruta Maya • Jamaica

SOUTH AMERICA

Argentina, Uruguay & Paraguay • Bolivia • Brazil • Brazilian phrasebook • Buenos Aires • Chile & Easter Island • Chile & Easter Island travel atlas • Colombia • Ecuador & the Galápagos Islands • Latin American Spanish phrasebook • Peru • Quechua phrasebook • Rio de Janeiro • South America on a shoestring • Trekking in the Patagonian Andes • Venezuela

Travel Literature: Full Circle: A South American Journey

ANTARCTICA

Antarctica

ISLANDS OF THE INDIAN OCEAN

Madagascar & Comoros • Maldives • Mauritius, Réunion & Seychelles

AFRICA

Africa - the South • Africa on a shoestring • Arabic (Moroccan) phrasebook • Cape Town • Central Africa • East Africa • Egypt • Egypt travel atlas • Ethiopian (Amharic) phrasebook • Kenya • Kenya travel atlas • Malawi, Mozambique & Zambia • Morocco • North Africa • South Africa, Lesotho & Swaziland • South Africa, Lesotho & Swaziland travel atlas • Swahili phrasebook • Trekking in East Africa • West Africa • Zimbabwe, Botswana & Namibia • Zimbabwe, Botswana & Namibia travel atlas

Travel Literature: The Rainbird: A Central African Journey • Songs to an African Sunset: A Zimbabwean Story

MAIL ORDER

Lonely Planet products are distributed worldwide. They are also available by mail order from Lonely Planet, so if you have difficulty finding a title please write to us. North American and South American residents should write to Embarcadero West, 155 Filbert St, Suite 251, Oakland CA 94607, USA; European and African residents should write to 10 Barley Mow Passage, Chiswick, London W4 4PH; and residents of other countries to PO Box 617, Hawthorn, Victoria 3122, Australia.

NORTH-EAST ASIA

Beijing • Cantonese phrasebook • China • Hong Kong • Hong Kong, Macau & Guangzhou • Japan • Japanese phrasebook • Japanese audio pack • Korea • Korean phrasebook • Mandarin phrasebook • Mongolia • Mongolian phrasebook • North-East Asia on a shoestring • Seoul • Taiwan • Tibet • Tibet phrasebook • Tokyo

Travel Literature: Lost Japan

MIDDLE EAST & CENTRAL ASIA

Arab Gulf States • Arabic (Egyptian) phrasebook • Central Asia • Iran • Israel & the Palestinian Territories • Israel & the Palestinian Territories travel atlas • Istanbul • Jerusalem • Jordan & Syria • Jordan, Syria & Lebanon travel atlas • Middle East • Turkey • Turkish phrasebook • Turkey travel atlas • Yemen

Travel Literature: The Gates of Damascus • Kingdom of the Film Stars: Journey into Jordan

ALSO AVAILABLE:

Travel with Children • Traveller's Tales

INDIAN SUBCONTINENT

Bangladesh • Bengali phrasebook • Delhi • Hindi/Urdu phrasebook • India • India & Bangladesh travel atlas • Indian Himalaya • Karakoram Highway • Nepal • Nepali phrasebook • Pakistan • Rajasthan • Sri Lanka • Sri Lanka phrasebook • Trekking in the Indian Himalaya • Trekking in the Karakoram & Hindukush • Trekking in the Nepal Himalaya

Travel Literature: In Rajasthan • Shopping for Buddhas

SOUTH-EAST ASIA

Bali & Lombok • Bangkok • Burmese phrasebook • Cambodia • Ho Chi Minh City • Indonesia • Indonesian phrasebook • Indonesian audio pack • Jakarta • Java • Laos • Lao phrasebook • Laos travel atlas • Malay phrasebook • Malaysia, Singapore & Brunei • Myanmar (Burma) • Philippines • Pilipino phrasebook • Singapore • South-East Asia on a shoestring • South-East Asia phrasebook • Thailand • Thailand travel atlas • Thai phrasebook • Thai audio pack • Thai Hill Tribes phrasebook • Vietnam • Vietnamese phrasebook • Vietnam travel atlas

AUSTRALIA & THE PACIFIC

Australia • Australian phrasebook • Bushwalking in Australia • Bushwalking in Papua New Guinea • Fiji • Fijian phrasebook • Islands of Australia's Great Barrier Reef • Melbourne • Micronesia • New Caledonia • New South Wales & the ACT • New Zealand • Northern Territory • Outback Australia • Papua New Guinea • Papua New Guinea phrasebook • Queensland • Rarotonga & the Cook Islands • Samoa • Solomon Islands • South Australia • Sydney • Tahiti & French Polynesia • Tasmania • Tonga • Tramping in New Zealand • Vanuatu • Victoria • Western Australia

Travel Literature: Islands in the Clouds • Sean & David's Long Drive

THE LONELY PLANET STORY

Lonely Planet published its first book in 1973 in response to the numerous 'How did you do it?' questions Maureen and Tony Wheeler were asked after driving, bussing, hitching, sailing and railing their way from England to Australia.

Written at a kitchen table and hand collated, trimmed and stapled, *Across Asia on the Cheap* became an instant local bestseller, inspiring thoughts of another book.

Eighteen months in South-East Asia resulted in their second guide, *South-East Asia on a shoestring*, which they put together in a backstreet Chinese hotel in Singapore in 1975. The 'yellow bible', as it quickly became known to backpackers around the world, soon became *the* guide to the region. It has sold well over half a million copies and is now in its 9th edition, still retaining its familiar yellow cover.

Today there are over 240 titles, including travel guides, walking guides, language kits & phrasebooks, travel atlases and travel literature. The company is the largest independent travel publisher in the world. Although Lonely Planet initially specialised in guides to Asia, today there are few corners of the globe that have not been covered.

The emphasis continues to be on travel for independent travellers. Tony and Maureen still travel for several months of each year and play an active part in the writing, updating and quality control of Lonely Planet's guides.

They have been joined by over 70 authors and 170 staff at our offices in Melbourne (Australia), Oakland (USA), London (UK) and Paris (France). Travellers themselves also make a valuable contribution to the guides through the feedback we receive in thousands of letters each year and on our web site.

The people at Lonely Planet strongly believe that travellers can make a positive contribution to the countries they visit, both through their appreciation of the countries' culture, wildlife and natural features, and through the money they spend. In addition, the company makes a direct contribution to the countries and regions it covers. Since 1986 a percentage of the income from each book has been donated to ventures such as famine relief in Africa; aid projects in India; agricultural projects in Central America; Greenpeace's efforts to halt French nuclear testing in the Pacific; and Amnesty International.

'I hope we send people out with the right attitude about travel. You realise when you travel that there are so many different perspectives about the world, so we hope these books will make people more interested in what they see. Guidebooks can't really guide people. All you can do is point them in the right direction.'

– Tony Wheeler

LONELY PLANET PUBLICATIONS

Australia
PO Box 617, Hawthorn 3122, Victoria
tel: (03) 9819 1877 fax: (03) 9819 6459
e-mail: talk2us@lonelyplanet.com.au

USA
Embarcadero West, 155 Filbert St, Suite 251,
Oakland, CA 94607
tel: (510) 893 8555 TOLL FREE: 800 275-8555
fax: (510) 893 8563
e-mail: info@lonelyplanet.com

UK
10 Barley Mow Passage, Chiswick,
London W4 4PH
tel: (0181) 742 3161 fax: (0181) 742 2772
e-mail: lonelyplanetuk@compuserve.com

France:
71 bis rue du Cardinal Lemoine, 75005 Paris
tel: 1 44 32 06 20 fax: 1 46 34 72 55
e-mail: 100560.415@compuserve.com

World Wide Web: http://www.lonelyplanet.com
or AOL keyword: lp